D0768908

The Rorschach Assessment
of Aggressive
and Psychopathic Personalities

The LEA Series in
Personality and Clinical Psychology
Irving B. Weiner, Editor

Gacono & Meloy • The Rorschach Assessment of Aggressive
and Psychopathic Personalities

The Rorschach Assessment
of Aggressive
and Psychopathic Personalities

Carl B. Gacono
Federal Medical Center, Fort Worth, Texas
University of California, San Francisco

J. Reid Meloy
Forensic Mental Health Division, San Diego County
University of California, San Diego

LEA LAWRENCE ERLBAUM ASSOCIATES, PUBLISHERS
1994 Hillsdale, New Jersey   Hove, UK

Lawrence Erlbaum Associates, Inc., Publishers
365 Broadway
Hillsdale, New Jersey 07642

Cover design by Kate Dusza. Cover art used with permission of the
Vincent van Gogh Foundation/van Gogh Museum, Amsterdam.

Library of Congress Cataloging-in-Publication Data

Gacono, Carl B.
   The Rorschach assessment of aggressive and psychopathic
personalities / Carl B. Gacono, J. Reid Meloy.
     p.   cm.
   Includes bibliographical references and indexes.
   ISBN 0-8058-0980-5
   1. Rorschach Test. 2. Aggressiveness (Psychology) 3. Antisocial
personality disorders. I. Gacono, Carl B. II. Meloy, J. Reid. III. Title.
   [DNLM: 1. Rorschach Test. 2. Aggression—psychology.
3. Antisocial Personality Disorder—psychology. WM 145 G122r 1994]
RC473.R6G33 1994
155.2'32—dc20
DNLM/DLC
for Library of Congress   94-11478
                                        CIP

Printed in the United States of America
10 9 8 7 6 5 4 3 2

*Dedicated to the
work and memory of
Robert Lindner, PhD*

Contents

Acknowledgments

Many people have contributed their time and energy to help us produce this book. We have acknowledged each of them throughout the book as his or her individual contribution was felt. There are two individuals, moreover, whose kindness, generosity, and effort permeate this entire project, and without whom it would not have been completed—Phil Erdberg, PhD, and Marilyn Clarke. Our deepest gratitude to you both.

The views expressed in this book are solely ours and do not necessarily reflect the views of the Federal Bureau of Prisons, the Universities of California at San Diego and San Francisco, or San Diego County Department of Health Services.

Foreword

The *Rorschach Assessment of Aggressive and Psychopathic Personalities* could not have been written 25 years ago. The authors' unswerving devotion and two significant developments in assessment and personality theory have made this work possible.

The first of these advances is with the Rorschach. As the authors note, Robert Lindner suggested early on that the Rorschach might prove uniquely useful in understanding antisocial and psychopathic personality. So did Samuel Beck, whose name is commemorated with a Society for Personality Assessment Award for which Dr. Gacono was the 1994 recipient. Sadly, neither of these early psychologists had the technology to take full advantage of their vision. The synthesis that John Exner has brought to the Rorschach and the computer technology that allows the thoughtful analysis of large-sample data now make it possible to realize the test's promise.

The second development has been in personality theory. Advances in psychoanalysis, particularly object relations theory and self psychology, have brought a much more precise conceptualization of borderline and psychotic-level personality organization. The pioneering work of Mahler, Kernberg, and Kohut foreshadowed what has now become a multifaceted, genuinely exciting literature of personality disorder.

It is these two advances—in the Rorschach and in personality theory—that Carl Gacono and Reid Meloy have brought together in this landmark book. They realized that the combination of the "new" Rorschach and the "new" psycho-analysis had the potential for bringing greater clarity to our picture of personality disorder than could have been previously achieved. Using analytic theory as the roadmap and the Rorschach as the camera, that is precisely what they have accomplished in *Rorschach Assessment of Aggressive and Psychopathic Personalities.*

It is the aggressive, antisocial segment of the personality disorder spectrum to which Gacono and Meloy apply this integration of assessment technology and personality theory. These are syndromes with which they—as clinicians doing assessment, treatment, and administration in a variety of inpatient, outpatient, and criminal justice settings—have over a decade of experience. Their experience insures an important focus. Throughout the extensive data presentations that form the book's core they never forget that it is the working clinician for whom they are writing.

The wide-ranging relevance of psychodynamic theory for understanding psychopathic function has been one of Dr. Meloy's most important insights. Much of the book's organization follows from that insight. The authors' presentation of child, adolescent, and adult female data emphasizes the importance of developmental and gender issues. Their inclusion of data on individuals with both schizophrenic and antisocial diagnoses allows us to consider the complexity of multilayered psychopathology.

From a substantive standpoint, Gacono and Meloy have developed the clearest picture yet available of the aggressive/antisocial part of the personality disorder continuum. From a methodological standpoint, it is important to note that they've done it by bringing together the hard-won Rorschach and personality theory advances of the last quarter-century. We can hope that this book is the first of many in which clinical researchers use sophisticated assessment and theory to bring the sort of clarity to other syndromes that Gacono and Meloy provide for the antisocial and psychopathic syndromes.

—Philip Erdberg

He who bears the brand of
Cain shall rule the earth.

—George Bernard Shaw
Back to Methuselah (1921) 1.2.

And I looked, and behold a pale horse:
and his name that sat on him was Death,
and Hell followed with him.

—Revelation 6:8

Introduction

This book represents for us the culmination of a decade of clinical research with aggressive and psychopathic personalities. Our thinking has been shaped by clinical experience and theoretical writings concerning the severe personality disorders. As collaborators our styles have been complementary. Reid Meloy has always been the theoretician and clinician firmly grounded in traditional psychoanalytic writings. His early career work was largely with schizophrenic patients in a variety of clinical settings, and then shifted to male and female adult criminal populations in maximum security settings. Carl Gacono's thinking sprung from clinical observations of conduct-disordered children during play therapy, adolescent delinquents in multifamily treatment groups, psychotherapy with antisocial personality disordered (ASPD) adults, and the administration of hundreds of Rorschachs and Revised Psychopathy Checklists (PCL–Rs).[1] Theories have provided descriptions for and incisive understanding of what we have observed with patients; and our observations, in turn, have prompted us to delineate and expand the boundaries of theory.[2]

---

[1]Later work at Atascadero State Hospital would include evaluating psychopaths, sexual homicide perpetrators, sadists, and schizophrenic ASPDs.

[2]Reid Meloy's first book integrated psychoanalytic and psychobiological knowledge to further understanding of the psychopath (Meloy, 1988). His second book probed violent relationships from the perspective of object relations and attachment theories (Meloy, 1992b). Carl Gacono has made a number of previous contributions to the Rorschach literature (Gacono, 1988, 1990, 1992; Gacono & Meloy, 1991, 1992, 1993; Gacono, Meloy, & Berg, 1992; Gacono, Meloy, & Heaven, 1990).

The chapters of this book evolved from empirical data, and in the style of Cleckley (1976), compose a clinical and research textbook where observation and theory converge. We hope our case examples and large-group studies provide clinicians with fascinating, sound, and useful data that will stand the test of time. For every question answered, however, several more beg to be asked.

When we coauthored our first article (Gacono & Meloy, 1988), and individually authored a dissertation (Gacono, 1988) and a book (Meloy, 1988), subsequent collaborative research was only a pleasant, unfulfilled inchoate wish. The strength of our friendship and commitment to the study of violence and psychopathy has sustained our 10-year collaboration. We have never had research grants, and continue to have none at present, but have managed to bootleg research time from our other clinical obligations. This Rorschach work has truly been a "labor of love," which only those fortunate enough to become enamored with the richness and complexity of those 10 inkblots will understand.

Our research subjects are a different story. We both have had extensive clinical experience with these loveless individuals held in county jails, state prisons, forensic hospitals, and private psychiatric hospitals. These subjects elicit extreme, and usually negative, countertransference reactions from both clinicians and society.

Adult institutions are distinguished by their relatively high frequency of psychopathic residents. Best estimates are that approximately 23% of male inmates and 11% of male forensic psychiatric inpatients would meet our criteria for psychopathy, or what has been traditionally known as the Cleckley psychopath (Cleckley, 1976/1941; Hare, 1991). Prevalence rates for women are three to five times less, given the gender-related aspect of psychopathy.[3]

These "failed" psychopaths, by virtue of their incarceration, have been the focus of a large amount of clinical attention during the past century, but not until relatively recently has there been an empirically sound measure of the construct *psychopathy* (Hare, 1980, 1985, 1991; see chapter 5 for a review). The PCL–R (Hare, 1991) has catalyzed research during the past decade by providing a reliable and valid method for classifying adults as psychopathic or not. The 20-item scale (see Table 1.1) functions well as an independent classification from which other dependent measures, such as the Rorschach, can be taken. It is this simple methodology that has shaped much of our work, and will inform future endeavors.

But isn't it enough to know that these are bad people who do bad things? We think not. The ascendancy of the socially deviant model of antisocial behavior, most apparent in the *DSM–II–IV* series of the American Psychiatric Association (APA, 1968, 1980, 1987, 1994), has supported the notion that to describe behavior of antisocial individuals is enough. But what this model has failed to satisfy is

---

[3] The lifetime risk of ASPD (*DSM–III–R*) is 4.5% for males and 0.8% for females, for a combined risk of 2.8% in the general population (Regier & Robins, 1991). Approximately one third of ASPD individuals will meet criteria for primary psychopathy.

TABLE 1.1
The Psychopathy Checklist–Revised

1. Glibness/superficial charm
2. Grandiose sense of self-worth
3. Need for stimulation/proneness to boredom
4. Pathological lying
5. Conning/manipulative
6. Lack of remorse or guilt
7. Shallow affect
8. Callous/lack of empthy
9. Parasitic lifestyle
10. Poor behavioral controls
11. Promiscuous sexual behavior
12. Early behavior problems
13. Lack of realistic, long-term goals
14. Impulsivity
15. Irresponsibility
16. Failure to accept responsibility for own actions
17. Many short-term marital relationships
18. Juvenile delinquency
19. Revocation of conditional release
20. Criminal versatility

Note. From Hare (1991). Copyright 1991 by Multihealth Systems Inc. Reprinted by permission.

clinical understanding of the disorder. A search for clinical knowledge leads to questions of motivation and meaning, prompting further inquiry into the thought organization, affective life, defensive operations, impulses, and object relations of psychopaths and other aggressive individuals.

Our work, then, becomes another logical contribution to understanding psychopathy and aggression. It is our best effort to psychometrically "map" the intrapsychic life of these subjects, and those aggressive children and adolescents we consider at risk for the later development of psychopathic character.

THE RORSCHACH

We selected the Rorschach as our dependent measure and primary investigative tool for a variety of reasons. First, we both have had extensive training in its administration and interpretation. Carl Gacono's graduate studies included Rorschach training with James Madero, PhD, utilizing the Comprehensive System, Kwawer's (1980) borderline object relations categories, and the Lerner and Lerner (1980) defense scales. Subsequently, he trained and consulted with Phil Erdberg and Paul Lerner. Reid Meloy was originally taught the Rorschach by Sidney Smith, PhD, during his graduate studies, utilizing the methodology of Rapaport, Gill, and Schafer (1945) and the form-level scoring of Martin Mayman, PhD. He subsequently was trained in the Comprehensive System through

Rorschach Workshops, his principal teachers being Phil Erdberg, John Exner, Jr., and Irving Weiner. Both of us received our doctorates in clinical psychology from United States International University.

Second, the Rorschach itself is ranked eighth among psychological tests used in a national survey of outpatient mental health facilities (Piotrowski & Keller, 1989). It is the second most widely used test with adolescent patients, and is the most popular projective technique with this population (Archer, Maruish, Imhof, & Piotrowski, 1991). It is also the second most widely used psychological test by members of the Society for Personality Assessment, an international organization of psychological scientists and practitioners (Piotrowski, Sherry, & Keller, 1985). Watkins (1991) reviewed 30 years of survey studies (1960–1990) of psychological assessment and found that the Rorschach was one of the most frequently used and consistently mentioned psychological tests in most clinical settings, was one of the most popular instruments, along with the Minnesota Multiphasic Personality Inventory (MMPI), to research, and has received continuing emphasis in most clinical psychology training programs. In forensic evaluations, psychiatrists will specifically request the use of the Rorschach approximately 25% of the time (Rogers & Cavanaugh, 1983). It is a psychological test that has weathered the vicissitudes of time and opinion quite well.

Third, the five most common scoring systems for the Rorschach have been integrated and standardized over the past 30 years by John Exner, Jr., culminating in the Comprehensive System, a reliable and valid interpretive methodology for understanding the Rorschach. We would like to acknowledge Dr. Exner's enormous contribution to Rorschach science, and our indebtedness to his accomplishments concerning the Rorschach and personality structure.

Fourth, developments parallel to the Comprehensive System have occurred within the psychoanalytic community. Psychoanalytically trained psychologists have charted new territory by attempting to understand the content of the Rorschach with empirical methods consistent with psychoanalytic theory. These methods have generally focused upon object relations (Blatt & Lerner, 1983; Kwawer, 1979, 1980), defenses (Cooper, Perry, & Arnow, 1988; Lerner & Lerner, 1980), development and psychopathology (Urist, 1977), and thought organization (Athey, 1974; Meloy & Singer, 1991). Much of the psychoanalytic Rorschach research since the late 1970s is signified in four books (Kissen, 1986; Kwawer, Lerner, Lerner, & Sugarman, 1980; Lerner, 1991; Lerner & Lerner, 1988).

Fifth, our work has attempted to integrate both a *structural* and *content* understanding of the Rorschach (Erdberg, 1993) by applying several different scoring systems and methods to our research protocols. We think this approach, wherein the Comprehensive System (Exner, 1986a) is used to understand *psychostructure* and various psychoanalytic methods are used to understand *psychodynamics*, is most fruitful, and has yielded both important nomothetic (Gacono et al., 1992) and idiographic (Gacono, 1992; Meloy, 1992b; Meloy & Gacono, 1992b) findings. Our approach is illustrated in Fig. 1.1.

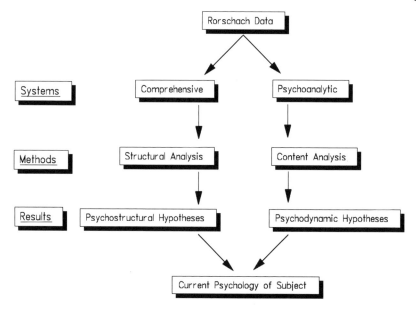

FIG. 1.1.   Approach to the Rorschach data.

Sixth, self-report measures with criminal populations are notoriously unreliable (Hare, 1991). In both clinical and research settings, when the subject is a forensic patient, the psychologist is wise to minimize the use of self-report tests. Only those tests with robust measures of distortion, such as the MMPI and MMPI–2 (Minnesota Multiphasic Personality Inventory, Version 2), should be considered. Self-report tests with high face validity, such as the Beck Depression Inventory, should be assiduously avoided, unless they are being purposefully used to measure distortion by comparing them with other less obvious measures. The Rorschach is unique in the sense that it is a perceptual-associative-judgmental task that partially bypasses volitional controls, yet yields important data, some of which are projected material (Meloy, 1991b). We have also found, contrary to our expectations, that psychopaths generally produce a normative amount of Rorschach responses, at least in a research setting. We have purged our group samples of protocols with less than 14 responses without great heartache, because they were few in number. An individual protocol with fewer than 14 responses, however, still yields important data about the subject when Lambda is not elevated (< .85).

Seventh, the Rorschach is the most empirically defensible instrument to access data concerning a subject that is both psychological and preconscious, or unconscious. This *level* of access is consonant with our notion that psychopathy, and other personality disorders, will only be understood when an inclusive "levels" approach is undertaken (Gacono & Meloy, 1988, 1993; Gacono et al., 1992; Stone & Dellis, 1960). This approach is illustrated in Table 1.2, and suggests a multimethod study of personality that recognizes the social, psychological, and biological dimensions of such a complex construct.

TABLE 1.2
A Multimethod "Levels" Model of Understanding Personality

Level	Method	Research Example
I. Behavior	Observation	Robins (1966)
		Hare (1991)
II. Conscious Cognitions	Self-Report Measures	Yochelson & Samenow (1977a, 1977b)
III. Unconscious Structure and Function	Projective Testing	Gacono & Meloy (1992)
IV. Biology	GSR, EEG, HR, RCBF, CAT, PET, MRI, BEAM, ERP	Hare (1991) Raine & Dunkin (1990)

In this table, both the level and method columns could be generalized to any personality disorder, although the representative research column is limited to the study of psychopathy. As noted, our work has focused at the third level of unconscious structure and function. Histrionic personality disorder, for example, could also be studied with this multimethod, and, to a certain degree, was by Horowitz (1991).

And eighth, the time is right for exploring claims of early researchers (Lindner, 1943; see Appendix A) who, although frustrated in their attempts to empirically test their assertions, believed that the Rorschach was a valuable aid in making the diagnosis of psychopathic personality.

APPROACH TO THE DATA

We approached the Rorschach data from four different perspectives: development and pathogenesis, interpretation, construct validity, and individual differences.

Development and Pathogenesis

Extant research suggests that psychopathy is a stable trait (Hare, 1991) that shows little change across the adult life span (Hare, McPherson, & Forth, 1988). This prompted us to begin to search for intrapsychic risk factors in childhood and adolescence that might predict psychopathy in adulthood. Although a conduct disorder diagnosis in childhood or adolescence predicts an antisocial personality disorder in adulthood (Robins, 1972), and certain central and peripheral autonomic measures in adolescence appear to predict criminality in adulthood (Raine, Venables, & Williams, 1990), most conduct-disordered children and adolescents do not become ASPD adults, let alone psychopaths.[4] Is there a way to identify with

---

[4]Approximately 25% of CD children will meet criteria for ASPD when they reach adulthood (Regier & Robins, 1991). If only one third of ASPD adults are primary psychopaths, we can estimate that only 8% of CD children are at risk for primary psychopathy in adulthood.

the Rorschach the relatively small proportion of conduct-disordered children and adolescents at risk for psychopathic character in adulthood? This question led to the gathering of Rorschach data on samples of conduct-disordered children (see chapter 2) and adolescents (see chapter 3), and a beginning search for indices that might help identify the psychopathically at-risk subjects.

Similarly the pathogenesis of psychopathy is gender related and also may be differentially expressed in mentally ill subjects with concurrent character pathology (Meloy, 1988). We have therefore included chapters on a sample of female prisoners' Rorschachs (see chapter 4), and a sample of schizophrenic ASPDs (see chapter 6) for comparison to our ASPD male sample (see chapter 5). There is little published research on the female psychopath (Hare, 1991), and none on the schizophrenic psychopath. Our hope is that the data in these chapters describe the psychological operations of these heretofore unexamined groups, and prompt further comparative research with other samples. The term *schizopath*, and research concerning schizotaxia (Meehl, 1962, 1989) and schizotypy (Henderson & Kalichman, 1990), find relevance in our work with the schizophrenic psychopath.

In chapter 9 the Rorschachs of a sample of sexual homicide perpetrators are presented and discussed. Their protocols highlight the Rorschach's sensitivity in discriminating one extremely aggressive sexual disorder from other aggressive antisocial disorders. The final chapter (10) extends our thinking on the relationship between various levels of the psychopathic mind.

Interpretation

Our interpretive approach to the Rorschach data, as mentioned earlier, is both *psychostructural* and *psychodynamic* (see Fig. 1.1). The psychostructural data are derived through scoring and interpretation using the Comprehensive System (Exner, 1986a). We have utilized the Rorschach Scoring Program, Version 2 (RSP–2; Exner, Cohen, & Mcguire, 1990) and the Rorschach Interpretive Assistance Program, Version 2 (RIAP–2; Exner, 1990a) for computerized scoring and the generation of clinical hypotheses. Group descriptive data were generated by Philip Erdberg, PhD.

The psychodynamic data are derived through three scoring methods, all of which we have found to have satisfactory interjudge reliability: Primitive interpersonal modes of relating (Kwawer, 1980) is a categorization of Rorschach responses that are preoedipal and pathognomonic of a borderline or psychotic personality organization; and two interrelated defense scales (Cooper et al., 1988; Lerner & Lerner, 1980) score a variety of neurotic, borderline, and psychotic defenses as manifested in Rorschach content. We have found the Cooper et al. method more useful because it is not limited to whole human responses (Gacono, 1988).

Additional experimental Rorschach scores centering on intrapsychic aggressive drive derivatives (Gacono, 1988, 1990; Meloy & Gacono, 1992a) are also noted for select samples and cases. Chapter 8 is devoted to the scoring and interpretation of our aggression indices. The measurement of aggression and narcissism is central to understanding aggressive character pathology; therefore chapter 7 explores pathological narcissism and the Rorschach reflection response.

All of the psychoanalytic scoring methods assume that personality has both a level of organization and a particular character style (Kernberg, 1975, 1984). Our work has empirically supported these theoretical formulations, and we continue to find it clinically quite meaningful, as do others (Acklin, 1992; Lerner, 1991; Murray, 1992; Peterson, 1992b).

Construct Validity

Our earlier articles explored various aspects of psychopathy that we believed needed further construct validation: borderline personality organization (Gacono, 1988, 1990), narcissism and hysteria (Gacono et al., 1990), a lack of attachment and anxiety (Gacono & Meloy, 1991; Weber, Meloy, & Gacono, 1992), and aggression (Meloy & Gacono, 1992a). This book continues the construct validation of psychopathy and is based on the dynamic interplay between empirical findings and theory: Each becomes an incremental building block, or a discriminating marker, for the other, depending on our empirical results and theoretical creativity.

Our real-world anchors for both our Rorschach data and theorizing are the behavioral and trait measures we have used for subject selection. These measures include *DSM–III–R* diagnostic categories, PCL–R quantitative ratings, and specific behaviors, such as sexual homicide. As Lanyon and Goodstein (1971) wrote, "construct validity is the gradual accumulation of supporting evidence garnered from a variety of research findings, arranged to demonstrate a *network of relationships* among the measure in question and other relevant concepts" (pp. 131–132).

Individual Differences

We consider ourselves both lumpers and sorters. We value nomothetic (group) research to understand similarities, and we treasure idiographic (individual) research to understand differences (Meloy & Gacono, 1992b, 1993). Eysenck (1967) has been the most vocal advocate of this dual approach to personality research, and we ally with his position. It was most recently apparent to us, for example, when we investigated the aggression response and the Rorschach (Meloy & Gacono, 1992a). We found no significant nomothetic (group) differences between psychopaths and nonpsychopaths, except for the sadomasochistic response (SM); but did find the various aggression indices a useful source of data for understanding drive derivatives and object relations in any one forensic case. Idiographic examination is consistent with the original intent of the Rorschach method that valued individual nuances and facets as essential for valid interpretation (Klopfer & Kelley, 1942; Rapaport, Gill, & Schafer, 1945). Unfortunately, an informal review of current psychological assessment journals will produce few case studies, and the overwhelming preferences among journal editors are nomothetic, comparative studies.

In our attempt to balance these research approaches, we present both nomothetic and idiographic data in each chapter when appropriate and available. This should appeal to both the Rorschach researcher's interest in group differences and the Rorschach clinician's curiosity about the individual case.

Descriptive and Inferential Statistics

Our book is replete with descriptive statistics of both group and individual Rorschach data. But we have intentionally limited the inferential statistics to only underscore certain theoretical points in the narrative. We made this decision for two reasons: First, inferential comparison of our various groups to other control groups was beyond the original intent and scope of the data gathering; and second, the intent of our book is to provide the reader with normative and descriptive Rorschach data to further research or clinical acumen. In this sense, our book lays the groundwork for many subsequent scientific articles concerning the Rorschach and psychopathy. Our work becomes the compulsive person's dream (JRM) or nightmare (CBG): It has just begun, or will it ever end?

We include an article written by Robert Lindner, PhD, over 50 years ago (see Appendix A). A graduate of Cornell University in 1938 with a doctorate in psychology, he completed psychoanalytic training and was analyzed by Theodor Reik. He eventually took a job at Lewisburg Federal Penitentiary in Pennsylvania, and there wrote his first book in 1944, *Rebel Without a Cause: The Hypnoanalysis of a Criminal Psychopath*. During World War II, he continued to work throughout the Federal Bureau of Prisons, and eventually practiced psychoanalysis in the Baltimore area. He was one of the few nonphysicians to be trained as a psychoanalyst, was shunned by the medical establishment, and a year before he died, saw his most famous work published, *The Fifty Minute Hour*. Robert Lindner was hospitalized at Johns Hopkins with a congenital heart defect at the age of 41. He died on February 27, 1956. His untimely death deprived the psychological community of a clinically astute mind and a first-rate researcher. His popular books overshadowed his less well known scholarly papers concerning the Rorschach. Although unable to empirically demonstrate his assertions, Lindner (1943) believed the Rorschach could be used as an aid for diagnosing psychopathic personality. We continue on the path that he walked for a very short time, and dedicate this book to his memory.

CHAPTER 2

The Child Antisocial Pattern

There is an American ballad in which a murderer to be hanged on the gallows before the eyes of the community, instead of feeling duly chastened, begins to berate the onlookers, ending every salvo of defiance with the words, "God damn your eyes." Many a small child, shamed beyond endurance, may be in a chronic mood (although not in possession of either the courage or the words) to express defiance in similar terms.

—Erikson (1950, p. 253)

Skillful clinicians fortunate enough to work with conduct-disordered (CD) children often find the experience both gratifying and illuminating. A psychodynamic conceptualization of developmental processes is particularly useful for understanding the CD child. Part-object relations, primitive defensive operations, and primary process manifest on a symbolic but readily observable level through the child's play (A. Freud, 1936, 1974; Halpern, 1953; Klein, 1946, 1963; Russ, 1988; Waelder, 1933). These pre-oedipal psychodynamics provide a poignant view of inner turmoil (Rabinovitch, 1949). Psychodynamics may resonate with the clinician's own unanalyzed and sometimes forgotten parts. For some, resonance leads to empathy. Others devalue and distance from the child as primitive processes evoke their forgotten demons.[1]

---

[1] In certain cases distancing is a result of realistic and necessary precautions rather than countertransference. Winnicott (1958a) wisely expressed caution related to a child patient who became a psychopathic adult: "Nevertheless I am afraid to follow-up his case for fear that I should become involved again with a psychopath, and I prefer that society should continue to take the burden of his management" (p. 306).

The CD child struggles with narcissistic vulnerability (Aichhorn, 1925; Smith, 1994; Willock, 1986) in ways similar to the ASPD adult. "To cope with the hurt, angry, frightening belief that no one really cares about them, they act as if they do not care about anybody else" (Willock, 1986, p. 63; 1987). Evident from the first contact, narcissistic vulnerability in the child must be acknowledged and respected by the clinician. Six-year-old Tommy came to his second therapy session and asked with puzzled hope, "Where did you get that drawing?" The drawing had come from another child patient on the unit. Tommy's fragile narcissism, now dependent on this potential relationship with the therapist as object, was threatened. He wanted reassurance that he was special to his therapist. The doctor replied, "Well Tommy, it's true I do talk with other children during the week. However, for the hour you come to see me you are the most important little boy I see," reinforcing the constraints of reality while bolstering Tommy's need to feel uniquely valued. Discrepancies within Tommy's psychological testing later revealed small, inadequate human figures, constricted but anxious Rorschach responses, and TAT (thematic apperception test) themes pervaded with grandiosity. Not infrequently therapists are greeted by competing voices when entering a children's psychiatric unit, "Do you need me? Do you need me now?" These CD children are unable to acknowledge their need for the therapist as object (T = 0) and must project. To do otherwise risks vulnerability to further disappointments.

Some CD children are hypothesized to come from overindulged (spoiled) backgrounds, whereas others have been severely deprived or abused (Aichhorn, 1925; Levy, 1950; Spitz, 1949). In some cases, the overindulged pattern forms the template for an adult narcissistic personality whereas the deprived becomes an antisocial personality (Gacono, 1988).[2] Deprivation may begin before birth with the child being unwanted (Willock, 1986). In both cases part-object relationships exist between mother and child. The child is treated as an extension of the parent. Severe disappointments in early attachment figures are apparent.

Aggressive drives in CD, "borderline" (Leichtman & Shapiro, 1980), and "prepsychotic" (Rausch de Traubenberg & Boizou, 1980) children reign over softer libidinal ones, whereas normal processes of identification, internalization, and attachment are disrupted (Bowlby, 1973, 1982; Meloy, 1988; Morrison, 1978; Olesker, 1980). Egos are deficient without self-soothing capacities. Part-object attachments, splitting mechanisms, and shame predominate over whole-object relations, repression, and the experience of guilt and gratitude. "Such children relate to others indiscriminately as need satisfying objects or enter into intense, controlling, dependent or hostile dependent relationships" (Leichtman & Shapiro, 1980, p. 350). The deprived child's superego suffers from a deficiency in identification (Karpman, 1949) whereas the overindulged child's superego impairment results from a strong identification with the idealized part maternal

---

[2]Underlying biological substrates likely play a role in this differentiation as well.

object (Aichhorn, 1925; Karpman, 1959; Levy, 1950). The superego does not become internalized but remains dependent on the environment (Friedlander, 1945). "Healthy ego and superego formation and functioning both lie somewhere between the Scylla and Charybdis of excessive indulgence on the one side, and excessive frustration on the other" (Teicholz, 1978, p. 843). When 7-year-old Heidi, who had been severely physically and sexually abused, was evaluated, primitive splitting and severe affective lability made standardized testing impossible. During a diagnostic play interview the precocious child's affect and perceptions of the examiner rapidly shifted. Her personal questioning offered hope of attachment, "Are you married? Do you live alone?" Physical and verbal aggression negated a potential bond while protecting a divided ego. Trying to spit on and kick the examiner, she screamed, "You fucking jerk. You asshole!" Eventually Heidi physically separated herself from the examiner, retreating to safety underneath the office desk and ashamed by her loss of control. This "borderline" child, at the mercy of primitive superego precursors and frightened by attachment, made herself the devalued and discarded object (Willock, 1986).

Unlike the antisocial adult who for the most part has abandoned his search for an idealized object (Aichhorn, 1925; Kohut, 1971; Winnicott, 1958a), most CD children have not given up. Only the most severely psychopathic or autistic children are unable to idealize, a necessary process for attachment (Rabinovitch, 1949; Spitz, 1949). Idealization stimulates the feeling of hope and potential for further disappointment. Bonding difficulties may manifest through the child's inability to attach to toy objects and play. When bonding is absent the CD child will race from one toy to another, never developing a coherent play theme. The therapist will feel drained by the child's emptiness. Four-year-old David was restricted in his ability to attach and commented on the doctor's conversation with Mr. Potatohead, "That's Mr. Potatohead. He's not real, can't talk." Limiting the number of potential play objects may help to determine if distractibility or a lack of bonding is the main consideration.

An infantile grandiose self-structure may take on organizing functions not available to other borderline children. The CD child may begin to fantasize himself to be superior while adapting an identification with the aggressor (Bilmes, 1967; A. Freud, 1936). Later his passivity will be transformed into active, aggressive, and perhaps sadistic behavior. Evidence of aggressive identifications is often revealed on the Rorschach. The identification of the severe CD child, like Lucifer in Milton's *Paradise Lost*, proclaims "Here at least we shall be free; th'Almighty hath not built here for his envy, will not drive us hence: Here we may reign secure, and in my choice to reign is worth ambition though in Hell: Better to reign in hell, than serve in heaven" (Milton, 1968, p. 54).

When attachment does develop, the child is extremely vulnerable and interpersonally sensitive to disruptions. At the end of his third session Tommy requested to take a toy car from the therapist's office. The importance of protecting this "transitional object" from harm was discussed at length with him.

Tommy agreed to bring "speedy" (the little VW bug) to every session. Away from the sessions "speedy" was placed at the back of his dresser drawer. Tommy spent much time caring for "speedy" and painting the little car with designs. On days when he felt out of control the little car would race across the therapist's desk, mirroring the anxious attachment that Tommy felt. The doctor prevented the car from falling off the edge of the table as he interpreted Tommy's need to feel safe. Eventually Tommy requested that "speedy" accompany him on home visits. Disrupted attachments increase already abundant shameful feelings because the CD child will feel more shame around his attachment needs (Bilmes, 1967). Splitting may facilitate the child hating the person on whom he would depend (Aichhorn, 1925; Bowlby, 1984; Redl & Wineman, 1951; Spiegel, 1966).

Aggression and regression occur in response to threatened attachments (Leichtman & Shapiro, 1980). Tommy kept a treasured picture of himself and the therapist. Pictures were important to him. He often expressed distress over his lack of evocative recall (Russ, 1988), "not remembering what people looked like." As therapy approached termination, he asked, "Would the picture [with the therapist] be ruined if someone spit on it?" Tommy feared that his angry and hurtful feelings might destroy the soothing, but fragile, internalized image of his therapist. In most CD children aggression stimulated by object loss is primarily constructive and only secondarily destructive (Bender, 1943; Willock, 1986; Winnicott, 1958b). It is a cry for help that signals both object loss and a fear of ego disintegration. At times stealing may symbolize an attempt to retake what has been lost (Winnicott, 1958a). By adulthood, however, stabilized defenses and cognitive skills (Piaget, 1965) allow anger to be used to protect the grandiose self-structure (Kernberg, 1975), and secondarily to intimidate and control the external object world (Bursten, 1972, 1973; Gacono & Meloy, 1988; Meloy, 1988).

At what point does the CD child give up idealized yearnings and his expression of hope? To date no longitudinal Rorschach studies have assessed shifts in idealization patterns throughout the childhood period. Prior to age 7, however, there is emotional discomfort and anxiety concerning dependency needs (Bowlby, 1973; Sontag, 1959). Somewhere during latency and into adolescence instinctual desires become "invariably more important than satisfactions gained from an object relationship" (Friedlander, 1945, p. 190). Evidence for a decreased interest in object ties is suggested by T-less protocols in abused and CD children (Exner, 1986a; Exner & Weiner, 1982).

In this chapter we review the conduct disorder diagnostic criteria (APA, 1987). The Rorschachs of normal and CD children are discussed from a developmental perspective. We then present and discuss Comprehensive System data for 60 CD children. The object relations (Mutuality of Autonomy Scale scores; Urist, 1977) of these troubled children are statistically compared with a group of nonpatient children (Tuber, 1989b). The chapter ends with the tragic case study of Damion, a 9-year-old CD child at risk for the later development of adult ASPD and possibly psychopathy.

THE CONDUCT DISORDER DIAGNOSIS

The conduct disorder diagnosis (see Table 2.1) is one of three childhood disorders included in the Disruptive Behavior Disorders section of *DSM–III–R* (APA, 1987). A persistent pattern (duration greater than 6 months) of violating others' rights and major age-appropriate societal norms distinguishes CD from the other two disorders, attention-deficit hyperactivity and oppositional defiant. According to *DSM–III–R*, in conduct disorder,

> [P]hysical aggression is common. Children or adolescents with this disorder usually initiate aggression, may be physically cruel to other people or to animals, and frequently deliberately destroy other people's property (this may include fire setting). They may engage in stealing with confrontation of the victim, as in mugging, purse snatching, extortion, or armed robbery. At later ages, the physical violence may take the form of rape, assault, or, in rare cases, homicide.
>
> Covert stealing is common. This may range from borrowing others' possessions to shoplifting, forgery, and breaking into someone else's house, building, or car. Lying and cheating in games or in schoolwork are common. Often a youngster with this disorder is truant from school, and may run away from home. (p. 53)

Although the 13 items comprising the CD criteria are listed in descending order of discriminating power, psychologically diverse children can receive a CD diagnosis. A combination factorial indicates that there are 8,100 possible combinations of 3 or more criteria out of 13 that would yield a diagnosis of conduct disorder (Nancy McGreevy, personal communication, October 1992). A CD diagnosis based on a history of physical fighting, cruelty to animals, using a weapon in more than one fight, and forcing someone into sexual activity is likely to belong to a quite different child than one who is classified as CD by virtue of running away from home at least two times, being often truant from school, and having stolen without confrontation of the victim on more than one occasion. The heterogeneity of the CD diagnosis has been, in part, addressed by designating three subtypes: group type, solitary aggressive type, and undifferentiated type,[3] and rating the disorder as mild, moderate, or severe. The CD diagnosis appears to be gender related as 9% of males and 2% of females under the age of 18 receive this diagnosis. Gender differences relate to biological differences in aggression and social conditioning (Meloy, 1988, 1992b).

Assessing what motivates a CD child's disruptive behavior is essential for separating character from neurotic conflict[4] and making treatment or dispositional

---

[3]CD group type includes conduct problems occurring primarily in group activities with peers where aggressive physical behaviors may or may not occur. The essential feature of the solitary aggressive type is a pattern of physical aggression toward others initiated by the child outside of a group context. The undifferentiated subtype presents a mixture of features not fitting either of the other types (APA, 1987).

[4]The ability of structural data to differentiate character from neurotic problems prior to age 12 is uncertain. Clinicians should rely on historical information. After age 12 elevated egocentricity ratios, evidence of poor impulse control, es > EA, elevated S, lower pure H, and poor form quality

TABLE 2.1
Diagnostic Criteria for Conduct Disorder

A. A disturbance of conduct lasting at least 6 months, during which at least three of the following have been present:
 1. Has stolen without confrontation of a victim on more than one occasion (including forgery).
 2. Has run away from home overnight at least twice while living in parental or parental surrogate home (or once without returning).
 3. Often lies (other than to avoid physical or sexual abuse).
 4. Has deliberately engaged in fire setting.
 5. Is often truant from school (for older person, absent from work).
 6. Has broken into someone else's house, building, or car.
 7. Has deliberately destroyed others' property (other than by fire setting).
 8. Has been physically cruel to animals.
 9. Has forced someone into sexual activity with him or her.
 10. Has used a weapon in more than one fight.
 11. Often initiates physical fights.
 12. Has stolen with confrontation of a victim (e.g., mugging, purse snatching, extortion, armed robbery).
 13. Has been physically cruel to people.
B. If 18 or older, does not meet criteria for antisocial personality disorder (APA, 1987, p. 55).

recommendations (Exner & Weiner, 1982; Morrison, 1978). This is particularly difficult prior to age 5 (Leichtman & Shapiro, 1980). Exner and Weiner proposed five behavioral categories that aid the classification of childhood behavioral problems: by-products of psychosis, organic problems, sociological antecedents, neurotic issues, and character problems.

When social antecedents motivate dyssocial behavior CD children usually belong to a deviant subculture. Solitary antisocial acts are not expected. The neurotic child is motivated by underlying conflict. Loss, the need to be admired, distress, and mild family problems precipitate problem behaviors. Capacity for interpersonal closeness is maintained in both deviant social and neurotic types (Exner & Weiner, 1982).

By contrast, character problems reflect an "asocial orientation" (Exner & Weiner, 1982, p. 340). These children are detached loners (Bowlby, 1982). Group affiliation is generally superficial, possibly motivated by secondary gain. Problem behaviors result from a disregard for the rights and feelings of others and inability or unwillingness to control behavior. These children show little concern for the effects of their behavior on others and may volitionally use their aggression to obtain what they want (Weiner, 1975, 1982). The Exner and Weiner character-disordered child most closely resembles the CD solitary aggressive type, and those at highest risk for developing psychopathy.

consisting primarily of unusual answers suggest character problems (Exner & Weiner, 1982). The neurotic record will indicate stabilized and premature use of resources, elevated M (Campo, 1988), elevated EA (unless situational stress elevates es), elevated T, C', V, Y, m (more distress), FC > CF + C, and low Afr. Exner (1988a) also stressed the presence of Level 1 versus Level 2 special scores in nonpatient children.

We think these severely conduct-disordered children (psychopathic) can be distinguished by latency age.[5] They are characterized by aggressively sadistic behavior, a complete absence of attachment capacity, lack of remorse, shame, or empathy, severe identity problems, and grandiosity. It is important to remember, however, that most CD children are not at risk to develop psychopathic character, although CD in childhood is a prerequisite for ASPD in adulthood (APA, 1987, 1994).

CHILDREN'S RORSCHACHS

Although some authors believe the Rorschach to be valid beginning at age $2\frac{1}{2}$ or 3 (Ames, Learned, Metraux, & Walker, 1952), most agree that by age 5 to 7 the test is useful (Exner & Weiner, 1982; Leichtman, 1988; Levitt & Trauma, 1972). At any age, testing borderline children warrants special attention. CD children can be untestable, testable with modification of standard instructions, or testable with standard Comprehensive System administration procedures. Young children (ages 3 to 7) are sensitive to disruptive effects of the unstructured, affectively stimulating Rorschach blots. The test raises anxieties threatening ego integrity (Leichtman & Shapiro, 1980). Bobby, a 6-year-old, untestable, CD child, saw snakes on Card III. He began to wriggle his body and hiss, stating, "They're going to bite you." Bobby was not able to complete the Rorschach test. When asked if he needed staff intervention to help feel safe, he requested that the examiner hold him. Despite never being completed or scored, this brief Rorschach experience (Lerner, 1991; Schachtel, 1966) provided important information relevant to Bobby's psychodynamics and treatment. With the untestable child, history, behavioral observations, and diagnostic play interviews provide information not available through standard Rorschach administration (ages 3 to 7). Through the diagnostic play interview the "untestable child's" psychodynamics are revealed.

Distractibility, short attention span, and proneness to boredom contribute to some CD children's difficulties completing a valid Rorschach. The borderline child reacts to testing and the examiner in a chaotic, intense, and primitive manner (Leichtman & Shapiro, 1980). In these cases the examiner should consider conducting the inquiry directly after the free association to each response. Ames, Metraux, Rodell, and Walker (1974), whose childhood samples began at age 2, supported this revised administration and suggested that more useful records could be obtained in this manner (see also Leichtman, 1988). Although Exner and Weiner (1982) recommended caution in choosing altered testing procedures, they did not exclude the possibility with certain "difficult clients" (p. 30). When

---

[5]Identification of prominent psychopathic traits may coincide with the stabilization of certain Rorschach variables between 12 and 14.

the inquiry follows directly after each response, children do produce significantly more responses (20.4 vs. 16.2, $p < .05$; Leura & Exner, 1977). The only statistical differences in structural data were increased D and F answers (Leura & Exner, 1977). Leura and Exner did not analyze content differences.

Obtaining the illusive "valid" 14-response protocol (Exner, 1988b) with some CD children can be problematic. Despite the effects of R on structural summary data (Meyer, 1993) discarding the <14-response protocol eliminates useful data. Many of these Rorschachs *are* clinically valid. Understanding the reason for constriction in conjunction with careful content analysis often yields information relevant to the referral question. Rigid adherence to the 14-response rule, not always appropriate with adult ASPDs (Gacono & Meloy, 1992; Gacono et al., 1992), may be equally inappropriate with younger children as they normatively produce fewer mean responses than do adults (Ames et al., 1974; Exner & Weiner, 1982).

INTERPRETATION

Ames et al. (1952) stated, "Projective techniques, if carefully administered and skillfully interpreted in the perspective of adequate age norms, can throw light on each of these three factors: 1) the child's level of development, 2) his innate individuality, and 3) the kind of adjustment he is making to his life situation" (p. 1).

Many Rorschachers who work primarily with adults are reluctant to test children. They do not understand that the same principles of interpretation apply to both populations. Exner and Weiner (1982) emphasized that "Rorschach behavior means what it means regardless of the age of the subject" (p. 14). Interpretation becomes meaningful when data are compared to age-appropriate developmental norms.

Between the ages of 3 and 12 the child's biology and psychology undergo significant change. Defensive operations and object relations mature. Language develops. Cognitive schemata shift from concrete operations to increasing conceptual and abstracting ability (Piaget, 1965). Rorschachs manifest equivalent variability through childhood and latency:

> Some of the perceptual-cognitive features measured by the test, such as perceptual accuracy, appear to be quite stable or consistent very early in the developmental years. Others appear to remain unstable until mid-adolescence or adulthood and some, mainly related to situational stress, remain unstable indefinitely. (Exner & Weiner, 1982, p. 38)

Predictions prior to age 14–16 are difficult to make with certainty (Exner, Thomas, & Mason, 1985). Children generally produce fewer responses (R) than do adults. Fewer than 17 Rs is not uncommon before age 15. Greater than 25 Rs is unusual under age 13. Whole responses predominate over details (lowest percentage of detail responses between ages 3 and 6; Ames et al., 1974) until age 12. The child's expected W:D:Dd ratio is 5:4:1 (Ames et al., 1974). As they decrease in frequency W responses become better articulated (Ames et al., 1974). Between ages 5 and 7 DQv are not uncommon. After age 7 DQ+ increases (Exner & Weiner, 1982).

Erlebnistypus (EB; M:WSumC) stabilizes between ages 14 and 18. Introversive styles persist whereas extratensives change (ages 8 to 14). When experience actual (EA) increases, it remains so, although 50% of all subjects do not show more EA by age 14. The experience base (es) is unstable. FM and T remain consistent whereas clob[6] varies. Inanimate movement is unexpected between 2 and 10 years (Ames et al., 1974). FD begins to increase by age 8 (Exner & Weiner, 1982).

Although animal movement (FM) is present, human movement (M) does not occur until late childhood, surpassing FM in adolescence (Campo, 1988). M doubles in frequency from 12 years to adulthood (Viglione, 1990). M– is unexpected in nonpatient children (Viglione, 1990).

Color form (CF) occurs more frequently than form color (FC). By midadolescence FC begins to exceed CF+C. Once this shift occurs the pattern persists. However, only 50% of children exhibit this at age 14. Color naming (Cn) is found in $2\frac{1}{2}$- to 3-year-olds and rarely after.

At 9 years of age reflections are unusual and personals decrease. Records containing > 2 morbids (MOR) decrease between 8 and 10 years. Pure H, infrequent in children, gradually increases. Percentage of animal content (A%) approaches 50% throughout childhood. Prior to age 8 plants and inanimate objects predominate over human objects.

Extended form quality (X+%) begins to stabilize as early as age 8 (Exner et al., 1985; Viglione, 1990). Pure form (F+%) increases through childhood. Between 8 and 10 years Sum6 special scores > 4 decrease. Level 1 rather than Level 2 special scores are produced by nonpatient children (Exner, 1988a). Populars (P) are fairly constant throughout childhood.

CONDUCT-DISORDERED RORSCHACHS (*N* = 60)[7]

We gathered a sample of conduct-disordered children's Rorschachs from two private, nonprofit inpatient hospitals in northern and southern California (*N* = 60). Half of the sample were randomly drawn from a pool of 483 inpatient records in the course of data gathering for a doctoral dissertation (Weber, 1990). These

---

[6]Clob designated the use of dysphoric shading (darkness) as color (Ames et al., 1974).

[7]We thank Drs. Jacqueline Singer and Carey Weber for their contribution of protocols to this sample.

Rorschachs were administered by predoctoral interns trained in the Comprehensive System as part of the inpatient admission psychological evaluation to a southern California hospital. The diagnosis of conduct disorder was confirmed by Weber and Meloy's review of historical data and inpatient information. CD children with an additional comorbid diagnosis were eliminated from the sample. The other half of the sample were drawn from 700 clinical records of a clinical psychologist whose practice included evaluations at a northern California hospital. Dysthymic and psychotic diagnoses were eliminated from this sample, and the CD diagnosis was confirmed by review of historical records and other inpatient information.

All protocols were administered between 1986 and 1992. Only protocols containing ≥ 14 responses were included in the final sample ($N = 60$). All protocols were rescored by Meloy and Singer. Twenty protocols were selected at random to determine percentage of agreement across scoring categories and total agreement: location 98%, DQ 97%, determinants 91%, FQ 93%, content 92%, Z score 95%, special score 83%, total agreement 65%.

The age of the sample ranged from 5 to 12 ($M = 9.75$, $SD = 1.6$). There were 52 males and 8 females. Two thirds ($N = 40$) of the sample were solitary aggressive subtype (*DSM–III–R*; APA, 1987). Average IQ was 102 ($SD = 14$). The racial/ethnic makeup of the group was as follows: 73% (44) White, 13% (8) Black, 10% (6) Hispanic, and 4% (2) unknown. The CD group had a 43% (26) rate of documented sexual or physical abuse, and a 13% (8) rate of *diagnosed* ADHD.

Descriptive statistics and select ratios, percentages, and derivations are presented in Tables 2.2 and 2.3. Admittedly, the Rorschach data for this sample are developmentally "collapsed"—variables that change substantially between ages 5 and 12 are averaged, and actual variability is lost because small numbers did not allow for the development of separate CD norms for each age group. Nevertheless, we comment on certain variables that differ markedly from 9-year-old children (Exner, 1990b) because this is the average age of the CD sample. In reviewing the data, we have kept in mind findings that indicate that the majority of Rorschach variables do not stabilize until "the interval between 14 and 16" (Exner et al., 1985, p. 13).

Core Characteristics. The CD children produced R ($M = 20.37$) at the same frequency as normal 9-year-olds ($M = 20.53$). Greater variance, probably due to the greater age range, was evident. As noted in Table 2.3 most CD children produce high Lambdas (65% > .99, $M = 2.16$, $SD = 3.4$). This finding contrasts sharply with the expected pattern for normal 9-year-olds ($M = .81$, $SD = .37$). Lambda averages in normal children between 5 and 12 range from .49 to .86 (Exner, 1990b). Skewed Lambdas with a predominance of high Lambdas would be expected in CD populations as both high and low Lambdas have been associated with disruptive acting out in children (Exner & Weiner, 1982).

The majority of the CD children are ambitents and extratensives (82%). Only 18% are introversives (see Table 2.3). They are not, however, devoid of normal

TABLE 2.2
Structural Data for 60 Conduct-Disordered Children

Variable	Mean	SD	Min	Max	Freq	Median	Mode	SK	KU
R	20.37	5.07	14.00	33.00	60	19.50	16.00	0.71	−0.42
W	10.85	4.56	1.00	23.00	60	10.00	9.00	0.34	0.20
D	7.05	5.24	0.00	23.00	57	6.00	4.00	1.38	2.06
Dd	2.47	1.53	0.00	7.00	55	2.00	2.00	0.62	0.31
Space	2.03	1.56	0.00	6.00	48	2.00	2.00	0.44	−0.55
DQ+	5.17	3.53	0.00	18.00	54	5.00	8.00	0.73	1.47
DQo	13.70	5.24	3.00	28.00	60	13.00	11.00	0.52	0.41
DQv	1.33	1.77	0.00	9.00	38	1.00	−0.00	2.49	7.83
DQv/+	0.17	0.56	0.00	3.00	6	0.00	0.00	3.70	14.04
FQX+	0.02	0.13	0.00	1.00	1	0.00	0.00	7.75	60.00
FQXo	7.67	3.35	1.00	15.00	60	7.50	5.00	0.37	−0.51
FQXu	3.72	2.36	0.00	9.00	56	3.00	2.00	0.48	−0.51
FQX−	8.23	3.05	3.00	18.00	60	8.00	6.00	0.75	0.66
FQXnone	0.73	1.57	0.00	9.00	19	0.00	−0.00	3.38	13.96
MQ+	0.02	0.13	0.00	1.00	1	0.00	0.00	7.75	60.00
MQo	1.02	1.23	0.00	5.00	33	1.00	−0.00	1.27	1.16
MQu	0.42	0.67	0.00	2.00	19	0.00	−0.00	1.36	0.58
MQ−	0.85	1.26	0.00	5.00	27	0.00	−0.00	1.76	2.82
MQnone	0.00	0.00	0.00	−0.00	0	0.00	−0.00	−	−
Space−	0.90	1.05	0.00	4.00	32	1.00	−0.00	1.11	0.80
M	2.30	2.08	0.00	7.00	45	2.00	−0.00	0.66	−0.65
FM	2.57	2.05	0.00	9.00	52	2.00	2.00	1.13	1.55
m	1.32	1.70	0.00	8.00	35	1.00	−0.00	1.76	3.51
FM+m	3.88	2.92	0.00	14.00	56	3.00	3.00	1.17	1.57
FC	0.83	1.47	0.00	6.00	23	0.00	−0.00	2.30	5.09
CF	1.42	1.50	0.00	6.00	41	1.00	−0.00	1.27	1.18
C	0.75	1.14	0.00	6.00	26	0.00	−0.00	2.20	6.56
Cn	0.03	0.18	0.00	1.00	2	0.00	−0.00	5.33	27.36
FC+CF+C+Cn	3.03	2.34	0.00	11.00	53	3.00	3.00	1.05	1.28
WgSumC	2.96	2.22	0.00	10.00	53	2.50	1.00	0.77	0.53
Sum C'	1.05	1.36	0.00	6.00	31	1.00	−0.00	1.50	2.36
Sum T	0.17	0.53	0.00	3.00	7	0.00	−0.00	3.80	15.99
Sum V	0.08	0.28	0.00	1.00	5	0.00	0.00	3.09	7.83
Sum Y	0.47	1.02	0.00	5.00	16	0.00	−0.00	2.85	8.61
Sum Shd	1.77	2.12	0.00	10.00	40	1.00	−0.00	1.63	2.98
Fr+rF	0.23	0.50	0.00	2.00	12	0.00	−0.00	2.10	3.79
FD	0.45	0.72	0.00	3.00	20	0.00	−0.00	1.57	1.92
F	11.18	4.29	3.00	24.00	60	11.00	12.00	0.58	0.41
Pairs	4.13	2.99	0.00	12.00	54	4.00	3.00	0.69	0.12
Ego	0.23	0.16	0.00	0.61	54	0.21	−0.00	0.56	−0.22
Lambda	2.16	3.40	0.22	18.00	60	1.15	1.00	3.77	14.43
EA	5.26	3.01	0.00	13.00	58	5.00	3.00	0.42	−0.51
es	5.65	3.70	0.00	15.00	59	5.00	3.00	0.58	−0.51
D Score	−0.13	1.16	−4.00	2.00	60	0.00	−0.00	−0.41	1.16
Adj D Score	0.13	0.93	−2.00	2.00	60	0.00	−0.00	0.12	0.05
SumActvMov	4.20	2.89	0.00	13.00	56	4.00	3.00	0.67	0.20
SumPassMov	1.98	1.80	0.00	8.00	49	2.00	1.00	1.36	1.96
SumMactv	1.53	1.53	0.00	7.00	41	1.00	−0.00	1.16	1.61
SumMpass	0.77	1.09	0.00	5.00	27	0.00	−0.00	1.77	3.50

(Continued)

TABLE 2.2
(Continued)

Variable	Mean	SD	Min	Max	Freq	Median	Mode	SK	KU
IntellIndx	0.68	0.96	0.00	4.00	28	0.00	−0.00	1.85	3.66
Zf	12.42	4.92	1.00	26.00	60	13.00	11.00	0.27	0.47
Zd	−0.57	4.36	−9.00	11.50	59	−1.00	0.50	0.29	0.10
Blends	2.10	1.72	0.00	7.00	51	2.00	1.00	0.84	0.01
CSBlnd	0.27	0.63	0.00	4.00	13	0.00	−0.00	3.84	19.80
Afr	0.49	0.19	0.18	1.00	60	0.45	0.50	0.80	0.35
Populars	3.88	1.92	1.00	8.00	60	3.50	2.00	0.33	−0.90
X + %	0.37	0.12	0.03	0.63	60	0.40	0.36	−0.42	0.05
F + %	0.42	0.17	0.00	0.71	59	0.42	0.50	−0.31	−0.28
X − %	0.41	0.13	0.17	0.75	60	0.40	0.40	0.19	−0.07
Xu %	0.18	0.10	0.00	0.40	56	0.18	0.18	0.07	−0.50
S − %	0.10	0.12	0.00	0.50	32	0.08	−0.00	1.16	0.92
IsoIndx	0.15	0.14	0.00	0.52	46	0.12	−0.00	0.97	0.19
H	1.75	1.55	0.00	6.00	46	2.00	2.00	1.06	1.10
(H)	1.32	1.38	0.00	6.00	38	1.00	−0.00	1.15	1.38
Hd	1.40	1.52	0.00	7.00	37	1.00	−0.00	1.17	1.60
(Hd)	0.45	0.85	0.00	5.00	20	0.00	−0.00	3.22	13.91
Hx	0.05	0.29	0.00	2.00	2	0.00	−0.00	6.15	39.25
H + (H) + Hd + (Hd)	4.92	2.88	0.00	16.00	57	5.00	5.00	0.96	2.56
A	9.32	3.48	3.00	19.00	60	9.00	9.00	0.72	0.67
(A)	0.67	1.14	0.00	7.00	24	0.00	−0.00	3.22	15.09
Ad	1.27	1.39	0.00	5.00	34	1.00	−0.00	0.76	−0.52
(Ad)	0.18	0.47	0.00	2.00	9	0.00	−0.00	2.63	6.51
An	0.32	0.62	0.00	3.00	15	0.00	0.00	2.25	5.62
Art	0.40	0.78	0.00	4.00	17	0.00	−0.00	2.62	8.16
Ay	0.22	0.45	0.00	2.00	12	0.00	−0.00	1.95	3.16
Bl	0.43	0.67	0.00	3.00	21	0.00	0.00	1.63	2.74
Bt	0.72	1.17	0.00	7.00	26	0.00	−0.00	3.04	13.51
Cg	0.98	1.05	0.00	4.00	35	1.00	−0.00	0.94	0.51
Cl	0.18	0.83	0.00	6.00	5	0.00	0.00	6.18	41.83
Ex	0.17	0.56	0.00	2.00	5	0.00	0.00	3.09	7.83
Fi	0.60	0.81	0.00	3.00	26	0.00	0.00	1.27	1.02
Food	0.42	1.03	0.00	7.00	16	0.00	0.00	4.76	28.53
Geog	0.00	0.00	0.00	0.00	0	0.00	0.00	−	−
HHold	0.35	0.66	0.00	2.00	15	0.00	−0.00	1.68	1.48
Ls	0.68	1.05	0.00	4.00	24	0.00	−0.00	1.68	2.28
Na	0.72	1.14	0.00	5.00	23	0.00	−0.00	1.80	3.18
Sc	1.52	1.76	0.00	7.00	36	1.00	−0.00	1.24	0.99
Sx	0.07	0.31	0.00	2.00	3	0.00	−0.00	5.11	27.62
Xy	0.03	0.18	0.00	1.00	2	0.00	−0.00	5.33	27.36
Idio	1.38	1.66	0.00	9.00	40	1.00	1.00	2.13	6.60
DV	0.65	0.75	0.00	3.00	30	0.50	0.00	0.93	0.27
INCOM	1.87	1.55	0.00	6.00	48	2.00	1.00	0.77	−0.05
DR	0.50	0.85	0.00	4.00	20	0.00	−0.00	2.03	4.53
FABCOM	0.67	0.88	0.00	3.00	27	0.00	0.00	1.19	0.58
DV2	0.03	0.18	0.00	1.00	2	0.00	0.00	5.33	27.36
INC2	0.35	1.05	0.00	6.00	9	0.00	−0.00	3.82	15.97
DR2	0.02	0.13	0.00	1.00	1	0.00	0.00	7.75	60.00

(Continued)

21

TABLE 2.2
(Continued)

Variable	Mean	SD	Min	Max	Freq	Median	Mode	SK	KU
FAB2	0.40	0.69	0.00	3.00	18	0.00	0.00	1.79	2.89
ALOG	0.12	0.32	0.00	1.00	7	0.00	0.00	2.45	4.14
CONTAM	0.03	0.18	0.00	1.00	2	0.00	0.00	5.33	27.36
Sum6SpSc	3.83	2.21	0.00	9.00	56	4.00	2.00	0.18	−0.70
Sum6SpScLv2	0.80	1.44	0.00	8.00	24	0.00	−0.00	2.92	10.88
WSum6SpSc	13.73	11.03	0.00	60.00	57	11.00	5.00	1.59	3.98
AB	0.03	0.18	0.00	1.00	2	0.00	−0.00	5.33	27.36
AG	0.72	1.11	0.00	5.00	23	0.00	−0.00	1.68	2.82
CFB	0.02	0.13	0.00	1.00	1	0.00	−0.00	7.74	60.00
COP	0.55	0.75	0.00	2.00	24	0.00	−0.00	0.96	−0.51
CP	0.05	0.22	0.00	1.00	3	0.00	0.00	4.24	16.49
MOR	1.38	1.94	0.00	12.00	35	1.00	−0.00	3.15	14.64
PER	0.30	0.77	0.00	5.00	13	0.00	−0.00	4.34	24.09
PSV	0.85	0.92	0.00	4.00	34	1.00	−0.00	0.99	0.93

stress tolerance and controls. Seventy-eight percent have AdjD $\geq$ 0 ($M = .13$, SD = .93), and fare slightly better than normal latency age children ($M = -.10$, SD = .41). Our data do not suggest that CD children, on average, are deficient in the processing of external feedback in situations of frustration (Weiner, Levy, & Exner, 1981). Nonvolitional affect exceeds nonvolitional ideation in only 20% of our sample. These CD children appear to be able to organize their behavior in a predictable manner, and are not overwhelmed with affective or ideational "noise."

Affect.   The affect modulation of our CD sample averages slightly less than 1:3 (.83:2.17). This is similar to our adolescent (see chapter 3) and adult ASPD (see chapters 4 & 5) averages, and worse than normal 9-year-old children (1.89:3.22). The latter finding, however, may be due to the "collapsing" of the data, because modulation of affect shows marked developmental improvement during childhood and early adolescence. For instance, the FC:CF+C ratio between 6- and 7-year-old normal children changes from 1:4.5 to 1:2 (Exner, 1990b). It seems apparent that affect modulation may stop improving for most antisocial samples during early latency age. This may be paradoxically due to enduring pre-Oedipal defenses that keep affect out of consciousness (e.g., splitting, projection, denial)—and result in less WgtSumC for the CD sample ($M = 2.96$, $SD = 2.22$) when compared to normal 9-year-olds ($M = 5.13$, $SD = 1.07$). Avoidance of emotionally provoking external stimuli is also quite apparent (Afr = .49, $SD = 0.19$) when compared to normals (Afr = 0.79, $SD = 0.13$). Variance is similar. Pure C responses still occur in almost half of the CD children (43%), whereas these measures of unmodulated emotion have diminished in frequency to 16% by age 9 in normals. At age 7, however, Pure C is still present in 60% of normals (Exner, 1990b).

TABLE 2.3

CD Children's ($N = 60$) Group Means and Frequencies for Select Ratios, Percentages, and Derivations

$R = 20.37$	$L = 2.16$	$(L > .99 = 65\%)$

EB = 2.30 : 2.96	EA = 5.26
eb = 3.89 : 1.77	es = 5.66 (FM+m < SUMShading ... 12 20%)
D = -0.13 AdjD = 0.13	

EB STYLE

Introversive	11	18%
Super-Introversive	8	13%
Ambitent	28	47%
Extratensive	21	35%
Super-Extratensive	14	23%

EA − es DIFFERENCES:D-SCORES

D Score > 0	15	25%
D Score = 0	25	42%
D Score < 0	20	33%
D Score < -1	6	10%
AdjD Score > 0	18	30%
AdjD Score = 0	29	48%
AdjD Score < 0	13	22%
AdjD Score < -1	2	3%

AFFECT

FC:CF+C = .83 : 2.17		
Pure C = .75		(Pure C > 0 = 43%;Pure C > 1 = 18%)
FC > (CF+C) + 2	2	3%
FC > (CF+C) + 1	5	8%
(CF+C) > FC + 1	27	45%
(CF+C) > FC + 2	20	33%

SumC' = 1.05	SumV = .08	SumY = .47

Afr = .49	(Afr < .40 = 32%; Afr < .50 = 53%)
S = 2.03	(S > 2 = 35%)
Blends:R = 2.10 : 20.37	
CP = .05	

INTERPERSONAL

COP = .55	(COP = 0, 60%; COP > 2 = 0%)
AG = .72	(AG = 0, 62%; AG > 2 = 8%)
Food = .42	
Isolate/R = .15	
H:(H)+Hd+(Hd) = 1.75 : 3.17	(H = 0, 23%; H < 2 = 48%)
(H)+(HD):(A)+(Ad) = 1.77 : .85	
H+A:Hd+Ad = 11.07 : 2.72	
Sum T = .17	(T = 0, 88%; T > 1 = 3%)

(Continued)

TABLE 2.3
(Continued)

SELF-PERCEPTION

$3r+(2)/R$ = .23   (72% < .33; 10% > .44)
$Fr+rF$ = .23   ($Fr+rF$ > 0 = 20%)
FD = .45
An+Xy = .35
MOR = 1.38   (MOR > 2 = 13%)

IDEATION

a:p = 4.20 : 1.98   (p > a+1 = 5%)
Ma:Mp = 1.53 : .77   (Mp > Ma = 13%)
M = 2.30   (M− = .85; M none = .00)
FM = 3.88   m = 1.32
2AB+(Art+Ay) = .68   (2AB+Art+Ay > 5 = 3%)
Sum6 = 3.83   (Sum6 > 6 = 25%)
WSum6 = 13.73   (Level 2 Special Scores > 0 = 40%)

MEDIATION

Populars = 3.88   (P < 4 = 50%; P > 7 = 3%)
X+% = .37
F+% = .42
X−% = .41
S−% = .10
Xu% = .18

X+% > .89	0	0%
X+% < .70	60	100%
X+% < .61	59	98%
X+% < .50	50	83%
F+% < .70	58	97%
Xu% > .20	21	35%
X−% > .15	60	100%
X−% > .20	57	95%
X−% > .30	47	78%

PROCESSING

Zf = 12.42
Zd = −0.57   (Zd > +3.0 = 17%; Zd < −3.0 = 25%)
W:D:Dd = 10.85:7.05:2.47   (Dd > 3 = 25%)
W:M = 10.85:2.30
DQ+ = 5.17
DQv = 1.33   (DQv + DQv/+ > 2 = 20%)

CONSTELLATIONS

SCZI = 6... 6	6%	DEPI = 7...1	2%	CDI = 5... 4	7%
SCZI = 5...12	20%	DEPI = 6...2	3%	CDI = 4...16	27%
SCZI = 4...20	33%	DEPI = 5...9	15%		

S−Constellation Positive	0	0%
HVI Positive	8	13%
OBS Positive	0	0%

Chronic oppositionalism (S) surprisingly shows little difference when compared to normal children ($M = 2.03$, $SD = 1.56$). Painful rumination (V), however, is present in a small proportion (8%) of CD children, a finding that is completely absent in normal 9-year-olds. Only six subjects in all of Exner's childhood samples (ages 5–12) produced a V response. Felt helplessness, or anxiety (Y), is noticeably less in the CD children ($M = 0.47$, $SD = 1.02$, 27%) when compared to other 9-year-olds ($M = 0.83$, $SD = 0.85$, 73%), and suggests the first signs of regulatory mechanisms that aid in discharging affect (see chapter 10) and the absence of anxiety in the adult psychopath. For all children low frequencies and percentages of the shading variables (Ames, Metraux, & Walker, 1959) may be linked to group styles for modulating affect, like the CD children, as well as developmentally determined abilities for expressing dysphoric affect. Both would effect Rorschach manifestations in regard to appearance (frequency/proportion) and nature (content) of variables.

We think there is a biopsychosocial axis between autonomic hyporeactivity (biology), reduced levels of anxiety (psychology), and chronic detachment (social) that first becomes apparent during early latency age in the at-risk-for-psychopathy child. Only 12% of our CD sample produced T, a measure of normative attachment, whereas 88% of 9-year-olds evidence this robust measure. Autonomic hyporeactivity in early adolescence has been shown to predict criminality (Raine, Venables, & Williams, 1990) in early adulthood, but no studies of the ANS patterns of latency age CD children have been published. Prospective studies do not address cause and effect, nor issues of heritability.

Interpersonal (Object) Relations. CD children do not expect cooperative interactions with others (60% COP = 0), unlike normal 9-year-olds (3% COP = 0). When COP does appear it is mostly spoiled, suggesting the CD child's problematic and distorted interpersonal relationships (Gacono & Erdberg, 1993). Most CD children do not manifest aggressive responses (AG = 38%) anywhere near as frequently as normals (AG = 91%). We think this is due to the acting out of aggression, rather than symbolization of it, in CD children. AG responses in normal children are quite stable, and range from 80% to 100% in 5- to 12-year-olds (Exner, 1990b).[8] These tensions of aggression are likely ego dystonic due to superego structuralization during the Oedipal period. Likewise some CD nonborderline children whose experience of aggression is ego alien theoretically might produce these AG responses in greater frequency than normals. CD children have fewer Rorschach AG responses, but if their protocols are scored for our other aggression scores (Meloy & Gacono, 1992a), we get the following frequencies: AgContent 93%, AgPast 33%, and AgPot 17%. AG (Exner, 1986a) *should not* be used to predict real-world aggression in CD subjects, and may

---

[8] The 6-year-old children in Exner's (1990b) normative sample only produced a 25% frequency of AG responses. This appears to be an anomaly that remains unexplained.

actually be negatively correlated with such behavior due to the ego syntonic nature of these impulses (see chapter 8).

The representation of others as whole, real, and meaningful objects (Pure H) shows deficits in CD children ($M = 1.75$, 77%) when compared to normal 9-year-olds ($M = 2.87$, 99%). Quasi-human and part human objects dominate the internal world of the CD child ($M = 3.17$), although both normal and CD children average about five "all human content" responses per protocol. We would expect part-object dominated internal representations in CD children, consistent with borderline children (Leichtman & Shapiro, 1980) and borderline personality organization (Kernberg, 1984). Good and bad part objects do not integrate unless object constancy is achieved, and splitting will regressively prevent such higher level ego functioning and tripartite structuring (ego, id, superego) of the child's personality. The monkey-on-the-back nature of primitive defenses adaptively support the developing antisocial personality, while defensively preventing maturation of personality.

Self-Perception. Despite the general absence of the Rorschach manifestations of unpleasant feelings,[9] CD children do compare themselves negatively to others (72% egocentricity < .33) and are not positively self-absorbed like normal 9-year-olds (EgoC $M = 0.57$, $SD = 0.12$).[10] Reflection response frequency is virtually identical between our CD sample and normals, and will occur in one out of five records in both groups. Narcissistic defenses have not yet crystallized, and defensive grandiosity is markedly absent in most CD children's Rorschachs. The grandiose self-structure (Kernberg, 1975) may develop later than originally theorized (Meloy, 1988) in psychopathy, although emotional detachment, part-object representations, and a lack of the expectation of positive interaction with others may be the early latency age precursors for such psychopathology. A negative turning inward has begun at this age, which is eventually transformed into a positive and expansive identification with the aggressor (A. Freud, 1936).

Ideation. The thinking of the CD child shows, on average, the same amount of formal thought disorder as the normal 9-year-old (WSum6SpSc $M = 13.73$). There are more occasional indicators of severe cognitive slippage, however, with 40% of the CD children producing one or more Level 2 scores. A greater amount of nonvolitional ideation in response to anxiety (m) is also apparent ($M = 1.32$, $SD = 1.70$). M– responses, like in the adult antisocial samples, are frequent (45%) when compared to normal latency age children (5%). Already there is a tendency

---

[9]Depression in children is frequently masked by temper tantrums, psychophysiological reactions, hyperactivity, and asocial and aggressive behavior. Blended affect is expected among CD children as they tend to simultaneously exhibit high levels of both angry and depressed affect (Sanders, Dadds, Johnston, & Cash, 1992).

[10] These Rorschach findings are consistent with the CD child's tendency to devalue self or exhibit "elevated internally focused negative cognitions" (Sanders et al., 1992, p. 503).

toward fantasy abuse (Mp > Ma = 13%), but this is not outside the range for normal children (10%–15%) between ages 5 and 12. There is slightly less human movement productivity (M) than the expected three M responses per protocol. Nonvolitional ideation in response to unmet needs (FM) is more than one standard deviation below normal (M = 2.57, SD = 2.05) in CD children when compared to all latency age groups. We begin to see in the CD child the cognitive markers of psychopathy: grossly deficient or failed empathy (M–), occasionally severe perceptual distortions and associative derailments (Level 2 scores), a sense of being shot at (m),[11] and rapid discharge of need states (FM). Formal thought disorder (WSum6) in the CD child is not yet distinguishable from the normal latency age child (range 8.86–14.88). The problem is that it does not improve as the CD child grows older (see chapter 3).

Mediation.   CD children are divorced from conventional reality. They see fewer popular responses (M = 3.88) than normal latency age children (M = 5.78). In fact 50% see less than four popular responses per protocol (as noted in Table 2.3), percepts seen in one of every three Rorschach records (Exner, 1986a). CD children's perceptual convergence is likewise grossly idiosyncratic (X+% M = 37) with or without other determinants (F+% M = 42). We are struck by the severe impairments in reality testing of these young subjects (X–% M = 41) when compared to normal 9-year-olds (M = 8)—a measure that is remarkably stable after age 4, and varies between 7% and 11%, on average, into adulthood for most nonpatients. This CD children's mean is comparable to adult inpatient schizophrenics (M = 37; Exner, 1990b), and underscores the crucial clinical importance of impaired reality testing in these children, despite the absence of a diagnosable psychotic disorder on Axis I.

Conduct disorder is not just a behavioral problem. The aggressive activity of these children is likely a manifest expression of severe affective, perceptual, and associational abnormality. Our best reality-testing index out of all the subjects was 17%, still worse than most borderline personality disordered adults who average 13% on this measure (Exner, 1986b). CD children cannot clearly distinguish between internal and external stimuli, and their reactivity to the world is likely a response to their own projective and introjective oscillations. They will not be able to accurately locate the origin of thoughts and feelings, but should be able to recognize a boundary between inside and outside. If the boundary is lost, confusion becomes fusion, and the child is psychotic.

Processing.   The CD children put as much effort into integrating percepts (Zf M = 12.42, SD = 4.92) as do normal latency age children (M = 11.16, SD = 1.54). They also do it, on average, successfully (Zd M = –.57). Twenty-five percent are

---

[11]This subjective childhood experience of "being shot at" evolves into a pervasive sense of being victimized as an adult. The ASPD then sees himself as a victim entitled to victimize others.

underincorporators. These are likely the ADHD subsample (13%). Like children in general, but more so (normals, W:M = 10.33:3.12) for the CD children (10.85:2.30), aspirations outstrip abilities. Unlike normals this measure of grandiosity does not decrease with age in antisocial populations, although it is not an obvious abnormality during latency. Once again, this variable, like affect modulation, appears to developmentally fix in early latency and does not further mature.

In summary, the CD child is likely to show gross abnormalities in certain areas (reality testing, ideation, negative self-assessment, perceptual unconventionality, part-object dominance, low anxiety, chronic detachment, affect avoidance, ego syntonic aggression, rapid discharge of need states); normal functioning in other areas (stress tolerance and controls, use of fantasy, Rorschach productivity, narcissism, oppositionalism, visual perceptual organization) that may worsen over time and development; and normal functioning *for a child* that does not change with time and development (grandiosity, unmodulated affect) and appears fixed at an early latency age period (Kegan, 1986). This latter category of psychological structure *becomes* abnormal as a function of chronological growth and emotional immaturity.

OBJECT RELATIONS IN THE CD CHILD

The Mutuality of Autonomy (MOA) scale was developed and validated by Urist (1977) who based it on the borderline and narcissistic psychoanalytic theory of both Kohut (1971) and Kernberg (1975). Urist's original intent was to "demonstrate the structural argument that individuals tend to experience self–other relationships in consistent, enduring characteristic ways that can be defined for each individual along a developmental continuum" (p. 3). This continuum ranged from primary narcissism to object-relatedness, and Urist assumed that the Rorschach would mirror the subject's experience and definition of interpersonal relations.

The scale depicts seven modes of interaction that range from mutually autonomous activity (1) to overpowering envelopment and incorporation (7). The data generated are ordinal, and responses are scored when two objects, whether human, animal, or inanimate, are related. Many scorable responses involve movement and a Z score (Exner, 1991), although when a second object is implied, but not seen, it is a scorable response (Coates & Tuber, 1988). Interrater reliability for the instrument has consistently ranged between 70% and 90% (Tuber, 1989b). The seven points on the ordinal scale can be summarized as follows:

1. Separate, autonomous interaction.
2. Separate, autonomous parallel activity.
3. Dependent activity.
4. Reflected activity.

5. Malevolent control.
6. Destructive imbalance.
7. Overpowering envelopment.

Coates and Tuber (1988) incisively noted that aggression is independent of this object relations scaling, but the *nature* of the aggression would determine where on the scale the response was located. A rating of 1, for example, would be given to the response (Card III): "Two people arguing over the rules of a game of chess"; whereas a rating of 6 would be given to the response (Card II): "One bear has crushed the head of another bear, and here's the blood pouring out." The MOA as a reliable measure of self and object representations is deeply embedded in the history of the Rorschach as a tool to access the internal representational world of the patient (Piotrowski, 1957; Rorschach, 1942; Schachtel, 1966).

The validation of the MOA with children has focused on separation-anxiety disorder (Goddard & Tuber, 1989), depression (Goldberg, 1989), borderline psychopathology and attention-deficit disorder (Thomas, 1987), later adjustment (Tuber, 1983), gender identity (Coates & Tuber, 1988; Ipp, 1986; Tuber & Coates, 1989), children with imaginary companions (Meyer & Tuber, 1989), children anticipating surgery (Tuber, Frank, & Santostefano, 1989), and findings in non-clinical samples derived from a larger study of suicidal children and adolescents (Santostefano, Rieder, & Berk, 1984; Tuber, 1989a, 1989b) and elementary school children (Ryan, Avery, & Grolnick, 1985).

Tuber (1992) reviewed the impressive research concerning the reliability and validity of the MOA with children, and concluded that it is "an ordinal scale depicting differing modes of object experience of varying severity" (p. 189). He emphasized, however, that the MOA is measuring varying levels of adaptive and psychopathological object relations, and is not, contrary to Urist's (1977) original expectations, measuring development (see Blatt, Tuber, & Auerbach, 1990). It appears to be a quite useful tool for exploring the dynamics of internalized object representations in both normal and clinical samples of children.

We compared the MOA scores for our sample of CD children ($N = 60$) to Tuber's (1989b) normal sample of children ($N = 40$) to explore the Scale's usefulness in discriminating and understanding this childhood disorder. The demographics and initial results are presented in Table 2.4.

Although the gender characteristics of the two samples differ, the age range and distribution within the samples is virtually identical. Tuber (1989b) noted significant gender differences on MOA scores in his normal children's sample, but with our small number of female subjects ($N = 8$), we were unable to do similar comparisons to see if such differences would hold true in this population. When gender differences were significant in the normal sample, we only used the normal male subjects ($N = 19$) for comparison to our mostly (87%) male CD subjects.

Prior research has demonstrated that IQ does not correlate with major MOA measures (Tuber, 1989b). Intelligence does differ between these two samples,

TABLE 2.4
Comparison of MOA (Urist, 1977) Scores for Conduct-Disordered ($N = 60$)
and Nonpatient ($N = 40$; Tuber, 1989b) Children

Demographics	CD Subjects	Nonpatients
Age	9.75 (SD 1.6) 5–12	10.5 (SD 2.3) 6–13
Male	52	19
Female	8	21
IQ	101.88 (SD 13.97)	110.88 (9.36)
	Rorschach Findings	
Total R	1202	807
Mean R	20.37 (SD 5.07)	20.18 (SD 9.46)
Total MOA Scores	259	193
% MOA Scores	22	24
Range of MOA Scores	0–14	1–15
Mean Number MOA Scores	4.32 (SD 2.69)	4.65 (SD 3.3)[a]
HORS	1.95 (SD 1.42)	2.74 (SD 1.59)[a]
LORS	4.72 (SD 2.08)	5.00 (SD 1.20)[a]
Mean MOA	3.33 (SD 1.56)	3.83 (SD 1.07)[a]

[a]Male subjects only for nonpatient sample ($N = 19$) due to gender differences.

however, with the normal children demonstrating a mean IQ (110.88) higher than the CD children (101.88). The normal children came from predominately technical/professional, intact working families, whereas the CD children, all hospitalized within private, inpatient facilities when tested, were from predominately middle-class, not intact families. The parental status of the CD group was as follows: 45% (27) divorced, 28% (17) married, 22% (13) never married or single, and 5% (3) unknown. As we noted earlier, the racial/ethnic status of the CD group was as follows: 73% (44) White, 13% (8) Black, 10% (6) Hispanic, and 4% (2) unknown. The CD group also had a 43% (26) rate of documented sexual or physical abuse, and a 13% (8) frequency of diagnosed ADHD. Two thirds (66%) of the CD group met criteria for solitary aggressive subtype.

There were no significant differences between the groups for mean number of Rorschach responses, proportion of MOA responses, range of MOA scores, mean number of MOA scores per subject, the mean for the highest MOA score (HORS), the mean for the lowest MOA score (LORS), and the mean MOA score. There was a counterintuitive trend for the CD subjects to produce somewhat *higher*, or less psychopathological, scores when the data are analyzed in this manner.

Table 2.5 analyzes the data from a different perspective, looking at both proportion of subjects who produced scores at various levels, and proportion of frequencies of scores at various levels.

Although the proportion of subjects who produced the highest MOA scores (1–3) did not vary, significantly more CD subjects produced at least one Response 4 (reflected activity) ($p < .02$) and a worst response at Level 7 ($p < .05$). These

TABLE 2.5
Comparison of MOA (Urist, 1977) Proportionate Scores for Conduct-Disordered
($N = 60$) and Nonpatient ($N = 40$) Children

Proportion of Subjects	CD	Normals	X2	p
Best response 1 or 2	.77	.75	–	NS
At least one response 3	.45	.50	–	NS
At least one response 4	.22	.025	6.04	< .02
Worst response 5–7	.70	.60	1.06	> .20
Worst response 7	.13	0	5.24	< .05
Proportion of Frequencies				
Responses 1 and 2	.40	.50	4.12	< .05
Response 3	.14	.16	–	NS
Response 4	.05	.02	–	NS
Responses > 5	.41	.33	3.98	< .025
Response 5	.17	.25	4.23	< .05
Response 6	.21	.07	13.03	< .001
Response 7	.03	0	6.68	< .01
Malevolent (5–7) scored 5	.41	.77	20.83	< .0005
Malevolent (5–7) scored 6	.50	.23	12.69	< .0005
Malevolent (5–7) scored 7	.09	0	4.17	< .05

Note. Chi-square nonparametric statistic is nondirectional.

data suggest that CD subjects are more likely to represent objects as a source of narcissistic mirroring or an overwhelming, omnipotent, and malevolent force.

The data that analyze proportion of frequencies are also significant in predicted directions. Responses 1 and 2 are significantly more frequent in normal children ($p < .05$), suggesting a greater capacity for the representation of autonomous objects and parallel activity. Responses 3 and 4 show no differences, but the malevolent responses (5–7) are significantly more frequent in the CD subjects when analyzed from a variety of perspectives. Most remarkable is the finding that normal children, when they do represent objects in a malevolent manner, will do so at Level 5, displaying a theme of malevolent control (77%). Only on occasion do they resort to a Level 6 representation (23%), destructive imbalance, and never to a Level 7 representation (0%), overpowering envelopment. On the other hand, the CD children derive most of their malevolent scores (59%) at a Level 6 or 7, and only 41% at a Level 5. In fact, 9% of their malevolent scores are at a Level 7. Some examples of scores from the CD sample include:

Level 1. (Card III) Two people talking to each other. (Inquiry) Holding onto a table, standing up, faces talking to each other.

Level 2. (Card VIII) These look like ground sloths climbing up a mountain. (Inquiry) Nice and furry head and tail, the way the illustrator did it.

Level 3. (Card II) An elephant standing up. (Inquiry) The back, ears, and you can see them holding the bullet together.

Level 4. (Card VIII) It's a wolf staring, see its statue in the water. (Inquiry) Look like a wolf right here, rocks, water, it's looking for food, looking in the water if it's hungry.

Level 5. (Card VI) Look like a fox, a furry fox that's flying from his prey, I mean from his predator. (Inquiry) Can see whiskers, this is the head and body (?) because the way that it's flying (touches card).

Level 6. (Card I) A lady with no head, with wings, raising her arms. (Inquiry) Her old head was right here, it was cut off, she's a sorceress, here's the wings. Her arms would be here if she weren't raising them.

Level 7. (Card II) An explosion, volcano, eruption, the cut-away side. (Inquiry) Cut-away side of molten lava blowing out all over the place, sorry for my language (?) red, look like man crawling because his feet got tore off.

The results of this study using the Mutuality of Autonomy Scale (Urist, 1977) further validate its use as a measure of object relations in children. CD children, when compared to nonpatient children of the same age, produce significantly more narcissistic, malevolent, and destructive object relational percepts on the Rorschach, suggesting that their internal representations of self and others are governed by these same troublesome and psychopathological characteristics. These data also lend validity to the hypothesis that aggressive and antisocial behavior among children, defined by the conduct-disordered diagnosis, will also be expressed representationally in a perceptual, associative, and judgmental task such as the Rorschach.

This study poses several suggestive findings for further research: First, the Rorschach test, when scored using the MOA scale, may be able to differentiate between normal and CD children; second, proportional measures of level of object relations are statistically more powerful than average or distributional measures in these populations; and third, CD children produce more narcissistic, potentially intrusive, and toxic modes of object experience (Tuber, 1992) on the Rorschach.

DAMION, A CONDUCT-DISORDERED CHILD AT RISK FOR PSYCHOPATHY[12]

Damion is an attractive, dark-complexioned 9-year-old boy born in a South American country. Although physically small, he is socially sophisticated. Damion's childhood was marked by inconsistencies, including place of residence. He resided in his parents' home, various orphanages, and at times lived on the streets. Adopted at age 6, Damion was underweight, malnourished, and infested with parasites. Various "marks" on his body provided evidence of physical and

---

[12]Appreciation is extended to Jacqueline Singer, PhD, for contributing material for this case study.

sexual abuse initiated by his natural parents. Damion now lives in the United States with his adoptive mother and his 15-year-old adoptive sister. He is enrolled in the third grade and receives resource specialist services for reading, despite speaking fluent English.

In 1991, at age 9, Damion was first hospitalized on a children's psychiatric unit. His presenting problems included: running away from home, lying, fire setting, uncontrollable fits of anger, initiating physical fights with his sister, and threatening to kill his family. These behaviors were consistent with a diagnosis of severe conduct disorder, solitary aggressive type. He exhibited dangerous and thrill-seeking behaviors and made suicidal threats. These included trying to jump out of a moving vehicle and running across a busy street (possibly with the intent to harm himself). Damion was hospitalized four times over a 1½-year period between 1991 and 1993.

During his first admission Damion was involved in a range of activities including school, individual psychotherapy, family therapy, and music, recreational, and occupational therapies. Damion had difficulty following directions, responding in an oppositional manner to the staff. He readily provoked peers with subtle remarks or gestures, and then consistently denied responsibility for his behavior. Provocative and manipulative behavior was noted to provide a mask for a child with a poor sense of self.

Damion used individual psychotherapy to recount in detail his early abusive and deprived history. Stories of physical and sexual abuse and living unchaperoned on the streets were related to overwhelming and intense anger. There appeared to be no end to his rage, which was directed at whomever was present. Imipramine helped Damion contain his aggression and brighten his mood. His suicidal impulses also diminished.

Damion was briefly discharged to home with plans for continued day treatment. Within 10 days the escalation of anger and rage resulted in readmittance to the inpatient setting. Damion had threatened to kill day treatment staff. On the weekend prior to this second hospitalization he had also threatened to kill his mother when she refused to purchase a toy he wanted for Christmas. Damion had also run away from home. Signs of an agitated depression were noted at admission. Damion felt both helpless and hopeless.

During the 2 months of his second hospitalization, Damion's behavior was even more erratic than the previous admission. Homicidal threats predominated. Rage was triggered by both reminiscences of early abuse as well as current frustrations. Even minor events provoked rage. Damion's rage stimulated fantasies of obtaining a gun in order to kill a staff member. Although violence toward others in both fantasy and deed helped with self cohesion, any obstacle threatened it. Recompensation through violence is a *sine qua non* of the psychopathic process, and, as Meloy (1988) noted, separates the psychopath from more benign narcissistic disorders.

Often cruel, the severity of Damion's provocative and manipulative behavior at times required physical restraint and separation from the milieu. Isolated from others and without participants for projective-introjective cycles and sadistic interactions, he became more stable (see Response 14 on his Rorschach protocol, Table 2.6).

Damion could present a veneer of charm and cooperation. Periods of cooperation were unexpected and confusing to staff. On the surface receptive behaviors seemed inconsistent with Damion's general demeanor. Closer inspection, however, revealed that they were self-serving, occurring at specific and predictable times. Damion's charm intensified in expectation of a weekend pass or other favor. His self-esteem appeared greater when he was charming.

Staff members believed Damion maintained the capacity to distinguish between right and wrong. Damion's "poor judgment," rather than stemming from a deficit, appeared to result from a lack of concern for others and indifference to the consequences of his behavior.

Because Damion presented severe and mixed symptomatology during his second hospitalization a number of medications were considered. Weight loss, believed to be related to a loss of appetite and depression, was not impacted by antidepressant medications. When the medications were decreased, Damion's appetite improved. An antipsychotic, thiothixene, was considered to treat Damion's violent outbursts and possibly an underlying paranoid process. Informed of the potential long-range side effects, however, Damion's mother refused to provide consent for a trial on this neuroleptic.

Damion's adoptive mother had little conscious recognition of the severity of his problems. Patterns of "enabling," suggesting projective identification cycles between mother and Damion, were apparent. Through denying the severity of Damion's problems his mother protected projected parts of herself. It was suspected that Damion's mother suffered from a paranoid disorder as well (see Reiner & Kaufman, 1974).[13]

Damion was discharged from the hospital to attend a day treatment program closer to his home. No medications were prescribed at the time of discharge, although Damion remained without overt depression, suicidal gestures, or assaultive behavior. Damion's behavioral adjustment lasted for approximately 2 weeks. Without the structure of the inpatient setting or medications, his behavior began to deteriorate. He was "out of control." Damion's oppositionalism increased. A suicidal threat led to a third hospitalization, which lasted 6 days.

Despite his history of positive response to medications, Damion's mother remained resistant to their use. Following a mild earthquake, Damion's disruptive behavior increased. Occurring the day prior to discharge, the tremor did not alter release plans. Damion returned home as planned.

Damion's day treatment lasted 5 days before he was rehospitalized. Behaviors were similar to previous admissions. Vacillations between severe depression and paranoia required Damion's assignment to a single room. Relationships with

---

[13]Reiner and Kaufman (1974) noted the high frequency of personality disorders among the parents of delinquents.

others were colored by entitlement and behavioral manipulation as if the entire unit existed solely to serve Damion's needs.

Damion threatened peers and seemed to delight in his power to intimidate others. Damion shared with a staff member how he would enjoy seeing one of his peers die from having his throat cut. After this incident he shared that "he wanted to grow up to be an assassin." Damion was remorseless in his determination. Despite his rage, there was a cold and calculating quality to his threats. He defended his threats with extreme conviction and righteous indignation.

Violent fantasies surfaced during individual sessions. Damion described his detailed attempt to kill his sister with a sharpened pencil. He justified this behavior by explaining that she had chased him when he tried to run away from home. It was clear that if he succeeded in killing his sister, Damion would feel no remorse. Concurrently Damion's treating psychiatrist experienced the intensely negative countertransference reaction commonly felt when interacting with the psychopath in a treatment setting (Meloy, 1988).

Damion's mother finally consented to a trial treatment with thiothixene, and a dosage of 25 mg was initiated. Damion's behavior showed some improvement. Violent and assaultive behavior diminished; interactions with peers subsequently improved. Intervention on the part of Damion's mother, however, resulted in a decreased dosage of thiothixene. Damion's behaviors almost immediately returned to baseline severity. Because Damion's mother withdrew her consent, at the time of discharge Damion was without medication. As is often the case with the severe CD child, parents unconsciously and consciously reinforce circumstances that facilitate problem behaviors. They invest in the child's psychopathology.

DAMION'S RORSCHACH

Damion completed the Wechsler Intelligence Scale for Children–Revised (WISC–R), Rorschach, Thematic Apperception Test, and Projective Drawings during his first admission. He was cooperative with testing, although he sometimes had difficulty following directions. Damion, however, offered little historical information and would not discuss reasons for admittance to the hospital. Mental status revealed normal affect despite self-reports of anger and sadness. Frustration tolerance was adequate. Thinking processes were clear and goal directed with no psychotic thought evident. Judgment was observed to be poor.

Table 2.6 presents Damion's Rorschach protocol. Table 2.7 shows the sequence of scores, and Table 2.8 shows the structural summary, both generated by Rorschach Scoring Program, Version 2 (Exner, Cohen, & Mcguire, 1990).

Structural Interpretation

Damion produces a normative number of responses (R = 18). He is not guarded or rigid (Lambda = .50). His protocol is interpretatively valid. Although scoring within a standard deviation of the normal range for 9-year-olds (Lambda = .81,

TABLE 2.6
Damion's Rorschach Protocol

Free Association	Inquiry
Card I 1) Looks like a spider. catching something and it's in the web.	E: (Rpts S's response) S: 2 hands in it — ants don't have hands. Has a web like this. E: Spider? S: Very long and big stomach and big head. E: Web? S: Fortunate web do look like that they're big or can be small. This one is big.

Structural Scoring: W+ FMa− A,Id 4.0 INC,AG
Aggression Scores: AgC
Primitive Modes of Relating: Engulfment; MOA = 5
Defenses: Projective Identification.

| Card II 2) A butterfly dying and blood all over it. | E: (Rpts S's response)
S: First looks like butterfly all round and I pretend there's a white thing in middle. You can't see it but other butterflies know what it looks like and they don't look the same.
E: Blood?
S: Coming out because it's red. |

Structural Scoring: WS+ C'F.CF.FMp.mau A,Bl 4.5 MOR
Aggression Scores: AgPast
Primitive Modes of Relating: None.
Defenses: Projection.

| 3) Looks like black and white and red. | E: (Rpts S's response)
S: Outside is white and inside is white and outside is black and orange too. |

Structural Scoring: WSv Cn Id
Aggression Scoring: None
Primitive Modes of Relating: None.
Defenses: None categorized.

| Card III 4) Two ladies sitting down and getting something, and a bowtie on them. | E: (Rpts S's response)
S: They're standing like this and face looks like it's right here, getting something. |

Structural Scoring: D+ Mao 2 H,Cg P 4.0
Aggression Scores: None.
Primitive Modes of Relating: None. MOA = 2
Defenses: None categorized.

(Continued)

TABLE 2.6
(Continued)

Free Association	Inquiry
5) And a red light.	E: (Rpts S's response) S: It's a string hanging down with a big long thing.

Structural Scoring: Do FC.mpu Hh
Aggression Scores: None.
Primitive Modes of Relating: None.
Defenses: None categorized.

6) And a red bowtie.	E: (Rpts S's response) S: Right here and here—can't see it red they show it red they show it black, red and looks like bowtie.

Structural Scoring: Do CFo Cg
Aggression Scores: None.
Primitive Modes of Relating: None.
Defenses: None categorized.

Card IV 7) Looks like a monster with a tail and small arms and big feet.	E: (Rpts Ss response) S: Looks like a monster face is small feet are real big can tell looks like a monster and looks like a tail and small hands are black if you see anything that's black it sure looks like it.

Structural Scoring: Wo FC'o (A) 2.0
Aggression Scores: AgC
Primitive Modes of Relating: None.
Defenses: None categorized.

Card V 8) Butterfly with big wings a ferocious butterfly.	E: (Rpts S's response) S: Because it has these big things and big long ones and things hanging out of it.

Structural Scoring: Wo FMpo A P 1.0 INC,AG
Aggression Scores: AgC
Primitive Modes of Relating: None.
Defenses: Massive Denial.

9) And a bee.	E: (Rpts S's response) S: Bees have one of these so they can sting people and they have big butterfly's—big wings.

Structural Scoring: Wo Fo A 1.0
Aggression Scores: AgC
Primitive Modes of Relating: None. MOA = 5
Defenses: None categorized.

(Continued)

TABLE 2.6
(Continued)

Free Association	Inquiry
Card VI 10) A caterpillar.	E: (Rpts S's response) S: Just looks like it looks like a straight line with caterpillars inside of it. E: Inside? S: It's so huge.

Structural Scoring: W+ F− A 2.5 ALOG
Aggression Scores: None.
Primitive Modes of Relating: Metamorphosis & Transformation.
Defenses: None categorized.

| 11) And a wolf. | E: (Rpts S's response)
S: Little things here and big ears and big fluffy stuff and paw and feets and butt, butt.
E: Fluffy?
S: Has stuff on it like black stuff (touches card). |

Structural Scoring: Wo FTu A 2.5 DV
Aggression Scores: AgC
Primitive Modes of Relating: None.
Defenses: None categorized.

| Card VII   12) Two ladies. | E: (Rpts S's response)
S: Hair, arms, butts and feets. |

Structural Scoring: Wo Fu 2 H,Sx 2.5 DV
Aggression Scores: None.
Primitive Modes of Relating: None.
Defenses: Devaluation.

| 13) Two little girls. | E: (Rpts S's response)
S: Skirt, legs and arms and big cute hair. |

Structural Scoring: Wo Fu 2 H 2.5
Aggression Scores: None.
Primitive Modes of Relating: None.
Defenses: None categorized.

| Card VIII 14) It's a wolf staring see it's statue in the water. | E: (Rpts S's response)
S: Looks like a wolf right here and rocks and water. It's looking, see it's looking for food looks in water if it's hungry. |

Structural Scoring: W+ FMp.Fro A,Na P 4.5 DV
Aggression Scores: None.
Primitive Modes of Relating: Narcissistic Mirroring. MOA = 4
Defenses: None categorized.

(Continued)

TABLE 2.6
(Continued)

Free Association	Inquiry
Card IX 15) Looks like a storm.	E: (Rpts S's response) S: It is—it looks like it. Orange and it's white and it's like a mirror right beside it.

Structural Scoring: WSv C'.C Na
Aggression Scoring: AgC
Primitive Modes of Relating: None.
Defenses: None categorized.

16) A mirror.	E: (Rpts S's response) S: Just looks like it because everything looks so natural and the same.

Structural Scoring: Ddv F− Hh
Aggression Scores: None.
Primitive Modes of Relating: Narcissistic Mirroring. MOA = 4
Defenses: None categorized.

Card X 17) Looks like a jet with outer space persons.	E: (Rpts S's response) S: Actually it doesn't.

Structural Scoring: D+ Fo 2 (H),Sc 4.0
Aggression Scores: None.
Primitive Modes of Relating: None.
Defenses: Devaluation, Denial.

18) Looks like bull cows and they're running away from the storm.	E: (Rpts S's response) S: Fluffy and have horns on them grey stuff on them. E: Storm? S: Pink stuff it looks like a storm because it's pink and looks like a cloud.

Structural Scoring: D+ FMa.FT.CFu 2 A,Na 4.0
Aggression Scores: AgC, AgPot
Primitive Modes of Relating: Violent Symbiosis, Separation, Reunion. MOA = 7
Defenses: Projective Identification.

SD = .37), Damion's disruptive behaviors were consistent with those noted for children producing skewed Lambdas, either high or low (Exner & Weiner, 1982). Damion integrates at a normal level (Zf = 13), however he does it in a haphazard manner (Zd = −2.5). We postulated a percentage of the underincorporators (Zd ≤ −3.0) within our CD sample (25%) might also meet the criteria for ADHD. This diagnosis was not ruled out for Damion.

TABLE 2.7
Damion's Sequence of Scores

Card I	1) W+ 1	FMa−		A,Id		4.0	INC1,AG	(AgC,Engulfment)
Card II	2) WS+ 1	C′F.CF.FMp.mau		A,Bl		4.5	MOR	(AgPast)
	3) WSv 1	Cn		Id				
Card III	4) D+ 1	Mao	2	H,Cg	P	4.0		
	5) Do 2	FC.mpu		Hh				
	6) Do 3	CFo		Cg				
Card IV	7) Wo 1	FC′o		(A)		2.0		(AgC)
Card V	8) Wo 1	FMpo		A	P	1.0	INC,AG	(AgC)
	9) Wo 1	Fo		A		1.0		(AgC)
Card VI	10) W+ 1	F−		A		2.5	ALOG	(Metamorphosis & Transformation)
	11) Wo 1	FTu		A		2.5	DV	(AgC)
Card VII	12) Wo 1	Fu	2	H,Sx		2.5	DV	
	13) Wo 1	Fu	2	H		2.5		
Card VIII	14) W+ 1	FMp.Fro		A,Na	P	4.5	DV	
Card IX	15) WSv 1	C′.C		Na				(AgC)
	16) Ddv 99	F−		Hh				
Card X	17) D+ 11	Fo	2	(H),Sc		4.0		
	18) D+ 11	FMa.FT.CFu	2	A,Na		4.0		(AgC,AgPot)

Damion's percepts are less conventional (P = 3) than other 9-year-olds (M = 5.78; Exner, 1990b) but similar to our CD sample. Like other CD children Damion is less concerned with perceptual accuracy (X+% = 39; F+% = 33) and demonstrates impairment in reality testing (X−% = 17). His WSum6 (12.0) is normative for children. There are no Level 2 special scores or contaminations (CON). The presence of one ALOG alone, unexpected in adults, may or may not indicate severe thinking disturbance in a 9-year-old boy. Combined with poor perceptual accuracy, however, it probably indicates the severity of Damion's cognitive problems and is predictive of future ones. Damion is not positive for any constellations.

Like 35% of the CD sample and 40% of nonpatient 9-year-olds (Exner, 1990b), Damion evidenced an extratensive style. He has fewer organized resources (EA = 6.0) than expected (Exner [1990b] nonpatient 9-year-olds, EA = 8.25). M is less than normative and consistent with an absence of delay. His eb (FM+m = 7) is elevated indicating unorganized resources and the press of unmet needs. Damion feels assaulted from within and without. Fewer resources and poor controls (D = −2, AdjD = −1) suggest tenuous defenses unable to manage impulses. If Damion's development continues on the current course, D and AdjD would increase in late adolescence as his defensive operations and object relations work in concert.

Damion is chronically angry and behaviorally oppositional (S = 3). Even in comparison to nonpatient 9-year-olds, he has difficulty modulating affect (FC:CF+C = 1:5) with a tendency to be explosive (C = 1). Damion's FC:CF+C ratio is made more atypical as two of the CFs occur in complex blends (C′F.CF.FMp.mau; FMa.FT.CFu) whereas his pure C is combined with a C′ and

TABLE 2.8
Damion's Rorschach Structural Summary

Determinants

Location Features	Blends	Single	Contents	S-Constellation
				..$FV+VF+V+FD > 2$
			H = 3, 0	..Col-Shd Bl > 0
Zf = 13	C'F.CF.FM.m	M = 1	(H) = 1, 0	..Ego < .31, > .44
ZSum = 39.0	FC.m	FM = 2	Hd = 0, 0	..MOR > 3
ZEst = 41.5	FM.Fr	m = 0	(Hd)= 0, 0	..Zd > + − 3.5
	C'.C	FC = 0	Hx = 0, 0	..es > EA
W = 12	FM.FT.CF	CF = 1	A = 8, 0	..CF+C > FC
(Wv = 2)		C = 0	(A) = 1, 0	..X+% < .70
D = 5		Cn = 1	Ad = 0, 0	..S > 3
Dd = 1		FC' = 1	(Ad)= 0, 0	..P < 3 or > 8
S = 3		C'F = 0	An = 0, 0	..Pure H < 2
		C' = 0	Art = 0, 0	..R < 17
DQ		FT = 1	Ay = 0, 0	x.....TOTAL
.....(FQ−)		TF = 0	Bl = 0, 1	
+ = 7 (2)		T = 0	Bt = 0, 0	*Special Scorings*
o = 8 (0)		FV = 0	Cg = 1, 1	
v/+ = 0 (0)		VF = 0	Cl = 0, 0	Lv1 Lv2
v = 3 (1)		V = 0	Ex = 0, 0	DV = 3 × 1 0 × 2
		FY = 0	Fd = 0, 0	INC = 2 × 2 0 × 4
		YF = 0	Fi = 0, 0	DR = 0 × 3 0 × 6
		Y = 0	Ge = 0, 0	FAB = 0 × 4 0 × 7
		Fr = 0	Hh = 2, 0	ALOG = 1 × 5
Form Quality		rF = 0	Ls = 0, 0	CON = 0 × 7
		FD = 0	Na = 1, 2	SUM 6 = 6
		F = 6	Sc = 0, 1	WSUM6 = 12

	FQx	FQf	MQual	SQx			
+ =	0	0	0	0		Sx = 0, 1	AB = 0 CP = 0
o =	7	2	1	0		Xy = 0, 0	AG = 2 MOR = 1
u =	6	2	0	1		Id = 1, 1	CFB = 0 PER = 0
− =	3	2	0	0			COP = 0 PSV = 0
none =	2	—	0	2	(2) = 5		

Ratios, Percentages, and Derivations

R = 18   L = 0.50

					FC:CF+C = 1 : 5	COP = 0	AG = 2
					Pure C = 1	Food = 0	
EB = 1:	5.0	EA =	6.0	EBPer = 5.0	Afr = 0.38	Isolate/R = 0.33	
eb = 7:	5	es =	12	D = −2	S = 3	H:(H)Hd(Hd) = 3: 1	
		Adj es =	11	Adj D = −1	Blends:R = 5:18	(HHd):(AAd) = 1: 1	
					CP = 0	H+A:Hd+Ad = 13: 0	

FM = 5	:	C' = 3	T = 2				
m = 2	:	V = 0	Y = 0				
				P = 3	Zf = 13	3r+(2)/R = 0.44	
a:p		= 4: 4	Sum6 = 6	X+% = 0.39	Zd = −2.5	Fr+rF = 1	
Ma:Mp		= 1: 0	Lv2 = 0	F+% = 0.33	W:D:Dd = 12: 5: 1	FD = 0	
2AB+Art+Ay		= 0	WSum6= 12	X−% = 0.17	W:M = 12: 1	An+Xy = 0	
M −		= 0	Mnone = 0	S−% = 0.00	DQ+ = 7	MOR = 1	
				Xu% = 0.33	DQv = 3		

SCZI = 1   DEPI = 4   CDI = 3   S-CON = N/A   HVI = No   OBS = No

Note. From Exner (1990a). Copyright 1990 by John E. Exner, Jr. Reprinted by permission.

Wsv. He has more affect than he can handle. Aggression is problematic (AG = 2). Given poor controls and an active style (Ma:Mp = 1:0) he is likely to act out this impulse. Much of his energy is expended avoiding (Afr = .38) and constraining affect (SumC' = 3; FC' = 1, C'F = 1, C' = 1), neither of which he does successfully.

CD children do not usually produce T (88% are T·= 0). Damion's 2 Ts may indicate discomfort with skin contact (Schachtel, 1966) and affectional hunger rather than affectional relatedness (both are spoiled Ts). His affectional hunger creates disruption, the extent of which are discussed via sequence and content analysis. As he develops will his Ts disappear? Or like our sexual homicide perpetrators (see chapter 9), will his affectional hunger, in part, fuel violence during latency, and later sexual violence? Keep in mind at age 9 he has already demonstrated homicidal fantasy, threatened to kill, and physically assaulted female family members. For this he shows no anxiety or remorse (Y = 0, V = 0).

Despite normative pure H, cooperativeness is not expected (COP = 0). Pathologically narcissistic (Fr = 1; W:M = 12:1), Damion is still less self-absorbed (egocentricity = .44) when compared to other 9-year-olds (M = .57, SD = .12). He experiences himself as damaged (MOR = 1). The lack of PERs support unstable defenses in this 9-year-old CD and the absence of the smooth functioning defenses of omnipotence and grandiosity. Perhaps Damion finds some solace in isolation (Isolate/R = .33).

Interpretation of Scoring Sequence

Damion's protocol is comprised primarily of Ws (W:D = 12:5). His scoring sequence reveals the interplay of impulse and defense. His perceptual accuracy is "stably unstable" throughout the protocol. At times recovery occurs (Cards III & X) when he relaxes his need to integrate the whole (produces Ds rather than Ws). On other cards (II & IX) the press of needs and difficulty with their integration are evident, despite on IX defensively resorting to a Dd (FQx−).

He begins Card I with an integration of the whole blot (W+). The press of needs (FMa−), possibly aggression (AG), impedes the integrative process (FQx−, INC). Card II, the first with chromatic color, continues attempted control (S) of need states (FMp, m) through integration. The results, however, are similar. Constraint is minimally effective (C'F, FQxu) and affect is poorly modulated (CF). Hostility and helplessness (S, m) evolve from a sense of damaged and injured self (MOR, Bl). Further deterioration occurs on Response 3 as WSv is accompanied by a Cn. When combined with his Zd = −2.5 this unexpected Cn provides further speculation concerning a biologically based cognitive deficit. Recovery occurs on Card III (FQz = o, u, o; FC). Perhaps the use of a popular and reliance on Ds aid perceptual accuracy. Integrating details is less taxing than including all aspects of the whole.

Cards IV and V represent Damion's last "pocket" of recovery (all o form quality). Like Card I, evidence of the disruptive effects of aggression on thinking

(AG, INC) occur. The popular, however, facilitates adequate perceptual accuracy. Cognitive slippage (ALOG, DV) is severe on Card VI as relational needs are stimulated (FTu). Response 10 is most severely impaired (FQx–, ALOG). The W is accompanied by DQx+, once again demonstrating his difficulty integrating the whole.

A sex (Sx) response, virtually absent in both nonpatient 9-year-olds (0%) and CD children (5%), occurs on Card VII. Sexual impulses not expected during a normal latency may prematurely trouble Damion. FQxu accompanies both responses on Card VII, not unexpected in a child as the need to integrate the whole takes away from finer discriminations in perceptual accuracy. On Card VIII he recovers a modal reflection (see chapter 9) whose interpretation awaits content analysis. Self-focusing without a human object (A, Na), aided by a popular, helps organize the response. Still a DV occurs.

The dysphoric elements of Card IX are overwhelming (DQv, FQx–). On Response 15 disorganization occurs (Wsv, C) despite attempted constraint (C'). Damion's only Dd is produced on 16 as a desperate attempt to control affect. This defensive manuever is not successful (FQx–). Card X suggests partial recovery. He ends the task, however, in the same manner he began, with unmet needs (FMa.FT) and poorly modulated affect (CF). In real life Damion's struggle with affective discharge and affective constraint closely mirror his Rorschach scoring sequence.

Interpretation of Content

Content analysis suggests an inner object world characterized by fears of engulfment (Responses 1 & 18), aggressive and damaged objects (1, 2, 7, 8, 9, 11, 14, 15, & 18), and the need for mirroring (14 & 16). Card I begins with "a spider catching something in its web." Projective identification creates an object world that is dangerous and potentially engulfing. Damion's malevolent transformation of objects (Gacono, 1992) occurs on Card V where projective material transforms a benign "butterfly with big wings" into a "ferocious butterfly." Aggressive imagery, such as a bee ("that can sting people"), wolves, and storms are produced throughout Damion's protocol. In fact 39% of his responses contain AgC. Abundant, aggressive imagery suggest identification with the aggressor as a developing, defensive process. His life experience correlates with the process of aggression (Card I) leading to a sense of being assaulted or damaged: "a butterfly dying and blood all over it" (Card II).

Unlike 88% of our CD sample who produce T-less protocols, Damion produces two Ts. Both Ts also contain aggressive "spoilers." Rather than soft teddy bears, Damion produces texture with a "wolf" and "bull cows running away from a storm." Affectional hunger is suffused with aggression. Interpersonal interactions are potentially damaging. Damion's perception of others is filtered through devaluation, like "outer space persons" (Response 17).

Response 14 is particularly revealing. A wolf (aggressive imagery) "staring see its statue in the water . . . it's looking, see it's looking for food looks in water if it's hungry." The predator looking for prey. Like Narcissus looking in the pond, Damion will emotionally wither before he finds sustenance through mirroring. Mirroring in his 9-year-old personality is ineffective. The juxtaposition (Card IX) of "storm" (15) and "mirror" (16) represents the failure of narcissistic defenses to manage overwhelming affect. The mirror without object may represent his infancy during which no one validated his existence. Like a mirror awaiting an object to reflect, Damion's self was a blank slate on which no one wrote. The sad nature of this experience is indicated by his acceptance: "It just looks like it because everything looks so natural and the same" (16).

Damion's MOA scores are consistent with psychopathology and other content analysis. His worse mean MOA score (4.5) is more pathological than either normal ($M = 3.88$) or most CD children ($M = 3.33$). Eighty-three percent of his MOA scorable responses fall within a pathological range (Levels 4, 5, 6, or 7) and he produces one very psychopathological Level 7 score.

Summary

Damion's Rorschach is consistent with a child who displays significant psychopathic personality precursors. The etiology of his disorder is likely both biological and environmental. His protocol is rich in displaying symbolic correlates of observed behaviors. His Rorschach is suffused with poorly integrated libidinal and aggressive drives. Without adequate resources or mature defenses, he lacks the ability to tolerate dysphoric affect. The development of this capacity, if possible in this case, would require attachment to others and the development of self-soothing processes. Paradoxically, potential attachments are too threatening as they further stimulate affect. Damion's own projective material turns potential "helpers" into enemies. Despite his affectional hunger, attachment is not possible. Narcissistic withdrawal and aggressive/sadistic acting out protect his damaged self from inner and other bad objects.

The effects of long-term residential treatment combined with medication might offer hope of some remediation in these areas. Certainly with every child appropriate therapeutic intervention should be made available. Inconsistencies in Damion's treatment, fueled by family dynamics, however, make change unlikely. Because of his aggression, Damion currently cycles in and out of residential treatment. His adoptive mother continues to be an object of ambivalence. Development of the requisite, strong therapeutic alliance necessary to mediate his attachment difficulties remains illusory.

Given the chronic nature of his condition, coupled with the mother's severe denial (to see Damion's psychopathology clearly would affront her narcissism—Damion as a projected ideal object representation) suggests a poor prognosis for change and the likelihood of Damion becoming a severe antisocial personality in adulthood. Should Damion be incarcerated as an adult he, like others, may initiate litigation demanding psychological services. Unfortunately, by then it will be too late.

The Adolescent
Antisocial Pattern

*Living as he does somewhere between the regressive dependency of
childhood and the progressive independence of adulthood, struggling against
each to forge an identity of his own, the adolescent has occupied something
of a nosological no man's land.*

—Rubenstein (1980, p. 441)

The importance of adolescence as an "at-risk" time for the development of
psychopathology was highlighted in a special edition of the *American Psychologist* (American Psychological Association, 1993). Since research in the 1970s
(Petersen et al., 1993), attention has shifted from adolescence as a transitional
stage to a distinct developmental one (Sugarman, Bloom-Feshbach, & Bloom-Feshbach, 1980). "Few developmental periods are characterized by so many
different levels—changes due to pubertal development, social role redefinitions,
cognitive development, school transitions, and the emergence of sexuality"
(Eccles et al., 1993, p. 90).

The developmental turmoil of adolescence is sometimes confused with or
exacerbated by psychopathology (Weiner & Del Caudio, 1976). When present,
however, psychological difficulties in adolescence frequently develop into
adulthood psychiatric disorders (Petersen et al., 1993). As Sugarman et al. (1980)
noted, "Seldom do borderline adolescents resolve severe difficulties themselves
and enter adulthood in the neurotic or higher range of character pathology" (p.
472). Adolescent "character problems," however, are relegated to Axis I (APA,
1994), suggesting developmental flux and a hope of modification. At age 18 and

45

thereafter, personality disorder diagnoses appear on Axis II (APA, 1994), reflecting their chronicity and the stabilization of character traits.

The clinician can be misled into believing that a full clinical syndrome (personality disorder) is not, in some cases, present by adolescence and even childhood (see Bleiberg, 1984; P. Kernberg, 1981, 1989, 1990; Smith, 1994). Weiner and Del Caudio (1976) cautioned against the too frequently exercised practice of overdiagnosing "situational disorders" (adjustment disorders) in adolescents when more severe psychopathology existed. An adjustment disorder diagnosis obfuscates the clinical picture and subsequent treatment interventions. With both children and adolescents the clinician must carefully delineate between state and trait-related problems. A psychodynamic assessment of personality functioning is crucial for the CD adolescent when psychopathy level[1] contributes to treatment prognosis or other specific predictive questions, such as risk of violence.

PSYCHOPATHY AND ADOLESCENCE

John was a 16-year-old Hispanic gang member whose escalating violent behavior toward both family and strangers resulted in numerous incarcerations in juvenile hall. As a final remedial step before incarceration in the California Youth Authority, John was placed in a residential treatment home. John met the criteria for a diagnosis of Conduct Disorder (CD), undifferentiated, severe type (APA, 1987; see chapter 2 for CD criteria). His level of personality functioning was clearly borderline. John was an adolescent with a crystallizing psychopathic character.

The structure of the residential setting helped contain John's physical violence. Aggression was reduced to verbal outbursts and threats. John could sometimes be found hiding in the closet after rageful episodes, sucking his thumb. Concerned with his regressive incidents, treatment staff ordered a psychiatric evaluation, but a trial of psychotropic medications was postponed. Instead John was prescribed psychotherapy. Group and weekly individual sessions began, and the group method taught coping skills (i.e., anger management, problem solving, alteration of criminal thinking). Individual psychotherapy facilitated ego integration and identity formation. Shortly after the onset of treatment, John's regressive incidents diminished.

Aggressive and sexual impulses in psychopathic adolescents do not become dormant during the latency period. Regulated by pre-Oedipal defenses, they remain unsublimated. Aggressive drives are at the forefront of psychic functioning; fueled

---

[1]Adaptations of the PCL–R for adolescent offenders are currently underway (Adelle Forth, personal communication, January 1993; David Kosson, personal communication, June 1993). Preliminary findings have been positive, suggesting the scale's usefulness with adolescent offenders (Forth, Hart, & Hare, 1990).

by narcissistic vulnerabilities, they act as an impetus to behavioral violence. It is not uncommon to evaluate conduct disordered children ages 7–10 who are violent and/or sexually acting out. These behaviors often mark the disorder.

John's violence began early. At age 6 his rage erupted because another youngster had a toy he coveted. This was the earliest of several examples John related, suggesting the influence of envy within his personality: his wish to destroy the goodness he perceived in others (Klein, 1946). John believed he made a decision at that time. Because he would never have what others had, he was entitled to take, and justified in assaulting the child. John's easily provoked rage led to murderous fantasies. Violence helped him repair his internal object relations (Meloy, 1988). He openly expressed his desire to "beat someone up" whenever he felt bad. This included violent fantasies toward staff. He described his rage as an "inner blackness," his affective experience as emptiness. John sincerely felt little concern for others and experienced a complete and total absence of remorse (developmentally an impossibility for him [Meloy, 1988]).

Without the necessary childhood templates, the psychopathic adolescent is unable to complete the task of adolescence and establish an integrated ego identity (Erickson, 1950). Residual part self and object representations, impaired internalization processes, aggressive identifications, and bonding deficits from childhood (Meloy, 1988; Weber, 1990) impede the process of positive identification that would aid in identity formation. Because attachment capacity and the ability to idealize (Aichhorn, 1925; Winnicott, 1958a) have prognostic significance, they must be carefully assessed for each adolescent.

For severe CD adolescents (psychopathic) major childhood disappointments and a predominance of shame have extinguished the capacity for interpersonal attachment, if it was psychobiologically possible in the first place (see chapter 2). These adolescents take on aggressive identifications (A. Freud, 1936) which compensate for vulnerability, protect the self from shameful feelings (the underbelly of narcissism), and provide justification for ruthless behaviors. As Bilmes (1967) noted, "One may identify with what is evil but never with what is shameful . . . the more we associate it with evil—the more dramatic and heroic a model it becomes for certain of our youth. We create a highly idealized and desirable image" (p. 123).

Gender identity confusion is also common in adolescent psychopathy (Eissler, 1949). One 15-year-old female psychopathic subject appeared much calmer when staff allowed her to dress as a male and called her "Al" instead of "Alice." John's identifications were both predatory and feminine. His symbiotic identification with mother and inability to separate from her, in part, fueled his rage. He was furious at his own passivity and feminine identification. Unable to separate from the maternal object and grieve his loss, the CD youth may choose to massively deny his attachment and strike a "cool pose" (Majors & Billson, 1992). Raised in a single-parent home lacking a father, John maintained a fragile, idealized "part-attachment" to his family. He would not tolerate anyone talking about or inquiring of his family, and even casual questions provoked his rage. Any suggestion of reality threatened his precariously maintained idealized maternal and familial part objects. He resisted any involvement in treatment by his mother or family, because it threatened his internalized representations of them as "all good" objects, and might necessitate the integration of their split off "all bad" qualities (Kernberg, 1975).

Adolescence reawakens the need to separate (Rubenstein, 1980) in normal teenagers. For the psychopathic adolescent, however, these needs have never slept. Object relations theory (Jacobson, 1964) posits adolescence as a second individuation stage (Blos, 1979; Mahler, Pine, & Bergman, 1975). John was unable to acknowledge attachment to anyone, and by any measure John was detached. Yet paradoxically, John's fragile cathexis to an internalized and idealized part object was an important source of stabilization. As in narcissistic psychopathology, the pseudo-autonomy of social behavior masked a strong dependency on idealized part objects to ward off devalued part objects.[2]

Initial sessions focused on "why he should trust the therapist," and "why he should change." John associated the idea of change with weakness and being controlled. At times he stated that his individual sessions were his favorite "group." Any observations from his treating doctor that the sessions were important to him or that he demonstrated prosocial behavior, however, were first adamantly denied, and then followed by paranoid ideation.[3] Splitting and primitive denial were evident because John lacked conscious awareness of his inconsistencies and could not tolerate them in thought. They were quickly evacuated through paranoid projection.

Over time John would confront others in group. He continued to separate staff into all good and all bad objects. Devaluation helped ward off potential attachment to staff or the therapist. When asked "why he couldn't carry around staff (internally) like he did his mother," he replied, "then I would be angry all the time."[4] Despite his devaluation of the therapist he would come to group early and help arrange the chairs. When the therapist appeared early for a session (to

---

[2]In some cases, idealized internal objects represent others, such as mother or father; in other cases, the idealized internal object may only represent the self, a form of secondary narcissism (S. Freud, 1914). In the latter, a gross incapacity to bond is usually evident because the idealized residue of a prior attachment (the internalized part object) is gone. Or perhaps was never there.

[3]As Meloy (1988) theorized, ". . . any clinical attempts to modify the ideal self in a more socially adaptive or affectional direction would cause a disidentification with the idealized object and a reactivation of the idealized object as an aggressive introject within the grandiose self-structure. This would phenomenally be experienced by the psychopathic character as a subjective sense of being under attack . . ." (pp. 52–53).

[4]It is much easier to maintain an Mp than an Ma. Day-to-day living with real objects (people) that are internalized as whole, real, and meaningful representations means that multiple and varied feelings will be experienced, and may need to be expressed (Ma). If, however, internalized objects are few in number and devoid of real-world connections, such as an idealized memory of mother (Mp), then affects and ambivalence remain at a greater psychological distance, and the internal object becomes a haven of fantasy. Living is more comfortable, but done at a great price: the asocial or antisocial tendency. John did not want his actual mother around.

shoot pool in the game room), John would offer to rack up the pool balls. Behavior on home passes improved.

The lack of evocative recall, a measure of object constancy, was evident. During individual sessions John verbalized his inability to remember what others looked like. He lived in the here and now. Consideration of a future stimulated the possibility of hope—a feeling that created envy, potential disappointments, and subsequent rage. John was surprised that the therapist showed up every week on time. He was never certain that the therapist would be there until the moment of physical appearance. Normal adolescents cognitively progress from concrete to formal operations (Inhelder & Piaget, 1958), evidencing a greater capacity to distance from the present through the use of abstract or symbolic thought. For youth such as John this progression never occurs. Like the adult psychopath they remain prisoners of the present (Meloy, 1988), unable to project into the future and foresee the consequences of their actions, and lacking a capacity to reflect upon the past in any meaningful way, the latter requiring certain mnemonic and object constancy attainments.

Two months prior to the therapist's vacation an impending session to be missed became a topic of discussion. John denied that the absence would mean anything. He only became angry and began to question why he should trust the therapist when any implication that the sessions had value was made.

The vacation day came and went. John refused to attend his next session. The second scheduled session lasted only 30 minutes. He berated the therapist and then remained ragefully silent. Unfortunately, as is often the case, the most inexperienced staff work with the most difficult youth. John's splitting was unwittingly reinforced. His behavior got worse. He began to disregard rules with only minor consequences from the staff. John reoffended on a home pass, assaulting an elderly man with a baseball bat. Perhaps with some relief, John was subsequently remanded to the California Youth Authority (a prison for adolescents). At least now he could spend his days not having to struggle with internal fears and anxieties.

ADOLESCENT RORSCHACHS

Marguerite Hertz pioneered the Rorschach exploration of adolescent development (Hertz, 1935, 1940, 1941; Hertz & Baker, 1943a, 1943b). She noted changes specific to childhood and adolescence. During mid- to late adolescence, age-related Rorschach variability begins to diminish (Ames et al., 1959; Rubenstein, 1988).

Although variables stabilize at different rates (Exner et al., 1985), when patterns for identified ratios appear during adolescence, they tend to endure (Exner & Weiner, 1982). Introversion and extratension stabilize after ages 8 and 10–12, respectively (Exner & Weiner, 1982). When the FC frequency exceeds CF+C, or EA becomes greater than es, they generally remain so. The same stability does not exist for es > EA when elevations in es are influenced by situationally affected determinants (m and Y). FC dominance, however, is only present in less than half of subjects by age 14 (Exner & Weiner, 1982). This ratio of FC> CF+C may not occur until the late teens (Exner & Weiner, 1982) or later (Ames et al., 1959) for the majority of nonpatients.

Ames et al. (1959) compared ranges for child (ages 5–10) and adolescent (ages 10–16) protocols. For this age range (5–16) a gradual increase in the total number of responses is expected. Response productivity (child R = 14–19; adolescent R = 19–23) is comprised of more Ds (child D% = 33%–48%; adolescent 41%–51%) whereas W% (child 42%–58%; adolescent 43%–51%) remains fairly constant. W:D shifts from 1:1 in childhood to 1:1.5 in adolescence. Due to the increase in other determinants such as M (child 0.4–1.7; adolescent 1.8–2.6) and FM (child 1.1–1.9; adolescent 1.6–2.5), F% (child 52%–70%; adolescent 56%–63%) decreases. FM > M begins to shift in adolescents. Movement responses are primarily extensor (44%), followed by static (33%), conflicted (15%), and flexor passive (8%).[5] C′ is noticeably absent. F+% increases during adolescence (child 78%–89%; adolescent 90%–93%), then decreases slightly in adulthood (< 80%). A% (adolescent 41%–49%) remains fairly consistent whereas H% (adolescent 18%–19%) increases. Ames et al. (1959) noted that, "The Rorschach responses of adolescents and preadolescents, on the other hand, do not differ dramatically from those of adults" (p. 7). Similarities become particularly apparent by age 16.

Gender

In the children's chapter (chapter 2) we emphasized developmental aspects of conduct disorder and their Rorschach manifestations. In this chapter we place equal importance on considering adolescent gender and identity issues. We believe sensitivity to these issues may be particularly relevant when examining Rorschachs within clinical populations.[6]

Gilligan (1982) postulated different gender-related developmental tracks. She observed that feminine identity is based on a continuous process related to attachment. Females separate from mother and then identify with her. Male identity is based on a discontinuous process equated with separation and detachment. An

---

[5]"Rorschach identifies two stances taken by the actor in the perceived movement: extensor (more literally, "stretch"; the German is *streck*) and flexor ("bend or bow"; German *beuge*) . . . Stance is identified from S's language according to whether the direction of the movement is toward the center of the blot's axis, centripetal on flexor; or away from the blot's axis, centrifugal or extensor" (Beck, Beck, Levitt, & Molish, 1961, p. 77). Beck et al. also identified "mixed" (elements of extensor and flexor) and "static" movement responses. The static responses were similar to Exner's (1986a) passive response, involving motionless, rigidly fixed movement, that is, "a little boy standing."

[6]In a sample of 1,710 high school students, Lewinsohn, Hops, Roberts, Seeley, and Andrews (1993) discovered a greater prevalence rate for males (> 2× more likely) than females in the Disruptive Behavior Disorders category (APA, 1987). Males were more often diagnosed as ADHD, almost 3× as likely to receive a conduct disorder diagnosis and > 3× as likely to receive the oppositional defiant disorder than females. We would expect some sensitivity of the Rorschach in elucidating aspects of these striking behavioral differences.

identity defined in the negative, by what is not feminine, the male process leads to increased competition and aggression. "From very early, then, because they are parented by a person of the same gender . . . girls come to experience themselves as less differentiated than boys, as more continuous with and related to the external object-world, and as differently oriented to their inner object-world as well" (Chodorow, 1978, p. 167). Identity precedes intimacy for males; for females they are intertwined (Gilligan, 1982). Attachment-based differences are critical when studying antisocial and narcissistic disturbances in both women and men, personality disorders noted for their "independent styles" (Millon, 1981). We would expect certain Rorschach variables to reflect gender differences (also see chapter 4).

Exner and Weiner (1982) attributed little to Rorschach manifestations of gender differences during childhood and adolescence because they discovered few significant statistical findings. They did note increased Y and egocentricity in girls during adolescence. Their empirical findings are seemingly at odds with developmental theory and differ markedly from the findings of Ames et al. (1959) who placed significance on gender differences beginning in adolescence:

> Though the behavior of boys and girls has been observed to differ in many respects during the earliest years . . . so far as the Rorschach is concerned sex differences in the first 10 years are small in comparison to age differences. We anticipate that sex differences would increase and stabilize during the years from 10 to 16 perhaps equaling age differences as a source of variation in the Rorschach response. (p. 5)

In the Ames et al. (1959) adolescent samples girls generally produced more responses ($p < .01$). Locations, virtually equal through childhood, differed with boys, producing a greater W% ($p < .01$), but less D% ($p < .05$) and Dd% ($p < .01$). Girls also produced more S.

F% was not significantly different and decreased in girls after age 13. By age 16, 50% of the girls produced F% similar to adults. Boys produced the highest F% at age 15, decreasing afterwards. F+% was slightly higher in girls ($p < .05$). M varied throughout adolescence with a greater productivity in girls ($p < .05$). FM was variable, with boys producing more until age 14 and then girls producing more afterwards. Inanimate movement (m) was infrequently produced by both genders. Girls produced more static and moderate extensor responses whereas boys exceeded in the mixed or conflicted category. Ames et al. suggested that Rorschach patterns indicated girls matured earlier than boys.

Girls produced more FC and CF ($p < .05$). Seventy-five percent use some form of color by age 16. Throughout the 10–16 year age range only 12% of subjects produced pure C. Consistent with Exner and Weiner's (1982) finding, they also produced more F(C).[7] The use of black, FC', C'F, FClob, and ClobF was infrequent for either gender (Ames et al., 1959).

---

[7]Rapaport used F(C) to designate the use of shading to specify important inner details or for color-form responses that referred to texture (Exner, 1986a).

Content differences included more (H) for boys and greater H% ($p < .01$) for girls. A% was variable to equal across genders. Boys produced more animal than human reflection responses, whereas the reflections of girls involved more scenes, mirrors, and trees.[8] Both genders chose Card X most often as the best liked card. Girls' consistent choice of Card IV as the most disliked was interpreted as indicating problems with body image, not with father (Ames et al., 1959). Boys varied in this area.

The Ames et al. (1959) findings suggest that gender should be considered as an independent variable in Rorschach research. We believe gender differences may be statistically significant within clinical populations in general and character-disordered populations in particular (Berg, Gacono, Meloy, & Peaslee, 1994; Gacono et al., 1992). Psychopathology may exacerbate basic differences that do not meet the threshold for statistical significance in normal populations, and are not empirically noticed in the natural environment. Authors who have discussed (Helfgott, 1992) and studied (Hare, 1991; Peaslee, Fleming, Baumgardner, Silbaugh, & Thackrey, 1992, see chapter 4) psychopathy in women also suggest gender-based differences.[9]

Differential expressions of aggression, a fundamental construct of both psychopathy and antisocial personality disorder, add to the rationale for considering gender as an independent variable. Violence patterns differ with males being significantly more violent than females. They disproportionately select strangers as victims, although both genders are more likely to be violent toward family members or friends. Women are almost exclusively violent toward members of their family, and it is usually for defensive purposes. These gender differences, stable across culture, race, age, and socioeconomic status, are fundamentally psychobiological, although shaped by the prevailing social and cultural ethos (Ellison, 1991; Meloy, 1992b).

A preliminary examination of the violence histories available for a subsample of our CD adolescents ($N = 74$), 56 males and 18 females, revealed a greater prevalence of violence toward others among the male subjects. Seventy-five

---

[8]This finding is consistent with our findings of different card choice in males and females who produce reflections. Also, some cards are more conducive to producing human (Cards III, VII) than animal (Card VIII) content (see chapter 7).

[9]Perhaps gender differences related to attachment form the template for the greater prevalence of conduct disorder in males. Sugarman et al. (1980) observed that borderline adolescent females manifest hysterical/infantile features and the males manifest obsessive/paranoid traits. We would add our observations of the prominent narcissistic features in male offenders and hysterical/borderline features in female offenders. MMPI findings (Graham, 1990) also support gender differences consistent with clinical observations. High scores on Scale 3 (hysteria) are more common in women (p. 58). Both men and women with high scores on Scale 4 (psychopathic deviate) may act aggressively, but females "are likely to express aggression in more passive, indirect ways" (p. 63). Female hospitalized psychiatric patients who elevate on Scale 5 (masculinity-femininity) tend to be diagnosed as psychotic (p. 67). Guze et al. (1971a) additionally found a familial association between histrionic and antisocial personality disorders that was gender related.

percent of the males ($N = 42$) and 44% of the females ($N = 8$) evidenced violence histories ($x^2 = 3.89$, $p < .025$), suggesting a gender ratio of 2:1 for violence in CD adolescents. Although significantly different in the CD sample, this ratio is much lower than would be expected when normal males and females are compared (10:1). It is consistent with Raine and Dunkin's (1990) hypothesis that there may be a heavier psychobiological loading for psychopathy, in this case androgenic, in psychopathic women when compared to psychopathic men. Beginning with our adolescent sample, sensitivity to possible gender differences is acknowledged through presentation of the data as well as a separate chapter devoted to the antisocial female (see chapter 4).

CONDUCT DISORDER AND THE RORSCHACH

The *severe* conduct-disordered pattern (psychopathy) in adolescence represents one behavioral manifestation of borderline pathology.[10] Sugarman et al. (1980) posited two types of borderline adolescents that we believe also apply to the CD adolescents. One type was similar to the adult borderline psychotic (Schafer, 1954) or borderline schizophrenic (Knight, 1954). Preoccupation with maintaining self–other boundaries, disturbances in self- and object relations, and personality structure were noted. Ego deficits manifest either *directly* (uninhibited) or in an *inhibited* mode on the Rorschach. The "uninhibited" (Sugarman et al., 1980, p. 473) or expressive borderline psychotic adolescent produced a variety of contamination, confabulatory, and fabulized special scores. Response content contained primitive drive-laden material (Sugarman et al., 1980).

The guarded and constricted nature of the "inhibited" (Sugarman et al., 1980, p. 474) borderline psychotic adolescent protocol makes assessment difficult. Hyperalertness, vigilance, and resistance during the testing process suggest the ego's vulnerability to regressive pull. Records may contain low R, whereas achromatic shading is used to delineate the form of percepts associated with the use of projective identification (Lerner & Lerner, 1980).

In both the uninhibited and inhibited borderline psychotic adolescent, human responses are produced in the form of quasihuman [(H)], quasihuman detail [(Hd)], and human detail (Hd) content. Few pure human (H) content are produced, if any. Part-object attachments are also suggested by a low frequency of human movement (M) and a predominance of animal content (A). When M is produced

---

[10]Sugarman et al. (1980) noted that "borderline personality organization" should not be applied to adolescents, because it implies a stable and enduring structure. It "risks premature conceptual closure and jeopardizes sophisticated and integrated psychodynamic understanding of these youngsters" (p. 472). Other authors would disagree (e.g., P. Kernberg, 1990). We suggest caution in diagnosing children and adolescents but do believe that the failure to acknowledge the presence of borderline personality organization in younger clients may interfere with them receiving appropriate treatment interventions.

it is usually popular (Cards III & VII) with poor form quality. When M occurs on other cards it contains an idiosyncratic or self-referential quality with unusual or minus form level. These patterns are consistent with the CD adolescents. Their pure H and COP are produced in lower than normative frequencies and mostly spoiled (Gacono & Erdberg, 1993). Decreases in synthesis responses (DQ+) suggest difficulties evolving from concrete to formal operations. F+% is less than normative.

Rorschach content is pregenital (Sugarman et al., 1980). Imagery may contain primitive modes of relating (Kwawer, 1980). "One might then hypothesize that the tension aroused by the wish to separate will be evidenced by Rorschach imagery in which the desire for fusion and denial of separateness will be seen" (Rubenstein, 1980, p. 453). This aggressive imagery is contained in Kwawer's symbiotic merging and violent symbiosis, separation, reunion responses. Uninhibited and inhibited styles characterize the true borderline adolescent (Sugarman et al., 1980).

The second type of borderline adolescent group exhibits borderline features (Sugarman et al., 1980), but is not borderline psychotic. The aggression of these pseudoborderline adolescents lacks the behavioral intensity of the previous group, and is rarely feared or found to be homicidal. Their Rorschachs reveal more ego strength. Boundary disturbance is rare. Thought disorder indices will generally be less severe (absence of contaminations and confabulations) and fabulized combinations or incongruous combinations will be of the Level 1 type (Exner, 1986a). These adolescents are more vulnerable to the conscious experience of depression. Anatomy and X-ray responses may appear, indicating the discharge of affects into the soma (Sugarman et al., 1980).

Although all ASPDs appear to manifest some degree of borderline personality organization, both theoretically (Kernberg, 1975) and empirically (Gacono & Meloy, 1992), the relation of borderline pathology to CD adolescents is unknown. Because a conduct disorder (CD) diagnosis is necessary to receive an adult antisocial personality disorder (ASPD), the psychoanalytic developmental relationship between the two also informs current nomenclature (*DSM* series; APA, 1952, 1968, 1980, 1987, 1994).

A COMPARISON OF CD AND DYSTHYMIC ADOLESCENTS

We conducted a preliminary study to ascertain if, as Robins (1966, 1970, 1972) suggested, similarities in personality structure existed between conduct disorder and adult antisocial personality. Utilizing a subsample of our CD adolescents (*N* = 48), we studied their attachment capacity, presence of anxiety, and internal representations of others as whole, real, and meaningful objects (Weber, 1990; Weber et al., 1992). Texture (T, TF, FT), diffuse shading (Y, YF, FY), and pure human content responses (H) were compared between 48 CD subjects and 30 dysthymic (D) control subjects in a private inpatient psychiatric setting. Both groups contained male and female adolescents. Subjects were between the ages of 13 and 16 (CD, $M = 14.6$; D, $M = 15.3$) and free of functional psychosis or mental retardation (Weber, 1990; Weber et al., 1992).

Consistent with predictions, the dysthymic subjects produced a significantly greater frequency of T ($p < .01$), Y ($p < .05$), and pure H ($p < .05$). In sharp contrast to what is normatively expected, only 29% (14 subjects) of the CD group produced a T response. Exner's (1990b) nonpatient adolescents between ages 13 and 16 produce frequencies of texture ranging from 80% to 92%. The dysthymic sample produced T responses at a frequency (63%) closer to nonpatients. Diffuse shading (Y) was produced less frequently in the CD group (52%) than in dysthymic subjects (80%) or inpatient depressives (68%; Exner, 1986a). When compared to dysthymic subjects (97%) CDs produced less pure H (67%).

Would the CD group reflect similar heterogeneity as the adult ASPDs (Gacono & Meloy, 1992)? The CD group was divided into mild, moderate, and severe categories (APA, 1987; see chapter 3 for criteria). No significant differences were obtained for between-group comparison; however, for both Y and T, expected trends were apparent. Fifty-six percent ($N = 9$) of the mild subjects, 50% ($N = 8$) of the moderate subjects, and 37% ($N = 6$) of the severe subjects produced Y (Weber et al., 1992). T was produced at the following frequencies: severe CDs 19% ($N = 3$), moderate CDs 31% ($N = 5$), and mild 37% ($N = 6$). Findings for pure H were counterintuitive. Sixty-nine percent ($N = 11$) of the mild CDs, 75% ($N = 12$) of the moderate CDs, and 87% ($N = 14$) of the severe CDs produced at least one pure H. Concerning the texture findings, we concluded:

> The difference in the frequency of T responses suggests that conduct-disordered adolescents have proportionally less interest in affectional relatedness than dysthymic adolescents. It also may indicate etiological and developmental differences between conduct disorder and dysthymia. Attachment failure in conduct disordered adolescents may prevent the internalization of good objects and subsequent positive identifications (Meloy, 1988). (Weber et al., 1992, p. 22)

Lower T and pure H responses for the CD subjects when compared to dysthymic subjects suggests a greater desire for interpersonal relatedness among the depressed adolescents. Consistent with previous research on delinquency and human content (Exner, Bryant, & Miller, 1975), the low frequency of H in the CD sample may indicate an indifference to others as whole, real, and meaningful objects, and an absent capacity to internally represent others as such. Decreased anxiety and helplessness, as well as an inability to tolerate these experiences, is suggested by the lower frequency of Y among the CD subjects. For some of these CDs, the beginning stabilization of certain regulatory defensive operations such as acting out and grandiosity in warding off threats to internalized object relations may be indicated (see chapter 10), rather than the neurotic use of signal anxiety to manage internal conflict (see Fig. 3.1).

Despite the likelihood of greater heterogeneity among the CD adolescent subjects than among the incarcerated ASPD subjects we have utilized in our samples, similarities in the quantitative analysis of select variables among the child, adolescent, and adult samples support a developmental continuum for the antisocial pattern. These similarities include, but are not limited to, attachment deficits, lessened anxiety, and deficits in whole-object internalization. We now look further.

ADOLESCENT CONDUCT-DISORDERED SAMPLE (*N* = 100)[11]

Adolescent protocols with < 14 responses were eliminated from the CD sample. The final adolescent CD sample is composed of 100 subjects—79 males and 21 females—from various inpatient and residential treatment settings in California and Iowa. Forty-eight percent were gathered during the course of a doctoral dissertation (Weber, 1990) from a random pool of 483 patients admitted to a private adolescent psychiatric hospital in San Diego, California. Thirty-one percent were gathered by a clinical psychologist during the course of treatment at a residential center in Fresno, California. And 21% were gathered in Iowa by two clinical psychologists from several residential treatment centers.

Sixty-four percent of the subjects are White, 11% Black, 18% Hispanic, 5% Asian, and 2% other. The age range is 13–17 (*M* = 14.8, *SD* = 1.22). Seventeen percent were 13 years old, 27% were 14 years old, 20% were 15 years old, 29% were 16 years old, and 7% were 17 years old. All subjects met criteria for conduct disorder (*DSM–III–R*; APA, 1987) as determined by records review (San Diego subjects) and clinical interview and records review (Fresno and Iowa subjects). All subjects were free of an additional Axis I diagnosis as determined by records review or clinical interview. Rorschachs were administered using the Exner Comprehensive System and all protocols were scored initially by the examiners and rescored by us. Rorschach variables, ratios, and indices were generated using the Rorschach Scoring Program Version 2 (Exner et al., 1990). Table 3.1 presents the Comprehensive System data for the CD sample. Tables 3.2 and 3.3 show the group structural summary data for males and females respectively. Group Rorschach data were generated by Philip Erdberg, PhD.

Response Frequency and Style.   Both the male and female CD adolescents produced a normative amount of responses (*M* = 21.58, *SD* = 7.50), with the males producing slightly fewer responses (*M* = 20.37) than the females (*M* =

---

[11]We wish to thank Drs. Carey Weber, Thomas Shaffer, Eva Christianson, Jeanne Simms, and Gregory Meyer for their generous contribution of protocols to this sample.

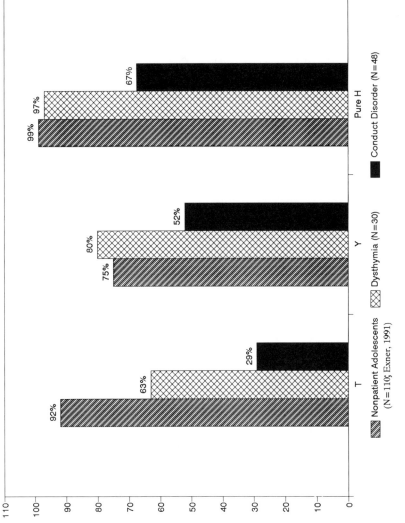

FIG. 3.1. Texture, diffuse shading, and pure human content in conduct-disordered adolescents. The dysthymic group produced a significantly greater frequency of T, $p < .01$; Y, $p < .05$; and pure H, $p < .05$; responses than did the conduct-disordered group.

TABLE 3.1
Structural Data for Adolescent Conduct-Disordered Subjects ($N = 100$)

Variable	Mean	SD	Min	Max	Freq	Median	Mode	SK	KU
R	21.58	7.50	14.00	55.00	100	20.00	14.00	2.01	5.17
W	10.04	4.80	1.00	24.00	100	10.00	9.00	0.62	0.46
D	8.03	5.80	0.00	31.00	99	7.00	6.00	1.73	3.61
Dd	3.51	3.47	0.00	18.00	83	3.00	0.00	2.06	5.71
Space	2.54	2.04	0.00	11.00	90	2.00	2.00	1.53	3.34
DQ+	4.92	3.03	0.00	14.00	94	5.00	3.00	0.54	0.12
DQo	14.63	6.66	6.00	43.00	100	13.50	14.00	1.77	4.35
DQv	1.41	1.76	0.00	8.00	63	1.00	0.00	1.76	3.16
DQv/+	0.62	1.05	0.00	6.00	37	0.00	0.00	2.36	7.11
FQX+	0.01	0.10	0.00	1.00	1	0.00	0.00	10.00	100.00
FQXo	8.70	3.19	2.00	18.00	100	8.00	8.00	0.81	1.03
FQXu	6.21	3.06	1.00	14.00	100	5.50	5.00	0.68	0.07
FQX−	6.52	4.50	0.00	27.00	98	6.00	5.00	1.90	5.32
FQXnone	0.14	0.43	0.00	3.00	12	0.00	0.00	4.00	20.49
MQ+	0.01	0.10	0.00	1.00	1	0.00	0.00	10.00	100.00
MQo	1.44	1.30	0.00	6.00	72	1.00	0.00	0.97	1.01
MQu	1.02	1.08	0.00	4.00	60	1.00	0.00	0.89	−0.10
MQ−	0.81	1.02	0.00	4.00	51	1.00	0.00	1.38	1.52
MQnone	0.02	0.14	0.00	1.00	2	0.00	0.00	6.96	47.42
Space−	1.22	1.34	0.00	6.00	65	1.00	0.00	1.42	1.96
M	3.30	2.43	0.00	10.00	87	3.00	3.00	0.69	0.16
FM	2.87	2.04	0.00	9.00	91	2.00	2.00	0.82	0.45
m	1.36	1.44	0.00	7.00	67	1.00	0.00	1.38	2.28
FM+m	4.23	2.58	0.00	12.00	95	4.00	3.00	0.59	0.00
FC	0.61	0.83	0.00	5.00	46	0.00	0.00	2.04	7.11
CF	1.83	1.71	0.00	7.00	73	2.00	0.00	1.06	1.04
C	0.17	0.49	0.00	3.00	13	0.00	0.00	3.45	13.44
Cn	0.00	0.00	0.00	0.00	0	0.00	0.00	−	−
FC+CF+C+Cn	2.61	2.04	0.00	8.00	82	2.00	2.00	0.68	0.01
WgSumC	2.39	1.97	0.00	7.50	82	2.00	0.00	0.78	0.14
Sum C'	1.10	1.71	0.00	12.00	53	1.00	0.00	3.36	16.92
Sum T	0.17	0.45	0.00	2.00	14	0.00	0.00	2.73	7.03
Sum V	0.35	0.69	0.00	3.00	25	0.00	0.00	2.09	3.99
Sum Y	0.48	0.81	0.00	3.00	33	0.00	0.00	1.81	2.73
Sum Shd	2.10	2.46	0.00	18.00	74	1.00	0.00	3.11	16.84
Fr+rF	0.51	0.89	0.00	4.00	33	0.00	0.00	2.01	3.64
FD	0.61	0.83	0.00	3.00	43	0.00	0.00	1.28	0.94
F	11.36	5.43	2.00	31.00	100	11.00	8.00	0.95	1.59
Pairs	5.72	3.37	0.00	16.00	96	5.00	4.00	0.57	0.05
Ego	0.34	0.17	0.00	0.95	98	0.32	0.25	0.51	0.71
Lambda	1.66	2.03	0.13	14.00	100	1.09	1.00	3.94	18.90
EA	5.69	3.42	0.00	16.50	96	5.50	4.00	0.64	0.57
es	6.33	3.90	0.00	27.00	97	6.00	6.00	1.65	6.91
D Score	−0.21	1.08	−4.00	3.00	100	0.00	0.00	−0.73	2.40
Adj D Score	0.05	1.02	−3.00	3.00	100	0.00	0.00	0.19	1.11
SumActvMov	4.85	3.05	0.00	17.00	96	4.00	4.00	1.03	1.70
SumPassMov	2.68	2.21	0.00	13.00	85	2.00	2.00	1.58	4.55
SumMactv	1.99	1.68	0.00	6.00	76	2.00	0.00	0.57	−0.55
SumMpass	1.31	1.57	0.00	9.00	60	1.00	0.00	1.87	5.28

(Continued)

TABLE 3.1
(Continued)

Variable	Mean	SD	Min	Max	Freq	Median	Mode	SK	KU
IntellIndx	1.03	1.62	0.00	8.00	45	0.00	0.00	2.01	4.14
Zf	12.11	5.22	1.00	27.00	100	12.00	13.00	0.50	0.54
Zd	−0.91	4.77	−12.50	10.50	89	0.00	0.00	−0.29	−0.13
Blends	2.57	1.98	0.00	10.00	86	2.00	2.00	1.00	1.34
CSBlnd	0.33	0.60	0.00	3.00	28	0.00	0.00	2.23	6.21
Afr	0.53	0.23	0.21	1.25	100	0.45	0.33	1.05	0.53
Populars	4.69	1.72	1.00	10.00	100	5.00	4.00	0.50	0.80
X + %	0.42	0.13	0.13	0.85	100	0.43	0.50	0.10	0.01
F + %	0.42	0.18	0.00	1.00	99	0.40	0.50	0.73	1.11
X − %	0.29	0.13	0.00	0.60	98	0.28	0.24	0.06	−0.48
Xu%	0.29	0.10	0.06	0.57	100	0.29	0.29	0.02	0.09
S − %	0.19	0.20	0.00	1.00	65	0.15	0.00	1.17	1.75
IsoIndx	0.20	0.16	0.00	0.76	90	0.18	0.00	1.24	1.84
H	2.32	1.95	0.00	8.00	85	2.00	1.00	0.95	0.23
(H)	1.21	1.54	0.00	10.00	60	1.00	0.00	2.49	10.23
Hd	1.68	1.84	0.00	11.00	74	1.00	1.00	2.23	7.20
(Hd)	0.49	0.72	0.00	3.00	38	0.00	0.00	1.46	1.81
Hx	0.17	0.45	0.00	2.00	14	0.00	0.00	2.73	7.03
H + (H) + Hd + (Hd)	5.70	3.51	0.00	25.00	98	5.00	4.00	2.09	8.50
A	9.08	3.95	3.00	25.00	100	8.50	9.00	1.41	3.36
(A)	0.52	0.70	0.00	3.00	41	0.00	0.00	1.17	0.72
Ad	1.77	1.92	0.00	9.00	71	1.00	0.00	1.66	3.28
(Ad)	0.15	0.41	0.00	2.00	13	0.00	0.00	2.83	7.86
An	0.67	1.03	0.00	5.00	42	0.00	0.00	2.04	4.53
Art	0.33	0.73	0.00	3.00	22	0.00	0.00	2.48	5.84
Ay	0.32	0.63	0.00	3.00	24	0.00	0.00	2.05	3.81
Bl	0.21	0.59	0.00	4.00	15	0.00	0.00	3.81	18.14
Bt	0.96	1.20	0.00	5.00	53	1.00	0.00	1.41	1.79
Cg	0.87	1.97	0.00	4.00	56	1.00	0.00	1.01	0.39
Cl	0.24	0.51	0.00	3.00	21	0.00	0.00	2.55	8.25
Ex	0.27	0.60	0.00	3.00	21	0.00	0.00	2.67	7.98
Fi	0.46	0.78	0.00	4.00	33	0.00	0.00	2.06	4.84
Food	0.27	0.58	0.00	3.00	22	0.00	0.00	2.68	8.56
Geog	0.09	0.32	0.00	2.00	8	0.00	0.00	3.80	15.26
HHold	0.64	0.90	0.00	4.00	46	0.00	0.00	1.95	4.45
Ls	0.80	1.05	0.00	5.00	50	0.50	0.00	1.63	2.81
Na	0.95	1.27	0.00	6.00	52	1.00	0.00	1.77	3.31
Sc	0.72	1.10	0.00	6.00	43	0.00	0.00	2.15	5.82
Sx	0.31	0.60	0.00	3.00	25	0.00	0.00	2.08	4.48
Xy	0.05	0.26	0.00	2.00	4	0.00	0.00	5.78	35.93
Idio	0.79	1.08	0.00	6.00	49	0.00	0.00	1.93	5.01
DV	1.03	1.27	0.00	7.00	59	1.00	0.00	2.10	6.41
INCOM	1.66	1.58	0.00	9.00	76	1.00	1.00	1.56	3.95
DR	0.78	1.45	0.00	9.00	41	0.00	0.00	3.22	12.84
FABCOM	0.86	1.05	0.00	4.00	51	1.00	0.00	1.24	1.16
DV2	0.03	0.22	0.00	2.00	2	0.00	0.00	7.99	66.48
INC2	0.37	0.73	0.00	3.00	25	0.00	0.00	2.11	3.93
DR2	0.07	0.29	0.00	2.00	6	0.00	0.00	4.57	22.49

(Continued)

TABLE 3.1
(Continued)

Variable	Mean	SD	Min	Max	Freq	Median	Mode	SK	KU
FAB2	0.23	0.53	0.00	3.00	19	0.00	0.00	2.69	8.46
ALOG	0.10	0.36	0.00	2.00	8	0.00	0.00	3.90	15.58
CONTAM	0.01	0.10	0.00	1.00	1	0.00	0.00	10.00	100.00
Sum6SpSc	4.44	3.31	0.00	21.00	94	4.00	4.00	1.94	6.45
Sum6SpScLv2	0.70	1.13	0.00	6.00	40	0.00	0.00	2.15	5.35
WSum6SpSc	14.27	12.63	0.00	69.00	96	11.00	6.00	1.84	4.56
AB	0.19	0.53	0.00	2.00	13	0.00	0.00	2.74	6.37
AG	0.58	0.91	0.00	4.00	35	0.00	0.00	1.51	1.63
CFB	0.01	0.10	0.00	1.00	1	0.00	0.00	10.00	100.00
COP	0.95	1.06	0.00	5.00	59	1.00	0.00	1.30	1.91
CP	0.05	0.22	0.00	1.00	5	0.00	0.00	4.19	15.90
MOR	1.39	1.50	0.00	8.00	69	1.00	1.00	1.71	3.85
PER	1.19	1.70	0.00	8.00	53	1.00	0.00	2.02	4.27
PSV	0.35	0.63	0.00	3.00	28	0.00	0.00	1.85	3.31

24.09). The CD adolescents are high Lambda subjects (L>.99 = 59%–62%), in contrast to normal 15-year-old subjects (L>.99 = 7%). With an average Lambda of 1.66, we would interpretively expect resilient defenses against affect and a simple, item-by-item approach to problem solving in this diagnostic group.

Core Characteristics. CD adolescents, on average, are ambitents, with no clearly defined problem-solving orientation (to self or others). Forty-eight percent of the males and 57% of the females are ambitents, unlike normal 15-year-old subjects where 21% are ambitents. Surprisingly, a greater proportion of CD subjects are introversive (37% males, 33% females) than extratensive (15% males, 10% females). Both male and female CD adolescents are deficient in psychological resources (EA = 5.77 for males, 5.40 for females) when compared to normal 15-year-olds (EA M = 8.82, SD = 2.34).

Despite these shortcomings, both D and AdjD are normal, on average, for both male and female CD adolescents (D M = −0.16 males,−0.38 females; AdjD M = 0.14 males, −0.29 females). Most are not overwhelmed by feeling badly (FM+m < Sum shading 16% males, 19% females). And less than 10% of our sample are grossly disorganized and unpredictable in their stress tolerance and controls (AdjD < −1). These findings are consistent with the patterns noted in CD children (see chapter 2) and adult ASPD males (see chapter 5), and underscore the centrality of organized, predictable, and controlled behavior in antisocial samples, regardless of age or gender.

Affects. CD adolescents modulate affect poorly. Average FC:CF+C ratios are .57:2.08 (1:4) for males and .76:1.71 (1:2.5) for females. Nonpatient 15-year-olds average 3.14:2.88. There is a striking gender difference here. Male

TABLE 3.2
CD Male Adolescents (N = 79) Group Means and Frequencies for Select Ratios,
Percentages, and Derivations

$R = 20.37$	$L = 1.67$	$(L > .99 = 59\%)$

EB = 3.32 : 2.45		EA = 5.77
eb = 4.15 : 2.10		es = 6.25 (FM+m < SUMShading ... 13 16%)
D = −0.16	AdjD = 0.14	

EB STYLE

Introversive	29	37%
Super-Introversive	21	27%
Ambitent	38	48%
Extratensive	12	15%
Super-Extratensive	8	10%

EA - es DIFFERENCES:D-SCORES

D Score > 0	15	19%
D Score = 0	45	57%
D Score < 0	19	24%
D Score < −1	8	10%
AdjD Score > 0	19	24%
AdjD Score = 0	46	58%
AdjD Score < 0	14	18%
AdjD Score < −1	4	5%

AFFECT

FC:CF+C = .57 : 2.08		
Pure C = .18		(Pure C > 0 = 13%; Pure C > 1 = 4%)
FC > (CF+C) + 2	1	1%
FC > (CF+C) + 1	2	3%
(CF+C) > FC + 1	32	41%
(CF+C) > FC + 2	21	27%

SumC' = 1.14	SumV = .35	SumY = .47

Afr = .53	(Afr < .40 = 33%; Afr < .50 = 61%)
S = 2.62	(S > 2 = 41%)
Blends:R = 2.75 : 20.91	
CP = .04	

INTERPERSONAL

COP = 1.02	(COP = 0, 39%; COP > 2 = 9%)
AG = .65	(AG = 0, 62%; AG > 2 = 5%)
Food = .25	
Isolate:R = .21	
H:(H)+Hd+(Hd) = 2.24 : 3.28	(H = 0, 16%; H < 2 = 44%)
(H)+(Hd):(A)+(Ad) = 1.69 : .71	
H+A:Hd+Ad = 10.97 : 3.30	
Sum T = .14	(T = 0, 87%; T > 1 = 1%)

(Continued)

TABLE 3.2
(Continued)

SELF-PERCEPTION

$3r+(2)/R = .36$	$(47\% < .33; 28\% > .44)$
$Fr+rF = .59$	$(Fr+rF > 0 = 37\%)$
$FD = .57$	
$An+Xy = .78$	
$MOR = 1.48$	$(MOR > 2 = 18\%)$

IDEATION

$a:p = 4.99 : 2.48$	$(p > a+1 = 6\%)$
$Ma:Mp = 2.14 : 1.18$	$(Mp > Ma = 22\%)$
$M = 3.32$	$(M- = .86; M$ none $= .02)$
$FM = 2.65 \qquad m = 1.51$	
$2AB+Art+Ay = 1.00$	$(2AB+Art+Ay > 5 = 9\%)$
$Sum6 = 4.38$	$(Sum6 > 6 = 27\%)$
$WSum6 = 14.53$	(Level 2 Special Scores $> 0 = 42\%$)

MEDIATION

Populars $= 4.75$ $(P < 4 = 19\%; P > 7 = 6\%)$
$X+\% = .41$
$F+\% = .43$
$X-\% = .29$
$Xu\% = .29$
$S-\% = .19$

$X+\% > .89$	0	0%
$X+\% < .70$	78	98%
$X+\% < .61$	74	94%
$X+\% < .50$	58	73%
$F+\% < .70$	74	94%
$Xu\% > .20$	64	81%
$X-\% > .15$	65	82%
$X-\% > .20$	61	77%
$X-\% > .30$	35	44%

PROCESSING

$Zf = 12.70$	
$Zd = -1.42$	$(Zd > +3.0 = 15\%; Zd < -3.0 = 34\%)$
$W:D:Dd = 10.49:7.27:3.15$	$(Dd > 3 = 35\%)$
$W:M = 10.49 : 3.32$	
$DQ+ = 5.25$	
$DQv = 1.42$	$(DQv + DQv/+ > 2 = 34\%)$

CONSTELLATIONS

SCZI = 6... 3	4%	DEPI = 7... 0	0%	CDI = 5...11	14%
SCZI = 5... 9	11%	DEPI = 6... 5	6%	CDI = 4...18	23%
SCZI = 4...17	22%	DEPI = 5...12	15%		

S-Constellation Positive 3 4%
HVI Positive 7 9%
OBS Positive 0 0%

TABLE 3.3
CD Female Adolescents (N = 21) Group Means and Frequencies for Select Ratios,
Percentages, and Derivations

$R = 24.09$	$L = 1.61$	$(L > .99 = 62\%)$

EB = 3.24 : 2.17		EA = 5.40
eb = 4.52 : 2.09		es = 6.62 (FM+m < SUMShading ... 4 19%)
D = −0.38	AdjD = −0.29	

EB STYLE

Introversive 7		33%
Super-Introversive 5		24%
Ambient 12		57%
Extratensive 2		10%
Super-Extratensive 2		10%

EA - es DIFFERENCES:D-SCORES

D Score > 0 1	5%
D Score = 0 13	65%
D Score < 0 7	33%
D Score < −1 2	10%
AdjD Score > 0 2	10%
AdjD Score = 0 12	57%
AdjD Score < 0 7	33%
AdjD Score < −1 2	10%

AFFECT

FC:CF+C = .76 : 1.71		
Pure C = .14		(Pure C > 0 = 14%; Pure C > 1 = 0%)
FC > (CF+C) + 2 0		0%
FC > (CF+C) + 1 2		10%
(CF+C) > FC + 1 10		48%
(CF+C) > FC + 2 2		10%
SumC' = .95	SumV = .33	SumY = .52
Afr = .56		(Afr < .40 = 29%; Afr < .50 = 33%)
S = 2.24		(S > 2 = 33%)
Blends:R = 1.90 : 24.09		
CP = .09		

INTERPERSONAL

COP = .67	(COP = 0, 48%; COP > 2 = 5%)
AG = .33	(AG = 0, 76%; AG > 2 = 0%)
Food = .33	
Isolate/R = .15	
H:(H)+Hd+(Hd) = 2.62 : 3.71	(H = 0, 10%; H < 2 = 38%)
(H)+(Hd):(A)+(Ad) = 1.71 : .53	
H+A:Hd+Ad = 13.00 : 4.00	
Sum T = .29	(T = 0, 81%; T > 1 = 10%)

(Continued)

TABLE 3.3
(Continued)

SELF-PERCEPTION

$3r+(2)/R = .28$	$(62\% < .33; 14\% > .44)$
$Fr+rF = .19$	$(Fr+rF > 0 = 19\%)$
$FD = .76$	
$An+Xy = .71$	
$MOR = 1.05$	$(MOR > 2 = 10\%)$

IDEATION

$a:p = 4.33 : 3.43$	$(p > a+1 = 14\%)$
$Ma:Mp = 1.43 : 1.81$	$(Mp > Ma = 33\%)$
$M = 3.24$	$(M- = .62; M \text{ none} = .00)$
$FM = 3.71 \qquad m = .81$	
$2AB+Art+Ay = .42$	$(2AB+Art+Ay > 5 = 14\%)$
$Sum6 = 4.67$	$(Sum6 > 6 = 24\%)$
$WSum6 = 13.29$	(Level 2 Special Scores $> 0 = 33\%$)

MEDIATION

Populars $= 4.48$	$(P < 4 = 29\%; P > 7 = 5\%)$	
$X+\% = .44$		
$F+\% = .41$		
$X-\% = .28$		
$Xu\% = .28$		
$S-\% = .18$		

$X+\% > .89$	0	0%
$X+\% < .70$	21	100%
$X+\% < .61$	21	100%
$X+\% < .50$	11	52%
$F+\% < .70$	20	95%
$Xu\% > .20$	18	86%
$X-\% > .15$	17	81%
$X-\% > .20$	14	67%
$X-\% > .30$	7	33%

PROCESSING

$Zf = 9.90$	
$Zd = .98$	$(Zd > +3.0 = 19\%; Zd < -3.0 = 5\%)$
$W:D:Dd = 8.33:10.90:4.86$	$(Dv > 3 = 67\%)$
$W:M = 8.33 : 3.24$	
$DQ+ = 3.67$	
$DQv = 1.38$	$(DQv + DQv/+ > 2 = 19\%)$

CONSTELLATIONS

$SCZI = 6...0$	0%	$DEPI = 7...0$	0%	$CDI = 5...4$	19%
$SCZI = 5...2$	10%	$DEPI = 6...0$	0%	$CDI = 4...6$	29%
$SCZI = 4...3$	14%	$DEPI = 5...7$	33%		

S-Constellation Positive	0	0%
HVI Positive	2	10%
OBS Positive	0	0%

CD adolescents modulate affect as well as a 5- to 6-year-old, and the same as the adult male psychopath. CD adolescent females do better. Their affect modulation is comparable to a 7-year-old nonpatient. Affect modulation appears to stop getting better in early latency and remains fixated at this developmental point for most antisocial individuals, regardless of age.

Our data are consistent with Schachtel's (1951) data, which found a greater lability of color reaction among delinquents (FC:CF+C). Only 21.6% of his sample produced FC > CF+C (p. 167). This figure rose to 42% when only delinquents giving color responses were considered.

Our group produced a stronger color response (SumC = 2.61) than did his group (SumC = 1.7), but both samples are much less responsive to color than were normal 15-year-olds (SumC = 6.04, *SD* = 2.01). This supports the hypothesis that CD adolescents will consciously experience less affect than normals, but when felt, it will be less modulated, and is likely to be expressed in a coarser manner.

Pure C responses accentuate this clinical hypothesis. Schachtel (1951) found an 8% frequency for pure C responses in delinquents, compared to 5.6% in nondelinquents. Thirteen percent of our male subjects produced C ≥ 1, whereas 14% of our female subjects did. Only 3% of nonpatient 15-year-olds produce a pure C response, and none produce C > 1. Four percent of our CD males produce C > 1.

The constraint of affect (C') is normal in both male and female CD adolescents when compared to normals. Dysphoric feelings (V), however, are notable, with both males and females averaging .33–.35 responses per subject. Proportionality highlights this fact. Twenty-five percent of our male subjects and 24% of our female subjects produced a vista, in stark contrast to the 11% of normal 15-year-olds who do. The CD adolescent appears more than twice as likely as the normal adolescent to experience painfully introspective feelings as he or she negatively compares the self to others.

Anxiety (Y), or felt helplessness, is experienced less frequently (32% males, 38% females) and to a lesser degree (*M* = .47 males, .52 females) in CD adolescents than in normal 15-year-olds (75%, *M* = 1.30). Adolescence is not an anxious time for CD subjects, probably due to lower levels of autonomic arousal (Raine et al., 1990), fewer attachments, and less interest in others (Weber et al., 1992).

Adolescent CD males are slightly more avoidant of emotionally provoking stimuli than are females, but both are within a standard deviation of normal 15-year-olds (Afr *M* = 0.65, *SD* = 0.18). Sixty-one percent of the CD males, however, cluster below an Afr of .50, and show more variance on this index than do CD females or normals. Some affect avoidance should be clinically expected in this population, and being "swept away by affect" is clearly the exception to the rule. Both male and female CD adolescents are chronically angry and oppositional (S = 2.62 males, 2.24 females), distinctively different from normals (S = 1.44).

Our data also suggest a link between hysteria and psychopathy, an association that has been noted in the literature for 100 years (Meloy, 1988). Ten percent of our female CD subjects and 4% of our male CD subjects produce a color projection (CP) response, a rare occurrence that is completely absent in normal 15-year-olds. An overall CP hit rate of 5% in our sample of 100 subjects suggests a primitive hysterical defense, such as denial and dissociation, that appears linked to psychopathy. It is most apparent in our sexual homicide perpetrator sample (see chapter 9). Although perhaps not a sensitive indicator of hysteria, the CP response may be quite specific to primitive hysteria, and is clinically important whenever it emerges in a subject sample, even at a low frequency. Meloy (1988) hypothesized "that varieties of dissociability, both as characterological defense and ego-dystonic state, are fundamental to the psychopathic process" (p. 164).

CD subjects produce only half the blends of normal 15-year-olds, suggesting the simplicity of their psychological operations. They are also somewhat more confused by emotion than are normal adolescents. Color-shading blends occur among 17% of normals and 28% of CD adolescents.

Interpersonal (Object) Relations.   CD adolescents do not expect cooperative interactions with others. Like their younger counterparts, 39% of CD adolescent males and 48% of CD adolescent females produce no COP responses. Only 11% of normal 15-year-olds do not produce a COP.

Consistent with our child and adult samples, CD adolescents produce *fewer* aggression (Ag) responses than normals. Seventy-six percent of female and 62% of male CD adolescents produce no AG, a finding in only 16% of normals. This stable finding across our samples is best understood as an absence of tensions of aggressive impulses within antisocial adolescents. Rather than symbolizing and verbalizing such ego-dystonic impulses, the CD adolescent acts them out in an ego-syntonic, conflict-free manner. It is clear from our data that inferring real-world aggression from the *presence* of AG responses in antisocial samples is an error, despite Exner's (1986a) recommendation to do so in normals. He did not have the benefit of antisocial sample data. Our findings suggest the opposite may be true: AG responses in an antisocial patient may indicate ego-dystonic aggressive impulses that are mentally represented and may suggest a *positive* prognostic indicator. Our experimental aggression scores, however, are well represented in both male and female CD adolescents.

As indicated in Table 3.4, Ag Content is most common (86%–87%), followed by Ag Past (29%–43%) and Ag Potential (18%–33%). We do not have adolescent nonpatient data with which to compare these frequencies, so we are unable to make any comparisons or draw any conclusions. There does appear to be a balance, however, between percepts that identify an aggressor (AgPot) and those that identify a victim (AgPast). These probably represent shifting identifications within the CD adolescent, and may also infer certain sadistic (AgPot) or masochistic (AgPast) aims (see chapter 8).

TABLE 3.4
Means, Standard Deviations, and Frequencies for Aggression
Scores in 100 Conduct-Disordered Male and Female Adolescents

Category	CD Males (N = 79)				CD Females (N = 21)			
	M	SD	Frequency	Maximum	M	SD	Frequency	Maximum
Aggressive Movement (AG)	.65	.96	30 (38%)	4	.33	.66	5 (24%)	2
Aggressive Content (AgC)	3.18	2.80	69 (87%)	15	2.62	2.33	18 (86%)	9
Aggressive Past (AgPast)	.65	1.00	34 (43%)	4	.33	.58	6 (29%)	2
Aggressive Potential (AgPot)	.25	.65	14 (18%)	4	.52	.87	7 (33%)	3

Food responses, suggesting dependency needs, are normal in our sample, whereas the Isolate/R is elevated at .21. This is almost 1 SD (standard deviation) higher than normal 15-year-olds ($M = .15$, $SD = .07$), and implies a tendency toward social isolation—the antisocial individual's inclination "to attach more readily to the nonhuman environment, either in fantasy or in material reality" (Meloy, 1988, pp. 401–402).

The object relational world of the CD adolescent is also disturbed and abnormal. We expect and want three pure H responses from a normal 15-year-old. CD adolescents average two, and a large proportion of males (44%) and females (38%) produce fewer than two. Relational attitudes are unlikely to be reality based, and are imbued with fantasy. Sixteen percent of CD males and 10% of CD females produce no pure H responses.

We also expect H>(H)+Hd+(Hd) in normal adolescents, with an average ratio of 3.42:2.15—an empirical measure of a whole-object–dominated representational world. In CD adolescents, part objects reign. CD males average 2.24:3.28 and females average 2.62:3.71. The predominance of part-objects in the CD adolescent is a marker of pre-Oedipal personality organization. The integration of good and bad split objects into whole, integrated objects has not yet occurred, a defining characteristic of neurotic personality organization (Kernberg, 1984). This "lack of synthesis of contradictory self and object images" (Kernberg, 1975, p. 28) is both a result of, and perpetuates, splitting as a genotypic defense, lending to the CD adolescent certain, characteristic borderline features (Sugarman et al., 1980).

What are the psychodynamics between these internal objects? Table 3.5 indicates that most of the CD sample produce at least one primitive mode of relating response (Kwawer, 1980). For the males, the most common psychodynamic is narcissistic mirroring (37%), followed by boundary disturbance (29%) and violent symbiosis (28%). These frequencies are virtually identical to our ASPD males (see chapter 5). The CD females, however, produce violent symbiosis (29%), boundary disturbance (24%), and birth-rebirth (24%) most

TABLE 3.5
Means, Standard Deviations, and Frequencies for Kwawer's (1980) Primitive
Modes of Relating in 100 Conduct-Disordered Male and Female Adolescents.

Category	CD Males (N = 79)				CD Females (N = 21)			
	M	SD	Frequency	Maximum	M	SD	Frequency	Maximum
Engulfment	—	—	4 (5%)	1	—	—	2 (9%)	1
Symbiotic Merging	.25	.49	18 (23%)	2	.14	.36	3 (14%)	1
Violent Symbiosis	.48	.97	22 (28%)	5	.43	.81	6 (29%)	3
Birth & Rebirth	.10	.38	6 (8%)	2	.29	.56	5 (24%)	2
Malignant Internal Processes	.19	.46	13 (16%)	2	.19	.40	4 (19%)	1
Metamorphosis & Transformation	.13	.37	9 (11%)	2	.29	.71	4 (19%)	3
Narcissistic Mirroring	.58	.97	29 (37%)	4	.19	.40	4 (19%)	1
Separation Division	.16	.41	12 (15%)	2	.14	.36	3 (14%)	1
Boundary Disturbance	.37	.64	23 (29%)	3	.24	.44	5 (24%)	1
Womb Imagery	—	—	2 (2%)	1	.14	.48	2 (9%)	2
Total Object Relations Categories	2.29	2.30	64 (81%)	11	2.14	2.30	16 (76%)	9

often. This latter category is most likely gender related and representationally linked to the continuous nature of feminine identification (Gilligan, 1982). CD males produce very few categories that infer a regressive identification with the maternal object (engulfment, birth-rebirth, womb imagery: 2%–8%). The fact that 81% of our male and 76% of our female sample produced at least one of Kwawer's (1980) categories, and average two, is further empirical evidence of the borderline psychodynamics of the CD adolescent (Sugarman et al., 1980).

A capacity for attachment is strikingly absent in CD adolescents. Eighty-seven percent of the males and 81% of the females produce no T responses. Although a small proportion (10%) of the females are affectionally hungry (T > 1), only 1% of the males are. T = 1 is found in 92% of nonpatient 15-year-olds. The ubiquity of this finding in all our antisocial samples in this book, except for the sexual homicide perpetrators, is a central and developmentally stable measure of chronic emotional detachment. It is expected in an antisocial patient, regardless of age. On the other hand, the presence of one T response in a nonpsychopathic antisocial patient's Rorschach protocol is a positive prognostic finding.

Self-Perception. CD adolescents, particularly females, compare themselves negatively to others. Forty-seven percent of the males and 62% of the females produce egocentricity < .33. Only 6% of nonpatient 15-year-olds do this. Indices of pathological narcissism (Rf > 0) are twice as prominent in CD males (37%) as in CD females (19%). This latter finding, however, is not abnormal, because nonpatient 15-year-olds average 0.50 reflection responses per subject, and frequencies between nonpatients and our sample are similar. Characterological narcissism does not distinguish CD adolescents from their peers; but the former's relative inability to introspect in a balanced manner (FD = 43%) when compared to normals (FD = 75%) may predict the eventual solidification of narcissistic defenses against a negative self-concept and a felt sense of self-injury (MOR *M* = 1.39, 69%).

Ideation. Although the CD adolescents produce M within the normal range (*M* = 3.32 males, 3.24 females), it is below average for nonpatient 15-year-olds (*M* = 4.35, *SD* = 2.17). M– frequency is 51% in our CD sample, in stark contrast to its low frequency (12%) in normals. This reality-testing impairment that accompanies human movement is consistent with our other antisocial samples, and infers the perceptual problems that surround the CD adolescent's reasoning, judgment, deliberation, and delay of gratification. There is also a demonstrable retreat into fantasy (Mp > Ma) in 22% of the male CDs and 33% of the female CDs, greater than the expected 15% frequency in nonpatient 15-year-olds.

Both male and female CD adolescents show less nonvolitional ideation in response to primitive need states (FM) than do normals, another consistent finding across groups, except for the sexual homicide perpetrators (see chapter 9). Instinctual discharge, or immediate gratification, is a structural characteristic of these developing antisocial personalities. Ideational helplessness (m) is normal.

CD adolescents are not prone to intellectualize (2AB+Art+Ay>5 = 9%–14%), but when they do think, they evidence moderate and pervasive thought disorder. WSum6 for the CD males is 14.53 and for the females is 13.29—a gross deviation from normals (*M* = 4.71, *SD* = 3.33). This finding is also consistent with our other samples, and underscores the clinical importance of formal thought disorder in this population: cognitive slippage that is unlikely to be detected during a routine mental status exam.

Mediation. The translation of external stimuli into meaningful percepts is likewise a problem for these youth. Although they give conventionality its just dues (Populars *M* = 4.75 males, 4.48 females), their perceptions are highly idiosyncratic with and without affect (X+% *M* = 42, F+% *M* = 42). Their reality testing is severely impaired (X–% *M* = 29) when compared to normal 15-year-olds (X–% *M* = 7). In fact, it is worse than our adult samples, but better than our children's sample. It appears as if reality testing gradually improves in antisocial patients with age, but eventually settles within the borderline range (X–% 15–25) once adulthood is reached. Only 19% of our CD adolescents had X–% < 15.

Processing. The CD adolescents put as much energy into organizing and synthesizing percepts as do normals (Zd *M* = 12.11), but do it less effectively (Zd *M* = –0.91). They are disproportionately underincorporators (34%) if they are males, but not so if they are females (5%), when compared to normal 15-year-olds (15%). This is a marked gender difference. They also strive beyond their abilities (W:M > 3:1) if they are males, but not if they are females. Female CD adolescents produce slightly more D responses than W responses, a finding in the normal range, but male CD adolescents do not. This economy of approach to the Rorschach also appears to be a gender difference, but may not be clinically significant.

Taken together, the cognitive operations of the CD adolescent are clearly impaired, but are likely to be overlooked in a clinical setting in the absence of another Axis I disorder. Clinicians should note that the perceptual and associative abilities of the CD adolescent, whether male or female, are impaired and disorganized. They are likely to be frustrated by therapeutic approaches that emphasize change through the use of cognitive skills, regardless of their measured IQ.

The constellations deserve attention. One out of five of the CD adolescents were positive on the SCZI. One out of three of the CD adolescent females were positive on the DEPI. And one out of four of the entire sample were positive on the CDI. None of the normal 15-year-olds was positive for the SCZI or DEPI, whereas 10% were positive for the CDI.

These findings are striking, because all CD subjects were screened to rule out a comorbid schizophrenic or mood disorder. In light of these findings, we offer the following treatment suggestions for CD adolescents:

1. Perceptual and thinking problems must be addressed, despite their absence during a routine mental status exam. Low-dose neuroleptic medications may be of benefit to many CD patients to help "glue together" their cognitive operations.

2. A depressive component, especially in CD female adolescents, should be carefully assessed and treated, probably most effectively with both pharmacotherapy (such as serotonergic agonists) and psychotherapy. Overt aggression should not be allowed to mask such a mood disorder, and may be a result of it.

3. Grossly deficient social skills will be present in one out of four CD adolescents, and may need a day treatment or residential approach to ameliorate these interpersonal inadequacies. Skills for daily living (ADLs) should also be carefully assessed.

4. A constant, mostly nurturant object is crucial to therapeutic success if the chronic emotional detachment of the CD adolescent is to be impacted. In some cases this lack of bonding may be biogenic; in other cases it may be the result of neglectful and abusive parenting. Therapeutic optimism should not give way to therapeutic nihilism (Meloy, 1988). As Freud (Aichhorn, 1925) wrote:

> Analysis has revealed that the child lives on almost unchanged in the sick patient as well as in the dreamer and the artist; it has thrown a flood of light on the instinctual forces and impulses which give the childish being its characteristic features; and it has traced the paths of development which proceed to maturity. (p. 5; foreword to *Wayward Youth* by Aichhorn)

JASON, AN ADOLESCENT PSYCHOPATH[12]

Jason was a tall, 15-year-old, Asian youth. When adopted at age $1\frac{1}{2}$, he moved to the United States with his new parents. Jason's discipline was severe and abusive. Beginning at age 7, his adoptive parents slapped him, hit him with sticks, and pulled his hair. Despite harsh discipline, Jason was "reported" to be a good student with no behavioral problems through the eighth grade.

Problems emerged in the ninth grade. Jason skipped school, ran away from home, hung out on the street, and was involved in joyriding, fighting (at times he had a knife), and theft. He also accumulated $4,000 in charges on his parents' credit cards. Despite other delinquent behaviors, Jason denied substance or alcohol abuse. During this period his school grades dropped. He additionally indicated a fascination with knives and reported collecting them: "My first knife was a butterfly knife."

At age 14 Jason was arrested and charged with attempted auto theft, auto burglary, and possession of stolen property. This arrest led to an initial psychological evaluation and a first Rorschach. Unaware of the extent of delinquency, and specifically a history positive for fighting and aggression, the evaluating psychologist diagnosed Jason as conduct disorder, group type (socialized, nonaggressive).

Six months after the first assessment, the same psychologist would have a second opportunity to evaluate Jason. Between evaluations Jason reports attempts at increased control on the part of his parents: "My parents were pretty strict, they got stricter and stricter after we went to counseling. They wanted to keep a close eye on me." During the 6-month interval Jason ran away from home four or five times. Jason's second Rorschach was administered while in custody. He had severely stabbed his mother and murdered his father. A meat cleaver and knife were used in the matricidal assault and patricide.

Probation reports suggested that the assault was predatory. Jason described the violence: "I came back home after school around 3:30. When I got home, my father got this letter from the school saying I was absent a few days—which I never was. My dad started getting angry with me . . . He did not slap me, but he kind of pointed his finger at me . . . Then we left home, my father and I, and went to pick up my brother from baseball practice. Afterwards we drove home."

Jason continued, "When we got home, I was walking up and my dad was still talking to me about it. I was just thinking about what he had said, and it kind of got me angry . . . I started thinking about the past and what he did to me, then all of a sudden, I just thought, 'I want to do it right then.' "

Examiner, "Do what?"

Jason, "Kill him. So I took a shower, and then my brother took a shower. While I was taking my shower, I had a doubt in my mind first. I knew what was going to

---

[12]Appreciation is extended to Jonathan French and Andy Smith for their contribution of this fascinating adolescent case.

happen to me if I did this. But I decided, 'Yea, I'm going to do it.' So while my brother was taking his shower, I took out a 3-inch knife from a box in my room, and I was getting ready. I got all my clothes together. Once my brother finished— my brother went down to take his shower—so when he was taking his shower, I was in the kitchen." Jason had planned to "use the cleaver in my left hand, and get him [father] in the throat so he couldn't yell, and then stab him, and he would just drop to the floor and die." His mother, however, unexpectedly returned home. "I was waiting, but then all of a sudden my mom came home. She walked into the kitchen, and asked, 'What was I doing with the knife?' I hesitated at first, but had a cleaver in my hand, and with my left hand I swung at her left shoulder."

Examiner, "With what?"

Jason, "With the cleaver. I struck her left shoulder. She started yelling for help. So then my father heard and ran upstairs. My father saw my mother bleeding, and ran . . . he confronted me. He yelled and told me to 'Put down the knife.' I yelled back at him, 'No, no!' He replied, 'Why not?' I told him, 'Why don't you come on?' So we both collided coming toward each other. I stabbed him in the stomach a couple times, I think, I'm not sure. I dropped the cleaver on the floor. We started fighting in the living room. By that time my mother was already in the neighbor's house. While me and my father was fighting, my brother was in his room listening to music. After my father and I fought a little bit, I stabbed him some more in the back."

Examiner, "How many times?"

Jason, "One or two times. We stopped fighting and I ran all the way to the kitchen, and my father still followed me upstairs into his room. So I told my brother 'Come on and help me' and he said, 'No, I don't want to get involved.' I told him to get out of the house. Then my father came in and I stabbed him in the chest. My brother started running down the stairs all the way to the first floor. I ran down after him, and I saw him put on his shoes. Then I ran into the shower to wipe off all the blood."

Jason continued, "My father came into the room, because the bathroom was connected to the two rooms. When my father came in I saw him pick up a pool cue stick. So I picked up this metal piece. He swung, I swung, but dropped the thing. So he swung and hit my head twice. I swung with my fist and hit his head. Then he fell down. I ran back up the stairs, back to my room. I changed my socks and my shirt. I broke into my father's room (Jason's parents kept their room locked due to his stealing) because I wanted to get the car keys, so I could get away. But I didn't find them. I looked out the window and saw a police car. So I knew I wouldn't have a chance to escape. So I just lied face down on my father's bed waiting for a policeman. So the policeman came in, points the gun at me. One officer grabbed my shirt and ran me against the wall, nearly choking me. Then he put the handcuffs on me, and we walked outside. I saw my father lying there."

Jason denies ever thinking about killing his father prior to the offense. When asked if he had any doubts about killing his father he responded in a tangential manner, "Father helped me a lot in school and taught me a lot of things, like tennis." Jason believed he could get away with the murder, "Yea, with my parents dead—I would take the phone line off, so no one would call, and change the locks." He planned to tell relatives that his parents were on vacation. Jason indicated that he had planned to murder his mother and stuff the bodies in a crawl space in the house. His main concern had been the possibility of his brother inheriting his parents' money and "He would take the money and spend it."

Jason viewed his current incarceration as a temporary inconvenience and believed that he "would be going on with his life shortly." When asked how he felt given all that had happened, his only concern was that he "needed some nice new clothes and a good place to live." When asked how he felt about what happened, he replied, "I feel that somehow in the future I'll have a new life." He reported that, "I'm pretty sure he's [father] up in heaven," and, "My mother is still alive, and I hope she understands why I did it—because of what she did to me—She punished me, and did not let me do what I wanted to do, and all that stuff. I hope I'll be sentenced to the Youth Authority [California Juvenile Prison] for about 5 to 6 years, and maybe during my sentence time I can get a good education at becoming a mechanic."

Mental status indicated an alert and oriented adolescent. Intelligence was estimated to be average. Memory was intact, although he had a tendency to be vague and evasive about specific events in his personal history. Jason's ability to express immediate emotions or feelings was severely restricted. Shallow affect was noted. When he described painful or pleasant experiences his emotional and physical expression was one of indifference. Talking about murder or love was as easy as talking about breakfast.

The psychologist wrote:

> Jason views himself as a loner who needs autonomy and strength. He sees himself as mistreated and abused by others. Consequently, he justifies hurting others because he believes that he has been hurt by others. He sees people as generally oppressive and thus deserving of being exploited ... He feels entitled to break the rules or the law. His calmness inside allows him to lie to others purposefully for personal gain, or physically harm another person without feeling any nervousness, doubt, or remorse.

Jason's diagnosis was changed to conduct disorder, undifferentiated type, severe.

Jason's Rorschachs

Tables 3.6, 3.7, and 3.8 contain Jason's prehomicide Rorschach protocol, sequence of scores, and structural summary. Tables 3.9, 3.10, and 3.11 show his posthomicide Rorschach protocol, sequence of scores, and structural summary. Sequence of scores and structural summaries were generated with Rorschach Interpretation Assistance Program (RIAP) Version 2 (Exner et al., 1990).

TABLE 3.6
Jason's Prehomicide Rorschach Protocol

Card I   1) Fly.

E: (Rpts S's response)
S: Wings, antennas.

Structural Scoring: Wo Fu A 1.0
Aggression Scores: None.
Primitive Modes of Relating: None.
Defenses: None Categorized.

2) Crab.

E: (Rpts S's response)
S: Because of these four things here.
E: (?)
S: Holes.
E: (?)
S: On the crab I remember seeing one on the body.
E: (?)
S: Claws, body.

Structural Scoring: WSo Fo A 3.5 PER,MOR
Aggression Scores: AgC
Primitive Modes of Relating: None.
Defenses: Devaluation.

3) A bat.

E: (Rpts S's response)
S: Wings, two feet holding together.
E: (?)
S: Usually when I watch a movie and see a bat, the two feet are holding together.

Structural Scoring: Wo FMpo A P 1.0 PER
Aggression Scores: None.
Primitive Modes of Relating: None.
Defenses: Rationalization.

Card II   4) Looks like 2 bears.

E: (Rpts S's response)
S: Shape of a bear—two sides.
E: (?)
S: Same shape as I see on TV.

Structural Scoring: Do Fo 2 A P PER
Aggression Scores: None.
Primitive Modes of Relating: None.
Defenses: None Categorized.

5) A butterfly.

E: (Rpts S's response)
S: I guess I see these two as wings, head, antennas.

(Continued)

TABLE 3.6
(Continued)

E: Butterfly?
S: Wings, head, antennas.

Structural Scoring: Wo Fo A 4.5
Aggression Scores: None.
Primitive Modes of Relating: None.
Defenses: None Categorized.

Card III   6) Looks like a frog.

E: (Rpts S's response)
S: Arms, eyes.
E: (?)
S: Because I seen them on TV, big body.

Structural Scoring: Do 1 F− A PER,INC
Aggression Scores: None.
Primitive Modes of Relating: None.
Defenses: None Categorized.

Card IV   7) Looks like a dragon.

E: (Rpts S's response)
S: The head of a dragon.
E: (?)
S: Two eyes, spikes.

Structural Scoring: Do 1 Fu (Ad)
Aggression Scores: AgC
Primitive Modes of Relating: None.
Defenses: None Categorized.

Card V   8) Looks like a snail with wings.

E: (Rpts S's response)
S: Two antennas and wings.
E: (?)
S: They look spread out.
E: Spread out?
S: Like when he flaps.

Structural Scoring: Wo FMau A 1.0 INC
Aggression Scores: None.
Primitive Modes of Relating: None.
Defenses: Massive Denial.

      9) And a butterfly.

E: (Rpts S's response)
S: Antennas and wings going upward.
E: (?)
S: Horizontal.

Structural Scoring: Wo Fo A P 1.0
Aggression Scores: None.
Primitive Modes of Relating: None.
Defenses: None Categorized.

(Continued)

TABLE 3.6
(Continued)

Card VI 10) Looks like a machine gun.	E: (Rpts S's response) S: Handles, trigger, barrel.

Structural Scoring: Wo F− Sc 2.5
Aggression Scores: AgC
Primitive Modes of Relating: None.
Defenses: None Categorized.

Card VII 11) Looks like 2 girls' faces.	E: (Rpts S's response) S: Mouth, nose, hair braided. E: Braided? S: It goes with the face.

Structural Scoring: Do 1 Fo 2 Hd P ALOG
Aggression Scores: None.
Primitive Modes of Relating: None.
Defenses: None Categorized.

12) And a butt.	E: (Rpts S's response) S: Legs and butt (laughs).

Structural Scoring: Do 4 F− Hd,Sx
Aggression Scores: SM
Primitive Modes of Relating: Boundary Disturbance.
Defenses: None Categorized.

Card VIII 13) It looks like a mountain to me.	E: (Rpts S's response) S: A bunch of rocks—and these look like animals trying to climb up the mountain. E: (?) S: I think they were part of the mountain. E: Rocks? S: I've seen the shape of a mountain.

Structural Scoring: W+ FMau 2 A,Ls P 4.5 PER
Aggression Scores: None.
Primitive Modes of Relating: Symbiotic Merging.
Defenses: None Categorized.

Card IX 14) Looks like a city with a dome.	E: (Rpts S's response) S: A castle (lisps) with a tower, and this is a glass dome. E: (?) S: You can barely see this part right here—covering it. And these things sticking out.

(Continued)

TABLE 3.6
(Continued)

E: (?)
S: Usually when you look through a glass, you see some little blurry stuck.
E: (?)
S: I guess the ink dries up and it gets blurry—makes it look like you can see through it.
E: (?)
S: When the color changes.

Structural Scoring: D+ 2 FVu Sc 2.5 DV
Aggression Scores: None.
Primitive Modes of Relating: Boundary Disturbance.
Defenses: None Categorized.

Card X   15) Looks like a place for rodents.

E: (Rpts S's response)
S: These look like insects, cockroaches, spiders, a regular insect.

Structural Scoring: Wo Fo A P 5.5 DR
Aggression Scores: AgC
Primitive Modes of Relating: None.
Defenses: Devaluation.

TABLE 3.7
Jason's Prehomicide Sequence of Scores

Card I	1 Wo	Fu		A		1.0	
	2 WSo	Fo		A		3.5	PER,MOR
	3 Wo	FMpo		A	P	1.0	PER (AgC)
Card II	4 Do 6	Fo	2	A	P		PER
	5 Wo	Fo		A		4.5	
Card III	6 Do 1	F−		A			PER,INC
Card IV	7 Do 1	Fu		(Ad)			(AgC)
Card V	8 Wo	FMau		A		1.0	INC
	9 Wo	Fo		A	P	1.0	
Card VI	10 Wo	F−		Sc		2.5	(AgC)
Card VII	11 Do 1	Fo	2	Hd	P		ALOG
	12 Do 4	F−		Hd,Sx			(SM)
Card VIII	13 W+	FMau	2	A,Ls	P	4.5	PER
Card IX	14 D+ 2	FVu		Sc		2.5	DV
Card X	15 Wo	Fo		A	P	5.5	DR (AgC)

TABLE 3.8
Jason's Prehomicide Structural Summary

Location Features	Determinants — Blends	Determinants — Single	Contents	S-Constellation
				NO..FV+VF+V+FD > 2
			H = 0, 0	NO..Col-Shd Bl > 0
Zf = 10		M = 0	(H) = 0, 0	YES..Ego < .31, >.44
Zsum = 27.0		FM = 3	Hd = 2, 0	NO..MOR > 3
ZEst = 31.0		m = 0	(Hd) = 0, 0	YES..Zd > +− 3.5
		FC = 0	Hx = 0, 0	YES..es > EA
W = 9		CF = 0	A = 10, 0	NO..CF+C > FC
(Wv = 0)		C = 0	(A) = 0, 0	YES..X+% < .70
D = 6		CN = 0	Ad = 0, 0	NO..S > 3
Dd = 0		FC' = 0	(Ad) = 1, 0	NO..P < 3 or > 8
S = 1		C'F = 0	An = 0, 0	YES..Pure H < 2
		C' = 0	Art = 0, 0	YES..R < 17
DQ		FT = 0	Ay = 0, 0	6 ..... TOTAL
...... (FQ−)		TF = 0	Bl = 0, 0	
+ = 2 (0)		T = 0	Bt = 0, 0	Special Scorings
o = 13 (3)		FV = 1	Cg = 0, 0	
v/+ = 0 (0)		VF = 0	Cl = 0, 0	Lv1 Lv2
v = 0 (0)		V = 0	Ex = 0, 0	DV = 1 × 1 0 × 2
		FY = 0	Fd = 0, 0	INC = 2 × 2 0 × 4
		YF = 0	Fi = 0, 0	DR = 1 × 3 0 × 6
		Y = 0	Ge = 0, 0	FAB = 0 × 4 0 × 7
		Fr = 0	Hh = 0, 0	ALOG = 1 × 5
		rF = 0	Ls = 0, 1	CON = 0 × 7
	Form Quality	FD = 0	Na = 0, 0	SUM 6 = 5
		F = 11	Sc = 2, 0	WSUM6 = 13

	FQx	FQf	MQual	SQx
+ =	0	0	0	0
o =	7	6	0	1
u =	5	2	0	0
− =	3	3	0	0
none =	0	−	0	0

Contents (continued):
Sx = 0, 1
Xy = 0, 0
Id = 0, 0
(2) = 3

AB = 0   CP = 0
AG = 0   MOR = 1
CFB = 0   PER = 5
COP = 0   PSV = 0

Ratios, Percentages, and Derivations

R = 15   L = 2.75

EB = 0: 0.0	EA = 0.0	EBper = N/A	
eb = 3: 1	es = 4	D = −1	
	Adj es = 4	Adj D = −1	

FM = 3 : C' = 0   T = 0
m = 0 : V = 1   Y = 0
a:p = 2: 1   Sum 6 = 5
Ma:Mp = 0: 0   Lv2 = 0
2AB+Art+Ay = 0   WSum6 = 13
M− = 0   Mnone = 0

FC:CF+C = 0 : 0   COP = 0   AG = 0
Pure C = 0   Food = 0
Afr = 0.25   Isolate/R = 0.07
S = 1   H:(H)Hd(Hd) = 0: 2
Blends:R = 0:15   (HHd):(AAd) = 0: 1
CP = 0   H+A:Hd+Ad = 10: 3

P = 6   Zf = 10   3r+(2)/R = 0.20
X+% = 0.47   Zd = −4.0   Fr+rF = 0
F+% = 0.55   W:D:Dd = 9: 6: 0   FD = 0
X−% = 0.20   W:M = 9: 0   An+Xy = 0
S−% = 0.00   DQ+ = 2   MOR = 1
Xu% = 0.33   DQv = 0

SCZI = 1   DEPI = 4   CDI = 4*   S-CON = 6   HVI = No   OBS = No

Note. From Exner (1990a). Copyright 1990a by John E. Exner, Jr. Reprinted by permission.

TABLE 3.9
Jason's Posthomicide Rorschach Protocol

Card I	1) Looks like a bat . . . These little white spots . . . look like spots on the back, yea.	E: (Rpts S's response) S: Wings, body, tail, two hands. E: Bat? S: It kind of resembles like a bat. E: (?) S: It's black, two wings—from what I've seen on TV, it kind of resembles one. E: Spots? S: Yea.

Structural Scoring: WSo FC'o A P 3.5 INC,PER
Aggression Scores: None.
Primitive Modes of Relating: None.
Defenses: None Categorized.

	2) Top part looks like a cliff or	E: (Rpts S's response) S: These two right here. E: (?) S: Looks like square-shaped, but kind of out of shape, not perfect.

Structural Scoring: Dv 7 Fu Ls
Aggression Scores: None.
Primitive Modes of Relating: None.
Defenses: Devaluation.

	3) Bottom part looks like a bee's eyes.	E: (Rpts S's response) S: The two . . . on TV, I've seen bees' eyes. E: (?) S: When you look through a bee's eyes, it's not just one thing—but lots and lots.

Structural Scoring: Ddso 26 Fu 2 Ad PER,DR
Aggression Scores: AgC
Primitive Modes of Relating: Boundary Disturbance.
Defenses: Projection.

Card II	4) I see two elephants.	E: (Rpts S's response) S: The black parts. E: (?) S: Big, head's big, big ears and the trunk.

Structural Scoring: Do 6 Fo 2 A P
Aggression Scores: None.
Primitive Modes of Relating: None.
Defenses: None Categorized.

(Continued)

TABLE 3.9

(Continued)

5) Red part looks like a bug.

E: (Rpts S's response)
S: Looks more like those red beetles bugs—they're very, very small.
E: (Lady bug?)
S: Yea.

Structural Scoring: Do 3 FCu A DV
Aggression Scores: None.
Primitive Modes of Relating: None.
Defenses: None Categorized.

6) Top part of the red looks like finger prints.

E: (Rpts S's response)
S: They have lines shaped like a finger print.

Structural Scoring: Dv 2 F− 2 Id
Aggression Scores: None.
Primitive Modes of Relating: None.
Defenses: None Categorized.

7) Looks like a space craft.

E: (Rpts S's response)
S: This is the fire—when the fire pushes it.
E: (Fire?)
S: Like on TV—the white part is not so red. It looks like a picture of a fire. It connects the spaceship.
E: (?)
S: Light red. And this is the front part right here—looks like the head.

Structural Scoring: Ds+ 5 ma.CF.YFo Sc,Fi,Art 4.5 PER,DV
Aggression Scores: None.
Primitive Modes of Relating: Symbiotic Merging.
Defenses: Isolation.

Card III   8) Looks like two monkeys.

E: (Rpts S's response)
S: Looks like chimpanzees—small, big head, back is bended, feet are more like human feet.
E: (Bent?)
S: The monkey is going like this (demonstrates).
E: (?)
S: That's the way he stands.

Structural Scoring: Do 9 FMpo 2 A INC
Aggression Scores: None.
Primitive Modes of Relating: None.
Defenses: Massive Denial.

(Continued)

TABLE 3.9
(Continued)

9) Red part looks like a nose.

E: (Rpts S's response)
S: Right here.
E: (?)
S: In the middle it looks like this, and the dark part of the red is kind of slanted down.
E: (?)
S: The dark part comes away from the other red color and makes it look like it's curved.

Structural Scoring: Do 3 F− Hd
Aggression Scores: None.
Primitive Modes of Relating: None.
Defenses: None Categorized.

10) Entire thing looks like a crab.

E: (Rpts S's response)
S: One time I caught a crab and looked under it and it reminds me of a crab.
E: (?)
S: There's some spaces left that looks like a crab, and these two look like the crab's eyes.

Structural Scoring: WS+ F− A 5.5 PER
Aggression Scores: None.
Primitive Modes of Relating: None.
Defenses: Projection.

Card IV   11) Looks like a dragon.

E: (Rpts S's response)
S: In Chinese customs. I've seen it on paper−this looks like his eyes, head, tail.

Structural Scoring: Wo Fu (A),Art 2.0 PER
Aggression Scores: AgC
Primitive Modes of Relating: None.
Defenses: None Categorized.

12) Looks like a person sleeping.

E: (Rpts S's response)
S: Feet, legs, body, two arms, head up here−it had no eyes, so it looks like he's sleeping or he's dead or something.

Structural Scoring: Do 7 Mpo H P ALOG,MOR
Aggression Scores: None.
Primitive Modes of Relating: None.
Defenses: Projection.

(Continued)

TABLE 3.9
(Continued)

13) Two black cats on the side.

E: (Rpts S's response)
S: Two little white spots. Looks like eyes.
E: (Cat?)
S: Head, body, tail.
E: (?)
S: Two of them.

Structural Scoring: Ddso 99 FC′ − 2 A
Aggression Scores: None.
Primitive Modes of Relating: None.
Defenses: Projection.

Card V   14) Looks like a butterfly with a snail's head.

E: (Rpts S's response)
S: Wings, body of a snail.

Structural Scoring: Wo Fu A 1.0 INC2
Aggression Scores: None.
Primitive Modes of Relating: Symbiotic Merging.
Defenses: Massive Denial.

Card VI   15) Top part looks like a cat's head.

E: (Rpts S's response)
S: Nose, whiskers, fur.
E: (?)
S: It got grey, black and a little white.

Structural Scoring: Do 3 FC′u Ad
Aggression Scores: None.
Primitive Modes of Relating: None.
Defenses: None Categorized.

16) Bottom part looks like a Mac 10 pistol.

E: (Rpts S's response)
S: I've seen what a Mac 10 looks like—It's a black gun, real small, size of a pistol; handle.

Structural Scoring: Do FC′u 2 Sc PER
Aggression Scores: AgC.
Primitive Modes of Relating: None.
Defenses: None Categorized.

17) Put together it looks like a guitar.

E: (Rpts S's response)
S: One of those heavy metal guitars— head, body—looks like two guitars connected together.
E: (?)
S: It's been built to have two guitar strings in it.

Structural Scoring: Wo Fu Sc 2.5
Aggression Scores: None.
Primitive Modes of Relating: None.
Defenses: None Categorized.

(Continued)

TABLE 3.9
(Continued)

Card VII 18) Looks like two Playboy bunny
heads.

E: (Rpts S's response)
S: I have seen them on T.V., kind of
like a bar or casino where they wear
those fake bunny ears.
E: (?)
S: These look like the mouth and nose.

Structural Scoring: Do 1 Fo 2 Hd,Art P PER
Aggression Scores: None.
Primitive Modes of Relating: None.
Defenses: None Categorized.

19) Bottom part looks like this, ah . . .
well, to me it looks like (points) a
woman's genitals.

E: (Rpts S's response)
S: Right here.
E: (?)
S: It just looks like it.
E: (?)
S: Inside legs and the dark part here,
looks clean.
E: (?)
S: It looks white right there.

Structural Scoring: Do 6 YF.C'Fo Hd,Sx PER
Aggression Scores: None.
Primitive Modes of Relating: None.
Defenses: None Categorized.

20) In the middle it looks two mean
bunnies.

E: (Rpts S's response)
S: Bunny eyes, white eyes — looks like
he's grinning.
E: (Mean?)
S: When he's grinning he has a mean
face — looks like he's mean.

Structural Scoring: Do 3 Mp.FC'o 2 Ad FAB
Aggression Scores: SM, AgC
Primitive Modes of Relating: None.
Defenses: Projection, Massive Denial.

Card VIII 21) Looks like a mountain.

E: (Rpts S's response)
S: Top part, middle, bottom — connected
all together.

Structural Scoring: Wv Fu Ls 4.5
Aggression Scores: None.
Primitive Modes of Relating: None.
Defenses: None Categorized.

(Continued)

TABLE 3.9
(Continued)

22) On the side it looks like two bears.

E: (Rpts S's response)
S: They're big. Four feet, back part is not a full line. Looks like a bear's fur.
E: (?)
S: All this up and down.
E: (Fur?)
S: On the edge.

Structural Scoring: Do 1 Fo 2 A P
Aggression Scores: None.
Primitive Modes of Relating: None.
Defenses: None Categorized.

23) The bottom looks like water.

E: (Rpts S's response)
S: Looks like mixed chemicals in it so it changed color and everything.
E: (?)
S: It looks wavy—as if it was glittering from the sun.
E: (?)
S: All these different shades.
E: (Chemicals?)
S: Yea—because if it was water, it would be clear. But chemicals change colors.
E: (Wavy?)
S: It's not in a straight line.

Structural Scoring: Dv 2 C.Y Na
Aggression Scores: None.
Primitive Modes of Relating: None.
Defenses: None Categorized.

24) Inside middle looks like trees.

E: (Rpts S's response)
S: Because it's green, and it's straight up and everything, and it looks branchy at the top.

Structural Scoring: Do 5 CF− Bt DV
Aggression Scores: None.
Primitive Modes of Relating: None.
Defenses: None Categorized.

25) The very top looks like a grey mountain.

E: (Rpts S's response)
S: Because the color is grey—it's triangle shaped.

Structural Scoring: Dv 4 C'Fo Ls
Aggression Scores: None.
Primitive Modes of Relating: None.
Defenses: None Categorized.

(Continued)

TABLE 3.9
(Continued)

Card IX 26) Looks like in the middle a sword.

E: (Rpts S's response)
S: It doesn't look straight—but it's going toward the sharp point.

Structural Scoring: Do 5 Fu Sc
Aggression Scores: AgC
Primitive Modes of Relating: None.
Defenses: None Categorized.

27) From the bottom and middle it looks like a castle.

E: (Rpts S's response)
S: All these lines make it look like windows, the middle part looks like those old time castles with those skinny buildings.
E: (?)
S: That's the tower.

Structural Scoring: Do F− Id,Ay
Aggression Scores: None.
Primitive Modes of Relating: None.
Defenses: None Categorized.

28) Top part looks like a dome.

E: (Rpts S's response)
S: One of those clear domes—like covering the castle.
E: (Clear?)
S: Looks like a perfect circle.
E: (Covering?)
S: Tower looks like it's under the dome.
E: (?)
S: Just looks like a perfect circle.

Structural Scoring: Dso 8 FDo Id
Aggression Scores: None.
Primitive Modes of Relating: Boundary Disturbance.
Defenses: Idealization.

Card X 29) Looks like there's a lot of insects.

E: (Rpts S's response)
S: . . . . .

Structural Scoring: Wo Fo A 5.5
Aggression Scores: None.
Primitive Modes of Relating: None.
Defenses: None Categorized.

30) On the side it looks like micro organisms.

E: (Rpts S's response)
S: Organisms, I've seen them through a microscope.

(Continued)

TABLE 3.9
(Continued)

E: (?)
S: Looks like all these organisms like big under the microscope.
E: (?)
S: Little arms and little small bodies and things like that.

Structural Scoring: Dv Fu A PER, INC
Aggression Scores: None.
Primitive Modes of Relating: Metamorphosis and Transformation.
Defenses: Isolation.

31) At the top it looks like two beetles.

E: (Rpts S's response)
S: Two.
E: (?)
S: This white part looks like beetles' mouths and the beetles' eyes.
E: (?)
S: Body and antennas.

Structural Scoring: DS+ 8 Fo 2 A 6.0
Aggression Scores: None.
Primitive Modes of Relating: None.
Defenses: None Categorized.

32) At the bottom it looks like two worms.

E: (Rpts S's response)
S: Worms are like squirming, skinny— looks like they moved around a lot.
E: (?)
S: The green.

Structural Scoring: Do 4 FMa.FCo 2 A
Aggression Scores: None.
Primitive Modes of Relating: None.
Defenses: None Categorized.

33) In the middle it looks like two yellow eyes.

E: (Rpts S's response)
S: Right here.
E: (?)
S: Bright yellow, looks like the outside part, and the two orange spots look like the inside part.

Structural Scoring: Do 2 CF− Ad INC
Aggression Scores: None.
Primitive Modes of Relating: None.
Defenses: Projection.

TABLE 3.10
Jason's Posthomicide Sequence of Scores

Card I								
1	Wso		FC'o		A	P	3.5	PER,INC
2	Dv	7	Fu		Ls			
3	DdSo	26	Fu	2	Ad			PER,DR (AgC)
Card II								
4	Do	6	Fo	2	A	P		
5	Do	3	FCu		A			DV
6	Dv	2	F−	2	Id			
7	Ds+	5	ma.CF.YFo		Sc,Fi,Art		4.5	PER,DV
Card III								
8	Do	9	FMpo	2	A			INC
9	Do	3	F−		Hd			
10	Ws+		F−		A		5.5	PER
Card IV								
11	Wo		Fu		(A),Art		2.0	PER (AgC)
12	Do	7	Mpo		H	P		ALOG,MOR
13	Ddso	99	FC'−	2	A			
Card V								
14	Wo		Fu		A		1.0	INC2
Card VI								
15	Do	3	FC'u		Ad			
16	Do		FC'u	2	Sc			PER, (AgC)
17	Wo		Fu		Sc		2.5	
Card VII								
18	Do	1	Fo	2	Hd,Art	P		PER
19	Do	6	YF.C'Fo		Hd,Sx			PER
20	Do	3	Mp.FC'o	2	Ad			FAB, (SM,AgC)
Card VIII								
21	Wv		Fu		Ls			
22	Do	1	Fo	2	A	P		
23	Dv	2	C.Y		Na			
24	Do	5	CF−		Bt			DV
25	Dv	4	C'Fo		Ls			
Card IX								
26	Do	5	Fu		Sc			(AgC)
27	Do		F−		Id,Ay			
28	Dso	8	FDo		Id			
Card X								
29	Wo		Fo		A		5.5	
30	Dv		Fu		A			PER,INC
31	Ds+	8	Fo	2	A		6.0	
32	Do	4	FMa.FCo	2	A			
33	Do	2	CF−		Ad			INC

TABLE 3.11
Jason's Posthomicide Structural Summary

Location Features	Determinants		Contents	S-Constellation
	Blends	Single		

Location Features	Blends	Single		Contents		S-Constellation
						NO..FV+VF+V+FD > 2
				H = 1, 0		YES..Col-Shd Bl > 0
Zf = 8	m.CF.YF	M = 1		(H) = 0, 0		NO..Ego < .31, >.44
ZSum = 30.5	YF.C'F	FM = 1		HD = 3, 0		NO..MOR > 3
ZEst = 24.0	M.FC'	m = 0		(Hd) = 0, 0		YES..Zd > +- 3.5
	C.Y	FC = 1		Hx = 0, 0		YES..es > EA
W = 7	FM.FC	CF = 2		A = 12, 0		YES..CF+C > FC
(Wv = 1)		C = 0		(A) = 1, 0		YES..X+% < .70
D = 24		Cn = 0		Ad = 4, 0		YES..S > 3
Dd = 2		FC' = 4		(Ad) = 0, 0		NO..P < 3 or > 8
S = 7		C'F = 1		An = 0, 0		YES..Pure H < 2
		C' = 0		Art = 0, 3		NO..R < 17
DQ		FT = 0		Ay = 0, 1		7.....TOTAL
......(FQ-)		TF = 0		Bl = 0, 0		Special Scorings
+ = 3 (1)		T = 0		Bt = 1, 0		
o = 24 (5)		FV = 1		Cg = 0, 0		Lv1 Lv2
v/+ = 0 (0)		VF = 0		Cl = 0, 0		DV = 3 × 1 0 × 2
v = 6 (1)		V = 0		Ex = 0, 0		INC = 4 × 2 1 × 4
		FY = 0		Fd = 0, 0		DR = 1 × 3 0 × 6
		YF = 0		Fi = 0, 1		FAB = 1 × 4 0 × 7
		Y = 0		Ge = 0, 0		ALOG = 1 × 5
Form Quality		Fr = 0		Hh = 0, 0		CON = 0 × 7
		rF = 0		Ls = 3, 0		SUM 6 = 11
	FQx FQf MQual SQx	FD = 1		Na = 1, 0		WSUM6 = 27
+ = 0 0 0 0		F = 16		Sc = 4, 0		
o = 14 5 2 4				Sx = 0, 1		AB = 0 CP = 0
u = 11 8 0 1				Xy = 0, 0		AG = 0 MOR = 1
- = 7 3 0 2				Id = 3, 0		CFB = 0 PER = 9
none = 1 - 0 0		(2) = 11				COP = 0 PSV = 0

Ratios, Percentages, and Derivations

R = 33	L = 0.94			FC:CF+C = 2 : 4	COP = 0	AG = 0
				Pure C = 1	Food = 0	
EB = 2: 5.5	EA = 7.5	EBper = 2.8		Afr = 0.65	Isolate/R = 0.18	
eb = 3:11	es = 14	D = -2		S = 7	H:(H)Hd(Hd) = 1: 3	
	Adj es = 12	Adj D = -1		Blends:R = 5:33	(HHd):(AAd) = 0: 1	
				CP = 0	H+A:Hd+Ad = 14: 7	
FM = 2 : C' = 7	T = 0					
m = 1 : V = 1	Y = 3		P = 5	Zf = 8	3r+(2)/R = 0.33	
a:p = 2: 3	Sum 6 = 11		X+% = 0.42	Zd = +6.5	Fr+rF = 0	
Ma:Mp = 0: 2	Lv2 = 1		F+% = 0.31	W:D:Dd = 7:24: 2	FD = 1	
2AB+Art+Ay = 4	WSum6 = 27		X-% = 0.21	W:M = 7: 2	An+Xy = 0	
M- = 0	Mnone = 0		S-% = 0.29	DQ+ = 3	MOR = 1	
			Xu% = 0.33	DQv = 6		

SCZI = 2	DEPI = 6*	CDI = 3	S-CON = 7	HVI = No	OBS = No

Note. From Exner (1990). Copyright 1990a by John E. Exner, Jr. Reprinted by permission.

Jason's first protocol is constricted, commonly produced during a forensic evaluation. Despite an adequate number of responses (R = 15), the record's structural validity is questionable. Low R (R = 15), high Lambda (L = 2.75), restricted EA (0), no blends, Afr = .25, PER = 5, and so on, in the context of the testing circumstances caution against interpreting structural data alone. A guarded and defensive approach (Lambda = 2.75, PER = 5) to the Rorschach task is indicated. Content analysis reveals aggressive identifications (AgC = 4), primitive modes of relating (boundary disturbance and symbiotic merging), and the following defenses: massive denial, devaluation, and rationalization. Concerning the nature of his psychopathology, the first record reveals only the tip of the iceberg. Jason's prehomicide protocol (R = 15) manifests many of the features of Sugarman et al.'s (1980) inhibited borderline whereas the posthomicide protocol (R = 33) looks like an uninhibited record. Both records offer interpretative problems; the first due to the absence of information whereas the second exhibits the effects of inflation.

Both pre- and posthomicide protocols are included for the reader's perusal and comparison. We highlight differences and similarities between them, although focus on the latter for our primary interpretation.

Structural Interpretation of Jason's Posthomicide Protocol

Jason's second Rorschach yields twice as many responses (R = 33) as his first protocol (R = 15), and more than expected in nonpatient 15-year-olds (M = 21.94, SD = 4.21; Exner, 1990b). Complex affective states (Blends = 5; es = 14; Color shading blends = 3) press for expression. Both protocols exhibit less than adequate organized resources; es is greater than EA in both. EA (= 7.5) in the posthomicide protocol would be adequate in the context of an average length protocol, however, within the lengthy record it is less than expected.

Impulses disrupt Jason's controls, more so on the second protocol (D = −2; AdjD = −1) where situational affects exist (Y = 3). Sexual preoccupation may be a source of anxiety (YF.C'Fo Hd,Sx, PER, response 19) and, given incarceration, restraint (C'F). He is prone to ruminate (FV = 1; FD = 1), despite his shallow presentation. An upsurge of affect has resulted in increased levels of constraint (C' = 7), none of which was evident in the prehomicide protocol (C' = 0).

Jason's experience style is pervasively extratensive (EB = 2:5.5). This raises special problems, as information from the environment is distorted (X+%, X−%, F+%), modified by egocentricity (PER = 9) and unconventional (P = 5). His perceptual accuracy with (X+% = 42) and without (F+% = 31) affect is poor, as is his reality testing (X−% = 21). Cognitive slippage is pervasive, more so on the posthomicide protocol (WSum6 = 27), and at times severe (ALOG = 1; INC2 = 1). SCZI is not positive.

The posthomicide protocol reveals less integration than expected in nonpatient 15-year-olds (Zf = 8; nonpatients = 12.68; SD = 2.59; Exner, 1990b), and overincorporation (Zd = +6.5). This differs from the first protocol, which evidenced inefficient processing (Zf = 10, Zd = –4.0). Jason's Lambda is elevated (L = .94), similar to 62% of our CD sample, but not invalidating, as was the case with his first protocol (L = 2.75). A high Lambda is consistent with Jason's rigid defenses against affect and a simple, item-by-item approach to problem solving.

Jason does not have the capacity for bonding at present (T = 0 in both protocols), does not see others as real, whole, and meaningful objects (Protocol 1, M = 0, H = 0; Protocol 2, M = 2; H = 1), and does not expect positive interactions with others (COP = 0). Part objects (Hd = 3) predominate his inner world. His two Mps, produced with adequate FQxo but spoiled by moderate (FAB) and severe (ALOG) cognitive slippage, add support for impaired interpersonal relations. Relationships are characterized by his needs to control and self-aggrandize (Protocol 1, PER = 5; Protocol 2, PER = 9). Detachment rather than pathological dependency (Food = 0) is suggested.

Although the prehomicide protocol suggests affective avoidance (Afr = .25), the posthomicide record does not (Afr = .65). Difficulties modulating affect (FC:CF+C = 2:4), explosiveness (C = 1), and a lack of delay (M = 2) are consistent with his demonstrated behaviors. Jason is chronically angry and oppositional (S = 7) and currently troubled by dysphoric and confusing affect (V = 1; Y = 3; C' = 7; ColShad blend = 3 [One C.Y blend]; DEPI = 6; S-CON = 7). His affect is poorly modulated, poorly constrained, and severely disruptive.

Jason's W:M (7:2) suggests grandiosity and aspirations that exceed abilities. His low egocentricity ratio (.33) is similar to 47% of our CD males. It is consistently lower (Protocol 1 = .20; Protocol 2 = .33) than expected in nonpatient 15-year-olds (M = .44, SD = .10; Exner, 1990b). Both protocols exhibit normal morbids (MOR = 1), but painful self-evaluation (FV = 1), perhaps self-pity, with the posthomicide protocol also containing an FD. Introspection in Jason is available but dominated by dysphoric affect. Coupled with the absence of reflections, elevated PER (=9), and general disorganization noted throughout the protocol, Jason can be described as a poorly functioning psychopath (Protocol 1, CDI = 4; Protocol 2 DEPI = 6) whose defenses are currently not working to bolster grandiosity.

The interpretation of sequence and content that follows is limited to the posthomicide protocol only.

Interpretation of Sequence of Scores

Like Damion's protocol in chapter 2, Jason's sequence is marked by a stable instability. Perceptual accuracy evidences variability throughout the protocol. Sixty percent of each card's final response end with u or –FQx; including indices of cognitive slippage, 80% end with a "spoiled" response. Only Card VII demonstrates adequate FQx on each of its three responses. Impulse reigns over defenses throughout Jason's sequence. Ultimately defense fails as Jason's final response (#33) contains both a CF– and an INC.

Location choice is also variable. Five cards (I, IV, V, VIII, X) begin with Ws whereas five begin with Ds. Three cards end with Ws (III, V, VI). When he does produce a Dd it is the result of a W to D to Dd progression (Cards I, IV). Both of his Dds, produced on the final responses of their respective cards, contain impaired FQx. In these cases, narrowing down the stimulus field does not aid perceptual accuracy. Popular responses usually aid in organizing perceptual accuracy, but in Jason's case they do so only 60% of the time. Two of his populars contain either mild (INC) or severe (ALOG) cognitive slippage.

Jason's sequence is characterized by affective constraint and attempted impulse control. Five of his cards (I, II, III, IV, IX) end with space responses (S), three with C' (IV, VII, VIII), whereas 90% of the cards contain at least one. He begins the Rorschach with strained defenses (Response 1; S, FC', INC) and ends with failed ones (Response 33; CF–, INC).

Interpretation of Content

Content analysis supports a "true" rather than "pseudo" borderline adolescent protocol (Sugarman et al., 1980). Primitive modes of relating (boundary disturbance, symbiotic merging, and metamorphosis and transformation) and primitive defensive operations (devaluation, projection, and massive denial) frequent the record. They support the presence of borderline personality organization and pervasive distortions of the internal object world. Distortions manifest in forced combinations that deny the constraints of reality, "Chimpanzees—small, big head, back is bended, feet are more like human feet" (#8), "butterfly with a snail's head" (#14), as well as content that does not match stimulus properties (F+%, X+%, X–%).

Despite his history of violence he fails to produce any AG. Aggressive content (AgC = 5), "bee" (#3), "dragon" (#11), "Mac 10 pistol" (#16), "sword" (#26), is frequently produced. Three of the five AgC occur with PERs, suggesting aggressive identifications. Jason's object orientation is sadistic (SM = 1) rather than masochistic (AgPast = 0). The nature of his sadism is revealed in Response 20, "In the middle it looks like two bunnies . . . bunny eyes, white eyes—looks like he's grinning . . . When he's grinning he has a mean face—looks like he's mean." Sadism is denied and projected as Jason places it in the object; "grinning, mean bunny."

Jason's SM response differs from those that contain pleasurable affect in the presence of devalued, morbid, or aggressive content (see chapter 8). In the latter response sadism is neither projected nor denied. Jason's SM response is paradigmatic of the relationship between his aggression and real-world behavior. In conjunction with aggressive imagery and the frequent use of projection throughout, the record suggests that responsibility for aggression is projected. Jason perceives others as the aggressors, and therefore feels justified in aggressing against them. Within his intrapsychic world it is interpreted as self-defense.

Summary

Jason's prehomicide Rorschach protocol is relevant to a point we have made previously (Gacono et al., 1992; Gacono & Meloy, 1992) and continue to stress throughout this book. When evaluating the constricted records of antisocial and psychopathic individuals, the constriction itself requires explanation before the protocol is dismissed as invalid. The examiner is encouraged to look within the context of the testing situation, Lambda, and other Rorschach variables when interpreting the source of constriction. Within the forensic context a 13-response protocol (see Paul's protocol in chapter 7) can be interpretatively valid when low Lambda, increased Ws, elevated blends, and so forth, suggest characterological constriction, whereas at times those with 14–20 responses may not be.

Response frequency should not be the only consideration when assessing constriction. Constriction can occur with a normative number of responses.[13] Additionally, one rejected card does not necessarily invalidate the protocol. Rather, the cause for the rejection needs explanation.

Jason's Rorschachs are consistent with the patterns described by Sugarman et al. (1980). With the absence of T, COP, and a paucity of M and pure H they do not reflect a large capacity for therapeutic change. Rather, their severity and chronicity reveal a 15-year-old adolescent developmentally well on his way to manifesting a full-blown psychopathic character. The only positive prognostic indicators are the presence of anxiety ($Y = 3$) and some capacity for insight ($FD = 1$)—both perhaps contributing to a major mood disorder ($DEPI = 6$) at the time of the second testing. If interventions are delayed, or unavailable, defensive recompensation to an emotionally comfortable psychopathic character is predicted.

---

[13]This is the case in our sexual homicide sample (see chapter 9). Nine of the original protocols, all with ≥ 14 responses, were interpretatively invalid due to interpersonal factors related to the testing situation.

The Antisocial Female

When the Himalayan peasant meets the he-bear in his pride, he shouts to scare the monster, who will often turn aside. But the she-bear thus accosted rends the peasant tooth and nail, for the female of the species is more deadly than the male.

—Rudyard Kipling, "The Female of the Species"

The participation of females in crime has increased over the past 20 years (Simon & Sharma, 1979; Wilson & Herrnstein, 1985),[1] but the prototypical criminal remains young and male. Men are 10 times more likely to commit crimes than women. Furthermore, the disproportionate number of male arrests and reported crimes have not been linked to a gender bias:

> When respondents were asked if they reported crimes to the police, half of those victimized by males, but only one-third of those victimized by females, said yes. The discrepancy, however, seems to have had more to do with the seriousness of the crime than the sex of the criminal. Male victims of serious personal crimes were more likely to report a female than a male assailant, while female victims had the reverse bias. On balance, reporting to the police showed no clear sex difference, once seriousness was taken into account. (Wilson & Herrnstein, 1985, p. 113)

Increases in female crimes in the past were largely accounted for by property crimes (Ward, Jackson, & Ward, 1969). Currently on the federal level, however,

---

[1]Between 1981 and 1991 the proportion of females in federal prisons increased from 5.4% to 7.4%. This represents a 254% increase in real numbers (1,400 to 5,000) over the 10-year period. The growth rate for males was 147% for the same period (Kline, 1992).

drug-related offenses now account for the largest increases. Twenty-six percent of federally incarcerated women were convicted of drug-related offenses in 1981 whereas 63.9% of the 1991 female inmates committed drug offenses (Kline, 1992). Drug offenses provide the highest rates for federal inmates regardless of gender.[2]

The style of offending for violent crimes differs between genders (Ward et al., 1969). A substantial body of research on violence indicates a correlation with male gender (Meloy, 1988). Socialization and modeling patterns have not satisfactorily explained differences in aggression across gender. Maccoby and Jacklin (1980) postulated that sex differences were found too early in life to be attributed to differential socialization and noted the correlation between aggression and hormones. Upon reviewing the violence literature Wilson and Herrnstein (1985) concluded, "While aggression is often situationally controlled and the forms it takes are shaped by learning, the durability, universality, and generality of the relative aggressiveness of males cannot plausibly be blamed entirely on arbitrary sex roles" (p. 121).[3] In one recent study in a sample of 4,462 men, testosterone correlated with a variety of antisocial behaviors. Socioeconomic status (SES), however, proved to be a moderating variable, with weaker testosterone–behavior relationships among higher SES subjects. The testosterone effect size, moreover, was small, and accounted for appreciable variance only at extreme levels of the male hormone (Dabbs & Morris, 1990).

Gender differences also exist for the diagnosis of antisocial personality disorder (ASPD; APA, 1987). The ASPD classification, common among chronic offenders, has been a predominately male diagnosis. Base rate estimates among American adults are 1% to 3% for males and less than 1% for females (APA, 1987). Prison populations reflect similar differences for the ASPD diagnosis. Sixty percent to 80% of male prison inmates meet the ASPD criteria whereas only 40% to 60% of female offenders do (Peaslee et al., 1992). The paucity of research with female ASPDs (Helfgott, 1992; Martinez, 1972; Peaslee et al., 1992; Strachan, 1993) may in part be explained by these lower base rates.[4] The size of our female antisocial personality disordered sample ($N = 38$) reflects this trend.

---

[2]We recognize that federal policy during this decade focused on rigid, determinant sentencing of drug offenders, which was arguably a failed approach to curb drug use, particularly among non-White groups. This does not, however, explain the disproportionate increase in female offenders, which paralleled an increase in female violent offenders at the state level.

[3]Different gender-related violence patterns were observed for men and women across two federal prisons samples. Violence among women was often related to relationship issues such as a lesbian love triangle; whereas men engaged in violence over territorial issues, perceived put-downs, and violations of personal space (personal communication, Jean Stiehler, M.A., September 1993).

[4]The lower number of female offenders result in less female institutions. Institutions serve as sites for both established and doctoral-level research. Within the federal correctional system, for example, 11% ($N = 8$) of federal prison camps and federal correctional institutes house female offenders, whereas 89% ($N = 68$) are designated for males (1993). The U.S. penitentiaries maintain inmates with extensive criminal records, long sentences, histories of violence, or histories of sophisticated criminal activity. All six of these maximum security institutions contain only male offenders.

Despite gender-based and diagnostic differences, histories of male and female offenders appear quite similar. In their study of 500 women offenders, Glueck and Glueck (1934) found factors that predisposed women to crime were generally the same as those for men, including "feeblemindedness," psychopathic personality, and marked emotional instability. Half the women studied had illegitimate pregnancies, over half had been prostitutes, and most had hostile attitudes toward their children (Glueck & Glueck, 1934). Not unlike male offenders, family histories of female offenders have been characterized by parental loss and deprivation due to divorce, mental illness, alcoholism, foster home placements, and neglect (Cloninger & Guze, 1970a, 1970b; Harmon, Rosner, Wiedlight, & Potter, 1983; Robertson, Bankier, & Schwartz, 1987). Consistent with a personality disorder diagnosis, the antisocial adult, regardless of gender, exhibits deficits in personal, social, and occupational functioning.

HYSTERIA, PSYCHOPATHY, AND ANTISOCIAL PERSONALITY

The association between hysteria and psychopathy has been studied for nearly a century (Meloy, 1988). The syndromes have been linked through histories of criminal behavior (Moravesik, 1894), commingling traits (Kraepelin, 1915), shared psychodynamics (Chodoff, 1982; Meloy, 1988, 1992a; Rosanoff, 1938; Vaillant, 1975), and similar neuropsychology (Flor-Henry, 1974; Tucker, 1981). Robins (1966) found adolescent females in treatment for antisocial behaviors were later diagnosed as adult hysterics. Hysterical personality traits remained throughout the life span, but subjects rarely continued patterns of antisocial behaviors into adulthood (Robins, 1966). Lilienfeld, Van Valkenburg, Larntz, and Akiskal (1986) found links between histrionic personality structure (HPD) and the development of antisocial personality (male) or somatization disorder (female) dependent on the sex of the individual. Cloninger and Guze (1970a, 1970b) gathered evidence for the commingling of the two disorders in a study of 66 female criminals. Hysteria or sociopathy was noted in 80% of the subjects with 26% of the cases including both. Thirty-nine percent had a single diagnosis of sociopathy, whereas 15% had the sole diagnosis of hysteria. By including the antisocial and histrionic personality disorders in Cluster B, the dramatic, emotional, erratic cluster, *DSM–III–R* and *DSM–IV* (APA, 1987, 1994) continued the trend toward acknowledging similarities between ASPD and HPD.

Studies tentatively show that hysterics and psychopaths[5] tend to marry each other and produce hyperactive children who later demonstrate antisocial or

---

[5]A psychopath as measured by the Hare Psychopathy Checklist–Revised score ($\geq$ 30) will meet the DSM–III–R criteria for ASPD (APA, 1987) slightly more than 90% of the time. Within most prison populations, however, only a third of the inmates diagnosed as ASPD will meet the threshold for severe or primary psychopathy (PCL–R = $\geq$30).

histrionic personality depending on their sex (Spalt, 1980). The dynamics of these relationships suggest complementary object relations and defensive operations (Meloy, 1988, 1992b). Denial and other primitive defenses in the hysteric function to maintain object ties to a less than ideal object. Primitive defenses in the psychopath function to bolster grandiosity and encourage the projected omnipotence from the hysterical partner. By implication different object relational paradigms are present (see Meloy, 1992b).

Although ASPD and psychopathy are a predominately masculine diagnosis and classification respectively, HPD (see Table 4.1) is more often diagnosed in females. These disorders share the traits of impulsivity, egocentricity, and shallow affect. Helfgott (1992) described their relationship:

> The words in the description of HPD refer to exhibitions of excessive emotionality. The words in the description of ASPD refer to irresponsible and aggressive behavior. Both disorders represent people with shallow affect and the inability to bond with others to the point of extreme self-centeredness and lack of empathy. The major difference between the two is that HPDs usually don't harm others. (p. 69)[6]

Is the HPD the female equivalent of psychopathy? Perhaps in its most severe form. The literature does not, however, provide a definitive answer. This is partially due to the interchangeable misuse of the terms psychopathy and antisocial personality disorder (Arkonac & Guze, 1963; Cadoret, 1978; Cadoret & Caine, 1981; Chodoff, 1982; Cloninger & Guze, 1970a, 1970b, 1973a, 1973b; Guze, Woodruff, & Clayton, 1971a, 1971b; Robins, 1966). The problem that plagues offender research unrelated to gender has been the choice of criteria for inclusion in "psychopathy" groups. Often the "psychopaths" in one study are only remotely similar to those in another. When reviewing or citing literature in the area of psychopathy the researcher must first judge the appropriateness of the independent measure.

As we have stressed throughout this text, psychopathy does not equal ASPD. The ASPD diagnosis correlates highest with one aspect of psychopathy: its behavioral expression. Antisocial personality, in turn, does not equal psychopathy. Psychopathy as measured by the PCL–R is comprised of two primary factors: Factor 1, aggressive narcissism, a trait dimension; and Factor 2, chronic antisocial lifestyle, a behavioral dimension. This is particularly relevant to a comparative literature review. Most self-report measures (e.g., MMPI) used as inclusion criteria for psychopathic groups demonstrate the highest correlations (.28–.31) with the PCL–R Factor 2 (Hare, 1991) rather than the trait domain, Factor 1. Narcissistic and hysterical traits evidence the highest correlations with Factor 1, whereas ASPD and Factor 2 are more closely related (Hart & Hare, 1989).

---

[6]It should be noted that some male rapists (see Gacono, 1992, for a case example) meet the criteria for HPD and do harm others. Often they concurrently meet the criteria for ASPD.

TABLE 4.1

DSM–III–R Criteria for Histrionic Personality Disorder

A pervasive pattern of excessive emotionality and attention seeking, beginning by early adulthood and present in a variety of contexts, as indicated by at least four of the following:

1. Constantly seeks or demands reassurance, approval, or praise.
2. Is inappropriately sexually seductive in appearance or behavior.
3. Is overly concerned with physical attractiveness.
4. Expresses emotion with inappropriate exaggeration; e.g., embraces casual acquaintances with excessive ardor, uncontrollable sobbing on minor sentimental occasions, has temper tantrums.
5. Is uncomfortable in situations in which he or she is not the center of attention.
6. Displays rapidly shifting and shallow expression of emotions.
7. Is self-centered, actions being directed toward obtaining immediate satisfaction; has no tolerance for the frustration of delayed gratification.
8. Has a style of speech that is excessively impressionistic and lacking in detail; e.g., when asked to describe mother, can be no more specific than, "She was a beautiful person." (p. 349).

Note. The disorder is apparently common, and is diagnosed much more frequently in females than in males. In many cases somatization disorder and histrionic personality disorder coexist. Borderline personality disorder is also often present.

Reviewing the literature with this understanding suggests that hysteria is the core personality domain in psychopathic females as narcissism is in psychopathic males. Like narcissism in males, it could be a necessary but not sufficient component of psychopathy.

Level of personality organization must also be considered. Whereas borderline or psychotic organization is expected in psychopaths and ASPDs (Kernberg, 1975), this would not be the case for all hysterics (Gabbard, 1990; Meloy, 1992b). Higher level hysterics utilize repression rather than splitting as their primary defense mechanism. These neurotic hysterics evidence mature ego functions and maintain the capacity for empathy and attachment. The female psychopath, by contrast, would evidence either borderline or psychotic personality organization with associated ego and superego impairment and a reliance on splitting and other primitive mechanisms. Object relations would be severely impaired. She may or may not meet the criteria for ASPD due to suspected gender differences in the manifest behavioral expression (Hare, 1991; Karpman, 1941; Peaslee et al., 1992).

Would gender differences surface on the Rorschach? Exner (1990b) did present the adult nonpatient norms by gender. He did not, however, discuss differences among the heterogeneous characterological sample ($N = 180$) either by gender or diagnosis. This discussion would be particularly relevant to gender-based differences for narcissistic and hysterical traits among male and female psychopaths. Ephraim, Occupati, Riquelme, and Gonzales' (1993) Rorschach findings supported a gender-related basis for hysterical and narcissistic traits in a nonpatient population. Women produced internal organs, sexual female anatomy, oral anatomy, childish, and rejection and denial responses at significantly higher frequencies than men. Men were more likely to produce responses in the categories of explosion, pretentiousness, and science. Pretentiousness is related to grandiosity or narcissism. Internal organs reflecting bodily concerns (somatization) and denial are associated with hysteria.

Women produced more rejection denial (denial of previous percept) and counterphobia (attempts to suppress, undo, or otherwise transform threatening, depressive, or ugly content: e.g., "animals fighting? No, they are playing") responses than men (Ephraim et al., 1993, p. 74). They wrote:

> Some clinicians consider the use of diminutives as indicative of hysteria. From a less pathological perspective that takes into account gender-role behaviors, the higher frequency of childish, oral anatomy and fusion contents in female protocols could be related to the distinctive focus on nurturance and dependency that accompanies female gender-role socialization. (Ephraim et al., 1993, p. 73)

In discussing the differences between narcissism and hysteria it is always desirable to distinguish core personality from traits. As we previously wrote, "Narcissism and hysteria are personality or character traits that determine the severity and expressive nature of psychopathy" (Gacono et al., 1990, p. 277). The discussion of gender-related Rorschach differences among psychopathological groups and psychopaths in particular provides room for further exploration.

THE ANTISOCIAL FEMALE IN RELATION TO PSYCHOPATHY AND BORDERLINE PERSONALITY DISORDER

Early studies of female offenders generally used poorly delineated criterion groups (Martinez, 1972; Peaslee et al., 1992). Treating women offenders as a homogeneous group failed to account for psychopathy as an independent measure. Martinez's (1972) unpublished study was an exception. She used a checklist based on Cleckley's criteria as an independent measure for psychopathy.[7] She compared three groups—psychopathic ($N = 15$), mixed ($N = 15$), and nonpsychopathic ($N = 15$) females—on a number of demographic and testing variables. Martinez found psychopathic females (P) to differ from nonpsychopathic females (NP) in age of first offense (P = 20, NP = 31; $p < .01$) and criminal versatility (only 7% of the P group were first offenders whereas 33% of the NP group were). Each group included two subjects convicted of murder. The psychopathic murderers were recidivists, whereas the nonpsychopaths were first-time offenders. Martinez hypothesized physiological gender differences, but similar behaviors for male and female psychopaths.

---

[7]Martinez's (1972) master's thesis was conducted prior to the development of the PCL and PCL–R.

Peaslee et al.'s (1992) research was particularly relevant to understanding female psychopathy.[8] The project contained four different sections. The researchers sought to (a) examine the relationship between female offenders and PCL–R scores, (b) study the intrapsychic functioning of the female offender, (c) compare female and male offenders manifesting different levels of psychopathy on Rorschach variables relating to narcissism, hysteria, anxiety, and attachment, and, (d) compare male and female offenders with moderate and severe levels of psychopathy on Rorschach variables measuring cognitive ideation and mediation.

Section 1. As measured by the PCL–R, is psychopathy the same in male and female offenders? Subjects were 64 female inmates at a state prison for women in Wyoming. They were incarcerated for 26 different offenses, both violent and nonviolent. Wechsler Adult Intelligence Scale–Revised (WAIS–R) IQ and Wide Range Achievement Test (WRAT) scores were used to exclude borderline or lower intellectual functioning. In order to complete the PCL–R, inmate files were reviewed, correctional staff were interviewed, and each subject participated in a semistructured interview. The first 20 subjects were interviewed by two raters with adequate interrater agreement (r = .93). The final PCL–R score for these subjects was an average of two ratings. The remaining PCL–R scores were based on one rater.

The total PCL–R score determined a subject's inclusion in the high (PCL–R ≥ 27), medium (PCL–R = 20–26), or low (PCL–R < 20) psychopathy group. Subjects in each group equaled 16 (25%), 28 (44%), and 20 (31%), respectively. The mean PCL–R score for the sample was 21.3 (*SD* = 7.6): low psychopathy, 12.3 (*SD* = 5.5), medium psychopathy, 22.6 (*SD* = 1.8), and high psychopathy, 30.3 (*SD* = 2.2). Peaslee et al. (1992) noted consistency between the distribution of these mean scores and scores in male offender groups (Hare, 1991).

We examined the relationship between the total PCL–R scores across gender by independent samples *t*-test comparison of Peaslee et al.'s (1992) female total PCL–R score with Hare's (1991) pooled male sample from seven prison populations (*N* = 1,192; *M* = 23.6, *SD* = 7.9). The males' mean score was significantly higher than the females' (z = 2.35, p = .02). This significant finding might have been spurious. It could have resulted from (a) the effects of a large *N* on *t*-test analysis, (b) an atypical female sample due to sampling bias, (c) variation within a normal range (the female score is within the range reported by Hare [1991] for male samples, 20.4–25.8),[9] or (d) actual gender difference. PCL–R ranges are needed from additional female prison populations.

Comparative analysis of Factor 1 and Factor 2 scores shed light on the differences noted for female total PCL–R scores. We utilized independent samples

---

[8]Peaslee (1993) would provide additional analysis of these data in her doctoral dissertation, which was unavailable as we wrote this chapter.

[9]The Peaslee et al. (1992) sample is similar to Neary's (1990) female sample (*N* = 120), 21.1 (*SD* = 6.5) and a female sample (*N* = 40), 24.9 (*SD* = 7.2) reported by Strachan, Williamson, and Hare (1990).

t tests to compare males and females on their separate Factor scores. Whereas Hare's (1991) males produced Factor 1 scores (aggressive narcissism) significantly lower (M = 8.93, SD = 3.93; z = 3.93, p = .0001) than the females (M = 10.8, SD = 3.7), the inverse relationship occurred for Factor 2 scores (females, M = 8.9, SD = 4.10; males, M = 11.69, SD = 3.90; z = 5.32, p = .000000). Perhaps these scores provide evidence for a gender-related difference in the behavioral expression of psychopathy (Hare, 1991; Peaslee et al., 1992). As Hare noted concerning two previous studies with females:

> Although these data are preliminary, they suggest that there may be sex differences in the behavioral manifestations of psychopathy. However, given that there are sex-based differences in socialization, it would not be surprising to find that the way in which psychopathy is "expressed" is different in women than it is in men, even if there are no sex differences in the core personality structure of the disorder. (p. 64)

The females' lower Factor 2 scores are consistent with a decreased prevalence of the ASPD diagnosis among them, because the ASPD diagnosis correlates more strongly with this factor than Factor 1. In the Peaslee et al. (1992) sample, 65% met the criteria for ASPD or personality disorder not otherwise specified with antisocial and histrionic features (hence fewer met the full criteria for antisocial personality disorder). A higher frequency for subjects meeting ASPD criteria might be expected in a typical male prison population. This initial study awaits replication.

Section 2.   What are the underlying personality characteristics of the female offenders? Forty-seven subjects were randomly selected from the 64 female offenders (FOs) used in Section 1. Rorschachs were administered following Comprehensive System procedures (Exner, 1986a) by examiners blind to the subjects' PCL–R scores. Percent agreement for variables analyzed fell within acceptable ranges (85%–100%). Rorschach variables with nonparametric properties were analyzed with a Yates-corrected independent samples chi-square. Those with normal distributions were analyzed using the independent samples *t* test. Female subjects were compared to the Exner (1990b) nonpatient females (N = 350) for the following operations: affect (Afr, SumY, SumC, SumC′, S, blends, and DEPI), interpersonal and self-perception (SumT, PER, COP, MOR, FD, SumV, Fr+rF), stress tolerance and controls (D-score, AdjD score, and CDI), information processing (Zf, Zd, Lambda), and cognitive ideation and mediation (X+%, X–%, F+%, Xu%, S–%, Wsum6, Level 2 special scores).

Affect.   The FOs were more likely to be positive on the depression index (*p* < .05) and affectively more avoidant than the nonpatients (Afr, *p* < .01). The FOs also produced less color (WSum C, *p* < .01). The FOs were less internally complex and possibly more impoverished (Blends, *p* < .01). Significant differences were not found for SumY or SumT; however, trends were noted. These female offenders were proportionately more anxious (57% of FOs and 36% of normals produced at least 1 Y) and evidenced less affective constraint (57% of FOs and 75% of normals produced at least 1 C'). Frequencies for space (S) were virtually equivalent (FOs, 79%; Normals, 81%).

Stress Tolerance and Control. Female offenders were more likely to be positive on the CDI ($p < .01$). Forty-five percent of the offenders were positive compared to 3% of normal females. D Scores were more likely to be less than zero for the offenders ($p < .01$). No significant differences were found for AdjD scores, although trends were apparent (30% of FOs were less than zero vs. 13% of normals).

Self- and Interpersonal Perception. No significant differences were found for PER, SumV, or MOR. Sixty-four percent of the offenders, however, did produce MORs compared to 48% of normal females. Female offenders were more ($p < .01$) self-focused (26% produced reflections, 7% normals), but less ($p < .01$) prone to objective introspection (FD produced by 40% of offenders, 80% normals). They were also less ($p < .01$) bonded (68% T = 0) and less interested in positive human interaction (53% produced COP, 81% normals). The Peaslee et al. (1992) female findings were consistent with the detachment, egocentricity, and guarded interpersonal relationships we noted in ASPD males.

Cognitive Style and Thought Disorder. No significant differences were noted for Zf or Zd. The mean Zd score for FOs was slightly in the minus direction ($M = -.19$, $SD = 4.04$). As we expected, and consistent with a simplistic, affectively avoidant style, Lambdas were higher ($p < .01$) in the offenders ($M = .76$, normals $M = .59$). The female offenders also evidenced mild but pervasive thought disorder and differed significantly ($p < .01$) on F+% (FOs, $M = 62$, $SD = 17$; Normals, $M = 70$, $SD = 18$), X+% (FOs, $M = 58$, $SD = 12$; Normals, $M = 79$, $SD = 08$), X-% (FOs, $M = 21$, $SD = 9$; Normals, $M = 6$, $SD = 5$), WSum6 (FOs, $M = 10.60$, $SD = 9.70$; Normals, $M = 3.20$, $SD = 2.70$), and SumLevel2 (FOs, $M = 12.42$, $SD = .85$; Normals, $M = .04$, $SD = .20$). They did not differ significantly on Xu% or S-%.

The female offenders display internal operations distinct from normal females. The affectively and interpersonally impoverished Rorschachs of these women are consistent with the behavioral histories noted by Glueck and Glueck (1934) for women offenders. Their test protocols reveal reality-testing problems and thought disorder levels consistent with borderline personality organization. Peaslee et al. (1992) concluded:

> In summary, these data highlight the internal characteristics of the female offender and provide support for borderline personality organization (Kernberg, 1975) as evidenced by primitive defenses, emotional immaturity, a narcissistically flavored

identity, with concomitant lack of attachment, and periodic fragmentation in thought processes. (pp. 26–27)

Section 3.   Would female offenders grouped by psychopathy level differ with respect to attachment capacity (SumT, COP), anxiety (SumY), narcissism (PER, Pair, Fr+rF), or hysteria (IMP)? If psychopathy was used as an independent measure, would males and females differ? Peaslee, Fleming, Baumgardner, Silbaugh, and Thackrey (1992) used the 47 female subjects described in the preceding section for their within-gender comparison (Section 2). Thirty-two females scored above 19 on the PCL–R and were utilized in between-gender comparisons. Thirty-nine male subjects were obtained from our original ASPD sample and have been described elsewhere (Gacono et al., 1990; Gacono & Meloy, 1991). The males were incarcerated at the time of testing, met the criteria for ASPD, and were free of a diagnosis of schizophrenia, bipolar disorder, or mental retardation.

PCL–R scores were used to form three female groups for within-gender comparisons. Twelve subjects were placed in the high-psychopathy group (PCL–R $\geq$ 27), 19 in the medium-psychopathy group (PCL–R = 20–26), and 12 in the low-psychopathy group (PCL–R < 20). Gender comparisons involved four offender groups. Peaslee et al. (1992) used a medium split procedure to form both male and female groups.[10] Twenty males were placed in the severe psychopathy group (PCL–R $\geq$ 30) and 19 in the moderate group (PCL–R = 20–29). Twelve females formed the severe (PCL–R $\geq$ 27) and 20 the moderate (PCL–R = 20–26) group. Kruskal–Wallis analysis was used to assess group differences. Mann–Whitney U was utilized for pairwise comparisons.

Differences were not obtained for the female subjects compared across psychopathy level. Peaslee et al. (1992) did report a nonsignificant trend in the direction of less SumY in the moderate- and high-psychopathy groups. Because we did not have access to Peaslee et al.'s (1992) frequencies for Fr+rF, SumT, SumY, and IMP, we were unable to subject them to chi-square analysis. For these four variables a significant difference of presence or absence has clinical meaning that may be more relevant than possible differences in proportions. For example, in most of our samples a large percentage of subjects who produce one

---

[10]Peaslee et al.'s (1992) choice of $\geq$ 27 as a cutoff score for their female primary psychopathy group when comparing across gender is curious. The medium split method has been used (infrequently) in other studies with all male subjects where the psychopathy range was skewed to the low end. This procedure can increase the number of subjects in the high group for better statistical comparison. The lower cutoff does not effect a comparison of mean PCL–R scores between groups (total PCL–R score comparison) or comparison of subgroups within a larger group (high, moderate, low). We, however, caution against the use of different cut-off scores when independent group comparisons are made with dependent variables such as Rorschach variables. Findings are suspect as the independent measure may not be equal. For example, comparing females, PCL–R $\geq$ 27, with males, $\geq$ 30, on specific Rorschach variables assumes that Peaslee et al.'s (1992) female sample is representative of PCL–R distributions in women offenders. Based on the scores for two other female samples cited by Hare (1991), this would be a premature conclusion.

Fr or rF produce more than one (see chapter 7). T in our sexual homicide sample also has a bimodal distribution—either absent (T = 0) or greater than 1 (see chapter 9).

Males and females differed on variables related to narcissism (Fr+rF, PER; p < .05) and attachment (SumT; p < .05); males were more narcissistic and more detached. Differences were not found for pairs, impressionistic (IMP) responses, COP, or SumY.

As Peaslee et al. (1992) observed:

> ... the male group with severe psychopathy was notably more egocentric and defensive than the males with moderate psychopathy, more defensive than the females with severe psychopathy, but notably indistinct on these variables from the females with moderate psychopathy. However, the male group with severe psychopathy evidenced a profound lack of capacity for attachment, statistically different from all other groups ... These results support a similarity in intrapsychic structure between male offenders with moderate psychopathy and female offenders with moderate or severe psychopathy. However, as evidenced by these data, the Rorschach manifestation of severe psychopathy in female inmates is qualitatively distinct from what is observed in male offenders with severe psychopathy. (Peaslee et al., 1992, pp. 33–34)

Based on their Rorschach findings, Peaslee et al. (1992) concluded that severely psychopathic females presented internalized operations more conducive to treatment intervention than the severely psychopathic males. Although level of psychopathy was not considered in their observations (Sims, 1992; Jean Stiehler, personal communication, September 1993), female offenders in general come to therapy because of dependency issues and tend to continue therapy for longer periods of time than males: ". . . women tend to suffer from anxiety and depressive disorders as a result of their situation. They are more likely than men to participate over the long term in group discussions led by a staff member . . . Most women display a genuine commitment to these groups and are motivated to take what they have learned back to the community . . ." (Sims, 1992, p. 45).

Concerning gender and violence Peaslee et al. (1992) concluded, "violent behavior notable among severe male psychopaths may be an unlikely behavioral correlate of severe female psychopathy" (p. 36).

Section 4. Would higher levels of psychopathy independent of gender display greater evidence of thought disorder and cognitive slippage? The same subjects from Section 3 used for the between-gender comparisons (females = 32; males = 39) were compared for X+%, F+%, Xu%, X–%, S–%, Level 2 special scores, Sum6, and WSum6. Although level of psychopathy was not a significant moderator for these variables, females produced significantly greater F+% and lower X–%, whereas males were higher for Level 2 special scores, Sum6, and WSum6.

What do the Peaslee et al. (1992) findings tell us about psychopathy in females? First, there is a likely gender difference. After replication in other female prisons, adjustments to the PCL–R may be required for assessing psychopathy in women (further work with female offenders is currently underway; Hare, 1991; Strachan, 1993[11]; Adelle Forth, personal communication, May 1993). Second, the Rorschach suggests patterns for female offenders differing from nonpatient females and similar to character-disordered subjects. Third, the Rorschach is likely sensitive to some of the cross-gender differences in psychopathy. The dangers of comparing moderate- and severe-psychopathy groups have to be kept in mind. Most significant differences have been found between low and severe levels. Hare designated the middle ranges as a mixed group containing some psychopaths and nonpsychopaths. Hence, differences between moderate and severe groups are always an unexpected surprise (Gacono, 1990). And fourth, the female offenders' internal worlds suggest a base line of borderline personality organization.

BORDERLINE AND ANTISOCIAL FEMALES

Given the finding of borderline personality organization (Knight, 1954) among the female offenders, how would they compare to nonoffending borderline personality-disordered females? We sought to explore the relationship between ASPD and borderline personality disorder (BPD) women by comparing select structural (see Table 4.2), object relations (see Table 4.3), and aggression indices (see Table 4.4) between a sample of outpatient BPDs ($N = 32$) and the Peaslee et al. (1992) incarcerated ASPDs ($N = 38$)[12] (Berg, Gacono, Meloy, & Peaslee, 1994).

---

[11]Strachan (1993) found in her doctoral dissertation that the PCL–R was very appropriate for use with female offenders. Psychometric properties were excellent, indicating a homogeneous and unidimensional scale. Factor analysis yielded the same two-factor structure. In her sample of 75 incarcerated female offenders in a Canadian prison, the mean PCL–R score was 24.49 ($SD = 7.45$), and 31% scored ≥ 30. Alpha coefficient for the study was .87, and single rating intraclass correlation coefficient was .92 (average rating .96). The mean Factor 1 score was 9.95 ($SD = 3.25$) and the mean Factor 2 score was 10.90 ($SD = 4.14$). The PCL–R scores correlated .41 ($p < .001$) with a diagnosis of ASPD in her sample, but Factor 1, in isolation, did not correlate (.02). Prototypicality ratings of three personality disorders and the PCL–R were as follows: histrionic (.45), narcissistic (.42), and borderline (.47)—all significant at $p < .006$. Most interesting, and consistent with the psychodynamics of psychopathy surrounding attachment failures (Meloy, 1988), the psychopathy ratings of the women were strongly related to the failure to parent even when the effects of drug abuse and prostitution were removed (.62, $p < .001$).

[12]Subjects for the ASPD group were the 32 females (PCL–R ≥ 20) used by Peaslee et al. (1992) and an additional 6 subjects from the files of Meloy or Gacono. All female subjects met the criteria for antisocial personality disorder or personality disorder NOS with antisocial and histrionic features. To ensure greater homogeneity we chose only those female subjects who scored ≥ 20 on the PCL–R. In our clinical experience with males, seldom do incarcerated subjects who meet the criteria for antisocial personality disorder score lower than 18–20 on the PCL–R (Gacono & Hutton, 1994).

TABLE 4.2
Select Structural Variables for Antisocial and
Borderline Personality Disordered Females

Variable	Antisocial (N = 38)			Borderline (N = 32)		
	M	SD	Frequency	M	SD	Frequency
Controls						
DScore	−.6	1.5	38	0	2.3	32
ADjD Score*	−.16	1.0	38	.5	1.9	32
Lambda	.83	.48	38	.73	.96	32
FC***	.68	.87	18	2.2	2.1	25
Affective States						
CF**	2.1	1.8	31	3.5	2.3	30
C	.47	.60	16	.4	.7	10
Afr	.52	.19	38	.55	.26	32
SumT**	.39	.75	11	1.3	1.3	32
SumC'	1.39	1.17	28	2.0	1.9	24
SumV	.97	1.38	22	.8	1.2	16
SumY	1.03	1.40	19	1.1	1.3	18
MOR	1.66	1.24	30	2.8	2.5	27
IMP	.4	1.0	10	.8	1.0	15
Self- and Other Relatedness						
Pairs**	6.29	3.77	37	9.9	4.9	32
Reflections	.47	.92	10	.5	1.1	9
EgoC ratio	.40	.20	37	.46	.14	32
PER	1.84	1.85	28	1.6	1.9	19
COP	.84	.92	21	1.1	1.5	17
FD	.32	.52	11	.5	.7	12
Perceptual Accuracy						
X+%***	.56	.12	38	.40	.13	32
F+%**	.58	.16	38	.43	.24	29
X−%	.17	.09	37	.20	.11	21
Xu%***	.25	.11	38	.37	.12	32
Content						
Sex	.71	.80	21	1.3	2.3	13
Blood**	.13	.34	5	.9	1.2	12
Anatomy	1.16	1.17	25	1.6	2.5	15

Note. This table contains unpublished data from Berg, Gacono, Meloy, and Peaslee (1994).
*$p \leq$ .05 Mann–Whitney U analysis. **$p \leq$ .01 Mann–Whitney U analysis. ***$p \leq$ .001 Mann–Whitney U analysis.

TABLE 4.3

Means, Standard Deviations, and Frequencies for Kwawer's (1980)
Primitive Modes of Relating in Antisocial and Borderline
Personality Disordered Females

Category	M	SD	Frequency		M	SD	Frequency	
	Antisocial Personality (N = 38)				Borderline Personality[a] (N = 32)			
Engulfment	–	–	1	(3%)	.25	.81	4	(13%)
Symbiotic Merging	.37	.85	9	(24%)	.38	.55	11	(34%)
Violent Symbiosis	.45	.65	14	(37%)	.74	1.20	12	(38%)
Birth & Rebirth	.16	.55	4	(10%)	.16	.37	5	(16%)
Malignant Internal Processes	.50	.69	15	(40%)	.77	1.00	15	(47%)
Metamorphosis & Transformation[b]	.16	.44	5	(13%)	.4	.70	11	(34%)
Narcissistic Mirroring	.53	.99	10	(26%)	.80	1.60	9	(28%)
Separation Division	.18	.46	6	(16%)	.38	.76	8	(25%)
Boundary Disturbance[c]	.26	.45	10	(26%)	.87	1.1	15	(47%)
Womb Imagery	.10	.39	3	(1%)	.09	.39	2	(6%)
Total Object Relations Categories[c]	2.79	2.80	30	(79%)	4.90	4.4	26	(81%)

Note. Frequencies equal the number of subjects who produced at least one response in a given category.

[a]BPD females were previously described in Berg, Gacono, Meloy, and Peaslee (1994).

[b,c]Mann–Whitney U analysis revealed BPDs produced a greater proportion of metamorphosis and transformation responses ($p \leq .05$), greater amounts of boundary disturbance, and total object relations categories ($p \leq .01$).

TABLE 4.4

Means, Standard Deviations, and Frequencies for Aggression Scores in
Antisocial and Borderline Personality Disordered Females

Category	M	SD	Frequency		M	SD	Frequency	
	Antisocial Personality (N = 38)				Borderline Personality[a] (N = 32)			
Aggressive Movement (AG)[b]	.71	.80	20	(53%)	1.6	2.2	22	(69%)
Aggressive Content (AgC)	2.21	1.49	32	(84%)	2.6	2.0	29	(91%)
Aggressive Past (AgPast)	.74	1.00	17	(45%)	1.3	1.5	16	(50%)
Aggressive Potential (AgPot)	.34	.71	9	(24%)	.6	1.3	7	(22%)

Note. Frequencies equal the number of subjects who produced at least one in a given category.

[a]BPD females were previously described in Berg, Gacono, Meloy, and Peaslee (1994).

[b]Mann–Whitney U analysis revealed BPDs produced more AG than the ASPD females ($p \leq .05$).

BPD females produced a significantly greater ($p \leq .01$) amount of Kwawer's (1980) primitive modes of relating (object relations; $M = 4.90$, $SD = 4.4$) than did ASPD ($M = 2.8$, $SD = 2.8$), although frequencies were similar (81% of the BPDs and 79% of the ASPDs produced at least one). The total object relations means for the ASPD females were more similar to a sample of NP-ASPD[13] males (2.24, $SD = 2.74$) than P-ASPD males ($M = 5.0$, $SD = 2.39$). This would be expected because the majority of the ASPD females were likely not psychopathic (PCL–R ≥ 30). We wrote:

> Although most of the BPD females demonstrated a capacity for attachment, the high incidence of primitive object relations (Kwawer, 1980) is illustrative of the pre-oedipal nature of their internal world. Objects are perceived in relation to each other; however, these relations are characterized by disturbances in symbiotic merging, violent separation and reunion, malignant internal processes, metamorphosis and transformation, and boundary disturbance, the latter two being significantly higher in the borderline sample. These findings also confirm the essentially ego dystonic internalized object world for the borderline patient, both male and female, when compared to the antisocial patient. The latter group is characterized by a more alloplastic character structure which is less internally conflicted, probably more identified with what were once aggressive introjects, and acts out against others, rather than the self, to maintain a representational homeostasis (Meloy, 1988). (Berg et al., 1994, p. 17)

Like ASPD males and BPD males, texture was infrequently produced by the ASPD females (29%) and significantly differentiated ($p \leq .01$) them from the BPD females (69%). The paucity of T provides some concurrent validation for detachment in antisocial females (Maas, 1966). Unlike the P-ASPD males and BPD males who differed significantly with respect to egocentricity ratio, reflections, and personals (P-ASPD, Ego $M = .47$, $SD = .23$, Reflections = 50%, PER, $M = 3.32$, $SD = 2.46$; BPD, Ego $M = .40$, $SD = .19$, Reflections = 33%, PER, $M = 1.67$, $SD = 2.56$), our female ASPDs and BPDs did not. Egocentricity ratios were, however, higher for BPDs ($M = .46$, $SD = .14$) than ASPDs ($M = .39$, $SD = .19$). Reflection frequencies (BPD = 28%; ASPD = 26%) were very similar. Elevations of PER and the diminution of cooperative movement (BPD, $M = 1.1$, $SD = 1.5$; ASPD, $M = 0.7$, $SD = .9$) in both groups when compared to normals suggest rigid character pathology that does not expect cooperative interpersonal experiences (Berg et al., 1994).

Greater adjusted D scores ($p \leq .05$) and FC ($p \leq .001$) in the BPDs (AdjD, $M = .5$, $SD = 1.9$; FC, $M = 2.2$, $SD = 2.1$) when compared to the ASPDs (AdjD, $M = -.16$, $SD = 1.0$; FC, $M = .68$, $SD = .87$) suggest the BPDs' greater capacity for controlling and directing behavior and, at times, modulating affect. Better

---

[13] These data were reported in Gacono et al. (1992). NP-ASPD designates nonpsychopathic antisocial personality disorder (PCL–R < 30) and P-ASPD psychopathic antisocial personality disorder (PCL–R ≥ 30).

controls in the BPDs, however, coexisted with more unmodulated affect, because CF responses were also significantly greater in the BPDs ($p < .01$). The BPDs also evidenced more idiosyncratic reality testing (see Table 4.2).

More internal conflict in the BPD subjects was suggested by greater proportions of Kwawer's (1980) indices, AG scores ($p \leq .05$; BPD, $M = 1.6$, $SD = 2.2$, 69%; ASPD, $M = 0.7$, $SD = .8$, 53%), and Blood content responses ($p \leq .001$; BPD, $M = 0.9$, $SD = 1.2$; ASPD, $M = 0.1$, $SD = .3$). The amount of Sx and An responses did not differ significantly (X^2 nonsignificant) between groups, although trends in frequencies were apparent. Consistent with the hysteria and somatization noted in both groups, more Sx and An (ASPD, Sx = 55%, An = 66%; BPD, Sx = 41%, An = 47%) were produced than normatively expected (Exner [1990b] nonpatient females produced Sx = 5% and An = 35%). This finding also parallels the work of DeVos (1952) and Thiesen (1952) in their use of combined sex-anatomy content to measure the inability of the subject to repress primitive, unacceptable impulses. This content combination, although infrequent, has discriminated schizophrenic samples from normals, and may add to our understanding of both borderline and psychotic personality organization (Taulbee & Sisson, 1954).

Both female groups evidenced a high degree of uncomfortable affects (C'; ASPD, $M = 1.4$, $SD = 1.2$, Freq. = 74%; BPD, $M = 2.0$, $SD = 1.9$, Freq. = 75%) when compared to P-ASPD males (C', $M = .73$, $SD = .94$, Freq. = .55). Dysphoria and depression (MOR; ASPD, $M = 1.6$, $SD = 1.2$; BPD, $M = 2.8$, $SD = 2.5$) were apparent in both. Unsublimated drive material fills the intrapsychic world of these two groups. ASPD females use acting out to discharge drives whereas BPDs internalize them:

> Both groups are significantly psychopathologic when affect states, object relations, and perceptual accuracy are measured. The damage, dysphoria, and anxiety of both groups is only distinguished by the borderline female's capacity to bond and a greater amount of affect, positive treatment indicators that also portend a tumultuous tie to the psychotherapist. Object relations will be pre-oedipal in both groups, but much more apparent in the borderline female. Symbiotic rather than autistic developmental themes are likely (Mahler, Pine & Bergman, 1975). Both groups will be characterologically rigid, self-absorbed, and likely to express a narcissistic sense of entitlement: the borderline female's wish to be taken care of, the antisocial female's wish to take. (Berg et al., 1994, pp. 18–19)

THE ANTISOCIAL FEMALE SAMPLE (N = 38)[14]

We analyzed Rorschach data from a sample of 32 women incarcerated in the Wyoming Prison for Women. Six of the female protocols were taken from our private files. All the women were administered the Rorschach using the Exner

[14]Appreciation is extended to Donna Peaslee, PhD, for donating the majority of protocols to this sample.

Comprehensive System, and no protocols with fewer than 14 responses were included. The women met a variety of DSM–III–R Axis II diagnoses, including narcissistic, histrionic, antisocial, and borderline personality disorder. All were convicted felons and scored $\geq$ 20 on the PCL–R, placing them in the moderate to severe range of psychopathy. This sample was not randomly gathered, and is too small to be considered anything other than a descriptive Rorschach sampling of female offenders. It should not be used for any normative purposes, but sheds additional light on the internal world of the female offender when compared to the other findings in this chapter.

The women ranged in age from 21 to 45 years (M = 29.47, SD = 6.50). Seventy-one percent of the sample were White, 16% Black, 11% Hispanic, and 3% unlisted. Half of the sample reported at least a high school education. See Tables 4.5 and 4.6 for details.

Core Characteristics. The female offenders (FOs) produced a normative amount of responses (M = 20.08, SD = 7.42) when compared to nonpatient females (M = 22.14, SD = 3.94), although with a greater range and variance. Deviations that we note from the nonpatient female database (Exner, 1991) are not the result of R frequency differences.

Lambda is elevated (M = .83) and 37% of the women have a Lambda > .99. This can be interpreted as both a defense against affect and a propensity toward a simple, item-by-item problem solving style. Volitional psychological resources are almost one standard deviation below the mean (EA M = 6.66, SD = 2.99) when compared to nonpatient women (EA M = 8.35, SD = 2.10). Nonvolitional ideation and affect are normal, however, resulting in a mean D of −.60 and an AdjD of −.16. Despite this slight imbalance, a majority of the sample have D scores $\geq$ 0 (66%) and AdjD is even more pronounced (74% $\geq$ 0). Only two (5%) of our subjects evidence noticeable impairments in their ability to organize their psychological operations in a predictable manner (AdjD < −1). This is the same proportion as nonpatient females (Exner, 1990b). Forty-two percent of the female offenders are ambitents, an expected finding in psychiatric populations. Most striking is the degree of pervasive and rigid extratension (24%) and introversion (29%), almost three times the frequency when compared to nonpatient women.

Affect. The FOs, like their antisocial male counterparts, do not modulate affect well. Their FC:CF+C is almost 1:4, on average, comparable to our male psychopathic sample, and worse than male ASPDs in general (1:3) and nonpatient females (2:1) in particular. Forty-two percent also have a tendency toward emotional explosiveness (C > 0), a finding in only 7% of nonpatient women. Despite these affective problems, color articulation is far less frequent (SumC = 3.29) than normals (SumC = 6.27). This suggests an avoidance of affect (Afr = .52), which may be a way to unconsciously manage an immature and labile

TABLE 4.5
Structural Data for 38 Antisocial Females

Variable	Mean	SD	Min	Max	Freq	Median	Mode	SK	KU
R	20.08	7.42	14.00	43.00	38	18.50	14.00	2.02	3.92
W	8.71	3.50	4.00	18.00	38	8.50	5.00	0.61	−0.09
D	9.24	5.98	1.00	26.00	38	8.00	10.00	1.10	1.22
Dd	2.13	2.00	0.00	8.00	30	2.00	1.00	1.24	1.32
Space	1.68	1.51	0.00	8.00	32	1.00	1.00	2.22	7.65
DQ+	5.76	2.94	0.00	14.00	37	6.00	5.00	0.64	1.17
DQo	11.60	5.28	3.00	28.00	38	11.00	8.00	0.99	1.19
DQv	2.00	3.06	0.00	18.00	27	1.00	−0.00	4.09	20.73
DQv/+	0.71	0.96	0.00	3.00	17	0.00	−0.00	1.22	0.50
FQX+	0.05	0.23	0.00	1.00	2	0.00	0.00	4.17	16.27
FQXo	10.87	3.48	5.00	20.00	38	10.00	9.00	0.59	−0.18
FQXu	5.08	3.44	1.00	21.00	38	4.00	4.00	2.95	12.02
FQX−	3.60	3.02	0.00	16.00	37	3.00	2.00	2.31	7.24
FQXnone	0.47	0.72	0.00	3.00	14	0.00	−0.00	1.66	2.90
MQ+	0.05	0.23	0.00	1.00	2	0.00	−0.00	4.17	16.27
MQo	2.24	1.65	0.00	5.00	30	2.00	−0.00	0.05	−1.25
MQu	0.74	0.68	0.00	2.00	23	1.00	1.00	0.39	−0.77
MQ−	0.39	0.82	0.00	4.00	10	0.00	−0.00	2.81	9.46
MQnone	0.05	0.32	0.00	2.00	1	0.00	0.00	6.16	38.00
Space−	0.47	0.95	0.00	4.00	10	0.00	−0.00	2.27	5.03
M	3.47	2.39	0.00	10.00	35	3.00	3.00	0.79	0.73
FM	3.05	1.72	1.00	7.00	38	3.00	3.00	0.48	−0.64
m	1.58	1.52	0.00	6.00	29	1.00	1.00	1.26	1.32
FM+m	4.63	2.62	1.00	11.00	38	4.50	2.00	0.51	−0.42
FC	0.68	0.87	0.00	3.00	18	0.00	0.00	1.20	0.79
CF	2.13	1.76	0.00	7.00	31	2.00	1.00	0.80	0.33
C	0.47	0.60	0.00	2.00	16	0.00	−0.00	0.88	−0.13
Cn	0.00	0.00	0.00	0.00	0	0.00	0.00	−	−
FC+CF+C+Cn	3.29	1.86	0.00	8.00	35	3.00	3.00	0.30	0.16
WgSumC	3.18	1.87	0.00	8.50	35	3.00	4.50	0.39	0.50
Sum C'	1.39	1.17	0.00	4.00	28	1.00	1.00	0.53	−0.51
Sum T	0.39	0.75	0.00	3.00	11	0.00	−0.00	2.37	5.95
Sum V	0.97	1.38	0.00	6.00	22	1.00	1.00	2.30	5.53
Sum Y	1.03	1.40	0.00	5.00	19	0.50	−0.00	1.43	1.14
Sum Shd	3.79	3.28	0.00	15.00	35	3.00	1.00	1.48	2.61
Fr+rF	0.47	0.92	0.00	3.00	10	0.00	−0.00	1.93	2.66
FD	0.32	0.52	0.00	2.00	11	0.00	−0.00	1.40	1.13
F	8.53	4.56	2.00	20.00	38	7.00	7.00	0.91	0.27
Pairs	6.29	3.77	0.00	20.00	37	5.00	5.00	1.49	3.70
Ego	0.40	0.20	0.00	0.81	37	0.37	0.29	0.38	−0.58
Lambda	0.83	0.48	0.14	2.14	38	0.80	0.27	0.71	0.16
EA	6.66	2.99	1.50	14.50	38	6.75	5.50	0.38	−0.06
es	8.42	4.90	2.00	22.00	38	7.50	9.00	1.02	0.96
D Score	−0.60	1.55	−6.00	2.00	38	0.00	−0.00	−1.49	3.29
Adj D Score	−0.16	1.00	−3.00	2.00	38	0.00	−0.00	−0.69	2.61
SumActvMov	4.18	2.62	0.00	9.00	37	4.00	1.00	0.34	−0.81
SumPassMov	3.95	2.08	1.00	10.00	38	4.00	3.00	0.61	0.55
SumMactv	1.68	1.45	0.00	6.00	28	1.50	−0.00	0.70	0.40
SumMpass	1.79	1.74	0.00	6.00	26	1.50	−0.00	0.76	−0.36

(Continued)

TABLE 4.5
(Continued)

Variable	Mean	SD	Min	Max	Freq	Median	Mode	SK	KU
IntellIndx	2.03	2.01	0.00	8.00	25	2.00	−0.00	0.81	0.33
Zf	11.18	3.55	5.00	22.00	38	11.00	8.00	0.98	1.54
Zd	−1.24	3.39	−6.50	8.00	34	−1.75	−3.50	0.71	0.16
Blends	3.63	2.25	0.00	8.00	36	3.00	2.00	0.35	−0.81
CSBlnd	0.63	1.00	0.00	4.00	15	0.00	−0.00	1.85	3.23
Afr	0.52	0.19	0.15	1.09	38	0.49	0.56	0.93	1.46
X + %	0.56	0.12	0.35	0.79	38	0.57	0.64	−0.14	−0.82
F + %	0.58	0.16	0.30	1.00	38	0.57	0.50	0.39	0.10
X − %	0.17	0.09	0.00	0.37	37	0.14	0.14	0.60	−0.21
Xu%	0.25	0.11	0.07	0.53	38	0.23	0.21	1.08	0.81
S − %	0.12	0.26	0.00	1.00	10	0.00	−0.00	2.43	5.83
IsoIndx	0.24	0.18	0.00	0.79	36	0.20	0.05	1.19	1.15
H	2.21	1.69	0.00	7.00	32	2.00	2.00	0.88	0.76
(H)	1.32	1.25	0.00	4.00	27	1.00	1.00	0.92	0.06
Hd	0.95	1.37	0.00	6.00	20	1.00	−0.00	2.21	5.43
(Hd)	0.34	0.67	0.00	2.00	9	0.00	−0.00	1.76	1.75
Hx	0.24	0.59	0.00	2.00	6	0.00	−0.00	2.41	4.65
H + (H) + Hd + (Hd)	4.82	2.85	1.00	14.00	38	4.00	4.00	1.23	1.85
A	8.21	2.97	4.00	16.00	38	7.00	7.00	0.83	0.37
(A)	0.66	0.78	0.00	3.00	19	0.50	0.00	1.06	0.75
Ad	1.55	1.43	0.00	5.00	28	1.00	1.00	0.92	0.25
(Ad)	0.08	0.27	0.00	1.00	3	0.00	−0.00	3.25	9.05
An	1.16	1.17	0.00	4.00	25	1.00	1.00	0.94	0.12
Art	0.39	0.82	0.00	3.00	9	0.00	−0.00	2.19	4.13
Ay	1.00	1.09	0.00	4.00	22	1.00	−0.00	0.92	0.16
Bl	0.13	0.34	0.00	1.00	5	0.00	0.00	2.27	3.33
Bt	1.00	1.23	0.00	5.00	22	1.00	−0.00	1.65	2.85
Cg	1.39	1.33	0.00	4.00	26	1.00	−0.00	0.68	−0.61
Cl	0.50	0.65	0.00	3.00	17	0.00	−0.00	1.58	4.23
Ex	0.08	0.27	0.00	1.00	3	0.00	−0.00	3.25	9.05
Fi	0.63	0.82	0.00	3.00	17	0.00	−0.00	1.11	0.45
Food	0.10	0.31	0.00	1.00	4	0.00	0.00	2.68	5.46
Geog	0.08	0.27	0.00	1.00	3	0.00	0.00	3.25	9.05
HHold	0.42	0.68	0.00	2.00	12	0.00	−0.00	1.37	0.62
Ls	0.79	0.90	0.00	3.00	21	1.00	0.00	1.13	0.75
Na	1.05	1.68	0.00	8.00	16	0.00	−0.00	2.28	6.85
Sc	0.63	0.88	0.00	3.00	16	0.00	−0.00	1.32	0.96
Sx	0.71	0.80	0.00	3.00	21	1.00	0.00	1.25	1.72
Xy	0.13	0.41	0.00	2.00	4	0.00	−0.00	3.38	11.78
Idio	1.08	1.44	0.00	6.00	21	1.00	−0.00	1.86	3.66
DV	1.45	1.35	0.00	6.00	28	1.00	1.00	1.20	2.03
INCOM	1.89	1.52	0.00	5.00	32	1.50	1.00	0.77	−0.26
DR	1.47	1.87	0.00	8.00	27	1.00	1.00	2.42	6.52
FABCOM	0.76	0.85	0.00	3.00	21	1.00	0.00	1.04	0.67
DV2	0.08	0.27	0.00	1.00	3	0.00	0.00	3.25	9.05
INC2	0.21	0.66	0.00	3.00	4	0.00	0.00	3.25	10.07
DR2	0.42	1.69	0.00	10.00	5	0.00	0.00	5.32	29.99

(Continued)

111

TABLE 4.5
(Continued)

Variable	Mean	SD	Min	Max	Freq	Median	Mode	SK	KU
FAB2	0.26	0.55	0.00	2.00	8	0.00	−0.00	2.06	3.51
ALOG	0.08	0.36	0.00	2.00	2	0.00	−0.00	4.85	24.25
CONTAM	0.00	0.00	0.00	0.00	0	0.00	0.00	–	–
Sum6SpSc	5.66	3.72	0.00	19.00	37	5.00	3.00	1.45	3.29
Sum6SpScLv2	0.97	2.61	0.00	15.00	13	0.00	−0.00	4.59	23.52
WSum6SpSc	18.47	23.16	0.00	137.00	37	11.00	8.00	3.98	19.00
AB	0.32	0.70	0.00	3.00	8	0.00	−0.00	2.44	5.85
AG	0.71	0.80	0.00	3.00	20	1.00	0.00	0.92	0.27
CFB	0.00	0.00	0.00	0.00	0	0.00	0.00	–	–
COP	0.84	0.92	0.00	3.00	21	1.00	0.00	0.77	−0.35
CP	0.05	0.23	0.00	1.00	2	0.00	0.00	4.17	16.27
MOR	1.66	1.24	0.00	4.00	30	2.00	1.00	0.25	−0.87
PER	1.84	1.85	0.00	8.00	28	1.00	1.00	1.29	1.89
PSV	0.16	0.37	0.00	1.00	6	0.00	0.00	1.95	1.92

emotional responsiveness to stimuli, an interpretation also applicable to adult male ASPDs.

Although their affective constraint (C′) is normal, they are prone to dysphoria and remorse (V M = 0.97, Freq. = 58%), much more so than nonpatient females (V M = 0.27, Freq. = 22%). They are also more anxious (Y M = 1.03) than normals (Y M = 0.56), but not more frequently so. The amount of nonvolitional affect is almost identical to normal women (SumShading M = 3.79). Only a small proportion (18%) would be considered chronically characterologically angry (S > 2). Blends are less expectable.

Interpersonal (Object) Relations.   The FOs do not expect cooperation from others (COP M = .84, 45% COP = 0). Only 19% of nonpatient women produce no COP responses. They do not necessarily isolate more than other women (Isolate/R = .24), but they do evidence less oral dependency (Fd > 0 11%) than do normals (Fd > 0 23%).

Tensions of ego-dystonic aggression, like our other antisocial samples, are less than normal women (AG M = .71 vs. 1.19) and occur less frequently (AG = 0 47% vs. 36%). We think this is due to a predisposition to act out aggressive impulse in an ego-syntonic manner, rather than contain, channel, and perhaps sublimate (at the neurotic level) the drive. Other aggression indices are apparent, most noticeably AgC (84%). AgPast responses are twice as frequent as AgPot responses (see Table 4.4), and suggest an identification with the prey/victim rather than the predator/victimizer (Meloy & Gacono, 1992a). No SM scoring was done for this sample.

Like their male antisocial counterparts, the FOs are less likely to mentally represent others as whole, real, and meaningful human beings (Pure H = 2.21). Their object relations are also part–object dominated ([H]+Hd+[Hd] M = 2.61).

TABLE 4.6
Female Antisocial Personality Disorders ($N = 38$) Group Means and
Frequencies for Select Ratios, Percentages, and Derivatives

$R = 20.08$	$L = .83$	$(L > .99 = 37\%)$

EB = 3.47 : 3.18	EA = 6.66
eb = 4.63 : 3.79	es = 8.42
D = −0.60 AdjD Score = −0.16	

EB STYLE

Introversive	11	29%
Super-Introversive	8	21%
Ambitent	16	42%
Extratensive	11	29%
Super-Extratensive	9	24%

EA - es DIFFERENCES:D-SCORES

D Score > 0	4	11%
D Score = 0	21	55%
D Score < 0	13	34%
D Score < −1	7	18%
AdjD Score > 0	6	16%
AdjD Score = 0	22	58%
AdjD Score < 0	10	26%
AdjD Score < −1	2	5%

AFFECT

FC:CF+C = .68 : 2.60		
Pure C = .47		(Pure C > 0 = 42%; Pure C > 1 = 5%)
FC > (CF+C) + 2	1	3%
FC > (CF+C) + 1	2	5%
(CF+C) > FC + 1	21	55%
(CF+C) > FC + 2	16	42%

SumC' = 1.39	SumV = .97	SumY = 1.03

Afr = .52	(Afr < .40 = 21%; Afr < .50 = 50%)
S = 1.68	(S > 2 = 18%)
Blends:R = 3.63 : 20.08	
CP = .05	

INTERPERSONAL

COP = .84	(COP = 0, 45%; COP > 2 = 5%)
AG = .71	(AG = 0, 47%; AG > 2 = 3%)
Food = .10	
Isolate:R = .24	
H:(H)+Hd+(Hd) = 2.21 : 2.61	(H < 2, 34%; H = 0, 16%)
(H)+(Hd):(A)+(Ad) = 1.66 : .74	
H+A:Hd+Ad = 10.42 : 2.50	
Sum T = .39	(T = 0, 71%; T > 1 = 5%)

(Continued)

TABLE 4.6
(Continued)

SELF-PERCEPTION

$3r+(2)/R = .40$ $(45\% < .33; 34\% > .44)$
$Fr+rF = .47$ $(Fr+rF > 0 = 26\%)$
$FD = .32$
$An+Xy = 1.29$
$MOR = 1.66$ $(MOR > 2 = 26\%)$

IDEATION

$a{:}p = 4.18 : 3.95$ $(p > a+1 = 32\%)$
$Ma{:}Mp = 1.68 : 1.79$ $(Mp > Ma = 34\%)$
$M = 3.47$ $(M- = .39; M \text{ none} = .05)$
$FM = 3.05 \qquad m = 1.58$
$2AB+Art+Ay = 2.03$ $(2AB+Art+Ay > 5 = 26\%)$
$Sum6 = 5.66$ $(Sum6 > 6 = 39\%)$
$WSum6 = 18.47$ $(\text{Level 2 Special Scores} > 0 = 34\%)$

MEDIATION

$Populars = 5.21$ $(P < 4 = 26\%; P > 7 = 18\%)$
$X+\% = .56$
$F+\% = .58$
$X-\% = .17$
$Xu\% = .25$
$S-\% = .12$

$X+\% > .89$	0	0%
$X+\% < .70$	35	92%
$X+\% < .61$	24	63%
$X+\% < .50$	12	32%
$F+\% < .70$	29	76%
$Xu\% > .20$	26	68%
$X-\% > .15$	16	42%
$X-\% > .20$	11	29%
$X-\% > .30$	3	8%

PROCESSING

$Zf = 11.18$
$Zd = -1.24$ $(Zd > +3.0 = 11\%; Zd < -3.0 = 34\%)$
$W{:}D{:}Dd = 8.71{:}9.24{:}2.13$ $(Dd > 3 = 18\%)$
$W{:}M = 8.71 : 3.47$
$DQ+ = 5.76$
$DQv = 2.00$ $(DQv + DQv/+ > 2 = 34\%)$

CONSTELLATIONS

SCZI = 6...	0	0%	DEPI = 7...	2	5%	CDI = 5... 3	8%
SCZI = 5...	3	8%	DEPI = 6...	7	18%	CDI = 4...10	26%
SCZI = 4...	2	5%	DEPI = 5...	5	13%		

S-Constellation Positive 1   3%
HVI Positive 0   0%
OBS Positive 0   0%

This sharply contrasts with the whole-object relations of the nonpatient female (H:[H]+Hd+[Hd] = 3.17:1.96), empirical Rorschach measures of the integrated objects at a neurotic level of personality and the split objects at a borderline level of personality.[15] Sixteen percent of the FOs produced no pure H responses, a finding in only 1 out of 100 nonpatient female subjects.

Whole-object relations developmentally parallel normative attachment (Meloy, 1992b). Consequently a finding of T = 0 (a Rorschach variable usually unrelated to the perception of human or humanlike objects) in 71% of the FOs is not surprising. These women are chronically emotionally detached like our other antisocial samples, and do not show the abnormal, bimodal distribution that emerges in our sexual homicide sample (T > 1). Only 11% of nonpatient women produce no T responses. This finding would predict attachment failures in the real world, most noticeably a failure to parent *despite the absence of clinical depression*. Strachan (1993) did find this in her sample of female psychopaths.

Object relations in the FOs are also marked by primitivity. Seventy-nine percent produce at least one primitive mode of relating (PMR; Kwawer, 1980; as noted in Table 4.3), the most common category being malignant internal processes (40%), followed by violent symbiosis (37%), narcissistic mirroring (26%), and boundary disturbance (26%). Malignant internal processes is also elevated in BPD females (47%) and sharply contrasts with its frequency in male ASPDs (17%) and primary psychopaths (15%). It may be the one Kwawer category most influenced by gender, and is consistent with the established familial relationship between somatization disorder and ASPD in women (Lilienfeld et al., 1986). Somatic concern is also more apparent in our FOs sample (An+Xy = 1.29) than the nonpatient female (An+Xy = .44). Almost three primitive modes of relating responses are expected in a female offender Rorschach.

Self-Perception. The majority of the FOs perceive themselves in an abnormal manner—they either compare themselves negatively to others (45%) or are quite self-absorbed (34%). Although almost four times as likely to produce a reflection response than nonpatient females (26% vs. 7%), most of the FOs would not be considered pathologically narcissistic. They do not, however, have a capacity for psychological mindedness (FD freq. = 29%), unlike the majority of women (FD = 80%).

Morbids are elevated in our sample (*M* = 1.66, MOR > 2 26%), an expected finding at a borderline level of personality. When accompanied by a reflection response, Morbids hint at the inner damaged, disregarded, and loathsome self

---

[15]We recognize the theoretical leaps in our analysis between part objects and whole objects on the Rorschach and split objects and whole objects in developmental object relations theory (Kernberg, 1975). Nevertheless, we find the empirical data striking in its consistency with theory (see the interpersonal cluster data for our other samples).

that is defended against by the much more clinically evident grandiose self—the narcissistic duality of contemporary object relations theory (Svrakic, 1989).[16]

Ideation. FOs show less capacity for empathic and deliberate thinking than do nonpatient females ($M = 3.47$ vs. 4.07). M− responses are also more frequent in the FOs (26%) than in the nonpatient female (4%), but less so than in the male ASPDs. Passive withdrawal into fantasy and dependency on others do not mark the majority of women in our offender sample (Mp>Ma = 34%), and they do not use intellectualization as a defense. Formal thought disorder is a problem, and, like the male samples, is moderate and pervasive (WSum6 = 18.47). Although our data suggest that reality testing improves with age across antisocial samples, the organization of thought does not. Thirty-four percent of the FOs produced at least one Level 2 special score, most likely a fabulized combination. Rather than derail (DR) in the service of self-aggrandizement like antisocial males, female offenders appear more likely to juxtapose objects in impossible real-world relationships, perhaps a formal thought disorder driven by a compensatory fantasy that replaces the need to bond. This may be a subtle, gender-related difference in the perceptual-associative problems of male and female antisocial subjects. Rorschach indices suggestive of schizophrenia (ALOG, CONTAM) in FOs are unlikely in the absence of a diagnosed major mental disorder.

Cognitive Mediation. FOs see fewer popular percepts than normals, and their perception is idiosyncratic and unconventional (X+% = 56, F+% = 58). Their reality testing, however, is less impaired (X−% = 17) than male antisocials. It is still comparable to other borderline personality disordered individuals (Exner, 1986b). Only 21% of the FOs have reality testing in the normal range (X−% ≤ 15), in contrast to 97% of nonpatient females. Although reality testing appears to improve with age in antisocial populations, it does not reach a neurotic level where the origination of internal and external stimuli is clear and undistorted by unconscious drives and fantasies. This important liability may improve with treatment (Weiner & Exner, 1991).

Cognitive Processing. The FOs organize and synthesize percepts efficiently (Zf = 11.18) but not very effectively (Zd = −1.24). Thirty-four percent of our sample are underincorporators, a quite treatable condition (Exner, 1991).

---

[16]Svrakic (1989) systematically elaborated the structure, emotions, cognitions, superego elements, and interpersonal activity of the narcissistic personality disorder. The grandiose self is characterized by grandiosity (free-floating or structured) and exhibitionism, whereas the real self is marked by inferiority, insecurity, pursuit of metamorphosis, fatigue of living, hypochondriasis, and polarization (splitting) of experience. Interpersonal relations of the grandiose self are characterized by mirroring in external objects, lack of empathy, entitlement, seductivity, addiction to flattery, and pathological intolerance of criticism; the real self is marked by envy and aggression toward objects, a search for the transformational object, and selective interpersonal repulsion.

Hypervigilance (HVI+ = 0) and undue attention to detail (Zd>+3.0 = 11%) are not characteristic problems. And unlike their male counterparts, female offenders' aspirations do not outstrip their abilities (W:M = 8.71:3.47). This predicts less frustration, failure, and grandiose striving in female offenders when compared to antisocial males.

Constellations. The most salient constellation for the FOs is DEPI—36% scored positive. On the basis of this index, one out of three female offenders would be expected to manifest symptoms of major depression. Only one of our subjects, however, was positive on the suicide constellation. The female offender appears more likely to act out her measured dysphoria against others rather than herself.

Conclusions. The Comprehensive System Rorschach data on a small, nonrandom sample of female offenders are consistent with the extant body of research that we have summarized earlier in this chapter. The female offender's prototypical personality structure is marked by unmodulated affect, a part-object–dominated representational world, emotional detachment, and an abnormally undervalued or overvalued sense of self. She is not chronically angry, but evidences a ruminative dysphoria that, despite its presence, she is able to manage without a loss of destructive controls toward self or others. She does this by avoiding emotion in others and in herself, but at the price of somatic preoccupation and a sense of internal damage. Her cognitive problems are noticeable on testing, but unlikely to be picked up during a clinical interview—her reality testing is in the borderline range and her formal thought disorder is moderate and pervasive. She is more likely to be motivated for psychotherapy than her male counterpart, because she feels badly; yet the treatment outcome is guarded due to her lack of attachment and cognitive misreading of the psychotherapist's behaviors.

KAREN, A FEMALE SEXUAL PSYCHOPATH[17]

Karen was born in 1943 in Boston, Massachusetts, the second sibling of three in an intact French-Catholic family. Her father worked in the movie house business as a "troubleshooter" and her mother was a housewife. The family traveled throughout the country.

Karen's descriptions of her childhood were vague, idealized, and contradictory. In retrospect, little factual information was available concerning her early years. Descriptions of her parents included the word *normal*, with her mother perceived as "aloof but loving," and her father "warm and affectionate." Her use of splitting

---

[17]This case example is an adapted and expanded version of "Case 1: Serial Sexual Homicide," pp. 232–249, presented in Meloy (1992b) and reprinted with permission of Jason Aronson, Inc. The authors and Dr. Judith Meyers evaluated Karen.

was apparent in her characterization of mother as both the "light of the family" and "an ogre with eyes in the back of her head." She generally characterized her parents as "very warm, loving, caring, and giving people" when asked if they had provided for her needs as a child. There do not appear to have been any significant childhood illnesses or injuries, although she does report an early onset of puberty (age 11).

When Karen was 15 years old, her mother died of cardiac arrest. She described her father's reaction: "He was dependent on my mother. She was the sun and my father rotated around her. After she died, there was nowhere to shine." The night of her mother's death, Karen's father came into her bedroom and attempted to orally copulate her. "I was the shining star in my father's eyes ... I didn't know I had been sexually abused. I was confused and angry. It was wrong. My mother had just died." She rebuffed him, and he went to her sister.

Karen began sexually acting out. On one occasion she danced nude on the roof of her house. At other times she would peek through the bedroom windows of her neighbors. Exhibitionism and voyeurism would remain paraphilic constants in her sexual history.

Her father emotionally abandoned Karen, and she began to lose control of her life. Eighteen months after her mother's death, he remarried and was spurned on his wedding night. He made his first suicide attempt shortly thereafter and killed the house cat, smearing its blood on the walls of their home. The children were placed in foster care and then went to live with their uncle. She remembers, "It was a degrading process."

When Karen was 18, her father committed suicide by hanging and she was raped by her boyfriend's brother. Two days later, the assailant committed suicide. These became the second and third formative events that linked, or paired, sexuality and death in Karen's mind. "I was lonely and unhappy. There was no guidance and control. No affection. I related sexuality with affection. I had frequent sexual intercourse with whomever, whenever. I always had animosity in my feelings for men. In retrospect, I can see that I didn't select well-integrated men. I fostered my own neurosis."

She first married at age 18 to a man she had known for 12 days. It lasted for another 6. He pressed her into prostitution, physically assaulted her, and wanted to sodomize her. "He was a street creep, a transient—but charming and good looking." Her second relationship was with an impotent man who wrote pornographic novels. It lasted for 8 years, and he sent her to nursing school, where she became a licensed vocational nurse. "There was intense rapport, but no sex." She described him as the "best of friends," but he left her after 2 years and went to Portland. She followed him, and they remained together for another 6 years.

During these latter years, when Karen was in her mid-20s, she met and married her second husband, Jack. She described him as "exclusively homosexual." Their marriage was "uncomfortable and strange." They separated five times, and their union produced two boys. Karen is diabetic, and both pregnancies were medically risky. She had pneumonia following the first child's birth, had a subsequent miscarriage, and the second child was taken by cesarean section at 8 months.

As this marriage deteriorated—not a surprising outcome given her previous object relational patterns and attachment histories with men—she met Daniel on December 28, 1979. Daniel was 10 years her junior but befriended her in their apartment complex. Karen, eager for male company now that she was separated from her husband, was captivated. "He had total control over me. I had a lack of will. He had a soft, drowning, sensuous voice." Over the course of their 8-month relationship, however, there was mounting tension. Once living together, their domestic life was chaotic. Daniel would teach her two sons mock knife fighting. On several occasions he came home at night and fell on the floor, exhausted and covered with blood. He also appeared to be an alcoholic.

But the sexual relationship was unusually exciting. "We had fantasies. Incredibly neat sexual fantasies. Part of the fantasies involved capturing young women and subduing them, using them sexually. And from there he branched out to this business of necrophilia and killing people. I was thinking it was just pure fantasy and I didn't think there was any possibility of him delving into it. We fantasized together, sometimes during sex, sometimes having no sex at all—we'd just lay in bed and describe possible sex scenes for different things to do." She eventually sent her two boys to live with their paternal grandmother "for their own safety." Karen was taking 10 mg of Librium, as needed, to manage her anxiety.

Offenses. On June 20, 1980, she and Daniel picked up a girl named Cathy in Hollywood. They had not decided who would kill the girl, but if Karen wanted to do it, she would speak a code word and Daniel would let her. While Cathy orally copulated Daniel in the front seat of his car, he signaled Karen to hand him the .25-caliber revolver. She drew it from her purse and gave it to him. He shot Cathy in the head. While Daniel drove, Karen held the dying girl on her lap and removed her clothing and jewelry. She had $7 in her pocket. They dumped her body in an isolated area of Los Angeles, and nicknamed her "river rat" because she had been thrown near a stream. On March 3, 1981, sheriff's deputies found the remains of a young woman matching the general description of Cathy.

Karen's description of Cathy's murder is revealing: "She didn't die right away. She kept breathing hard and I'm sitting in the back and he, see, he's yelling at me. 'Alright, I know you're nervous. But, cool, be cool, remember your abc's.' and I sat back there and said I'm fine. This was the first. He shot her once and she collapsed in the front seat. She bled like a stuck pig all over my blouse. Her head was in my lap. And he didn't want to shoot her again. It was obviously a terminal shot, but she was doing a lot of huffing and puffing and I kept checking her pulse rate which was strong and steady and good, and she might have survived.

I think there is a possibility she could have been saved. He reached—we always kept what we call the kill bag in the car, which contains paper towels, clean plastic bags, we haven't handled . . . usually rubber gloves of some sort. Lately we've added a knife and things of that sort. He's telling me to strip her, strip her down. So I got all her jewelry off, everything off, underneath a jacket in the front seat. And if you don't think it isn't a bitch to get a dress off of a dead girl who isn't cooperating in the least bit . . . anyway, in the front seat of the damn car with a man freaking out beside me nervous as hell. I wasn't. This astounded me because this . . . because I hadn't been involved with him before. I wasn't the least bit nervous. I was very cool. I wasn't turned on to it. I wasn't turned off with it. I was intellectually interested in the outcome."[18]

This would be the first of several sexual murders committed by the pair. Shortly before they were arrested on August 11, 1980, they were venturing out almost every night looking for someone to kill. They fantasized about capturing young women, subduing them, and sexually using them. The plan was to make the killings look progressively more gruesome. They wanted to kill Black prostitutes because of "their smugness." On one occasion Karen assisted in the molestation of an 11-year-old girl. Karen took photographs of her orally copulating and engaging in other sexual acts with Daniel. She also molested her.

They called the girls that were to be killed "bitches, botches, or butches." On June 23, 1980, Daniel murdered a prostitute named Exxie and decapitated her. Karen suggested to him that he dismember the woman so that the murder would look as "psychotic as possible" and the police would look for "some nut" rather than them. Daniel brought the victim's head home to Karen. They put it in the refrigerator and froze it. They had discussed this in fantasy, and when he did it, they "had alot of fun with her." Karen said, "Where I had my fun with the head was the makeup. I took a lot of cosmetics and would make up the face. I treated her like a Barbie doll. But one of her eyelids kept folding in a strange manner. She was still half frozen. After I painted her face, Daniel would take her head into the shower. He would stuff his penis into her mouth. He would masturbate in her mouth in the shower. We used to pick her up by the hair. Daniel would swing it back and forth by the hair."[19] Karen and Daniel were careful not to touch the box that they bought for the head, which might leave fingerprints. They disposed of it by dumping it in an alley.

By August 1, 1980, Karen was extremely concerned about her own safety with Daniel. She sought out a man named Jim, a former lover, and found him in a bar with another woman. He told her to wait. After several hours, she finally

[18]This material is taken from the transcript of the criminal interrogation following Karen's arrest.

[19]During the clinical interview, Karen told us that Daniel always wanted her to put makeup on the contusion on the victim's head, "so no one would think that he hurt her." When confronted with the gross illogic of this statement, Karen used it to rationalize that Daniel was not sadistic because he killed the victims before he sexually assaulted or mutilated them.

was able to confess her involvement in the murders. "I had in my mind for Jim to hide me. It was not specific." She also consumed four mixed drinks and a "handful" of Librium. Jim told Karen he was going to the police, so she decided to kill him.

Karen waited in her car near Jim's van until he left the bar. She put her gun in her waistband, a pair of leather gloves and a cleaning rag in her pocket, and her knife in her purse. When Jim returned, she entered the van with him. He told her, "You caused me to lose the other girl. I want you to take care of this." She performed fellatio on him. He slapped her and told her she "was fucking crazy."

She then engaged in oral/anal sex, and while Jim was facing away from her, she drew her gun, put it to the back of his head, and fired. She checked his pulse, which was still steady and regular. Then she shot him a second time in the head, "just to make sure he was dead." Karen sat there and looked at him for a period of time, thinking, "Dan will sure be mad at me." She then stabbed him in the back about six times. Using a fish deboning knife that she kept in her "kill bag" in her car, she decapitated him for the purpose of getting the bullets out of the van. She did not realize that the pistol ejected the spent cartridges. She reported that she really didn't have any conscious feelings as she was decapitating him. "It wasn't me. But I still had to function. I had to decide what to do. It was nauseating, revolting." She described a state of depersonalization, with no conscious awareness of affect.

Karen then sliced the victim's buttocks "to make the murder more gruesome, like a sexual pervert type thing." She put the victim's head in a plastic bag, which she dropped in the street when she fled the van. She put the head back in the bag and took it home, and Dan helped her dispose of both the head and the knife she had used. She later told the police, "Now that I've done it, it was really kind of interesting. It sure as hell is not like going to the beach or barbecuing. Does it gross you out to think that a woman could climb in, kill a friend of hers, somebody that she cares about, not in anger, not in passion, not in any normal relation that you would expect, and then behead him? What really surprised me, of course, was my advantage of having been blind for a while so that I could know how to deal in the dark. That van was pitch black. I really am thoroughly amazed that I didn't become messier than hell. When I left that van I was clean. I shouldn't have been. But the way the situation was, I was doing my very best to make it like it was a psycho killing, rather than somebody who was hitting, a personal thing. . . ."

One week after her murder of Jim, Karen confessed to the police and was arrested. During her first contact with the police in her apartment, she revealed some of her own psychodynamics: "The situation started out as a fantasy that just got badly out of control . . . Daniel is really . . . a . . . a real doll and I do love him. So part of me feels like a real shit for telling on him. On the other hand, there is a man out there who is going around killing people who has no sense of or regard for anything.[20] It doesn't matter if the prostitutes are young girls. He is not picking on old ladies. His criteria, believe it or not, for whether or not they die, is whether or not they give a decent blow job. I don't know enough psychology to say whether or not I'm paranoid schizophrenic. I'm obviously not paranoid. Whether or not I'm schizophrenic, I don't know. Sane people don't go around killing people. I don't want to face the gas chamber. I can't stay with Daniel because he will ultimately hurt me. But he hasn't struck me. He's never injured me. I've never seen him strike anybody. In which case that wouldn't be so bad either, if you understand. The way he did it was a nice, quick, clean show . . ."

Karen pled guilty to two counts of first-degree murder and admitted to a use allegation. The special circumstances (multiple murder and witness killing) that could have condemned her to death, or life without possibility of parole, were dropped. She was sentenced to 52 years to life in prison.

Clinical Interview. We evaluated Karen 8 years after her relationship with Daniel during a day-long visit to the California Institute for Women. Karen presented as a short, slightly obese 45-year-old woman who was remarkable for her lack of distinguishing features. She wore glasses for cataracts. Her cropped, brown hair framed a face that was pleasant, round, and plain. She appeared neither masculine nor particularly feminine.

Karen was an articulate woman and relished the attention we gave her. She described her history with rich detail and was never embarrassed or hesitant when discussing the most sensitive material. She was, however, quite emotionally labile. She would escalate into uncontrollable giggling and, during the Rorschach, slammed one of the cards (VI) on the table in a moment of dramatic outburst. When we began the interview, she assertively wanted to know all about our credentials, in turn, to decide if we were worth talking to. She responded, however, to limit setting in a quick, meek fashion. Throughout the course of our time together, which totaled 8 hours, she was very sensitive to the amount of attention she was receiving. She even interpreted Reid Meloy's withdrawal of attention from her during one of the self-report tests, the Minnesota Multiphasic Personality Inventory (MMPI), as sadistic.

Karen's mental status exam revealed no indications of psychotic process. There were no evident delusions, hallucinations, or formal thought disorders on clinical exam, and she had no history of psychotropic medications during her years in prison. The content of our interview focused on a detailed recounting of her life and criminal history with Daniel, which was described earlier. Her telling of her story was generally consistent with other data from the Los Angeles

---

[20] This is a striking example of splitting. She alternately conceives of Daniel as both a good and bad man, but not at the same time. Her verbiage sounds like she is talking about two completely different people.

County District Attorney's Office,[21] although she tended to minimize, and take less responsibility for, the acts of serial violence she performed. This is not unusual and underscores the importance of comparing the recall of the individual's crimes (the Systematic Self-Report of Violence, SSRV; Meloy, 1992b) with other, independent accounts.

Evaluation Procedures. We tested Karen with the Quick Test (QT; Ammons & Ammons, 1977), MCMI–II (Millon Clinical Multiaxial Inventory II), MMPI, Thematic Apperception Test (TAT), Human Figure Drawings (DAP), Early Memories (EMs), and the Rorschach. All of these instruments were completed during the 1-day interview. Karen's intelligence was reliably estimated to be in the bright normal range (IQ 110–119). This is consistent with her educational achievement and work history as a nurse.

The MCMI–II showed marked elevations (BR > 85) on the avoidant, self-defeating, schizotypal, and borderline personality scales, and less on the passive–aggressive personality (BR = 81) and dysthymic (BR = 84) scales. Although the profile suggested that Karen was exaggerating her psychopathology (Disclosure BR 93, Debasement BR 94), these elevations may also be associated with an acute episode of emotional turmoil. This latter hypothesis, however, was not supported by the Rorschach. The MCMI–II described a woman who had a history of disappointments in relationships, and a tendency to precipitate self-defeating encounters with others. She was also likely to experience periods of marked emotional, cognitive, and behavioral dysfunction.

She expected others to be rejecting and disparaging, and despite her longing for warmth and affection, she withdraws to maintain a safe distance from others. Her surface apathy conceals an intense sensitivity, which may be expressed in bursts of anger toward those she sees as nonsupportive. There is also a likely history of self-damaging acts and suicidal gestures; "innumerable wrangles and disappointments with others occur as she vacillates among self-denial, sullen passivity, self-destructive activities, and explosive anger."

The expectation of ridicule and derision is seen in Karen's tendency to exaggerate disinterest by others into complete condemnation. She then responds with impulsive hostility. Constraint is followed by outbursts that are, in turn, followed by remorse and regret.

The MCMI–II also identified a major depression, dysthymic disorder, and a generalized anxiety disorder, all part of her enduring character structure. Treatment recommendations, according to this instrument, focused on the rapid implementation of pharmacotherapy or supportive psychotherapy to ameliorate her Axis I symptoms of depression and anxiety. Once she was stabilized, long-term psychotherapeutic work could begin to bolster her low self-esteem, but would likely be responded to with limit testing and withdrawal. Karen would

---

[21]We would especially like to thank David Guthman for his help.

be deterred from psychotherapy because the rekindling of hope would remind her of past failed relations, and the humiliations that resulted. Certainly her history reflects such a plethora of disappointments. She would likely struggle to maintain a safe distance from others to keep a level of adjustment to which she was accustomed.

Karen produced a valid "bad apple" MMPI profile, with clinical elevations on Scale 4 (T = 81), Scale 8 (T = 77), Scale 6 (T = 73), and Scale 9 (T = 70).[22] Validity scales showed no distortion in the direction of malingering (fake bad) or dissembling (fake good). Supplemental scales gave a more complete clinical picture of Karen. There was a wide discrepancy between her dependency scale (T = 71) and her dominance scale (T = 45), suggesting an individual who is inclined to subsume her needs to the wishes of others, and who will not take an active, initiating role in her behavior. Although Scale 2 was not clinically elevated (T = 65), the Harris and Lingoes Brooding subscale (D5) was in the clinical range (T = 72), and supported Karen's propensity to ruminate about slights and her melancholic state of mind. Although one would expect elevations on Scale 3, Karen's hysteria score was normative (T = 52). She did, however, show an elevation on HY5, inhibition of aggression (T = 67), suggesting a tendency to deny and inhibit angry or hostile impulses, and perhaps be gratified if others act out these impulses in her presence.

Scale 4 elevations were impressive and consistent with an antisocial history prior to incarceration. Familial discord (T = 69), authority problems (T = 69), social alienation (T = 74), and self-alienation (T = 70) all suggest that Karen has psychopathic characteristics that predominate the clinical picture. The one subscale that was not elevated, social imperturbability (T = 47), is consistent with Karen's inability to maintain her Faustian bargain with Daniel during the killings, and her subsequent confession. Her psychopathy is also supported by her elevated narcissism-hypersensitivity subscale (T = 70, MF1), and amorality subscale (T = 72, MA1).

Although Karen showed no clinical indication of psychosis, there were elevations on the persecutory ideas subscale (T = 75) and the poignancy subscale (T = 76). These scales are consistent with her hypervigilant search for insult and feelings that she has been singled out for persecution, respectively. Likewise, several of the Scale 8 (Schizophrenia) subscales were elevated: emotional alienation (T = 76) and lack of ego mastery, conative (T = 74). There were no elevations on the subscale that would suggest psychotic perceptions (hallucina-

---

[22]As Scales 4, 8, 6, and 9 elevate, the risk to others increases. These scales, in concert, have also been associated with morbid fantasy, sadomasochism, unbonded sexuality, and a history of sexual abuse. It is the "villain and victim" profile (Alex Caldwell, personal communication, October 1992). Jeffrey Dahmer, a necrophile who also engaged in dismemberment and cannibalism of multiple victims in an infamous Wisconsin case tried in 1992, also produced this profile.

tions). Karen's introversive personality, despite her superficial assertiveness, was evidenced by her elevated O scale (T = 65), and an extreme elevation on the inferiority and personal discomfort subscale (T = 92, SI1).

The overall impression from the MMPI is that of a character-disordered woman who is antisocial, unconventional and rebellious, mistrustful of others, and extremely alienated from the world around her. She is mildly depressed and anxious, quite introverted, and prone to form impulsive, dependent attachments to individuals who will mistreat her. She is not psychotic, but her perceptions and associations will reflect a certain amount of persecutory expectation.

Karen's TAT, a measure of her self- and object relations, captures some of her more conscious attitudes toward herself, others, and the world around her:

Card 15. "A morbid one. This is time realizing its own mortality. That's it, the beginning, middle, and end. (Inquiry?) Trapped, desperate. He's running out of his own essence. Time. He doesn't know how to stop it. Every middle-aged man and woman saw time slipping away and didn't know how to stop it. I could have told you he was a casket salesman (laughter)." [SM response]

Card 5. "Mother's come upstairs. She's calling her son. Time to go to school. You'll be late. (How does she feel?) Harried and put upon. (How does he feel?) Sleepy. He is a lazy, little asshole, bastard kid. 'Mom, I'm sick.' Another cliche. (What's the ending?) She pulls the bedclothes off, tickles his feet until he wakes up."

Card 3BM. "Total despondency. This woman has been crushed by life and all its enormity. Whatever has been—total devastation. Off in the corner is her friend watching her, hurting for her and with her. Until this one is ready to pull back into life. For a while she's closed out her support. She knows it's there. She takes strength from knowing her friend is there. They'll hold and console each other. They'll share with each other. (What is the item on the floor?) A set of keys. A carrot with a bite out of it."

Card 13MF. "His inflatable doll just sprung a leak. (laughter; SM) Geez. I think he just shot his wife. He did something to her. He's feeling extreme remorse. Why or what got out of control. (Ending?) I don't know. It's not over, though."

Card 18GF. "Two spinster sisters spent their lives together. Both are afraid to face the world. Both are reclusive, interdependent with a tremendous amount of mutual hatred and rage. Forty-five years of togetherness. One woman is banging her sister's head against the banister. The sister who lives will become reclusive and miserable in her own self. She will die a lonely old age. Her situation does not improve. She blames her sister and her friends for her problems. They've festered and grown bigger."

Card 12M. "He is sort of a faith healer. She is sick in her bed. She's turned to her religious practitioner in the hope that he can help her. It's her last hope. He's laying on his hands. He orders her to heal. (Ending?) He fails. He doesn't get his fee and goes off to live somewhere else. Her faith stays resolute. She still maintains her hope."

The TAT findings, although not to be relied upon in forensic evaluations or testimony because of the lack of reliability, validity, and norms,[23] are a rich source of object relational and emotional hypotheses. In these responses, themes of anger toward the self, dependency needs, hopefulness, despair, and the expectation of failure are obvious. There is also the hint of sadism and perversion in her laughter to Cards 15 and 13MF, references to both death and sex that have been immutably linked throughout Karen's history. This test lends further support to the centrality of hostility and dependency in Karen's object relations.

We interpret Karen's Human Figure Drawings displayed in Figs. 4.1 and 4.2 with similar cautions. Their convergence with other test data, however, allow some additional comments about object relations and identity problems.

Karen expressed confusion as to the gender of her first drawing, a female figure. "I didn't give that one a sex. What will it be, male or female? I guess it's femaleish." Confusion over the gender of figures is not uncommon for individuals organized at a borderline or psychotic level. Karen's confusion was likely linked to her own uncertain identity and self-reported bisexuality. Egocentricity or self-absorption at the expense of planning was suggested by the size of the figure. It filled the entire page, not leaving room for feet.

Both figure drawings suggest problems with aggression, stubbornness, and passive-aggressiveness. The word bubbles for each drawing were particularly revealing. Figure 4.1 stated, "I'm not getting off this world! If you don't like it you can leave"; and Fig. 4.2, "So what!". Splitting is also suggested by the discrepancies between her Fig. 4.1 descriptors, "decisive, strong-willed, self- reliant, knows where she's going," and Fig. 4.2, "receptive, patient, reliable, blind as a bat, misses details."

We then assessed Karen's earliest memories. Karen recalled her earliest memory of her mother: "I was 4 years old and my mother had an old-fashioned wringer washer. I pulled up the sheets and got my arms caught in the wringer. She freed me and they took me to a doctor and X-rayed my arms." Karen's second earliest memory of mother: "Mom is holding my hand. We're standing

---

[23]Drew Westen's (1991) work on the empirical measurement of object relations using the TAT is the one exception.

FIG. 4.1.   Karen's first human figure drawing.

between studio lights in one of the Hollywood movie theaters. We role played as little actresses then." Her earliest memory of father: "My sister and I are in the back seat of our car. Dad is outside. He said, 'these are my daughters, Karen and Victoria.' " Like her memories of mother, Karen's earliest memory without her parents also contains the theme of sudden, unexpected injury with the second memory narcissistically compensating through a focus on appearance (the maternal memory contained reference to "role playing as little actresses"): "I was 20 months old and my brother was bouncing on his bed. I climbed up. He said, 'Don't do it, you'll fall.' I did and broke my collarbone."; and the second, "Sitting in a little chair with a bonnet on. I don't remember if it was white or pink." Karen's early memories provide clues to an adult histrionic personality style that compensates for painful affect.

FIG. 4.2.   Karen's second human figure drawing.

KAREN'S RORSCHACH

The Rorschach is the final test we administered to Karen, and it marks the last stop on the psychometric journey from conscious self-report (MCMI–II, MMPI) through attachment and object relational themes (TAT, DAP, EMs) to unconscious personality structure and psychodynamics (Rorschach). These tests provide levels of analysis of a patient's psychology that can then be ordered, and compared, on a continuum from conscious to unconscious (Stone & Dellis, 1960). Table 4.7 shows Karen's Rorschach protocol. Table 4.8 presents her sequence of scores, and Table 4.9 shows the structural summary, both generated by Rorschach Scoring Program, Version 2 (RIAP–2; Exner, Cohen, & Mcquire, 1990).

Structural Interpretation

Karen's Rorschach yielded 16 responses, a valid but constricted protocol. A structural analysis of Karen's psychological operations indicates that she has a normal amount of psychological resources (EA = 8.5), but does not have a delineated problem-solving style (EB = 5:3.5). Her stress tolerance and controls are normal (D = 0, AdjD = 0). The only abnormally elevated characteristic on the nonvolitional side of her operations is a heightened physiological need state at the time of testing, manifested as unwanted thoughts (FM = 5). Nonpatient

TABLE 4.7
Karen's Rorschach Protocol

Free Association	Inquiry
Card I 1) A Wile E. Coyote in an aggressive mode. Wile E. Coyote is the one that chases the Roadrunner on the cartoons. My initial impression is a carnivore. Is that an unusual response? He needs eye balls.	E: (Rpts S's response) S: These look like eyes that are hostile, angry, white orbs. These look like pupils, appear to be ears. E: (Hostile?) S: Without going into details of cartoons, there is a way of drawing the eyes that looks angry. My first impression was aggression. Wile E. Coyote about to attack the Roadrunner. Yes there is a large aggressive part of me. He looks like a carnivore ready to strike. All I see is the eyes and a hostile mouth, what else is there to see? I wish I could see doves mating. Something soft and gentle. Something that's not hostile.

Structural Scoring: Wso FMp.C'Fo (Ad),Art 3.5 AG,DR,PER
Aggression Scores: AG, AgC, AgPot.
Primitive Modes of Relating: None.
Defenses: Higher Denial, Projection, Projective Identification, Rationalization, Splitting.

2) A young animal looking at reflection in a pool of water. I see a baby elephant, ears up. A little trunk here.	E: (Rpts S's response) S: I saw what I want to see, a baby elephant looking at his standing reflection. Here is the back, legs, ears, and the face, here's the trunk. E: (Reflection?) S: This line separates it and gives the impression of a reflection in water.

Structural Scoring: W+ FMp.Fro A,Na 4.0 DR
Aggression Scores: None.
Primitive Modes of Relating: Narcissistic Mirroring.
Defenses: Omnipotence.

Card II 3) I see two baby bears dancing and playing patty cake.	E: (Rpts S's response) S: Here the little ear, another ear. They're squashed down or crouched down. Their little foot paws crowding against each other.

Structural Scoring: D+ 6 Mao (2) A P 3.0 COP,FAB,DV
Aggression Scores: None.
Primitive Modes of Relating: None.
Defenses: Pollyannish Denial.

(Continued)

TABLE 4.7
(Continued)

Free Association	Inquiry
4) Second thing again. A little elephant. He's got a playmate. Their little noses are and they're trying to kiss. It must be fun trying to interpret these things.	E: (Rpts S's response) S: Elephants' trunks brushing against each other. They look up like they are trying to kiss.

Structural Scoring: D+ 6 Mao (2) A P 3.0 COP,FAB,DR
Aggression Scores: None.
Primitive Modes of Relating: None.
Defenses: Pollyannish Denial, Intellectualization.

Card III	5) Two aborigine women over a cooking pot.	E: (Rpts S's response) S: Whether they are aborigine or not, they look like mature women. They have an elongated neck. There is a tribe of women that used to elongate their necks. Here are breasts and this looks like a cooking pot. They look cheerful enough. E: (Mature women?) S: Dressed in conventional clothing. Half clothed. It appears as if they got those necklaces on their elongated necks. It's not that I'm seeing them as nude, but seeing them as tribal people.

Structural Scoring: D+ 1 Mp+ (2) H,Sx,Cg,Ay P 3.0 DR
Aggression Scores: None.
Primitive Modes of Relating: None.
Defenses: Intellectualization, Pollyannish Denial, Higher Denial.

Card IV	6) I don't think you'll like the answer to this one. The only thing that comes to mind is a smudge on a carpet. What happens when a six-year-old spills on a carpet.	E: (Rpts S's response) S: Principally because I couldn't see an image in it. But later I did. It was an image that tickled me and I couldn't take it seriously. E: (Smudge?) S: It looks like a chocolate milk stain, the only thing I could think of.

Structural Scoring: Wv/+ C' Fd,Hh 2.0 DR
Aggression Scores: None.
Primitive Modes of Relating: Symbiotic Merging.
Defenses: Reaction Formation, Hypomanic Denial, Rationalization.

(Continued)

TABLE 4.7

(Continued)

Free Association	Inquiry
7) I do see something but it's funny. If I told you what I see I don't think you would see it as valid. Back view of Sasquatch on a motorcycle riding away.	E: (Rpts S's response) S: Another name for Bigfoot. Here's big feet. The feet are huge. Motorcycle handles, bars of the motorcycle. Rear wheel. He's hunched like this. His head is down a little.

Structural Scoring: W+ Mao (H),Sc P 4.0 FAB,DR
Aggression Scores: None.
Primitive Modes of Relating: None.
Defenses: Reaction Formation.

Card V 8) A Butterfly.	E: (Rpts S's response) S: Butterflies have little antennae, little feet, little wings. And he looks like a little butterfly.

Structural Scoring: Wo Fo A P 1.0
Aggression Scores: None.
Primitive Modes of Relating: None.
Defenses: Higher Denial.

9) A bat, something flying away.	E: (Rpts S's response) S: Same reason. They are shaped like bat wings. Looks like more insectoid than mammalian. So my real impression was a butterfly. It could be a bat. I don't have any negative feeling for a bat. Its just a little animal flying away. It could be Jimmy the cricket doing a dance. Flying wings moving up and down, an animal that is sedentary wouldn't have wings like this unless it was fearful of a predator.

Structural Scoring: Wo FMao A P 1.0 DR2,ALOG
Aggression Scores: AgV (aggression vulnerability)
Primitive Modes of Relating: None.
Defenses: Intellectualization, Higher Denial, Pollyannish Denial, Projection, Splitting.

Card VI 10) What do they call it? A manta ray. Those things that want to fly, it looks like a manta ray.	E: (Rpts S's response) S: A large fish shaped like it's got wings. That are flying, looks like a large fish first, large tail with Indian feathers.

Structural Scoring: Wo FMau A 2.5 INC,DR
Aggression Scores: None.
Primitive Modes of Relating: None.
Defenses: Massive Denial.

(Continued)

TABLE 4.7
(Continued)

Free Association	Inquiry
11) Or a filet of fish ready to put on a frying pan.	E: (Rpts S's response) S: I'm not seeing the tail with Indian feathers. Just the filet of fish. E: (Filet?) S: Side by side. It's been deboned, (Laughs) sorry I shouldn't have said that term. He'll be ready to go into the frying pan or perhaps is already in the pan. E: (Deboned?) S: I knew you were going to hit me on that. No spine, no substance, no form, a blob! A piece of fish to be cooked. Or perhaps a Fudgsicle that's been allowed to set in the sun and melt.

Structural Scoring: Dv 1 Fu Fd DR,MOR
Aggression Scores: AgPast, SM.
Primitive Modes of Relating: Violent Symbiosis, separation, & reunion, Boundary Disturbance.
Defenses: Projection.

Card VII 12) Looks like a couple of Indian women, gossiping.	E: (Rpts S's response) S: Like women anywhere. When they get together will tend to gossip. There are their faces. Indian feathers on the top of their head. Hands are in a position like they're expressing a point.

Structural Scoring: W+ Mpu (2) H,Cg,Ay 2.5 DR,COP
Aggression Scores: None.
Primitive Modes of Relating: None.
Defenses: Devaluation.

Card VIII 13) I don't know but the colors are pretty.	E: (Rpts S's response) S: Pretty colors run together, they have no form. The use of colors, they're pleasing, nice soft pastels.

Structural Scoring: Wv C Id
Aggression Scores: None.
Primitive Modes of Relating: Boundary Disturbance.
Defenses: Intellectualization.

14) An animal, beaver or badger. Looks like he's walking near a pool and his reflection is in it. Some kind of woodland animal climbing.	E: (Rpts S's response) S: I saw a ship but it didn't fit. Primary thing, these animals. And a ship sail but a beaver wouldn't be climbing a ship sail except in the cartoons. When I turned him sideways about to stand on a tree limb.

(Continued)

TABLE 4.7
(Continued)

Free Association	Inquiry
	E: (Water?)
	S: Shimmering, feel fluid, not solid, like a mirror image.
	E: (Shimmering?)
	S: Edges of parts of drawings looks watery. When you look at the edge of the paper.

Structural Scoring: W+ FMa.Fro A,Na P 4.5 DR
Aggression Scores: None.
Primitive Modes of Relating: Narcissistic mirroring.
Defenses: Rationalization.

Card IX 15) A moose, a moose in the forest.	E: (Rpts S's response)
	S: How could you see anything else but a moose?! (Laughingly slams card down on the table) How can you expect me to explain to you why I see a moose? These look like bushes.
	E: (Bushes?)
	S: (Laughs) These green leaves. This part I have no explanation for. Back view of a moose. These are antlers. Head turned slightly. The shape of the face with racks above.

Structural Scoring: D+ 2 CF− Ad,Bt 2.5 DR
Aggression Scores: None.
Primitive Modes of Relating: None.
Defenses: Omnipotence, Hypomanic Denial.

Card X 16) A palette for a set of water paints.	E: (Rpts S's response)
	S: You got all these different colors. When I use my water colors. Pink looks like bled a little part. Initially it looked like blue crabs with green feathers, but I had to throw that out. Looks like smeared colors.

Structural Scoring: Wv CFu Art PER,DR
Aggression Scores: None.
Primitive Modes of Relating: Boundary Disturbance.
Defenses: Hypomanic Denial.

TABLE 4.8
Karen's Rorschach Sequence of Scores

Card I	1	WSo	FMp.C'Fo		(Ad),Art		3.5	PER,AG,DR
	2	W+	FMp.Fro		A,Na		4.0	DR
Card II	3	D+ 6	Mao	(2)	A	P	3.0	COP,FAB,DV
	4	D+ 6	Mao	(2)	A	P	3.0	COP,FAB,DR
Card III	5	D+ 1	Mp+	(2)	H,Sx,Cg,Ay	P	3.0	DR
Card IV	6	Wv/+	C'		Fd,Hh		2.0	DR
	7	W+	Mao		(H),Sc	P	4.0	FAB,DR
Card V	8	Wo	Fo		A	P	1.0	
	9	Wo	FMao		A	P	1.0	DR2,ALOG
Card VI	10	Wo	FMau		A		2.5	INC,DR
	11	Dv 1	Fu		Fd			DR,MOR
Card VII	12	W+	Mpu	(2)	H,Ay,Cg		2.5	DR,COP
Card VIII	13	Wv	C		Id			
	14	W+	FMa.Fro		A,Na	P	4.5	DR
Card IX	15	D+ 2	CF−		Ad,Bt		2.5	DR
Card X	16	Wv	CFu		Art			PER,DR

females average 3.67 FM responses ($SD = 1.27$; Exner, 1990b). Elevated FMs in the sexual homicide perpetrator suggest primitive need states that nonvolitionally press for gratification and are experienced as obsessions (as noted in chapter 9).

Karen's affects are characterized by grossly unmodulated emotion (FC:CF+C = 0:3) and a tendency toward emotional explosiveness (C = 1), which we observed. Although she avoids emotionally provoking stimuli (Afr = .33), she is not defended against internal affect (Lambda = .14). There is no indication of a chronically angry character pattern (S = 1), and a surprising absence of confused, remorseful, painful, or dysphoric feelings states (C' = 2, V = 0, T = 0, Y = 0, no Color/Shading blends). She shows no desire or capacity to form an emotional bond with others (T = 0), a characteristic found in only 11% of nonpatient females, but ubiquitous in ASPD females (71% produce T-less protocols) and psychopathic males (Gacono & Meloy, 1991). The paucity of pure H [H = 2, (H) = 1] in her record further supports deficient desire or capacity to perceive others as whole and meaningful objects. A normative frequency for M (5) is misleading. Final interpretation must wait for a qualitative analysis of each response.

Karen appears to exhibit an expectation of cooperativeness (COP = 3) and an inordinate desire to depend on others (Food = 2). Upon closer examination of her COPs, one discovers that all three are qualitatively spoiled. Two contain animal objects and Level 1 Fabcoms; the third, although with human interaction, contains u form quality and devaluation. Reexamining the five Ms indicates they are also spoiled (all contain a FAB or DR and two contain both). Karen's expectation of cooperativeness might be reinterpreted as an inability to fathom the nuances of interpersonal experience and, like other psychopaths who lack the necessary emotional prerequisites for relationships, superficial charm.

TABLE 4.9
Karen's Rorschach Structural Summary

Location Features	Determinants		Contents	S-Constellation
	Blends	Single		
				NO..FV+VF+V+FD > 2
		H = 2, 0		NO..Col-Shd Bl > 0
Zf = 13	FM.C'F	M = 5	(H) = 1, 0	YES..Ego < .31, > .44
ZSum = 36.5	FM.Fr	FM = 2	Hd = 0, 0	NO..MOR > 3
ZEst = 41.5	FM.Fr	m = 0	(Hd)= 0, 0	NO..Zd > +- 3.5
		FC = 0	Hx = 0, 0	NO..es > EA
W = 11		CF = 2	A = 7, 0	YES..CF+C > FC
(Wv = 2)		C = 1	(A) = 0, 0	YES..X+% < .70
D = 5		Cn = 0	Ad = 1, 0	NO..S > 3
Dd = 0		FC' = 0	(Ad)= 1, 0	NO..P < 3 or > 8
S = 1		C'F = 0	An = 0, 0	NO..Pure H < 2
		C' = 1	Art = 1, 1	YES..R < 17
DQ		FT = 0	Ay = 0, 2	4.....TOTAL

DQ		FQ-
+ = 8	(1)	
o = 4	(0)	
v/+ = 1	(0)	
v = 3	(0)	

Single (continued):

TF = 0	Bl = 0, 0
T = 0	Bt = 0, 1
FV = 0	Cg = 0, 2
VF = 0	Cl = 0, 0
V = 0	Ex = 0, 0
FY = 0	Fd = 2, 0
YF = 0	Fi = 0, 0
Y = 0	Ge = 0, 0
Fr = 0	Hh = 0, 1
rF = 0	Ls = 0, 0
FD = 0	Na = 0, 2
F = 2	Sc = 0, 1
	Sx = 0, 1
	Xy = 0, 0
	Id = 1, 0
(2) = 4	

Form Quality

	FQx	FQf	MQual	SQx
+ =	1	0	1	0
o =	8	1	3	1
u =	4	1	1	0
- =	1	0	0	0
none =	2	-	0	0

Special Scorings

	Lv1	Lv2
DV =	1 × 1	0 × 2
INC =	1 × 2	0 × 4
DR =	12 × 3	1 × 6
FAB =	3 × 4	0 × 7
ALOG =	1 × 5	
CON =	0 × 7	
SUM 6 = 19		
WSUM6 = 62		

AB = 0		CP = 0	
AG = 1		MOR = 1	
CFB = 0		PER = 2	
COP = 3		PSV = 0	

Ratios, Percentages, and Derivations

R = 16   L = 0.14

EB = 5: 3.5	EA = 8.5	EBPer = N/A
eb = 5: 2	es = 7	D = 0
	Adj es = 7	Adj D = 0

FM = 5 :	C' = 2	T = 0
m = 0 :	V = 0	Y = 0
a:p	= 6: 4	Sum 6 = 19
Ma:Mp	= 3: 2	Lv2 = 1
2AB+Art+Ay = 4		WSum6 = 62
M-	= 0	Mnone = 0

FC:CF+C = 0 : 3	COP = 3		AG = 1
Pure C = 1	Food	= 2	
Afr = 0.33	Isolate/R	= 0.31	
S = 1	H:(H)Hd(Hd)	= 2: 1	
Blends:R = 3:16	(HHd):(AAd)	= 1: 1	
CP = 0	H+A:Hd+Ad	= 10: 2	

P = 7	Zf = 13	3r+(2)/R = 0.63
X+% = 0.56	Zd = -5.0	Fr+rF = 2
F+% = 0.50	W:D:Dd = 11: 5: 0	FD = 0
X-% = 0.06	W:M = 11: 5	An+Xy = 0
S-% = 0.00	DQ+ = 8	MOR = 1
Xu% = 0.25	DQv = 3	

SCZI = 2	DEPI = 3	CDI = 2	S-CON = 4	HVI = No	OBS = No

Note. From Exner (1990a). Copyright 1990 by John E. Exner, Jr. Reprinted by permission.

Isolation (Isolate/R = 0.31), pathological narcissism (Fr = 2),[24] self-absorption (Egocentricity = .63), and a propensity to self-aggrandize and identify with the aggressor (PER = 2; Gacono et al., 1990) form a constellation of intrapsychic processes that function in a defensive manner, providing respite from the slings and arrows of problematic interpersonal relations. Karen does not fully understand her role in these interactions as she lacks the capacity to reflect in a balanced and introspective manner (FD = 0). Despite self-focus and a hysterical personality style, her Rorschach does not indicate psychosomatic preoccupation (An+Xy = 0), a counterintuitive finding.

Karen's cognitive processing is notable for her propensity to scan the environment haphazardly and miss important visual cues (Zd = −5.0). She attempts to visually organize as much as others (Zf = 13) but does a poor job of it, seeking and failing to grasp the entire percept at once. She also tends to unconventionally perceive the world and attach idiosyncratic meaning to its components (X+% = 56), yet her reality testing is unimpaired. In fact, it is normal for nonpatient females (X−% = 6). On the other hand, she shows indications of pervasive and severe formal thought disorder (WSum6 = 62, only one Level 2 score, a DR2), most of them related to tangential or circumstantial responses (DR = 13). She does have one indicator that is pathognomonic of schizophrenic thought (ALOG = 1), and is only produced by 5% of our ASPD female sample and 4% of nonpatient females (Exner, 1991). Karen did not score positive for any of the constellations.

Karen's structural data reveal a personality that is marked by contradiction and conflict, yet not in a state of emotional distress: dependency on others and disinterest in them; pathological narcissism and the expectation of cooperativeness; personal isolativeness and normal stress tolerance; unmodulated affects and normal controls.

Interpretation of Scoring Sequence

Karen begins Card I with a white space (S) response. Not unexpected, however, when produced within a FMp.C'Fo blend and special scores, PER, AG, and DR, it becomes noteworthy. That Response 1 suggests difficulties with hostility and aggression would be an understatement. The extent to which she experiences shock from Card I is telling. She quickly produces primitive and only partially constrained (C'F) impulse. Aggression is indeed "a large part" of Karen (PER), which results in cognitive slippage (DR).

Karen's scoring sequence provides the perfect example of the interplay between impulse and defense (Schafer, 1954). Impulse predominates throughout this fluid Rorschach. Karen produces primarily Ws, indicative of her grandiosity

---

[24]Although 26% of our ASPD females produce one or more reflection responses, only 7% of nonpatient women do (Exner, 1991).

and attempts at maintaining control over all aspects of the blot (and herself). Most striking is the decrease in her ability to maintain control as perceptual accuracy (X+% = 56; F+% = 50) diminishes over the 10-card presentation. Putting together the pieces of the blot (W, DQ+) is too great a task from the onset. Cognitive slippage abounds.

On Responses 6, 11, 13, and 16 Karen surrenders to the press of impulse/needs, producing vague developmental quality (DQv) and formless responses. The absence of INCs and FABs, and presence of DRs (on these responses) signals her relief and perhaps the use of dissociation.[25] Her first DQv regression occurs on Card IV with Fd content. The second on Card VI also with Fd content and a MOR. Ignoring for a moment the content implications of these cards, DQvs with Fd content would suggest regression related to her inordinate desire to depend on others. Certainly her family history reveals the etiology of this frustration. A pure C′ appears on the first DQv response, suggesting her needs for dependency relate to a looseness of emotional control. Her third DQv response appears on Card VIII with a pure C. She describes this formless response, "The use of colors, they're pleasing, nice, soft pastels." Karen ends the Rorschach with a final DQv on Card X, giving into impulse, and distancing through denial.

Through the first nine responses perceptual accuracy is fairly well maintained. A formless percept is produced on Response 6; however, Karen quickly recovers perceptual accuracy on 7. Focusing on the external and conventional (67% of the first nine responses contain populars) aids perceptual accuracy but cannot prevent cognitive slippage. Despite adequate perceptual accuracy, the first nine responses contain special scores. She pays a toll for maintaining perceptual accuracy. At times Karen has been able to present a facade of normality in the absence of emotion (no C, C′) when sufficient and clear environmental cues exist (P). Over time her facade crumbles.

Karen's defenses collapse on Response 9 (ALOG and DR2). She never recovers. The remaining responses, 10 through 16, exhibit two DQvs and predominately impaired FQx (1 = o, 4 = u, 1 = −, and 1 = no form). Only Response 14 contains an ordinary FQx. Response 14 also contains a reflection and a popular. Self-focus withdrawn from the interpersonal context and combined with the conventional provides an immature but functional regulatory process. Response 15 continues a pattern of poorly modulated affect (CF−) followed by a similar ending on Card X (Wv CFu).

Interpretation of Content

Karen's Rorschach content is uniquely rich. It reveals her psychopathology and its characterological expression. The fluidity evident throughout her tangential and

---

[25]Glen Gabbard, MD, considers dissociation a defense against a parallel *traumatic* unconscious, whereas repression defends against a developmentally normal and *dynamic* unconscious (personal communication, July 1993).

lengthy responses (despite restricted R) suggests abundant and primitive needs pressing for expression. Her responses provide a poignant view of the interplay between defense, impulse, and object relations. Response 1 is remarkable from a content analytic perspective. Karen first perceives projected aggression, what has been termed *aggressive potential* (Gacono, 1990), and related to sadism (Meloy & Gacono, 1992a). It is suffused with a paranoid quality of piercing, staring predatory eyes (Meloy, 1988), which through projective identification she owns as part of herself (PER). While identifying with the aggressor (A. Freud, 1936), oral aggression becomes an explicit focus ("hostile mouth"). Attempting to minimize the threat, she produces it all within the context of a childlike, cartoon character, a measure of the degree to which hysterical denial can operate as a defense in psychopathic character. Finally, there is a primitive split through wish to a benign, yet sexual percept ("doves mating") that is not perceived, only conceived. Once again, the fusion of aggression and sexuality is evident in Karen's psychology, epitomized by her association with a man who linked sexuality and death in a most horrible manner.

Response 2 contains narcissistic mirroring (isolated self-soothing) and omnipotence used to recover from the assault of Card I. Her infantile and hysterical character is revealed through the choice of "baby elephant" (#2), "baby bears dancing and playing pattycake" (#3), and "little elephant. He's got a playmate" (#4). The diminutive content suggests a regressive quality when she attempts to reduce threatening impulses through pollyannish denial. Problems with interpersonal relations are suggested as the animals are "squashed" or "crouched down," "crowding against each other," and "brushing against each other."

Intellectualization is used in Responses 4 and 5. This defense might be unexpected except when viewed as an index of detachment and in its most primitive form, combined with splitting, as a tendency to depersonalize.[26] Correlates exist in Karen's unemotional, detached report of some of the most primitive aspects of the murders. One got the impression of observing an object under a microscope. The regressed, formless "smudge" and a "six-year-old spills on a carpet" follows. Content and defense follow that offer additional support for infantile, hysterical character structure: "Little antennae, feet, wings" (#8), "insectoid bat" turned into "Jimmy Cricket doing a dance" (#9), "I don't have any negative feeling for a bat," and, "unless it was fearful of a predator."

Massive denial is evident in "fish with Indian feathers" (Card VI). Response 11 with the word "deboned" and sadistic impulse (SM) is particularly interesting. Karen cut off the head of her victim with a fish deboning knife. "Boning" is also a vernacular term for sexual intercourse. Again the fusion of sexual and aggressive impulses are suggested. Their fusion leads to regression and possibly dissociation as the response ends with "no form . . . a blob—a Fudgsicle that's been allowed to set in the sun and melt."

---

[26]Meloy (1992a) found a similar pattern in the Rorschach of Sirhan Sirhan.

An opportunity for a positive interaction between human figures occurs on 12; however, Karen adds devaluation by suggesting that the women are "gossiping . . . like women everywhere." Similarly she struggles with her own feminine identity. Following Response 12 the remaining responses are noteworthy for content without form, the use of color, and recovery through mirroring. Content ends with smeared colors consistent with the regression noted throughout the record and a confusing and diffuse object world.

Summary

Karen is a woman organized at a borderline level of personality with predominantly masochistic, histrionic, and psychopathic character traits. Her psychology is dominated by two psychodynamic themes: the pairing of sexuality and death, and the centrality of dominance and submission. The linking of sexuality and death began with the three traumagenic events in adolescence: the death of her mother and sexual abuse by father, her rape and subsequent suicide of the perpetrator, and her father's suicide. This bizarre pattern was repeated in impulsive bonding with abusive, if not impotent, males (perhaps a reaction formation), and culminated in her intense attachment to a serial sexual murderer whose most delightful necrophilic act was to experience the vaginal contractions of a woman as she died at his hands. As Karen said, "He was the perfect partner for me."

The centrality of dominance and submission is also apparent in Karen's history, clinical interview, and psychological testing. She repeated the cycle of degradation begun by her father in a desperate search to undo it, only finding that mastery of the situation was beyond her grasp. She overtly identified with her masochistic character, and even carried this through in prison. Karen formed a sadomasochistic relationship with a woman in prison who was terminally ill with cancer. She would masturbate on the floor in front of her, dance nude for her, and allow herself to be beaten with a fly swatter. "I belonged to her and she could do with me as she pleased."

But Karen also had a sadistic aspect to her character that remained unconscious. She would seek out males that would act out her sadism, and thus gratify this passive–aggressive aspect of her own personality: the wish to hurt and control the withholding love object. This reached its pinnacle in the atrocities that she would witness Daniel commit, a voyeuristic deed in which she could watch herself as the prostitute, in fantasy, be humiliated and killed by the sadist time and again, and could identify and participate with him in the acts themselves. This is an unusual form of triangulated projective identification in which Karen placed devalued aspects of herself into the young prostitutes, and then could passively enjoy Daniel's dominance and control of them, including their annihilation, by identifying with him as the aggressor. This triangulation also suggests the Oedipal (Electra) theme of actually killing the mother during the act of mating with father so that the daughter can be with the father as a sexual and romantic equal. Karen repeated this act time and again with Daniel, a man whose psychopathy provided a real-world stage for Karen's most primitive impulses, and meant the end of her life as she knew it.

Karen's treatment in prison should focus on the alleviation of any depressive or anxious symptoms, neither of which rose to a clinical threshold at the time of our evaluation. Her character pathology is probably untreatable without an intensive form of psychotherapy or psychoanalysis, both of which would be unavailable to her. Any form of therapeutic alliance is unlikely, given the absence of indices of attachment capacity on the Rorschach and her propensity to form impulsive, sadomasochistic relations that have no enduring, empathic dimension.

Her risk of future dangerousness is probably extremely low, unless she formed a subsequent attachment to a male who could, once again, act out her unconscious sadism. Unfortunately, if Karen were released to the community, controlling this possibility would be extremely difficult. Her failure to learn from her experience is also disconcerting. She continues to receive an occasional letter from Daniel, who is now awaiting execution in San Quentin, and corresponds in return. Daniel also manages to telephone her sons, now young adults, each time they move, to remind them that he knows where they live—a psychopathic attempt to induce fear and omnipotently control others, even from Death Row.

CHAPTER 5

The Antisocial and Psychopathic Male

Conflict over the role of personality in criminality has not been resolved . . .
personality cannot be dismissed readily, as it is by many sociologists, and
the etiologic role cannot be assumed casually, as it is by many psychiatrists
and psychologists.

—Waldo and Dinitz (1967, p. 202)

The term *psychopathy* elicits strong reactions from most clinicians. We have found countertransference feelings, unless understood, to be detrimental to understanding the disorder. The glib, charming, shallow psychopath provides the perfect vessel to contain our projections, both good and bad. These narcissistic subjects define the limits of the psychotherapeutic endeavor. Clinicians who have narcissistic difficulties accepting the shortcomings of psychotherapy and their abilities to heal, are very sensitive to becoming caught in the psychopath's interpersonal web, and thus his psychodynamics. As Richards (1993) aptly wrote: "The abilities to recognize and accurately assess psychopathy and to adjust the approach to treatment accordingly are important skills for any therapist, but especially those working in dual diagnosis settings and correctional or forensic programs" (p. 292). Further, according to Richards:

> . . . [I]ndividuals who pursue the mental health disciplines tend to share certain characteristics, attitudes, and values. To generalize, mental health workers tend to be what may be called benign narcissists. They like to help and change others and derive satisfaction and a sense of efficacy from doing so. This helping in many cases may be a means of narcissistic repair, compensating for the therapist's own narcissistic liabilities. It is perhaps especially difficult for such persons to acknowledge and identify patients who might inherently be unable to benefit from

141

the therapist's kindness, attention, or diligent investment, or whose mode of narcissistic repair might be the obverse of the therapist, that is, destructive and victimizing toward others, rather than constructive and helpful. Especially for therapists not sufficiently aware of their own sadism and aggression, their kindness and desire to help may obscure their ability to detect the complete lack of compassion and attachment in others . . . [they] may not recognize the possibility that (given currently available understandings and treatment techniques) the severe psychopath for all intents and purposes may not be treatable. (pp. 308–309)

We use the term psychopathy, a traditional categorization, because it is conceptually bound to both trait and behavioral characteristics. A subject needs a significant quantity of characteristics from both domains to meet its inclusion criteria, hence it describes a more homogeneous group of subjects than designations such as antisocial personality disorder (*DSM–III–R*: APA, 1987; *DSM–IV*: APA, 1994), which are couched solely in behavioral criteria. Not synonymous, the terms are often interchangeably misused. In reality severely psychopathic individuals constitute a small group of subjects. Only one out of three inmate subjects diagnosed as antisocial personality disorder (ASPD) would meet the criteria. Whereas, depending on the security level of the prison, a large percentage of inmates (up to 75%) will meet the criteria for ASPD.

Empirically assessing the level of psychopathy allows the clinician to further delineate this heterogeneous group. Finer slicing of the ASPD pie yields important information for management and treatment. We do not advocate that the clinician discard current *DSM–IV* nomenclature (or ICD-10, World Health Organization, 1990), only that psychopathy level be considered when working with or studying offender groups (Gacono & Hutton, 1994; Meloy & Gacono, 1994).

In using the term psychopathic (as measured by the PCL–R) we acknowledge confidence intervals for the classification instrument and the individual differences inherent in any diagnostic entity. In other words, strict cutoffs can be used for research purposes, but ranges should be considered for clinical decision making. The next three sections of this chapter present information concerning psychopathy and antisocial personality disorder and their relationship. We then turn to a review of our Rorschach studies of adult male antisocial personality disorder and provide Rorschach data and their discussion for a sample of 82 ASPD and 33 psychopathic male felons. The chapter concludes with a case study of Travis, an adult male psychopath.

EVOLUTION OF PSYCHOPATHY AS A CLINICAL SYNDROME

Nearly 200 years ago, Phillipe Pinel, a French physician and pioneer in the field of mental disorders, encountered unusual cases not fitting any contemporary classification for mental disturbance. Characterized by relatively normal intellectual functions—perception, judgment, imagination, memory—but a pronounced disorder of affect, blind impulse to acts of violence, even murderous fury, he described the syndrome as *manie sans delire*—"madness without confusion" (Pinel, 1801). Other clinicians noted similar cases of "moral insanity" (Prichard, 1835) where clear thought coexisted with affective disturbance and incompatible antisocial behaviors (Esquirol, 1838; Rush, 1812). These cases were perplexing to the diagnostician. Presenting with many different "masks," the syndrome was difficult to classify.

Early practitioners believed degenerative processes underlay most mental disturbance (i.e., *dementia praecox*). Those who described psychopathy, influenced by this bias, also ignored information concerning personality (Lewis, 1974; Maudsley, 1874; Morel, 1839). Psychopathy became a wastebasket category for all personality deviation lying between the psychosis and neurosis (Karpman, 1948, 1950; Partridge, 1930). The poorly defined category produced a plethora of descriptive terms—constitutional inferior, constitutional psychopathic inferior, constitutional psychopathic personality, psychopathic personality, psychopathy, constitutional psychopathic state, moral imbecile, constitutional defective, defective delinquent, emotionally unstable or inferior, neurotic constitution, instinct character, sociopathic (Partridge, 1930)—which indicated the lack of a clearly defined syndrome. Many believed it was easier to describe what the disorder was not, rather than to develop a comprehensive definition of what it was (Savage, 1881).

Typologies for classifying criminal behavior in general and psychopathy in particular were as numerous as the terms (Partridge, 1930; Schafer, 1969). In retrospect, some attempts, like the phrenological profiles for inmates at the Eastern Penitentiary in Philadelphia (Barnes & Teeters, 1944), would now be perceived with some humor. They often reflected individual morals or the psychological *zeitgeist* of the period. The social context for defining psychopathy was embedded within a 19th-century concern for treating the mentally ill separate from nonmentally ill criminals (Schafer, 1969). Distinguishing the mentally ill from the behaviorally bad is a struggle that continues in many of our forensic state hospitals today. It raises numerous legal and ethical issues.

During the first half of the 20th century the concept of "psychopathic personality" emerged without the implication of constitutional inferiority (Rabin, 1979). Although biological roots were still hypothesized, Kraepelin's (1915) adoption of the term "psychopathic personality" led to a decline in the use of terms that suggested a degenerative process (Gacono, 1988). Despite an abundance of attention, severe psychopathy was thought to be a rare disorder (Partridge, 1930).

Eleven years after Partridge's (1930) review article identifying the confusion surrounding psychopathy, a seminal book on the psychopathic personality, *The Mask of Sanity* (Cleckley, 1976/1941), was published. Cleckley's text, which would appear in five editions after 1941, took steps to clarify the syndrome. He described 16 core characteristics for psychopathy (noted in Table 5.1), presented

TABLE 5.1
Cleckley's 16 Criteria for Psychopathy

---

1. Superficial charm and good "intelligence."
2. Absence of delusions and other irrational thinking.
3. Absence of "nervousness" or psychoneurotic manifestations.
4. Unreliable.
5. Untruthfulness and insincerity.
6. Lack of remorse and shame.
7. Inadequately motivated antisocial behavior.
8. Poor judgment and failure to learn from experience.
9. Pathological egocentricity and incapacity for love.
10. General poverty in major affective reactions.
11. Specific loss of insight.
12. Unresponsiveness in general interpersonal relations.
13. Fantastic and uninviting behavior with drink and sometimes without.
14. Suicide rarely carried out.
15. Sex life impersonal, trivial, and poorly integrated.
16. Failure to follow any life plan.

---

literary case studies, and discussed etiology and treatment. *The Mask of Sanity* would influence most subsequent theoretical and empirical work.

Cleckley expanded early organic and behavioral conceptualizations of psychopathy (Gacono, 1988). Although postulating a constitutional deficit, Cleckley's traits provided a dynamic description without links to a degenerative disorder. He believed the psychopath did evidence a semantic problem in that he was unable to process or internalize the affective components of human interaction (Cleckley, 1976, p. 238). The psychopath could recite the interpersonal words but never understand the music[1] (Johns & Quay, 1962).

Cleckley also argued that the core characteristics of psychopathy could be found within some individuals occupying some of society's most respected roles and settings. Others since Cleckley also believed that not all the psychopaths were in prison (Bursten, 1972, 1973; Millon, 1981). We agree, and are interested in psychopaths who manage their way into positions of power within society. These "power seekers" are often not arrested and therefore not referred for psychological evaluation. This makes studying the "noncriminal" psychopath difficult. Rorschach studies of some "white-collar" criminals might offer additional understanding. Weiner (1991) hypothesized, with some empirical support, that many "noncriminal "psychopaths manifest similar superego deficits as crimi-

---

[1]The lack of appreciation for the nuances of interpersonal relations was described by Theodore Bundy (an infamous serial killer who murdered in several states throughout the United States during the 1970s), "In my early schooling, it seemed like there was no problem in learning what the appropriate social behaviors were," he (Bundy) would one day tell an interviewer. "It just seemed like I hit a wall in high school." The wall, apparently no great barrier for his peers, was caused by a lack of empathic understanding for other people. "I didn't know what made things tick," Bundy would recall. "I didn't know what underlay social interactions." (Time-Life Books, 1993, p. 53).

nal psychopaths, but maintain more intact ego functions. This is consistent with our observations that these individuals may not meet the behavioral criteria for ASPD but do often meet the threshold criteria for other personality disorders (i.e., narcissistic or histrionic personality disorders) (Wulach, 1988).

HARE PSYCHOPATHY SCALES

The theoretical basis for empirically assessing psychopathy can also be attributed to Cleckley. The Hare Psychopathy Checklists (PCL, PCL–R; Hare, 1991; Hare, Hart, & Harpur, 1991) provide a standardized method for assessing criminal psychopathy. Both scales were designed to measure behaviors and core psychopathic personality characteristics. Like Cleckley, Hare postulated some biological substrates for psychopathy (see chapter 10 for a review), and his work and others have begun to measure them (Hare, 1991). PCL–R Items 6 (lack of remorse), 7 (shallow affect), and 8 (callous lack of empathy) form a constellation of variables that may be measuring Cleckley's semantic disorder and the inability of the psychopath to appreciate the nuances of interpersonal emotional experience (see Table 5.2). By comparing Tables 5.1 and 5.2 the reader can identify the similarities between the PCL–R criteria and Cleckley's 16 descriptors.[2]

The PCL–R consists of two stable, oblique factors that correlate (on average .56) in prison inmates (Hare et al., 1991). Factor 1 contains Items 1, 2, 4, 5, 6, 7, 8, and 16 (see Table 5.2) and is characterized by egocentricity, callousness, and remorselessness. It correlates with *DSM–III–R*'s (APA, 1987) narcissistic and histrionic personality disorders (Hare, 1991) and self-report measures of Machiavellianism and narcissism (Harpur, Hare, & Hakstian, 1989; Hart & Hare, 1989). Meloy (1992b) labeled this Factor 1 "aggressive narcissism," and Hare (1991) originally defined it as a callous and remorseless disregard for the rights and feelings of others.

Factor 2 contains Items 3, 9, 10, 12, 13, 14, 15, 18, and 19, and is characterized by an irresponsible, impulsive, thrill-seeking, unconventional, and antisocial lifestyle. Although both factors correlate with *DSM–III–R*'s (APA, 1987) antisocial personality disorder, Factor 2 demonstrates the strongest relationship. Factor 2 also correlates with the presence of criminal behaviors, lower socioeconomic background, lower IQ and less education, and self-report measures of antisocial behavior (Hare, 1991; Harpur et al., 1989). Hare labeled Factor 2 "chronic antisocial behavior."

PCL–R scores can range from 0 to 40. Subjects receive a score of 0, 1, or 2 for individual scale items. Zero designates an absence of the trait. One means some elements of the item apply, a partial match. Two indicates a reasonably

---

[2] The original PCL contained 22 items. Two items found to be nonessential were eliminated to form the PCL–R. The scales are virtually identical with respect to reliability and validity (Hare, 1991).

TABLE 5.2

The Hare Psychopathy Checklist–Revised (PCL – R)

1. Glibness/superficial charm.[a]
2. Grandiose sense of self-worth.[a]
3. Need for stimulation/proneness to boredom.
4. Pathological lying.[a]
5. Conning/manipulative.[a]
6. Lack of remorse or guilt.[a]
7. Shallow affect.[a]
8. Callous/lack of empathy.[a]
9. Parasitic lifestyle.
10. Poor behavioral controls.
11. Promiscuous sexual behavior.
12. Early behavior problems.
13. Lack of realistic, long-term goals.
14. Impulsivity.
15. Irresponsibility.
16. Failure to accept responsibility for own actions.[a]
17. Many short-term marital relationships.
18. Juvenile delinquency.
19. Revocation of conditional release.
20. Criminal versatility.

[a]Items designated represent Factor 1.

good match to the item criteria. The mean PCL–R score for a combined prison population (based on six samples, $N = 1,065$; Hare, 1991) is 23.37 ($SD = 7.96$). Forensic psychiatric populations (four samples, $N = 440$; Hare, 1991), as expected, produce slightly lower mean PCL–R scores ($M = 20.56$; $SD = 7.79$). Although a score of ≥ 30 has been most frequently used to designate primary psychopathy, other cutoff scores have been used for clinical work and research. Impressive findings have demonstrated physiological, personality, and behavioral differences between psychopathic and nonpsychopathic offenders, and prompted our strong recommendation to use the scale whenever offenders are studied (Gacono & Meloy, 1992). Psychopathy level is a necessary independent measure for offender research and clinical evaluations for triers of fact.

Psychological assessment methods have often been criticized due to the lengthy training and administration time required to use them. With moderate amounts of clinician training, however, the PCL–R has proven to be a reliable, valid, and efficient method for both research (Hare, 1991) and clinical/forensic assessments of psychopathy (Gacono, in press; Gacono & Hutton, 1994; Serin, 1992).

While the PCL–R requires a thorough evaluation of a subject's behavioral history, the Rorschach provides rich information concerning reality testing, object relations, defensive operations, stress tolerance and controls, affects, and thought. The two instruments complement most forensic assessments where issues of motivation, prediction, and personality functioning arise (Gacono, 1990; Gacono & Hutton, 1994; Meloy & Gacono, 1994).

DSM SERIES

Cleckley influenced a second line of classification contained in the first *Diagnostic and Statistical Manual of Mental Disorders* (*DSM*; APA, 1952). In the first *DSM* sociopathic personality replaced psychopathic personality.[3] It described a variety of conditions such as sexual deviation, alcoholism, and "antisocial" and "dyssocial" reactions. The "antisocial reaction" diagnosis was given to those individuals:

> . . . who are always in trouble, profiting neither from experience or punishment and maintaining no loyalties to any person, group, or code. They are frequently callous and hedonistic, showing marked emotional immaturity with lack of sense of responsibility, lack of judgment, and an ability to rationalize their behavior so that it appears warranted, reasonable, and justified. (APA, 1952, p. 38)

The antisocial reaction closely resembled the classic psychopath (Jenkins, 1960). The reactive aspect of the diagnosis, however, suggested a fundamentally learned response to the slings and arrows of the environment—the original premise of Birnbaum (1914) who coined the term *sociopath*.

The second *DSM* (*DSM–II*; APA, 1968) eliminated reactivity, presented several personality disorders, and subsumed antisocial and dyssocial reactions under the rubric of "antisocial personality" (ASPD). Often recognizable by adolescence, the personality disorders were characterized by deeply ingrained traits and maladaptive patterns of behavior perceptibly different from psychotic and neurotic symptoms. Antisocial personality disorders were distinguished by their unsocialized and antisocial behavior. Incapable of significant loyalty to individuals, groups, or social values, they were described as grossly selfish, callous, irresponsible, impulsive, and unable to feel guilt or to learn from experience and punishment. They demonstrated poor frustration tolerance and blamed others, while offering plausible rationalizations for their behavior (APA, 1968). These changes in *DSM–II* were spearheaded by Lee Robins, a sociologist at Washington University in St. Louis, and were based on her groundbreaking empirical study of delinquents (Robins, 1966). Robins' work provides a "social deviancy" model of antisocial personality in contrast to Cleckley's "personality" or trait model.

Although the *DSM–II* maintained some traits associated with traditional descriptions of psychopathy (Hare et al., 1991; Karpman, 1961; Millon, 1981), the fixed

---

[3]Unfortunately, clinicians still confuse the two terms—psychopath and sociopath—using them interchangeably. Further confusion has resulted from the substitution of antisocial personality disorder for sociopathic personality in *DSM–II* (APA, 1968). Although the three terms differ, sociopathic personality and antisocial personality disorder both belong to the same *DSM* family tree. We eschew the term sociopath because it was born from the belief that criminality was solely the result of a depriving environment, its popular life span was brief (1940s through 1960s) and reflected a psychiatric generation trained as psychoanalysts in the sociogenic model, and it is no longer in the official psychiatric nomenclature.

set of behavioral criteria in the *DSM–III* (APA, 1980) firmly endorsed a social deviance model (Robins, 1966) and eschewed most trait descriptions. The *DSM–III* and *DSM–III–R* (APA, 1987) criteria did not explicitly include traits such as selfishness, egocentricity, callousness, manipulativeness, and lack of empathy. The presence of these characteristics found in the criteria for narcissistic personality disorder are necessary for a diagnosis of severe psychopathy. The third revision emphasized an early onset (< age 15) of continuous and chronic antisocial behavior that persisted into adult life while eliminating reference to specific traits. Thus *DSM–III* and *DSM–III–R* moved further away from the psychopathic traits described by Cleckley and Hare. *DSM–IV* criteria for antisocial personality disorder, although simplified (seven items), firmly endorsed the social deviancy model (APA, 1994). The companion treatment chapter, however, does not (Meloy, in press).

The ASPD criteria describe a heterogeneous group of criminal personalities rather than criminal psychopaths (Gacono & Hutton, 1994). Approximately 60% to 75% of any prison population can be expected to meet ASPD criteria—a discriminant validity problem in forensic settings. Although ASPD correlates most closely with antisocial lifestyle (Factor 2; Hare, 1991), a subject must evidence sufficient traits from both factors of the PCL–R to be designated a criminal psychopath. Only 20% to 25% of a prison population would be expected to meet these more stringent criteria for psychopathy. Consequently only one out of three individuals diagnosed as ASPD are psychopaths.

The *DSM–III–R* (APA, 1987) acknowledged the possibility of an Axis I schizophrenic disorder coexisting with the Axis II antisocial disorder (see chapter 6). This was an important addition to the *DSM–III–R*. Practicing forensic clinicians were aware of such dual-diagnosed patients whose behaviors, despite active psychosis, were motivated by the characterological component of their personality (Meloy, 1988; Meloy & Gacono, 1992b). Careful assessment of concurrent Axis I and Axis II disorders in these patients provides hypotheses regarding the role of criminal responsibility. Specifically, are motivations linked to "badness" or "madness" or both?[4]

A positive addition to the *DSM–III–R* (APA, 1987) ASPD criteria was the inclusion of concepts such as "performing antisocial acts that are grounds for arrest," "conning others for personal profit or pleasure," and "lacks remorse (feels

---

[4]One patient, Dave, who carried a dual diagnosis of paranoid schizophrenia and antisocial personality (psychopathy level was severe), assaulted another patient in a state hospital. Dave calmly approached the victim, holding the weapon (pencil) in his left hand out of sight. He put his right arm over the victim's shoulder and began joking with him. When the victim relaxed, Dave stabbed the victim in the left side of his head, just missing the eye. As staff responded, Dave dropped both hands to his sides and calmly stated, "Everything's okay." Careful analysis of the assault indicated the victim had confronted Dave in a group session earlier in the day. The assault was not motivated by delusion or hallucination, but rather predisposed by Dave's psychopathic personality, and driven by rage as a defense against the narcissistic wound of being humiliated in front of others. Psychotic mechanisms may have lowered his threshold for violence if active at the time of the assault.

justified in having hurt, mistreated, or stolen from another)" (pp. 345–346). These are familiar character traits. Even with revisions, however, the fixed behavioral criteria have been criticized for their length and problems with content and construct validity (Hare et al., 1991). Empirical support for both gender and biological links[5] was also noted.

Heterogeneity among offenders, all who manifest behavioral criminality, has made classification of characterological antisocial patterns (antisocial reaction, or psychopath) and individuals manifesting antisocial behavior (dyssocial reaction) under one diagnostic category impractical (Gacono, 1988). Many authors have recommended the use of refined criteria for the disorder (psychopathy) or classifying antisocial behavior as secondary to the primary personality disorder (Arieti, 1963; Bursten, 1972, 1973; Gacono, 1988; Gibbs, 1982; Jarvinen, 1977; Kernberg, 1975; Millon, 1981; Tuovinen, 1974; Wulach, 1983).

Although within a given personality structure traits, attitudes, and behaviors are related (Gacono & Meloy, 1988, 1993; see chapter 10), diagnostic criteria based on trait and attitude *description* are conceptually at odds with those emphasizing symptoms and signs. Traits and attitudes emphasize continuity of behavior, while symptoms and signs emphasize discontinuity. Behavioral descriptors do not lend themselves to the type of understanding suggested by Brittain (1970) 25 years ago, "We cannot treat, except empirically, what we do not understand, and we cannot prevent, except fortuitously, what we do not comprehend" (p. 206).

A RORSCHACH PERSPECTIVE OF THE ADULT MALE ASPD

Could psychodynamic constructs associated with psychopathy be empirically tested? The unstructured stimuli of the Rorschach technique were chosen in an attempt to answer this question. The following section reviews our previously published studies with antisocial adult male subjects.

Gacono (1988, 1990) sought to test Kernberg's (1970, 1975) assertions that all antisocial personality disorders were organized at a borderline level of personality organization. He compared the object relations and defensive operations of 14 psychopathic antisocial personality disordered subjects (P-ASPD) and 19 nonpsychopathic antisocial personality disordered subjects (NP-ASPD). Those subjects scoring ≥ 30 on the PCL–R were placed into the psychopathic group (this cutoff was used in all of our subsequent research). All subjects were free of organic mental

---

[5] The 301.70 antisocial personality disorder is more common in males (1% to 3% of American adult population) than females (< 1% of American adult population). The antisocial diagnosis is 5 times more common among first-degree biological relatives of males with the disorder and 10 times more common in first-degree biological relatives of females than in the general population (APA, 1987).

disorder, functional psychosis or mental retardation (IQs $\geq$ 80; these inclusion criteria were also used for all our samples with the exception of the schizophrenic ASPDs and sexual homicide perpetrators).

Exner's (1973) Self-Focus Sentence Completion Test was completed as an independent measure of narcissism. All subjects' Rorschach protocols were scored for Kwawer's (1980) primitive modes of relating categories (borderline) and Lerner and Lerner (1980) defense indices. Object relations and defense indices were compared utilizing nonparametric analyses. Cooper and Arnow's (1986) defense indices, Gacono's impressionistic response, and our experimental aggression scores (see chapter 8) were descriptively displayed.

The level of narcissism, composite of H, Hd, (H), and (Hd) content, and proportion of defenses did not differ significantly between the P-ASPDs and NP-ASPDs. The entire ASPD sample (N = 33) did produce a mean Self-Focus score of 15.85 (SD = 3.24) similar to Exner's (1973) mean score of 15.20 obtained for a "sociopathic" sample. The ASPD Self-Focus score indicated a significant amount of group egocentricity. Gacono (1988) hypothesized that the self-focus measure failed to differentiate between groups in part because individual personality styles within the psychopathic group dictated the manner in which grandiosity manifested. One highly psychopathic subject (PCL–R = 38.5), for instance, whose predominant characterological style was paranoid, scored well below the mean. He produced statements such as "It's fun to daydream about a better world," and, "Someday I wish the world would see one another as one world family," which went beyond typical criteria for scoring self-focus.

Specific defenses did not appear to differentiate between the groups. The use of preoedipal defenses, however, characterized the entire ASPD sample (N = 33). The Lerner and Lerner (1980) scoring revealed a reliance on devaluation, primitive denial, and a paucity of idealization. Cooper and Arnow (1986) scoring, which does not rely solely on human content, produced more scoreable responses. Their system revealed the presence of splitting, projective identification, and devaluation among the ASPD subjects (Gacono, 1988). There was a paucity of neurotic level defenses.

Kwawer's (1980) primitive modes of relating were produced in a proportionally greater amount (p < .01) by the P-ASPD group. Psychopaths produced a mean Kwawer score of 2.50 (SD = 1.50), while the mean score obtained by the nonpsychopaths was 1.37 (2.01). These significant differences were particularly surprising. Using ASPD criteria as a second independent measure resulted in Gacono's (1988, 1990) sample including few low (< 20) PCL–R scorers.[6] His P-ASPDs and NP-ASPDs were comprised of high ($\geq$ 30) and moderate (20–29) scorers. Hare and his colleagues consistently found significant differences between the extreme levels of psychopathy, high ($\geq$ 30) and low (< 20) (Hare,

---

[6]In our clinical experience incarcerated (in prison) felons who meet the criteria for ASPD typically will not score less than 20 and rarely less than 16 on the PCL–R (Gacono & Hutton, 1994).

1991). Rorschach studies comparing such extremes on the psychopathy continuum might produce even more dramatic differences between variables.
Gacono (1990) concluded,

> The frequency of borderline object relations and defense categories lends credence
> to Kernberg's (1970) assertion concerning the prevalence of borderline personality
> organization among antisocial personality disordered individuals. The high level
> of narcissism found in these individuals also supports Kernberg's (1975) belief
> that an extreme form of pathological narcissism exists in those with antisocial
> personality disorders (who are prison inmates). Pathological narcissism is one
> component of psychopathy. (p. 596)

Gacono also hypothesized that the grandiose self-structure along with primitive
defenses served "an organizing function that allowed the psychopath to appear
better organized" (p. 597) than some borderline personality disordered subjects
whose "ego structure maintained a precarious adjustment, vulnerable to fragmentation in the form of brief psychotic episodes" (p. 597). Further validation of
this hypothesis would appear in subsequent studies (Gacono & Meloy, 1993).

In Gacono et al. (1990) we examined the relationship between psychopathy
and narcissism (Gacono, 1988; Harpur et al., 1989; Kernberg, 1975; Meloy,
1988) and hysteria (Guze, 1976; Guze, Woodruff, & Clayton, 1971a; Hart &
Hare, 1989; Meloy, 1988). The Rorschach protocols of P-ASPDs ($N = 21$) were
compared to those produced by NP-ASPDs ($N = 21$). Exner's (1986a) pair (2),
reflection (rF, Fr), and personal responses (PER) along with the egocentricity
ratio [3r+(2)/R] were used as measures of self-focus and pathological narcissism.
Meloy (1988) had previously hypothesized that the combination of pairs and
reflections represented an empirical measure of the grandiose self-structure in
psychopathic subjects. The impressionistic response[7] (IMP; Gacono, 1988, 1990)
was used as a measure of hysterical mechanisms (Shapiro, 1965).

The mean number of pair and impressionistic responses did not significantly
differ between the two antisocial groups. P-ASPDs did exhibit a significantly
greater mean number of reflection ($p < .05$) and personal ($p < .05$) responses.
The egocentricity ratios were also significantly different ($p < .01$) with the
P-ASPDs producing greater ratios ($M = .46$, $SD = .18$) than the NP-ASPDs ($M
= .30$, $SD = .14$). These differences provided some support for the pathological
narcissism in P-ASPDs. The low egocentricity ratio produced by the NP-ASPDs

---

[7]The impressionistic response (IMP) was reported in Gacono (1988, 1990) and Gacono et al.
(1990). Derived from David Shapiro's (1965) hysterical personality's "impressionistic" cognitive
style, the response identifies associations to the blot stimulated by color and containing abstract
concepts or events (Gacono et al., 1990). It is operationized by scoring achromatic (including shading)
or chromatic color and an abstraction (AB). Although we initially believed IMP might be specific
to the hysterical cognition of the primary psychopath, we now think it may be "a sensitive indicator
of the degree to which certain patients organized at a borderline level split off affect into rapid and
diffuse symbolization" (Gacono et al., 1992, p. 45).

when compared to both the P-ASPDs and Exner's (1985) nonpatients ($M = .39$) and character disorders (.42) stimulated further thinking concerning the effectiveness of regulating processes noted previously in the psychopaths (Gacono, 1988): "The low mean egocentricity ratios for the moderate psychopaths suggest a reduced effectiveness for bolstering grandiosity and warding off the disruptive effects of internal (anxiety) and external (incarceration) threat. The internal regulating mechanisms of the severe psychopath are less tenuous" (Gacono et al., 1990, pp. 275–276).

We observed a variety of reflection responses produced within the ASPD population that suggested a range of interpretations for this variable (see chapter 7). The quality of object relatedness represented by individual reflection responses varied. Not all reflections were created equal.[8] We described "confused reflections" and "reflection only" responses (Gacono et al., 1990). We also proposed the coding of a formless or "pure r." The pure r is not included in the Comprehensive scoring (Exner, 1986a) but is consistent with the differentiation of other determinants. The important relationship of the reflection response to character pathology is researched and discussed in chapter 7.

We expanded Exner's (1986a) interpretation of the PER as a defensive maneuver used by subjects needing to protect their self-image or as a means to fend off a possible challenge from the examiner (Gacono et al., 1990). PERs appear to represent within psychopathic populations an identification with the aggressor (A. Freud, 1936) and may signal the defensive use of omnipotence and projective identification. We believe the PER response is an important discriminating variable for psychopathy within antisocial samples. Among sexual homicide perpetrators (Meloy & Gacono, 1992b; Meloy et al., 1994; see chapter 9), PERs often occur in conjunction with projective identification and omnipotence, signaling the projection of self rather than object-representations (Gacono, 1992; Meloy, 1991a). We noted a differential, defensive use of the PER dependent on the psychopathy level of the subject:

> In lower levels of psychopathy, we observed the personal response to aid the subject defensively by providing a "last ditch" rationale for a self-perceived inadequate response or explanation. In these cases, self-reference becomes the final avenue for providing an explanation and maintaining grandiosity, but for the highly psychopathic individual, it is often the first choice. (Gacono et al., 1990, p. 275)

We concluded that narcissism and hysteria were personality traits that determined the severity and expressive nature of psychopathy and recommended that Rorschach variables be interpreted in the context of other test and historical data (Gacono et al., 1990).

---

[8] This reminds us of a timeless aphorism: "God created man. Sam Colt made them equal" (Score AgC, idealization).

Shallow affect, autonomic hyporeactivity, and deficits in the capacity for attachment have been fundamental constructs related to psychopathy (Cleckley, 1976; Hare, 1965, 1966, 1970; Meloy, 1988). Through a comparison of Rorschach texture (T, TF, FT), diffuse shading (Y, YF, FY), vista (V, VF, FV), D-scores (D), and Adjusted D-scores (Adj-D) between P-ASPDs ($N = 21$) and NP-ASPDs ($N = 21$), we investigated Rorschach manifestations of attachment and anxiety in the psychopath (Gacono & Meloy, 1991). Vista frequencies did not differ significantly between the groups. As expected, texture ($p < .01$) and shading ($p < .001$) frequencies were less in the P-ASPDs than in the NP-ASPDs. Although the D and adjusted D scores did not differ significantly, trends were noted. The P-ASPDs mean scores were all in the positive direction (D = .00, SD = .84; AdjD = .09, SD = .94), and more similar to Exner (1985) nonpatients (D = .02, SD = 1.83; AdjD = .31, SD = 1.37) than were the NP-ASPDs (D = −.33, SD = .73; AdjD = .05, SD = .67) whose D-scores moved in the negative direction.

We interpreted the presence of V in psychopaths as representing failed grandiosity (Fr, rF, r) and perhaps self-pity. Lower amounts of Y in the P-ASPDs coupled with the normal D and AdjD score patterns suggested the absence of anxiety and helplessness associated with primary psychopathy (Cleckley, 1976; Fagan & Lira, 1980; Hare, 1970) and, consistent with lower egocentricity ratios for NP-ASPDs (Gacono et al., 1990), the tenuous nature or vulnerability of the grandiose self-structure (Kernberg, 1975) in NP-ASPDs. The virtual absence of T in the P-ASPD sample (5%) supported the profound detachment clinically observed in psychopaths (Reid, 1978).

Aggression plays a crucial role in the development and functioning of both conduct and antisocial personality disorder (see chapter 8). It has been identified as a discriminating variable between the psychopathic and narcissistic disorders (Kernberg, 1975; Meloy, 1988). Based on earlier observations and theoretical considerations (Gacono, 1988; Meloy, 1988), we realized the limitations of the Exner (1986a) aggressive movement response for capturing the range and intensity of aggressive drive derivatives produced by ASPD subjects on the Rorschach (see chapter 8). In Meloy and Gacono (1992a) we reintroduced our experimental aggression scores (first presented in Gacono, 1988, 1990), provided interrater reliabilities for the indices, and presented a list of content to guide the scoring of aggressive content (AgC).

Aggressive indices were compared between P-ASPDs ($N = 22$) and NP-ASPDs ($N = 21$). With the exception of the sadomasochistic (SM) response, which appeared more frequently in the P-ASPD sample ($p < .05$), no significant differences were found. The ASPD samples also produced less AG than did nonpatients (Exner, 1985). Although Meloy (1988) initially suggested an active censoring of this response in ASPD subjects, we now think that the ego-syntonic nature of the aggressive impulse and a pattern of acting out aggression for ASPDs contribute to its absence on the Rorschach (see chapter 8). We recommended the idiographic use of our new aggression scores and suggested the need for further nomothetic validation (Meloy & Gacono, 1992a).

Although our previous studies were influenced by Lindner's (1943) ideas, in Gacono and Meloy (1992) we first attempted to test his assertion that the Rorschach could aid in the diagnosis and understanding of psychopathy (see Appendix A). Means, standard deviations, and frequencies were presented for Lerner and Lerner (1980) and Cooper et al. (1988) defense indices (ASPD, $N = 43$), Kwawer's (1980) primitive object relations categories (P-ASPD, $N = 22$; NP-ASPD, $N = 21$), and Exner's (1986a) Comprehensive system data (ASPD, $N = 60$). The proportion of Kwawer's indices were compared statistically between groups. Similar to a prison population, approximately 22% of the ASPD sample ($N = 60$) were psychopaths. Consistent with Exner's (1990b) normative samples, only those protocols with ≥ 14 responses were included in the sample of 60.

Adequate interrater agreement was obtained for the Lerner and Lerner (1980) defense indices. Twenty randomly selected protocols revealed 85% agreement for composite devaluation, 83% for composite denial, and 100% for composite idealization (Lerner & Lerner, 1980). Fewer than five responses were obtained for splitting and projective identification; these were not included in the interrater reliability check. The Cooper et al. (1988) indices were used only as comparison data points and therefore not subjected to interrater reliability analysis.

We reported that the ASPD subjects ($N = 60$) relied on the use of devaluation, grandiosity, and other primitive defenses (Gacono & Meloy, 1992). Seventy-seven percent of the ASPDs produced at least one devaluation response (Lerner & Lerner, 1980, defenses), whereas 100% of the subjects produced at least one Cooper et al. (1988) devaluation response (50% produced ≥ 4 devaluation responses). Cooper et al.'s (1988) massive denial response was the second most frequently produced defense with 81% of the sample producing at least one. A comparison of P-ASPDs with NP-ASPDs revealed that P-ASPDs produced the Cooper et al. indices at the following frequencies: massive denial 91%, projective identification 77%, splitting 68%, omnipotence 68%, primitive idealization 50%, and higher level denial 27%, whereas NP-ASPDs produced projective identification 76%, massive denial 71%, omnipotence 57%, splitting 48%, primitive idealization 38%, and higher level denial 10%.

Our discovery of a paucity of idealization responses in the ASPD sample was noteworthy because idealization is necessary for both attachment and the development of mature compensatory mechanisms (H. Lerner, 1988; P. Lerner, 1991):

> The prevalence of devaluation and massive denial, with an absence of higher-level denial and idealization (in the ASPD subjects), may indicate their lack of compensatory mechanisms (H. Lerner, 1988) or pseudosublimatory channels (Kernberg, 1975), and their tendency to discharge impulses and conflicts directly through action (Lerner, 1991). This psychodynamic finding correlates with behaviors that demonstrate a lack of consistent career choice and difficulties maintaining employment, the PCL-R's second factor (antisocial lifestyle) and many of the *DSM-III-R*'s (APA, 1987) criteria. (Gacono & Meloy, 1992, p. 403)

When ASPDs do produce idealization responses, they are likely to be expressed through primitive idealization, nonhuman percepts, or combined with PER and Reflections suggesting self-idealization and other primitive defenses.

Interrater agreement was adequate for Kwawer's (1980) primitive modes of relating indices. Ninety-five percent agreement was obtained for the total object relations categories while individual categories yielded the following agreements: symbiotic merging 100%; violent symbiosis, separation, and reunion 100%; birth-rebirth 87%; malignant internal process 100%; and narcissistic mirroring 100%. Other categories contained fewer than five responses and were not analyzed for interrater agreement. Consistent with earlier findings, P-ASPDs produced a significantly greater proportion of primitive or pre-Oedipal object relations ($p < .001$). They also more frequently produced boundary disturbance ($x^2 = 5.79$; $p < .05$) and narcissistic mirroring ($x^2 = 6.25$; $p < .05$) responses and produced a significantly greater proportion of narcissistic mirroring ($p < .05$) responses than the NP-ASPDs.

Structural data also supported the pathological object relations in the ASPDs. Elevated reflections (38%), PERs ($M = 1.97$), and an average W:M ratio of 9.72:3.37 were consistent with pathological narcissism, omnipotence, and grandiosity. For P-ASPDs "aspirations superceded real world abilities," and, "Pleasure in fantasy was more desirable than the pain and endurance involved in effort toward responsible goals" (Gacono & Meloy, 1992, p. 401). The dearth of M also suggests deficient cognitive control over impulses, a lack of concern and interest in people, and a tendency to disregard others in the pursuit of selfish emotional gratification (Haramis & Wagner, 1980; Lerner, 1975; Wagner & Hoover, 1972). A lack of affectional relatedness (T, $M = .30$, Freq. = 22%), a higher frequency of Hd (67%), lower frequency of H (82%), and less COP (45%), coupled with narcissism, indicates interpersonal detachment and relationships characterized by part-object internal representations.

Problems with affective modulation were suggested by an FC to CF + C ratio of 1 to 2.5, which is proportionally the opposite of nonpatients (2:1). Lower F+% ($M = 53$) and X+% ($M = 53$) along with elevated X−% ($M = 23$) and Wsum6 ($M = 17.12$) suggested moderate, but pervasive thought disorder and serious reality-testing problems. Poor affect regulation and,

> responses characterized by tangential answers and unusual perceptions and combinations, primarily level 1 special scores, may contribute to understanding Cleckley's (1976, p. 238) phrase, "semantically disordered" psychopath. In general, thought disorder in the severe psychopath often is seen in loose and tangential elaborations that are personalized in a grandiose manner. (Gacono & Meloy, 1992, p. 402)

We concluded that our findings supported Lindner's (1943) hypotheses concerning the usefulness of the Rorschach for understanding psychopathy and the more generic ASPD. Patterns emerged that were able to differentiate P-ASPDs from NP-ASPDs consistent with theoretical constructs. Although our findings were by no means conclusive, they did demonstrate the application of advanced assessment techniques to the study of one personality disorder.

After investigating the Rorschach patterns in incarcerated psychopathic and ASPD subjects we saw a need for comparative studies with nonoffending clinical groups. Lindner (1943) believed that the Rorschach could separate the psychopath from other clinical groups although he did not specify other "personality disorders." Given the heterogeneity of Exner's (1990b) character-disordered sample, various researchers have identified the need for more refined character-disordered samples (Philip Erdberg, personal communication, July 1991). Would Rorschach analysis in its current state be up to the task? Could the Rorschach elucidate the nuances that differentiate similar personality-disordered groups?

We chose for comparison subjects who were theoretically similar to the ASPDs, their *DSM–III–R* (APA, 1987) Cluster B cousins: the narcissistic, borderline, and histrionic personality disorders. We compared select Rorschach variables of outpatient narcissistic personality disordered (NPD; N = 18) and borderline personality disordered (BPD; N = 18) subjects with those of P-ASPDs (N = 22) and NP-ASPDs (N = 21) (Gacono et al., 1992).[9]

Although both P-ASPDs and NPDs were highly narcissistic [elevated Fr, rF, r, and 3R+(2)/R], NPD subjects produced more indices of anxiety (Y, YF, FY) and attachment capacity (T, TF, FT) and fewer scores related to borderline object relations (Kwawer, 1980) and damaged identity (MOR, AgPast). BPDs were less narcissistic than P-ASPDs and NPDs. BPDs shared equal numbers of borderline object relations (Kwawer, 1980) with P-ASPD subjects; however, they were more anxious, produced more unsublimated aggressive (AG) and libidinal (Sx) material, and evidenced greater potential for attachment.

NP-ASPDs were less borderline than P-ASPDs or BPDs, less narcissistic than NPD and P-ASPDs, produced less evidence of attachment capacity than the outpatient groups, but more than P-ASPDs, and were similar to BPDs in their proneness to anxiety. Consistent with Lerner's (1991) theories, the outpatient groups produced more idealization responses than the incarcerated ASPD groups. We wrote, "Behavioral descriptions offered for these three Cluster B personality disorders, when used in conjunction with information such as level of personality organization (Kernberg, 1984), level of psychopathy (Hare, 1980, 1985), and outpatient versus inpatient research settings, may have greater intrapsychic specificity than previously thought" (Gacono et al., 1992, p. 32). Further, "[t]he Rorschach ... continues to impress us as a potent tool for understanding the intrapsychic world of the borderline organized patient and the variety of characterological styles that are presented to clinicians" (Gacono et al., 1992, pp. 46–47).

---

[9]Unfortunately, we did not have a sample of histrionic personality disordered patients to study. In fact, to our knowledge, we know of no published Rorschach data concerning HPD patients.

In the following section, Rorschach data from 82 ASPD subjects are examined with the hope of adding to our understanding of the antisocial disorder. Comprehensive System data (Exner, 1986a) are presented along with scoring for object relations (Kwawer, 1980) and our aggression indices for use when subjects are evaluated within forensic settings.

THE MALE ANTISOCIAL PERSONALITY DISORDER SAMPLE (*N* = 82)[10]

Our sample of 82 males were all incarcerated in various forensic hospitals and state prisons in California. All the Rorschachs were administered by us or Thomas Heaven, PhD. The Rorschachs were rescored by us, and any scoring disagreements were resolved through consultation with Phil Erdberg, PhD. Data were analyzed using the Rorschach Scoring Program 2 (Exner, Cohen, & Mcguire, 1990) and other descriptive software programs. No protocols were accepted into the final subject pool unless they produced ≥ 14 responses. Twenty protocols were eliminated for this reason.

Forty-five of the subjects (Gacono & Meloy, 1992) were randomly gathered for the dissertations of Gacono (1988) and Heaven (1988). The additional 37 protocols were gathered during the routine course of forensic evaluations at Atascadero State Hospital, a maximum security forensic hospital in central California. All protocols were gathered during the years 1985–1992. Screening criteria for admission to the sample included a diagnosis of antisocial personality disorder (*DSM–III–R*; APA, 1987) as agreed on by two researchers through interview and record data; and no diagnosis by history or mental status exam of a functional psychosis, organic mental disorder, or mental retardation. Individuals with a history of alcohol or substance abuse were not excluded from the sample, although no subjects were actively using psychotropic chemicals at the time of testing.

The racial composition of the sample was as follows: 68% White (56), 15% Black (12), 15% Hispanic (12), 2% other (2). The age range of the sample was 18 to 48 (*M* = 29.96, *SD* = 7.36). We considered both reported marital status and exact intelligence scores unreliable, although all individuals in the sample had IQs ≥ 80, eliminating any low IQ confounding variables.

Forty percent (*N* = 33) of the sample were primary psychopaths as determined by scores on the PCL–R (Hare, 1991). This is slightly higher than the predicted one third of ASPD males meeting the criteria for primary psychopathy (≥ 30

[10]Appreciation is extended to the California State Department of Corrections, Richard J. Donovan Facility, San Diego, and California Department of Mental Health, Atascadero State Hospital, Atascadero, for approving research proposals that allowed our data to be gathered. Special thanks to Dr. Thomas Heaven, who as Dr. Gacono's research partner began gathering ASPD Rorschach protocols in 1985.

PCL–R score). The data concerning the primary psychopaths are discussed following the overall sample analysis.

Tables 5.3 and 5.4 list the Comprehensive System variables and select ratios, percentages, and derivations for the sample of 82 ASPD males.

Core Characteristics. The sample of ASPD males produced a normative amount of responses ($M = 21.41$, $SD = 8.42$) with more variance than one would expect in nonpatient males. The sample is dominated by high Lambda subjects ($M = .94$, $SD = .60$), with Lambda $> .99$ in 37%. This finding is consistent with two clinical characteristics of ASPD males: first, their noticeable defenses against affect; and second, their simplistic, item-by-item approach to problem solving. This latter characteristic is related to their inability to foresee the long-term consequences of their behavior, measurable with four of the PCL–R criteria (poor behavioral controls, lack of realistic goals, impulsivity, and irresponsibility). It is likely that high Lambda in this context foreshadows long-term self-destruction, despite successful short-term manipulations, because eventual aversive consequences are not foreseen. As Willy Sutton said to the judge when asked why he kept robbing banks, "Your Honor, that's where they keep the money." This finding may also be a psychological correlate of frontal lobe problems in antisocial behavior, but measures of this cortical abnormality among criminals have yielded mixed results (Hare, 1991; Kandel & Freed, 1989; Lueger & Gill, 1990; Miller, 1987).

Psychological resources (EA) are also significantly below average ($M = 6.65$, $SD = 3.30$) in this sample when compared to nonpatient males ($M = 9.31$, $SD = 2.16$). Nonvolitional affect and ideation (es), however, are also below the mean for nonpatient males ($M = 8.21$, $SD = 2.58$), rendering an average D score ($-.37$) and adjusted D score ($.11$) that predict normative stress tolerance and controls.[11] ASPD males do not appear to have disorders of cognitive or emotional impulse control, on average, but still may have behavioral impulse problems, as measured by PCL–R Item 14 (see Table 5.2). This tripartite distinction among impulse measures appears to be theoretically and empirically meaningful (Rivers, 1993).

Although 67% of the sample produce D scores ≥ 0 and 82% produce adjusted D scores ≥ 0, a small proportion of ASPDs will be expected to show unpredictable, disorganized behavior (20% AdjD < 0). This is, however, the exception to the rule, and compels clinicians to think carefully before they assume impulse control problems in an antisocial individual. A recent study found that high-violence ASPD males addicted to cocaine performed *better* on the Wisconsin Card Sorting Test (WCST) than did low-violence ASPD males addicted to cocaine. The WCST

---

[11]When faced with increased stimulus complexity, however, high Lambda and less than average psychological resources predict maladaptive coping responses on the part of ASPD patients despite the presence of "adequate controls." This may partially explain why their "controls" appear better while in prison.

TABLE 5.3
Structural Rorschach Data for Antisocial Personality Disordered Males ($N = 82$)

Variable	Mean	SD	Min	Max	Freq	Median	Mode	SK	KU
R	21.41	8.42	14.00	52.00	82	19.00	14.00	1.70	2.68
W	9.34	4.11	2.00	26.00	82	8.00	5.00	1.09	2.23
D	9.68	6.79	2.00	37.00	82	8.00	7.00	1.79	4.08
Dd	2.39	2.44	0.00	10.00	62	2.00	0.00	1.23	0.98
Space	2.39	1.85	0.00	8.00	72	2.00	1.00	0.91	0.44
DQ+	5.28	2.73	0.00	12.00	78	5.00	4.00	0.31	−0.05
DQo	13.72	7.17	5.00	38.00	82	11.50	9.00	1.60	2.35
DQv	1.88	2.10	0.00	9.00	55	1.00	0.00	1.36	1.55
DQv/+	0.54	0.82	0.00	4.00	31	0.00	0.00	1.74	3.45
FQX+	0.06	0.24	0.00	1.00	5	0.00	0.00	3.74	12.27
FQXo	10.98	4.30	3.00	30.00	82	10.00	10.00	1.45	4.03
FQXu	4.85	3.19	0.00	14.00	81	4.50	2.00	0.73	−0.11
FQX−	4.90	3.82	0.00	22.00	81	4.00	3.00	2.10	5.64
FQXnone	0.62	1.03	0.00	5.00	32	0.00	0.00	2.23	5.49
MQ+	0.02	0.15	0.00	1.00	2	0.00	0.00	6.28	38.40
MQo	2.04	1.29	0.00	6.00	71	2.00	2.00	0.32	0.08
MQu	0.55	0.92	0.00	4.00	29	0.00	0.00	2.01	4.14
MQ−	0.66	0.89	0.00	5.00	39	0.00	0.00	2.02	6.27
MQnone	0.02	0.15	0.00	1.00	2	0.00	0.00	6.28	38.40
Space−	0.79	1.00	0.00	4.00	41	0.50	0.00	1.33	1.41
M	3.29	2.05	0.00	10.00	76	3.00	3.00	0.51	0.33
FM	3.05	1.86	0.00	10.00	77	3.00	3.00	0.80	1.44
m	1.34	1.57	0.00	10.00	54	1.00	0.00	2.53	10.77
FM+m	4.39	2.59	0.00	13.00	80	4.00	3.00	0.88	0.77
FC	0.85	0.93	0.00	3.00	45	1.00	0.00	0.77	−0.43
CF	1.93	1.98	0.00	9.00	60	1.00	0.00	1.61	3.40
C	0.67	0.90	0.00	4.00	38	0.00	0.00	1.53	2.25
Cn	0.01	0.11	0.00	1.00	1	0.00	0.00	9.05	82.00
FC+CF+C+Cn	3.46	2.42	0.00	11.00	74	3.00	2.00	0.97	1.29
WgSumC	3.36	2.48	0.00	11.00	74	3.00	2.00	0.92	0.86
Sum C'	1.24	1.36	0.00	6.00	52	1.00	0.00	1.37	2.18
Sum T	0.28	0.63	0.00	3.00	17	0.00	0.00	2.67	7.65
Sum V	0.46	0.71	0.00	3.00	30	0.00	0.00	1.64	2.74
Sum Y	1.49	2.04	0.00	11.00	51	1.00	0.00	2.24	6.03
Sum Shd	3.48	3.01	0.00	16.00	72	3.00	3.00	1.46	2.91
Fr+rF	0.67	1.13	0.00	5.00	29	0.00	0.00	1.88	3.11
FD	0.40	0.61	0.00	2.00	28	0.00	0.00	1.24	0.53
F	9.58	5.36	0.00	25.00	81	8.50	6.00	1.15	1.36
Pairs	5.85	3.79	0.00	26.00	81	5.00	4.00	2.28	9.19
Ego	0.38	0.18	0.00	0.93	81	0.33	0.30	0.77	0.92
Lambda	0.94	0.60	0.00	2.50	81	0.77	1.00	1.06	0.57
EA	6.65	3.30	1.00	17.00	82	6.50	6.50	0.48	−0.07
es	7.87	4.44	1.00	22.00	82	7.50	5.00	1.10	1.25
D Score	−0.37	1.24	−5.00	2.00	82	0.00	0.00	−1.40	3.78
Adj D Score	0.11	0.90	−3.00	3.00	82	0.00	0.00	0.09	2.17
SumActvMov	5.18	3.04	1.00	14.00	82	5.00	2.00	0.76	0.32
SumPassMov	2.50	1.84	0.00	8.00	74	2.00	1.00	0.70	−0.09
SumMactv	2.01	1.58	0.00	6.00	69	2.00	1.00	0.65	−0.44
SumMpass	1.28	1.22	0.00	6.00	58	1.00	1.00	1.15	1.73

(Continued)

TABLE 5.3
(Continued)

Variable	Mean	SD	Min	Max	Freq	Median	Mode	SK	KU
IntellIndx	2.56	3.59	0.00	25.00	58	1.00	0.00	3.52	18.52
Zf	11.50	4.20	1.00	25.00	82	11.50	12.00	0.68	1.17
Zd	−0.75	3.80	−9.00	7.00	78	−0.50	−2.00	−0.05	−0.56
Blends	3.35	2.34	0.00	10.00	77	3.00	3.00	0.91	0.69
CSBlnd	0.68	0.90	0.00	4.00	39	0.00	0.00	1.51	2.21
Afr	0.53	0.26	0.15	1.57	82	0.50	0.42	1.46	3.38
Populars	4.94	2.00	1.00	9.00	82	5.00	4.00	0.30	−0.34
X + %	0.53	0.14	0.20	0.85	82	0.52	0.50	−0.01	−0.55
F + %	0.53	0.22	0.00	1.00	79	0.51	0.50	−0.02	0.26
X − %	0.22	0.11	0.00	0.50	81	0.20	0.14	0.73	0.06
Xu%	0.22	0.10	0.00	0.42	81	0.22	0.07	0.01	−0.94
S − %	0.15	0.20	0.00	1.00	41	0.03	0.00	1.45	2.60
IsoIndx	0.20	0.15	0.00	0.60	75	0.15	0.00	0.88	0.27
H	2.17	1.55	0.00	6.00	67	2.00	2.00	0.36	−0.34
(H)	0.96	1.21	0.00	5.00	42	1.00	0.00	1.27	1.03
Hd	1.38	1.49	0.00	6.00	55	1.00	1.00	1.28	1.25
(Hd)	0.32	0.63	0.00	3.00	20	0.00	0.00	2.12	4.48
Hx	0.15	0.47	0.00	3.00	9	0.00	0.00	3.99	18.34
H + (H) + Hd + (Hd)	4.83	2.77	0.00	13.00	80	4.00	4.00	0.79	0.74
A	8.56	3.92	3.00	22.00	82	8.00	5.00	1.40	2.38
(A)	0.58	0.77	0.00	3.00	36	0.00	0.00	1.21	0.92
Ad	2.10	1.90	0.00	9.00	69	2.00	1.00	1.44	2.29
(Ad)	0.11	0.35	0.00	2.00	8	0.00	0.00	3.38	11.83
An	0.69	0.96	0.00	4.00	37	0.00	0.00	1.67	3.03
Art	0.94	1.42	0.00	6.00	39	0.00	0.00	2.00	3.90
Ay	0.62	0.88	0.00	4.00	36	0.00	0.00	1.82	3.97
Bl	0.38	0.78	0.00	4.00	20	0.00	0.00	2.42	6.37
Bt	1.05	1.18	0.00	6.00	52	1.00	1.00	1.73	3.97
Cg	1.05	1.08	0.00	4.00	52	1.00	0.00	1.00	0.47
Cl	0.30	0.60	0.00	3.00	21	0.00	0.00	2.54	8.05
Ex	0.21	0.49	0.00	2.00	14	0.00	0.00	2.38	5.04
Fi	0.49	0.83	0.00	5.00	29	0.00	0.00	2.65	10.14
Food	0.29	0.58	0.00	2.00	19	0.00	0.00	1.86	2.45
Geog	0.21	0.58	0.00	3.00	12	0.00	0.00	3.41	12.56
HHold	0.44	0.74	0.00	3.00	27	0.00	0.00	1.91	3.63
Ls	1.01	1.23	0.00	6.00	46	1.00	0.00	1.64	3.41
Na	0.63	0.97	0.00	5.00	33	0.00	0.00	1.94	4.55
Sc	0.87	1.14	0.00	5.00	41	0.50	0.00	1.65	3.05
Sx	0.65	0.85	0.00	4.00	37	0.00	0.00	1.37	2.00
Xy	0.12	0.53	0.00	4.00	6	0.00	0.00	5.73	37.40
Idio	1.12	1.38	0.00	8.00	50	1.00	0.00	2.28	7.88
DV	1.16	1.79	0.00	12.00	45	1.00	0.00	3.34	16.18
INCOM	1.30	1.28	0.00	5.00	57	1.00	1.00	1.13	1.02
DR	1.58	2.18	0.00	12.00	46	1.00	0.00	2.10	5.94
FABCOM	0.54	0.83	0.00	4.00	30	0.00	0.00	1.71	3.12
DV2	0.01	0.11	0.00	1.00	1	0.00	0.00	9.05	82.00
INC2	0.15	0.39	0.00	2.00	11	0.00	0.00	2.66	6.86
DR2	0.13	0.41	0.00	2.00	9	0.00	0.00	3.22	10.33
FAB2	0.38	0.70	0.00	3.00	23	0.00	0.00	2.02	4.01

(Continued)

TABLE 5.3
(Continued)

Variable	Mean	SD	Min	Max	Freq	Median	Mode	SK	KU
ALOG	0.10	0.40	0.00	3.00	6	0.00	0.00	5.38	33.97
CONTAM	0.06	0.29	0.00	2.00	4	0.00	0.00	5.20	28.94
Sum6SpSc	4.74	4.07	0.00	19.00	74	3.50	3.00	1.38	2.13
Sum6SpScLv2	0.67	1.02	0.00	4.00	33	0.00	0.00	1.71	2.63
WSum6SpSc	15.65	13.68	0.00	69.00	76	13.00	0.00	1.17	1.72
AB	0.50	1.36	0.00	10.00	20	0.00	0.00	4.93	30.23
AG	0.60	0.87	0.00	4.00	33	0.00	0.00	1.58	2.43
CFB	0.02	0.15	0.00	1.00	2	0.00	0.00	6.28	38.40
COP	0.74	0.89	0.00	3.00	40	0.00	0.00	0.86	−0.36
CP	0.02	0.15	0.00	1.00	2	0.00	0.00	6.28	38.40
MOR	1.66	1.81	0.00	8.00	55	1.00	0.00	1.37	1.70
PER	2.11	2.06	0.00	8.00	60	1.00	0.00	0.89	0.05
PSV	0.28	0.53	0.00	2.00	20	0.00	0.00	1.74	2.23

is one measure of frontal lobe performance and rapid adjustment to environmental cues (Rosse, Miller, & Deutsch, 1993).

The experience style of the sample is evenly distributed between introversives (30%) and extratensives (29%), but a large proportion of ASPD males (40%) are ambitent. A proportional increase in this absence of a clear problem-solving style is expected in psychiatric reference groups (Exner, 1990b). Thirty-three percent of our sample exhibit a rigid, inflexible style, either introversive or extratensive, in contrast to the 24% of nonpatient males who do (Exner, 1986a). Meloy (1988) predicted a dominance of extratensives or ambitents among psychopaths, but this does not appear to be the case among ASPD males. A relationship between *extroversion* and criminality has been established (Eysenck, 1967), but should not be equated with Exner's term *extratensive*, although similarities between the terms do exist.

Affect. Affect modulation is considered to be notoriously poor among criminals in prison settings, and is confirmed by our data. The FC:CF+C ratio averages 1:3, and 46% produce a pure C response (*M* = .67). Thirteen percent produce C>1. Nonpatient males' FC:CF+C averages about 2:1, with only 7% producing a pure C (*M* = .08) and 1% producing C>1 (Exner, 1986a). Despite these stark contrasts, ASPD males articulate only half the color responses (SumC = 3.46) that nonpatient males do (SumC = 6.80), and are more affectively avoidant (Afr = .53) than are nonpatient males (Afr = .70). ASPD males are well defended against both internal and external emotionally provoking stimuli. The composite finding of both unmodulated affect and average controls has previously led us to hypothesize that ASPD males use affect in a deliberate manner to control objects in their environment (Gacono & Meloy, 1992). This feeling of "walking on eggshells" around the antisocial male, and fear that his affect may be provoked

TABLE 5.4
ASPD Male (N = 82) Group Means and Frequencies for Select Ratios,
Percentages, and Derivations

$R = 21.41$	$L = .94$	$(L > .99 = 37\%)$

EB = 3.29 : 3.36	EA = 6.65
eb = 4.39 : 3.48	es = 7.87 (FM+m < SUMShading ... 25 30%)
D = −0.37 AdjD = 0.11	

EB STYLE

Introversive	.25	30%
Super-Introversive	.15	18%
Ambitent	.33	40%
Extratensive	.24	29%
Super-Extratensive	.12	15%

EA − es DIFFERENCES:D-SCORES

D Score > 0	.13	16%
D Score = 0	.42	51%
D Score < 0	.27	33%
D Score < −1	.10	12%
AdjD Score > 0	.21	26%
AdjD Score = 0	.46	56%
AdjD Score < 0	.15	18%
AdjD Score < −1	2	2%

AFFECT

FC:CF+C = .85 : 2.60
Pure C = .67   (Pure C > 0 = 46%; Pure C > 1 = 13%)

FC > (CF+C) + 2	0	0%
FC > (CF+C) + 1	4	5%
(CF+C) > FC + 1	.45	55%
(CF+C) > FC + 2	.27	33%

SumC' = 1.24   SumV = .46   SumY = 1.49

Afr = .53   (Afr < .40 = 30%; Afr < .50 = 49%)
S = 2.39   (S > 2 = 39%)
Blends:R = 3.35 : 21.41
CP = .02

INTERPERSONAL

COP = .74   (COP = 0, 51%; COP > 2 = 4%)
AG = .60   (AG = 0, 60%; AG > 2 = 4%)
Food = .29
Isolate/R = .20
H:(H)+Hd+(Hd) = 2.17 : 2.66   (H = 0, 18%; H < 2 = 33%)
(H)+(Hd):(A)+(Ad) = 1.28 : .69
H+A:Hd+Ad = 10.75 : 3.48
Sum T = .28   (T = 0, 79%; T > 1 = 5%)

(Continued)

TABLE 5.4
(Continued)

SELF-PERCEPTION

$3r+(2)/R = .37$	$(48\% < .33; 29\% > .44)$
$Fr+rF = .67$	$(Fr+rF > 0 = 35\%)$
$FD = .40$	
$An+Xy = .81$	
$MOR = 1.66$	$(MOR > 2 = 22\%)$

IDEATION

$a:p = 5.18 : 2.50$	$(p > a+1 = 18\%)$
$Ma:Mp = 2.01 : 1.28$	$(Mp > Ma = 28\%)$
$M = 3.29$	$(M- = .66; M \text{ none} = .02)$
$FM = 3.05 \qquad m = 1.34$	
$2AB+(Art+Ay) = 2.56$	$(2AB+Art+Ay > 5 = 28\%)$
$Sum6 = 4.74$	$(Sum6 > 6 = 38\%)$
$WSum6 = 15.65$	(Level 2 Special Scores $> 0 = 40\%$)

MEDIATION

$Populars = 4.94$	$(P < 4 = 24\%; P > 7 = 12\%)$
$X+\% = .53$	
$F+\% = .53$	
$X-\% = .22$	
$Xu\% = .22$	
$S-\% = .15$	

$X+\% > .89$	0	0%
$X+\% < .70$	70	85%
$X+\% < .61$	54	66%
$X+\% < .50$	34	41%
$F+\% < .70$	66	80%
$Xu\% > .20$	46	56%
$X-\% > .15$	50	61%
$X-\% > .20$	38	46%
$X-\% > .30$	15	18%

PROCESSING

$Zf = 11.50$	
$Zd = -0.75$	$(Zd > +3.0 = 15\%; Zd < -3.0 = 26\%)$
$W:D:Dd = 9.34:9.68:2.39$	$(Dd > 3 = 23\%)$
$W:M = 9.34 : 3.29$	
$DQ+ = 5.28$	
$DQv = 1.88$	$(DQv + DQv/+ > 2 = 41\%)$

CONSTELLATIONS

$SCZI = 6 \ldots 5$	6%	$DEPI = 7 \ldots 4$	5%	$CDI = 5 \ldots 8$	10%
$SCZI = 5 \ldots 2$	2%	$DEPI = 6 \ldots 8$	10%	$CDI = 4 \ldots 10$	12%
$SCZI = 4 \ldots 6$	7%	$DEPI = 5 \ldots 15$	18%		

S-Constellation Positive	4	5%
HVI Positive	8	10%
OBS Positive	0	0%

by others, serves his defensive fantasies of omnipotent control and reinforces his grandiosity.

Thirty-nine percent of our sample are chronically oppositional, negativistic, and angry (S > 2). Space responses, on average, are almost one standard deviation above the mean when compared to nonpatient males ($M = 1.61$, $SD = 1.19$), and only 13% of the latter group elevate > 2. Blends are roughly equivalent to normals.

Affective constraint (C') in ASPD males ($M = 1.24$, $SD = 1.36$) is comparable to nonpatient males ($M = 1.58$, $SD = 1.07$). Dysphoric affect (V), however, is more frequent (37%) in ASPD males than nonpatient males (17%), as is felt helplessness (Y). ASPD males appear to be more anxious ($M = 1.49$) than nonpatient males (.59), but the frequency of a Y response in these two groups is more comparable (62% vs. 42%). The sum total of affect outside conscious awareness and beyond volitional control is virtually identical in the two groups. This is also true for nonvolitional ideation in response to unmet needs (FM) and ideational helplessness (m).

Interpersonal (Object) Relations.   Although this is the least validated cluster in the Comprehensive System, findings are suggestive. ASPD males do not expect cooperation from others (51% COP = 0, $M = .74$) unlike nonpatient males (23% COP = 0, $M = 1.99$). When they do produce COP it is often spoiled (Gacono & Erdberg, 1993). Any other finding would be counterintuitive, and only 4% of ASPD males yield COP > 2.

Aggressive responses, however, are less than expected (60% AG = 0, $M = .60$) when compared to other males (31% AG = 0, $M = 1.17$), if one does not account for the ego syntonic nature of aggressive impulse in ASPDs (see chapter 8). Less aggression *occurring in the present* has been a consistent finding throughout most of our antisocial samples when compared to normals. More detailed measures of symbolized aggression are necessary. Table 5.5 illustrates the aggression scores for our sample. Ninety-six percent produced at least one category, most likely an aggressive content ($M = 3.08$, $SD = 2.28$). AgPast responses are also expected (61%) and may suggest a "victim" or masochistic identification or an unwanted introject,[12] the former more likely in a nonpsychopathic ASPD. The SM response, although an underestimation,[13] was still scored in one out of five protocols, and warrants careful investigation for real-world sadomasochistic acts when it occurs in a protocol. Research concerning sadism and psychopathy is beginning (Holt, 1994).

ASPD males do not assume, by and large, a schizoid stance toward their object world (Klein, 1946). Almost one fourth (23%) show dependency needs

---

[12]We use the traditional psychoanalytic distinction between identification and introject; the former is felt as a part of the self; the latter is experienced internally, but is felt in relation to the self (Meloy, 1985a, 1988).

[13]The scoring of SM requires observation of pleasurable affect on the part of the subject. The SM response may have occurred on some protocols and not have been recorded.

TABLE 5.5

Means, Standard Deviations, Frequencies for Aggression Scores
in Antisocial Personality Disorder and Psychopaths

Category	Antisocial Personality Disorder (N = 82)				Psychopaths (N = 33)			
	M	SD	Frequency	Maximum	M	SD	Frequency	Maximum
Aggressive Movement (AG)	.60	.87	33 (40%)	3	.58	.79	14 (42%)	3
Aggressive Content (AgC)	3.08	2.28	74 (90%)	9	2.63	2.19	29 (88%)	7
Aggressive Past (AgPast)	1.07	1.17	50 (61%)	4	.79	.96	18 (55%)	4
Aggressive Potential (AgPot)	.38	.60	26 (32%)	2	.36	.65	9 (27%)	2
Sadomasochism[a] (SM)	.27	.55	18 (22%)	2	.30	.53	9 (27%)	2
Total Aggression	5.40	3.53	79 (96%)	15	4.64	3.20	32 (97%)	15

[a]SM figures are an underestimation of the true distribution of scores. SM scoring requires that the subject's affect be noted during the Rorschach administration (see chapter 9). We can only be certain of SM scores that were specifically designated and have no way of assessing the presence of SM on protocols where it was not scored.

(Fd M = 0.29), more so than do nonpatient males (15%), and are no more lonesome and isolated (M = .20, SD = .15) than their normal counterparts (Isolate/R). Object representations, however, tell a different story. Part objects or quasi-human whole objects are more prevalent and dominate the ASPD males' intrapsychic world [H:(H)+Hd+(Hd) = 2.17:2.66] when compared to nonpatient males (3.62:2.09), and one third of the ASPD sample produce H < 2. This is very unusual in other males (7%) and suggestive of their interpersonal difficulties.[14] We also see a tendency toward paranoid perception of others in the ASPD sample (H+A:Hd+Ad = 10.75:3.48) with a ratio less than four to one. Only 10% are positive on the HVI, however, a measure that suggests a characterological predisposition to clinical paranoia.

Internal objects of the ASPD male show a dearth of whole, real, and meaningful representations of others. This finding is consistent with an expected abundance of borderline object relations in our sample (see Table 5.6), a measure of the way in which these predominately part objects interact. Ninety-four percent of the sample produce at least one primitive mode of relatedness (PMR; Kwawer, 1980), with the most common being violent symbiosis (50%), narcissistic mirroring (35%), and boundary disturbance (33%). The most primitive category, engulfment, rarely appears (6%), and suggests a psychotic object relation when it does (Kernberg, 1984; Meloy & Gacono, 1992b). The absence of at least one PMR in an ASPD protocol is quite unexpected, and is clinically very important. Most ASPDs produce several (M = 3.44, SD = 2.78).

Attachment capacity is markedly absent in 79% of the sample (T = 0). Although this validated measure of bonding interest is expected to decrease in most psychiatric samples (Exner, 1990b), the nonpatient males rarely evidence such detachment (12% T = 0). The nonpatient and ASPD males samples are indistinguishable, however, when it comes to affectional hunger (T > 1), a rare finding in both groups.

Self-Perception.   The ASPD has an ambivalent and conflicted sense of self-worth. Almost half of our sample compare themselves negatively to others (48% Egocentricity < .33), in contrast to 13% of nonpatient males. Morbid responses are also elevated (M = 1.66, MOR>2 = 22%). Yet 35% produce a reflection response, an indicator of pathological narcissism. This failed grandiosity probably contributes to their dysphoric rumination (V) and mild somatic preoccupation (An+Xy M = .81). These findings, taken together, lend empirical support to the widely accepted notion of a duality in narcissistic disorders: a clinically obvious grandiose self, and a hidden, unloved, disregarded, loathsome, and injured self. These findings may also be a product of the incarcerated status of our sample because, by definition, they have failed to be successful criminals. Comparison to a sample of ASPDs on probation or parole would be very useful to explore this potential situation

---

[14]In Rorschach terminology the psychopath could be described as a (H) living in a pure H world.

TABLE 5.6

Means, Standard Deviations, and Frequencies for Kwawer's (1980) Primitive Modes of Relating in Antisocial Personality Disorder and Psychopaths

Category	M	SD	Frequency	Maximum	M	SD	Frequency	Maximum
			Antisocial Personality Disorder (N = 82)				Psychopaths (N = 33)	
Engulfment	.08	.36	5 (6%)	2	.09	.38	2 (6%)	2
Symbiotic Merging	.34	.69	20 (24%)	3	.51	.83	11 (33%)	3
Violent Symbiosis	.83	1.12	41 (50%)	5	.64	1.03	14 (42%)	5
Birth & Rebirth	.19	.43	15 (18%)	2	.21	.42	7 (21%)	1
Malignant Internal Processes	.19	.46	14 (17%)	2	.18	.46	5 (15%)	2
Metamorphosis & Transformation	.29	.62	19 (23%)	3	.24	.44	8 (24%)	1
Narcissistic Mirroring	.67	1.13	29 (35%)	5	.85	1.15	15 (45%)	4
Separation Division	.16	.46	10 (12%)	2	.21	.55	5 (15%)	2
Boundary Disturbance	.51	.84	27 (33%)	3	.61	.90	13 (39%)	3
Womb Imagery	.18	.50	11 (13%)	2	.18	.53	4 (12%)	2
Total Object Relations Categories	3.44	2.78	77 (94%)	15	3.70	2.72	30 (91%)	11

confound, and delineate the state versus trait aspects of concurrent grandiosity and self-injury.

Only 34% of the ASPDs show a capacity for balanced introspection (FD), while 78% of nonpatient males do. One colleague (Errol Leifer, PhD, personal communication, February 1993) described this lack of a capacity to reflect upon the past (FD) and lack of a capacity to foresee consequences (elevated Lambda) as the perfect existentialist position of the ASPD. Meloy (1988) described them as prisoners of the present.

Ideation. The thinking of the ASPD male is moderately disorganized (WSum6 $M = 15.65$), but with great variance ($SD = 13.65$). The presence of formal thought disorder is clinically significant because all of our subjects were screened to eliminate any Axis I psychotic disorders. The ASPD male usually does not think in a logical or sequential manner,[15] and may act on the basis of irrelevant or tangential thought. These Aristotelian failures, moreover, will not be noticed during a routine mental status exam. Subtle measures such as the Rorschach are necessary to understand a particular ASPD patient's thinking problem.

Although most formal thought disorder can be expected to occur at Level 1 and be dominated by DV, DR, and INCOM responses (Kleiger & Peebles-Kleiger, 1993; Meloy & Singer, 1991), 40% produce one clearly bizarre Level 2 response. The DR+PER combination is also likely, and can be interpreted as a circumstantial or tangential response in the service of self-aggrandizement.

The M– response, very rare in nonpatient males (3%), is quite common (48%), if not expected, in ASPD males. A serious pathognomonic indicator that may suggest, especially with passive movement, a delusional process, the M– response links empathic failure and lost reality testing. It begs the question of whether a stable attachment history in childhood contributes to adequate reality testing in normals.

M is constricted in this population ($M = 3.29$, $SD = 2.05$), yet the Ma:Mp ratio (2:1) is not clinically significant. Mp exceeds Ma in 28% of the sample, but this is also expected in psychiatric reference groups (Exner, 1990b). Nonpatient males rarely utilize this passive-dependent abuse of fantasy (7%). Behavioral flexibility (a:p) in the ASPDs is virtually the same as other males, although 18% are always in need of more data before they will act ($p < a+1$). None of the nonpatient males evidence this characteristic.

Mediation. The translation of external visual stimuli into meaningful internal percepts is generally idiosyncratic and seriously impaired for most ASPD males. A lack of perceptual convergence (X+%) is the norm (85% X+ < 70) with or

---

[15]One psychopathic young man murdered his girlfriend in San Diego, California, and decided he needed to flee the country. He began driving to Canada and was arrested about 30 miles north of the city. When interviewed 2 days later by JRM, he was asked why he didn't go to Mexico, because Canada was 2,000 miles away and Mexico was a 10-minute drive. He responded, "But doc, I don't speak Spanish."

without other thoughts or emotions (80% F+% < 70). Reality testing (X–%) is impaired at a borderline level (> 15) for 61% of the sample, and surprisingly, at a psychotic level (> 30) for 18% of this nonmentally ill group of males. Thirty-nine percent also show no clinically significant impairment in reality testing. S–% is not clinically elevated and needs validation to determine what it means, if anything. ASPDs produce fewer populars ($M = 4.94$) than do normals ($M = 6.90$), a further measure of perceptual unconventionality.

Processing. ASPD males organize percepts as frequently as normal males and appear to do it almost as efficiently (Zd $M = -.75$). There are also proportionally more underincorporators (26%) than among normal males (5%), which may be adult sequelae of ADHD, a comorbid diagnosis with conduct disorder in some children. The ASPD males do not economize well (W:D $M =$ 1:1) yet dwell disproportionately on unusual details (Dd>3 = 23%) when compared to normal males (5%). They perceptually reach beyond their grasp, yet also get sidetracked by the details. This failed striving is apparent in their aspiration ratio (W:M = 9.34:3.39), which is on the cusp of grandiosity (> 3:1).

THE PSYCHOPATHIC MALE SAMPLE

We extracted from our ASPD sample ($N = 82$) all of the primary psychopaths (PCL–R $\geq$ 30, $N = 33$) and present their Comprehensive System data in Table 5.7. Although we did not inferentially compare the ASPD and psychopathic samples since the psychopaths were included in the larger ASPD group, certain distinguishing characteristics are noteworthy. We compared independent samples of psychopathic and nonpsychopathic males in previous studies (Gacono, 1988, 1990; Gacono et al., 1990; Gacono & Meloy, 1991; Gacono & Meloy, 1992).

Affect. The affect modulation of the psychopaths is poorer than ASPD males in general (FC:CF+C = 1:4). They are more affectively avoidant (Afr = .48). Felt helplessness or anxiety is less (Y = 1.0), and in this sample is comparable to nonpatient males. SumShading is also low ($M = 2.76$, $SD = 2.37$) and when considered with the other affect findings provides evidence of the shallow affect noted in psychopaths.

Interpersonal (Object) Relations. The Kwawer (1980) primitive modes of relating (PMR) for the psychopaths (as noted in Table 5.6) indicate that narcissistic mirroring responses (45%), unlike ASPDs in general, are more frequent than violent symbiosis (42%) or boundary disturbance (39%) responses. Symbiotic merging frequency also increases from 24% in the ASPDs to 33% in the psychopaths. At least one Kwawer category should be expected in 9 out of 10 (91%) psychopathic Rorschach protocols.

TABLE 5.7
Structural Rorschach Data for Psychopathic Males ($N = 33$)

Variable	Mean	SD	Min	Max	Freq	Median	Mode	SK	KU
R	21.45	8.51	14.00	52.00	33	19.00	14.00	2.05	4.69
W	8.94	3.13	5.00	15.00	33	8.00	5.00	0.46	−1.02
D	10.03	7.39	2.00	37.00	33	9.00	9.00	1.95	4.81
Dd	2.48	2.33	0.00	9.00	28	2.00	1.00	1.28	1.11
Space	2.36	1.71	0.00	7.00	30	2.00	1.00	0.83	0.23
DQ+	5.30	2.69	0.00	12.00	31	5.00	4.00	0.18	0.37
DQo	13.54	7.76	7.00	38.00	33	10.00	8.00	1.97	3.42
DQv	1.97	2.07	0.00	7.00	23	1.00	0.00	1.06	0.18
DQv/+	0.64	0.82	0.00	3.00	15	0.00	0.00	1.15	0.67
FQX+	0.03	0.17	0.00	1.00	1	0.00	0.00	5.74	33.00
FQXo	11.12	4.53	5.00	30.00	33	10.00	8.00	2.32	8.69
FQXu	4.70	3.35	1.00	14.00	33	4.00	2.00	1.01	0.59
FQX−	4.85	3.73	1.00	18.00	33	4.00	2.00	1.82	3.84
FQXnone	0.76	1.23	0.00	5.00	14	0.00	0.00	2.12	4.57
MQ+	0.03	0.17	0.00	1.00	1	0.00	0.00	5.74	33.00
MQo	1.85	1.33	0.00	5.00	27	2.00	2.00	0.38	−0.31
MQu	0.54	0.87	0.00	4.00	13	0.00	0.00	2.28	6.83
MQ−	0.70	0.81	0.00	3.00	18	1.00	0.00	1.38	2.21
MQnone	0.00	0.00	0.00	0.00	0	0.00	0.00	−	−
Space−	0.70	0.95	0.00	4.00	15	0.00	0.00	1.59	3.03
M	3.12	1.95	0.00	7.00	31	3.00	1.00	0.33	−0.75
FM	3.24	2.19	0.00	10.00	31	3.00	3.00	1.05	1.55
m	1.33	1.86	0.00	10.00	21	1.00	0.00	3.29	14.49
FM+m	4.58	2.99	0.00	13.00	32	4.00	2.00	0.94	0.76
FC	0.64	0.74	0.00	2.00	16	0.00	0.00	0.72	−0.79
CF	1.82	1.81	0.00	9.00	25	2.00	0.00	2.00	6.62
C	0.76	1.03	0.00	4.00	16	0.00	0.00	1.61	2.40
Cn	0.00	0.00	0.00	0.00	0	0.00	0.00	−	−
FC+CF+C+Cn	3.21	2.30	0.00	11.00	30	3.00	2.00	1.26	2.75
WgSumC	3.27	2.43	0.00	11.00	30	2.50	2.00	1.10	1.71
Sum C'	1.24	1.37	0.00	6.00	22	1.00	1.00	1.63	3.40
Sum T	0.12	0.41	0.00	2.00	3	0.00	0.00	3.69	14.03
Sum V	0.39	0.56	0.00	2.00	12	0.00	0.00	1.03	0.12
Sum Y	1.00	1.27	0.00	4.00	18	1.00	0.00	1.35	0.87
Sum Shd	2.76	2.37	0.00	9.00	26	2.00	0.00	1.02	1.14
Fr+rF	0.85	1.15	0.00	4.00	15	0.00	0.00	1.23	0.58
FD	0.45	0.67	0.00	2.00	12	0.00	0.00	1.19	0.31
F	10.03	6.14	2.00	25.00	33	9.00	6.00	1.28	1.08
Pairs	6.24	4.50	1.00	26.00	33	6.00	4.00	2.93	11.48
Ego	0.41	0.18	0.14	0.90	33	0.40	0.25	0.86	0.28
Lambda	1.03	0.69	0.13	2.50	33	0.78	0.38	0.81	−0.43
EA	6.39	3.38	1.00	17.00	33	6.00	4.00	1.00	1.57
es	7.33	4.31	1.00	22.00	33	8.00	5.00	1.18	2.89
D Score	−0.30	1.45	−5.00	2.00	33	0.00	0.00	−1.28	2.58
Adj D Score	0.09	1.13	−3.00	3.00	33	0.00	0.00	−0.19	1.58
SumActvMov	5.12	3.31	1.00	13.00	33	5.00	3.00	0.81	0.02
SumPassMov	2.58	1.92	0.00	6.00	29	2.00	1.00	0.31	−1.27
SumMactv	1.67	1.53	0.00	6.00	26	1.00	1.00	1.10	0.83

(Continued)

TABLE 5.7
(Continued)

Variable	Mean	SD	Min	Max	Freq	Median	Mode	SK	KU
SumMpass	1.45	1.12	0.00	4.00	27	1.00	1.00	0.69	−0.08
IntellIndx	2.82	4.57	0.00	25.00	25	1.00	1.00	3.81	17.73
Zf	11.33	3.26	4.00	19.00	33	12.00	12.00	−0.10	0.94
Zd	−1.20	4.28	−9.00	7.00	31	−1.50	3.00	−0.04	−0.90
Blends	2.91	2.02	0.00	9.00	31	3.00	1.00	0.93	1.31
CSBlnd	0.64	0.99	0.00	4.00	13	0.00	0.00	1.83	3.37
Afr	0.48	0.19	0.20	1.00	33	0.47	0.33	0.75	0.46
Populars	5.06	2.19	1.00	9.00	33	5.00	6.00	0.18	−0.77
X+%	0.54	0.14	0.25	0.79	33	0.56	0.63	−0.19	−0.62
F+%	0.56	0.23	0.00	1.00	32	0.56	0.50	0.03	0.25
X−%	0.22	0.12	0.06	0.50	33	0.19	0.13	0.89	0.25
Xu%	0.21	0.11	0.06	0.41	33	0.19	0.07	0.23	−1.15
S−%	0.11	0.15	0.00	0.50	15	0.00	0.00	1.06	−0.12
IsoIndx	0.18	0.15	0.00	0.56	28	0.15	0.00	0.79	0.10
H	2.09	1.59	0.00	6.00	25	2.00	3.00	0.29	−0.29
(H)	1.03	1.33	0.00	5.00	18	1.00	0.00	1.54	1.92
Hd	1.18	1.45	0.00	6.00	20	1.00	0.00	1.64	2.85
(Hd)	0.33	0.59	0.00	2.00	9	0.00	0.00	1.65	1.84
Hx	0.18	0.58	0.00	3.00	4	0.00	0.00	3.99	17.61
H+(H)+Hd+(Hd)	4.64	2.69	1.00	13.00	33	4.00	4.00	1.67	2.93
A	9.06	4.51	3.00	22.00	33	8.00	8.00	1.49	2.49
(A)	0.51	0.79	0.00	3.00	12	0.00	0.00	1.53	1.84
Ad	2.15	2.17	0.00	9.00	29	1.00	1.00	1.79	3.16
(Ad)	0.09	0.29	0.00	1.00	3	0.00	0.00	2.98	7.34
An	0.91	1.23	0.00	4.00	16	0.00	0.00	1.46	1.45
Art	0.91	1.53	0.00	6.00	14	0.00	0.00	2.12	4.15
Ay	0.64	0.93	0.00	4.00	15	0.00	0.00	2.06	5.08
Bl	0.27	0.57	0.00	2.00	7	0.00	0.00	2.06	3.41
Bt	0.91	0.91	0.00	3.00	21	1.00	1.00	0.97	0.47
Cg	0.94	0.90	0.00	3.00	21	1.00	1.00	0.67	−0.25
Cl	0.42	0.79	0.00	3.00	10	0.00	0.00	2.27	5.30
Ex	0.15	0.44	0.00	2.00	4	0.00	0.00	3.11	9.82
Fi	0.27	0.45	0.00	1.00	9	0.00	0.00	1.07	−0.91
Food	0.27	0.57	0.00	2.00	7	0.00	0.00	2.06	3.41
Geog	0.06	0.24	0.00	1.00	2	0.00	0.00	3.86	13.74
HHold	0.61	0.83	0.00	3.00	15	0.00	0.00	1.58	2.52
Ls	0.79	0.86	0.00	3.00	18	1.00	0.00	0.75	−0.32
Na	0.51	0.87	0.00	3.00	11	0.00	0.00	1.77	2.47
Sc	0.88	1.11	0.00	5.00	18	1.00	0.00	1.85	4.75
Sx	0.61	0.70	0.00	2.00	16	0.00	0.00	0.74	−0.59
Xy	0.06	0.24	0.00	1.00	2	0.00	0.00	3.86	13.74
Idio	1.24	1.12	0.00	4.00	23	1.00	1.00	0.63	−0.36
DV	1.03	1.47	0.00	6.00	17	1.00	0.00	1.96	4.08
INCOM	1.09	1.16	0.00	4.00	21	1.00	0.00	1.11	0.72
DR	1.97	2.57	0.00	12.00	21	1.00	0.00	2.23	6.47
FABCOM	0.64	0.99	0.00	4.00	13	0.00	0.00	1.83	3.37
DV2	0.00	0.00	0.00	0.00	0	0.00	0.00	−	−
INC2	0.12	0.33	0.00	1.00	4	0.00	0.00	2.43	4.17

(Continued)

171

TABLE 5.7
(Continued)

Variable	Mean	SD	Min	Max	Freq	Median	Mode	SK	KU
DR2	0.21	0.48	0.00	2.00	6	0.00	0.00	2.31	5.04
FAB2	0.30	0.58	0.00	2.00	8	0.00	0.00	1.84	2.54
ALOG	0.06	0.24	0.00	1.00	2	0.00	0.00	3.86	13.74
CONTAM	0.15	0.44	0.00	2.00	4	0.00	0.00	3.11	9.82
Sum6SpSc	4.94	4.12	0.00	17.00	30	4.00	2.00	1.02	0.91
Sum6SpScLv2	0.64	1.02	0.00	4.00	12	0.00	0.00	1.74	2.72
WSum6SpSc	16.91	14.04	0.00	46.00	30	14.00	0.00	0.56	−0.74
AB	0.64	1.83	0.00	10.00	8	0.00	0.00	4.49	22.45
AG	0.48	0.71	0.00	2.00	12	0.00	0.00	1.16	0.03
CFB	0.03	0.17	0.00	1.00	1	0.00	0.00	5.74	33.00
COP	0.73	0.88	0.00	3.00	16	0.00	0.00	0.88	−0.28
CP	0.03	0.17	0.00	1.00	1	0.00	0.00	5.74	33.00
MOR	1.36	1.58	0.00	5.00	20	1.00	0.00	1.18	0.55
PER	2.15	1.70	0.00	6.00	27	2.00	1.00	0.40	−0.92
PSV	0.27	0.45	0.00	1.00	9	0.00	0.00	1.07	−0.91

Aggression responses show decreasing trends across all categories, except SM, when only measured in psychopaths (see Table 5.7). This is consistent with our alloplastic hypothesis that ego-syntonic aggression will be less readily verbalized in a Rorschach response, and may actually predict *more frequent* real-world aggression in psychopathic samples (Hare & McPherson, 1984). We expect, however, more frequent sadomasochistic (SM) responses in psychopathic protocols (Meloy, 1992b).

Attachment capacity in psychopaths is virtually nonexistent with 91% producing $T = 0$ protocols. The chronic detachment of the psychopath is clinically expected because relations are defined by power gradients rather than affectional needs (Meloy, 1988).

Self-Perception.   Elevated morbid responses (MOR > 2) decrease slightly in psychopaths (18%), whereas reflection responses increase to 45%. Although indices of self-injury (MOR) and pathological narcissism (Rf) appear together in a small proportion of psychopaths, trends are in the direction of a less conflicted sense of self and a more smoothly functioning grandiosity. The grandiose self-structure of the psychopath appears more resilient to the insults of reality than the comparable structure in the ASPD male who is not psychopathic (Gacono, 1988; Gacono et al., 1990; Gacono & Meloy, 1991, 1993).

Ideation.   M− responses in the psychopath are more frequent (55%) than in ASPD males in general. Likewise the Ma:Mp ratio approaches 1:1, with more psychopaths than ASPDs producing Ma<Mp protocols (39%). This abuse of fantasy in a large proportion of psychopaths, accompanied by a relatively poor grasp of reality, may be (a) a structural indicator of unconscious yearnings for

dependence (Exner, 1986a); (b) a capacity for rehearsal fantasy associated with acts of predatory violence (Meloy, 1988); (c) a risk marker for acts of predation in general (Meloy & Gacono, 1992a; Skoler, 1988); or (d) a finding with no specific meaning for psychopaths. Further research is needed. The psychopath, however, appears to be less inclined to delay action to gather further data than do ASPD males in general (p>a+1 = 6% in psychopaths).

Mediation. Psychopaths are proportionally more underincorporative (33%) than ASPD males in general.

The descriptive differences noted here between our psychopathic subsample and the larger ASPD sample are generally consistent with previous findings that compared psychopaths and nonpsychopaths (Gacono & Meloy, 1992). Future Rorschach research will likely identify subgroups of offenders that are primary psychopaths. To date our research, however, has identified at least one group manifesting a constellation of five variables: T = 0, Y ≤ 1, Fr+rF > 0, egocentricity ratio > .45, and PER ≥ 3. This group of psychopaths often produces proportionally greater numbers of Kwawer's (1980) PMRs.

TRAVIS, A MALE PSYCHOPATH[16]

Travis was a 41-year-old White male evaluated in a maximum security facility after being transferred from minimum security due to potential escape risk and assaultive behavior. Travis openly and frequently bragged about feigning psychiatric symptoms in order to avoid prison (PCL–R Item 5; see Table 5.8). His boasts were consistent with a current diagnosis of malingering, the lack of psychiatric symptoms, and the absence of prescribed psychotropic medications.

Like many psychopaths, Travis reported a childhood history of physical abuse and sadistic treatment. By self-report his father was physically abusive. Travis was incorrigible as a child, frequently fighting, shoplifting, and skipping school (PCL–R Item 12). Had he been diagnosed in childhood, Travis would have been classified as 312.00 Conduct-Disorder, solitary aggressive type (APA, 1987). His lengthy criminal history, primarily comprised of burglaries, began with an arrest at the age of 7 for shoplifting. As an adult Travis primarily supported himself through sales of marijuana and burglaries.

---

[16]Our appreciation is extended to the Rorschach Study Group at Atascadero State Hospital (1991–1993); Drs. Thomas Bade, Richard Morey, Joseph Jenson, Michael Philips, Robert Bodholt, Eric Speth, David Dennis, William Huet, and Alan Roske. Along with Dr. Andy Smith they rescored many of the protocols in our individual case studies. Both friends and colleagues, their participation in the analysis of protocols led to numerous insights concerning the links between Rorschach data and offenses patterns for these subjects. Additional thanks to Drs. Garrett Esseres and Karen Sheppard for their work with the PCL–R at Atascadero State Hospital.

Travis's adult *DSM–III–R* (APA, 1987) diagnosis included Axis I: V65.20, Malingering; 305.90, Psychoactive Substance Abuse NOS; and Axis II: 301.81, Narcissistic Personality Disorder; 301.70, Antisocial Personality Disorder. Themes from his earliest memories were consistent with antisocial (Davidow & Bruhn, 1990; Hankoff, 1987) and narcissistic pathology. Travis' earliest memory of father was aggressive: "Seeing him killing snakes that were infested in the front of the house. No feeling that I am aware of." His earliest memory of mother involved being gazing and being gazed upon: "I recall, as I laid in my baby's crib, looking up and seeing a woman's face looking down upon me. My feeling at this time is that she must have been my mother. There also seems to have been some sort of bright light coming from her face, which now prevents me from recalling exact facial features. However, it seems that her hair was either dirty blond or of a light brown color. Would like to have been picked up."[17] He received a PCL–R score of 37.8 (see Table 5.8), placing him in the severe range of psychopathy (Gacono & Hutton, 1994; Hare, 1991).

Travis' intellectual functioning fell within the average range. Interestingly, staff perceived Travis to be intellectually well above average. Not uncommon in the relationship between staff and narcissistic patients, they are imbued with qualities superior to their actual attributes. While projecting their omnipotence onto the psychopath, staff introject the psychopath's countertransference of impotence (Lasch, 1978). He feels better, and they do too. Countertransference patterns form the template for staff manipulation and splitting.

Overvaluation of the charming psychopath also has real-world correlates. The psychopath may spend inordinate amounts of energy honing a few criminal skills, hence excelling at them.

More likely to be behavioral problems in prison than nonpsychopaths (Hare, 1991), psychopaths within the less secure facility are particularly disruptive.[18] Travis was not an exception. He was routinely involved in "loan sharking/strong

---

[17]There is no empirical support for visual memory recall at this age (< 1 year). It is probable that this "memory" is a wishful mirroring fantasy by the idealized maternal object, often the only authentic attachment (albeit in fantasy) that the psychopath has. This maternal fantasy is often consciously experienced as a search for an idealized woman who is corrosively devalued once the real relationship has begun. By keeping the desire for a return to a maternal symbiosis unconscious, the psychopath can endow the conscious fantasy of an idealized woman with erotic and sexual feelings without violating the oedipal taboo.

[18]Our preliminary findings from a sample of 17 hospital patients who malingered the insanity defense (all had a *DSM–III–R* Axis I diagnosis of malingering, were not prescribed psychotropic medications, and either acknowledged or boasted about feigning psychiatric symptoms) revealed that they represented major management problems within the less secure hospital setting. As a group their mean PCL–R score = 34.72 (all were above 30). Diagnostically all had an Axis II diagnosis of ASPD. Assaultive and manipulative behavior was typical. All 17 had been verbally and physically assaultive in the institution with 6 requiring specialized treatment plans to control their aggression. Manipulative behavior included getting staff to bring in drugs and sexual acting out (six were involved with or married female staff). They were generally considered escape risks with two being successful. After release they didn't fare much better. Of the six who had been released by the court, four eloped from their conditional release programs. One of the subjects' whereabouts is still unknown.

TABLE 5.8
Travis' Psychopathy Checklist–Revised (PCL–R) Scores

1. Glibness/superficial charm	2
2. Grandiose sense of self worth	2
3. Proneness to boredom/need for stimulation	2
4. Pathological lying	2
5. Conning/Manipulative	2
6. Lack of Remorse	2
7. Shallow affect	1
8. Lack of empathy	2
9. Parasitic lifestyle	2
10. Poor behavioral controls	2
11. Promiscuous sexual behavior	omit
12. Early behavioral problems	2
13. Lack of realistic long-term goals	2
14. Impulsivity	2
15. Irresponsibility	2
16. Failure to accept responsibility for actions	2
17. Many marital relationships	1
18. Juvenile delinquency	2
19. Poor risk for conditional release	2
20. Criminal versatility	omit
Total score	34
Prorated score	37.8

arming" of lower functioning inmates. He demonstrated sadistic behavior toward peers. Noted for verbally threatening staff and peers, Travis was suspected of a ganglike assault on a psychotic inmate. The inmate was too frightened to testify against him.

Travis was frequently found with manufactured weapons and other contraband. He boasted about his ability to pick locks. He frequently obtained fraudulent access to peers' lockers and, at times, staff offices. One time he obtained staff addresses and phone numbers which he used in the service of intimidation. So disruptive was his behavior that a specialized treatment plan was devised to prevent his harming other patients or staff.

Monitoring violence potential and teaching increased control over aggression were the goals of Travis' treatment. The team psychologist was chosen to supervise a very structured plan of management. This would include being involved in any necessary physical restraint procedures. Staff splitting was virtually eliminated as only designated staff could interact with Travis. Precursors to sadism and violence were identified. When they occurred Travis was offered least restrictive options such as a PRN medication or voluntary room seclusion.

Initially, room seclusion was necessary. Early interventions met with angry denial of responsibility. Travis was left locked in his room under medical supervision until he could verbalize alternatives to instigating behaviors. When calm, he came out of his room under less confining wrist restraints. Being in wrist restraints in front of staff and schizophrenic inmates was experienced as humiliation. After a period of appropriate interaction Travis could be released from wrist restraints. Although Travis' emotional reactions were directed toward several staff, the treating psychologist became the object of a growing narcissistic transference.

Initially, Travis attempted to include the psychologist in sadomasochistic interactions. One time he approached the psychologist stating, "You enjoy this don't you" (placing him in room seclusion). His grin suggested that, through projective identification, the psychologist had become the container for his sadism. Responses by the psychologist did not foster the negative transference, "Not really, but I believe what I have to offer as a competent professional is to help you learn new ways for dealing with your anger." Interruptions in the projective cycle caused Travis to appear perplexed and confused. On another occasion Travis, with a sadistic grin, queried, "You would probably like to be there when I get the gas chamber." Psychologist, "Possibly, but I wouldn't be celebrating. Rather, I would be sad that you chose to waste your life in such a worthless and irresponsible manner." This met with equal confusion. Travis was unable to recruit the doctor into reenacting his sadistic relationship to his father.

Despite his sadism and psychopathy, an idealizing narcissistic transference also developed rapidly with the psychologist. Travis would place stickers and tape notes on the psychologist's door. He would boast that upon release his psychologist was going to work for him in the spiritual center he would open. Verification of his transference occurred with statements like, "The doctor was like a father I never had."

Time between seclusion began to decrease. Not able to act out his aggression or split staff, Travis became anxious, increasing the dispensing of PRN ibuprofen. Behavior and dress began to conform to the facility codes. Eventually Travis would be transferred to a less secure facility. We would like to highlight aspects of Travis's Rorschach that demonstrate psychopathic character and antisocial orientation and offer insight into potential management/treatment strategies with such a subject in a secure setting.

Travis' Rorschach

Table 5.9 presents Travis' Rorschach protocol. Table 5.10 shows the sequence of scores, and Table 5.11 shows the structural summary, both generated by Rorschach Scoring Program, Version 2 (Exner, Cohen, & Mcguire, 1990). Travis had previously refused psychological testing. This was his first Rorschach.

Structural Interpretation

Travis' Rorschach yielded 16 responses, a valid but constricted protocol. His constriction is more characterological than guarded or defensive (Lambda = .78). Comprised primarily of Ws (76%), constriction is unlikely related to grandiosity (W:M = 12:5) but may reflect a need to maintain imaginary control over all

TABLE 5.9
Travis' Rorschach Protocol

Card I	1) A butterfly.	E: (Rpts S's response) S: This here is the body. Butterfly looks pretty.

Structural Scoring: Wo Fo A P 1.0
Aggression Scores: None.
Primitive Modes of Relating: None.
Defenses: None categorized.

	2) A moth. A deformed moth. How does that sound? I'm getting dramatic.	E: (Rpts S's response) S: It's torn apart here. Especially the claws made me think it was deformed. Something dying, falling apart. Two faces here.

Structural Scoring: Wo FMpo A 1.0 MOR,DR,INC
Aggression Scores: AgC, AgPast
Primitive Modes of Relating: Violent Symbiosis, Separation & Reunion; Boundary Disturbance.
Defenses: Devaluation, omnipotence, projection.

Card II	3) Two cartoon characters putting their hands together like they're engaged in a dance.	E: (Rpts S's response) S: See the faces up here. Cartoonish, hands coming together. Especially the feet coming together, hands are in a form of prayer. E: Cartoonish? S: The faces have ski masks on. E: Ski masks? S: Has things here and on the mouths (subject points to shaded area). Reminds me of the time I had a ski mask on and everyone was looking at me.

Structural Scoring: W+ Mao (2) (H),Cg 4.5 COP,PER
Aggression Scores: None.
Primitive Modes of Relating: None.
Defenses: Devaluation, denial.

Card III	4) This looks pretty. These are musical things in the background. A mixture of a man and woman at the same time with breasts. Touching this table designed in the shape of a face.	E: (Rpts S's response) S: This looks like a musical design. A bow tie here. A man and a woman in one see the breasts and the penises. Table looks like a face with ear muffs coming down over the eyes. Fred Astaire type. E: Musical?

(Continued)

TABLE 5.9
(Continued)

S: This reminds me of my sister, she
owns a ballroom in Chicago. She
tried to teach me ballroom dancing.
People there in black tuxedos and
ties . . . etc.

Structural Scoring: W+ Mao (2) H,Sx,Hh P 5.5 PER,INC2
Aggression Scores: None.
Primitive Modes of Relating: Symbiotic Merging.
Defenses: Massive Denial, splitting, idealization.

    5) A bow tie in the middle.

E: (Rpts S's response)
S: Yeah.

Structural Scoring: Do 3 Fo Cg
Aggression Scores: None.
Primitive Modes of Relating: None.
Defenses: None categorized.

Card IV   6) It looks like some kind of animal
here. Exotic creature, that has been
flayed. Like you would find on
another planet like a bear rug.

E: (Rpts S's response)
S: Tail, head like an anteater, tail here.
Like a carpet, cleaned out. This is
the fur out here, this here (points to
outline).

Structural Scoring: Wo Fo (Ad) 2.0 MOR
Aggression Scores: AgPast
Primitive Modes of Relating: None.
Defenses: Idealization, splitting, projection.

Card V   7) This looks like a bat of some sort.

E: (Rpts S's response)
S: At first saw this as a aura. I saw a
man here with antennas coming out,
vetoed it, saw it as a bat.
E: Bat?
S: Wings, antennalike ears.

Structural Scoring: Wo Fo A P 1.0 DR
Aggression Scores: None.
Primitive Modes of Relating: None.
Defenses: Rationalization.

Card VI   8) Violin.

E: (Rpts S's response)
S: The first thing that popped into my
head.

Structural Scoring: Wo F− Id 2.5
Aggression Scores: None.
Primitive Modes of Relating: None.
Defenses: None categorized.

(Continued)

TABLE 5.9
(Continued)

9) Flayed squirrel, tail back here.

E: (Rpts S's response)
S: A squirrel that's been laid out. Tail, front legs, back legs.
E: Flayed?
S: Opened out.
E: I'm not sure I see it as you do?
S: Tail, head seems to be missing, took the head off just wanted furry part.
E: Furry?
S: Stringy part like hair.

Structural Scoring: Wo mpo Ad 2.5 MOR
Aggression Scores: AgPast
Primitive Modes of Relating: Violent Symbiosis, Separation & Reunion.
Defenses: Projection, devaluation.

Card VII 10) Twins being born. Ponytails sticking up in the air.

E: (Rpts S's response)
S: Coming out of a vagina, something in early fifties. It's the way they used dress. Engaged in a dance of life. Identical twins.

Structural Scoring: W+ Mau (2) H,Sx,Cg 2.5 AB,INC2,FAB2
Aggression Scores: None.
Primitive Modes of Relating: Birth & Rebirth, Womb Imagery.
Defenses: Massive Denial.

Card VIII 11) Now this looks like an animal. A colorful planet, the water down there, with its reflection in the water. It's reaching out from a rock, to a stump, can't figure out why it's going over there. It has its own reason. This is real pretty.

E: (Rpts S's response)
S: There's the rock here it's reaching over.
E: You said colorful?
S: Coloring, see the face, eyes. Where the nose comes down. Trying to figure out if it went over there just to see it's own reflection.
E: Water?
S: The reflection makes it look like a reflection.

Structural Scoring: W+ Fr.CF.FMao A,Na P 4.5 DR2
Aggression Scores: None.
Primitive Modes of Relating: Narcissistic Mirroring.
Defenses: Rationalization, idealization.

Card IX 12) It looks like a shrimp of some sort. Transparent shrimp, you can see through it and see its organs and its functions.

E: (Rpts S's response)
S: Internal organs, seems transparent. Shrimp, can be seen through. There is a similarity because I looked and inside a shrimp, like a jellyfish.

(Continued)

TABLE 5.9
(Continued)

Structural Scoring: Wv FD− A,An 5.5 PER,DV
Aggression Scores: None.
Primitive Modes of Relating: Boundary Disturbance.
Defenses: Omnipotence.

Card X   13) Two little creatures here, getting
together over the empty space. They
look identical, trying to communicate with each other. A chasm down
here, if they fall something down
here will catch them.

E: (Rpts S's response)
S: Face of a fish. Coming together for
agreement. A disagreement brought
them together. Hanging over a cliff.
Danger doesn't exist. Something will
catch them if they fall. It's interesting, may affect the whole communication. This is a device or life form
itself. Part of the agreement they are
making, have to put one foot over
the edge if you should fall something to catch you. A fishface of a
fish watching them.

Structural Scoring: WS+ Mau (2) (A),Ls 6.0 DV,COP,FAB
Aggression Scores: None.
Primitive Modes of Relating: Womb Imagery.
Defenses: Higher denial, intellectualization.

14) Here are two crabs.

E: (Rpts S's response)
S: Green part is a claw, little things
here.

Structural Scoring: Do 1 Fo (2) A P
Aggression Scores: AgC
Primitive Modes of Relating: None.
Defenses: None categorized.

15) Here are life forms of their own
maybe branches.

E: (Rpts S's response)
S: Can't make it into any life form
itself.

Structural Scoring: Do 15 Fu Bt DV
Aggression Scores: None.
Primitive Modes of Relating: None.
Defenses: None categorized.

16) Device floating in the air or another
creature.

E: (Rpts S's response)
S: All these things come together to watch
these two interact, at least for them
maybe it affects everything else.

Structural Scoring: D+ 3 mp.Mpu Id,(A) 4.5 DR
Aggression Scores: None.
Primitive Modes of Relating: Boundary disturbance.
Defenses: None categorized.

TABLE 5.10
Travis' Rorschach Sequence of Scores

Card						P		
Card I	1	Wo	Fo		A	P	1.0	
	2	Wo	FMpo		A		1.0	MOR,DR,INC
Card II	3	W+	Mao	(2)	(H),Cg		4.5	COP,PER
Card III	4	W+	Mao	(2)	H,Sx,Hh	P	5.5	PER,INC2
	5	Do 3	Fo		Cg			
Card IV	6	Wo	Fo		(Ad)		2.0	MOR
Card V	7	Wo	Fo		A	P	1.0	DR
Card VI	8	Wo	F−		Id		2.5	
	9	Wo	mpo		Ad		2.5	MOR
Card VII	10	W+	Mau	(2)	H,Sx,Cg		2.5	AB,INC2,FAB2
Card VIII	11	W+	Fr.CF.FMao		A,Na	P	4.5	DR2
Card IX	12	Wv	FD−		A,An		5.5	PER,DV
Card X	13	WS+	Mau	(2)	(A),Ls		6.0	DV,COP,FAB
	14	Do 1	Fo	(2)	A	P		
	15	Do 15	Fu		Bt			DV
	16	D+ 3	mp.Mpu		Id,(A)		4.5	DR

aspects of the stimulus field (blot). In the process of scanning, Travis is efficient ($Zd = -.50$) but does not pay great attention to details ($Dd = 0$).

Four-square analysis indicates that Travis has fewer ($EA = 6.0$) psychological resources than would be expected in nonpatient males ($EA = 9.30$, $SD = 2.16$). His limited resources are not currently overtaxed with affect ($T = 0$, $Y = 0$, $C' = 0$, $V = 0$, $es = 4$) or nonvolitional ideation ($FM = 2$, $m = 2$), and therefore do not impair his organization and controls ($D = 0$, $AdjD = +1$). Psychopathic defenses such as grandiosity ($Rf = 1$) and acting out ($AG = 0$) may facilitate rapid discharge of affect ($C' = 0$; $FC:CF+C = 0:1$) allowing for smooth psychological operations under most circumstances.

Travis is pervasively introversive, an unusual finding in psychopaths. Both EA and es contain predominately movement responses (9 of 10), 2 of which are little m and can be interpreted as his sense of being "shot at." Distinguished from the Jungian introversive, Travis' introversive style suggests gratification through an inner life, likely imbued with peculiar (his single Mp occurs with an mpu blend) and narcissistic fantasy ($Fr = 1$; $3r+(2)/R = .50$; $DR = 4$; $MOR = 3$) that may be interpreted as an affectless rumination about his grandiose failures.

Travis' affects are not characterized by a tendency toward emotional explosiveness ($C = 0$) and are virtually absent. There is no indication of a chronically angry character pattern ($S = 1$) or affective constraint ($C' = 0$). Affect in others is normatively processed ($Afr = .60$). Affective states suggesting dysphoria are notably absent ($C' = 0$, $V = 0$, $Y = 0$, no Color/shading blends). Sexual preoccupation is present ($Sx = 2$) and characterized by gender ambiguity (Response 4) and hysterical regression (Response 10).

Travis appears to exhibit an expectation of cooperativeness in interpersonal interactions ($COP = 2$). Upon closer examination, however, both COPs are

TABLE 5.11
Travis' Rorschach Structural Summary

Location Features	Determinants — Blends	Determinants — Single	Contents	S-Constellation
				NO..FV+VF+V+FD > 2
			H = 2, 0	NO..Col-Shd Bl > 0
Zf = 12	Fr.CF.FM	M = 4	(H) = 1, 0	YES..Ego < .31, > .44
ZSum = 37.5	m.M	FM = 1	Hd = 0, 0	NO..MOR > 3
ZEst = 38.0		m = 1	(Hd)= 0, 0	NO..Zd > +− 3.5
		FC = 0	Hx = 0, 0	NO..es > EA
W = 12		CF = 0	A = 6, 0	YES..CF+C > FC
(Wv = 1)		C = 0	(A) = 1, 1	YES..X+% < .70
D = 4		Cn = 0	Ad = 1, 0	NO..S > 3
Dd = 0		FC' = 0	(Ad)= 1, 0	NO..P < 3 or > 8
S = 1		C'F = 0	An = 0, 1	NO..Pure H < 2
		C' = 0	Art = 0, 0	YES..R < 17
DQ		FT = 0	Ay = 0, 0	4.....TOTAL
......(FQ−)		TF = 0	Bl = 0, 0	
+ = 6 (0)		T = 0	Bt = 1, 0	Special Scorings
o = 9 (1)		FV = 0	Cg = 1, 2	
v/+ = 0 (0)		VF = 0	Cl = 0, 0	
v = 1 (1)		V = 0	Ex = 0, 0	

	Lv1	Lv2
DV	= 3 × 1	0 × 2
INC	= 1 × 2	2 × 4
DR	= 3 × 3	1 × 6
FAB	= 1 × 4	1 × 7
ALOG	= 0 × 5	
CON	= 0 × 7	
SUM 6	= 12	
WSUM6	= 39	

Single (cont.): FY = 0, YF = 0, Y = 0, Fr = 0, rF = 0, FD = 1, F = 7

Contents (cont.): Cl = 0, 0 · Ex = 0, 0 · Fd = 0, 0 · Fi = 0, 0 · Ge = 0, 0 · Hh = 0, 1 · Ls = 0, 1 · Na = 0, 1 · Sc = 0, 0 · Sx = 0, 2 · Xy = 0, 0 · Id = 2, 0

AB = 1			CP = 0	
AG = 0			MOR = 3	
CFB = 0			PER = 3	
COP = 2			PSV = 0	

Form Quality

	FQx	FQf	MQual	SQx
+ =	0	0	0	0
o =	10	5	2	0
u =	4	1	3	1
− =	2	1	0	0
none =	0	−	0	0

(2) = 5

Ratios, Percentages, and Derivations

R = 16   L = 0.78

EB = 5: 1.0	EA = 6.0	EBPer = 5.0		
eb = 4: 0	es = 4	D = 0		
	Adj es = 3	Adj D = +1		

FM = 2 :	C' = 0	T = 0	FC:CF+C = 0 : 1 COP = 2 AG = 0
m = 2 :	V = 0	Y = 0	Pure C = 0 Food = 0
a:p = 5: 4	Sum6 = 12		Afr = 0.60 Isolate/R = 0.25
Ma:Mp = 4: 1	Lv2 = 4		S = 1 H:(H)Hd(Hd) = 2: 1
2AB+Art+Ay = 2	WSum6 = 39		Blends:R = 2:16 (HHd):(AAd) = 1: 3
M− = 0	Mnone = 0		CP = 0 H+A:Hd+Ad = 8: 2

P = 5	Zf = 12	3r+(2)/R = 0.50
X+% = 0.63	Zd = −0.5	Fr+rF = 1
F+% = 0.71	W:D:Dd = 12: 4: 0	FD = 1
X−% = 0.13	W:M = 12: 5	An+Xy = 1
S−% = 0.00	DQ+ = 6	MOR = 3
Xu% = 0.25	DQv = 1	

SCZI = 2	DEPI = 3	CDI = 2	S-CON = 4	HVI = No	OBS = No

Note. From Exner (1990a). Copyright 1990 by John E. Exner, Jr. Reprinted by permission.

spoiled. His first COP (Response 3) contains a quasi-human content and a PER; his second (Response 13) contains a quasi-animal content, S, Fu, and a DV and FAB special scores. Travis' perceptions of interpersonal relationships are shaded by narcissistic self-focus, tainted by devaluation, and limited by inordinate needs to control others (PER = 3). Somewhat isolative (.25), Travis shows no capacity to form an emotional bond (T = 0). The paucity of pure H (H = 2) in his record further supports a deficient desire or capacity to perceive others as whole and meaningful objects.

Travis' self-focus (3r+(2)/r = .50), pathological narcissism (Fr = 1), and propensity to self-aggrandize (PER = 3) may function defensively to counteract a basic sense of being damaged (MOR = 3). He is not insightful concerning this duality, and whatever his capacity for introspection, it is filtered through a distorted mirror (FD–, PER,DV).

Despite pervasive thought disorder (WSum6 = 39) Travis is not schizophrenic (SCZI = 2, M– = 0, ALOG = 0, CON = 0). Rather his thinking is spoiled by idiosyncratic word choice (DV = 3), self-indulgent rambling (DR = 4), and peculiar integrations (INC = 3; FAB = 2). Integration stretches his resources (five of six DQ+ evidence special scores). Perceptual accuracy (X+% = 63, F+% = 71) and reality testing (X–% = 13) are mildly impaired and typical of character pathology rather than schizophrenia. Travis did not score positive for any of the constellations.

Travis' structural data reveal a personality with less than normative resources, yet free of affect; a personality where adequate controls are bolstered by narcissistic defenses which, although intrapsychically effective, predict vacuous interpersonal relations.

Interpretation of Scoring Sequence

Travis is unable to maintain adequate perceptual accuracy for all 10 cards. His primitive defenses are only partially effective as impulse gradually affects perceptual accuracy. Eighty-nine percent of the first nine responses yield adequate FQx (o or +) compared to only 29% of the final seven. Travis does not end on a positive note. Aided by a popular, he manages one adequate FQx response out of four produced to Card X. He finishes with an mp.Mpu blend on the final response (#16). The scoring sequence suggests a qualitatively different interpretation of his "normal controls" (D = 0, AdjD = +1). His inability to maintain perceptual accuracy over the 10 cards sheds light on the tenuous nature of his limited resources (EA = 6.0) when subjected to the continual stress of an ambiguous task. This may be particularly relevant when the stimulus is affect provoking.

Travis begins the Rorschach with an adequate, popular, pure F response. Five populars appear in the record, all with good form quality. Problems surface quickly as percepts (FMp; MOR) stimulated on Response 2 result in an inappropriate combination (INC) and derailment from the task (DR). The COP produced on Response 3 is tainted by quasi-human content and a PER. The Sx content on Response 4, despite a popular, results in major cognitive slippage (INC2). He recovers on Response 5, relying on the bland and ordinary (Do).

Card IV again elicits a sense of damaged self (MOR). The use of a popular does not prevent loose thinking (DR) on Card V. Affected by the pull of Card VI, Travis produced –FQx on Response 8 whereas Response 9 suggests a sense of helplessness (mp) and contains a third MOR. Sexual content (Sx) appears with severe disorientation (FQxu, AB, INC2, FAB2) on Card VII. Narcissistic defenses (Fr.CF) and a popular aid a partial recovery on VIII (o FQx, but DR2).

After Card VIII perceptual accuracy suffers. Response 12 contains his only DQv produced with an FD– and An content. Travis had difficulty integrating the dysphoric colors of Card IX. Three of the four responses on Card X evidence u FQx.

Interpretation of Content

Structural and sequence analysis aids in understanding Travis' resources, controls, and the nature and extent of his severe and pervasive thought disorder. Content analysis vividly portrays Axis II pathology, highlighting the commingling of narcissistic and hysterical traits within psychopathic character structure.

Rather than relying on single indices or signs, Travis' protocol lends itself to interpreting content patterns. The presence of a single narcissistic mirroring response (generally a reflection) may not necessitate an interpretation of pathological narcissism. Travis' reflection response, which contains a CF, and content, ". . . It's reaching out . . . can't figure out why it's going over there . . . Trying to figure out if it went over there just to see it's own reflection," suggest a greater intensity of self-absorption than might occur in a simple modal reflection not indicative of pathological narcissism (see chapter 7). Personalized content, "Reminds me of the time I had a ski mask on and everyone was looking at me" (#3), "This reminds me of my sister, she owns a ballroom in Chicago. She tried to teach me . . ." (#4), "There is a similarity because I looked inside a shrimp . . ." (#12), "identical twins" (#10), and a sense of being observed, "A fishface of a fish watching them" (#13; also #3 again) support exaggerated self-focus and the need for mirroring. The ventral sensitivity of Travis' narcissism is his damaged identity, "a deformed moth . . . torn apart here" (#2), "Exotic creature that has been flayed" (#6), "Flayed squirrel" (#9), suffused with aggression. Travis is a poorly integrated narcissistic disorder. His Rorschach suggests failed grandiosity. Additionally, the use of omnipotence and devaluation are common narcissistic defenses.

Similar hysterical traits are suggested by an impressionistic style, ". . . Saw an aura . . ." (#7), ". . . Engaged in a dance of life . . ." (#10), and the pull of color, "Looks pretty . . ." (#4), "A colorful planet . . . This is real pretty . . ." (#11). Not relying on the narcissistic defenses of devaluation and omnipotence, Travis' protocol contains idealization, "Exotic creature . . ." (#6; also see #4 and

#11) and denial, "Hands are in a form of a prayer" (#3, see also #13). Consistent with his FD, Travis evaluated his Rorschach performance accurately, "I'm getting dramatic" (#2).

The primitivity of Travis' defensive operations are revealed through the use of splitting and exemplified by the presence of massive denial on Responses 3 and 10 where he offers, "A mixture of a man and woman at the same time with breasts," and, "Twins being born. Ponytails sticking up ... engaged in a dance of life." Content such as "... dying, falling apart." (#2), "... saw an aura ..." (#7), "Transparent shrimp, you can see through it ..." (#12), "Device floating in the air ..." (#16) reflect tenuous defenses and weak and fluid boundaries.

Content of Card X is particularly interesting in light of the developing narcissistic transference with the examiner (his treating psychologist). It could indicate preconscious associations to their relationship ("Two little creatures here, getting together over the empty space ... trying to communicate with each other ... if they fall something down here will catch them ... A disagreement brought them together. Hanging over a cliff. Danger doesn't exist. Something will catch them if they fall ... Part of the agreement they are making, have to put one foot over the edge ... ," and later, "... All these things come together to watch these two interact, at least for them maybe it affects everything else") or simply another way of maintaining control through devaluation of the examiner—perhaps both.

Summary

Like Karen's protocol (see chapter 4) Travis' contains all levels of defense: neurotic, borderline, and psychotic. Defenses such as rationalization and higher denial, when supported by splitting and primitive forms of denial, are more likely to suggest lower levels of personality organization. Greater distortion in cognition processes (WSum6) and an increased absurdity of rationalizations are expected in psychopaths rather than neurotics. Neurotics might demonstrate defensive stability and less cognitive slippage through the use of repression rather than a predominance of splitting, omnipotence, projection identification or devaluation.

Travis' protocol is positive for all five variables associated with psychopathy (T = 0, Y = 0, Fr > 0, Egocentricity ratio = .50, PER = 3). Additionally, the production of nine PMRs (Kwawer, 1980) suggests a severe narcissistic disorder (antisocial) organized at a borderline level. Travis' Rorschach provides clues to the possibility of a narcissistic transference that would later be observed. The presence of an FD– might signal a capacity, although distorted, for introspection. Dysphoric affect was not indicated; however, the disorientation on Card IX and the presence of two ms might suggest the potential for affect that is currently split off or discharged. The presence of higher level defenses along with three idealization responses (infrequently produced in ASPDs) bodes well for a potential narcissistic transference, as do several themes suggesting the need for mirroring. Therapeutic structure in the treatment milieu and the treating psychologist's refusal to enter into sadistic/masochistic interactions with Travis, despite this expectation (spoiled COPs; AgPast = 3; Violent Symbiosis = 1), were crucial for transference development. Regressive content such as womb imagery and birth-rebirth, not suffused with aggression, might suggest a softer, needing quality to his narcissism.

Not all psychopaths have the capacity for the type of transference exhibited by Travis. Some develop only the most primitive and predatory relationship to the therapist (Meloy, 1988). Travis' frustration tolerance increased. He learned additional strategies for managing his aggression. Possibly Travis was able to internalize parts of the treating psychologist. Although significant changes occurred during his institutional management, he remained severely narcissistic and psychopathic. Only time will tell if our "treatment" was corrective or just created a better functioning psychopath.

CHAPTER 6

The Antisocial
Schizophrenic Male

*I am your God and you will bow under me feet . . . Look and see you fools,
you will not proceed much further . . . How dare you turn away my invitations
of mercy . . . Do not fear the fear of man—fear me, for I have you in my
snare (p. 3).*

—David Koresh, leader of the Branch Davidians, Waco, Texas,
reported in the *Los Angeles Times*, April 20, 1993

Forensic psychologists often struggle with the clinical differentiation of madness
and badness. The antisocial personality disordered individual (bad) is generally
held accountable for her or his actions, while the psychotic patient (mad) may
not be. Motive and intent, however, may be fueled by character pathology (bad),
psychosis (mad), or both. The need for measurable demarcation may have, in
part, influenced the *DSM–III* (APA, 1980) to disallow a concurrent diagnosis of
schizophrenia and antisocial personality disorder.

This rather curious and misguided attempt to bring clarity to the interface
between a biochemical disorder of the brain and severe character pathology was
aborted 7 years later in *DSM–III–R* (APA, 1987). Criteria in the revised *DSM–III*
and *DSM–IV* (APA, 1994) allow for the concurrent diagnosis of schizophrenia and
antisocial personality disorder (ASPD), a change consistent with clinical observations attesting to the presence of these dual-diagnosed subjects. These schizophrenic ASPDs challenge the clinicians' assessment skills as their actions must be
carefully evaluated when issues of madness and badness need clarification. It is
beyond the scope of the *DSM* series, however, to answer questions concerning

etiology, the relationship between biology and psychodynamics, and effective treatment.

In this chapter we explore the relationship between schizophrenia, psychopathy, and ASPD.[1] Meloy's (1988) theoretical integration of psychopathic character and psychotic personality organization is used as a template for our discussion. We present Rorschach data from 80 dual-diagnosed (schizophrenia and ASPD, some of which were also psychopathic) subjects, comparing select variables to ASPD males ($N = 82$; see chapter 5) and Exner's (1990b) inpatient schizophrenic sample ($N = 320$). Personality differences between the schizophrenic ASPDs and schizophrenics who do not have the behavioral histories that warrant an ASPD diagnosis are suggested by these latter comparisons. The personality differences elaborated by our findings are consistent with behavioral data that indicate a positive relationship between previous arrest history (antisocial behavior) and future violence (Cirincione, Steadman, Robbins, & Monahan, 1992; Link, Andrews, & Cullen, 1992; Rice & Harris, 1992) and the predictive value of historical data such as alcohol abuse, past aggressive behavior, level of supervision, and level of psychopathy among schizophrenic samples (Rice & Harris, 1992).[2] These studies suggest that characterological elements fuel violent and chronic criminal behavior.

We conclude this chapter with the presentation of two case studies. The first case, Sam, was a schizophrenic ASPD whose psychopathic personality structure organized his paranoid schizophrenia. The nature and extent of Sam's psychopathology was not evident upon initial meeting. Sam met criteria for both ASPD and primary psychopathy (PCL–R ≥ 30) and offered a rather bland and constricted Rorschach. The second case, Ed, was a schizophrenic ASPD whose character style became evident when psychotic symptoms were controlled through administration of psychotropic medications. Ed met the *DSM–III–R* (APA, 1987) criteria for ASPD but was not psychopathic by PCL–R criteria. We now begin with a brief look back at the Rorschach and schizophrenia.

THE RORSCHACH AND SCHIZOPHRENIA

The Rorschach assessment of schizophrenia has been a concern since the test's beginnings. In *Psychodiagnostics* (1921/1942) Rorschach focused on differential

---

[1]The interested reader is referred to chapter 5 for the antisocial personality disorder (ASPD) criteria and to chapters 5 and 7 for a review of the differences between ASPD and psychopathy.

[2]Rice and Harris (1992) found that the Psychopathy Checklist–Revised (PCL–R) correlated significantly with both general ($p < .001$) and violent ($p < .01$) recidivism in their schizophrenic sample, suggesting character pathology among their subjects, demonstrating the predictive validity of the PCL–R with schizophrenic offenders, and supporting the clinical importance of assessing for degree of psychopathy in forensic psychiatric patients.

diagnosis and included 188 schizophrenics as subjects (46% of his original sample). In America Rorschach and schizophrenia research first appeared in the psychiatric literature in 1935 (Dimmick, 1935–1936; Hackfield, 1935). Shortly thereafter three major publications gave impetus to the use of the test in understanding schizophrenia: Beck's (1938) monograph, *Personality Structure in Schizophrenia*; Rickers-Ovsiankina's (1938) comparative study of normal and schizophrenic patients; and Benjamin and Ebaugh's (1938) validity study of the Rorschach (Weiner, 1966). These early works were subjected to rigorous review (Beck, 1938, 1943; Klopfer & Kelly, 1942).

Other significant contributions followed. Rapaport, Gill, and Schafer (1946/1948) devoted a portion of their classic text to the Rorschach and the differential diagnosis of schizophrenia, particularly in relation to cognitive functions. They cited as one of three conditions under which a psychosis could be diagnosed, "if the Rorschach test record is clearly psychotic, whether the other tests support this diagnosis or remain inconclusive" (p. 524).

Schafer (1948) pointed out, in his case study sequel to his book with David Rapaport and Merton Gill, that "the test responses of almost all schizophrenic subjects are greatly shaped by enduring, nonschizoid aspects of premorbid character make-up" (p. 62). Here we see a wise clinical insight that we want to underscore in this chapter: Our essential task is to define the manner in which the schizophrenia and the character structure interact to determine the individual's behavior. Schafer defined character as continuous adjustment efforts when confronting problem situations. His case book delineated the Rorschach expression of unclassified, paranoid, incipient and simple schizophrenia, and "schizophrenic character" (p. 86), what we would now refer to as borderline personality disorder.

Schafer's third book (1954), *Psychoanalytic Interpretation in Rorschach Testing*, focused on the interpersonal, thematic, and defense analyses of the Rorschach process, and thus subsumed diagnoses under these major dynamic and structural variables. He wrote,

> it would be necessary and desirable to clarify the ways in which and the extent to which schizophrenic Rorschach phenomena are abortive or hypertrophied forms of such normal psychic phenomena as dreams, daydreams, fluctuations of concentration efficiency, sporadic defensive ineffectiveness, momentary or circumscribed loss of clarity about one's social role or about the line between fact and fantasy. (p. 429)

It was from this psychodynamic and psychostructural orientation of Schafer and others (Sherman, 1960), that Weiner's (1966) consummate text entitled, *Psychodiagnosis in Schizophrenia*, was born. His premise was that schizophrenia is a phenomenological diagnosis based on observable ego impairments in six functional areas: thought processes (focus, reasoning, concept formation), relation to reality (reality testing, reality sense), object relations, defensive operations, autonomous functions, and synthetic functions. Using the Rorschach, Draw a Person, and Wechsler Adult Intelligence Scale (WAIS), he reviewed the research and assessment literature and provided the benchmark text for the psychological testing of schizophrenia. That same year Schachtel (1966) touched upon schizophrenia to illustrate the perceptual hold, the problem of fluidity, and the disintegration of form and color responses on the Rorschach. Both of these books are, unfortunately, out of print; but as Peterson (1992a) commented concerning Schachtel's book, they "should never be out of the mature Rorschacher's mind" (p. 647).

Exner (1986a) used the schizophrenic core characteristics of disordered thinking and inaccurate perception to develop his Schizophrenia Index (SCZI). He was guided by previous research, some of which we have already mentioned (Beck, 1965; Piotrowski & Lewis, 1950; Rapaport et al., 1946/1948; Theisen, 1952; Watkins & Stauffacher, 1952; Weiner, 1966). The most recent version of his Schizophrenia Index (Exner, 1991) is composed of perceptual and thinking measures, and consists of 10 variables spread across six tests:

1. $X+\% < .61$ and $S-\% < .41$ or $X+\% < .50$.
2. $X-\% > .29$.
3. Sum $FQ- >$ SumFQu or Sum $FQ- >$ Sum $(FQo + FQ+)$.
4. Sum Level 2 Special Scores > 1 and Fabcom2 > 0.
5. Sum6 Special Scores > 6 or Weighted Sum 6 Special Scores > 17 (cutoffs adjusted for children).
6. $M- > 1$ or $X-\% > .40$.

Modifications from the earlier version of the SCZI include the addition of the $S-\%$ and the demarcation of Special Scores into two levels. As a result of 50 discriminant function analyses, the aforementioned index provided the lowest false positive and highest true positive rates for diagnosing schizophrenia. Exner (1991) used a "Monte Carlo" procedure in his analyses, which consisted of five random drawings of 100 subjects each from five clinical pools: first-admission schizophrenics; first-admission major affective disorders; outpatients; adolescent behavior disorders; and adult nonpatients.

Scrutiny of his data indicates true positive rates for schizophrenia ranging from 78%–88%, and false positive rates ranging from 0%–11% (the highest rate was from the affective disordered group). Likewise, false negative rates ranged from 12%–22% and true negative rates ranged from 89%–100%. The SCZI is most robust when the patient scores positive on all six tests; false positive rates at this level did not exceed 1%. Clinicians should be cautious, however, when using the SCZI in chronic schizophrenic populations, as we demonstrate with our data.[3] Exner (1991) also sounded a cautionary note in his data concerning inpatient schizophrenics (N = 320), approximately half of whom were from private and public hospitals. This sample, randomly drawn from a pool of 1,100 records, was half female and half male, and ranged in age from 18 to 55. Eighty-five percent were White. The SCZI produced an 82% true positive rate and an 18% false negative rate in this sample, hit rates at the low end of previous data. Exner noted, however, that this sample should not be considered normative. We use his sample for comparative purposes later in this chapter, but with these limitations in mind.

Another continuing problem in the Rorschach diagnosis of schizophrenia is the confounding effects of drug-induced psychosis, particularly chronic amphetamine use. In the *DSM–III–R* (APA, 1987), the most salient diagnosis is "amphetamine or similarly acting sympathomimetic delusional disorder" (292.11), marked by the rapid development of persecutory delusions and associated with distortions of body image (reality sense) and tactile hallucinations of bugs or vermin crawling under the skin (formication). The differential diagnosis between schizophrenia and this disorder is usually easier in an acute setting, but with the cessation of drug use, amphetamine delusional disorder can persist, on occasion, "for over a year" (p. 137). Although there is some evidence that individuals who become chronically psychotic following the repeated ingestion of stimulants were "psychosis prone" prior to drug use (Meloy, 1992c), data that may render a differential question moot, deciding whether a patient has paranoid schizophrenia or a chronic delusional disorder due to amphetamine use can be quite challenging. Exner (1991) acknowledged this problem and warned that individuals scoring positive on the SCZI may be chronic users of amphetamine rather than schizophrenics (RIAP–2).

Weiner (1966) noted that Rorschach indices are not specific to paranoid disturbances, just as paranoid mechanisms are not specific to paranoid schizophrenia. Fantasy content in Rorschach responses that infer paranoid disturbances are experienced external threat, need for protection, and homosexual concern (Wheeler's [1949] signs). Although Weiner was confident that the Rorschach could differentiate between paranoid and nonparanoid schizophrenia, he was concerned about the former's confusion with amphetamine-induced psychosis. In two earlier articles, however, Weiner (1964, 1965) researched this question

---

[3]Gold and Hurt (1990) found that haloperidol treatment resulted in a significant decline in thought disorder scores using WAIS verbalizations during a month of treatment in a small sample of schizophrenic patients (N = 19). Formal thought disorder appears to be trait related and a genetic risk factor for developing psychosis (Arboleda & Holzman, 1985; Meloy, 1984). It is also responsive to dopamine antagonists, unlike intellectual impairments, which appear to be related to structural brain abnormalities (Seidman, 1983). We would expect a diminution of special scores on the Rorschach in schizophrenic patients during long-term hospitalization (> 1 month), but little change in measurable IQ.

and found that amphetamine psychosis produced a differential F+% and a degree of affective discharge that was not consistent with paranoid schizophrenia.

At any rate, the current actuarial state of the science is (a) the Rorschach can differentiate schizophrenic from nonschizophrenic conditions with substantial accuracy *if a drug-induced psychosis has been previously ruled out*; and (b) the Rorschach cannot differentiate between the various subtypes of schizophrenia. Our conclusions, however, do not preclude the use of other clinical indices from the Rorschach, such as the identification of paranoid mechanisms through thematic content, to answer diagnostic questions in a more refined manner.

Rorschach research with schizophrenic subjects during the past decade has been modest, with instead a growing emphasis on character disturbance and, particularly, borderline personality disorder. Perusal of the *Journal of Personality Assessment*, a major scientific forum for the dissemination of Rorschach research, reflects this changing emphasis as only 19 studies between 1985 and 1993 employed the Rorschach as a research instrument and schizophrenic patients as subjects. Most of the studies involved group comparisons ($N = 15$), and several were case studies ($N = 4$). The research addressed perceptual, associative, defensive, object relations, or boundary disturbance aspects of the disorder (Acklin, 1992; Archer & Gordon, 1988; Colligan & Exner, 1985; Cooper et al., 1988; Curran & Marengo, 1990; Edell, 1987; Exner, 1986b; Gold & Hurt, 1990; Harder, Greenwald, Ritzler, Strauss, & Kokes, 1988; Johnson & Quinlan, 1993; Kahn, Fox, & Rhode, 1988; Kleiger & Peebles-Kleiger, 1993; Mason, Cohen, & Exner, 1985; Meloy & Gacono, 1992b; Meloy & Singer, 1991; Murray, 1992; Perry, Viglione, & Braff, 1992; Peterson, 1992b; Wilson, 1985).

PSYCHOSIS AND PSYCHOPATHY

Meloy (1988) psychoanalytically explored the relationship between psychopathic character and psychotic personality organization. He delineated the particular identity, defensive, and reality-testing aspects of this developmentally low level of antisocial expression. Psychopathic character and psychotic personality organization, from a developmental-object relations perspective (Kernberg, 1984), provide a two-dimensional, perhaps orthogonal, view of the patient's habitual modes of relating.

Identity Disintegration. Fusion of self- and object representations, both perceptual and conceptual (Meloy, 1985a), obliterate any boundaries at a psychotic level of personality (Frosch, 1983). In psychopathy, a delusional identification with the aggressor emerges. This "stranger self-object" (Grotstein, 1982), a preconceived fantasy in normal development that helps the infant anticipate the presence of the predator (stranger anxiety) in the real world, becomes a component of the grandiose self-structure in psychopathy; and with psychosis, "malignantly grows to fantastic and delusional proportions" (Meloy, 1988, p. 257).

Delusions that accompany psychopathic character are distinguished by a lack of superego constraint, sadistic pleasure if they are acted out, dissembling or concealment when situationally warranted, identification with evil and its metaphors, increased self-esteem as a result of the grandiose content, and dysphoria when the delusion is lost, usually a result of involuntary medication. Mp- responses on the Rorschach may be most sensitive to the presence of delusion (see Case 1, this chapter).

Psychotic Defenses. Although borderline and psychotic level defenses are similar, the latter function to protect the individual from further ego disintegration (Kernberg, 1975). For instance, projective identification of self-representations may denote a psychotic level of personality, whereas projective identification of object representations may denote a borderline or neurotic level of personality (Goldstein, 1991; Meloy, 1991a; Meloy & Gacono, 1992b). When representational aspects of the self are attributed to and identified with the other, both the concept of the self as a contained entity demarcated from other selves, and the percept of the self, for example, as a listener of one's own thoughts, is lost. Consequently, such a primitive defense, in the service of ego protection, also becomes a catalyst for psychotic experience: Other selves as objects no longer exist, and sensory-perceptual symptoms, such as auditory hallucinations, appear.

Kwawer's (1980) primitive modes of relating, originally conceptualized as preoedipal, and ranging back to intrauterine experience, provide a useful template for viewing the collapse of demarcating defenses and the regressive emergence of more autistic object relations. We would expect that schizophrenic ASPD males would produce more of Kwawer's (1980) autistic level categories (womb imagery, birth-rebirth, malignant internal processes) than the ASPD males in their Rorschach responses, the latter organized at a borderline level of personality (Gacono, 1990).

Defensive collapse in psychosis is also clinically evident in an increase of formal thought disorder, measurable on the Rorschach through some of the special scores, Sum6, WSum6, and Level 2 scoring. The psychodynamic links between formal thought disorder and the defenses are the primary process mechanisms of condensation and displacement. Meloy (1986) noted that formal thought disorder can be conceptualized as (a) a condensing of abstract, functional, and concrete representations that violates conceptual boundaries of Aristotelean logic, and (b) a displacement from abstractions (connotations) to object and functions (denotations) to phonemes (verbalizations). Without "higher level" borderline defenses that work, such as projection and introjection, phenotypic expressions of splitting, which in turn has its genesis in the differentiation of pleasure from pain, inner space collapses.

Reality Testing. The general absence of reality testing is the third measurable characteristic that distinguishes borderline from psychotic personality organization. Reality testing is the ability to distinguish between interoceptive and exteroceptive stimuli: what is *within* from what is *without*. The Rorschach measure is X–%, and it significantly differentiates schizophrenic from borderline adults (Exner, 1986b). To produce a form minus response, internal fantasy overrides the constraints of the stimulus blot, and any percept goes—cognitive mediation breaks down and external visual contours become irrelevant to the articulated content. As Meloy (1988) noted, psychopathy developmentally implicates the *conceptual* fusion of self- and object representations through the gratification of narcissistic wishes (my wants subsume your wants); but with the addition of psychosis, *perceptual* fusion also occurs, both intrapsychically and interpersonally (there are only wants).

THE SCHIZOPHRENIC ASPD SAMPLE

Our sample ($N = 80$) of males with a diagnosis of both schizophrenia and antisocial personality disorder (*DSM–III–R*) was gathered during the years 1989–1993 from three hospitals in California. Ten of the subjects were gathered from Napa State Hospital, and 38 of the subjects were gathered from the California Medical Facility at Vacaville as part of an ongoing research project investigating the neuropsychological characteristics of this population.[4] Napa State Hospital is a large, medium to minimum security civil and forensic state hospital within the California Department of Mental Health. Vacaville is a large, maximum security prison hospital within the California Department of Corrections. The remaining 32 subjects were gathered from Atascadero State Hospital during the course of ongoing clinical work. Atascadero is a maximum security mental hospital within the California Department of Mental Health. The total sample should not be considered random, and consequently the generalizability of our data should be done with caution.

All subjects met the following inclusion and exclusion criteria: male gender, IQ > 80, no diagnosis of organic mental disorder, a diagnosis of one of the schizophrenia subtypes (predominantly paranoid), a diagnosis of antisocial personality disorder, both diagnoses confirmed by review of medical records independent of the study, and the production of a valid Rorschach protocol (R ≥ 14) administered according to the Comprehensive System (Exner, 1986a). All Rorschachs were rescored by the authors with occasional consultation by Dr. Phil Erdberg. Scoring disagreements were discussed and resolved by the authors.

The sample is composed of 48 (60%) Whites, 25 (31%) Blacks, 5 (6%) Hispanics, and 2 (3%) Asians. Ages range from 18 to 65 ($M = 31$, $SD = 10$). Ninety-nine percent of the sample completed high school.

Tables 6.1 and 6.2 contain a summary of the Comprehensive System scoring characteristics of the sample and a list of all scored variables. Tables 6.3 and

---

[4]We would like to thank the California State Department of Mental Health for permission and Drs. Myla Young, Michael Mattei, and their associates for their generous efforts in providing us with this portion of the sample.

TABLE 6.1
Comprehensive System Data for Schizophrenic ASPD Males ($N = 80$)

Variable	Mean	SD	Min	Max	Freq	Median	Mode	SK	KU
R	22.20	8.64	14.00	56.00	80	20.00	14.00	1.93	4.17
W	11.24	5.91	3.00	45.00	80	10.00	9.00	2.73	13.03
D	8.40	6.71	0.00	38.00	78	7.00	1.00	1.61	3.97
Dd	2.56	3.05	0.00	16.00	60	2.00	0.00	2.29	6.56
Space	1.85	1.74	0.00	7.00	60	2.00	0.00	1.13	1.07
DQ+	5.91	3.56	0.00	15.00	77	6.00	2.00	0.52	−0.16
DQo	13.31	7.47	2.00	48.00	80	11.50	9.00	1.90	5.40
DQv	2.44	2.10	0.00	8.00	61	2.00	0.00	0.69	−0.33
DQv/+	0.54	0.94	0.00	4.00	28	0.00	0.00	2.28	5.46
FQX+	0.01	0.11	0.00	1.00	1	0.00	0.00	8.94	80.00
FQXo	8.31	3.84	2.00	19.00	80	8.00	7.00	0.67	0.14
FQXu	5.70	4.71	0.00	21.00	76	5.00	3.00	1.51	2.20
FQX−	7.54	4.28	1.00	22.00	80	6.50	6.00	1.25	2.03
FQXnone	0.64	0.96	0.00	4.00	32	0.00	0.00	1.68	2.68
MQ+	0.01	0.11	0.00	1.00	1	0.00	0.00	8.94	80.00
MQo	1.40	1.36	0.00	6.00	55	1.00	0.00	1.04	1.00
MQu	0.79	0.99	0.00	4.00	43	1.00	0.00	1.65	2.81
MQ−	1.49	2.01	0.00	10.00	48	1.00	0.00	2.07	4.78
MQnone	0.02	0.22	0.00	2.00	1	0.00	0.00	8.94	80.00
Space−	0.81	1.09	0.00	5.00	38	0.00	0.00	1.52	2.30
M	3.71	2.93	0.00	11.00	71	3.00	1.00	0.67	−0.46
FM	2.59	2.44	0.00	12.00	64	2.00	0.00	1.29	1.89
m	1.59	1.65	0.00	7.00	54	1.00	0.00	1.10	0.75
FM+m	4.17	3.16	0.00	16.00	75	4.00	4.00	1.25	2.48
FC	0.74	1.04	0.00	5.00	35	0.00	0.00	1.66	3.21
CF	1.95	1.48	0.00	6.00	67	2.00	1.00	0.64	−0.07
C	0.55	0.82	0.00	3.00	30	0.00	0.00	1.43	1.26
Cn	0.09	0.40	0.00	3.00	5	0.00	0.00	5.79	38.39
FC+CF+C+Cn	3.32	1.75	0.00	7.00	77	3.00	3.00	0.34	−0.28
WgSumC	3.14	1.74	0.00	7.50	77	3.00	1.00	0.32	−0.31
Sum C'	1.46	1.42	0.00	7.00	58	1.00	1.00	1.27	2.04
Sum T	0.50	1.01	0.00	6.00	24	0.00	0.00	3.06	12.05
Sum V	0.36	0.81	0.00	4.00	16	0.00	0.00	2.40	5.64
Sum Y	0.71	0.97	0.00	4.00	37	0.00	0.00	1.55	2.26
Sum Shd	3.04	2.69	0.00	12.00	70	2.00	1.00	1.43	2.17
Fr+rF	0.57	1.21	0.00	6.00	22	0.00	0.00	2.64	7.23
FD	0.34	0.63	0.00	3.00	21	0.00	0.00	2.01	3.98
F	10.91	6.66	2.00	42.00	80	10.00	9.00	1.79	5.36
Pairs	7.17	4.47	0.00	22.00	78	6.00	5.00	0.91	0.90
Ego	0.40	0.21	0.00	1.29	78	0.38	0.35	1.04	3.28
Lambda	1.17	0.92	0.13	5.00	80	0.91	0.50	1.92	4.65
EA	6.86	3.56	1.00	16.50	80	6.00	2.00	0.71	0.12
es	7.21	4.42	0.00	20.00	79	7.00	7.00	0.79	0.34
D Score	−0.15	1.37	−5.00	3.00	80	0.00	0.00	−1.18	2.90
Adj D Score	0.17	1.31	−4.00	4.00	80	0.00	0.00	−0.57	2.57
SumActvMov	5.31	3.69	0.00	18.00	77	5.00	5.00	0.97	1.00
SumPassMov	2.57	2.20	0.00	11.00	65	2.00	0.00	1.13	1.86
SumMactv	2.30	2.08	0.00	8.00	63	2.00	0.00	0.98	0.37

(Continued)

TABLE 6.1
(Continued)

Variable	Mean	SD	Min	Max	Freq	Median	Mode	SK	KU
SumMpass	1.41	1.70	0.00	6.00	46	1.00	0.00	1.19	0.48
IntellIndx	2.47	3.24	0.00	19.00	54	1.00	0.00	2.48	8.71
Zf	12.77	5.33	5.00	42.00	80	12.00	12.00	2.44	10.84
Zd	−0.94	4.83	−14.00	9.00	75	−0.50	−2.50	−0.29	−0.24
Blends	3.07	2.67	0.00	10.00	67	2.00	2.00	0.94	0.05
CSBlnd	0.54	0.87	0.00	4.00	30	0.00	0.00	2.12	5.25
Afr	0.46	0.20	0.16	1.43	80	0.44	0.27	1.72	5.73
Populars	4.24	1.93	0.00	9.00	79	4.00	4.00	0.45	−0.11
X + %	0.38	0.13	0.10	0.71	80	0.37	0.29	0.25	−0.21
F + %	0.40	0.19	0.00	0.88	77	0.40	0.50	0.20	−0.08
X − %	0.35	0.18	0.06	0.80	80	0.32	0.29	0.85	0.54
Xu%	0.24	0.13	0.00	0.58	76	0.22	0.14	0.33	−0.40
S − %	0.12	0.17	0.00	0.83	38	0.00	0.00	1.78	3.44
IsoIndx	0.21	0.15	0.00	0.60	73	0.18	0.00	0.56	−0.37
H	2.45	2.15	0.00	9.00	66	2.00	1.00	0.99	0.68
(H)	1.35	1.33	0.00	6.00	58	1.00	1.00	1.34	1.80
Hd	1.40	1.88	0.00	10.00	52	1.00	0.00	2.74	9.69
(Hd)	0.37	0.77	0.00	3.00	19	0.00	0.00	2.14	3.91
Hx	0.25	0.65	0.00	3.00	13	0.00	0.00	2.88	8.26
H + (H) + Hd + (Hd)	5.57	3.42	0.00	18.00	79	5.00	6.00	0.95	1.33
A	8.94	4.71	2.00	28.00	80	8.00	7.00	1.29	2.54
(A)	0.50	0.93	0.00	6.00	27	0.00	0.00	3.22	15.11
Ad	1.37	1.59	0.00	8.00	55	1.00	1.00	2.24	6.68
(Ad)	0.05	0.22	0.00	1.00	4	0.00	0.00	4.21	16.12
An	1.11	1.39	0.00	6.00	43	1.00	0.00	1.49	2.39
Art	0.69	1.10	0.00	5.00	31	0.00	0.00	1.89	3.54
Ay	0.71	0.97	0.00	4.00	35	0.00	0.00	1.38	1.68
Bl	0.67	1.00	0.00	4.00	32	0.00	0.00	1.55	1.91
Bt	1.14	1.44	0.00	7.00	44	1.00	0.00	1.58	2.83
Cg	1.36	1.57	0.00	7.00	51	1.00	0.00	1.55	2.52
Cl	0.40	0.61	0.00	2.00	27	0.00	0.00	1.26	0.58
Ex	0.11	0.39	0.00	2.00	7	0.00	0.00	3.70	13.79
Fi	0.44	0.67	0.00	3.00	28	0.00	0.00	1.52	2.04
Food	0.47	0.97	0.00	5.00	22	0.00	0.00	2.52	6.82
Geog	0.11	0.32	0.00	1.00	9	0.00	0.00	2.50	4.36
HHold	0.79	1.09	0.00	5.00	40	0.50	0.00	2.01	4.87
Ls	0.62	1.14	0.00	7.00	32	0.00	0.00	3.36	14.43
Na	0.94	1.25	0.00	6.00	44	1.00	0.00	1.93	4.15
Sc	1.25	1.72	0.00	7.00	42	1.00	0.00	1.66	2.39
Sx	0.94	1.85	0.00	9.00	35	0.00	0.00	3.36	12.10
Xy	0.10	0.30	0.00	1.00	8	0.00	0.00	2.72	5.52
Idio	1.30	1.83	0.00	11.00	46	1.00	0.00	2.64	9.92
DV	1.02	1.25	0.00	5.00	45	1.00	0.00	1.42	1.64
INCOM	1.42	1.64	0.00	7.00	49	1.00	0.00	1.27	1.24
DR	1.66	1.61	0.00	6.00	52	1.00	0.00	0.61	−0.65
FABCOM	0.70	1.00	0.00	4.00	35	0.00	0.00	1.58	2.10
DV2	0.14	0.38	0.00	2.00	10	0.00	0.00	2.82	7.89
INC2	0.57	1.00	0.00	5.00	28	0.00	0.00	2.26	5.66

(Continued)

TABLE 6.1
(Continued)

Variable	Mean	SD	Min	Max	Freq	Median	Mode	SK	KU
DR2	1.10	1.65	0.00	7.00	37	0.00	0.00	1.78	2.72
FAB2	1.12	1.82	0.00	11.00	38	0.00	0.00	2.91	11.55
ALOG	0.47	0.89	0.00	5.00	24	0.00	0.00	2.49	8.14
CONTAM	0.16	0.56	0.00	4.00	9	0.00	0.00	4.88	28.77
Sum6SpSc	5.45	3.66	0.00	16.00	71	5.00	5.00	0.54	0.22
Sum6SpScLv2	2.94	3.21	0.00	16.00	58	2.00	0.00	1.82	4.50
WSum6SpSc	32.22	26.49	0.00	132.00	73	27.50	0.00	1.23	2.11
AB	0.54	1.24	0.00	8.00	21	0.00	0.00	3.63	16.91
AG	0.85	1.22	0.00	5.00	34	0.00	0.00	1.40	1.17
CFB	0.04	0.19	0.00	1.00	3	0.00	0.00	4.96	23.20
COP	1.32	1.43	0.00	6.00	52	1.00	0.00	1.19	0.94
CP	0.07	0.38	0.00	3.00	4	0.00	0.00	6.36	45.06
MOR	2.25	2.21	0.00	9.00	57	2.00	0.00	0.89	−0.03
PER	1.01	1.42	0.00	7.00	40	0.50	0.00	1.80	3.62
PSV	0.37	0.75	0.00	5.00	23	0.00	0.00	3.45	17.42

6.4 contain comparisons of select variables between ASPD males and schizophrenic ASPD males and between schizophrenic males and schizophrenic ASPD males, respectively.

Core Characteristics.   Response frequency is normal ($M = 22.20$, $SD = 8.64$) when compared to nonpatient males (Exner, 1991), inpatient schizophrenics ($M = 23.44$, $SD = 8.66$), and ASPD males ($M = 21.41$, $SD = 8.42$). This precludes our concern that an abnormally deviant average response frequency confounds other variables, although this sample has a greater skewness (1.93) and kurtosis (4.17) than does Exner's inpatient schizophrenic sample.

Half of the sample are high Lambdas (> .99), similar to schizophrenics, suggesting that their problem-solving style is simplistic (Lambda $M = 1.17$). They are also, on average, ambitents; but 25% are extratensives, marking the influence of psychopathic character as an alloplastic orientation to objects on an expected introversive disorder such as schizophrenia. Only 11% of inpatient schizophrenics are extratensive (Exner, 1991).

Volitional resources are limited (EA $M = 6.86$), but with a diminution of es ($M = 7.21$), both D ($M = -.15$) and AdjD ($M = .17$) are essentially normal. In fact, 81% of the sample have an AdjD ≥ 0, calling into question a commonly held clinical belief that stress tolerance and controls in this population are inadequate. They are not. Only 6% have an AdjD < -1.

Affects.   Emotions are weak (SumC $M = 3.32$) and highly defended against (Lambda = 1.17). Modulation of affect is expectedly poor, with an average FC:CF+C = 1:3. This is consistent with psychopathy, and is strikingly different

TABLE 6.2

Schizophrenic ASPD Males (N = 80) Group Means and Frequencies for Select Ratios, Percentages, and Derivations

R = 22.20	L = 1.17	($L > .99 = 46\%$)

EB = 3.71 : 3.14	EA = 6.86
eb = 4.17 : 3.04	es = 7.21 (FM+m < SUMShading . . . 23 29%)
D = −0.15 AdjD = 0.17	

EB STYLE

Introversive 29	36%	
Super-Introversive 17	21%	
Ambient 31	39%	
Extratensive 20	25%	
Super-Extratensive 16	20%	

EA − es DIFFERENCES:D-SCORES

D Score > 0 20	25%
D Score = 0 39	49%
D Score < 0 21	26%
D Score < −1 8	10%
AdjD Score > 0 .27	34%
AdjD Score = 0 .38	47%
AdjD Score < 0 .15	19%
AdjD Score < −1 5	6%

AFFECT

FC:CF+C = .74 : 2.50	
Pure C = .55	(Pure C > 0 = 38%; Pure C > 1 = 14%)
FC > (CF+C) + 2 2	3%
FC > (CF+C) + 1 4	6%
(CF+C) > FC + 1 42	54%
(CF+C) > FC + 2 32	41%

SumC′ = 1.46	SumV = .36	SumY = .71

Afr = .46	(Afr < .40 = 41%; Afr < .50 = 59%)
S = 1.85	(S > 2 = 28%)
Blends:R = 3.07 : 22.20	
CP = .07	

INTERPERSONAL

COP = 1.32	(COP = 0, 35%; COP > 2 = 19%)
AG = .85	(AG = 0, 57%; AG > 2 = 14%)
Food = .47	
Isolate:R = .21	
H:(H)+Hd+(Hd) = 2.45 : 3.12	(H = 0, 17%; H < 2 = 45%)
H+A:Hd+Ad = 11.39 : 2.77	
Sum T = .50	(T = 0, 70%; T > 1 = 11%)

(Continued)

198

TABLE 6.2
(Continued)

SELF-PERCEPTION

Egocentricity = 0.50	(36%, > 33; 36% > .44)
Fr+rF = 0.57	(Fr+rF > 0 = 28%)
FD = 0.34	
An+Xy = 1.21	
MOR = 2.25	(MOR > 2 = 36%)

IDEATION

a:p = 5.31 : 2.57	(*p* > a+1 = 9%)
Ma:Mp = 2.30 : 1.41	(Mp > Ma = 24%)
M = 3.71	(M− = 1.49; M none = .02)
FM = 2.59 m = 1.59	
2AB+Ay+Art = 2.47	(2AB+Ay+Art > 5 = 29%)
Sum6 = 5.45	(Sum6 > 6 = 59%)
WSum6 = 32.22	(Level 2 SpSc > 0 = 72%)

MEDIATION

Populars = 4.24	(P < 4 = 38%; P > 7 = 7%)
X+% = .38	
F+% = .40	
X−% = .35	
S−% = .24	
Xu% = .12	

X+% > .89	0	0%
X+% < .70	79	99%
X+% < .61	75	94%
X+% < .50	65	81%
F+% < .70	74	93%
Xu% > .20	44	55%
X−% > .15	71	89%
X−% > .20	65	81%
X−% > .30	43	54%

PROCESSING

Zf = 12.77	
Zd = −0.94	(Zd > +3.0 = 70%; Zd < −3.0 = 29%)
W:D:Dd = 11.24:8.40:2.56	(Dd > 3 = 22%)
W:M = 11.24:3.71	
DQ+ = 5.91	
DQv = 2.44	(DQv + DQv/+ > 2 = 53%)

CONSTELLATIONS

SCZI = 6. . .19	24%	DEPI = 7. . . 3	3%	CDI = 5. . .12	15%
SCZI = 5. . .13	16%	DEPI = 6. . . 5	9%	CDI = 4. . .17	21%
SCZI = 4. . .12	15%	DEPI = 5. . .16	20%		

Suicide Constellation Positive 6	7%
HVI Positive 8	9%
OBS Positive 0	0%

TABLE 6.3

Comparison of Select Variables Between ASPD Males ($N = 82$) and
Schizophrenic ASPD Males ($N = 80$)

Variable	Findings	p
Pure H	n.s.	
WSum 6	$Z = 4.98$	ASPD $<$ 0.000 (two tail)
AG	n.s.	
Pure C	n.s.	
Egocentricity Index	n.s.	
Populars	$Z = 2.27$	ASPD $>$ .02 (two tail)
X + %	$Z = 7.07$	ASPD $>$ 0.000 (one tail)
F + %	$Z = 4.029$	ASPD $>$ 0.0000 (one tail)
X − %	$Z = 5.53$	ASPD $<$ 0.000 (one tail)
S − %	n.s.	
Xu%	n.s.	
Afr	$Z = 1.923$	ASPD $>$ .05 (two tail)
AgC		ASPD $>$ .015
M −	n.s.	
Hx	n.s.	
Lv2 SpSc	$X^2 = 17.11$	ASPD $<$ 0.0000
Alog	$X^2 = 13.81$	ASPD $<$ .0002
Contam	n.s.	
SCZI+	$X^2 = 27.21$	ASPD $<$ 0.0000
CDI+	$X^2 = 4.01$	ASPD $<$ .04
DEPI+	n.s.	
Total P.M.R. (Kwawer, 1980)	n.s.	

TABLE 6.4

Comparison of Select Variables Between Schizophrenic Inpatients ($N = 320$;
Exner, 1991) and Schizophrenic ASPD Males in Forensic Hospital ($N = 80$)

Variable	Findings	p
Total R	n.s.	
T	n.s.	
Rf	$X^2 = 10.40$	ASPD $>$ .001
Y	$X^2 = 4.27$	ASPD $<$ .04
Per	n.s.	
Egocentricity	n.s.	
W	$Z = 3.40$	ASPD $>$ .0003
D	n.s.	
Pure H	$Z = 2.61$	ASPD $<$ .009
WSum 6	$Z = 3.50$	ASPD $<$ .0005

from Exner's (1991) schizophrenic sample (1:1), which is still worse than nonpatient males (2:1). Thirty-eight percent of our sample produce at least one pure C response. When affect is felt, it is likely to be unmodulated, with expression similar to that of an early latency age child.

C' is similar to schizophrenics ($M = 1.46$), but only one out of five subjects produce a vista response ($M = .36$). Our sample does not dysphorically ruminate, and the majority do not feel badly (FM+m<Sum Shading = 29%).

Anxiety, a noticeable presence in schizophrenia (Y $M = 2.12$; Exner, 1991), is dampened considerably by the addition of ASPD (Y $M = .71$), and to a significant degree ($X2 = 4.27, p = .04$). This finding is consistent with psychopathy (Gacono & Meloy, 1991), and the characterological attenuation of this feeling in the midst of an anxiety-producing biochemical disorder such as schizophrenia is quite remarkable. It provides additional support for the notion that antisocial character is a way of being generally devoid of helpless and anxious emotion—even in the throes of a major mental disorder. It also supports our hypothesis that antisocial defenses serve a regulatory, perhaps "numbing," function that wards off feelings stimulated by perceived threats (Gacono & Meloy, 1991, 1993).

Schizophrenic ASPDs are also avoidant of external, emotionally provoking stimuli (Afr $M = .46$), and more so than ASPD males ($Z = 1.923$, $p = .05$). Forty-one percent have Afr < .40. They are surprisingly less oppositional and angry (S = 1.85) than are schizophrenics (S = 2.77), which may be a product of their long-term hospitalization and capacity to discharge affective tension. Blends are not expected ($M = 3.07$).

Interpersonal (Object) Relations. Schizophrenic ASPD males anticipate more cooperation from others (COP $M = 1.32$, COP 0 = 35%) than either schizophrenics or ASPD males, but not to the degree that normal males do ($M = 1.99$, 23%).

Aggression scores, on the other hand, reflect the same pattern that we have seen in all of our antisocial samples. Schizophrenic ASPDs produce *less* AG ($M = .85$, AG 0 = 57%) responses than do nonpatient males and schizophrenic inpatients ($M = 1.26$, AG 0 = 50%). This is likely due to the direct expression of ego-syntonic aggression, rather than its Rorschach symbolization. Deliberate censoring by our subjects is possible, but unlikely, because AG responses are infrequent across all antisocial age groups (see chapter 8), and are more likely a product of alloplastic character (Ferenczi, 1930), wherein the "environment is altered through flight or defense" (Meloy, 1988, p. 246).

Table 6.5 lists all aggression scores for this sample. Ag Content (AgC) is most frequent (78%), although significantly less ($p = .015$) than ASPD males. It is followed by AgPast (50%), AG (43%), AgPot (39%), and SM (6%).[5]

---

[5]This SM percentage is unreliable, because we do not know if SM was scored for all 80 protocols. We think it underestimates the frequency of SM responses in this sample.

TABLE 6.5
Aggression Scores for Schizophrenic ASPDs ($N = 80$)

	Mean	SD	Maximum	Frequency
Aggression	.89	1.32	5	34 (43%)
Aggressive Content	2.23	1.96	11	62 (78%)
Aggressive Past	1.03	1.31	5	40 (50%)
Aggressive Potential	.54	.78	3	31 (39%)
Sadomasochism	.08	.31	2	5 (6%)
Total Aggression	4.79	4.0	17	74 (93%)

Ninety-three percent of the sample produce at least one of the five aggression scores, similar to our other groups. The relative balance of AgPot and AgPast responses is consonant with internalized object and self-representations that oscillate between prey and predator (Gacono, 1992; Meloy, 1988, 1992; Meloy & Gacono, 1992a, 1992b)—an affectionless and atavistic internal world.

The schizophrenic ASPD male is not orally dependent (Fd $M = .47$, 28%) and is somewhat isolative (Isolate:R = .21). His object relations are dominated by quasihuman or part objects (H: (H) + (Hd) +Hd = 2.45:3.12), and the representation of others as whole, real, and meaningful human beings (Pure H) is significantly less common than schizophrenic inpatients ($Z = 2.61$, $p = .009$). Pure H between ASPD males and schizophrenic ASPD males is not significantly different, underscoring the characterological shaping of object relations despite the presence of a chronic mental disorder that alters both percepts and concepts (Meloy, 1985a). The manifest psychotic symptoms of these internal object relations are hallucinations and delusions, respectively.

The nature of the schizophrenic ASPD male's object relations are noted in Table 6.6.

TABLE 6.6
Kwawer (1980) Primitive Modes of Relating for Schizophrenic ASPDs ($N = 80$)

	Mean	SD	Maximum	Frequency
Engulfment	.05	.22	1	4 (5%)
Symbiotic Merging	.44	.79	4	24 (30%)
Violent Symbiosis	.96	1.30	6	42 (53%)
Birth–Rebirth	.26	.50	2	15 (19%)
Malignant Internal Process	.49	.81	4	27 (34%)
Metamorphosis–Transformation	.25	.54	2	16 (20%)
Narcissistic Mirroring	.59	1.21	6	23 (29%)
Separation–Division	.14	.38	2	10 (13%)
Boundary Disturbance	.55	.88	4	28 (35%)
Womb Imagery	.14	.38	2	10 (13%)
Total P.M.R.	3.81	3.09	12	71 (89%)

Eighty-nine percent of the sample produce at least one Kwawer (1980) score, and each subject averages almost four, a finding of no significant difference when compared to our ASPD sample. These data lend empirical support to the concept of preoedipal personality organization within this sample. Contrary to our earlier prediction, however, the more regressive responses—birth-rebirth (19%), engulfment (5%), and womb imagery (13%)—do not dominate these clinical findings. Instead, in descending order of frequency, we find violent symbiosis (53%), boundary disturbance (35%), malignant internal processes (34%), symbiotic merging (30%), and narcissistic mirroring (29%). Malignant internal processes may be the category most specific to schizophrenia because it does not stand out among ASPD samples without a major mental illness (17% frequency among ASPD males, see chapter 5). It may represent a psychotic reality sense of the deterioration of internal organs or a somatic preoccupation noted in earlier Rorschach research with schizophrenics (Weiner, 1966).

The violent symbiosis and narcissistic mirroring categories have the greatest means, and further confirm earlier findings that separation-individuation tasks are suffused with both aggression and a need to find the self in the other in antisocial patients—a continuous wish to smash the mirror that cannot be just set aside. In Kohutian terms, frustration of the child's grandiose and exhibition-istic desires leads to a fixation at the developmental period when grandiosity, shame proneness, and narcissistic rage dominate. Psychopathy appears to mobilize one of three subtypes of mirroring called a merger transference: the demand for unquestioned dominance over objects (Kohut, 1977).[6]

The capacity to bond to others is quite diminished in this sample, an expected finding, but no less so than in schizophrenic inpatients ($T = 0$, 70% in both groups). Although detachment does not distinguish this group from schizophren-ics, it further extends the detachment finding in all of our antisocial samples. Regardless of the presence or absence of mental disorder, psychopathically disturbed individuals will be emotionally detached. The presence of one T response is unexpected and a positive prognostic finding in any antisocial patient. It predicts the formation of a therapeutic alliance (Gerstley et al., 1989).[7]

The link between weak affects, attachment, and object relations in antisocial individuals was cogently spelled out by Bursten (1989):

---

[6]The other two subtypes of mirroring in external objects are twinship transferences (expecting others to feel and act the same as the self) and true mirror transferences (expecting others to admire and approve of the self). These latter transferences are less likely in psychopathy, and more obvious in benign narcissistic disorders.

[7]One psychopathic patient, however, produced a T on his protocol that was a source of rage in his real world of objects. He had raped his sister and physically abused his wife. This inability to extinguish T may be an impetus to violence, particularly toward women, when it is colored by additional, erotic feelings. A paranoid cast may be attached to these affectional-sexual feelings through the mechanism of projective identification (e.g., "that bitch is controlling me"). This affective-defen-sive dynamic is apparent in some sexual homicide perpetrators (see chapter 9).

I speculate that the depth of affects of people with manipulative [antisocial] personalities has always been limited. While their genetic programs are written in such a way that they possess many of the affects of other narcissistic people, those with manipulative personalities are incapable of elaborating them intensely. This could be the result of genetic limitations, a lack of full development because of the way the early infantile affects were nourished, or both . . . affects are part and parcel of social contexts. It is quite possible that the weak affects go along with weak relationships. (p. 582)

The schizophrenic ASPD male nicely illustrates this theoretical notion with an expected SumC < 4, T = 0, and pure H < 3.

Self-Perception. Almost three fourths of schizophrenic ASPD males are deviantly self-absorbed, comparing themselves negatively to others (36%) or inordinately self-inflated (36%). This egocentricity index distribution, however, is nearly identical to schizophrenic inpatients (Exner, 1990b). What distinguishes the schizophrenic ASPD from the schizophrenic patient without ASPD is his pathological narcissism—reflection responses are significantly more frequent (28% vs. 13%, X2 = 10.40, p = .001). This finding extends the validity of Skoler's (1988) similar finding—elevated reflection responses and egocentricity ratios— when he compared schizophrenic patients considered a serious threat to the president of the United States by the Secret Service to Exner's (1991) schizophrenic sample. Notwithstanding the limitations of these statistical comparisons to an independent reference group, it appears that pathological narcissism is a measurable core characteristic of schizophrenic offenders. It is also consistent with the common clinical observation that grandiosity often distinguishes the schizophrenic patient in a forensic/criminal setting from the schizophrenic patient in a civil setting (Meloy, 1988). As Bursten (1989) wrote, "it may well be that the sense of self is the only integrity they possess" (p. 581).

Schizophrenic ASPD generally do not think about themselves in a balanced, introspective manner, despite their focus on the self (FD 26%). They are not somatically preoccupied (An+Xy M = 1.21), a finding from the Comprehensive System that is inconsistent with our earlier Kwawer (1980) inference. There is, however, a marked sense of self-injury or damage (MOR M = 2.25) that is greater than schizophrenic inpatients (MOR M = 1.47). This finding, when interpreted with the elevated reflection response, suggests a psychodynamic of *failed* grandiosity— perhaps a primary motivation for chronic, antisocial behavior, or the result of it. Consistent with this finding, Skoler (1988) noted significantly greater depression and suicide index scores among schizophrenic offenders who threatened the president than among schizophrenic reference groups (Exner, 1991). Skoler's sample also had a high incidence of suicide gestures and attempts (personal communication, February 1994). We also see this psychodynamic in the simplistic striving (W) of the schizophrenic ASPD, significantly greater than schizophrenic inpatients (Z = 3.40, p = .0003). Complex accomplishment through sustained effort does not distinguish our sample and is made worse by schizophrenia.

Ideation. The thinking of the schizophrenic ASPD male is expectedly disorganized (WSum6 = 32.22) and clearly bizarre (Level 2 SpecScores > 0 = 72%). When compared to schizophrenic inpatients, however, formal thought disorder is significantly less (Z = 3.50, p = .0005). This may be an artifact of comparing schizophrenics in an acute hospital setting (Exner, 1991) to schizophrenics in a chronic institutional setting, or a cognitive organizing effect of antisocial character upon schizophrenia. Further research is necessary.

When the schizophrenic ASPD subjects are compared to ASPD subjects, almost all ideational measures are significantly different as expected.[8] Contamination responses, however, are not. This finding lends support to Meloy and Singer's (1991) contention that Contaminations are an insensitive indicator of schizophrenia due to their relative infrequency, whereas ALOGs are much more useful. ALOGs did significantly distinguish our schizophrenic ASPDs from ASPDs (X2 = 13.81, p = .0002). Despite the moderate and pervasive formal thought disorder found in ASPD subjects, schizophrenia makes it much worse (Level 2 SpSc, X2 = 17.11, p = .0000).

Schizophrenic inpatients produced more M responses (M = 6.0) than did schizophrenic ASPDs (M = 3.71). We would expect this measure of empathy to be less in antisocial samples, and it is. M– is proportionately the same, occurring in slightly less than half the M responses. This reality-testing failure around the perception of human movement was not significantly different from our ASPD sample. Schizophrenic ASPDs also appear less behaviorally passive (a:p = 5.31 : 2.57) when compared to schizophrenics (5.51 : 4.25).

Nonvolitional ideation is unremarkable in this sample, whether in response to instinctual needs (FM = 2.59) or anxiety (m = 1.59). One instinctual desire, sexual preoccupation, is apparent in almost half of our sample (44%), a finding virtually identical to schizophrenic patients (46%).

Mediation.   Schizophrenia is primarily a disorder of thinking and perception (Weiner, 1966). The Comprehensive System measures of perception further confirm this clinical fact. They empirically demonstrate the degree to which this biochemical disorder significantly worsens the already apparent perceptual deficits within psychopathy (see chapters 2–7). When compared to ASPD males, schizophrenic ASPD males are less perceptually conventional (Populars, Z = 2.27, p = .02); less perceptually convergent (X+%, Z = 7.07, p = .0000) even without affect (F+%, Z = 4.029, p = .0000); and show much more impairment in reality testing (X–%, Z = 5.53, p = .0000). The latter finding in schizophrenic ASPDs (M = 35, SD = 18) is virtually identical to other schizophrenic inpatients (M = 37, SD = 14), including all distribution characteristics. The majority of schizophrenics, whether antisocial or not, will score > 30% on this variable.

---

[8]Saccuzzo, Braff, Sprock, and Sudik (1984) found the DV response discriminated between schizophrenic spectrum patients and controls, as did a visual backward masking procedure.

Both association (ideation) and perception (mediation) are made significantly worse when schizophrenia affects the brain of the premorbidly cognitively impaired psychopathic individual. This is a testament to the devastating effect of this biochemical disorder. Schizophrenia will usually manifest in a genetically vulnerable individual at least a decade after the first symptoms of conduct disorder, if both diagnoses are eventually made in the same patient. Although schizophrenia has been found to occur with a greater frequency in ASPD individuals (Regier & Robins, 1991), it appears to be independent when more precise measures of psychopathy are used (Hart & Hare, 1989). Both disorders appear to arise from a nonadditive gene-environment interaction (Quality Assurance Project, 1991). It is probable that schizotaxia, what Meehl (1962) called an inherited neural integrative defect, gives rise to a personality structure called the schizotype (Rado, 1956), of which Meehl (1989) estimated that 10% develop schizophrenia. This personality structure, marked by ambivalence, aversive drift, autism, cognitive slippage, and numerous other traits is fully phenotypically expressed in our sample as schizophrenia. We speculate that psychopathy, likewise a personality structure with a heritable component (Meloy, 1988), is also fully phenotypically expressed in the primary psychopath, but remains partially hidden when heterogeneous samples of ASPD males are studied (Regier & Robins, 1991). When both occur in one individual, significantly worse cognitive slippage occurs (WSum6)—as do many other traits and behaviors.[9]

Processing.   The majority of our schizophrenic ASPD sample are as efficient and effective in the initial processing of sensory input as normals. Zf is normative ($M = 12.77$) and Zd is only slightly below normal ($M = -.94$). Striving beyond one's capacities emerges once again in this sample (W:M > 3:1), unhindered by schizophrenia—a consistent finding in other antisocial samples and a marker for the resilience of pathological narcissism.

The Constellations.   Only slightly more than one half of our sample are positive for the SCZI ($55\% \geq 4$). This is strikingly different from the Exner (1990b) samples, and may reflect the chronicity of our population. One third (32%) are positive for the DEPI, and 36% are positive for the CDI. Erdberg (personal communication, July 1993) found no relationship between psychopathy, schizophrenia, and the CDI, and suggested the latter may be a general, global factor that is measuring social inadequacy, similar to Spearman's (1927) G factor for intelligence.

---

[9]For instance, Henderson and Kalichman (1990) focused on chaotic sexuality and presented several lines of evidence that suggested a subpopulation of sex offenders that fit the characteristic pattern of schizotypy. Meehl (1989) recently predicted that a very large majority of psychopaths are schizotaxic and endorsed a Cleckley (1976) model rather than a social deviance (APA, 1987) model for describing antisocial traits.

Conclusions. The schizophrenic ASPD, when psychometrically mapped by the Comprehensive System, the Kwawer (1980) variables, and experimental aggression scores (Meloy & Gacono, 1992a), shows structural and dynamic characteristics consistent with both disorders. Like the psychopathic patient, he is generally devoid of insight and anxiety, and emotionally detached. He does not modulate affect well, and it is weakly experienced, highly defended against, and avoided in others. He is not cognitively or emotionally impulsive,[10] and appears able to organize his behavior in a predictable manner if he wants to, at least when he is not acutely psychotic. His problem-solving style, however, is not clearly developed or complex. He strives beyond his capacities to dilute complicated questions and choices into simple answers.

He is self-absorbed, but his grandiosity is scarred by a continual sense of failure and self-injury. The schizophrenia may actually open the wound of the vulnerable, devalued self, heretofore protected by the umbrella of the grandiose or false self, an accepted structural duality in narcissistic psychopathology (Svrakic, 1989). He is likely to be quite sensitive and prone to feelings of shame and perceived humiliation, as the grandiose self is deflated and the wounded self is exposed.

His capacity for predatory violence (Meloy, 1988) is likely to be large and easily stimulated for the following reasons: an absence of bonding (T); minimal or no anxiety (Y); autonomic hyporeactivity to aversive stimuli (poor passive avoidance learning); decreased empathy (M); decreased representation of others as whole, real, and meaningful individuals (Pure H); an alloplastic adaptation (Ferenczi, 1930); ego-syntonic aggressive impulse (AG scores); sexual preoccupation (Sx); entitlement (Rf); a sense of self-injury (MOR); psychotic reality testing (X−%); borderline or psychotic personality organization (Kwawer categories); and severe formal thought disorder (WSum6).[11]

In short, the schizophrenic ASPD is an extremely dangerous individual in any clinical setting. These structural and dynamic characteristics of psychopathy, coupled with the further cognitive insults of schizophrenia, provide templates for a variety of motivations that may result in violent behaviors toward clinicians and other patients: (a) retaliation for a perceived insult or emotional wound, (b) preemptive aggression against a paranoid threat, (c) aggression in the service of a sexual or sadistically sexual impulse, (d) expansion of a territorial imperative

---

[10] There appear to be three measurable domains of impulse control: cognitive, emotional, and motor. Rivers (1993) found no significant relationship between histories of violence and these three areas of impulse control when she compared two groups of violent and nonviolent male prisoners. The prisoners, however, had significantly less impulse control than a demographically matched comparison group. We think AdjD is measuring a blend of cognitive/emotional impulse control, rather than motor control, a logical conclusion given the variables used to construct AdjD. With this sample, like our other groups, unmodulated affect is used in a deliberate and volitional manner to manipulate actual objects in the environment, thus enhancing fantasies of omnipotent control. This finding is consistent with structural and dynamic theory concerning psychopathy (Meloy, 1988).

[11] Recent research has established the importance of psychotic symptoms in the risk of violence among the mentally ill (Monahan, 1992).

in the midst of psychotic decomposition,[12] (e) instrumental seeking of other hedonic or sympathomimetic pleasures, such as legal or illegal drugs, (f) varieties of delusional pursuit, (g) and psychotic identification with the aggressor, usually a religious, cinematic, or cosmic figure identified as evil (Satan, Darth Vadar, the Terminator, etc.).

We offer the following clinical treatment suggestions:

1. Although the Axis I condition of schizophrenia is medically treatable in most cases, especially with the availability of second generation neuroleptics such as clozapine, the Axis II condition is usually not. Successful treatment of the schizophrenia may result in a better organized psychopathic individual. There is no clearcut clinical answer to this vexing problem, but it does raise important ethical issues for staff consideration and discussion.

2. Attempts to treat this patient should only be made if the considered approach has proven efficacy and can be done in a setting that ensures the safety of the clinician and other patients. A common clinical error is treating this patient in a setting that cannot contain his atavistic personality structure and vulnerability to psychosis, such as an outpatient clinic (see Meloy, 1988).

3. A careful assessment of the severity of psychopathy should be done using the PCL–R (Hare, 1991; Ogloff, Wong, & Greenwood, 1990). The schizophrenic who is also a primary psychopath (PCL–R $\geq$ 34; Gacono & Hutton, 1994; Meloy & Gacono, 1994) should only be treated psychopharmacologically, and should not be engaged in any individual or group psychotherapy, or therapeutic community. One 10-year outcome study found *higher* rates of violent reoffense in treated psychopaths when compared to untreated psychopaths (Rice, Harris, & Cormier, 1992), some of whom were also schizophrenics.

On the other hand, the schizophrenic ASPD who is nonpsychopathic can be viewed with greater therapeutic optimism. Nonpsychopathic criminals do show a treatment response (Gerstley et al., 1989; Rice et al., 1992), probably due to their capacity to bond and experience anxiety. We would expect the same in the nonpsychopathic ASPD patient with his schizophrenia in remission. Psychopathy measurement can be done with confidence in a male forensic psychiatric population (Gacono & Hutton, 1994; Hart & Hare, 1989).

4. CNS serotonin has been strongly linked to chronic antisocial behavior—specifically, assaultiveness, emotional dysregulation, and deficits in passive-avoidance learning (Lewis, 1991). There may be a role for serotonin agonists in the medical treatment of certain dangerous behaviors resulting from Axis II character pathology, especially psychopathy. No controlled studies have been published to date. Such biochemical management, in addition to therapeutic

---

[12]The collapse of internal space during psychosis may demand a compensatory increase in actual physical space from other objects.

containment (Meloy, 1985b), may be the future treatment direction for the schizophrenic psychopath.[13]

5. Clinicians should be exceedingly careful with this patient and closely monitor their countertransference reactions (Meloy, 1988). This is especially true if the clinician has had a lengthy history of positive identifications with schizophrenic patients in other settings. The most dramatic and telling counter-transference reaction with any psychopathic patient is a sudden, visceral fear response when in his presence: "he made the hair stand up on my neck." Meloy discussed this atavistic response and its phylogenetic roots as being unconsciously caught in a prey-predator dynamic. It should not be dismissed and may signal a real, immediate danger.

SAM, AN ANTISOCIAL SCHIZOPHRENIC MALE PSYCHOPATH

Sam was a 27-year-old White male with a *DSM–III–R* diagnosis of schizophrenia, paranoid type, chronic, and antisocial personality disorder, severe. His obtained score on the PCL–R was > 30, placing him in the severe range of psychopathy. His intellectual functioning, assessed with the Wechsler Adult Intelligence Scale–Revised (WAIS–R; Wechsler, 1981), fell within an average range: VIQ = 98, PIQ = 118, and FSIQ = 106. He was medicated at the time of testing. Sam had been convicted of several nonsexual serial murders. Further historical information has been withheld in the interest of maintaining confidentiality.

Sam's Rorschach

Table 6.7 shows Sam's Rorschach protocol. Table 6.8 presents his sequence of scores, and Table 6.9 shows the structural summary, both generated by Rorschach Scoring Program, Version 2 (RIAP–2; Exner et al., 1990).

Structural Interpretation[14]

Sam's Rorschach yielded 15 responses, a valid (Lambda = .50) but constricted protocol. His psychological resources (EA = 6.5), although within one standard deviation of those expected in inpatient schizophrenics (Exner, 1990b; EA =

---

[13]Some schizophrenic ASPD patients will be perceived to be better functioning than they are due to the organizing effects of psychopathy and the inpatient structure. Medication reduction or elimination in these patients should be done with great caution, especially if there has been a history of violent crime.

[14]Among Exner's (1990b) nonpatient, character-disordered, and schizophrenic samples, Comprehensive System Variables for the schizophrenics exhibit the largest variance (standard deviations). This limitation is considered when comparisons are made between Sam's structural data and the Exner (1990b) inpatient schizophrenic sample.

TABLE 6.7
Sam, an Antisocial Schizophrenic Male Psychopath

I   1. Butterfly, this is the main part, and his eyes, little antennas and the wings.

     E: What made it look like that?
     S: Here wings, this was the eyes, little antenna, the body.
     E: Eyes?
     S: That's how a butterfly looks like if you've ever caught one. I used to catch them as a kid.

Comprehensive Scoring: Wo Fo A P 1.0 PER
Aggression Scoring: None
Primitive Modes of Relating: None
Defenses: None categorized

    2. A snowflake but the wrong color, not white, gray here, darkest black.

     E: What made it look like that?
     S: I come from Michigan, used to play in snow.

Comprehensive Scoring: Wv C′F− Na PER
Aggression Scoring: None
Primitive Modes of Relating: None
Defenses: Isolation

    3. Kind of looks like hips. Don't know name of it. Structure of person's hip or X ray. That's what I told them before and I've had this test 4–5 times from different people.

     E: What made it look like that?
     S: If you've ever seen those things in the doctor's office. I've seen a skeleton before.
     E: X ray?
     S: Because it's different grayish colors. That was a long time to get past the first one.
     E: A long time?
     S: I just went down to X ray.

Comprehensive Scoring: Wv YFo An PER, DR
Aggression Scoring: None
Primitive Modes of Relating: None
Defenses: Omnipotence

II   4. Oh man. You ever see a semitruck. They get a thing on the back looks like a fifth wheel. Fifth wheel on a semi. They look like, just like that. That's about all.

     E: What made it look like that?
     S: Looks just like it. Sets like this on an angle. Backs under these. Makes a big jolting sound when it backs up. My stepfather's a truck driver.

Comprehensive Scoring: WSo F− Sc 4.5 PER
Aggression Scoring: None
Primitive Modes of Relating: None
Defenses: None categorized

(Continued)

TABLE 6.7
(Continued)

	5. Another species of a butterfly. Head, antenna and wings. Different species got red, black and gray.	E: What made it look like that? S: Looked the same as the first one. I just said that because it has different colors.

Comprehensive Scoring: Wo FC′.FCo A 4.5
Aggression Scoring: None
Primitive Modes of Relating: None
Defenses: None categorized

III	6. That one—two people. These are people right here bending down to pick up a basket, parcel here. Right side up.	E: What made it look like that? S: Didn't use these (people). Head, chest, arms going down. Both look the same. Whatever, picking up a box or parcel.

Comprehensive Scoring: D+1 Mao 2 H,Hh P 3.0 COP
Aggression Scoring: None
Primitive Modes of Relating: None
Defenses: None categorized

	7. Person going like this. Arms, eyes, shoulders, chest.	E: What made it look like that? S: Chest, arms, eyes, the black spots, rest are facial features. E: Chest? S: He's like this, chest here.

Comprehensive Scoring: DdSo 99 Mp− Hd 4.5
Aggression Scoring: None
Primitive Modes of Relating: None
Defenses: Projection

IV	8. Looks like baby Godzilla in a movie. The one that blows smoke rings out.	E: What made it look like that? S: You ever seen it? It does look like that. Here is a big back, scaly. Legs and arms, parts of tail. (Scaly) Colors look like a bear. If you ever seen Godzilla, that's what he looks like. Upside down. Thin, except upside down.

Comprehensive Scoring: Wo FTo (A),Art 2.0 PER,INC
Aggression Scoring: AgC
Primitive Modes of Relating: None
Defenses: Hypomanic denial

V	9. A moustache. Geraldo, that's the kind of moustache (laughs).	E: What made it look like that? S: Looks just like it here. Right here, real thick. Curly ends here.

(Continued)

TABLE 6.7
(Continued)

E: Moustache?
S: That pretty much says it.

Comprehensive Scoring: Wv Fu Hd
Aggression Scoring: None
Primitive Modes of Relating: None
Defenses: Idealization, Omnipotence

10. Some kind of bat. These are bugs,   E: What made it look like that?
wings, his feet, antennalike ears,   S: These were wings, feet, head, little
head.   features. Head of a bat. This was
his feet.

Comprehensive Scoring: Wo Fo A P 1.0
Aggression Scoring: None
Primitive Modes of Relating: None
Defenses: None categorized

VI   11. Looks like a rug to me. Bearskin, a   E: What made it look like that?
pelt, a pelt. Head, whiskers, skin   S: We used to have a rug like that
from part of a head. Some kind of   dyed green. Didn't have this. This is
wild animal.   the head part of a lion, whiskers,
when they skinned it.

Comprehensive Scoring: Wo Fo Ad P 2.5 PER
Aggression Scoring: AgPast
Primitive Modes of Relating: None
Defenses: Projection

VII   12. I said at jail, someone going like   E: What made it look like that?
this, two thumbs up. Someone hitch-   S Yea, that's what it looks like. These
hiking, going like this. That's it. I   are thumbs and fist going like this.
do a lot of hitchhiking.   The arms and the shoulder.

Comprehensive Scoring: W+ Mp− Hd 2.5 PER
Aggression Scoring: None
Primitive Modes of Relating: None
Defenses: None categorized

VIII   13. I don't know this kind of, like a   E: What made it look like that?
flower. Upside down it looks like a   S: A flower, petal's pink part, green
flower, goes in the ground, pink   part bud, and stem coming out of
petal, green bud.   the ground.
Right side up I can't see anything
up. Looks like a flower to me.

Comprehensive Scoring: Wo CFo Bt 4.5
Aggression Scoring: None
Primitive Modes of Relating: None
Defenses: None categorized

(Continued)

TABLE 6.7
(Continued)

IX	14. Another bad one. I don't have any idea. A splotch of ink story—according to the doctor at the jail.	E:	What made it look like that?
		S:	Couldn't see anything, coudn't picture it as anything. Really it wouldn't be a splotch. This is green, orange, pink.

Comprehensive Scoring: Wv CF− Id
Aggression Scoring: None
Primitive Modes of Relating: None
Defenses: Devaluation, Omnipotence

X	15. That's, oh man, could be anything. Another type of a flower like you see. Could be anything. Just colors. Like flowers, maybe setting there in a backyard.	E:	What made it look like that?
		S:	All the colors, yellow, orange, blue, green, black, gray. Flower with a stem here.

Comprehensive Scoring: Wv C′F.CFo Bt
Aggression Scoring: None
Primitive Modes of Relating: None
Defenses: None categorized

8.63, $SD = 5.39$) and similar to our schizophrenic ASPDs ($M = 6.86$), are below average for nonpatients. Sam tends toward underincorporation, although not significantly so, and does not manifest a clearly delineated problem-solving style (EB = 3:3.5; an ambitent). Despite adequate stress tolerance and controls (D = 0, AdjD = 0) he is likely to have difficulty meeting normal environmental demands (CDI = 4). With an increase in complexity, inadequate resources and the lack of a clearly defined problem-solving style would further stress his limited coping abilities. Elevated constellations (CDI = 4, SCZI = 4, and DEPI = 5) also suggest severe impairment and a high probability of a major mental disorder with both cognitive and affective components.

Perhaps interpersonal isolation (Isolate/R = .27) and affective avoidance (Afr = .25) are immature strategies Sam relies on for coping. Certainly interpersonal problems are suggested by the quality of his three Ms (two of which are − form) and the low frequency of H (H = 1). Affective avoidance may in part stem from modulation problems (S−% = 40%; YF = 1; FC:CF+C = 1:3, one CF−). Sam's FC:CF+C ratio is similar to our schizophrenic ASPDs (.74:2.50). In conjunction with other structural data the elevated S−% may also suggest the likelihood of psychotic breaks with reality during fits of rage. In the context of reduced R two space responses (S) may indicate chronic hostility and oppositionalism, whereas elevated C′ (C′ = 3) suggests efforts at emotional constraint that may only be partially effective (two are C′F, one with − form).

Consistent with psychopathic structure Sam is grandiose (W:M = 13:3) and likely paranoid as he expends much of his energy in observing and omnipotently

TABLE 6.8
Sam's Rorschach Sequence of Scores

CARD	NO	LOC	# DETERMINANT(S)	(2)	CONTENT(S)	POP	Z	SPECIAL SCORES
I	1	Wo	1 Fo		A	P	1.0	PER
	2	Wv	1 C'F−		Na			PER
	3	Wv	1 YFo		An			PER,DR
II	4	WSo	1 F−		Sc		4.5	PER
	5	Wo	1 FC'.FCo		A		4.5	
III	6	D+	1 Mao	2	H,Hh	P	3.0	COP
	7	DdSo	99 Mp−		Hd		4.5	
IV	8	Wo	1 FTo		(A),Art		2.0	PER,INC
V	9	Wv	1 Fu		Hd			
	10	Wo	1 Fo		A	P	1.0	
VI	11	Wo	1 Fo		Ad	P	2.5	PER
VII	12	W+	1 Mp−		Hd		2.5	PER
VIII	13	Wo	1 CFo		Bt		4.5	
IX	14	Wv	1 CF−		Id			
X	15	Wv	1 C'F.CFo		Bt			

SUMMARY OF APPROACH

I:W.W.W	VI:W
II:WS.W	VII:W
III:D.Dds	VIII:W
IV:W	IX:W
V:W.W.	X:W

controlling all aspects of his environment (PER = 7).[15] A number of variables suggest he does this poorly (Zf = 10; Zd = −1.0; Wv = 5). Paranoia is also suggested by a H+A:Hd+Ad ratio < 4:1. There is an absence of reflections and his egocentricity ratio (Ego = .07; schizophrenic ASPDs = .40) is less than expected: Both of these variables suggest the absence of pathological narcissism and a negative comparison of self to others.

Despite little interest in others as whole and meaningful objects (H:Hd = 1:3), bonding capacity (T = 1) and expectations of cooperativeness (COP = 1) are both

---

[15]We have previously found PERs to be a discriminating variable in psychopathy (Gacono et al., 1990, 1992).

TABLE 6.9
Sam's Rorschach Structural Summary

Location Features	Determinants Blends	Determinants Single	Contents	S-Constellation
				NO..FV+VF+V+FD > 2
		H = 1, 0	YES..Col-Shd Bl > 0
Zf = 10	FC'FC	M = 3	(H) = 0, 0	YES..Ego < .31, > .44
ZSum = 30.0	C'F.CF	FM = 0	Hd = 3, 0	NO..MOR > 3
ZEst = 31.0		m = 0	(Hd)= 0, 0	NO..Zd > + − 3.5
		FC = 0	Hx = 0, 0	NO..es > EA
W = 13		CF = 2	A = 3, 0	YES..CF+C > FC
(Wv = 5)		C = 0	(A) = 1, 0	YES..X+% < .70
D = 1		Cn = 0	Ad = 1, 0	NO..S > 3
Dd = 1		FC' = 0	(Ad)= 0, 0	NO..P < 3 or > 8
S = 2		C'F = 1	An = 1, 0	YES..Pure H < 2
		C' = 0	Art = 0, 1	YES..R < 17
DQ		FT = 1	Ay = 0, 0	6.....TOTAL
......(FQ−)		TF = 0	Bl = 0, 0	
+ = 2 (1)		T = 0	Bt = 2, 0	Special Scorings
o = 8 (2)		FV = 0	Cg = 0, 0	
v/+ = 0 (0)		VF = 0	Cl = 0, 0	Lv1 Lv2
v = 5 (2)		V = 0	Ex = 0, 0	DV = 0 × 1 0 × 2
		FY = 0	Fd = 0, 0	INC = 1 × 2 0 × 4
		YF = 1	Fi = 0, 0	DR = 1 × 3 0 × 6
		Y = 0	Ge = 0, 0	FAB = 0 × 4 0 × 7
		Fr = 0	Hh = 0, 1	ALOG = 0 × 5
Form Quality		rF = 0	Ls = 0, 0	CON = 0 × 7
		FD = 0	Na = 1, 0	SUM6 = 2
FQx FQf MQual SQx		F = 5	Sc = 1, 0	WSUM6= 5
+ = 0 0 0 0			Sx = 0, 0	
o = 9 3 1 0			Xy = 0, 0	AB = 0 CP = 0
u = 1 1 0 0			Id = 1, 0	AG = 0 MOR = 0
− = 5 1 2 2				CFB = 0 PER = 7
none = 0 − 0 0		(2) = 1		COP = 1 PSV = 0

Ratios, Percentages, and Derivations

R = 15 L = 0.50	FC:CF+C = 1: 3	COP = 1 AG = 0
	Pure C = 0	Food = 0
EB = 3: 3.5 EA = 6.5 EBPer = N/A	Afr = 0.25	Isolate/R = 0.27
eb = 0: 5 es = 5 D = 0	S = 2	H:(H)Hd(Hd) = 1: 3
Adj es = 5 Adj D = 0	Blends:R = 2:15	(HHd):(AAd) = 0: 1
	CP = 0	H+A:Hd+Ad = 5: 4
FM = 0 : C' = 3 T = 1		
m = 0 : V = 0 Y = 1	P = 4	Zf = 10 3r+(2)/R = 0.07
a:p = 1: 2 Sum6 = 2	X+% = 0.60	Zd = −1.0 Fr+rF = 0
Ma:Mp = 1: 2 Lv2 = 0	F+% = 0.60	W:D:Dd = 13: 1: 1 FD = 0
2AB+Art+Ay = 1 WSum6 = 5	X−% = 0.33	W:M = 13: 3 An+Xy = 1
M− = 2 Mnone = 0	S−% = 0.40	DQ+ = 2 MOR = 0
	Xu% = 0.07	DQv = 5

SCZI = 4*	DEPI = 5*	CDI = 4*	S-CON = 6	HVI = No	OBS = No

within a normal range. Spoiling of the FT response [INC and (A)] begs the question of just what is the target of Sam's affectional desire. His real-world criminal behaviors indicated that human interactions were used to ritualistically gratify sadistic fantasies (Dietz, Hazelwood, & Warren, 1991). A single COP and H appear on Response 6 and, absent overt spoiling (poor form, special scores), reveal a superficial normality (produced with a popular). Further interpretation of these indices await sequence and content analysis.

The most significant aspect of both interpersonal impairment and thought disorder are revealed by Sam's human movement (M) responses. The first, an Ma on Response 6, aided by a popular, occurs with adequate form; the second and third, however, are Mp– responses with Hd content. Coupled with an Ma:Mp ratio of 1:2, his human movement responses suggest gross distortions in perception and should alert the clinician to the abuse of fantasy and the possibility of delusions, perhaps deliberately concealed by the patient. Both of these hypotheses were supported by subsequent clinical data that indicated that the patient habitually fantasized about dismembering bodies (Hd) in a sadistic manner. His X–% (33%) indicates psychotic reality testing despite perceptual accuracy (X+% = 60%; F+% = 60%), more similar to character disorder norms (Exner, 1991; X+% = 58%; F+% = 59%) than schizophrenic ASPDs in general (X+% = 38%; F+% = 40%). Cognitive slippage, normally evident through an elevated WSum6, is not present (WSum 6 = 5). However, the schizophrenic constellation (SCZI = 4) is positive. Formal thought disorder may be less clinically apparent in paranoid schizophrenia when compared to other schizophrenic subtypes.

Interpretation of Scoring Sequence

Sam begins Card 1 with an adequate response aided by a popular. Although 54% of the 11 responses without populars exhibit less than adequate form quality, 100% (N = 4) of his responses with populars evidence adequate form. At times Sam is able to use the environment to produce an appropriate but perhaps superficial response. Cards I and II provide clues concerning Sam's approach to the ambiguous Rorschach task. PERs are produced on the first four responses. In addition to a paranoid or defensive posture toward the task and examiner (Exner, 1986a), an attitude of omnipotence rather than inadequacy is suggested, the latter often being associated with the responses of nonpsychopathic subjects who produce PERs (Gacono et al., 1990).

Responses 2 and 3 are also Ws but with vague developmental quality. Determinants and defenses reveal Sam's coping style in response to the ambiguous task. He first unsuccessfully attempts to constrain (C'F–) and isolate affect (Response 2). Failing this, he conquers a temporary feeling of anxiety (YF) through control (An, PER) and retreat into omnipotence (Response 3). Sam becomes invulnerable.

Initial shock (F–) and subsequent affective constraint (WS; FC'.FC) are evident on Card II. Response 4 highlights a Rorschach pattern found in some ASPDs where constrained hostility results in impaired perceptual accuracy (Gacono & Meloy, 1992). Expressed aggression (AgC, AgPast, AgPot) at times can aid in restoring perceptual accuracy.

Card III begins with a pure H and a manageable popular. This successful pull for human imagery results in rapid deterioration as paranoia surfaces on Response 7 when DdS is combined with Mp– and Hd content (defensive projection is also notable).

Card IV contains an FT spoiled by (A), AgC, and an INC. Card V (Response 9) continues a process that began with Response 8. Usually a popular bat or butterfly is seen on Card V; however, Sam's initial response (#9; Wv Fu Hd) suggests a continued theme of impaired and part-object relations. Idealization and omnipotence (on 8) are linked to recovery on Response 10, which also includes a popular. The single response on Card VI is also organized with a popular, showing adequate form quality with an AgPast score.

Card VII represents a decompensation (– form) and delusional content (Mp–; Hd). Freed from human content (Bt on Response 13), Sam recovers while demonstrating problems with affect modulation. The affect laden stimulus on Card IX, however, triggers deterioration (Wv CF–). Sam's final response represents a partial recovery (o form) while once again highlighting his difficulties with affect (Wv CF) and its constraint (C'F).

Interpretation of Content

Sam's protocol is notable for the absence of Kwawer (1980) primitive modes of relating, an unlikely finding in both schizophrenic ASPD and ASPD males (see chapters 5 & 6). This does not negate the usefulness of content in expanding our understanding of Sam's object world. A high number of vague (developmental quality = v) percepts, "snowflake," "hips/X ray," "moustache," "splotch," and "flower" (Responses 2, 3, 9, 14, 15) attest to boundary disturbance problems and perceptual fluidity.

An analysis of Sam's defenses (Cooper et al., 1988) is useful. Isolation, a neurotic defense, is produced on Response 2. It is used as an initial coping strategy for handling the aggressive identifications from Response 1. Isolation leads to omnipotence (#3), a frequently utilized defense for Sam (Responses 3, 9, & 14) and expected in the records of psychopaths. Projection, found on Responses 7 and 11, is the second borderline defense utilized by Sam, and is consistent with the psychopathic proclivity to attribute blame and responsibility to others; and even more psychodynamically, to perceive threat from the environment through the projection of persecutory objects. Idealization in Response 9 coexists with omnipotence and in the context of Hd content is more likely to reflect immature levels of self-idealization rather than idealization of others. Devaluation (Response 14), a defense expected in narcissistic and borderline samples, counterbalances Sam's idealization.

The only psychotic defense, hypomanic denial, appears in Response 8, and is linked to a texture response that is spoiled by both aggressive content, albeit infantilized ("baby Godzilla"), and a negation (Meloy & Gacono, 1992a). A negated T response occurs when a scorable texture response appears, but the tactile sense is either incongruous or displeasurable. A "baby Godzilla" would not be "scaly" (note the reptilian inference). Although there are only two scorable aggressive responses (AgC, #8, AgPast, #11), the content for Response 1 highlights the predatory identification that Sam has behaviorally manifested. "That's how a butterfly looks like if you've ever caught one. I used to catch them as a kid." The predatory aspect of Sam's personality is ego syntonic (Meloy, 1988).

Summary

Besides the obvious danger of this patient to both staff and other patients, the most difficult management problem for the seasoned clinician is to keep the more naive and optimistic staff from viewing him as safe and cured when on medications. For instance, an itemized "sign" approach to his Rorschach using the Comprehensive System could suggest adequate stress tolerance and controls (AdjD = 0), normal bonding (T = 1), normal anxiety (Y = 1), no real aggression risk (AG = 0), and successful treatment of a schizophrenic thought disorder (WSum6 = 5). Such an approach would fail to understand the operative psychopathic dynamics apparent when a content analysis and sequence of scores interpretation are done. Failure to understand the aggressive identifications of the psychopath, whether psychotic or not, and his propensity for predatory violence (even when fueled by delusions, Mp–; see Meloy, 1988) could also contribute to serious misinterpretation of these data.

It is likely Sam's delusional fantasies persisted while he was in remission, but were sufficiently controlled and contained to be concealed from staff. These fantasies were primary drive mechanisms during his serial murdering (Prentky et al., 1989; see chapter 9), and continued to be. Case 1 is an excellent clinical example of the fact that, despite the wonders of modern biochemistry, this patient remained (a) a paranoid schizophrenic, (b) a primary psychopath, (c) a serial murderer, and (d) a continual danger, whether manifesting obvious psychotic symptoms or not.

ED, A NONPSYCHOPATHIC ANTISOCIAL
SCHIZOPHRENIC MALE

Ed is a 41-year-old Black male, with a diagnosis of schizophrenia, paranoid type, chronic, and antisocial personality disorder. Ed's score on the PCL–R was < 30. Ed is not a psychopath. In order to protect his anonymity we have withheld any additional historical information.

Ed's Rorschach

Clinicians reading Ed's protocol for the first time will be struck by their unpleasant, visceral reactions. From Response 6 on, we are privy to the violent, regressive, and sexually suffused internal world of the paranoid schizophrenic.[16] Oral, anal, genital, and phallic zones of libidinal interest are condensed with both sexual and aggressive drives. Ed's protocol is difficult to read because it overrides our own higher level defenses with graphic, primary process material—thoughts that, perhaps, could originate in ourselves. Only when spoken do such taboos marshall feelings of disgust and repulsion as an affective defense against their contemplation in the nonpsychotic individual.

Scoring a psychotic protocol like Ed's can be a difficult task. The clinician will find his own handwritten protocol a confusing mess, and will often resort to lines and arrows to somehow link, or tie together, various free associations and various inquiries. This is often diagnostic of a thought disorder where tangentiality and circumstantiality (and our drawn vectors that symbolize them) rule the day. Only when the record has been sorted out, and read several times to desensitize the visceral reaction, can an organized and systematic approach to interpretation begin.[17]

Table 6.10 presents Ed's Rorschach protocol. His scoring sequence and structural summary are included in Tables 6.11 and 6.12, respectively. The content of Tables 6.11 and 6.12 were generated with the RIAP–2 (Exner et al., 1990). This second case is in remarkable contrast to the first one as interpretation of structure, sequence, and content reveal.

Structural Interpretation

Ed produces a normative number of responses (R = 23) within a valid protocol (Lambda = .44). Although his resources are above average for both schizophrenics (EA = 8.63) or schizophrenic ASPDs (EA = 6.86), an ambitent problem-solving style (EB = 6:5.5), high levels of thought disorder (WSum6 = 66), less than adequate controls (D = −1), and impaired reality testing (X−% = 48%) make it highly unlikely that Ed is able to utilize them. The Comprehensive System data suggest (with reasonable certainty) a schizophrenic diagnosis. As we noted earlier in the chapter, false positive rates when the SCZI = 6 (Ed's score) do not exceed 1% (Exner, 1991).

Although Ed processes information (Zf = 13) at normative rates, he is an overincorporator (Zd = +6.0). Not necessarily an indicator of psychopathology, this information-processing trait is marked by a deliberate and careful attention to detail and is consistent with a paranoid orientation. Ed's whole responses are equal to

---

[16]Our colleague Philip Erdberg described the inner world of the ASPD schizophrenic as a "primordial ooze" (Philip Erdberg, personal communication, June 1993).

[17]We often finished a day of rescoring the schizophrenic ASPD Rorschachs from Atascadero State Hospital and the Medical Facility at Vacaville with pseudothought disorders of our own.

TABLE 6.10
Ed, a Nonpsychopathic Antisocial Schizophrenic Male

I   1. At first I thought it was a butterfly.   E: What made it look like a butterfly?

S: The wings.

Comprehensive Scoring: Wo Fo A P 1.0
Aggression Scoring: None
Primitive Modes of Relating: None
Defenses: None categorized

2. Two navels kissing.   E: What made it look like two navels?

S: The way they are humped up and the way this little hole is open it looks like they are kissing.

Comprehensive Scoring: Dd+22 Ma− 2 Hd 4.0 FAB2,DV′
Aggression Scoring: None
Primitive Modes of Relating: None
Defenses: Massive denial

3. Crab hands.   E: What made it look like crab hands?

S: Because they don't look like they have fingers. Just like crab hands.

Comprehensive Scoring: Ddo24 Fu2 Ad INC,ALOG
Aggression Scoring: None
Primitive Modes of Relating: None
Defenses: Massive denial

4. How pretty the lady's legs are.   E: What made it look like a lady's legs?

S: The shape and legs.

Comprehensive Scoring: Do Fo Hd
Aggression Scoring: None
Primitive Modes of Relating: None
Defenses: None categorized

5. This out here looks like birds, roosters, or hawks.   E: What made it look like birds?

S: Like a hawk with his wings open.

E: Hawk?

S: The head and back.

Comprehensive Scoring: Do7 Fo 2 A
Aggression Scoring: None
Primitive Modes of Relating: None
Defenses: None categorized

6. This is somebody taking a crap or somebody has got something stuck up in them. Drops of blood and somebody might have been emasculated. Homosexuals from behind.   E: What made it look like somebody?

S: There is something hanging down and it looks like something is hanging down and it looks like it is coming out of somebody's asshole and it looks like it is running down his leg.

(Continued)

TABLE 6.10
(Continued)

E: Blood?

S: This looks like the shape of a man's dick and it could be stuck in the homosexual ass and this is like blood. Like it is clotted.

E: Clotted?

S: It isn't drops, it is clots.

E: Emasculated?

S: It just looks like it was cut off.

Comprehensive Scoring: Dd+99 Ma.ma− Hd,Bl,Sx 4.0 MOR
Aggression Scoring: AgPast
Primitive Modes of Relating: Violent symbiosis, Malignant internal processes, Boundary disturbance
Defenses: Projection

II   7. Pretty gruesome. I don't want to say but it does look like a bleeding vagina and this way it looks like a bleeding vagina. These look like hands that are−fingers that are opening a woman's vagina like they are going to have oral copulation or something. And this way it looks like the fingers are opening− the woman is trying to direct him.

E: What made it look gruesome?

S: This.

E: Vagina?

S: The way the colors are and the way it comes out and the way the opening it looks like a vagina−a clitoris and opening here.

E: Blood?

S: Because of the color.

E: Color?

S: The red and the way it is shaded.

E: Shaded?

S: How the colors look with the shading black.

E: Hands?

S: That looks like fingers like they are opening the vagina.

Comprehensive Scoring: D+3 ma.CF.VF.Ma− 2 Sx,Bl,Hd 4.5 MOR
Aggression Scoring: None
Primitive Modes of Relating: Malignant internal processes
Defenses: Devaluation

    8. Or asshole and this way it looks like a bleeding asshole.

E: What made it look like an asshole?

S: Because this looks like an open asshole and this could be the blood. The color. The way the shades are colored and the way the texture looks like it could be shit coming out (touches card).

E: Blood?

S: I don't know, just the way it is shaded.

E: Shaded?

S: The color red.

(Continued)

TABLE 6.10
(Continued)

E: Texture?

S: The way the shading looks (touches card).

E: Shit?

S: The way it looks like a cut out anus.

E: Cut out?

S: I don't know.

Comprehensive Scoring: Dds+99 ma.FT.CF− Sx,Bl,Hd 4.5 MOR
Aggression Scoring: AgPast
Primitive Modes of Relating: Violent symbiosis
Defenses: Projection

III 9. This looks like two black Africans that cut two other black Africans' heads off. That looks like they got high heel boots on. They could be homosexuals. It looks like they have tits like homosexuals. It looks like they have hard-ons. And they are holding two people's heads—each one has a head.

E: What made it look like Africans?

S: This looks like the heads. And this is blood or part of the produce of cutting two black Africans' heads off.

E: African?

S: Because they are black and their heads are shaped like Africans'.

E: Blood?

S: The way it is shaped—the way—red drops.

E: Homosexual?

S: It looks like they could be taking a hormone and they have breasts.

Comprehensive Scoring: W+ FC′.Ma.CFu 2 H,Cg,Sx,Bl P 5.5 MOR,INC2,DV
Aggression Scoring: AgPast
Primitive Modes of Relating: Violent symbiosis
Defenses: Projection, Massive denial

IV 10. Like a giant bean stalk. A black giant bean stalk with a tail. And big feet. And tore off arms. And a headless looking "Acuphillia" the headless monsters.

E: What made it look like a bean stalk?

S: Because of the way it is angled—like if I look up at the top like it is a big piece of plant—not human—monster plant.

E: Tail?

S: Just the way the angle on the ink is on the paper.

E: Big feet?

S: Kind of an optical depth perception.

E: Ink?

S: It is black.

E: Torn off?

S: Because it looks like they are just hanging off like they were torn off.

Comprehensive Scoring: W+ FC′.FV− Bt,(Ad) 4.0 MOR,INC2,DV2
Aggression Scoring: AgPast
Primitive Modes of Relating: Violent symbiosis
Defenses: Projection, Massive denial, Devaluation

(Continued)

TABLE 6.10

(Continued)

V 11. This is a real butterfly. I think it is a burnt butterfly. It is a butterfly that got burned while trying to come out of his cocoon. This looks like a stingray or bat.

E: What made it look like a real butterfly?
S: The wings.
E: Burnt?
S: Because it looks like it was smooth (touches card).
E: Smooth?
S: It isn't smooth because it looks like it was made in a fire.
E: Fire?
S: Because it is ragged and rough.
E: Cocoon?
S: (touches card) Because it is burned. Because it is ragged and torn.
E: Stingray or bat?
S: Like those underwater mammals.
E: Mammals?
S: The two backs that are sticking out.

Comprehensive Scoring: Wo FTo A P 1.0 MOR,INC
Aggression Scoring: AgPast
Primitive Modes of Relating: Metamorphosis and transformation, Birth-rebirth
Defenses: Projection

VI 12. This is a penis. Like a flying penis with whiskers. Flying "Cocketail."

E: What made it look like a penis?
S: It looks like a penis, a male penis. These look like the testes.
E: Flying?
S: Because of these – like the condom is torn off.

Comprehensive Scoring: D+ ma– Hd,Sx 2.5 DV2,MOR,INC2
Aggression Scoring: None
Primitive Modes of Relating: Malignant internal processes, Violent symbiosis
Defenses: Massive denial

13. Like somebody is bent over like they just bent over and you can see like they are a two organ person.

E: What made it look like somebody?
S: This could be one organ and this could be another.
E: Another?
S: It looks like a woman organ.
E: Woman organ?
S: Because of the way it looks – it is open and this looks like a male organ.
E: Male organ?
S: Because it protrudes.

Comprehensive Scoring: Do Mp– Hd,Sx INC2
Aggression Scoring: None
Primitive Modes of Relating: Boundary disturbance
Defenses: Massive denial

(Continued)

223

TABLE 6.10
(Continued)

VII 14. This looks like a woman with her legs open getting ready to get ate out—like she is getting ready for me to eat her out.

E: What made it look like woman?

S: Because it has that look, because of how—maybe he couldn't see anything—could you see this? And this looks like her nylons—no nylons.

E: Nylons?

S: The way it looks—no, not nylons—the texture of the shading.

E: Texture?

S: (touches card)

Comprehensive Scoring: Wo Mp.FT— H,Cg,Sx 2.5 PER
Aggression Scoring: None
Primitive Modes of Relating: None
Defenses: Omnipotence

15. This also looks like clouds.

E: What made it look like clouds?

S: The way I have seen clouds in the sky. Storm clouds, dark.

Comprehensive Scoring: Wv C'Fo 2 Cl PER
Aggression Scoring: None
Primitive Modes of Relating: None
Defenses: None categorized

VIII 16. This looks like two squirrels.

E: What made it look like two squirrels?

S: They look like squirrels with fur (touches card).

E: Fur?

S: Because it is rough (touches card).

Comprehensive Scoring: DO FTo 2 A P
Aggression Scoring: None
Primitive Modes of Relating: None
Defenses: Isolation

17. Like an ice glacier and these are tigers or lions like the North Pole—the pink tigers on each side. This looks like some kind of exotic entrance to some kind of cavern or cave with gold or silver—like a gold find.

E: What made it look like an ice glacier?

S: See how these stick out.

E: Exotic entrance?

S: Because it looks like, it looks like a woman holding open her body to let someone in.

E: You mentioned a cave?

S: That is what I mean by exotic—like it is gold status. This is what makes it gold status.

E: Cavern or cave?

S: It looks like some rock—like it is a texture of some rock.

E: Texture?

S: The way the color is shaded.

(Continued)

TABLE 6.10
(Continued)

E: Shaded?
S: The way the colors blend—kind of yellow and red.

Comprehensive Scoring: W+ FT.CF− 2 A,Hd,Ls P 4.5 INC,DR2,FAB
Aggression Scoring: None
Primitive Modes of Relating: Womb imagery
Defenses: Isolation, Idealization, Pollyannish denial

IX   18. This is some kind of magic potent—like
         something coming out of a sorcerer's
         glass. And it has—I like the colors—it
         has a mystic type of look to it. Like
         some magical powers that are getting
         ready to make peace.

E: What made it look like magic potent?
S: This is the sorcerer's like you see in
   special effect. The way it is shaped and
   the way the color and shapes are blended together—like special effects. The
   color is like clouds of smoke.
E: Powers?
S: It looks mystic.

Comprehensive Scoring: Wv ma.CFu Cl AB
Aggression Scoring: None
Primitive Modes of Relating: Boundary disturbance
Defenses: Hypomanic denial

19. I see two pregnant women with hair on
    their stomachs.

E: What made it look like two women?
S: I don't think men could be pregnant.
E: Pregnant?
S: The way it sticks out.

Comprehensive Scoring: Ddo F− 2 H ALOG
Aggression Scoring: None
Primitive Modes of Relating: Birth-rebirth
Defenses: None categorized

20. Two heads of a skeleton.

E: What made it look like that?
S: This right here (outlines).

Comprehensive Scoring: Do F− 2 An INC
Aggression Scoring: None
Primitive Modes of Relating: Boundary disturbance
Defenses: Massive denial, Devaluation

X   21. Two seahorses.

E: What made it look like seahorses?
S: This blue seahorse.
E: Blue?
S: Like something out of the ocean.

Comprehensive Scoring: Do FCu 2 A INC
Aggression Scoring: None
Primitive Modes of Relating: None
Defenses: Pollyannish denial

(Continued)

TABLE 6.10
(Continued)

22. Two munchkins with hard-on clubs in their hands.	E: What made it look like munchkins?
	S: Because they look like they got feelers and legs and they look like they are hairy—like bowels and like cartoon characters.
	E: Hard on?
	S: The way the drops of ink are.
	E: Ink?
	S: It is dark and light and shading.

Comprehensive Scoring: D+ FTu 2 (H),Sx 4.0 DV2
Aggression Scoring: AgContent
Primitive Modes of Relating: Boundary disturbance
Defenses: Devaluation, Higher level denial

23. Some patterns of different types of crazy looking insects.	E: What made it look like insects?
	S: They just look like crazy looking insects like the type I would never find on this planet.
	E: Crazy?
	S: Because I can't make out anything else.

Comprehensive Scoring: Wo Fo A 5.5 ALOG,PER
Aggression Scoring: None
Primitive Modes of Relating: None
Defenses: None categorized

---

detail responses (W:D = 9:9), while elevations are noted on Dd responses (Dd = 5). In paranoid schizophrenia, this paradoxical juxtaposition of both elevated W and Dd may indicate both the striving, grandiose quality of initial perception, *and* the detailed search for the hidden meaning, the reading between the lines.

Ed's cognitive mediation is idiosyncratic and unconventional (F+% = 57%), and becomes more so when affects and ideation (X+% = 30%), both volitional and nonvolitional, enter the perceptual task. Reality testing, the differential between borderline and psychotic personality organization (Exner, 1986b; Kernberg, 1984), is grossly impaired and psychotic (X−% = 48%), and appears to be structurally, rather than dynamically based.[18] Ideation is also grossly impaired. Formal thought disorder is severe and pervasive (WSum 6 = 66), and primarily manifest in the absurd juxtaposition of part objects that do not exist in the real world (FAB = 2; INC = 9). Behavioral rigidity is also expected as a result of cognitive disorganization, and a plethora of M− responses, including

---

[18]Ed's reality-testing deficits are pervasive. Their severity outweighs any particular sequence interpretation of scoring, special scores, or determinants, all of which might be dynamically based. One would clinically expect this with a disorder such as schizophrenia wherein biochemistry is more important than psychodynamics in determining thinking problems.

TABLE 6.11
Ed's Rorschach Sequence of Scores

CARD	NO	LOC	#	DETERMINANT(S)	(2)	CONTENT(S)	POP	Z	SPECIAL SCORES
I	1	Wo	1	Fo		A	P	1.0	
	2	Dd+	22	Ma−	2	Hd		4.0	FAB2,DV
	3	Ddo	24	Fu	2	Ad			INC,ALOG
	4	Do		Fo		Hd			
	5	Do	7	Fo	2	A			
	6	Dd+	99	Ma.ma−		Hd,Bl,Sx		4.0	MOR
II	7	D+	3	ma.CF.VF.Ma−	2	Sx,Bl,Hd		4.5	MOR
	8	DdS+		ma.FT.CF−		Sx,Bl,Hd		4.5	MOR
III	9	W+	1	FC'.Ma.CFu	2	H,Cg,Sx,Bl	P	5.5	MOR,INC2,DV
IV	10	W+	1	FC'.FV−		Bt,(Ad)		4.0	MOR,INC2,DV2
V	11	Wo	1	FTo		A	P	1.0	MOR,INC
VI	12	D+		ma−		Hd,Sx		2.5	DV2,MOR,INC2
	13	Do		Mp−		Hd,Sx			INC2
VII	14	Wo	1	Mp.FT−		H,Cg,Sx		2.5	PER
	15	Wv	1	C'Fo	2	Cl			PER
VIII	16	Do		FTo	2	A	P		
	17	W+	1	FT.CF−	2	A,Hd,Ls	P	4.5	INC,DR2,FAB
IX	18	Wv	1	ma.CFu		Cl			AB
	19	Ddo		F−	2	H			ALOG
	20	Do		F−	2	An			INC
X	21	Do		FCu	2	A			INC
	22	D+		FTu	2	(H),Sx		4.0	DV2
	23	Wo	1	Fo		A		5.5	ALOG,PER

SUMMARY OF APPROACH

I:W.Dd.Dd.D.D.Dd   VI:D.D
II:D.DdS   VII:W.W
III:W   VIII:D.W.
IV:W   IX:W.Dd.D
V:W   X:D.D.W

two passive ones, suggest the presence of delusional thought content, more obvious in this case than in Case 1.

Ed is either not pathologically narcissistic or too disorganized to produce a reflection (Fr+rF = 0). He is, however, self-absorbed (3r+(2)/R = .52) and continuously ruminating (V = 2) about his deeply held sense of damage and self-injury (MOR = 7). Interpersonally he is isolative (Isolate/R = .26) with a schizoid relation to other objects. There is no expectation of cooperativeness from others (COP = 0), tensions of aggression (AG = 0), or dependency needs (Fd = 0). His internal representations are part-object dominated (H:Hd = 3:8), with a strong paranoid undercurrent and sexual preoccupation (Sx = 8).

Ed is internally assaulted by confusing and strong emotions (Blends = 8) such as affectional hunger (T = 6), dysphoria (es = 16; ColShading Blend > 0), and

TABLE 6.12

Ed's Rorschach Structural Summary

Location Features	Determinants		Contents	S-Constellation
	Blends	Single		

Location Features	Blends	Single	Contents	S-Constellation
				NO..FV+VF+V+FD > 2
			H = 3, 0	YES..Col-Shd Bl > 0
Zf = 13	M.m	M = 2	(H) = 1, 0	YES..Ego < .31, > .44
ZSum = 47.5	m.CF.VF.M	FM = 0	Hd = 5, 3	YES..MOR > 3
ZEst = 41.5	m.FT.CF	m = 1	(Hd)= 0, 0	YES..Zd > +− 3.5
	FC'.M.CF	FC = 1	Hx = 0, 0	YES..es > EA
W = 9	FC'.FV	CF = 0	A = 7, 0	YES..CF+C > FC
(Wv = 2)	M.FT	C = 0	(A) = 0, 0	YES..X+% < .70
D = 9	FT.CF	Cn = 0	AD = 1, 0	NO..S > 3
Dd = 5	m.CF	FC' = 0	(Ad)= 0, 1	NO..P < 3 or > 8
S = 1		C'F = 1	An = 1, 0	NO..Pure H < 2
		C' = 0	Art = 0, 0	NO..R < 17
DQ		FT = 3	Ay = 0, 0	7.....TOTAL
......(FQ−)		TF = 0	Bl = 0, 4	
+ = 9 (7)		T = 0	Bt = 1, 0	Special Scorings
o = 12 (4)		FV = 0	Cg = 0, 2	
v/+ = 0 (0)		VF = 0	Cl = 2, 0	Lv1 Lv2
v = 2 (0)		V = 0	Ex = 0, 0	DV = 2 × 1 3 × 2
		FY = 0	Fd = 0, 0	INC = 5 × 2 4 × 4
		YF = 0	Fi = 0, 0	DR = 0 × 3 1 × 6
		Y = 0	Ge = 0, 0	FAB = 1 × 4 1 × 7
		Fr = 0	Hh = 0, 0	ALOG = 3 × 5
Form Quality		rF = 0	Ls = 0, 1	CON = 0 × 7
		FD = 0	Na = 0, 0	SUM6 = 20
	FQx FQf MQual SQx	F = 7	Sc = 0, 0	WSUM6= 66
+ = 0 0 0 0			Sx = 2, 6	AB = 1 CP = 0
o = 7 4 0 0			Xy = 0, 0	AG = 0 MOR = 7
u = 5 1 1 0			Id = 0, 0	CFB = 0 PER = 3
− = 11 2 5 1				COP = 0 PSV = 0
none = 0 − 0 0		(2) = 12		

Ratios, Percentages, and Derivations

R = 23	L = 0.44		FC:CF+C = 1: 5	COP = 0	AG = 0
			Pure C = 0	Food = 0
EB = 6: 5.5	EA = 11.5	EBPer = N/A	Afr = 0.53	Isolate/R = 0.26
eb = 5: 11	es = 16	D = −1	S = 1	H:(H)Hd(Hd) = 3: 9
	Adj es = 5	Adj D = 0	Blends:R = 8:23	(HHd):(AAd) = 1: 1
			CP = 0	H+A:Hd+Ad = 11:10
FM = 0 : C' = 3	T = 6			
m = 5 : V = 2	Y = 0	P = 5	Zf = 13	3r+(2)/R = 0.52
a:p = 9: 2	Sum6 = 20	X+% = 0.30	Zd = +6.0	Fr+rF = 0
Ma:Mp = 4: 2	Lv2 = 9	F+% = 0.57	W:D:Dd = 9: 9: 5	FD = 0
2AB+Art+Ay = 2	WSum6 = 66	X−% = 0.48	W:M = 9: 6	An+Xy = 1
M− = 5	Mnone = 0	S−% = 0.09	DQ+ = 9	MOR = 7
		Xu% = 0.22	DQv = 2	

SCZI = 6*	DEPI = 6*	CDI = 2	S-CON = 7	HVI = No	OBS = No

228

perhaps remorse (V = 2). Although hampered by a clear sense of "being shot at" (m = 5), he is curiously absent any feelings of anxiety (Y = 0). Ed modulates affect poorly (FC:CF+C = 1:5), working hard to restrain (C' = 3) his feelings. The severity of his affective problems are revealed through decrements in perceptual accuracy and an elevated depression index (DEPI = 6). Although the suicide constellation is not positive (7), it is close. A concurrent mood disorder and suicidality should both be carefully assessed.

Interpretation of Scoring Sequence

Ed begins with a popular response (P) that is unremarkable. Populars generally facilitate adequate form quality, as they are easily recognized. Some schizophrenics, however, manage to spoil the form quality of even populars (see chapter 7). This is the case with Ed as only 40% (N = 2; Responses 1 & 16) of his popular responses are untarnished by inadequate perceptual accuracy or cognitive slippage; two others have u or − form (9 & 17), while a third (11) contains an INC.

Response 2, containing human content (Hd), indicates a complete loss of reality testing (Ma−) as well as severe cognitive slippage (FAB2). A psychotic disorder is suggested given the infrequency of Level 2 special scores in nonpsychotic individuals (2% in nonpatient males; Exner, 1991) and the presence of a psychotic defense, massive denial. Response 2 also introduces a defensive strategy employed ineffectively by Ed throughout the record. In order to reduce a potentially threatening stimulus (Hd), he defensively narrows the stimulus field (Dd). This strategy is ineffective on Response 2 (− form and FAB2) and elsewhere (3, 6, 8, 19). All five (100%) Dd responses evidence inadequate form quality (2, 6, 8, & 19 are − form). Content of these responses reveals an affective or interpersonal pull as four (80%) Dd responses contain H or Hd content, whereas two also contain Sx and Bl content. The fifth Dd (Response 3) contains Ad content with unusual form and severe cognitive slippage (ALOG). Recovery occurs on Response 4 despite the presence of Hd content. Adequate form continues on Response 5; however, the pull of Response 6 (Hd,Bl,Sx) causes an aborted attempt to successfully reduce threat (− form) by narrowing the stimulus field (Dd).

The disorganization caused by affect (Responses 7 & 8 contain Col Shading Blends, Sx,Bl, & Hd content and MORs) continues on Card II. The Dd (#8) once again is ineffective in managing affect stimulated by rumination (#7) and affectional need (#8). Ninety-two percent (11 of 12) of Ed's responses with H, Hd, or (H) content contain either − form quality (2, 6, 7, 8, 12, 13, 14, 17, 19), a severely pathological special score (2, 9, 12, 13, 17, 19, 22), or both (2, 9, 12, 13, 17, 19, 22). The presence of sexual content (Sx) on eight of the human content responses suggest pervasive sexual preoccupation. The emotions stimulated by Responses 7 and 8 are ego-dystonic and experienced as assaultive (both responses contain m).

Response 9 (Card III) reveals the failed use of a popular to recompensate (u form; INC2). Painful rumination (FV & MOR) and affective constraint (FC') are once again suggested by Response 10. The production of FC' on Responses 9 and 10 might be interpreted as Ed attempting to apply the affective "brakes" after the disruptions indicated on the two preceding responses.

Response 11 (Card V) contains a popular with an INC. Although Card V is typically a difficult card (bat or butterfly) to spoil, Ed succeeds. This response contains his second FT determinant and deserves comment. The production of six FT responses would be unexpected in psychopaths (Gacono & Meloy, 1991). Ed is not one. A qualitative analysis of his texture responses reveal that most are spoiled. Four (Responses 8, 14, 17, & 22) contain either u or − form quality with some variation of human content. The other two (11 & 16) have adequate form but are produced with populars and animal content. The variety of content, form quality, and special scores occurring with his texture responses are consistent with diffuse and primitive affectional hunger and suggest the disruptive effect of this emotional state on Ed's intrapsychic and interpersonal world.

Card VI contains two responses (12 & 13) both with − form, Hd and Sx content, and Level 2 special scores. Reality testing is lost on both (ma− and Mp−) as nonvolitional ideation prompted by anxiety becomes, perhaps, delusion. Bizarre juxtaposition of part objects once again defines Ed's formal thought disorder (INC2). Card VII (#14) begins with a sexualized tactile response (FT, H, Cg, & Sx content). Despite the lack of scorable aggression, this personalized response containing omnipotence and a Mp− is troubling. It raises questions concerning the presence and nature of his sexual delusions and warrants further evaluation by a clinician.[19] Partial recovery is revealed on Response 15 as adequate perceptual accuracy occurs; however, developmental quality and determinants (Wv C'F) suggest boundary disturbance and attempted affective constraint.

Card VIII begins with an adequate response (#16) aided by a popular. Influenced by affect (CF−) and affectional need (FT) deterioration occurs (#17) as Ed attempts to incorporate the whole (W). Ed's color shading blend (FT.CF−) is interesting, suggesting the diffuse and undifferentiated nature of his inner affective experience. A number of strategies are used to manage the dysphoric aspects of Card IX, but inadequate form quality and special scores indicate their failure.

Card X reveals more of the same. Ed's final response (#23) is almost a personal signature. Perceptual accuracy warrants an ordinary score, but "crazy" is introduced to define the insect's appearances. It is stated in the context of personal experience (PER) and illogic (ALOG). The pervasiveness of Ed's thought disorder and the ineffectiveness of his defenses are highlighted throughout the record. He fails to recover on most cards as the final response for every card contains either severe cognitive slippage or − form quality. Response 15 (Card

---

[19]Additionally, the content of this response, "like she is getting ready for me to eat her out" indicates Ed's perception, similar to some sex offenders, that "she really wanted it."

VII) is the only exception. This undifferentiated (Wv) and poorly modulated (C'F) response can hardly be considered indicative of recovery. Typical of the acutely psychotic subject the battle between impulse and defense is not much of a contest; the former overwhelms the latter with only minimal protest.

Interpretation of Content

Bizarre combinations, malevolent, damaged and diffuse object relations, and primitive defenses are revealed through an analysis of content. Ed disregards reality as part and whole objects are inappropriately combined. Percepts such as "Two navels kissing" (#1), "Crab hands" (#2), "It looks like they have tits like homosexuals ... they are holding two people's heads—each one has a head" (#9), "A black giant bean stalk with a tail" (#10), "Like a flying penis with whiskers, flying 'Cocketail' " (#12), "two organ people" (#13), "some kind of cavern or cave ... woman holding open her body ..." (#17), "Two heads of a skeleton" (#20), suggest a severe thought disorder. Almost half ($N = 10$; 44%) of Ed's percepts involve bizarre combinations.

A plethora of Kwawer's (1980) PMRs ($N = 13$; 57%) reveal the quality and nature of Ed's object relations. He exhibits a malevolent (violent symbiosis, separation, & reunion responses on 6, 8, 9, 10, & 12), dysphoric (malignant internal processes responses on 6, 7, & 12), and diffuse internalized object world (boundary disturbance responses on 6, 13, 18, 20, & 22). Ed's production of womb imagery (#17) and birth-rebirth (11, 19) responses suggest developmental issues related to the symbiotic phase. Their appearance is consistent with our earlier hypothesis predicting a greater prevalence of these indices among schizophrenic samples when compared to character-disordered groups. As reported earlier in this chapter, however, these were infrequently produced by either schizophrenic ASPDs or ASPDs and there was no significant differences between groups. Response 11 (metamorphosis and transformation) is particularly compelling from an object relations perspective, "I think it is a burnt butterfly. It is a butterfly that got burned while trying to come out of his cocoon." Note that this response contained an FT and MOR.

Ed's percepts contain a vulnerable and morbid quality as objects present as open, penetrated, or damaged (Fisher & Cleveland, 1958; AgPast = 5). Sexual themes and preoccupations predominate, sometimes combined with morbidity which focuses on the genitalia and the anus; a primary anal-narcissistic defensive structure and a fear of homosexual assault can be inferred. Shengold (1988) detailed this when he wrote:

> The anal defensive complex is returned to in subsequent psychic danger situations as a concomitant of a defensive regression toward narcissism ... The sphincter-like defensive power of reducing intensities enables the individual to modulate unpleasure and pain, to avoid overstimulation, and to diminish and evade conflict-ridden feelings associated with object-ties. If the defense goes too far ...

everything that evokes value and meaning can become undifferentiated stuff, and turn to excretable shit ... projected onto a defensive wall of indifference—a metaphor for the anal character structure ... that isolates from the world of others, and from the contradictory emotions that make for our humanity. (p. 24)

The frequent use of projection ($N = 5$) coupled with vulnerability and damaged self suggests a paranoid orientation. Response 6 is particularly revealing in this regard: The object has been aggressed against and damaged in a homosexual assault, and there is a condensing of fecal elimination ("taking a crap"), genital penetration ("something stuck up in them"), and genital destruction ("emasculated").[20] Additionally, Kwawer's (1980) PMR yield three scorable responses, indicative of objects violently struggling to separate, deteriorating internal organs, and confusion of boundaries.

Response 6 is a flight into heterosexual consensual sex, but the act is devalued through the inference that a "bleeding vagina" is "gruesome." This warrants a morbid (MOR) score given the patient's perception. The response introduces another widely held taboo that will probably elicit disgust in the examiner—the performing of cunnilingus while the woman is menstruating—and is a double condensation: the merging of procreation with eroticism and orality with genitality. Aggression, however, has been removed from consciousness.

Also of interest is the absence of overt sexual reference but hidden phallic-homosexual meaning, on Response 10. The neologism, "acuphillia," could be derived from the Latin *acus* meaning needle and the Greek *philos* meaning love.

Primitive defenses support Ed's bizarre combinations and disturbed object relations. Denial is most frequently used and appears in a number of forms: massive denial ($N = 7$), Pollyannish denial ($N = 2$), hypomanic denial ($N = 1$), and higher level denial ($N = 1$). Other defenses are also produced: projection ($N = 5$), devaluation ($N = 4$), omnipotence ($N = 1$), isolation ($N = 2$), idealization ($N = 1$).

Summary

Ed was chronically ill at the time of testing, and his protocol, when contrasted to Sam's (Case 1), demonstrates the great variability that can be seen across schizophrenic Rorschachs. The sexual preoccupation of this patient deserves further study, and application of the Morgan and Viglione (1992) sex response analysis would be useful to help delineate the risk of sexual offending. They reported that "sexually disturbed subjects produce more sexual responses under

---

[20]In cases such as this the clinician should note that delusional fear of homosexual assault by the paranoid schizophrenic patient does not rule out the possibility of real sexual victimization in the past, or the future. This risk is particularly warranted in maximum security prisons when mentally ill inmates are mixed with nonmentally ill inmates—the former are likely to be physically, emotionally, and sexually abused by the latter.

certain conditions than do closely matched but nonsexually disturbed subjects. General support is provided for the notion that sexual contents escape defenses in sexual disturbances and can be expressed in Rorschach responses under certain conditions" (p. 535). We had no data on this subject's sexual offense history, and his Rorschach awaits further analysis in this obvious area of clinical concern.

The Reflection Response

And when you look long into an abyss, the abyss also looks into you
—Nietzsche

W^{V+} M^P.V.r Id MORPot

Perhaps Nietzsche's abyss symbolizes the perfect mirror, reflecting the looker's emptiness. Lacking a capacity for object love, the potential for psychic deterioration (MORPot) hovers inchoate at its boundaries. In the original myth Narcissus' investment in self negated the possibility of object love. Unlike the neurotic for whom introspection might produce self-awareness and growth, Narcissus might have lived to an old age if he only could have looked beyond his own image. Narcissus, desired by many, loved no one but himself.

The story goes that one spurned admirer prayed to the gods that Narcissus love only himself and thereby not gain the thing he loved. The admirer's prayers were answered when thirsty Narcissus chanced upon a virgin spring. For the first time he perceived his own image reflected in the pool. Enamored and fearful the image would be lost should he divert his attention, Narcissus was unable to tear himself away from it. Unwilling to seek food or rest, in love with an insubstantial hope, an amorous illusion, propelled by the need to be reflected in the eyes of another, Narcissus sank into a psychic abyss and languished away. He left behind only a flower and an echoing nymph, symbols of what might have been.

The myth of Narcissus highlights many of the features associated with pathological narcissism: arrogance, self-centeredness, grandiosity, lack of empathy, uncertain body image, poorly differentiated self and object boundaries, absence of enduring object attachments, and a lack of psychological substance

(Nunberg, 1979). The nature of an individual's attachments reveals much about his psychological health. Object relations characterized by libidinal investment in self-representations at the expense of cathexis to object representations (Kernberg, 1975), mental activity designed to maintain structural cohesiveness with positive affective coloring of self-representations (Stolorow, 1975), or where the nature of the libidinal investment is idealization or self-aggrandizement (Kohut, 1971), are all considered narcissistic. As with the myth, these internalized object relations are not self-sustaining, but rather, subject to deterioration over time. Freud (1914) described the relationship between psychological health and object love: "A strong egoism is a protection against falling ill, but in the last resort we must begin to love in order not to fall ill, and we are bound to fall ill if, in consequence of frustration, we are unable to love" (p. 85).

Although often misunderstood, the concept of narcissism has been central to psychoanalytic theory (Teicholz, 1978). At various times the term has been applied to libidinal cathexis of the ego, a developmental stage, a type of object choice, the nature of libido (rather than target), specific internalized structure (grandiose self-structure; Kernberg, 1975), a mode of relating characterized by a lack of object relations, and, as part of a broader concept of self-esteem (Pulver, 1986). Originally used to describe a sexual perversion characterized by the treatment of one's own body as a sexual object (Ellis, 1927), Freud expanded upon the concept, discussing narcissism in economic terms and establishing its roots in drive theory (Freud, 1910, 1911). In 1914 he defined primary narcissism as the libidinal investment of the ego that occurred before an investment in external objects, and secondary narcissism as that which occurred after such investment was frustrated, resulting in a withdrawal of object cathexis and reinvestment in the ego. Freud's major contributions to the concept of narcissism were:

> . . . 1) a definition of (secondary) narcissism as a withdrawal of libido "from the outer world" and a redirection of the libido onto the ego; 2) the designation of the ego ideal as the "heir" or adult version of infantile narcissism; 3) the observation that there was a certain kind of object choice and object relation that must be labeled as narcissistic, based on the quality of need for that object and the psychic function served by it; 4) a recognition of "a very intimate connection" between "self-regard" and "narcissistic libido." (Teicholz, 1978, p. 833)

Freud's followers refined economic interpretations by identifying narcissism as a libidinal cathexis of the self rather than the ego, wherein self-representations rather than object representations were cathected (Hartmann, 1950; Reich, 1960). They elaborated and expanded upon "self" as part of the ego structure (Jacobson, 1964), the role of ego ideal and "ideal self" (Hartmann & Loewenstein, 1962), the differentiation and internalization of self- and object representations as stable, enduring structures (Jacobson, 1964), the role of identification in structuring self-representations and other ego functions (Meissner, 1972; Modell, 1968; Schafer, 1968), and the relation between structure and experience (Kohut, 1971; Modell, 1968). Freud's dichotomy between self-directed libido and object-directed libido was rejected as "attachments" to others were often observed in narcissistic patients. The quality of that attachment, however, served a regulatory function normally internalized and therefore carried out intrapsychically in healthy personalities (Teicholz, 1978). The other was not perceived as a separate entity, but as part of the self, used to protect the individual from intolerable negative self- and object representations (Teicholz, 1978). The etiology of pathological object ties lies in severe disappointments in the parenting relationship that prevented the integration of grandiose self-representations and idealized parent imagoes (Hartmann & Loewenstein, 1962; Kohut, 1971).

The developmental roots of narcissism also add to understanding some broader conceptualizations. Kohut (1971) postulated two *concurrent* lines of development: infantile narcissism leading to both higher forms of healthy narcissism and object love. Mahler (1958) conceptualized primary narcissism in two *consecutive* phases: normal autism (absolute primary narcissism) during an objectless period, and then normal symbiosis during which the infant behaves and functions as though he and his mother are a dual omnipotent unity within a common boundary. Our understanding of narcissim in aggression and antisocial personality is enhanced by both drive theory and developmental object relations theory.

NARCISSISM AND PSYCHOPATHY: THEORETICAL AND EMPIRICAL LINKS

Theoretical

Antisocial personality and *psychopathy* are behaviorally linked (see chapter 5) while *narcissism* and *psychopathy* are linked by character traits. At times the terms have been used interchangeably with narcissistic personality disturbance appearing in dynamic psychiatry as a synonym for psychopathy in descriptive psychiatry (Jarvinen, 1977). The relationship between narcissism and psychopathy is better understood as a continuum (Bursten, 1972, 1973; Kernberg, 1975; Millon, 1981).[1] The criminal psychopath represents a severe, aggressive variant of narcissistic disorder with a total absence of integrated superego (Gabbard, 1989; Gacono, 1988; Gacono & Meloy, 1988; Meloy, 1988).[2] Concerning this continuum, Weiner (1991) theorized, with some empirical support, that criminal psychopaths had both superego and ego impairments, while better functioning psychopaths in noncriminal settings had less ego impairments.

Meloy's (1988) seven criteria indigenous to psychopathic disturbance help distinguish between the benign and malignant narcissist (psychopath):

---

[1]These authors used the terms *antisocial* or *severe narcissist* when they were describing the psychopath.

[2]By definition the incarcerated criminal psychopath has failed. He generally has a history of violence toward others, felony offenses, and subsequent incarceration.

1. The predominance of aggressive drive derivatives and the gratification of aggression as the only significant mode of relating to others.

2. The absence of more passive and independent modes of narcissistic repair.

3. The presence of sadistic or cruel behavior, inferring the activation of primitive persecutory introjects, or "sadistic superego precursors" (Kernberg, 1984, p. 281).

4. The presence of a malignant ego ideal with developmental roots in a cruel and aggressive primary parental object.

5. The absence of a desire to morally justify one's behavior, which would imply the presence of superego precursors of a more socially acceptable ego ideal.

6. The presence of both anal-eliminative and phallic-exhibitionistic libidinal themes in the repetitive interpersonal cycle of goal conflict with others, the intent to deceive, the carrying out of the deceptive act, and the contemptuous delight when victory is perceived (Bursten, 1973).

7. The emergence of paranoid ideation when under stress, rather than a vulnerability to depressive affect.

Empirical

Rorschach findings suggest deficits for psychopaths in the areas of anxiety tolerance, affectional relatedness (Gacono & Meloy, 1991), and the operation of mature idealization (Gacono, 1990; Gacono & Meloy, 1992). Absent these traits the psychopath is developmentally incapable of mature object love. These abilities, although impaired, remain in the narcissistic personality (Gacono et al., 1992).

The factor structure of the Hare Psychopathy Checklist–Revised (PCL–R; Hare, 1991) contains two primary factors (Harpur et al., 1989). The first PCL–R factor, selfish, callous, remorseless use of others (Factor 1), was found to correlate with narcissistic and histrionic personality disorders in *DSM–III–R* (APA, 1987; Harpur et al., 1989; Hart & Hare, 1989). Guided by these findings, Meloy (1992b) labeled Factor 1 of the PCL–R, "aggressive narcissism." Our psychodynamic findings and Hare's trait/behavioral findings converge, indicating that pathological narcissism is a necessary but insufficient component of psychopathy.

DEVELOPMENTAL ASPECTS OF THE REFLECTION RESPONSE

How do we measure narcissism with the Rorschach? We can entertain the hypothesis that Narcissus sought the recognition of himself in the eyes of another (McDougall, 1980). Yet he found only his reflected image in a pool. We would imaginatively expect Narcissus' protocol to contain an egocentricity ratio[3] elevated by reflections, and increased frequency of Ws (Weiner, 1966) and personals (PER). On a more serious note, we find it remarkable that a "reflection" response from a 20th-century psychological test instrument, the Rorschach, is scientifically related to a psychopathology that finds its roots in a "reflection" myth over 2,000 years old.

Like the vista (V), texture (T), human movement (M), and other responses, the reflection (Fr) response contains both face and construct validity. Vista, for instance, relies on shading (anxiety) to produce depth (psychological insight, mindedness), while a necessary correlate of visual self-focus is looking upon the objectified self as a percept, perhaps reflected in a mirror. Viewing vistas and reflections as manifestations of self-focus is consistent with a continuum for narcissism (Exner, 1969; Gear, Hill, & Liendo, 1981; Kohut, 1971). Some Rorschach scoring systems have used the same coding for vista (V) and reflection (Fr) responses (Beck, Beck, Levitt, & Molish, 1961; Klopfer & Davidson, 1962). Although an apparent contradiction, on rare occasion a single response may contain elements of both variables: "(Card IV) Ah, a poor reflection of a sailboat (Fr). Yea, that's good enough . . . (Inquiry?) Yea, a poor reflection of a sailboat (devaluation). This is the mast here and this is the boat itself and this is the reflection on the water, but it's poorly done . . . Most people would think it is a doorway with a long dark hallway but I like my idea better. What is the right answer?" Indeed, content suggests a poor or failed reflection. Although not technically scorable for vista, this devalued "poor reflection" leads to more painful introspection, "a long, dark hallway," and the wish for more effective narcissistic operations, "I like my idea better." Whereas self-focusing in narcissistic disorders is designed to protect the self from negative representations, the presence of FQx− offers additional support for defensive failure. In this case perceptual accuracy (− form quality) suffered at the expense of mirroring.

Generally, reflections have been interpreted within the context of a developmental need for mirroring (Coonerty, 1986; Ipp, 1986; Kwawer, 1980; Lerner, 1988; Smith, 1980; Urist, 1977). The importance of mirroring during the later symbiotic phase, a time in which the infant begins to differentiate self- and object representations, was stressed by Mahler et al. (1975). Developing boundaries and separation between self- and object representations continue unimpeded into the practicing subphase of separation-individuation. Gradually the limitations in the goodness and power of the self- and parental objects are identified and introjected (Kohut, 1971).

The predominance of Kwawer's (1980) mirroring, symbiotic merging, violent symbiosis, and boundary disturbance responses in the protocols of psychopaths (Gacono & Meloy, 1992; see chapter 5) suggest developmental roots toward the

---

[3]Belter, Lipovsky, and Finch (1989) cautioned against linear interpretations between egocentricity ratio and self-worth. We concur with the need to examine other Rorschach variables before arriving at conclusions concerning the "qualitative aspects of the individual's self-evaluation" (Belter et al., 1989, p. 787).

end of the symbiotic period and through the practicing subphase of separation-individuation. Our Rorschach findings are consistent with Coonerty's (1986) formulations that placed boundary disturbance responses at preseparation-individuation, merging responses at early differentiation, and reflection responses at the practicing subphase.

The presence of "reflection only" or "confused reflection" responses in psychopathic records (Gacono et al., 1990) highlight these developmental issues. Their appearance signals disruptions in developmental mirroring, identity conflicts, and boundary disturbance, while presenting a template for understanding externalized object relations. Produced when the subject makes reference to the reflection of the object and not the object itself, the "reflection only" response suggests an early object relation in which the mirror, that is, the mother, was at one time more important than the self. Card VI: "A reflection off the water" (Inquiry?) "If you're on a lake sometime and looking at a bank, you will see the reflection of the bank" (What makes it look like a reflection?) "I think I just described it" (Gacono et al., 1990, p. 276). This response is symbiotically anchored because it contains the infantile twins of original narcissism[4]: grandiosity and omnipotence ("I think I just described it").

"Confused reflections" are also apparent in psychopathic records, as presented in the following partial response to Card III: ". . . a male gorilla watching his reflection in a pool," (Inquiry?) "Yea, that's interesting. If one was looking down into a pool you would see *themselves*, not a reflection." (Gacono et al., 1990, p. 276). They suggest unsuccessful differentiation from the parental object and subsequent identity disturbance. This same subject produced an elaboration on the inquiry of Card II containing a "broken mirror" and "crushed apples" (Gacono, 1992). Although infrequently produced, these two types of responses—reflection only and confused reflections—are particularly useful when assessing identity conflicts and the presence of boundary disturbance.

In nonpatient populations reflection responses present during childhood and adolescence diminish in adulthood, whereas in characterological and antisocial populations their frequency remains elevated (see Table 7.1). Consistent with developmental theory, moreover, *most* children, beginning at the age of 5 years, do *not* produce a reflection response, suggesting a successful passage through separation-individuation. Reflections are more likely to be produced by schizophrenics with a concurrent diagnosis of antisocial personality disorder when compared to Exner's (1990b) normative schizophrenic sample or schizophrenic offenders without the concurrent diagnosis of antisocial personality disorder (ASPD).[5] These patterns suggest a developmental fixation and strong ties to

---

[4]Original narcissism is associated with diffuse feelings of omnipotence and grandiosity experienced by the infant before self- and object differentiation has begun (Teicholz, 1978).

[5]A chi-square comparison of reflection frequencies between our schizophrenic ASPDs ($N = 80$) and Exner's (1990b) inpatient schizophrenics ($N = 320$) revealed that ASPD schizophrenics were significantly more likely to produce reflections ($X^2 = 10.40$, $p = .001$) than were the inpatient schizophrenics (see chapter 6).

TABLE 7.1
Frequency of Reflection Responses in Patient and Nonpatient Populations

Exner (1990b) Subjects			Gacono & Meloy Subjects		
Group	Frequency[a]		Group	Frequency	
Children			Conduct-Disordered		
5	(N = 90)	32%	5–12	(N = 60)	20%
6	(N = 80)	21%			
7	(N = 120)	18%			
8	(N = 120)	28%			
9	(N = 140)	19%			
10	(N = 120)	30%			
11	(N = 135)	21%			
12	(N = 120)	13%			
Adolescents					
13	(N = 110)	29%	13–17	(N = 100)	33%
14	(N = 105)	14%	Males	(N = 79)	37%
15	(N = 110)	24%	Females	(N = 21)	19%
16	(N = 140)	23%			
Adult			Adult Antisocial		
Males	(N = 350)	7%	Males	(N = 82)	35%
Females	(N = 350)	7%	Females	(N = 38)	26%
Schizophrenic	(N = 320)	13%	Schizophrenic	(N = 80)	28%
Character Disordered	(N = 180)	20%	Psychopaths[b]	(N = 22)	50%
Borderline[c]	(N = 84)	48%	Nonpsychopaths[b]	(N = 21)	14%
Schizotypal[c]	(N = 76)	10%	Sex Homicide	(N = 20)	45%
			Other Adult		
			Male Narcissistic[b]	(N = 18)	50%
			Male Borderline[b]	(N = 18)	33%
			Female Borderline[d]	(N = 32)	28%

[a]Frequency is the proportion of subjects in the sample that produced at least one reflection response. [b]Gacono, Meloy, and Berg (1992). [c]Exner (1986b). [d]Berg, Gacono, Meloy, and Peaslee (1994).

character structure, as does the tenacity of the reflection response to remain even after long-term psychodynamic psychotherapy (Weiner & Exner 1991).

INTERPRETATION

Early in his work Exner (1969) noted the importance of reflections. They were found to occur more frequently in overt homosexuals and offenders (Exner, 1969; Raychaudhuri & Mukerji, 1971) and were originally linked to narcissism. Within the Comprehensive System (Exner, 1986a) they were included, along with pairs, in formulating the egocentricity ratio[6] (Barley, Dorr, & Reid, 1985; Gordon & Tegtmeyer, 1982; Simon, 1985; Watson, 1985). Structural interpretations for reflections shifted from a specific link to narcissism (Exner, 1969) to the broader concept of self-focus (Exner, 1986a; Sugarman, 1980).

As the concept of narcissism has evolved to include a continuum of presentations, might not interpretations for individual reflections also vary? We believe this is the case. Bohm (1958) postulated that some reflections were more pathological than others. Viglione (1990) provided a different interpretation for reflections in a traumatized child over three Rorschach administrations. He interpreted the emergence of reflections in the records as an increased capacity for self-absorption in the service of previously absent self-soothing and parenting functions. In some conduct-disordered (CD) children the presence of reflections may indicate similar immature, self-soothing abilities without the desire for object ties (decreased M and H, T = 0).

What does the Rorschach reflection response tell us, and under which circumstances might it indicate the target of libidinal cathexis, the nature of the libidinal drive (idealizing and self-aggrandizing), an absence of object relations (narcissistic withdrawal/schizoid stance), or self-esteem?[7] As we have emphasized in our case studies throughout this book a combined analysis of structure, sequence, and content can provide answers to the quality (object relations and defensive implications) of an individual reflection response.

WHERE ARE REFLECTIONS PRODUCED?

Card choice provides one level for understanding the nature and process involved in producing a reflection response. Consistently throughout our clinical groups (as noted in Figs. 7.1 through 7.7) reflections are most likely to appear on Card VIII, followed by Card VII.[8] With some variability, they are least likely to be produced on Cards IV and V. Cards VII and VIII allow for populars to be reflected, whereas Cards IV and V are monochromatic and visually dense.

---

[6]Belter et al. (1989) interpreted the egocentricity ratio as representing a style of relating to self, including a willingness or propensity to engage in a process of self-evaluation. Gordon and Tegtmeyer (1982) viewed the egocentricity ratio as indicating a style of directing attention to oneself or external objects.

[7]Self-esteem and its regulation is considered to be a complex process involving both ego and superego functions. "The ego's role in self-esteem is to judge and evaluate the self-representations in comparison with the ego ideal. It is based on this comparative evaluation between the self-representations and the ego ideal that the individual develops a cognitive/affective attitude toward himself; and it is this cognitive/affective attitude toward the self that constitutes self-esteem ..." (Teicholz, 1978, p. 846).

[8]The female ASPDs were an exception as they produced the greatest frequency of reflections on Cards I and VII. The interpretation of this finding is left to the reader.

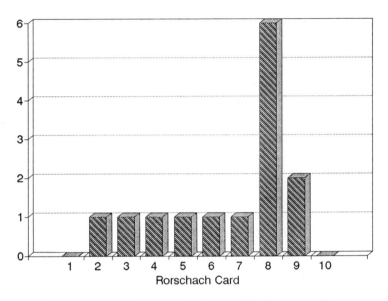

FIG. 7.1. Reflection responses ($N = 14$) in CD children ($N = 60$).

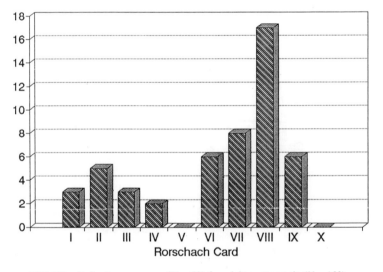

FIG. 7.2. Reflection responses ($N = 50$) for adolescent sample ($N = 100$).

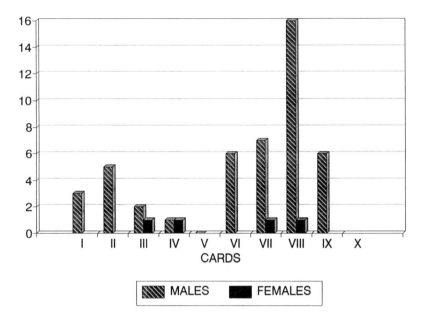

FIG. 7.3.   Reflection responses ($N = 50$) produced by CD adolescents ($N = 100$), by gender.

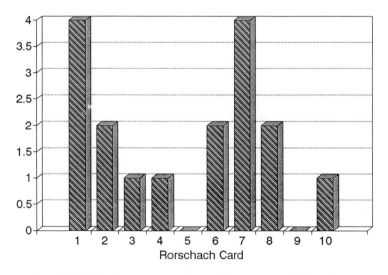

FIG. 7.4.   Reflection responses ($N = 17$) in female antisocials ($N = 38$).

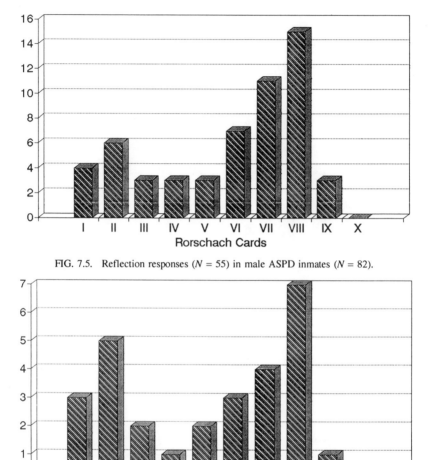

FIG. 7.5.   Reflection responses ($N = 55$) in male ASPD inmates ($N = 82$).

FIG. 7.6.   Reflection responses ($N = 28$) in psychopaths ($N = 33$).

Approximately one third of reflections were populars: schizophrenic ASPDs (30%), male ASPDs (29%), female ASPDs (39%), sexual homicide perpetrators (35%), male adolescent conduct disorders (28%), female adolescent conduct disorder (75%),[9] and conduct-disordered children (43%). Generally populars

---

[9] Only four reflection responses were produced by the adolescent females. Their reflections were closer to normal and less pathological than the adolescent males (Philip Erdberg, personal communication, June 1993). Watson (1985) found that adolescent inpatient males who produced more reflections scored higher on the Millon Adolescent Personality Inventory (MAPI) Scale 5 (narcissism). Females exhibited the opposite relationship: As their reflections increased, MAPI Scale 5 decreased.

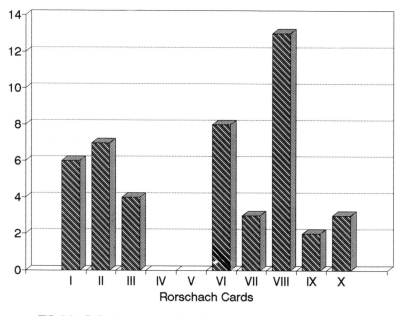

FIG. 7.7.   Reflection responses ($N = 46$) for schizophrenic sample ($N = 80$).

appear to aid subjects in organizing the reflection response. The exception occurs with the schizophrenic ASPDs ($N = 80$) who produced either − or u form quality (FQx) in 50% of their popular reflections.[10]

Some subjects produce multiple reflections. Seventy-seven percent of the sexual homicide perpetrators who produced a reflection had more than one (see chapter 9). Of all the subjects who produced reflections, 50% of the females and schizophrenic ASPDs, 48% of the male ASPDs, 34% of the adolescent males, 16% of the children, and 0% of the adolescent females produced multiple reflections. Multiple reflections in the record may have special interpretive significance. Combined with unusual card choice, as is the case with the sexual homicide perpetrators, they are likely to indicate a pathological process.

AN ANALYSIS OF 100 REFLECTION RESPONSES

Which determinants—form quality, content, and special scores—are likely to be produced with reflections? In order to obtain a representative sample of 100

---

[10]Within our samples ($N = 199$ reflections) − or u form quality reflections were produced with a popular only twice outside of the schizophrenic ASPD group. These two spoiled Ps occurred for one male adolescent and one sexual homicide subject. The sexual homicide subject may have been schizophrenic and, in time, the adolescent might be.

reflection responses we began by examining a mixed sample of 223 offender protocols. These were all the adult offender protocols in our files in 1990. Forty-one were female, 98 mixed ASPD males, 3 transsexual ASPDs, and 81 mixed psychotics. Ten females (24%) and 41 ASPD males (42%) produced reflection responses. None of the transsexual ASPDs produced reflections. Reflections were produced by 17 (21%) of the psychotics. The psychotic subjects were primarily ASPD schizophrenics ($N = 53$, 65%). Those subjects ($N = 7$) who were diagnosed as schizophrenic without the concurrent diagnosis of ASPD did not produce any reflections. Nine of the 15 reflections produced on Card VI were from convicted sex offenders.

Fifty subjects were chosen from the 68 subjects who produced reflection responses. The 50 subjects produced 105 reflections. Utilizing a random numbers table 105 responses was reduced to 100 (produced by 48 subjects).[11] Demographics for the 48 subjects are listed in Table 7.2.

Locations for these 100 responses can be seen in Figs. 7.8 and 7.9. Consistent with the other experimental groups, reflections are most likely to occur on Cards VIII and VII. While psychotics produced 39% of the total reflections, they produced 83% of the reflection responses on Cards IX and X. Tables 7.3 to 7.6 display an analysis of form level, special scores, content, and determinants found with the 100 reflections.

Form levels of reflection responses are usually ordinary (51%), but a significant proportion are minus form level (17%)[12] or contain no form (10%), that is, a pure reflection response (Gacono et al., 1990). Reality testing will be conventional in one of two reflection responses, suggesting the absence of mediational impairment when "mirroring" occurs in the perceptual field. The absence of mediational impairment tends to be card specific and related to affective pull and the amount of difficulty with which percepts can be readily integrated. On Card VIII easily produced populars help the subject affectively integrate the soft colors. Twenty-three (96%) of the 24 responses to Card VIII were o form quality. By contrast, the dysphoric blended colors of Card IX and sharper and more complex colors of Card X revealed two Fr, five rF, and five r, containing five −, two u, four no form, and only one o response. The populars on these two cards are not conducive to mirroring responses, and therefore do not provide the popular schemata for organizing these perceptions in the midst of affective stimuli in ordinary, or conventional ways. Poor form quality or severe cognitive slippage produced with reflections may indicate the defensive failure of self-focusing.

---

[11]Content and scoring for the 100 reflection responses are presented in Appendix B.

[12]Reflection responses with spoiled form quality (− or u) in our experimental groups were as follows: ASPD males (24%, −; 27%, u), conduct-disordered male adolescents (22%, −; 35% u), schizophrenic ASPDs (20% −; 35% u), conduct-disordered children (14% −; 14% u), sexual homicide perpetrators (6%, −; 35%, u), female ASPDs (5%, −; 16%, u), and conduct-disordered female adolescents (0%, − or u).

TABLE 7.2
Demographics for Subjects ($N = 48$)

Responses	19.9 (Mean)		7.71 (Standard Deviation)
Age	32.4 (Mean)		7.46 (Standard Deviation)
Race			
White	39	81%	
Black	6	13%	
Hispanic	1	2%	
Other	2	4%	
Gender			
Male	40	83%	
Female	8	17%	
Psychotic	15	31%	
Nonpsychotic	33	69%	

The pure form reflection response, perhaps a primary, or primitive form of narcissism at an autistic or symbiotic level of development, indicates the need for a pure or formless r response category in the Comprehensive System and further research. Both form and object are absent in the r response. A psychotic psychopath produced the following response on Card II: "Same thing a little bit of color added to it. This one here is more like a reflection, better practically same on both sides." (What makes it look like a reflection?) "Same on both sides." Perusal of the 10 pure r responses in our sample indicates that they are most likely to occur on Cards IX and X, and least likely to occur on Cards III

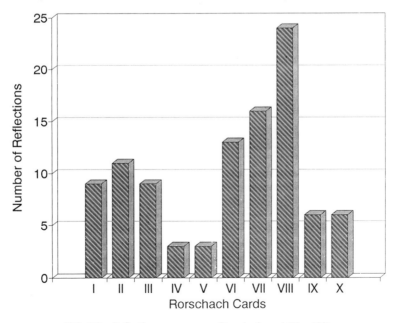

FIG. 7.8.   Reflection responses per Rorschach card ($N = 100$).

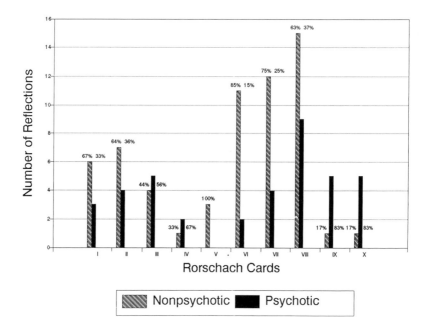

FIG. 7.9. Comparison of psychotic versus nonpsychotic subjects' reflection response frequencies (*N* = 100).

TABLE 7.3
Form Levels for 100 Reflection Responses

+	1%
o	51%
u	21%
−	17%
none	10%
Total[a]	100%

[a]Both psychotic and nonpsychotic subjects evidenced u, −, or no form quality in 48% of their responses (*N* = 29 and 19, respectively). Despite only producing 39% of the total reflection responses, psychotic subjects produced 70% of pure r (*N* = 7).

TABLE 7.4
Special Scores and Reflection Responses (*N* = 100)

Comprehensive		Experimental	
PER	8%	IMP	3%
DR1	15%	SM	1%
DV1	8%	AgC	4%
FAB1	7%	AgPot	3%
INC1	4%	AgPast	2%
DR2	4%	Omnipotence	11%
FAB2	2%	Other Kwawer	5%
MOR	6%		
AB	1%		

Note. 35% of the responses had one or more special (formal thought disorder) scores.

TABLE 7.5
Content of Reflection Responses (N = 100)

Primary		Secondary[a]	
A	41%	Na	29%
H	19%	Cg	5%
Na	14%	Ls	4%
Id	8%	Bl	3%
Cl	5%	Id	2%
Hd	3%	Sx	2%
Sc	2%	Ay	2%
(A)	2%	Sc	1%
Ls	2%	A	1%
Fd	1%	Hx	1%
Ad	1%	An	1%
Al	1%	Hh	1%
(H)	1%	Fi	1%
		Cl	1%
Total	100%	Art	1%

[a]Secondary content does not total 100% since most responses contained only one content.

and V. When rarely in a blend, the pure r occurs with pure C, a developmentally early and unmodulated affective response. Usually r has no other determinants. When there is definable content, on rare occasion, it is nonhuman (Na or Cl). Pure r appears to occur in an affect free, nonhuman psychological space descriptive of primary narcissistic reverie (S. Freud, 1914). In an otherwise pathological record the presence of pure r suggests the diffuse nature of the subject's inner self and object world.

Thought organization (Rapaport, 1951) is often impaired when a reflection response is given. Special scores indicating formal thought disorder are not unusual. One out of three reflection responses (35%) evidence it. The most likely manifestation is a DR response (19%) often accompanied by a personal (8%) and omnipotence (11%; Cooper et al., 1988). These data further support our hypothesis that formal thought disorder in narcissistic pathology is psychodynamically fueled by the need to self-aggrandize (PER) in a tangential or circumstantial (DR) manner (Gacono & Meloy, 1992). A PER produced with a reflection provides additional evidence for the interpretation of narcissistic libido. It suggests aggrandizement of the self-representation. The reflection/PER combination is particularly revealing in antisocial populations when occurring with grandiose or aggressive themes and percepts. Level 2 special scores occurred in only 6% of the 100 responses, suggesting the absence of more severe and bizarre forms of thought disorder in most reflection responses, and the defensive role of grandiosity for organizing personality structure in the psychotic subjects.

Content of reflection responses is usually whole animal (A) or whole human (H), accounting for 60% of the primary content. If secondary content occurs, it will most often be nature (Na, 29%). These data are a result of the "popular"

TABLE 7.6
Additional Determinants with Reflection Responses ($N = 100$)

None	
Fr/rF/r	27%

Animal Movement	
FMa	18%
FMp	10%
FMa.CF	4%
FMa.YF	1%
FMa.mp	1%

Human Movement	
Mp	13%
Ma	6%
Ma/p	1%
Ma.CF.ma	1%
Mp.CF	1%
Ma.C′F	1%

Inanimate Movement	
ma	1%
mp	1%
ma.CF	1%
mp.C	1%

Other	
CF	4%
C	4%
C′F	1%
VF	2%
TF	1%

| Total = | 100% |

reflection responses to Card III (humans), Card VII (humans), and Card VIII (animals). These three cards account for 49% of all reflection responses in our study. Content choice may have interpretive significance. For example, in a record containing less than adequate perceptual accuracy and indications of withdrawal (elevated isolate/R), an FMa.Fro blend (where the FQxo appears surrounded by poor form) on Card VIII containing A and Na content suggests the restorative functioning of self-focus absent affect, and affect stimulating human interaction.

Blends are ubiquitous in reflection responses (see Table 7.6). Seventy-three percent occur with a blend, often an active animal movement (18%), passive animal movement (10%), active human movement (6%), or passive human movement (13%). The Mp blend is curious, because it suggests the passive, "looking" quality of the reflecting act, and the reciprocal sense of being "looked upon" in a shameless, inactive way. It hints at the narcissistic quality of expectation without effort, the pleasure of being gazed upon by the self, a pseudoautonomous act of visualizing with a hint of unconscious autoerotic pleasure (only 2% of reflection responses have a secondary sex content). Although all movement active responses supercede movement passive responses (35:27), the ratio of Ma:Mp is 9:15. This may hint at the passive, wishful, dependent fantasy that unconsciously accompanies these blends when they occur.

Rarely is the reflection response accompanied by a sense of a damaged or injured self (MOR, 6%) or painful introspection (V, 2%), supporting Rothstein's (1984) definition of narcissism as a "felt quality of perfection" (p. 17), but betraying the ventral sensitivity of the narcissistic individual to experiences of shame (Lewis, 1991). However, the presence of both reflection and MOR responses in the protocols of male psychopaths (Fr/rF/r = 50%, MOR = 82%), male narcissistic personality disorders (Fr/rF/r = 50%, MOR = 50%), and sexual homicide perpetrators (Fr/rF/r = 45%, MOR = 80%) suggests the compensatory function of grandiosity in these individuals to manage an unconscious sense of self-injury.

Although an affective blend is found in only one out of five responses (22%), unmodulated or partially modulated affect is the rule. None of the responses were blended with form dominated affect. The FC:CF+C ratio of the entire reflection sample is 0:16 (Pure C = 5), clarifying the unmodulated nature of affect that accompanies a reflection response. Only 3% of the responses were blended with dysphoric or anxious affect (VF and YF), while another 2% were blended with constrained affect (C'F and FC'). Ideational helplessness was noted in only 6% of the responses (ma or mp). There were no color-shading blends in the entire sample, and the most common double determinants were FMa.CF (4%). Narcissism as a constellation of defenses against affect (Bromberg, 1979; Modell, 1975) is relevant to our clinical understanding.

SUMMARY

The modal reflection response will occur on Card VIII with a whole animal content. It will likely be a movement blend, accompanied by no special scores, with ordinary form level and a popular score. Although reflection responses are unexpected in any protocol, those deviating from this modal response probably have more clinical significance and deserve careful scrutiny in understanding the narcissistic psychodynamics of the patient. One of these modal reflections in an otherwise balanced record (containing normative COP, T, Pure H, ≤ 1 PER,

FC>CF+C, etc.) should not elicit an immediate interpretation of pathological narcissism.[13] When interpreted within the context of the entire protocol, analysis of reflections provides information concerning the self-focusing process, the nature of the libidinal drive, internalized object relations, and the defensive use of grandiosity and withdrawal. We emphasize the context of the entire protocol since reflections should never be interpreted in isolation from other structural data, determinants, content, form quality, or psychodynamic content analysis.[14]

PAUL, A PSYCHOPATHIC RAPIST

Paul was a 39-year-old violent rapist who had been incarcerated for 9 years. Paul had early childhood problems (PCL–R Item 12 = 2; see Table 7.7), significant juvenile arrests (PCL–R Item 18 = 2), a 30-year history of substance abuse, and a history of assault, all consistent with a diagnosis of 301.70 Antisocial Personality Disorder (*DSM–III–R*; APA, 1987). In addition to using substances he supported himself primarily through their sales and was involved in strong-armed tactics to enforce his trade. It was not uncommon for him to carry either a knife or gun. He carried the additional Axis I diagnoses of 302.90 Psychosexual Disorder, NOS, 304.90 Polysubstance Dependence, and Axis II diagnoses of 301.83 Borderline Personality Disorder and 301.81 Narcissistic Personality Disorder.

Paul scored a 32 on the PCL–R[15] (see Table 7.7) placing him in the low end of the severe range of psychopathy (Gacono & Hutton, 1994). His WAIS–R Verbal 90, Performance 87, and Full Scale 88, IQ scores were likely underestimating his true intellectual functioning as much scatter was evident throughout the test. Although he dropped out of high school, Paul received a graduate equivalency diploma.

---

[13]The examiner must pay careful attention to response content. As demonstrated by the following response, produced by a psychopathic subject (PCL = 36) to Card VIII, even a single reflection when imbued with omnipotence provides evidence of pathological narcissism. (Free association) "Color, write that down. This is a good one here. I see a cat or a mountain lion. Some kind of wild cat or mountain lion climbing on a ridge—sunset. His reflection, reflection of a cliff caught off a lake. It's right beside. Get all that? (Inquiry?) 'Cause I see a mountain lion, a cliff, a lake, he's walking over stones. This is a reflection. A nice sunset, too colorful. (Reflection?) I see the exact opposite. (Water?) Illusion, the white gives an illusion of water." WS+ FMa.Fr.CFo A,Na P 4.5 DR.

[14]Data from multiple sources can help elucidate the nature of a given reflection response. Recently a nonpsychopathic ASPD inmate completed the Rorschach and PCL–R. His Rorschach revealed one modal reflection produced on Card VIII. PCL–R Items 1 (glibness) and 2 (grandiosity) both received a score of 0. Further analysis of the Rorschach yielded 5 Ms, 3 Ys, an Afr = .25, and a positive CDI (= 4). Rather than having a dominating and merging narcissistic style, this inmate at times used self-focus and avoidance to manage strong affect often stimulated by his interpersonal relations.

[15]Extensive historical (record) data are necessary for scoring the PCL–R. Some studies have demonstrated that a valid assessment of psychopathy can be made from record data alone (Wong, 1988) but never when an interview is used as the sole information source. PCL–R items are directly linked to real-world behaviors and provide concurrent validity for the Rorschach indices discussed.

TABLE 7.7
Paul's Psychopathy Checklist–Revised (PCL–R)

1.[a] Glibness/superficial charm	1
2.[a] Grandiose sense of self-worth	2
3. Proneness to boredom/need for stimulation	2
4.[a] Pathological lying	2
5.[a] Conning/manipulative	2
6.[a] Lack of remorse	2
7.[a] Shallow affect	2
8.[a] Lack of empathy	2
9. Parasitic lifestyle	1
10. Poor behavior controls	2
11. Promiscuous sexual behavior	2
12. Early behavior problems	2
13. Lack of realistic long-term goals	1
14. Impulsivity	2
15. Irresponsibility	2
16.[a] Failure to accept responsibility for actions	2
17. Many marital relationships	0
18. Juvenile delinquency	2
19. Poor risk for conditional release	0
20. Criminal versatility	1
Total Score	32

[a]Items are Factor 1, aggressive narcissism. A score of 15 (16 possible for this factor) is consistent with a narcissistic personality disorder diagnosis.

Paul's committing offense involved the vaginal rape of a known female acquaintance. Although he strangled his victim she did not die. Paul described the rape as an "opportunity" during which he remembered being angry. When questioned about the effect of his behavior on his victim, Paul quickly reported how "the bitch bit my finger. It hurt for three months. I'm still doing time for it." At times Paul would become tearful when sharing details of his life and the offense. Careful examination revealed that rather than remorse, indicating guilt over harm caused to others, his affect was related to shame and self-pity. As noted in Table 7.7, he received PCL–R scores of 2 on both lack of remorse (Item 6) and lack of empathy (Item 8).

Can Paul's Rorschach and his four reflection responses help us understand the psychodynamics that fueled his committing offense? What can Paul's Rorschach tell us about possible borderline personality organization and pathological narcissism? Table 7.8 presents Paul's sequence of scores. Table 7.9 shows his structural summary.

Despite a reduced number of responses (R = 13) Paul's Rorschach is clinically valid (Blends/R = 4:13; Lambda = .86). He integrates as much as others (Zf = 12) and does so effectively (Zd = +1.5). Much of his energy is involved in overproducing Ws and provides partial explanation for the characterological

TABLE 7.8
Paul's Rorschach Sequences of Scores

CARD	NO	LOC	# DETERMINANT(S)	(2)	CONTENT(S)	POP	Z	SPECIAL SCORES
I	1	WSo	1 Fo		A		3.5	MOR (SM)
	2	Wo	1 Fo		A	P	1.0	DR (Omnipotence)
II	3	Wo	1 Fo		A		4.5	MOR,INC
								(Omnipotence)
III	4	D+	1 Mao	2	H,Cg,Ay		3.0	DR,PER,COP
	5	Do	3 Fo		A			DR
IV	6	Wo	1 Fo		Ad		2.0	
	7	W+	1 Ma.C'F.Fru		(H),Cl,Na		4.0	PER,DR2,AB
								(IMP,AgPot,
								Omnipotence)
V	8	Wo	1 Fo		A	P	1.0	DR
VI	9	W+	1 Ma.Fru		H,Na		2.5	(AgC)
VII	10	W+	1 Mau	2	H		2.5	COP,PER
VIII	11	W+	1 FMp.Fro		A,Na	P	4.5	MOR,DR,PER
IX	12	Wv/+	1 CF.rF−		Cl		5.5	
X	13	W+	1 CFu	2	Na,A	P	5.5	PER (AgC,
								Malignant Internal
								Processes)

constriction of the record. Elevated Ws, a product of his omnipotence and grandiosity, force an integration of all aspects of the blot, whereby imaginary (omnipotent) control is maintained. The W:M ratio (11:4) approaches 3:1 and is consistent with grandiosity (Weiner, 1966), as aspirations (fantasy) supercede abilities.

Paul's organization and predictability are currently good (D = +1, AdjD = +1). When interpreted within the context of a 13-response protocol and less than adequate resources (EA = 6.0), however, it is likely they will falter under stress as defensive strategies fail. We see some of this failure over the 10-card administration (perceptual accuracy failures, special scores). Perceptual accuracy and reality testing are adequate [F+% = 100 (F = 6); X−% = 8%] and when disruptions occur (X+% = 62) they are likely to be stimulated by affect and of character-disordered rather than psychotic proportions.

Although the record reveals the presence of formal thought disorder (Wsum6 = 23), special scores are comprised of six Level 1 scores (INC, DR = 5) and one Level 2 score without any of the severe indices (ALOG, CONTAM) pathognomonic of schizophrenia. For some sexual psychopaths, when adequate perceptual accuracy (F+%, X+%, & X−%) is found in combination with an elevated Wsum6 (comprised primarily of Level 1 special scores, mainly DRs),

TABLE 7.9
Paul's Rorschach Structural Summary

Location Features	Determinants		Contents	S-Constellation
	Blends	Single		

Location Features	Blends	Single	Contents	S-Constellation
				NO..FV+VF+V+FD > 2
			H = 3, 0	NO..Col-Shd Bl > 0
Zf = 12	M.C'F.Fr	M = 2	(H) = 1, 0	YES..Ego < .31, > .44
ZSum = 39.5	M.Fr	FM = 0	Hd = 0, 0	NO..MOR > 3
ZEst = 38.0	FM.Fr	m = 0	(Hd)= 0, 0	NO..Zd > +− 3.5
	CF.rF	FC = 0	Hx = 0, 0	NO..es > EA
W = 11		CF = 1	A = 6, 1	YES..CF+C > FC
(Wv = 0)		C = 0	(A) = 0, 0	YES..X+% < .70
D = 2		Cn = 0	Ad = 1, 0	NO..S > 3
Dd = 0		FC' = 0	(Ad)= 0, 0	NO..P < 3 or > 8
S = 1		C'F = 0	An = 0, 0	NO..Pure H < 2
		C' = 0	Art = 0, 0	YES..R < 17
DQ		FT = 0	Ay = 0, 1	4.....TOTAL

DQ

......(FQ−)				
+ = 6 (0)	FT = 0	Ay = 0, 1	
o = 6 (0)	TF = 0	Bl = 0, 0	
v/+ = 1 (1)	T = 0	Bt = 0, 0	Special Scorings
v = 0 (0)	FV = 0	Cg = 0, 1	
	VF = 0	Cl = 1, 1	Lv1 Lv2
	V = 0	Ex = 0, 0	DV = 0 × 1 0 × 2
	FY = 0	Fd = 0, 0	INC = 1 × 2 0 × 4
	YF = 0	Fi = 0, 0	DR = 5 × 3 1 × 6
	Y = 0	Ge = 0, 0	FAB = 0 × 4 0 × 7
	Fr = 0	Hh = 0, 0	ALOG = 0 × 5
	rF = 0	Ls = 0, 0	CON = 0 × 7
	FD = 0	Na = 1, 3	SUM 6 = 7
Form Quality	F = 6	Sc = 0, 0	WSUM6 = 23

Form Quality

	FQx	FQf	MQual	SQx
+ =	0	0	0	0
o =	8	6	1	1
u =	4	0	3	0
− =	1	0	0	0
none =	0	−	0	0

Sx = 0, 0	AB = 1	CP = 0
Xy = 0, 0	AG = 0	MOR = 3
Id = 0, 0	CFB = 0	PER = 5
(2) = 3	COP = 2	PSV = 0

This is a short record and may not be interpretively valid.
Ratios, Percentages, and Derivations

R = 13	L = 0.86		FC:CF+C = 0 : 2	COP = 2	AG = 0
			Pure C = 0	Food = 0
EB = 4: 2.0	EA = 6.0	EBPer = 2.0	Afr = 0.30	Isolate/R = 0.92
eb = 1: 1	es = 2	D = +1	S = 1	H:(H)Hd(Hd) = 3: 1
	Adj es = 2	Adj D = +1	Blends:R = 4:13	(HHd):(AAd) = 1: 0
			CP = 0	H+A:Hd+Ad = 11 : 1
FM = 1 : C' = 1	T = 0			
m = 0 : V = 0	Y = 0	P = 4	Zf = 12	3r+(2)/R = 1.15
a:p = 4: 1	Sum6 = 7	X+% = 0.62	Zd = +1.5	Fr+rF = 4
Ma:Mp = 4: 0	Lv2 = 1	F+% = 1.00	W:D:Dd = 11: 2: 0	FD = 0
2AB+Art+Ay = 3	WSum6 = 23	X−% = 0.08	W:M = 11: 4	An+Xy = 0
M− = 0	Mnone = 0	S−% = 0.00	DQ+ = 6	MOR = 3
		Xu% = 0.31	DQv = 0	

SCZI = 1	DEPI = 3	CDI = 2	S-CON = 4	HVI = No	OBS = No

255

impairments in *conceptual* accuracy indicative of narcissistic-borderline pathology (Meloy, 1985a) are suggested (Gacono, 1992). The DRs combined with five PERs and three omnipotence scores also suggest thinking problems associated with narcissistic object relations (Gacono & Meloy, 1992).

Paul is not troubled by dysphoric affect (Y = 0, V = 0, T = 0). His affect is shallow (PCL–R Item 7). What emotion he does experience is avoided (Afr = .30) and acted out (FC:CF+C = 0:2; Ma:Mp = 4:0), preventing any disruptive effects (X+% = 62). Although there is an absence of aggressive movement (AG = 0), self-representations include aggressive introjects (AgC = 2) more likely of a sadistic (S/M = 1; AgPot = 1) than masochistic (AgPast = 0) nature. These psychodynamics have historically shaped his acting out against others. More often than not, Paul's actions against others are volitional rather than unconsciously determined (Y = 0, D = +1, Adj D = +1). Once affect is stimulated, however, sadistic fantasy and primitive defenses such as dissociation (IMP = 1, Response 7) may provide avenues for affective violence (Meloy, 1988).

Three of the four Ms are u form quality; none are – form quality. Two are in Fr blends; the other two have PER special scores. Paul's two COPs are spoiled. They both contain PERs. This structural pattern strongly suggests the self-aggrandizing, omnipotent coloring of narcissistic libido and a pervasive lack of empathy (PCL–R, Item 8 = 2). He is both self-focused (EgoC = 1.15) and pathologically narcissistic (four reflections), as interactions are motivated by defensive need rather than affectional relatedness (T = 0). Three MORs represent the vulnerable underbelly of his narcissistic pathology. Their appearance may be the result of the subject's age and years of incarceration. The three MORs may also represent narcissistic wounds that fuel his affective rage. Paul's V-less protocol suggests a lack of remorse supported by both his verbalizations and a PCL–R score of 2 on "lack of remorse" (Item 6).

Paul's Ma:Mp ratio equals 4:0 and is consistent with his self report of an opportunistic rape; he also reports fantasies of murdering women, which is inconsistent with our hypothesis concerning rehearsal fantasy and a Mp > Ma ratio (Meloy & Gacono, 1992a; see chapter 9).

Four narcissistic mirroring (Responses 7, 9, 11, 12) and one malignant internal processes (Response 13) responses (Kwawer's, 1980, primitive modes of relating) suggest borderline object relations. Absent from the protocol are responses such as womb imagery or engulfment whose presence might suggest earlier developmental fixations (Gacono, 1992; Meloy & Gacono, 1992b).

Paul's reflection responses are particularly revealing (see Table 7.10). His first reflection occurs on Card IV, an unusual choice for a reflection. Cognitive processes are taxed (u form, DR2) during the articulation of this rather complex response. Rare in antisocial personality disorders, idealization (Lerner & Lerner, 1980) is present and, when occurring with a PER and omnipotence, suggests self-idealization and narcissistic libido (Gacono, 1988; Gacono & Meloy, 1992). Particularly disturbing is the suggestion of sadism (AgPot) combined with self-

TABLE 7.10

Paul's Reflection Responses

Card IV

(Free association?) (>) "From the side, oh what was his name? A picture of that Greek god with wings on his feet. These would be black clouds, it all looks like a reflection. (Inquiry?) The head on top, the wings. The rest of the figure would be black clouds, and there's trouble brewing in paradise. (Clouds?) I can think of nothing else that would go along with the picture, stands to reason, think of a god or goddess being in a cloud. He's flying into clouds. (Reflection?) Same thing someone gets angry, black clouds. I think of danger or anger. I'm a very angry person sometimes."

(7) W + Ma.C′F.Fru (H),Cl,Na 4.0 PER,DR2,AB,[AgPoT],
     [IMP],[Omnipotence]

Card VI

(Free association?) (>) This way, early in the morning, guy out fishing or hunting. Hunting and these here are shrubs, it's on the water, a reflection. (Inquiry?) Guy, rifle or fishing rod this boat these are shrubs.

(9) W + Ma.Fru H,Na 2.5 [AgC]

Card VIII

(Free association?) Looks like a bobcat. These are rocks he's perched on. This must be water down here because there's a reflection of the whole thing. (Inquiry?) Bobcat, perfect body of a cat too. Could be rocks, this could be a tree part. (Rocks?) My, I forgot the word, it doesn't look like any tree I've seen. This looks like dead part of tree assumed they were rocks. It's a mirrored image.

(11) W + FMp.Fro A,Na 4.5 PER,DR1,MOR

Card IX

(Free association?) Oh I can't think of anything off hand. So I'll have to say a cloud formation. (Inquiry?) I looked at it for awhile couldn't come up with anything else. 3 different groups here. They are also mirrored. (Groups?) Different colors.

(12) Wv + CF.rF − Cl 5.5

---

reference (PER), omnipotence, and personalized aggression (see chapter 8): "I'm a very angry person sometimes." The presence of aggressive self-representations and ego-syntonic aggression are indicated. Paul's self-esteem is overvalued and unrealistic. Attempts at constraint (C′F = 1) exist: however, Paul's rage is more likely to evoke primitive hysterical mechanisms such as dissociation (IMP) and denial.

Paul's second reflection occurs on Card VI. In antisocial populations sex offenders often produce reflections to this card. M with confusion around "hunting and fishing," "rifle and fishing rod" may suggest various intensities of masculine aggression and uncertainty concerning aggression, phallic identifications, and nurturance through feeding (food gathering). The absence of a PER in this conflicted response suggests an object rather than a self-representation if the response carries projective material.

The third reflection response occurs on Card VIII and contains o form quality. A DR1 and PER signal narcissistic psychopathology. The "perfect body" followed by the "dead part of tree" indicate self-representations that oscillate between idealization and devaluation, highlighting underlying splitting mechanisms (Cooper et al., 1988; Lerner & Lerner, 1980). A damaged self (MOR) is infrequently found with the reflection response, and in Paul's case suggests narcissistic vulnerability, defensive grandiosity, a passive sense of entitlement (FMp), and a stimulus for his rage. These psychodynamics parallel his motivations for his instance offense, and are consistent with our findings concerning a sample of sexual murderers (see chapter 9).

Paul's final reflection reveals the propensity for primitive hysterical mechanisms in this poorly modulated response (Wv+, CF.rF). Card IX's colors frequently pull for dysphoric affect in subjects, and reflections are more often produced by psychotics on this card (see Fig. 7.9). Paul's grandiose attempt to incorporate the entire blot (Wv+) results in distorted perceptual accuracy (– form), demonstrating the disorienting effect of strong negative emotion, possibly rage, on his introversive style (EB = 4:2).

CONCLUSION

Our nomothetic and idiographic investigation of the reflection response serves as a guide for examining other structural determinants such as texture or vista. It provides further construct validity for the reflection response as a marker of self-focusing (self-evaluation) and in antisocial samples, pathological narcissism. Moreover, its presence should be contextualized by frequency, location, form level, other determinants, and special scores to advance its meaning for a particular patient. Pure reflection, confused reflection, and reflection-only responses also deserve further study with an emphasis on object relations correlates. The pure reflection (r) response should be added to the Comprehensive System because it occurs in 10% of our random sample of reflection responses and may have significant, albeit primitive, meaning. "For now we see through a glass, darkly; but then face to face: now I know in part, but then shall I know even as I am known" (I Corinthians 13:12).

CHAPTER 8

The Aggression Response[1]

Violence sometimes may have cleared away obstructions quickly, but it has never proved itself creative

—Einstein

The ego's capacity for tolerating and channeling aggressive impulses serves a crucial role in both abnormal and normal development (A. Freud, 1936). When aggression and envy overwhelm infant libidinal drive, impairment occurs in the developmental process of defense formation and subsequent part- and whole-object integrations (Jacobson, 1964). Some conduct-disordered children, whose developing object relations are narcissistic, use grandiose fantasy, acting out, and identification with the aggressor (A. Freud, 1936) for coping with a generally mean and neglectful environment. The severity of adult psychopathy in these aggressive children can later, in part, be measured by their capacity for attachment (Gacono & Meloy, 1991; Meloy, 1988), ability to channel aggression through means other than acting out, and their degree of superego impairment (Weiner, 1991).

The relationship among intrapsychic aggression, primitive defenses, and object relations is relevant to the personality functioning of all individuals who carry a conduct disorder (see chapters 2 and 3) or antisocial personality disorder (see chapters 4, 5, and 6) diagnosis. Aggressive drive derivatives for conduct-disordered children, often ego-dystonic, are threatening to the integrity of the ego

---

[1]This chapter is a revised and expanded version of "The Aggression Response and the Rorschach" by R. Meloy and C. Gacono, 1992, *Journal of Clinical Psychology*, 48(1), pp. 104–114. It has been reprinted with permission of the Clinical Psychology Publishing Company, Inc.

(Winnicott, 1958a, 1958b). Lacking cognitive schemata, immature defenses operate to prevent ego disintegration. By adolescence the concurrent stabilization of primitive defensive operations and development of cognitive patterns (Gacono & Meloy, 1988; see chapter 10) aid in the management and channeling of intrapsychic aggression. For the dysthymic adolescent aggression is generally turned inward while maintaining object ties (Weber et al., 1992). The conduct-disordered adolescent, however, is less interested in object ties and will act out intrapsychic aggression against others as violence. Behavioral aggression thus parallels this intrapsychic shift, and is increasingly used in a conscious manner to control the environment.

For the adult antisocial personality, and particularly the psychopath, aggressive drives are channeled through primitive defenses supported by specific cognitive schemata (Gacono & Meloy, 1988). Together they aid in maintaining and restoring the grandiose self-structure (Bursten, 1972; Kernberg, 1975; Meloy, 1988). Ego-syntonic aggression is used by the adult psychopath in a deliberate, or at least partially conscious manner to intimidate and control others (Meloy, 1988). Although psychopaths may engage in both affective and predatory violence, predatory violence appears to be more frequent in psychopaths (Williamson, Hare, & Wong, 1987).

AGGRESSION AND THE RORSCHACH

The role of aggression and its manifest Rorschach derivatives are particularly relevant to the study of aggressive or acting-out personalities such as the borderline and antisocial disorders. For borderline personality disordered subjects, high frequencies of aggressive movement responses signal the ego-dystonic nature of intrapsychic aggression, whereas most antisocial subjects whose relationship to aggression is ego-syntonic produce less than normative frequencies[2] (Gacono et al., 1992; Meloy & Gacono, 1992a; see Table 8.1). Two exceptions to this finding are adult antisocial females and sexual murderers. Their productivity of AG responses, *despite* their real-world violence, may be due to several factors: Women are socialized to not be as aggressive as men, regardless of their individually different biological predispositions to aggress; and sexual murderers are, by measure anxious, dysphoric, and pathologically narcissistic. Both factors would contribute to an ego-*dystonic* relation to intrapsychic aggression despite its actual expression toward others.[3]

---

[2]A *t-test* comparison of our schizophrenic ASPDs ($N = 80$) and Exner's (1990b) inpatient schizophrenics revealed that the inpatients produced significantly more AG than did the ASPDs ($p = .02$).

[3]Ephraim et al. (1993) found similar patterns in their outpatient sample. Women were more likely to produce aggression responses of "all types."

TABLE 8.1
Comparison of Frequency of Aggression Responses

Exner (1990b) Subjects			Gacono & Meloy Subjects		
Group	Frequency[a]		Group	Frequency	
Children			Conduct-Disordered		
5	(N = 90)	91%	5–12	(N = 60)	33%
6	(N = 80)	25%			
7	(N = 120)	100%			
8	(N = 120)	80%			
9	(N = 140)	91%			
10	(N = 120)	100%			
11	(N = 135)	100%			
12	(N = 120)	82%			
Adolescents					
13	(N = 110)	77%	13–17	(N = 100)	35%
14	(N = 105)	85%	Males	(N = 79)	38%
15	(N = 110)	74%	Females	(N = 21)	24%
16	(N = 140)	76%			
Adult			Adult Antisocial		
Males	(N = 350)	69%	Males	(N = 82)	40%
Females	(N = 350)	64%	Females	(N = 38)	53%
Schizophrenic	(N = 320)	50%	Schizophrenic	(N = 80)	43%
Character Disorder	(N = 180)	31%	Psychopaths[b]	(N = 22)	41%
Borderline[c]	(N = 84)	52%	Nonpsychopaths[b]	(N = 21)	33%
Schizotypal[c]	(N = 76)	40%	Sex Homicide	(N = 20)	60%
			Other Adult		
			Narcissistic[b]	(N = 18)	50%
			Borderline[b]	(N = 18)	72%
			Borderline Females[d]	(N = 32)	69%

[a]Frequency is the proportion of subjects in the sample that produced at least one aggressive movement response. [b]Gacono, Meloy, and Berg (1992). [c]Exner (1986b). [d]Berg, Gacono, Meloy, and Peaslee (1994).

In a forensic setting, the question of the relationship between the Rorschach aggression response and behaviors of aggression toward self or others also finds merit in the ongoing controversy concerning the relevancy of psychometrics to violence assessment (Monahan, 1981). We recommend caution when making direct inferences between aggressive derivatives, especially the aggressive movement response (Exner, 1986a), and real-world behavior, because the data linking the two, at present, are equivocal.

Rapaport et al. (1946/1968) described the relationship between aggression and the Rorschach when they wrote that direct or implicit aggressive content in the

Rorschach implied "a great tension of aggressions within the subject" (p. 460). They were careful to not draw any inferences regarding the significance of this response to the subject's behavioral aggression. Schafer (1954) and Holt (1960) focused on the thematic analysis of aggressive content and did not limit interpretation to aggressive movement only (Exner, 1986a). Schafer emphasized the relationship of aggression to libidinal drives and orientation to the object; while Holt scored aggressive content in his primary process system along three points of an active–passive continuum: attacks, victims, and results. Empirical support for the theoretical formulations of Rapaport et al., Schafer, and Holt have been provided by Crain and Smoke (1981) who found that "well-adjusted" children produced aggression in the context of direct interactions whereas those children referred for psychological evaluations offered objects at the mercy of unknown or unreal attackers. They suggested, "Perhaps, even at this preliminary level of diagnosis, it is not enough simply to measure aggressive content globally, as the standard scales do. One may need to ask about the kind of aggression expressed" (p. 45). Our research has also supported these assertions as we found less than normative frequencies of Rorschach aggression responses among groups whose base rate for behavioral violence is high (Gacono, 1988, 1990; Heaven, 1988; Meloy & Gacono, 1992a). Trends in the Exner (1990b) normative samples also suggest that for those normal subjects where aggression produces *ego-dystonic tension*, frequencies of the aggressive movement response are greater than for character-disordered subjects who act out to express intrapsychic aggression that is ego-syntonic. The capacity for delay through inhibition or discharge in fantasy, the relationship of aggression to ego (syntonic/dystonic), and object-thematic content should all be considered when examining the relationship between Rorschach aggression responses and potential aggressive or violent behavior.

The Rorschach measurement of aggression and its correlations to behavior have also been of interest to other researchers when embedded in tension states (Elizur, 1949), destructive content (Finney, 1955; Rose & Bitter, 1980; Storment & Finney, 1953), white space (Carlson & Drehmer, 1984), color responses (Sommer & Sommer, 1958), hostile content (Murstein, 1956; Towbin, 1959; Walker, 1951), hostile and anxious content (Gorlow, Zimet, & Fine, 1952), aggressive drive and inhibitory controls (Rader, 1957), and differences between patients and nonpatients (Wirt, 1956). These findings, although demonstrating trends, were often equivocal as markers for behavioral aggression.

Despite clinical findings and theory supporting a broader examination of aggression, Exner (1986a) eliminated variations of aggressive content scoring in his Comprehensive System, and circumscribed the aggressive movement score (AG) to aggressive action that is only occurring in the present. In three subsequent studies Exner (1986a) reported mixed results concerning the relationship of the AG response to verbal and nonverbal measures of aggression in an experimental paradigm with inpatient groups (Kazaoka, Sloane, & Exner, 1978), in a naturalistic study of sixth-grade children (Exner, Kazaoka, & Morris, 1979), and a long-term "treatment effects" study of outpatients (Exner, 1986a). Exner concluded that these studies appeared to support the notion that elevations in AG signify an increased likelihood of aggressive behaviors.

We think that the elimination of other categories of aggression in the Comprehensive System, although solving the problem of interjudge reliability, has grossly reduced the usefulness of aggression responses to the Rorschach as a source of nomothetic comparison and idiographic understanding. This appears to be particularly true in samples of individuals with high base rates for physical violence such as primary or severe psychopaths (Hare & McPherson, 1984), and patients with unusual psychodynamic object fixations in their choice of victim, such as violent erotomanics (Meloy, 1992b) and sexual homicide perpetrators (Gacono, 1992; Meloy et al., 1994; see chapter 9).

Based on the work of Rapaport et al. (1946/1948), Schafer (1954), and Holt (1960), we developed four additional aggressive scoring categories (Gacono 1988, 1990; Meloy & Gacono, 1992a), in addition to the Comprehensive System AG response, which are useful for understanding aggression on the Rorschach. We think the aggressive content (AgC), aggressive past (AgPast), aggressive potential (AgPot), and sadomasochistic (S/M) responses hold promise for a deeper understanding of intrapsychic aggressive drives and object cathexis, and interpersonal violence and object attachment.

AGGRESSIVE CATEGORIES

Aggressive Movement (AG).   Any movement response in which the action is clearly aggressive and is occurring in the present (Exner, 1986a). Example: (Card III) "It's two people pulling a crab apart."

Aggressive Content (AgC).   Any content popularly perceived as predatory, dangerous, malevolent, injurious, or harmful. Example: (Card VI) "It's a gun"; second example: (Card IX) "It's a demon with claws" (this second percept would only receive one Ag Content score). We revised the originally published definition of AgC (Gacono, 1988, 1990) to improve interjudge reliability. Two groups of individuals, undergraduate college students and mental health professionals, were asked to rate 280 objects listed in the Comprehensive System workbook (Exner, 1985) and identified in psychopathic protocols according to our aggressive content definition.

The 85 objects listed in Table 8.2 were identified by a majority of at least one of the survey groups as content popularly perceived as predatory, dangerous, malevolent, injurious, or harmful. The results may serve as a guide for scoring AgC and as markers for the extrapolation of other objects that should be scored AgC.

TABLE 8.2
Rorschach Content Popularly Perceived as Aggressive as Rated by Undergraduate
Students and Mental Health Professionals, Frequencies and Percentages

Content	Students' Ratings (N = 31)		Mental Health Professional Ratings (N = 32)	
	Frequency	%	Frequency	%
Arrow	21	68	25	78
Axe	20	67	29	91
Barracuda	24	77	17	53
Bat	15	48	17	53
Battleship	22	71	24	75
Beast	20	67	18	56
Blade	22	71	28	88
Black Widow Spider	27	87	32	100
Bomb	26	84	31	97
Bullet	29	93	30	94
Cage	18	58	11	34
Claws	23	74	26	81
Club	10	32	22	69
Cobra	25	81	31	97
Cockroach	17	55	12	38
Copperhead	22	71	26	81
Crocodile	14	45	24	75
Demon	29	93	26	81
Devil	27	87	30	94
Devil's Sign	23	74	26	81
Dive Bomber	15	48	28	88
Dracula	25	81	30	94
Dragon	22	71	20	63
Explosion	31	100	31	97
Fangs	22	71	31	97
Fire	19	61	25	78
Fist	13	42	23	72
Forest Fire	23	74	29	91
Frankenstein	18	58	27	84
Garrote	3	10	25	78
Goblins	17	55	17	53
Gun	25	81	27	84
Hammer	5	16	18	56
Hatchet	25	81	26	81
Hurricane	29	93	27	84
Jackal	12	39	16	50
Jellyfish	17	55	13	41
Killer Whale	14	45	25	78
King Kong	16	52	17	53
Knife	28	90	32	100
Lion	12	39	22	69
Missile	28	90	27	84
Medusa	24	77	21	66

(Continued)

TABLE 8.2
(Continued)

Content	Students' Ratings (N = 31)		Mental Health Professional Ratings (N = 32)	
	Frequency	*%*	*Frequency*	*%*
Mummy	16	52	16	50
Monster	25	81	28	88
Mushroom Cloud (Explosion)	28	90	28	88
Needle	15	48	20	63
Noose	20	64	21	66
Nuclear Cloud	26	84	27	84
Nuclear Warhead	31	100	32	100
Panther	14	45	23	72
Pick	11	36	16	50
Pincers	18	58	23	72
Rats	10	32	19	59
Rattlesnake	27	87	31	97
Rifle	23	74	32	100
Saw	16	52	14	44
Scorpion	26	84	30	94
Shark	26	84	28	88
Sharp Teeth	20	64	23	72
Shot Gun	28	90	32	100
Sledgehammer	20	64	21	66
Snake	17	55	25	78
Spear	20	64	27	84
Spider	16	52	16	50
Spike	16	52	16	50
Sticker Bush	21	68	23	72
Syringe	15	48	21	66
Tarantula	24	77	32	100
Tiger	14	45	24	75
Tire-Iron	5	16	19	59
Tomahawk	21	68	26	81
Tornado	27	87	26	81
Torpedo	27	87	30	94
Torch	16	52	18	56
Vampire	26	84	30	94
Vampire Bat	25	81	28	88
Venus Fly Trap	6	19	16	50
Volcano (erupting)	31	100	28	88
Volcano	21	68	24	75
Wasp	23	74	24	75
Water Moccasin	21	68	27	84
Wolf	13	42	21	66
Wolfman	19	61	27	84
Yellow Jacket	21	68	19	59

Note. This content was selected from a sample of 240 objects listed in the Exner Workbook (Exner, 1985) and 40 additional objects identified in Rorschachs of psychopathic individuals. The items in this table were viewed as aggressive by greater than 50% of at least one of the survey groups.

Aggressive Potential (AgPot).   Any response in which an aggressive act is getting ready to occur. Usually the act is imminent (Gacono, 1988, 1990). Example: (Card X) "Two little alien creatures . . . being threatened to have their catch taken away from them by crablike creatures, real predators . . . they don't know these crab creatures are going to lop their heads off (laughs)." If the same two objects are involved in more than one act or potential act in a response, it should only be scored once. This category of aggression may implicate certain sadistic features in the subject, and finds its corollary in the "sadism" response of Schafer (1954) and the "attack (sadistic aggression)" response of Holt (1960).

Aggressive Past (AgPast).   Any response in which an aggressive act has occurred or the object has been the target of aggression (Gacono, 1988, 1990). Example: (Card X) "Looks like a bug here, someone used a drill press on him, blood here." This category of aggression may implicate certain masochistic features, and finds its corollary in the "masochism" response of Schafer (1954) and the "results of aggression" response of Holt (1960). It is often accompanied by a morbid score in the Comprehensive System (Exner, 1986a).

Sado-Masochism (SM).   Any response in which devalued, aggressive, or morbid content is accompanied by pleasurable affect expressed by the subject (Gacono, 1988, 1990; Meloy, 1988). Example: (Card VII) "A lady dancing and she got her head blown off (laughs)." The pleasurable affect is usually expressed through smiling or laughing, but the examiner should be careful to not misinterpret anxious behavior as pleasurable affect. A social desirability factor may also quickly inhibit the expression of pleasurable affect that accompanies this response, so the examiner *must look at* the examinee quickly and carefully. A marked lack of inhibition of the SM response, however, may signal the ego syntonic nature of the sado-masochistic impulse. The subject's identification with either the victim or the aggressor during the SM response on inquiry may also suggest the primacy of a sadistic or masochistic orientation to objects.

Occasionally subjects will combine the various indices of aggression in one response. All indices should be scored. For example: (Card II) "A bear getting shot (AG) . . . on one side this is the instant before he's shot (AgPot), this is the instant after (AgPast)."

INTERJUDGE RELIABILITY

Thirty Rorschach protocols of *DSM–III–R* antisocial personality disordered (APA, 1987) incarcerated adult males were randomly drawn from a larger subject pool ($N = 60$). The aggression categories were independently scored by the two authors to determine interjudge reliability. The interjudge reliability of the SM score was unable to be determined due to the Rorschach examiner's need to observe the examinee to score this variable, and the presence of only one examiner during the administration of these Rorschachs.

The interrater agreements for the Comprehensive System AG category (Exner, 1986a) and the three experimental aggressive scores are listed in Table 8.3. The AG agreement was 92%, the AgC agreement was 95%, the AgPot agreement was 100%, and the AgPast agreement was 96%. Other researchers have obtained equally high levels of agreement for our aggression categories (Margolis, 1992). Riquelme, Occupati, and Gonzalez (1991) found a percent agreement of 97% for both AgPast and AgPot in examining 40 randomly selected protocols obtained from a larger sample of 192 nonpatient subjects in Venezuela.

NOMOTHETIC APPLICATIONS

In order to test the sensitivity of our aggression scores we initially compared them in two groups of antisocial personality disordered (ASPD) incarcerated males, all serving time for various felonies in California institutions. The two groups were divided into psychopaths and nonpsychopaths, based on scores from the Hare Psychopathy Checklist–Revised (PCL–R; Hare, 1991), a reliable and valid measure of psychopathy in criminal populations (Hare et al., 1988; Schroeder, Schroeder, & Hare, 1983). Psychopathic and nonpsychopathic offenders have suggestively different histories of violence (Hare & Jutai, 1983; Hare et al., 1988). Hare and McPherson (1984) found in three studies that those individuals scoring ≥ 33 on the PCL (≥ 30 for PCL–R) were more likely to have a conviction for a violent crime, were more likely to use a weapon, and were more likely to verbally abuse, threaten, and fight while in prison, when compared to those individuals scoring < 33 on the PCL (PCL–R < 30).

The 43 male offenders selected for this comparison were free of an Axis I diagnosis of functional psychosis or organic mental disorder as determined by a review of records and a clinical interview. Subjects with an IQ > 80 were excluded. All subjects were taken from a mostly randomly selected population of ASPD individuals incarcerated in a California state prison or county detention facility.

The subjects were administered the Rorschach using the Comprehensive System rules (Exner, 1986a). Intelligence estimates were taken from scores on

TABLE 8.3
Agreement Between Raters for Aggressive Scoring

Score	Times Rated	Percent Agreement
Aggressive Movement	13	92%
Aggressive Content	107	95%
Aggressive Past	24	96%
Aggressive Potential	3	100%

the Shipley Institute of Living Scale (Shipley, 1940; Zachary, 1986) and the Wechsler Adult Intelligence Scale–Revised (WAIS–R; Wechsler, 1981). PCL–R scores were independently rated by each researcher, based on a clinical interview and records review. Interjudge reliability yielded a Spearman's Rho of .89. An average of the PCL–R scores for each rater produced the final PCL–R score.

Twenty-two individuals who scored > 30 on the PCL–R ($M = 33.15$) were assigned to the psychopathic group. Four were Black, 14 were White, and 4 were Hispanic. Average age was 30.4 years ($SD = 7.05$) and average IQ was 103.6 ($SD = 11.13$). Twenty-one individuals who scored < 30 on the PCL–R ($M = 23.93$) were assigned to the nonpsychopathic group. Seven were Black, nine were White, and five were Hispanic. Average age was 26.6 years ($SD = 6.11$) and average IQ was 100.5 ($SD = 8.94$). There was no significant difference in age or IQ for the two groups.

The aggression indices were scored blind to the PCL–R rating. Data were statistically analyzed using chi-square for significant differences between frequencies for the SM response only, and Mann–Whitney U analysis for significant differences for the other indices. Findings were considered significant if $p < .05$.

The results are presented in Table 8.4. No significant differences were found for any of the indices except for SM. The psychopaths produced a significantly greater frequency (41%) of sadomasochistic responses than did the nonpsychopaths (14%). Trends in the means of the aggression indices are apparent, however, except for AgPot, which showed virtually no difference in means or frequencies between groups. All subjects from both groups produced at least one aggressive score, with AgC most expectable.

When compared to nonpatient adults (see Table 8.5), however, both psychopaths and nonpsychopaths produced *less* aggressive movement responses (AG; Exner, 1990b), and *more* AgPast, AgPot, and AgC responses (Riquelme et al., 1991). Sixty-seven percent of the nonpatient sample (Exner, 1990b) produced at least one AG response ($M = 1.18$), while only 41% of the psychopaths and 33% of the nonpsychopaths produced one AG response ($M = .59$ and .43, respectively). As noted in Table 8.4, 59% of the psychopaths produced AgPast responses, 23% produced AgPot responses, 52% of the nonpsychopaths produced AgPast, 9% AgPot, and nonpatients produced AgPast and AgPot at the rate of 18% and 15% respectively (see Table 8.5). Comparing Tables 8.5 and 8.6 reveals that nonpatients average fewer AgC responses ($M = 1.70$, $SD = 1.01$) than psychopaths ($M = 3.95$, $SD = 2.55$), nonpsychopaths ($M = 3.10$, $SD = 2.09$), narcissists ($M = 3.22$, $SD = 1.86$), or borderline personality disorders ($M = 2.89$, $SD = 1.88$). The greater frequency of AgPast responses in the criminal samples is consistent with the higher rates of victimization in childhood of adult criminals (Robins, 1966) and early memories of delinquents of being injured and alone (Davidow & Bruhn, 1990). The nonsignificant trend toward more AgPot responses in psychopaths may signal the "conversion" of certain masochistic

TABLE 8.4
A Comparison of Means, Standard Deviations, and Frequencies
for Aggressive Rorschach Scores in Psychopaths and Nonpsychopaths

Category	Psychopaths (N = 22)				Nonpsychopaths (N = 21)			
	M	SD	Maximum	Frequency[a]	M	SD	Maximum	Frequency[a]
Aggressive Movement	.59	.85	3	9	.43	.68	2	7
Aggressive Content	3.95	2.55	9	21	3.10	2.10	8	20
Aggressive Past	1.00	1.15	4	13	1.00	1.34	5	11
Aggressive Potential	.41	.96	4	5	.14	.48	2	2
Sadomasochism	.52[b]	.68	2	9	.19[b]	.51	2	3
Total Aggression	6.57	4.27	16	22	4.90	3.41	14	21

[a]Frequencies equal the number of subjects who produced at least one response in a given category. [b]Chi-square analysis for SM response yielded significance $p < .05$ ($X^2 = 3.64$). No significant differences were obtained when the other aggressive categories were compared with Mann–Whitney U analysis.

TABLE 8.5
Aggressive Scores in Nonpatients

Category	Mean	SD	Maximum	Frequency	
Aggressive Movement[a]	1.18	1.18	5	466	(67%)
Aggressive Content[b]	1.70	1.01	6	131	(68%)
Aggressive Past[b]	.25	.61	4	35	(18%)
Aggressive Potential[b]	.16	.40	2	29	(15%)

[a]Exner (1990b) nonpatient adults (N = 700). [b]Riquelme et al. (1991) nonpatient adults (N = 192).

object relations to sadistic and compensatory object relations in this more severe psychopathology.

Gacono et al. (1992) compared object relations, defensive operations, and affective states among male narcissistic (N = 18), borderline (N = 18), and antisocial personality disordered subjects (N = 43). The ASPD subjects were divided into psychopaths (N = 22) and nonpsychopaths (N = 21) based on their PCL–R rating, a cutoff of $\geq$ 30 designating the psychopathic group. Although the groups did not produce significantly different (p > .05) frequencies or proportions of AG responses, trends were evident (see Table 8.6). BPDs produced the largest frequency of AG responses (72%), followed by NPDs (50%), P-ASPDs (41%), and NP-ASPDs (33%).

Although not subjected to statistical analysis among the groups, other aggression scores, Kwawer's (1980) borderline phenomena, specific structural indices, and hypothesized object relations paradigms were interpreted in this study:

> Specific object relations patterns, as measured by observation of Kwawer's (1980) individual categories and MOR and AgPast, suggest a self-identity that has been both damaged and aggressed against for both ASPD groups. The P-ASPDs present a malevolent, destructive internalized object world characterized by intense and violent intrapsychic conflict surrounding attachment and separation ... In comparison to P-ASPDs, NPDs self-identity is damaged (MOR = 67%), but possibly not the result of being aggressed against (P-ASPD, AgPast = 59%; NPD, AgPast = 28%). This may relate to actual early relationship paradigms. BPDs produced patterns consistent with a core damaged and aggressed against self-identity with an extremely malevolent, vulnerable, and conflicted internalized object world (AG = 72%; AgPast = 44%; MOR = 78%; malignant internal processes = 78%, violent symbiosis, separation, and reunion = 67%) ... BPDs experience their aggressive impulses as ego-dystonic, whereas P-ASPDs identify with aggressive introjects (Meloy, 1988) and experience these impulses as ego-syntonic. (Gacono et al., 1992, p. 46)

These findings were consistent with our theoretical considerations. The ego-syntonic, ego-dystonic distinction suggests that when aggressive impulses produce intrapsychic tension rather than elimination through rapid motoric discharge, they are more likely to be articulated on the Rorschach. The presence

TABLE 8.6

	Psychopathic ASPD			Nonpsychopathic ASPD			Narcissistic PD			Borderline PD		
Variable	Mean	SD	Frequency	Mean	SD	Frequency	Mean	SD	Frequency	Mean	SD	Frequency
Aggression												
Aggression (AG)	.59	.85	9	.43	.68	7	.78	1.21	9	1.39	1.33	13
Aggressive Content (AgC)	3.95	2.55	21	3.10	2.09	20	3.22	1.86	17	2.89	1.88	18
Aggressive Past (AgPast)	1.0	1.15	13	1.0	1.35	12	.39	.85	5	.83	1.46	8
Aggressive Potential (AgPot)	—	—	4	—	—	2	.39	.61	6	.89	2.16	6

Note. Frequencies equal the number of subjects in each group who produced at least one response in a given category (Gacono et al., 1992). The P-ASPD and NP-ASPD subjects are not identical to Table 8.4.

of fewer aggression responses among the conduct-disordered children in chapter 2 also supports this hypothesis, and does *not* support our more parsimonious thought that censoring is at work (Meloy & Gacono, 1992a), at least in children.

Margolis' (1992) dissertation was also relevant to our study of aggression and the Rorschach. She examined the Kwawer (1980) primitive modes of relating indices and the aggression scores in our sample of ASPD males. Additionally, Margolis attempted to replicate our survey on aggressive content (AgC) with a larger adult sample ($N = 200$) consisting of nonpatient, noncollege student, nonmental health professional, "normal" subjects.

Margolis (1992) first sought to answer whether, "the additional aggressive categories as proposed by Meloy and Gacono provide more sensitive information for scoring aggression that is excluded in using the current Comprehensive System?" (p. 7). Frequencies for the AG response in the ASPD sample were 59% AG = 0, 28% AG = 1, 10% AG = 2, and 4% AG = 3. When she included AgContent, AgPotential, and AgPast, along with AG, however, only 5% of the ASPDs produced Rorschachs without any aggression score. Margolis concluded "that individuals who have documented histories of aggression will have an increased amount of aggression scores on the Rorschach when a more comprehensive method for scoring is used" (p. 27).

Although her findings demonstrate that the use of our aggression indices increases an examiner's ability to quantify in a reliable manner a greater variety of manifest aggressive content and processes, without comparable nonpatient data and other real-world correlates of violence, questions of validity remain unanswered. Nonpatients without documented histories of aggression also produce increased amounts of aggression when the scoring of AgC, AgPot, AgPast is added to Exner's (1986a) AG movement response (see Table 8.5). Preliminary findings do, however, suggest low frequencies for AgPot, AgPast, and AgC in nonpatient populations (Riquelme et al., 1991).[4] Unlike AgPast, however, the AgPot score tends to have a low frequency of occurrence in even our ASPD populations. Without the necessary validity studies, including nonpatient comparison samples, we recommend that the interpretation of these aggression indices only be idiographic and within the context of the individual's entire protocol and history. We have found this case use to be extremely fruitful.

Margolis' (1992) second research question sought to ascertain whether the AgC list (see Table 8.2) could be replicated with a nonpatient, noncollege student, nonmental health worker survey population. She asked, "Are the words chosen for Meloy and Gacono's Aggressive Content List replicable with a more heterogeneous population, and are there any other words that should be included on the list?" (p. 7). Her results did produce substantially fewer content items than did our original surveys (only 30 objects were checked by $\geq$ 50% of the

---

[4]ASPD subjects were significantly more likely to produce AgPot ($x^2 = .017$, $p < .05$) and AgPast ($x^2 = .001$, $p < .05$) responses than did nonpatients (Margolis, 1992).

subjects). Unfortunately, as noted by Margolis, there were a number of methodological errors with her study, most important a change in the instructions given to subjects.

Our original instructions were meant to be objectified, requesting that a subject rate those objects *popularly* perceived as predatory, dangerous, malevolent, injurious, or harmful. By changing *popularly* perceived to *you* perceive to be predatory, dangerous, malevolent, injurious, or harmful, Margolis (1992) evoked a distinctly different cognitive set for subjects completing the survey.[5] The choice of *popularly* was meant to be ambiguous, allowing subjects to rate objects as to what *most* or *many* people consider to be aggressive. Subjects could externalize responsibility for their choice and would be less likely to worry about possible judgment from the examiner for answers given. Specific changes in the survey format were also noted by Margolis. Unfortunately, the Margolis study was a "replication" study in intention only. It tells us more about subject-examiner effects than about scoring aggressive content on the Rorschach.

IDIOGRAPHIC UNDERSTANDING

Varieties of aggressive responding to the Rorschach also provide a rich source for hypotheses concerning the quality, intensity, and directionality of aggressive drive derivatives toward certain self- and object representations. We would like to illustrate these psychodynamics through the case of Brinkley whose entire protocol was previously analyzed (Gacono, 1992) and is included as one subject in our sexual homicide sample (see chapter 9).

Brinkley is a 31-year-old White male incarcerated for the rape and murder of a stranger adult female when he was 27. Clinical interview and psychological testing reveal a severe, or primary psychopathic character organized at a borderline level of personality organization. Test indices include a PCL–R score of 34 (Hare, 1985), a 4 (T = 86), 5 (T = 82) MMPI high point pair (common among sex offenders), and a WAIS equivalent score (Shipley) of 110.

Brinkley produced a 13-response Rorschach protocol. Counting of the aggressive scores indicated one AG response, five AgC responses, five AgPot responses, four AgPast responses, and two SM responses. Examples of scoring the various indices include:

Card III: A woman that's had an abortion and she is having difficulty dealing with regrets afterwards (laughs) [score SM and AgPast]. This is great. Inquiry: As if suddenly they looked in the mirror and saw themselves. They realize it

---

[5]Censoring was suggested by comments from several subjects that although they felt that "other people might see these words as being aggressive, I don't see them in that way," and, "I must be really aggressive because I checked a lot of the words" (Margolis, 1992, p. 41).

takes two to tango. (?) The red bloody figures. The little bloody fetus. I don't get anything at all from the red in the middle.

Card IV: Your basic ten story childhood nightmare monster. It gives the illusion of great height and size [score AgC]. Inquiry: Brought back childhood nightmares. They're about to get trampled [score AgPot]. Nothing they can do about it, it's so high.

Card X: I have a busy one here. Ever hear of Frank Stella? I think he did this. Two little alien creatures who have caught a larger creature for game [AgPast]. Who are being threatened to have their catch taken away from them by crab like creatures [AgPot; AG], real predators [AgC]. On the hunting trip. I feel like a voyeur. Crab creatures offed them, not knowing their buddy had ate it [AgPast]. They don't know these crab creatures are going to lop their heads off [AgPot]. (laughs) [Score SM]. That's a Rorschach original.

The subject's final response (Card X) highlights the degree to which the sadomasochistic expression of his aggressive drive oscillates between self- and object representations and the past and the future.

> ... final response (#13) reveals a dramatic and fluid display of ego-syntonic aggression. It contains a variety of primitive defenses, such as idealization, splitting, projective identification, omnipotence (Cooper et al., 1988), aggressive scores, AG, AgC, AgPot, AgPast, and, SM, and demonstrates the presence of characterological sadism (Kernberg, 1982), a complete absence of empathy, and a strong identification with aggressive and predatory self-representations (A. Freud, 1936; Meloy, 1988). This final response reveals the predatory nature of his object world and is reminiscent of a statement from the Zodiac (a serial killer who terrorized the San Francisco Bay area in the late 1960's). "This is the Zodiac speaking. I like killing people because it is so much fun. It is more fun than killing wild game in the forest because man is the most dangerous animal of all ..." (Graysmith, 1976, p. 54). (Gacono, 1992, p. 14)

Identifications shift between "little creatures" and "real predators" and aggression shifts between an imminent act and one that has just occurred. Real-world behavior for this individual revealed physical fights and weapons use beginning at age 10, multiple suicide attempts beginning at age 12, prosecution for lewd and lascivious behavior with a 13-year-old nephew, a self-reported "date rape" at age 23, and the rape-homicide at age 27. There was also a period of rehearsal fantasy in which he ruminated about murdering a stranger female for 2 weeks prior to the instant offense.

Prentky et al. (1989) found support for the hypothesis of rehearsal fantasy as an internal drive mechanism for repetitive acts of sexual homicide. Meloy (1988) theorized that the Rorschach Ma<Mp ratio (Exner, 1986a) may be a psychostructural indicator for such fantasy abuse in sexual psychopaths, applying the "Snow

White" phenomenon identified by Exner (1986a) to this antisocial form of rehearsal fantasy. Brinkley had a Ma:Mp ratio of 1:2, providing some idiographic validation for this hypothesis, and further elaborating the nature of his intrapsychic aggression. Another dual-diagnosed (both psychotic and psychopathic) serial killer who experienced grandiose delusions and murdered seven victims—some were slashed, others strangled—produced a 15-response protocol with a Wsum6 = 0. His Rorschach included six PERs and an Ma:Mp ratio of 1:2. Although his perceptual accuracy was similar to character disorders (F+ = .67, X+ = .60), an analysis of his Mp responses revealed that both were of – form quality. The frequency of Mp>Ma is also elevated in the sexual homicide sample (see chapter 9).

Another idiographic use of the Rorschach aggression indices is based on the experimental work of Reis (1972, 1974), Flynn and his colleagues (Flynn, 1967; Flynn & Bandler, 1975) and Meloy's (1988) psychobiological model of human violence as either *affective* or *predatory*. Affective violence is an emotionally motivated behavior in reaction to an imminent threat. Predatory violence is an emotionless behavior that is planned and purposeful. Both forms of violence have somewhat distinctive biochemical and neuroanatomical pathways (Eichelman, Elliott, & Barchas, 1981).

We would expect that Rorschach corollaries of such modes of violence could be distinguished by both the aggressive scoring and the determinants. The articulation of predatory aggression in a Rorschach response would usually contain an AgPot in the absence of a color- or shading-dominated determinant. The articulation of affective aggression would usually not contain AgPot, but would include chromatic color- or shading-dominated determinants. Both forms of aggression, and these idiographic subtleties, are illustrated in responses to Card III and Card IV related earlier. Card III, the affective aggression response, would be determinant scored Mp.CFo without an AgPot. Card IV, the predatory aggression response, would be determinant scored FDo with one AgPot. Psychopathic individuals are both psychobiologically and psychodynamically predisposed to predatory aggression (Meloy, 1988), and we have anecdotally found a greater likelihood of "predatory" responses in psychopathic Rorschach protocols than in other populations.

In criminal forensic settings, individuals may also verbalize or infer certain weapons as AgC. BC, a 45-year-old female incarcerated for the shooting and decapitation of an exboyfriend (Meloy, 1992b; see chapter 4), gave the following response to Card VI:

A filet of fish ready to put in a frying pan. (Inquiry) I'm not seeing the tail with Indian feathers. Just the filet of fish (?) Side by side. It's been deboned (laughs), sorry I shouldn't have said that term. He'll be ready to go into the frying pan or perhaps is already in the pan. (?) I knew you were going to hit me on that. No spine, no substance, no form, a blob. A piece of fish to be cooked. Or perhaps a fudgesicle that's been allowed to set in the sun and melt.

When we reviewed her crime, we discovered that she had used a "deboning" knife to decapitate her victim. This remarkable response suggests a temporally stable, and highly cathected, object representation of her weapon and act that was evoked during the mediation and ideation phases of the Rorschach response process (Exner, 1986a) 7 years after the homicide. One sexual murderer who upon release from a maximum security institution would kill and torture (using a caliper) a child produced a "caliper" on his Rorschach several years *before* the murder. Another repeat sexual murderer who raped and strangled several female strangers produced a "monster with gooey dripping hands" 14 years after his last homicide. The production of Rorschach content consistent with the sexual murderer's fantasy life and internalized object representations is a frequent occurrence among this group.

DISCUSSION

Various Rorschach indices of aggression appear less promising for the nomothetic comparison of different groups than for the idiographic understanding of the quality, intensity, and directionality of aggressive impulses for a particular individual.

Our findings of no significant differences between nonpsychopaths and psychopaths on the aggressive scores, however, should be accepted with caution. Although psychopaths have significantly greater histories of violence (Hare & McPherson, 1984) than nonpsychopaths, we had insufficient data to determine whether our two groups of offenders were significantly different in real-world violent behavior. Therefore, our results may only parallel an actual insignificant difference in violence. Hare and McPherson were able to correctly classify 76.2% of their violent subjects through a direct discriminant analysis using the Psychopathy Checklist, with 22% false negatives and 30% false positives. Although both the PCL and PCL–R are highly useful behavioral trait instruments to infer a violent history, they should not be used alone as an independent measure of violence risk in criminal populations (Gacono & Hutton, 1994). We would likewise suggest that the mean or frequency of the various aggression responses not be used as a discriminating variable in the assessment of violence risk, especially in populations with low base rates for violence, until further research has been done.

The lesser mean amount of AG (Exner, 1986a) responses in psychopaths when compared to normals is not surprising, given theoretical assumptions related to ego-syntonic, ego-dystonic distinctions. Additionally, Meloy (1988) warned that the face validity of the AG response may prompt the psychopath to disregard, and not verbalize, his AG associations to the Rorschach. The ego-syntonic nature of aggression and violence in psychopaths may incline them to more easily recognize social or clinical situations in which aggressive responding should not occur, leading them to censor their responses (Exner, 1986a).

The psychopath's perception of aggression in an ambiguous stimulus situation like the Rorschach process also may not lead to a cognitively mediated associational link to aggression. It may instead be motorically channelled in a more alloplastic fashion without any fantasy elaboration. This would be more in keeping with the primitive defensive operations of psychopathy (Gacono & Meloy, 1988; Meloy, 1988) and has been supported in other subject pools of antisocial children and adolescents (see chapters 2 and 3).

The significantly greater frequency of SM responses in the severe psychopaths supports our thinking that this index may hold promise for the projective understanding of this troublesome human characteristic. Both psychodiagnostic and psychodynamic formulations suggest a link between sadism and antisocial character (APA, 1987; Meloy, 1988; Shapiro, 1981). Although probably not *sensitive* to the predominance of sadomasochism in personality, the SM index may be quite *specific* to this deeply endogenous characteristic. We have also observed in certain subjects a "projected" form of sadism. Rather than expressing pleasurable affect, as originally required for scoring the SM, these subjects attribute sadism to the Rorschach percept. For example one subject saw a human face, ". . . he's smiling like he's going to hit you." Another subject responded to Card III, "It's a fly. It's far out. I've been going to mental health counseling since 13 or 16." (Inquiry?) "A fly, got big eyes. When I was little used to pull flys eyes off." We recommend also scoring SM in responses where the object is presented as overtly sadistic. The sadomasochistic impulse may be either ego-syntonic or ego-dystonic and should be interpreted within the context of the patient's history to clarify its defensive or adaptive usage.

The idiographic usefulness of the various indices of aggression in understanding the subtle motivational and object relational meanings of intrapsychic aggression has been suggested. As we alluded to earlier and illustrated in the responses of subject Brinkley, the aggressive potential (AgPot) and the aggressive past (AgPast) may represent both an active–passive continuum of aggression, as noted by Holt (1960), and a predominant sadistic (AgPot) or masochistic (AgPast) position in relation to early developmental, and later adult objects (Schachtel, 1966). The AgPot, AG, and AgPast responses also denote a temporal sequence that may implicate certain instinctual tensions or aims (Fenichel, 1953). Although infrequent in ASPD samples, certain subjects produce aggressive responses notable for their sense of vulnerability. These aggressive vulnerability responses (AgV) such as, "It's a butterfly and here is where it needs to cover up so the predators can't attack it," like the AgPast response suggest masochistic rather than sadistic orientation.

The structural ratio Ma<Mp and its suggestive association with rehearsal fantasy in sexual homicide (Prentky et al., 1989) is a testable hypothesis for future research. It also may be linked to the Rorschach representation of predatory aggression (aggressive potential without chromatic color- or shading-dominated determinants) since by definition, it is a wishful, planned, purposeful, and

emotionless form of aggression. Affective aggression, however, is most likely to be perceived in the Rorschach given its real-world prevalence (Meloy, 1988) and the plethora of aggressive indices, shading responses, and chromatic color responses through which it could be verbalized.

AgC may represent an unusual and highly cathected individual weapon and act in certain forensic cases, as illustrated by subject BC, but more commonly may indicate an identification with aggressive objects in general. It may also implicate certain oral ("devouring mouths"; "vampire, spider, shark"; Lane & Chazan, 1989), anal ("exploding bombs"), or phallic ("cutting knives") psychosexual zones or modes (Erikson, 1950; Schafer, 1954). Examiners should pay special attention to any AgC that through elaboration is personalized by the subject, for example: "A giant swinging a club down. This has always been my favorite one"; "It's a sword in a stone. Wish I had lived in that time"; "It's a gun. I like guns." These responses are more likely to suggest a self-representation and should be interpreted within the context of its qualitative presentation rather than strict sign approaches (Klopfer & Kelley, 1942; Schachtel, 1966).

The various indices of aggressive responses to the Rorschach appear to be a rich source for understanding the structure and dynamics of an individual's intrapsychic aggression. Links to real-world behavior are suggestive, especially with individual cases, but have not been nomothetically demonstrated with any certainty. Our additional scoring categories should provide hypotheses for research concerning that "darkling plain, swept with confused alarms of struggle and flight, where ignorant armies clash by night" (Arnold, 1822–1888).

CHAPTER 9

Sexual Homicide

One sin, I know, another doth provoke; Murder's as near to lust as flame to smoke.

—Shakespeare, *Pericles*, I, I

That which is forbidden is always fascinating. And so it is with sexual homicide. The intentional killing of the object of one's desire was first clinically described by Krafft-Ebing in his forensic textbook, *Psychopathia Sexualis*, in 1886 (Krafft-Ebing, 1886/1965). But it would take more than 100 years before anything other than case studies would appear in the scientific literature.

Most virulent are the sexual homicides that become habitual, the so-called serial sexual homicides. Although historically documented for at least 500 years (Meloy, 1989), they appear to have increased in the latter half of this century.[1] The perpetrators become antiheroes of American culture and other, mostly western European, countries.

Ressler et al. (1988) completed the first empirical study of a small sample (*N* = 36) of sexual murderers. The data were gathered during 1979–1983 from

---

[1]Leyton (1986) constructed a historical sociology of multiple murder, and postulated three socioeconomic periods that spawned these acts: the preindustrial period of 15th-century Europe, the 19th-century industrial revolution, and the postindustrial closing of the middle class to many people in the mid-20th century. He considers one of the motivating factors for this form of homicide to be a nihilistic reversal of social values to protest against the established order. Although his theory is compelling, it remains only thoughtful speculation without further empirical data; much like the intriguing idea that 18th-century victims of legendary werewolves and vampires were actually victims of early sexual murderers.

official records and interviews with convicted and incarcerated sexual murderers in the United States. All of the sample were males, and 92% were White. Eighty-one percent had multiple victims, accounting for the deaths of 118 individuals, mostly women. This deviation from the normal pattern of homicide in which most victims are males underscores the female gender hating, or misogynistic nature of this crime (Cameron & Frazer, 1987; Meloy, 1988).

The perpetrators of this sexualized aggression, moreover, are the products of families in which sexual abnormality, criminal history, and psychiatric disturbance are ubiquitous. These data are summarized in Tables 9.1 and 9.2. Teasing out the relative contributions of nature and nurture awaits further research and much larger samples, but the data suggest that biology and environment interact and shape the eventual eroticized homicidal response to the victim, as is the case in most criminal behavior (Eysenck & Gudjonsson, 1989).

Table 9.1 summarizes select family background characteristics of the sample. All familial behaviors listed were present in a majority of the subjects except for physical abuse history (42%). Table 9.2 summarizes select childhood sexual experiences of the perpetrators. The majority reported rape fantasies, with half acknowledging the genesis of such fantasies in early adolescence. The other aberrant sexual experiences, although not reported by the majority, are greater than what one would expect among males in the general population. The classical pairing of sexual arousal and violence is a useful behavioral paradigm for understanding the later operant behavior of the sexual murderer (Meloy, 1988).

The act of sexual homicide, moreover, does not suddenly emerge from a vacuum. Table 9.3 summarizes the frequency (> 50%) of reported behaviors during childhood and adolescence among the subjects in the sample where data were available ($N = 28$). Although these data are compelling as indices of the stability of antisocial behavior across time, a few words of caution are necessary: The data are retrospectively self-reported by the subjects (introducing the variables of memory fallibility and/or conscious malingering) and there is no control group. In other words, even if the data are accurate, it does not mean that these behaviors are predictive of sexual homicide. Other groups, whether antisocial or not, may exhibit the same frequencies of behaviors and may not be significantly different from the sexual homicide sample. For instance, enuresis occurs at a very high frequency in this sample, 68% in childhood and 60% in

TABLE 9.1
Family Background Characteristics

- 72% Negative relation with male caretaker
- 69% Family alcohol history
- 66% Mother dominant parent
- 53% Family psychiatric history
- 50% Family criminal history
- 42% Physical abuse history

Note. Data are from an FBI study (Ressler et al., 1988).

TABLE 9.2
Childhood Sexual Experiences

- 61% Admitted rape fantasies
- 50% 12–14 years old: rape fantasies
- 43% Sexual abuse
- 35% Witnessed sexual violence
- 35% Witnessed parental sex
- 28% Sexual injury or disease

"Nobody bothered to find out what my problem was, and nobody knew about the fantasy world." (p. 28)

Note. Data are from an FBI study (Ressler et al., 1988).

adolescence. We have also found an enuretic history in a Rorschach case study of a mentally ill psychopath that we considered at risk for sexual homicide (Meloy & Gacono, 1992b). Nevertheless, 7% of males are enuretic at age 5 years, and 1% of males are enuretic at age 18 years (*DSM–III–R*; APA, 1987). Although the proportional frequencies are most likely significant when comparing sexual murderers to normal males, virtually all predictions of sexual homicide based on an enuretic history would be false positives given the extremely low base rate for the dependent variable we are trying to predict: sexual homicide. Aggregating the variables would help somewhat, but would not allow for accurate prediction given the low base rate and the concordance of these behaviors, as a group, with such diagnoses as conduct disorder (*DSM–III–R*).

The pattern suggested by the Table 9.3 variables, however, is intriguing. Perpetrators of sexual homicide in childhood and adolescence seem to be characterized by two behavioral patterns that alternate: reclusive, isolative, and withdrawn behavior in which fantasied objects are the primary source of *coerced* emotional gratification; and violent forays into the world of real objects wherein both people and things are aggressed against. Two case studies of homosexual serial homicide illustrate this pattern, one in the United States (Jackman & Cole,

TABLE 9.3
Frequency of Reported Behaviors ($N = 28$)

	Childhood	Adolescence
Isolation	71%	77%
Chronic lying	71%	75%
Enuresis	68%	60%
Rebelliousness	67%	84%
Nightmares	67%	68%
Destroying property	58%	62%
Fire setting	56%	52%
Stealing	56%	81%
Cruelty to children	54%	64%

Note. Data are from an FBI study (Ressler et al., 1988).

1992) and one in Great Britain (Masters, 1985). In fact, 28% of the sexual homicide sample committed a homicide while an adolescent, and were later released as an adult to eventually begin murdering again.

This FBI study (Ressler et al., 1988) led to further validation of a motivational model of sexual homicide that first appeared in Burgess, Hartman, Ressler, Douglas, and McCormack (1986). In this model, simplified and adapted in Fig. 9.1, certain sequential and interactive patterns coalesce to determine the eventual sexual homicide. We review and elaborate upon each pattern in turn.

Ineffective Social Environment.   The FBI data suggest that parents, or parental objects, of the sexual murderer do not nurture, protect, and consistently discipline the developing child. Attachment, or bonding, is selective or nonexistent, concordant with other literature on the relationship between attachment pathology and violence (Meloy, 1992b). Chronic detachment is also expected in samples of primary psychopaths (Gacono & Meloy, 1991). The ineffectiveness of the social environment is also suggested by the earliest memories of delinquents in which the self is perceived as weak and vulnerable, and parents are unavailable to help, or actually cause injury (Davidow & Bruhn, 1990).

Formative Traumatic Events.   Overwhelming experiences for the child, such as witnessing or being victimized by physical or sexual assault, lead to an essential trauma: "the loss of faith that there is order and continuity in life" (van der Kolk, 1987, p. 31). The trauma response is often biphasic, alternating between hyperarousal and intrusive thoughts, and emotional numbing and constriction. This inability to modulate physiological arousal may lead, ironically, to an addiction to the trauma. At a psychological level, real helplessness may stimulate compensatory aggressive fantasies to reassert against internalized objects a sense of dominance and control (Gacono, 1992; MacCulloch, Snowden, Wood, & Mills, 1983). At a biological level, inescapable stress depletes norepinephrine and dopamine levels in the central nervous system (CNS), leaving their receptors hypersensitive to subsequent stimulation. This can lead to a kindling effect (Goddard, McIntyre, &

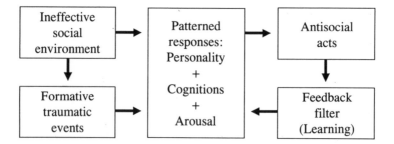

FIG. 9.1. Sexual homicide: Motivational model. Adapted from Burgess et al. (1986).

Leech, 1969) or behavioral sensitization. Opioid-induced analgesia, moreover, immediately follows various stressors that are intense, inescapable, and consciously perceived (van der Kolk, 1987). Thus trauma, and the shock of subsequent fear, is followed by an endorphin release that has the same effect as exogenous opioids (tranquilizing, anxiety relieving, antidepressing, and self-esteem elevating). We would suggest that the classical pairing of sexuality and violence in childhood, experienced as trauma with its attendant psychological and biological sequelae, would predispose an operant conditioning behavioral pattern in adolescence and adulthood. These later acts on the environment would be in the service of affective and physiological regulation, both to psychologically master the trauma and to evoke the endogenous opioid response immediately following the sexual violence. This sense of calm would be further enhanced by (a) postorgasmic euphoria, and (b) the absence of structuralized superego elements that could introduce conflicted feelings of guilt and remorse, but would most likely be missing in a psychopathically disturbed personality.

Patterned Responses: Personality. Ressler et al. (1988) cited a number of personality traits that arise from the childhood experiences of their sample: social isolation, preferred autoerotic activities and fetishes, rebelliousness, aggression, chronic lying, and a sense of entitlement. Relationships are primarily built upon fantasy, which provides imaginative emotional stimulation without the constraints of reality, yet imbued with narcissism. Many of these personality traits parallel the two factors of psychopathy (Hare, 1991), aggressive narcissism and chronic antisocial behavior.

Patterned Responses: Cognitions. Ressler et al. (1988) stressed the fixed, negative, and repetitive organization of thought in the sexual murderer, a style of "cognitive mapping and processing" (p. 73) that contributes to his antisocial stance. They hypothesized that the motivation is to control and dominate others as a substitute for "a sense of mastery of internal and external experience" (p. 73). One of our serial sexual homicide cases in which there were six male victims captures this intent through the perception of the seventh victim who escaped death. This is a portion of his testimony concerning his 4-day captivity during which he was restrained, tortured with disinfectant injections and electricity, and sexually assaulted:

> Q. Now during this time that you were a captive, tell us in your words what seemed to you, from your perspective, he was wanting most or enjoying most about his experience?
> A. Seemed to be enjoying the fact that I was powerless and that he had control totally.
> Q. Anything else that he seemed to be really interested in with you?
> A. The sex. It was nonnegotiable.

We understand these conscious cognitions as important pathways to behavior that are made fixed and repetitive with certain unconscious defenses (Gacono & Meloy, 1988), namely projection, projective identification, devaluation, and omnipotent control. These phenotypic defenses employ the genotypic mechanism of splitting and defend against actual memories of being victimized, devalued, and aggressed against, usually by the parental object. The theme of dominance and control in the FBI study is also consistent with a shift away from relations built upon affectional paradigms to relations constructed along power gradients, what Meloy (1988) called the prey–predator dynamic (see also Bailey, 1987).

The reliance on fantasy for emotional arousal also predicts a pattern of sexual behavior that will be entitled, detached, and dominating, in other words, sadistic. Such behavior is documented in a sample of sexually sadistic criminals (Dietz, Hazelwood, & Warren, 1990), which overlapped with the sexual murderer sample of Ressler et al. (1988). We would expect sexual sadism to be overtly manifest in a proportion of sexual homicides, but not all. Rehearsal fantasy has also been discussed by a number of authors (Brittain, 1970; Gacono & Meloy, 1988; MacCulloch et al., 1983; Meloy, 1988; Meloy & Gacono, 1992a, 1992b; Ressler et al., 1988; Revitch, 1965), but was only empirically tested in one study in which it was hypothesized to be a primary drive mechanism for serial sexual homicide. Prentky et al. (1989) found that it did discriminate between a sample of single ($N = 17$) and serial ($N = 25$) murderers, being more prevalent in the latter ($p = .001$). Both fetishism and transvestism were also significantly more predominant in the serial murderers' histories, two paraphilias that rely on fantasy to compensate for genital and gender dysphoria, respectively, and conceal within themselves hostility toward the maternal object (Stoller, 1975).

One problem that remains unresolved concerning rehearsal fantasy is the reason why, among sexual murderers at least, it must periodically be acted out against a real object, the hapless victim. Figure 9.2 is a *hypothetical* explanation, based on Hull's (1952) systematic behavior theory, which may shed light on this vexing problem.[2] The vertical (Y) axis is the intensity of the rehearsal fantasy, which is assumed to contain themes of dominance, degradation, and submission, and is a mixture of both sexuality and violence. This fantasy is classically paired with masturbation, and initially is both intense and completely gratifying. Over time, however, represented by the horizontal axis (X), the intensity of the rehearsal fantasy decreases as the frequency of its use for sexual gratification increases (this could be a rate increase, or simply repetition). As the intensity decreases, the *response tendency* increases, a measure of the motivation to act on the environment. At a frequency of five, again a hypothetical number, a threshold is passed where the response tendency exceeds the intensity of the rehearsal fantasy, and the likelihood of sexually aggressive behavior is only dependent on opportunity. The sexual murderer begins to look for a victim, an overt behavioral pattern that, in itself, may not be fully conscious. If a sexual homicide is completed

---

[2]Our thanks to David Keenan, PhD, for his guidance of our thinking in this area.

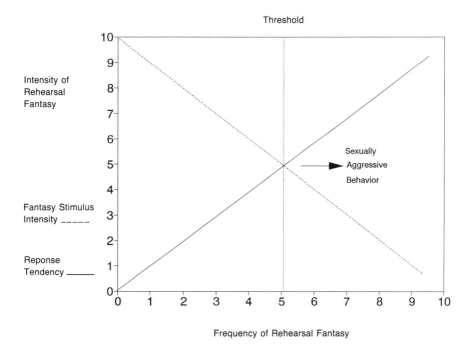

FIG. 9.2. Hypothetical relationship between rehearsal fantasy and acted out behavior (sexual aggression).

the mechanism would "reset," but the high arousal of the actual sexual violence would have less propensity to extinguish: These latter behavioral sequelae would account for the latency period between sexual homicides and the likelihood of the act being repeated.

Patterned Responses: Arousal. The arousal patterns of the sexual murderer pose some difficulty and inconsistency without further data. Ressler et al. (1988) hypothesized both sustained physiological arousal as a result of childhood trauma, consistent with posttrauma research (van der Kolk, 1987), and the need for high levels of stimulation, consistent with psychopathy research (Hare, 1991). Unfortunately these are contradictory hypotheses, unless one assumes a biphasic pattern of autonomic arousal, which suggests an "all or nothing" response to stress. This assumption is, in fact, consistent with the trauma research in which traumatized individuals respond to arousal with either unmodulated anxiety and aggression, or social and emotional withdrawal (Krystal, 1978). Attachment research with mammals has also measured the psychobiological *independence* of acute and chronic phase responses to separation distress, which may, nevertheless, occur at the same time (Hofer, 1987). Several hypotheses concerning the sexual murderer's arousal patterns come to mind: A biphasic response would characterize his arousal and attachment patterns, and would be manifest in general social and emotional withdrawal, punctuated by occasional unmodulated displays of arousal and aggression when stimulated; a chronic hyperarousal and affectional hunger that would need little kindling to be activated; a chronic hypoarousal and affectional detachment that would need high levels of stimulation to be activated. Each hypothesis may be true for certain sexual murderers, given the likely heterogeneity of a sample selected on the basis of one behavior. And all three hypotheses support the abnormal attachment paradigms and experiences that have been found in this population.

Antisocial Acts. Childhood and adolescent antisocial behavior (see Table 9.3) represents a displacement of aggression toward other children, animals, and property. Such acts become sexualized during puberty[3] and, if positively reinforced, predict their continuation and escalation into adulthood. Ressler et al. (1988) also noted that such behavior discourages friendships, and therefore reinforces isolation and narcissistic fantasy.

Feedback Filter (Learning). The serial sexual murderer learns from his mistakes, and works to make his internal fantasy concordant with the real world. After committing the first murder and not being caught, he is surprised; after committing the second murder, he is amazed; and after the third murder he is omnipotent.[4] If not apprehended, his grandiosity will blossom and his isolation will increase as he becomes wary of being caught. He also becomes a better criminal, and refines ways to avoid detection in both the planning and commission of the offense.

The Ressler et al. (1988) study advanced the understanding of sexual homicide. Unfortunately, no standardized psychological or neuropsychological testing accompanied the data gathering, and the internal world of the sexual murderer remains a speculative mystery. Manifest behaviors contribute to the development of inferences concerning psychological operations, which then need to be tested as hypotheses before definitive statements can be made.

THE RORSCHACH STUDY

With the exception of two case studies (Gacono, 1992; Meloy & Gacono, 1992b), there are no published Rorschach data of sexual murderers or individuals at risk for such behaviors. The Ressler et al. (1988) study, and these case studies, however, do facilitate the generation of *hypotheses* concerning the psychometric

---

[3]One rapist, prior to his first sexual assault, would break and enter into homes in his neighborhood when he knew a woman was asleep and alone in the house. He would describe the "rush when I quietly stood in her dark living room. I was in her space, and she didn't know it." He would then leave. Another sexual murderer broke into his teacher's home at age 12, placed her underwear on her bed, and stuck a knife through them.

[4]Our thanks to Bruce Harry, MD, for this cogent thought.

characteristics of a sample of sexual murderers. These hypotheses are also supported by recent Rorschach data concerning antisocial personality disordered (ASPD) and/or psychopathic subjects (Gacono & Meloy, 1992).

Pervasive Cognitive Deficits. Although the organizational efficiency and effort of perceptual processing would be expected to be normal, impairments in perceptual mediation are likely. Unconventional and idiosyncratic translation of the visual environment would predict X+% < 70 and F+% < 55, both at least one standard deviation below the mean for nonpatient males. Impaired reality testing is expected, with X–% > 15, and the likelihood of M– > 0. This latter measure, indicative of gross distortions in the perception of human movement, and likely containing projective content, begs the question of rehearsal fantasy surrounding sexual violence. We have previously speculated that Mp>Ma may be a structural indicator of a capacity for rehearsal fantasy in this population (Meloy, 1988; Prentky et al., 1989), and we would predict a significant proportion of a sample of sexual homicide perpetrators would be positive for this indicator (present in only 7% of nonpatient males; Exner, 1990b). Mp– responses may indicate delusional thought content.

Ideational problems are likely, with a plethora of Level 1 DR and INC responses. Sexual homicide perpetrators organized at a borderline level of personality, probably the majority, are inclined to fuse concepts rather than percepts (Meloy, 1985a), most obvious in their conceiving of others as an extension of their own grandiosity, yet not appearing clinically psychotic. Psychotic sexual homicide perpetrators would fuse both percepts and concepts, indicating a complete loss of reality testing and the inability to distinguish between internal and external stimuli (Meloy, 1985a). Level 2 special scores, suggestive of significant formal thought disorder at a psychotic level of personality, are unlikely in most sexual homicide perpetrators if our borderline hypothesis is correct.

WSum6 is likely to elevate in this population, suggesting pervasive but moderate formal thought disorder. Personal (PER) responses will often be scored with DR, linking the wish to self-aggrandize during the Rorschach, a narcissistic dynamic, with circumstantial disorganization of thought. Hysterical cognition (Shapiro, 1965), a likely component of the thinking of the sexual homicide perpetrator, will be measured by the presence of the impressionistic (IMP; Gacono, 1988) score, what we believe to be the rapid symbolization of affect that is split off or dissociated (Gacono et al., 1990).[5]

---

[5]IMP is scored when a chromatic or achromatic determinant occurs with an abstraction (AB) special score. The term is derived from Shapiro's (1965) "impressionistic" cognitive style in the hysteric. See Meloy (1988) for an elaboration of the 100-year literature on the relationship between hysteria and psychopathy, and Cahill (1986) for a case study wherein a sexual murderer chronically confused memory, dreams, and fantasies surrounding his killings. This latter individual produced an unscorable Rorschach, populated with only "flowers" and "bugs." In the hysteric, the sexual wanting that is obvious to others is consciously unknown to the self, a defense rooted in the usually eroticized relationship to the opposite sex parent.

Affect Tension and Dysphoria.   Anxiety in the sexual homicide perpetrator
is likely to be bimodally distributed, but abnormal. We would expect $Y = 0$ or
$Y > 1$. Dysphoria or chronic dysthymia will be manifest in several variables: V
> 0, elevated DEPI, and elevated color-shading responses, Rorschach indices of
a clinical characteristic that we think will probably distinguish the sexual
homicide perpetrator from the psychopathic personality.

Affect modulation will be poor (FC < CF+C), consistent with the modulation
problems in ASPDs who average 1:3 (Gacono & Meloy, 1991) on this ratio.
Emotional explosiveness is consonant with theory ($C > 0$), and the likely state
is chronic anger admixed with aggression ($S > 2$, AG > 1).

There will be a tension of aggressions (Rapaport, Gill, & Schafer, 1946/1948)
in these subjects, suggesting ego-dystonic impulses and emotions that are highly defended (Afr < .55, Lambda > .85) through the use of hysterical defenses
(CP > 0, IMP response) seen in the lower level histrionic personality disorder
(Gabbard, 1990). Occasional higher level defenses may be apparent, such as
isolation, but in most cases projection and projective identification will be
used to manage intolerable feelings of rage. Such defenses provide a primitive rationalization for the sexual aggression because the *victim* is perceived as
the aggressor (Gacono & Meloy, 1988). Devaluation will also be used to defensively manage affects, such as shame,[6] when narcissistic wounding is felt (MOR
+ AG). Devaluation also serves to manage envy of the good object, a particularly
common emotion in narcissistic psychopathology, and one that can prompt
inordinate aggression to render the once valued object unworthy of possession.
The mutilated corpse of the sexual homicide victim is a horrible example.[7]

---

[6]Janice Lindsay-Hartz, PhD, has differentiated shame from related affects such as embarrassment
and humiliation by associating it with *being* the negative self, rather than *failing to be* the ideal self
(paper presentation, American Psychological Association, Washington, 1992). This contrasts with
the primary psychopath, who will often positively identify with what others perceive as the negative,
or antisocial self-concept; in some cases, an infatuation with the idea of being perverse or a demon
(from the Latin *daemonium*, an evil spirit).

[7]Postmortem mutilation of the corpse is usually linked to the disorganized sexual murderer, and
the wound patterns focus on the primary or secondary genitals. In one case, the 20-year-old victim
was stabbed from behind as she entered her apartment with the perpetrator, a new acquaintance. This
first deep puncture wound severed her superior vena cava, spilling 2,000 cc of blood into her thorax
within minutes. He then slashed her throat, deep enough to sever her trachea. He then inflicted 15–20
puncture wounds across her breasts as she lay on the floor on her back. The final 30-in. wound was
done by literally sawing through her sternum and down to her pubus, penetrating the abdominal cavity
and injuring several organs. She was found within several hours with her hands wired behind her
back and her pants and panties removed. There was no evidence of sexual penetration of the victim.
The perpetrator was a same race 28-year-old male with a history of multiple rapes since age 14. He
had been released from prison, entered the army, and after his discharge returned to his home town.
He committed the sexual homicide 25 days after he had committed an assault and burglary of a
woman's apartment (she wrestled free of the wrist restraints and fled from her apartment), and 50
days after he had raped another woman in a garage, again binding her wrists. This is a striking
"lunar" cycling of sexual aggression. Often the disembowelment of the female victim, fueled by

In most cases affect will be avoided in the service of unbonded eroti-cism.[8]

Stress tolerance and control is likely to be quite satisfactory, or very poor, depending on the nature of the sexual homicide itself (organized or disorganized[9]; Ressler et al., 1988) and the degree of mental disorder or psychopathic character pathology. This would suggest a bimodal grouping for D and AdjD.

Pre-Oedipal Object Relations.   Identity disturbance is likely in this population, since it is expected with all individuals organized at a borderline or psychotic level of personality (Kernberg, 1984). Sexual confusion and gender dysphoria seem to fuel most paraphilias (Stoller, 1975), and will likely be the focus of identity issues among sexual homicide perpetrators. Symbiotic anxiety during sexual intercourse may stimulate homicidal aggression as a defense against regressive fusion with the maternal object (Stoller, 1974). Rorschach measures of such issues include reflection, reflection only, and confused reflection responses (Gacono et al., 1990), suggesting early narcissistic failures of idealization and grandiosity, sexual identity confusion on Card III, sexual content or reflection determinant responses to Card VI, and symbiotic or boundary disturbance responses (Kwawer, 1980) throughout the protocol. Engulfment and womb imagery responses would only be expected in psychotic sexual homicide perpetrators since they tap an autistic, rather than a symbiotic, developmental level (Mahler et al., 1975).

Perception is likely to conceive of the self as grandiose (Rf > 0, Egocentricity > .45, PER > 3) and deeply injured (MOR > 1, AgPast+MOR > 0), an inherent conflict and core psychopathology of this population. There are likely to be many aggressive introjects, manifested in aggressive potential (AgPot), sadomasochism (SM), and aggressive content (AgC) responses. These are *not*, however, identifications, and probably feed the internal dysphoria: Aggressive and persecutory objects are within the self, but not a part of the self. Unlike the smoothly functioning psychopath who identifies with these internalized aggres-sive objects and consciously conceives of himself as a predator, the sexual homicide perpetrator is likely to convey his pathos through a genuine, although ironic sense of himself as prey.

---

homicidal rage, is a means to gratify the wish for omnipotent control, and to look "within" the woman—a literal penetration of the skin boundary, and perhaps a wish to merge with her interior organs.

[8]Stoller (1975) agreed with this "conservative" thesis: "[U]nchecked sexuality dehumanizes erotic life and thus thwarts love . . . the need to dehumanize, which has its origins in traumatic, conflict-laden childhood experiences, is built from hostility" (p. 212).

[9]Organized sexual murders are identified by the following characteristics: planned offense, a stranger victim, personalizing of the victim, controlled talk during the crime, a controlled crime scene, the demand of submission, use of restraints, premorbid aggression, hiding and transporting the body, and no evidence or weapon left behind. The disorganized sexual murder consists of: a spontaneous offense, known victim, depersonalizing of the victim, minimal talk, a dyscontrolled scene, sudden violence, minimal restraints, postmortem sex, the body left at the scene in full view, and the weapon and evidence left behind.

Highly cathected objects of aggression may also appear among the Rorschach responses, and may have actually been used in the commission of crimes (see chapter 8). Malevolent transformations (Gacono, 1992) may also signify the conversion of benign into predatory objects (Card I: "It's a butterfly . . . with claws") and also signify the use of projective identification.[10]

The perception of others and internalized object relations would be characterized by an isolative, schizoid, yet aggressive style (COP = 0, or "bad" COP > 1, AG > 1, Isolate/R > .25), a conflicted dependency (Food > 0, ambivalent food responses [Gacono & Meloy, 1991]), and a part-object–dominated representational world (H < Hd) (see also Glasser, 1986).

A capacity for attachment, or bonding, would be bimodally distributed (T = 0, T > 1), and in the vast majority of subjects abnormal. T would be negated or suffused with aggression. The sexual murderer would be clinically viewed as emotionally detached or affectionally hungry. One 29-year-old sexual murderer responded to Card IX: "Two animals' claws reaching for each other." (Inquiry) "A hunting bird of prey because the talons are sharp. Reaching out to be together. One is lonely and wants a relationship with the other."[11]

Primitive object relations (Kwawer, 1980) would be expected to be present on most protocols, with an emphasis on destructive and malevolent separations and reunions. Pure H (< 2) might manifest, depending on the length of the protocol.

Primitive Defenses. Kernberg (1984) wrote that psychotic defenses are generally the same as borderline defenses, but serve a different purpose. Borderline defenses prevent conflict; psychotic defenses prevent decompensation. Prominent defenses in sexual homicide protocols are likely to include omnipotent control, projection, projective identification, devaluation, splitting, dissociation, and perhaps idealization (Cooper & Arnow, 1986). They will cluster at either a borderline or psychotic level of functioning.

Projective identification is central to understanding sexual homicide, since it involves both attribution and control: the projection of malevolent characteristics *into* the victim, a continued, linked identification with those characteristics, and a need to omnipotently control them (Gacono & Meloy, 1988; Grotstein, 1980; Klein, 1946). This latter impulse may stimulate pleasure, and clinically should be considered sadistic. Projective identification may function as either a borderline

---

[10]Van Gogh's "Death's Head Moth" (1889) on the cover of our book was used as an object of projective identification, perhaps a transitional one, in the movie *Silence of the Lambs*. It was placed in the mouths of victims as a cocoon, and paradoxically represented a malevolent transformation of incipient birth in the throes of death. Van Gogh bemoaned his own homicidal impulses when he painted the moth, conveyed in a letter to his brother Theo: "I had to kill it to paint it, and it was a pity, the beastie was so beautiful" (May 22, 1889; Auden, 1989, p. 359).

[11]Perhaps it is diagnostic of American society that the national symbol, an eagle, is a bird of prey, yet with the capacity for nurturing its young and affectional relatedness, at least to its biological offspring.

or psychotic defense (Goldstein, 1991; Meloy, 1991a). The projection of self-representations indicates its psychotic use; the projection of object representations signals its neurotic or borderline use. These may be distinguished on the Rorschach through the ego-dystonic or -syntonic quality of the response (Meloy & Gacono, 1992b). Projective identification is the vehicle for sexual murder; rage is the fuel (Gacono, 1992).

Idealization, rarely seen in psychopathic protocols (Gacono, 1988), and more likely an adaptive neurotic defense, will be manifest, if it occurs, as a failure. Likely content is (H) or (Hd) wherein the percept is dehumanized and distanced. A 53-year-old sexual murderer produced the following response to Card II: "Two people dancing . . . my first thought was two animals, bears, dancing but it could be people doing the same thing. It looks like they're banging their knees together and blood is spurting out." (Inquiry) "Notice the two hands, clapping hands, it's a high five type of thing, this is the body, this is where the knees hit together (?) because it was red (?) shock waves like in a cartoon." This response is notable for its decompensation from the percept of whole humans in cooperative interaction to aggression, blood, and dehumanization (scored W+ Ma.CF.mao 2 (H),Bl 4.5 COP,AG,Mor,DV1). This response also contains a "spoiled" COP. If idealization works, it will usually be linked to the self and contain personal content (PER) and a reflection determinant.

Neurotic defenses will generally fail in this population, indicated by their minus form quality and a sequential shift to an unusual or ordinary form quality response that contains a borderline defense. A vista response followed by aggressive movement may indicate acting out that is prompted by dysphoric affect (Gacono, 1992), an example of one way in which the sexual homicide itself may serve a defensive function to regulate affect. One neurotic defense that may manifest is isolation, and is probably related to sadistic detachment, a common behavior among sexually sadistic criminals (Dietz et al., 1990). A 34-year-old sexual murderer, who raped, electrocuted, and smothered a 15-year-old stranger female victim, gave the following response to Card I: "looks like an aerial photo of a continent. A satellite photo, islands, peninsulas, inlets." (Inquiry) "the outline, jagged edges, inlets, peninsulas." His intellectualization index was 8 and his isolation index (a measure of behavior, not defense, but in this case a corollary) was .53 in a 38-response protocol filled with similarly affectless, distancing responses like this one. Detachment, whether emotional or behavioral, and the use of isolation as a defense, appear in some "higher functioning" sexual sadists who have adaptive neurotic capacities (Shapiro, 1981).

Dissociation may also enhance and exaggerate normal feelings of detachment from surroundings, and we would look for the following Rorschach indices to suggest such dissociative propensities: C, CP, impressionistic response, Wv, Dv. As suggested earlier, dissociability is clinically tied to borderline and hysterical pathology, and is often present in psychopathic or so-called pseudopsychopathic character (Meloy, 1992b).

Pregenital Aggression and Sadism. We would expect elevations across all the aggression responses (AG, AgC, AgPast, AgPot) and the presence of sadomasochism responses (SM) in certain protocols if scored. The SM response, however, is probably not a sensitive indicator of this impulse. The ego-dystonic nature of the aggressive impulse, in its various manifestations, should produce AG responses at a normal frequency for nonpatient males ($M = 1.17$, $SD = 1.10$, Freq = 69%; Exner, 1990b). This contrasts with the significantly lower frequency of aggression responses in psychopathic protocols (see chapter 8). We would also expect a predominance of AgPast over AgPot responses, conveying a more conscious masochistic orientation to objects, despite the unconscious sadism. Such responses may oscillate throughout the protocol, inferring the object relational aspect of the impulse at any one time.

Sex responses should elevate in frequency when compared to nonpatient males (3.7%), and will convey a sexual preoccupation. Content in the protocols of sexual murderers, however, should be interpreted very cautiously unless they are extremely unusual, like sex responses, and are supported by validity data.

The presence of both a sexualized object and aggression in any one Rorschach response is highly unlikely, and would probably be censored by the examinee if it became conscious given the predictable criminal forensic setting in which the Rorschach was administered.

Method

Rorschach protocols were gathered nonrandomly from the authors' public and private forensic practices, and solicited from other colleagues,[12] during the period 1986–1992. All individuals were incarcerated in various prisons and forensic hospitals in the United States (California, Illinois, Florida, Massachusetts, and the District of Columbia). The only criteria for inclusion in the sexual homicide sample were positive evidence that a sexual homicide had been committed,[13] and the production of a valid Rorschach protocol (Exner, 1990a) following incarceration. Validity meant a protocol with at least 14 responses and administered according to the Comprehensive System rules (Exner, 1986a). We purposefully did not exclude individuals on the basis of mental retardation, mental illness, or neurological impairment to accurately represent the probable heterogeneity of this population. Twenty-nine protocols were originally gathered, but close scrutiny, and subsequent statistical testing, revealed that 9 of the protocols, gathered by one examiner, were significantly different from the others when key variables were compared. These

---

[12]We would like to thank the following individuals for their generosity in contributing protocols to this study: Lynne Kenney, PsyD, Reneau Kennedy, PhD, Paul Fauteck, PhD, and Maureen Christian, PhD.

[13]Positive evidence included physical evidence of sexual assault of the victim, sexual activity in close proximity to the victim, such as masturbation, or a legally admissable confession of sexual activity by the perpetrator.

protocols were thus eliminated from the study, and we discuss them in a subsequent portion of this chapter as they shed light on the Rorschach examiner–examinee relationship (Lerner, 1991; Schachtel, 1966).

The 20 remaining protocols were scored and rescored by us, and descriptive statistics (see Tables 9.4 and 9.5) were generated using the Rorschach Scoring Program–Version 2 (Exner et al., 1990). Additional scoring included the Kwawer (1980) primitive modes of relating categories (see Table 9.6), the predicted Cooper and Arnow (1986) defenses (see Table 9.7), and aggression scores (see Table 9.8).

Results

The sample included 18 male and 2 female subjects. Average age was 34.65 (*SD* = 9.33, range 18–53), and most of the subjects (90%) had at least a high school education. Fifteen of the subjects were White (75%), 2 were Black (10%), 2 were Hispanic (10%), and 1 was unknown (5%). At the time of testing 13 were single (65%), 4 were divorced (20%), 2 were married (10%), and 1 was unknown (5%).

The sexual homicide sample accounted for the deaths of at least 30 victims, most of whom were stranger females, consistent with other research (Ressler et al., 1988). None of the victims was married to or cohabitating with the perpetrators. Twenty percent (four) of the sample committed more than one sexual homicide. In cases where the race of the victims was known (13), 100 percent of the murders were intraracial. Age range of the known victims was 6–34 years.

Percentages of agreement for the Rorschach scoring were as follows: location 99.3%, developmental quality 99%, determinants 90.2%, form quality 99.3%, content 96.8%, Z score 98.7%, special scores 94.7%, and total agreement (for all variables) 85.5%.

The Rorschach results are listed in Tables 9.4–9.8. Results are discussed according to the hypotheses generated in the previous portion of this chapter.

Pervasive Cognitive Deficits. Unconventional and idiosyncratic translation of the visual environment is found because 95% of the sample produce X+% < 70 and 85% produce F+% < 70. Mean F+% is 53 (*SD* = 27). Impaired reality testing is also found, with Mean X–% = 20 (*SD* = 11). Fifty percent scored > 20 on this measure of reality-testing impairment, but only 10% scored > 30, supporting our borderline reality-testing hypothesis for most sexual murderers (60% scored X–% 15–30). M– responses were produced by 50% of the sample, and Ma<Mp occurred in 30% of the subjects (see Tables 9.4 and 9.5).

Most formal thought disorder occurred at Level 1, but 40% produced at least one Level 2 response, most likely a DR. Level 1 FABCOMs occurred in 45% of the subjects, whereas ALOGs, a more sensitive indicator of schizophrenia than are CONTAMs (Meloy & Singer, 1991), appeared in only 10% of the protocols. There were no CONTAMs. The majority of special scores indicating

TABLE 9.4
Rorschach Variables for Sample (N = 20) of Sexual Homicide Perpetrators

Variable	Mean	SD	Min	Max	Freq	Median	Mode	SK	KU
R	28.85	13.67	13.00	54.00	20	23.00	19.00	0.67	−1.06
W	8.55	3.55	2.00	14.00	20	8.50	7.00	−0.03	−0.76
D	15.70	11.05	5.00	37.00	20	11.00	5.00	0.67	−1.01
Dd	4.60	5.57	0.00	17.00	12	2.50	0.00	1.09	−0.07
Space	2.80	1.88	0.00	6.00	19	2.50	1.00	0.58	−0.78
DQ+	7.20	3.12	1.00	13.00	20	8.00	9.00	−0.37	−0.50
DQo	17.80	11.66	4.00	41.00	20	14.50	4.00	0.54	−0.80
DQv	3.15	2.50	0.00	9.00	18	2.50	2.00	1.00	0.43
DQv/+	0.70	1.13	0.00	4.00	8	0.00	0.00	1.88	3.24
FQX+	0.05	0.22	0.00	1.00	1	0.00	0.00	4.47	20.00
FQXo	14.35	6.66	7.00	30.00	20	12.00	12.00	1.04	−0.04
FQXu	8.05	6.06	2.00	19.00	20	5.00	3.00	0.77	−1.05
FQX−	5.70	3.28	0.00	11.00	19	6.00	4.00	−0.13	−1.01
FQXnone	0.70	1.26	0.00	5.00	7	0.00	0.00	2.38	6.57
MQ+	0.05	0.22	0.00	1.00	1	0.00	0.00	4.47	20.00
MQo	2.30	1.56	0.00	5.00	18	3.00	1.00	0.18	−1.09
MQu	1.30	1.03	0.00	3.00	15	1.00	1.00	0.28	−0.94
MQ−	0.70	0.86	0.00	3.00	10	0.50	0.00	1.21	1.14
MQnone	0.00	0.00	0.00	0.00	0	0.00	0.00	−	−
Space−	0.95	1.15	0.00	4.00	11	1.00	0.00	1.27	1.29
M	4.35	2.16	1.00	9.00	20	4.00	3.00	0.54	−0.38
FM	5.90	3.60	0.00	13.00	18	6.50	7.00	−0.02	−0.59
m	2.35	1.93	0.00	6.00	16	2.00	0.00	0.52	−0.63
FM+m	8.25	4.59	0.00	17.00	19	8.00	13.00	−0.03	−0.74
FC	1.85	1.84	0.00	5.00	16	1.00	1.00	0.86	−0.96
CF	2.60	2.35	0.00	9.00	17	2.00	2.00	1.30	1.56
C	0.55	0.76	0.00	2.00	8	0.00	0.00	1.02	−0.37
Cn	0.00	0.00	0.00	0.00	0	0.00	0.00	−	−
FC+CF+C+Cn	5.00	3.67	1.00	13.00	20	3.50	3.00	0.84	−0.43
WgSumC	4.35	3.25	0.50	11.50	20	3.50	0.50	0.95	0.25
Sum C′	1.70	1.38	0.00	5.00	15	2.00	2.00	0.60	0.34
Sum T	1.05	2.14	0.00	9.00	7	0.00	0.00	3.01	10.40
Sum V	0.85	1.35	0.00	5.00	10	0.50	0.00	2.30	5.21
Sum Y	2.30	3.63	0.00	12.00	11	1.00	0.00	1.87	2.75
Sum Shd	5.90	6.84	1.00	28.00	20	3.50	2.00	2.24	5.15
Fr+rF	0.85	1.04	0.00	3.00	9	0.00	0.00	0.64	−1.22
FD	0.35	0.59	0.00	2.00	6	0.00	0.00	1.52	1.64
F	10.10	7.59	0.00	25.00	19	8.50	13.00	0.53	−0.71
Pairs	8.50	5.28	2.00	26.00	20	8.00	5.00	1.94	5.69
Ego	0.43	0.21	0.14	1.08	20	0.41	0.26	1.45	3.94
Lambda	0.65	0.65	0.00	2.17	19	0.38	0.19	1.37	0.76
EA	8.70	4.05	1.50	17.00	20	7.75	5.50	0.53	−0.28
es	14.15	9.99	2.00	41.00	20	12.00	15.00	1.30	1.57
D Score	−1.95	2.93	−11.00	1.00	20	−1.00	0.00	−1.70	3.72
Adj D Score	−0.85	1.60	−5.00	1.00	20	0.00	0.00	−1.04	0.73
SumActvMov	7.55	3.65	1.00	14.00	20	6.50	6.00	0.17	−0.84
SumPassMov	5.05	3.82	0.00	13.00	19	4.50	1.00	0.86	0.22
SumMactv	2.50	1.50	0.00	5.00	18	3.00	3.00	−0.26	−1.17

(Continued)

TABLE 9.4
(Continued)

Variable	Mean	SD	Min	Max	Freq	Median	Mode	SK	KU
SumMpass	1.85	1.39	0.00	5.00	16	2.00	2.00	0.43	−0.11
IntellIndx	2.80	2.57	0.00	8.00	15	2.00	0.00	0.87	−0.01
Zf	12.70	3.45	6.00	20.00	20	12.50	10.00	0.18	−0.07
Zd	−2.25	3.49	−8.00	4.00	18	−1.50	−6.00	0.08	−1.04
Blends	5.25	4.06	1.00	17.00	20	4.00	1.00	1.30	2.29
CSBlnd	1.10	1.55	0.00	5.00	9	0.00	0.00	1.32	0.76
Afr	0.49	0.24	0.19	1.09	20	0.43	0.36	1.40	1.62
Populars	5.55	1.73	2.00	9.00	20	5.50	5.00	0.04	0.01
X+%	0.51	0.10	0.33	0.77	20	0.50	0.50	0.71	1.36
F+%	0.53	0.27	0.00	1.00	18	0.51	0.40	0.03	0.65
X−%	0.20	0.11	0.00	0.43	19	0.20	0.21	0.07	−0.11
Xu%	0.25	0.10	0.09	0.47	20	0.26	0.20	0.15	−0.39
S−%	0.15	0.19	0.00	0.67	11	0.11	0.00	1.51	2.13
IsoIndx	0.27	0.22	0.00	0.67	19	0.22	0.53	0.58	−1.18
H	2.65	1.35	1.00	6.00	20	2.50	2.00	0.86	0.70
(H)	1.10	1.16	0.00	4.00	12	1.00	0.00	0.90	0.33
Hd	2.10	1.92	0.00	6.00	15	1.50	0.00	0.59	−0.83
(Hd)	0.90	1.29	0.00	5.00	10	0.50	0.00	1.99	4.49
Hx	0.25	0.64	0.00	2.00	3	0.00	0.00	2.44	4.77
H+(H)+Hd+(Hd)	6.75	3.24	2.00	13.00	20	6.50	4.00	0.57	−0.55
A	10.20	4.62	3.00	22.00	20	10.00	9.00	0.69	0.86
(A)	0.75	0.97	0.00	3.00	9	0.00	0.00	0.95	−0.32
Ad	3.00	3.77	0.00	14.00	14	1.50	0.00	1.72	2.88
(Ad)	0.30	0.47	0.00	1.00	6	0.00	0.00	0.94	−1.24
An	1.15	1.46	0.00	4.00	11	1.00	0.00	1.18	0.04
Art	1.00	1.30	0.00	5.00	11	1.00	0.00	1.77	3.69
Ay	1.20	1.20	0.00	4.00	13	1.00	0.00	0.80	−0.06
Bl	0.40	0.82	0.00	3.00	5	0.00	0.00	2.26	4.90
Bt	1.05	1.19	0.00	3.00	11	1.00	0.00	0.72	−1.01
Cg	1.35	1.50	0.00	5.00	12	1.00	0.00	1.00	0.33
Cl	0.65	1.04	0.00	4.00	8	0.00	0.00	2.05	4.78
Ex	0.25	0.44	0.00	1.00	5	0.00	0.00	1.25	−0.50
Fi	0.55	0.76	0.00	2.00	8	0.00	0.00	1.02	−0.37
Food	0.55	0.89	0.00	3.00	7	0.00	0.00	1.59	1.85
Geog	0.10	0.31	0.00	1.00	2	0.00	0.00	2.89	7.04
HHold	0.55	0.83	0.00	3.00	8	0.00	0.00	1.69	2.96
Ls	1.65	2.21	0.00	7.00	12	1.00	0.00	1.54	1.33
Na	1.80	2.14	0.00	8.00	13	1.00	0.00	1.50	2.32
Sc	1.40	1.73	0.00	6.00	13	1.00	0.00	1.61	2.03
Sx	0.45	0.83	0.00	3.00	6	0.00	0.00	2.05	4.08
Xy	0.10	0.31	0.00	1.00	2	0.00	0.00	2.89	7.04
Idio	1.45	1.73	0.00	7.00	13	1.00	0.00	1.92	4.73
DV	2.05	2.14	0.00	8.00	15	1.50	0.00	1.36	1.73
INCOM	1.35	1.18	0.00	5.00	15	1.00	2.00	1.35	3.70
DR	2.75	3.31	0.00	12.00	13	1.50	0.00	1.42	1.83
FABCOM	0.75	1.02	0.00	3.00	9	0.00	0.00	1.22	0.45
DV2	0.00	0.00	0.00	0.00	0	0.00	0.00	−	−
INC2	0.20	0.52	0.00	2.00	3	0.00	0.00	2.74	7.40

(Continued)

TABLE 9.4
(Continued)

Variable	Mean	SD	Min	Max	Freq	Median	Mode	SK	KU
DR2	0.55	1.79	0.00	8.00	4	0.00	0.00	4.18	18.10
FAB2	0.15	0.37	0.00	1.00	3	0.00	0.00	2.12	2.78
ALOG	0.10	0.31	0.00	1.00	2	0.00	0.00	2.89	7.04
CONTAM	0.00	0.00	0.00	0.00	0	0.00	0.00	–	–
Sum6SpSc	7.00	4.98	0.00	18.00	18	5.50	5.00	1.03	0.86
Sum6SpScLv2	0.90	2.22	0.00	10.00	8	0.00	0.00	3.98	16.81
WSum6SpSc	21.65	18.72	0.00	71.00	18	15.50	12.00	1.28	1.39
AB	0.30	0.57	0.00	2.00	5	0.00	0.00	1.84	2.86
AG	0.85	0.93	0.00	3.00	12	1.00	1.00	1.19	1.09
CFB	0.00	0.00	0.00	0.00	0	0.00	0.00	–	–
COP	1.50	1.28	0.00	4.00	14	1.50	0.00	0.25	-1.09
CP	0.15	0.37	0.00	1.00	3	0.00	0.00	2.12	2.78
MOR	2.65	3.17	0.00	12.00	16	2.00	1.00	2.07	4.22
PER	2.95	3.78	0.00	13.00	14	2.00	0.00	1.72	2.23
PSV	0.15	0.37	0.00	1.00	3	0.00	0.00	2.12	2.78

formal thought disorder were Level 1 DV, DR, and INCOMs. These data lend further support to the borderline personality organization hypothesis for sexual murderers, and do not support speculation that these individuals are chronically psychotic.

WSum6 averaged 21.65 ($M = 18.72$), but ranged from 0 to 71 with a relatively normal distribution. Personals (PER) were also elevated ($M = 2.95$, $SD = 3.78$), supporting the link between DR and PER as a wish to self-aggrandize, which is then expressed circumstantially or tangentially to the task at hand. The mean number of PER+DR in each protocol was 1.0. Impressionistic responses occurred in 50% of the sample ($M = .90$, $SD = 1.07$), supporting the impressionistic cognitive style of the hysteric among sexual murderers.

Noticeably high elevations for both FM ($M = 5.9$, $SD = 3.60$) and m ($M = 2.35$, $SD = 1.93$) infer that nonvolitional ideation as a result of unmet needs (FM) and controllable helplessness (m) will distinguish this population from both ASPD males and psychopaths (see chapter 5). These findings further suggest that thinking problems in this population will be dynamically tied to affects and object relations, rather than structural deficits independent of personality, as we would see in schizophrenia. The FM elevation, interpreted as obsessional thinking, is also consistent with the sexual homicide literature, which suggests an obsessive-compulsive aspect to serial murder.

Affect Tension and Dysphoria. Anxiety is markedly present among our sample with a mean Y of 2.30 ($SD = 3.63$). Only 11 subjects (55%), however, produced a Y response, supporting our bimodal theory of anxiety, or felt helplessness, in this population. Either a sexual murderer is not anxious, or he

TABLE 9.5
Sexual Homicide Perpetrators ($N = 20$) Group Mean and Frequencies for
Select Ratios, Percentages, and Derivations

$R = 28.85$	$L = 0.65$	$(L > .99 = 20\%)$

$EB = 4.35 : 4.35$	$EA = 8.70$
$eb = 8.25 : 5.90$	$es = 14.15$ (FM + m $<$ SUMShading ... 4 20%)
$D = -1.95$ $AdjD = -0.85$	

EB STYLE

Introversive	6	30%
Super-Introversive	3	15%
Ambitent	8	40%
Extratensive	6	30%
Super-Extratensive	8	10%

EA − es DIFFERENCES:D-SCORES

D Score > 0	3	15%
D Score $= 0$	5	25%
D Score < 0	12	60%
D Score < -1	9	45%
AdjD Score > 0	3	15%
AdjD Score $= 0$	9	45%
AdjD Score < 0	8	40%
AdjD Score < -1	7	15%

AFFECT

FC:CF + C = 1.85 : 3.15	
Pure C = 0.55	(Pure C $> 0 = 40\%$; Pure C $> 1 = 15\%$)
FC $> (CF + C) + 2$ 1	5%
FC $> (CF + C) + 1$ 2	10%
$(CF + C) > FC + 1$ 9	45%
$(CF + C) > FC + 2$ 5	25%

SumC' = 1.70	SumV = 0.85	SumY = 2.30

Afr = 0.49	(Afr $< .40 = 45\%$; Afr $< .50 = 60\%$)
S = 2.80	(S $> 2 = 50\%$)
Blends:R = 5.25 : 28.85	
CP = .15	

INTERPERSONAL

COP = 1.50	(COP $= 0$, 30%; COP $> 2 = 25\%$)
AG = 0.85	(AG $= 0$, 40%; AG $> 2 = 10\%$)
Food = 0.55	
Isolate:R = 0.27	
H:(H) + Hd + (Hd) = 2.65 : 4.10	(H $= 0$, 0%; H $< 2 = 20\%$)
(H) + (Hd):(A) + (Ad) = 2.0 : 1.05	
H + A:Hd + Ad = 12.85 : 5.10	
Sum T = 1.05	(T $= 0$, 65%; T $> 1 = 25\%$)

(Continued)

TABLE 9.5
(Continued)

SELF-PERCEPTION

$3r+(2)/R = 0.43$	$(30\% < .33; 45\% > .44)$
$Fr+rF = 0.85$	$(Fr+rF > 0 = 45\%)$
$FD = 0.35$	
$An+Xy = 1.25$	
$MOR = 2.65$	$(MOR > 2 = 35\%)$

IDEATION

$a:p = 7.55 : 5.05$	$(p > a+1 = 15\%)$
$Ma:Mp = 2.50 : 1.85$	$(Mp > Ma = 30\%)$
$M = 4.35$	$(M- = 0.70; M\ none = .00)$
$FM = 5.90 \qquad m = 2.35$	
$2AB+(Art+Ay) = 2.80$	$(2AB+Art+Ay > 5 = 30\%)$
$Sum6 = 7.00$	$(Sum6 > 6 = 45\%)$
$WSum6 = 21.65$	$(Level\ 2\ Special\ Scores > 0 = 40\%)$

MEDIATION

Populars = 5.55	$(P < 4 = 10\%; P > 7 = 15\%)$
$X+\% = .51$	
$F+\% = .53$	
$X-\% = .20$	
$Xu\% = .25$	
$S-\% = .15$	

$X+\% > .89$	0	0%
$X+\% < .70$	19	95%
$X+\% < .61$	17	85%
$X+\% < .50$	9	45%
$F+\% < .70$	17	85%
$Xu\% > .20$	13	65%
$X-\% > .15$	14	70%
$X-\% > .20$	10	50%
$X-\% > .30$	2	10%

PROCESSING

$Zf = 12.70$	
$Zd = -2.25$	$(Zd > +3.0 = 5\%; Zd < -3.0 = 40\%)$
$W:D:Dd = 8.55:15.70:4.60$	$(Dd > 3 = 45\%)$
$W:M = 8.55 : 4.35$	
$DQ+ = 7.20$	
$DQv = 3.15$	$(DQv + DQv/+ > 2 = 60\%)$

CONSTELLATIONS

SCZI = 6...0	0%	DEPI = 7...0	0%	CDI = 5...0	0%
SCZI = 5...1	5%	DEPI = 6...3	15%	CDI = 4...6	30%
SCZI = 4...1	5%	DEPI = 5...4	20%		

S-Constellation Positive	1	5%
HVI Positive	3	15%
OBS Positive	0	0%

298

TABLE 9.6
Kwawer (1980) Primitive Modes of Relating for Sexual Homicide Perpetrators
(N = 20)

Category	Mean	SD	Frequency
Engulfment	.05	.22	1
Symbiotic Merging	.30	.47	6
Violent Symbiosis	1.05	1.73	8
Malignant Internal Process	.35	.93	4
Boundary Disturbance	.70	.80	10
Birth-Rebirth	.30	.57	5
Metamorphosis	.30	.57	5
Narcissistic Mirroring	.85	1.04	9
Separation-Division	.25	.64	3
Womb Imagery	.15	.37	3
Total Object Relations	4.20	2.42	18

TABLE 9.7
Selected Cooper and Arnow (1986) Defenses for Sexual Homicide Perpetrators
(N = 20)

Category	Mean	SD	Frequency	
Devaluation	2.85	3.01	17	(85%)
Projection	1.40	1.82	12	(60%)
Idealization	1.05	1.32	11	(55%)
Splitting	0.65	0.75	10	(50%)
Isolation	1.10	1.55	9	(45%)
Projective Identification	0.90	1.48	8	(40%)
Omnipotence	0.50	1.39	4	(20%)

TABLE 9.8
Aggression Scores, Impressionistic Score, and Color Projection Score
for Sexual Homicide Perpetrators (N = 20)

Category	Mean	SD	Frequency
Aggression (Exner, 1986a)	.85	.93	12
Aggressive Content	2.95	2.58	20
Aggressive Past	.95	1.64	7
Aggressive Potential	.90	1.48	9
Impressionistic	.90	1.07	10
Color Projection	.17	.38	3

experiences high levels of anxiety concerning uncontrollable stressors. The majority of these subjects, however, are not clinically depressed as measured by the DEPI $\geq$ 5 (35%). Yet half of them ruminate in a negative, dysphoric manner (Vista M = .85, SD = 1.35) and are confused about their emotions (Color Shading Blend M = 1.10, SD = 1.55).

Affect modulation is poor (FC:CF+C = 1.85:3.15), but markedly better than ASPD males in general (1:3) and psychopaths in particular (1:4). Pure C responses occurred in 40% of the subjects, and S > 2 in 50% of the subjects (see Table 9.5). The aggression response (AG) occurred in a majority of subjects (60%), quite similar to nonpatient males (Exner, 1990b). Ten percent produced AG > 2.

Trouble with affects is apparent, with the avoidance of external affect (Afr M = .49, SD = .24) prominent. Yet surprisingly the sexual homicide perpetrator, on average, is not a "high Lambda" individual (Lambda M = .65), and only 20% of the subjects produce Lambda > .99 (see Table 9.5). These individuals, despite their unpleasant affects, are not highly defended against them, and have not adopted a simplistic, item-by-item problem-solving style like the psychopath.

Three of the subjects (15%) produced a color projection response, an indicator of primitive hysterical defense. This is significantly greater than CP found in nonpatient males (X2 = 44.43, p < .0005) where the frequency is .6%. Only 2% of our ASPD sample (N = 82) produced a CP response, and only 4% of schizophrenics and 0% of character disorders produce CP (Exner, 1991). This finding is consonant with the impressionistic frequency noted earlier (50%), and the presence of primitive hysterical mechanisms in this population. A high Lambda defense against affects may be unnecessary if feelings are rapidly split off or dissociated.

Stress tolerance and controls are bimodally distributed. The majority of our sample behave in predictable, organized ways (AdjD $\geq$ 0 = 60%). Yet a significant minority (15%) have exceedingly poor impulse control (AdjD < −1) and do not organize their behavior in any predictable way. Sixty percent are disorganized due to situational stress at the time of testing (D < 0).

Pre-Oedipal Object Relations. Narcissistic psychopathology is expected in this population, with 45% producing at least one reflection response (M = .85, SD = .59). Symbiotic and boundary disturbances are also common (see Table 9.6). Fifty percent produced at least one boundary disturbance response, 40% a violent symbiosis response, and 30% a symbiotic merging response. Womb imagery and engulfment responses were found in a minority of subjects, supporting our notion that developmentally autistic responses would be exceptions to the symbiotic rule in a sample of sexual homicide perpetrators.

Despite elevated self-absorption (Egocentricity > .44) in 45% of the sample, there is also a sense of self-injury in 35% of the sample (MOR > 2). Six of the subjects (30%) produced the combination of RF > 0 and MOR > 1. Aggression scores also abound, with at least one of the aggression scores, usually aggressive content, in 100% of the protocols (see Table 9.8). Although we did not score SM responses in these protocols, 45% produced an aggressive potential response, and 35% produced an aggressive past response, inferring a sadistic or masochistic orientation to early objects, respectively (Meloy & Gacono, 1992a).

The isolative, schizoid, yet aggressive style receives some support because 30% of the sample produced COP = 0, there is a plethora of aggression responses, and the mean isolation index is .27 (SD = .22). Food responses are also common (35%) and H:(H)+Hd+(Hd) = 2.65:4.10 on average. The sexual homicide perpetrator has a part-object–dominated representational world, consistent with interest in part-object, as opposed to whole-object, pornography (Meloy, 1992b).

A capacity for attachment is abnormal in 90% of these subjects. Yet it is also bimodally distributed as we predicted. Sixty-five percent produce T = 0 and 25% produce T > 1. The sexual homicide perpetrator is emotionally detached or affectionally hungry.

Primitive object relations (Kwawer, 1980) appear at least once in 90% of the protocols, with several expected (M = 4.20, SD = 2.42).

Primitive Defenses. Table 9.7 summarizes the means and frequencies for seven defenses scored in the sexual homicide sample. The most frequent of these defenses, in descending order, are devaluation (85%), projection (60%), idealization (55%), splitting (50%), isolation (45%), projective identification (40%), and omnipotence (20%). The protocols average 8.45 of these defenses, with a range of 0–31. All of these defenses, except for isolation, would be considered borderline level in the Cooper et al. (1988) system.

These findings generally confirm our hypotheses that the sexual homicide perpetrator's defenses will cluster at the borderline level (although we did not score the protocols for all neurotic defenses), and such defenses should be expected in the Rorschach. Only one subject (5%) produced none of these defenses.

When descriptively compared to a sample (N = 43) of ASPD males (Gacono & Meloy, 1992), the sexual homicide perpetrator's defenses are quite similar. He does, however, appear to use omnipotence and projective identification less frequently, and isolation more frequently.

To preliminarily test Gacono's (1992) hypothesis that a vista response followed by aggression (AG, AgPot, AgPast, AgC, or SM)[14] may indicate the use of aggressive impulse to regulate dysphoric affect, we studied all the vista responses in the protocols in relation to the AG movement response only. There were 13 vista responses, 1 of which was followed by an aggressive movement response. This sequence occurred on Cards I and II: "If I really try I see a person with wings and his hands raised, body, legs, feet, and a skirt. (Inquiry) Here's the hands, the head, this part makes a body, legs and feet and the outer part, the

---

[14]*Any* aggressive imagery occurring *within* the vista response would also support this hypothesis.

lighter part is the skirt to see the body ... the head would be here, it's inside, the head is not clear, they're blowing, it's like an angel, its got the wings like an angel, I don't believe in angels." (W+ Mp.FV.mao (H),Cg 4.0 DR). And then the next response to Card II: "I could say it looks like two people dancing ... my first thought was two animals, bears dancing but it could be people doing the same thing. It looks like they're banging their knees together and blood is spurting out, of course, if the red wasn't there I wouldn't have thought of it." [W+ Ma.CF.mao 2 (H),Bl 4.5 COP,AG,MOR,DV]. This second response, which we used earlier in this chapter to illustrate a spoiled idealization, does appear to compensate for the prior vista response, and lends some support to Gacono's hypothesis. Any psychodynamic link between vista and aggression in sexual homicide samples needs further study of both within and between response patterns. Establishing a real-world correlate might be problematic.

A striking example of projective identification, a defense we have previously emphasized in sexual homicide (Gacono, 1992; Gacono & Meloy, 1988; Meloy, 1988, 1992b), was offered by a 34-year-old male who was awaiting trial for the murder of a woman he met in a bar. He had been previously convicted of the sexual murder of a cousin and served 10 years. He was out in the community for only a few months when the second sexual homicide occurred. He first told the Rorschach examiner that his initial victim was a man, but when later confronted with this lie, he justified his earlier statement by claiming that the first victim was so ugly that she looked like a man to him. After the second sexual homicide, the perpetrator left the victim's 2-year-old daughter in bed with the corpse of her mother. Here is his final response, Card X: "I got another picture of the Devil here. He got yellow eyes, bloodshot pupils, horns with huge ears on the side of his head and crustaceans feeding on him. Four crabs. (Inquiry) The brown is the crabs and the blue ones the horns. This piece is a hint of a nose. Open area is mouth and orange is tonsils. Bottom section is his two teeth. Canines curved inward. The rest is like his chin at the bottom. Something's feeding on him. He's been kicked to the curb and the animals are feeding on him. Being the Devil, always plotting and scamming, fire eyes, a state of anger. Last dregs of life there. He's gonna zap one of the crabs until something larger comes along, then the process starts all over again." (WS+ FMa.Mp.FC– 2 (Hd),A 6.0 MOR,AG,FAB2,DR [AgPot, AgC])

Klein wrote in 1946, "Much of the hatred against parts of the self is now directed towards the mother. This leads to a particular form of identification which establishes the prototype of an aggressive object relation. I suggest for these processes the term 'projective identification' " (p. 8). Both Lerner and Lerner (1980) and Cooper and Arnow (1986) looked for the following key elements to score projective identification on the Rorschach: (a) fantasies of placing hated or dangerous parts of the self into other objects, (b) fearful empathy with those objects, and (c) hyperalertness to external threat or attack, and rage. This final response abundantly illustrates this defense in a serial sexual murderer.

Pregenital Aggression and Sadism. Elevations across all the aggression responses are found (Table 9.8). Unlike the other antisocial samples in this book, the sexual homicide perpetrators approach nonpatient males in their frequency (60%) and number of aggressive movement responses ($M = .85$, $SD = .93$). We think this is due to the ego-dystonic nature of the aggressive impulse in this group, and the greater aggressive tensions in sexual homicide perpetrators when compared to both ASPD males and psychopaths.

Contrary to our prediction, AgPot responses slightly exceed AgPast responses, conveying a more conscious sadistic, rather than masochistic, orientation to objects. Sex responses do elevate in frequency (30%) when compared to nonpatient males (3.7%; Exner, 1991). Perusal of all the protocols yielded no responses in which a sex content occurred with an aggressive movement (Exner, 1986a) special score.

A significant proportion of the sample (30%) were positive for the coping deficit index.

Examiner Effects

The nine protocols that we eliminated from our sample were gathered from a maximum security sex offender treatment center as part of an approved research project. All nine Rorschachs were administered by a female psychologist with virtually no experience with this population, but competent in Rorschach administration. She was alone with the subject during the Rorschach administration in all cases except for once when she was accompanied by a male psychiatrist. The average PCL–R score for these 10 subjects, 9 of whom were sexual homicide perpetrators, was 30 (range 16–38). Four of the subjects scored < 30, and for research purposes would not be considered psychopaths. The remaining six would be considered primary psychopaths.

Scrutiny of these Rorschach protocols, when compared to the other initial 14 that were administered by a mixed-gender group, suggested significant differences. We then ran nonparametric tests of certain variables and confirmed significant differences in the direction of fewer responses for R ($p = .072$), T ($p = .025$), AG ($p < .025$), V ($p = .05$), and Y ($p < .025$). There was a trend for decreased Rf responses ($p = .08$). Lambda was significantly increased ($p = .02$) in the 9 protocols when compared to the other initial 14. General constriction in the protocols of these sexual homicide perpetrators, in the absence of any other real differences in this group when compared to the other subjects, suggested an examiner effect that went beyond a gender difference. In order to explore this hypothesis further we asked the examiner to recall her thoughts occurring during each subject's evaluation.

Our analysis of this examiner's retrospective thoughts and feelings suggest that emotions were stimulated in her in 60% of the Rorschach administrations, and these feelings could be characterized as anger, disgust, fear, or sadness.

Although we have no way of knowing for certain, it seems reasonable that her countertransference reactions to these mostly psychopathic and sexually aggressive individuals influenced the response process and led to a general constriction of symbolized affect and response frequency on the part of the subjects. The examinees' thoughts and feelings toward this examiner cannot be known, but the experiential process of the Rorschach in this context seemed very important (Schachtel, 1966). Normally we try to minimize examiner effects during the Rorschach by sitting side by side and speaking as little as possible to the examinee. The set and setting are designed so that the cards, rather than the examiner, will function as the primary projective vehicle. In this subset of protocols, it is likely that the affect generated in the examiner rendered the Rorschach cards a secondary object during the exam.

Evoked emotion in the Rorschach examiner may constrict both the response frequency and the use of affect by the examinee. In this context, the examinees may have sensed the examiner's unpleasant affect, and perhaps her negative judgment of them, and withdrawn from the task, resulting in more pure form, less use of shading, and fewer responses. It is also conceivable that for at least three of the subjects the examiner was caught in a prey–predator dynamic with the subject in which his instinctual aims were openly and sadistically directed toward her during the administration of the test. Most striking is the frightening return of one in her imagination late at night several months later. She may have fit this particular subject's victim pool most closely (Meloy, 1988) and became unconsciously wedded to him as a victim of destiny. She remembered thinking at the time of testing, "He seems enticing and yet dangerous to me."

We would recommend that researchers embarking on Rorschach studies of sexual aggressors be cognizant of their emotional reactions and countertransference vulnerabilities. It appears from our experience that such reactions may confound results and will usually result in more constricted protocols.

Comparison to a Psychopathic Sample[15]

We further tested the null hypothesis that individuals who commit a sexual homicide share the same personality structure as psychopaths. A comparison group of *nonsexually offending* psychopaths was chosen for the following reasons: the popular belief that all individuals who commit sexual homicide are "psychopaths"; the reliability and validity of an instrument to measure psychopathy (Hare, 1991); extant Rorschach research concerning psychopaths (Gacono & Meloy, 1992) and normal adults (Exner, 1990a); and the elimination of confounding paraphiliac attributes in an otherwise criminal and violent male comparison group.

---

[15]This portion of the chapter is an adapted version of "A Rorschach investigation of sexual homicide" by R. Meloy, C. Gacono, and L. Kenney, 1994, previously published in the *Journal of Personality Assessment, 62*, 58–67.

The sample of sexual homicide perpetrators contained two fewer subjects (N = 18) than did the sample discussed previously. At the time of this comparison we did not have 20 valid protocols.

The sample of primary psychopaths (N = 23) was selected at random from our large Rorschach sample of ASPD males (N = 82) described in chapter 5. This comparison group scored > 30 on the PCL–R and were not incarcerated for a sexual offense.[16] The psychopaths were free of a diagnosis of mental retardation, mental illness, or organic mental disorder.

Interjudge reliabilities for the PCL–R scores and Rorschach scores for the comparison group were previously determined (Gacono & Meloy, 1992). Select Rorschach variables were compared between groups based on previous research (Gacono & Meloy, 1991, 1992; Gacono et al., 1990; Meloy & Gacono, 1992a) and theory (Gacono, 1992; Meloy, 1988), and were grouped according to affects, cognitions, self-perception, and object relations. Variables were nonparametric and tested using either Mann–Whitney U (means comparison) or chi-square (frequency comparison). They were considered significantly different if $p < .05$.

Demographic characteristics of the samples are compared in Table 9.9. The sexual homicide sample is older than the psychopathic sample, and contains two female subjects. Ethnicity of the groups is comparable, although unlike other incarcerated populations in the United States, most perpetrators of sexual homicide are White. Education is comparable.

The sexual homicide sample accounted for the deaths of at least 30 victims, most of whom were stranger females, consistent with other research (Ressler et al., 1988). None of the victims was married or cohabiting with the perpetrators. Twenty-two percent (N = 4) of this sample committed more than one sexual homicide.

Spearman's Rho was .94 for interjudge reliability of the PCL–R for the comparison group. Percentages of agreement for the Rorschach scoring for the sexual homicide perpetrator group was the same as that noted earlier in the chapter for the sample of 20. Results of comparison of the Rorschach variables are listed in Table 9.10.

Total Responses. The sexual homicide sample produced significantly more Rorschach responses than did the psychopath sample ($p = .0058$). Because the frequency of many variables is dependent on R, differences are discussed with this limitation in mind. When a significantly greater frequency of a particular variable is produced by the group with fewer overall responses, it strongly suggests the characterological influence of the variable (Gacono & Meloy, 1992).

---

[16]We could not be sure, however, that there was absolutely no sexual offense in the history of these subjects.

TABLE 9.9
Demographic Data for Sexual Homicide Perpetrators ($N = 18$) and
Nonsexual Offending Psychopaths ($N = 23$)

	Sexual Homicide Perpetrators	Psychopaths
Age	35.3 (18–53)	29.7 (18–43)
Education	12.3 years	10.7 years
Male	89%	100%
Female	11%	0%
White	78%	61%
Black	11%	22%
Hispanic	6%	13%
Other/Unknown	5%	4%

Affects. Texture (T) responses, a measure of attachment capacity, were more frequently present ($X2 = 3.76$, $df = 1$, $p = .05$) in the sexual homicide sample (39%) than in the psychopathic sample (9%). Twenty-eight percent of the sexual homicide sample also produced $T > 1$, an abnormal finding in nonpatient populations that suggests a bimodal distribution for this variable among sexual homicide perpetrators. Elevated T (> 1), a measure of attachment hunger, was completely absent in the psychopathic controls ($X2 = 4.91$, $df = 1$, $p = .026$).

TABLE 9.10
Comparison of Select Rorschach Variables Between Sexual Homicide
Perpetrators ($N = 18$) and Primary Psychopaths ($N = 23$)

Variable	Sexual Homicide Perpetrators			Primary Psychopaths			p
	Mean	SD	Frequency	Mean	SD	Frequency	
Responses	30.00	13.91	18	19.04	5.93	23	.0058[a]
Affects							
T	1.17	2.23	7	.09	.29	2	
T = 0			11			21	.05[b]
T > 1			5			0	.026[b]
V	0.94	1.39	10	0.35	0.49	8	.18[a]
Space	2.72	1.78	17	2.48	1.78	20	
FM	6.11	3.60	16	2.87	1.74	21	.0019[a]
Cognitions							
WSum6	23.17	19.12	16	14.22	13.01	20	
X – %	21	12	17	20	10	23	
Self-Perception							
Rf	0.94	1.06	9	0.65	0.98	9	
PER	3.28	3.85	14	2.09	1.86	17	
Object Relations							
All H	7.00	3.22	18	4.26	2.09	23	.0029[a]
COP > 2			5			0	.007[b]

Note. Variables without *p* were not tested for significance. Frequency is the number of subjects who produced at least one of the variable, unless otherwise noted.
[a]Mann–Whitney *U*. [b]Chi-square.

Vista (V) responses, a measure of dysphoric or painful introspection, were not significantly different between the groups, but an apparent trend is suggested in the direction of the sexual homicide sample producing more ($M = .94$, $SD = 1.39$, $p = .18$).

Space responses (S), a measure of characterological anger or chronic negativism when S > 2, were found to be similar for both groups and clinically elevated in the predicted direction.

Animal movement (FM) responses, a measure of nonvolitional ideation resulting from unmet need states, were significantly greater in the sexual homicide sample than in the psychopathic sample ($M = 6.11$, $SD = 3.6$, $p = .0019$).

Cognitions. The WSum6 score, a weighted measure of formal thought disorder, was clinically elevated in both samples with a trend in the direction of a greater amount, and more variance, in the sexual homicide sample ($M = 23.17$, $SD = 19.12$). The X–%, a measure of reality-testing impairment, was grossly elevated and virtually the same in both groups.

Self-Perception. The reflection response (Rf), a measure of pathological narcissism, appeared with clinically elevated frequency (Rf > 0) in both the sexual homicide (50%) and psychopathic (39%) samples. The personal (PER) response, a measure of self-aggrandizement in forensic populations (Gacono et al., 1990), was also elevated (> 2) and similar in both samples, with greater variance among the sexual homicide perpetrators ($M = 3.28$, $SD = 3.85$).

Object Relations. The sexual homicide sample produced significantly more human content (All H), a general measure of interest in others, than did the psychopathic sample ($M = 7.0$, $SD = 3.22$, $p = .0029$). The sexual homicide sample also showed a greater frequency (28%) of cooperative movement responses (COP > 2), a measure of the expectation of cooperative human interaction, than did the psychopathic sample, which showed none (X2 = 7.28, df = 1, $p = .007$).

DISCUSSION AND CONCLUSIONS

Perpetrators of sexual homicide evidence abnormal personality structure when select Rorschach variables are used to measure affects, cognitions, self-perception, and object relations. Our sexual homicide sample ($N = 18$) generally showed more variance within Rorschach variables than did a comparative sample of primary psychopaths. This finding may be related to our choice to define a population for study on the basis of one extreme behavior, sexual homicide.

The remarkable response productivity of the sexual homicide sample, almost two standard deviations greater than the mean for nonpatient males ($M = 23.2$,

SD = 4.44; Exner, 1990b) confounds the findings of this study. Nearly 50% of the explainable variance in Rorschach data is accounted for by the number of responses (Meyer, 1992). Increased responses, however, are interpretively expected. Although the psychological operations of psychopaths facilitate discharge of affect and impulse, and bolster grandiosity, sexual homicide perpetrators seem to be overwhelmed, at times, by affect. Their defensive operations appear to function in a less efficient manner, and they have difficulty controlling the number of Rorschach responses as intrapsychic material presses for expression. Nevertheless, the structural findings are suggestive of certain characteristics of sexual homicide perpetrators when compared to psychopaths.

Eighty-nine percent of the sexual homicide sample evidence abnormal bonding or attachment capacities (T > < 1). A portion of these individuals, however, are hungry for attachment, rather than detached, in contrast to the primary psychopaths who are almost always chronically emotionally detached (Gacono & Meloy, 1991). Both groups are strikingly different from nonpatient males where normative attachment (T = 1) is evident in 88% of the population (Exner, 1990b). These findings further support the contributory factor of early childhood attachment problems in sexual homicide perpetrators (Ressler et al., 1988).

Both psychopaths and sexual homicide perpetrators appear to engage in dysphoric introspection (V), at least after incarceration, to a greater degree than normal males (*M* = .24, *SD* = .61; Exner, 1990b), and there is a trend toward more dysphoric rumination in the sexual homicide sample. This may be akin to failed grandiosity and self-pity as we previously hypothesized (Gacono & Meloy, 1992). This affective process, however, coexists with chronic characterological anger and negativism toward others (S > 2) in both samples, in contrast to the infrequent presence (13%) of this finding in nonpatient males (Exner, 1990b). Chronic anger appears to be a common mood trait in sexual homicide perpetrators, often manifest in crime scene behavior (Geberth, 1990; Ressler et al., 1988), but this emotion does not distinguish them from psychopaths.

A most striking difference between the groups is the suggestive data that sexual homicide perpetrators experience significantly more nonvolitional ideation (obsessional thoughts) due to the press of unmet need states (FM) than do psychopaths. In fact, the psychopaths experience less of this than do normal males (*M* = 3.73, *SD* = 1.09; Exner, 1990b). This unwanted ideation is prompted by unpleasant affect, and may motivate a common antecedent behavior, such as drug and alcohol use, prior to the sexual homicide (Ressler et al., 1988). Psychopaths, on the other hand, seem much more able to discharge affect and avoid this ideational "noise" in ways that support their generally alloplastic character (Fenichel, 1945; Ferenczi, 1930; Meloy, 1988). This finding is consistent with the sexual homicide research that has repeatedly mentioned the obsessive-compulsive and cyclical nature of serial sexual homicide (Revitch & Schlesinger, 1981). Our finding is the first group empirical measure of these unwanted thoughts, prompted by unmet and primitive sexual desire classically paired with violence. (Revitch & Schlesinger [1981] actually discuss a sexual murderer's Rorschach and note in his psychogram a grossly elevated FM response frequency.)

The two measures of cognitive functioning are abnormal in both groups. Although there is a trend toward more thought disorder (WSum6) in the sexual homicide sample, when we eliminated the two most extreme scores, the mean dropped to 17.22 (SD = 12.26), only slightly more than the psychopaths. Both groups, however, show moderate and pervasive formal thought disorder when compared to nonpatient males (M = 3.34, SD = 3.04), not unlike ASPD males (M = 17.12, SD = 13.83; Gacono & Meloy, 1991), but far less than inpatient schizophrenics (M = 44.69, SD = 35.40; Exner, 1990b). The quality of each of the thought disorders is somewhat different. The sexual homicide sample shows evidence of more frequently redundant, circumstantial, and irrelevant thoughts than do the psychopaths, and a somewhat greater frequency of clearly bizarre associations (44% vs. 30% Level 2 scores). These findings provide support for the deviant cognitive mapping and processing hypothesized as one motivational aspect of sexual homicide (Ressler et al., 1988).

The reality testing (X–%) of both groups is likewise impaired. It is much worse than normal males (M = 7, SD = 5; Exner, 1990b), almost the same as ASPD males (M = 23, SD = 11; Gacono & Meloy, 1992), and less than inpatient schizophrenics (M = 34, SD = 17; Exner, 1990b). This perceptual inability to accurately distinguish between internal and external stimuli may facilitate the sexual homicide perpetrator's use of fantasy as both a tool of projection and projective identification during the actual homicide itself (Gacono, 1992; Gacono & Meloy, 1988; Meloy, 1988, 1992b). Our results are consistent with the finding of rehearsal fantasy as a primary drive mechanism in sexual homicide, relatively unconstrained by the dictates of reality (Prentky et al., 1989).

Both sexual homicide perpetrators and psychopaths appear to be pathologically narcissistic (Rf), or at least inclined to self-aggrandize (PER), perhaps to shore up a threatened grandiose self-structure (Kernberg, 1984).[17] A sense of entitlement is ubiquitous in psychopathy, and appears to be so among sexual homicide perpetrators. This attitude of specialness, perhaps mixed with a sense of impunity, could disinhibit sexual and aggressive impulses aroused in the presence of a victim. Narcissistic traits among sexual homicide perpetrators and psychopaths have been noted elsewhere and are consistent with our findings (Hare, 1991; Ressler et al., 1988).

---

[17]Don Viglione (personal communication, March 1993), suggested that reflection responses may actually indicate a more callous, psychopathic trait, rather than just pathological narcissism. He also suggested a narcissistic triad consisting of reflections, personals, and elevated W:D. We have yet to test the W:D ratio as a discriminating variable, but it clearly is elevated in both ASPDs and psychopaths in particular. There does appear, however, to be a reflection "ceiling": We have yet to find a frequency greater than 50% in any sample of obviously narcissistic subjects, and have not found it in any other research.

The sexual homicide perpetrators show a greater genuine interest in other human beings (All H) when compared to psychopaths, although both groups are within one standard deviation of the finding for normal males ($M = 5.72$, $SD = 1.61$; Exner, 1990b). We also found a tendency for the sexual homicide perpetrators to more readily mentally represent others as whole, real, and meaningful individuals, a Rorschach measure of internalized object relations (Pure H) unreported in Table 9.9. These findings, along with a more frequent expectation of cooperativeness from others (COP > 2), suggests that sexual homicide perpetrators, despite the extreme violence of their crime(s), are whole-object seeking (Fairbairn, 1952/1986), unlike their psychopathic counterparts. There is genuine interest in others, at least sometimes.

These preliminary findings lend the first empirical support to a psychodynamic model that we propose to understand the act of sexual homicide itself (see Fig. 9.3). It is comprised of five dimensions: abnormal bonding, characterological anger, formal thought disorder, borderline or psychotic reality testing, and pathological narcissism (entitlement). We think these factors may play a large role in the psychogenesis of sexual homicide when the perpetrator is in the presence of a potential victim and is sexually aroused. Skin contact with the victim, the preferred mode of killing in these cases, and the victim's response, are one of many situational "wild cards" in this equation. The five dimensions, however, should be considered individual psychological operations that may predispose such activity. We would offer that these perceptions, attitudes, and feeling states become the phenomenological experience of the sexual homicide perpetrator, although he generally would not be conscious of them.

Our model is tentative, and has the following limitations: First, it may not be limited to sexual homicide, and may represent a more common psychodynamic pattern among sexual aggressors; second, the empirical basis of our model is limited due to its retrospective and inferential nature, but the Rorschach variables we selected for study generally have good temporal reliability (Exner, 1986a); and

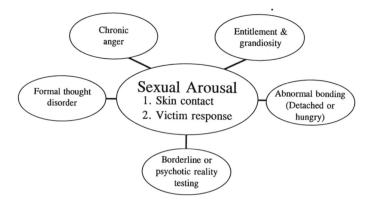

FIG. 9.3. Psychodynamics of sexual homicide.

third, the elevated frequency of R confounds the validity of our findings when compared to a psychopathic sample.

Our enthusiasm for the model, however, is supported by its consistency with the *motivational* model of Ressler et al. (1988), which attempted to understand the developmental antecedents of sexual homicide. We think our findings shed light on the psychodynamic shadows that portend this low-frequency but high-intensity act of sexual aggression.

> *I knew a man once did a girl in*
> *Any man might do a girl in*
> *Any man has to, needs to, wants to*
> *Once in a lifetime, do a girl in.*

—T. S. Eliot
"Sweeney Agonistes"
Collected Poems 1909–1935

CHAPTER 10

Toward an Integrated Understanding of the Psychopath[1]

> *"I did that," says my memory. "I did not," says my pride; and memory yields.*
>
> —F. Nietzsche, *Beyond Good and Evil*

The psyche can be accessed at different levels, depending on the context, the tool of access, and the conscious state of the subject (Frank, 1939; Stone & Dellis, 1960). Schafer (1954) proposed experiential markers for a levels continuum: dreaming, daydreaming, purposeful visualizing, and normal perceiving. Continua such as primitive to advanced, regressive to progressive, implicit to explicit (Schacter, 1992), unconscious to preconscious to conscious, all presuppose internal psychological operations that may occur at various ontogenetic, perhaps even phylogenetic (Bailey, 1987) levels. We view the relationship between unconscious defense process and conscious cognitive style as a "levels" phenomenon (Frenkel-Brunswik, 1953; Gacono & Meloy, 1988) and believe that the unconscious defenses are manifest in and can be inferred from assessment of the psychopath's conscious cognitive-behavioral style (including the psychopath's verbalizations).[2]

---

[1] This chapter expands our thinking summarized in two previously published articles (Gacono & Meloy, 1988, 1993). Adapted versions of "The Relationship Between Cognitive Style and Defensive Process in the Psychopath" (*Criminal Justice and Behavior, 15*(4), pp. 472–483; Sage Publications) and "Some Thoughts on Rorschach Findings and Psychophysiology in the Psychopath" (*British Journal of Projective Psychology*, 1993) are reprinted with permission. Appreciation is extended to Jacqueline Belevich, PhD, for suggesting revisions.

[2] The conscious cognitive-behavioral style of the psychopath results from (a) a complex of cognitive structures or beliefs, schemata, current concerns, and tacit assumptions that form cognitive errors (Meichenbaum, 1993), and, (b) supporting behaviors including verbalizations. In many cases the psychopath's thinking errors contain both cognitive deficiencies (absence of thought possibly related to a biological deficit) and cognitive distortions (faulty thinking) (Kendall, 1993).

Unconscious internal regulating mechanisms and primitive defenses help create and maintain the narcissistic object relations (Kernberg, 1974, 1975) found in the severe psychopath (Gacono, 1988, 1990; Meloy, 1988). An immature cognitive style (Piaget, 1965), observable in the form of specific thinking errors (Yochelson & Samenow, 1977a, 1977b), develops as a conscious cognitive correlate of primitive defenses. It manifests in attitudes and behaviors that bolster narcissistic self-perceptions.

Identified physiological patterns represent a third, psychobiological level of the psychopath's personality (Hare, 1965, 1970, 1978; Hare, Frazelle, & Cox, 1978; Ogloff & Wong, 1990; Raine, 1988; Raine & Dunkin, 1990; Raine et al., 1990; Venables, 1988). One aspect of the psychopath's physiology is evident in differential patterning of lower skin conductance level, and in some studies an underaroused EEG (electroencephelogram) profile and higher heart rate in anticipation of aversive stimuli when compared to nonpsychopaths (Hare, 1965, 1966, 1970, 1978; Hare et al., 1978; Mednick, Volavka, Gabrielli, & Itil, 1981; Ogloff & Wong, 1990; Raine & Dunkin, 1990). This pattern suggests a decreased sensitivity and active physiological "coping" in preparation for an aversive stimulus (Hare, 1978). Raine et al. (1990) also prospectively found that passive orienting responses were significantly less prevalent in 15-year-old males who had committed more criminal offenses when assessed again at age 24. The psychopath's ability to ward off anxiety or decrease dysphoric affects has obvious benefits in eliminating deterrents to criminal activity.

The functioning of the psychopath can best be understood from an integrated perspective. Three different "levels"—biological (arousal), largely unconscious (object relations; implicit memory), and largely preconscious or conscious[3]—regulate the inner world of these individuals (Gacono & Meloy, 1988, 1993). We think a constellation of differential autonomic patterns support psychodynamic mechanisms and a cognitive style that serve similar defensive functions. In this chapter we discuss the parallels and interactions between these three levels of personality. The concurrent validation of any one level in future research may provide construct validation for another. Our reasonable hope is that understanding the psychopath from a levels perspective will aid in the diagnosis and management of these individuals.

COGNITIVE STYLE AND PSYCHODYNAMICS

The influence of thinking on emotions and behavior has been of interest to psychology since its beginnings. One of the most thoroughly explored areas of

---

[3]Jacqueline Belevich, PhD, noted that our levels correlated with the neuropsychological concepts of arousal, implicit memory, and explicit memory, which are all viewed as aspects of "brain functioning." These "levels," however, are not limited to just these aspects of the central nervous system and may be active both simultaneously and sequentially.

personality (Butler, 1981; Ellis, 1962, 1993; Ellis, McInerney, DiGiuseppe, & Yeager, 1988; Meichenbaum & Cameron, 1974; Solomon, 1977; Walker, 1987; Walsh, 1986), cognitive models have formed the basis of several theories of criminality (Carroll & Weaver, 1986; Raimy, 1975; Redl & Wineman, 1951; Sykes & Matza, 1957; Yochelson & Samenow, 1977a, 1977b), and cognitive theorists have recently begun to acknowledge the importance of "unconscious processes" (Mahoney, 1993).[4]

Like other personality disorders (Berg et al., 1994; Gacono et al., 1992), many antisocial personality disordered (ASPD; APA, 1987) individuals share ongoing conscious styles of thinking and behaving that are dependent on specific unconscious internal regulating mechanisms (Bursten, 1972, 1973). These unconscious internal mechanisms (such as primitive defenses; see Kernberg, 1966, 1970; Klein, 1946) are rooted in the early phases of normal ego development and contain the linkages between early modes of cognitive-affective organization and major forms of psychopathology (Grala, 1980). They become maladaptive only in later development if they continue as the predominant mechanisms of defense (Kernberg, 1974, 1975; Lustman, 1977). For ASPDs who are also psychopathic, devaluation (100%) and massive denial (91%), both primitive defenses, predominate over mature defenses such as high denial (27%; as noted in Table 10.1) or repression.

Yochelson and Samenow (1977a, 1977b) were not the first to note cognitive patterns common to offenders; however, their cognitive model may be the most widely known. They considered psychoanalytic terminology inadequate for understanding the psychopath. They defined criminality in terms of irresponsibility, specific thinking errors, and general thinking patterns, interpreting all phenomena from a cognitive process level. Whereas authors such as Bursten (1972, 1973) considered psychodynamic theory integral for describing cognitive correlates of psychopathy, Yochelson and Samenow's dismissal of the theory and failure to acknowledge the interplay between unconscious defensive process and conscious thought detracted from their work. In our clinical experience, however, their criminal thinking patterns or, as we refer to them, *conscious cognitive-behavioral patterns*, can be consistently found in those adult clients we conceptualize as psychopathic (Gacono, 1985), as well as in the majority of clients diagnosed as ASPD.[5]

Central to Yochelson and Samenow's (1977a) cognitive-behavioral style of the psychopath was a process called the shut-off mechanism. They described this mechanism as a *psychological defense* operating more rapidly than repression,

---

[4]The April 1993 (61:2) edition of the *Journal of Consulting and Clinical Psychology* highlighted recent developments in cognitive theory and therapy.

[5]Gacono has found variations of these cognitive-behavioral patterns in 15- to 18-year-old conduct-disordered adolescents and psychodynamic correlates of these patterns in younger conduct-disordered children. Psychological testing frequently revealed specific aggressive themes including identification with the aggressor, and non-age–appropriate grandiosity mixed with themes of inner vulnerability, worthlessness, inadequacy, and helplessness (Gacono & Meloy, 1988).

TABLE 10.1
Rorschach Defensive Operations for 22 Psychopaths (PCL–R $\geq$ 30)

Defense	Mean	Standard Deviation	Frequency	
	Lerner and Lerner (1980) *Defense Categories*			
High Devaluation	.91	.92	13	(59%)
DV3	.32	.72	4	(18%)
DV4	–	–	2	(9%)
DV5	.36	.73	6	(27%)
High Idealization	.00	.00	0	(0%)
Low Idealization	–	–	2	(9%)
Denial 1	–	–	1	(5%)
Denial 2	–	–	4	(18%)
Denial 3	.55	.74	9	(41%)
	Cooper, Perry, and Arnow (1988) *Select Defense Categories*			
High Denial	–	–	6	(27%)
Massive Denial	2.32	1.46	20	(91%)
Splitting	1.32	1.46	15	(68%)
Projective Identification	1.82	1.59	17	(77%)
Omnipotence	1.55	1.57	17	(77%)
Devaluation	4.18	2.26	22	(100%)
Primitive Idealization	.95	1.25	11	(50%)
	Gacono (1990) and Gacono et al. (1990)			
Impressionistic Response (IMP)	.55	.80	9	(41%)

Note. Frequencies equal the number of subjects who produced at least one response in a given category. High devaluation includes Levels 1 and 2; high idealization includes Levels 1 and 2; low idealization includes Levels 3, 4, and 5. Five or fewer responses were produced in the Lerner and Lerner (1980) categories for splitting and projective identification, so these indices were not included in this table.

but then subsumed its process under a *cognitive operation*. The shut-off mechanism was at the core of the psychopath's cognitive style. It functioned in part to exclude aspects of personality that could either tarnish grandiose self-perceptions or contradict exploitive, ruthless behavior toward others. Splitting is the unconscious defensive process whose cognitive and behavioral manifestations Yochelson and Samenow noted with their term shut-off mechanism.

Splitting refers to a fragmented organization of the ego characterized by cognitive immaturity, limited synthetic or combinatory capacities, and an active separation of introjects and identifications of opposite valence (Kernberg, 1966). This genotypic or fundamentally "vertical" (Kohut, 1971) defense in all borderline personality organization is implicit in the mental mechanisms noted in Table 10.2

TABLE 10.2
Mental Mechanisms and Defensive Processes in Psychopathy

Mental Mechanisms[a]	Defense Processes
Shut-off	Splitting, denial, dissociation
Corrosion	Suppression
Cutoff	Splitting, denial, dissociation

[a]Mental mechanisms are from Yochelson and Samenow's (1977a) mental mechanisms, processes, and patterns.

(with the exception of suppression) and defensive processes in Table 10.3. At the most primitive level in the psychopath, splitting is phenotypically expressed as primitive denial.

Primitive defenses regulated by the grandiose self-structure ensure the psychopath's manipulative style (Bursten, 1972) and manifest themselves in the conscious cognitive-behavioral style noted in Table 10.3. Through splitting, the psychopath simultaneously contains highly unrealistic overvalued (grandiosity) and undervalued (worthlessness) representations of himself. Grandiosity is noted in virtually every area of the psychopath's thinking, including "criminal pride," "perfectionism," "uniqueness," and "pretentiousness" (Yochelson & Samenow, 1977b).

Yochelson and Samenow (1977a) labeled the psychopath's undervalued cognitive-affective complex[6] the "zero state" (p. 266). They described the experience of it as a self-perception containing three concurrent beliefs: (a) The individual is totally worthless, a "nothing," all bad (internal); (b) everyone else shares this dim view (external); and (c) this state of being will last forever (temporal). Unlike mature introjective depression and remorse, a developmental impossibility for the psychopath (Meloy, 1988), he experiences, at times, emptiness and shame.[7] These feelings, lacking the inclusion of the other as a separate internalized object, result from pathologically narcissistic object relations and involve a tarnished but idealized self-representation.

Extreme fear and subsequent avoidance of this inner state often serves as an impetus to acting out behavior prior to its actual experience (Wishnie, 1977). It is only when the grandiose self-structure fails or when the psychopath is prevented

---

[6]Cleckley (1976) described the undervalued cognitive-affective complex as an inner emptiness, whereas Wishnie (1977) discussed an inner state of anxiety.

[7]During the process of multifamily group treatment, Gacono discovered that conduct-disordered adolescents could readily verbalize their experiences of extreme envy and grandiosity coupled with inner boredom and emptiness. In response to the question of what they would be like without the part of them that was "superhuman" or better than anyone else, they replied, "Worthless, helpless"; "I would be like a guy in a three-piece suit, who goes to work everyday, nine to five"; "I would be helpless, vulnerable"; "It would be like death." One youth adamantly refuted an interpretation linking his depression and substance abuse until his "depression" was reframed as emptiness and boredom, at which time he dropped his head and became very depressed in appearance (Gacono & Meloy, 1988).

TABLE 10.3
Cognitive Style and Defensive Processes in the Psychopath

Conscious Cognitive-Behavioral Style[a]	Unconscious Defense Process
1. Criminal pride, uniqueness, pretentiousness, perfectionism	Idealization of self-representations, denial, omnipotence, devaluation of others
2. Ownership/entitlement	Omnipotence, denial of other's needs
3. Failure in empathy	Omnipotence, devaluation, dissociation
4. Victim stance	Projective identification
5. Refusal to be dependent	Omnipotence, projective identification, persecutory introjection
6. Lying	Denial, omnipotence, rationalization
7. Zero state	Affective emptiness, evacuation of good self- and object representations
8. Power thrust	Projective identification, omnipotent control
9. Anger	Projective identification, omnipotent control, denial
10. Sentimentality	Idealization of past self- and object representations
11. Nonpsychotic hallucinations	Introjection, dissociation
12. Sexuality	Projective identification, idealization, devaluation, omnipotent control

Other Areas of Criminal Thinking
Energy, fear, religion, suggestibility, loner, lack of time perspective, failure to endure adversity, poor decision making toward responsible living

[a]Conscious cognitive-behavioral styles and other areas of criminal thinking were adapted from Yochelson and Samenow's (1977a) criminal thinking errors and patterns. Often Yochelson and Samenow's terminology is unclear. Their failure to differentiate levels of experience and use of an idiosyncratic terminology not based on one of the major psychological schools of thought, such as learning theory or psychoanalytic theory, contribute to their lack of clarity. After more than 25 years we have yet to see any published studies concerning the reliability and validity of their methods of diagnosis and treatment.

from repairing his self-esteem through aggression and acting out that he or she is in danger of experiencing this state.

Unlike the shut-off mechanism or splitting, the *learned* process of "corrosion" (Yochelson & Samenow, 1977a, p. 413) is under the psychopath's conscious control. Like conscious suppression, corrosion allows the psychopath to think himself into a desired state. Through corrosion the psychopath systematically eliminates from his thoughts any external or internal deterrents until the desire to commit an act outweighs any fears. This conscious process also aids in maintaining an overvalued self-image. "Cut-off" refers to a rapid unconscious eradication, or dissociation, of fears from the mind. As noted in Tables 10.2 and 10.3, we view all dissociative phenomena as phenotypic expressions of splitting (Meloy, 1988).

Concrete thinking (Eissler, 1950; Glueck & Glueck, 1952) and "fragmentation" (Yochelson & Samenow, 1977a) are also indicative of cognitive immaturity in the psychopath. Concrete thinking is exemplified by the psychopath viewing others as part objects,[8] lacking empathy, experiencing extreme opposite and alternating views of a person over time, extrapolating from a few concrete events to form a global perception, and failing to learn from experience (Hare, 1980; Yochelson & Samenow, 1977a). Some psychopaths may present areas of faulty learning rather than an inability to learn.

Fragmentation refers to an extreme form of vacillation manifested by contradictions and fluctuations in the psychopath's thinking (Cleckley, 1976; Yochelson & Samenow, 1977a). Discrepancies between intentions and actual behavior, and behavior and self-perceptions, are examples of fragmentation. Yochelson and Samenow (1977a) believed cutoff produces the fragmented pattern within the psychopath's cognitive style. We think that fragmentation, however, is an inadequate term for describing contradictions in attitude, behavior, and self-perceptions due to splitting (68% produce scorable splitting responses, as noted in Table 10.1. Splitting is also inferred from other primitive defenses such as massive denial). Splitting and the other primitive defense processes remain unconscious, supporting cognitive mechanisms such as corrosion and cutoff (see Table 10.2), which are then manifested in the psychopath's cognitive-behavioral style (see Table 10.3).

Some empirical support for our levels hypothesis has been recently found by Helfgott (1991). She compared 60 *DSM–III–R* (APA, 1987) ASPD inmates with 40 college students. All subjects ($N = 100$) were male.[9] Each ASPD subject's correctional file was reviewed. Each subject completed a semistructured interview for scoring the PCL–R, a cognitive questionnaire (Cognitive Checklist; CC), and the Rorschach test. Psychopathy levels were designated ≥ 30 high, 20–29 midrange, and < 20 low. Helfgott used a goodness of fit to four of the following five Rorschach variables as a match for high psychopathy: $T = 0$, $Y = 0$, PER > 2, EGO $> .45$, and rF+Fr > 0. (See chapter 5.)

The CC was an *experimental* instrument devised by Helfgott (1991) for assessing 32 of Yochelson and Samenow's (1977a) criminal thinking errors. Each of the 32 thinking errors were assessed by 3 questions (96 total criterion questions) requiring different types of response (Likert scale, yes/no, and free writing[10]). For example, "energy" was assessed by the following: (a) Do you

---

[8] "Selfobjects" in a Kohutian (1971) sense; both terms imply the absence of a capacity to perceive others as whole, real, and meaningful persons in their own right. The concrete thinking would be manifest in object relations as an inability to *connotatively* describe others.

[9] Two cautions are needed when interpreting Helfgott's (1991) findings. She failed to match subjects on IQ. ASPD subjects' IQs ranged from 77 to 119 ($M = 94.94$; $SD = 10.06$). IQ estimates, however, were not available for the student controls. Intellectual functioning is particularly relevant as a baseline measure when evaluating cognitive style and also for Rorschach comparisons. Second, there is no indication that student records were available for scoring the PCL–R. Even though the mean scores for the student controls are not substantially different from those reported by Hare (1991) for a "normal" population, substantiated background data are a prerequisite for scoring the PCL–R.

[10] The method for answering the free-writing questions was based on Yochelson and Samenow's (1977a) "phenomenological reporting" of thinking errors.

get bored easily, especially when doing something you're not fond of? (rated from 1—never to 10—always), (b) "Do you have difficulties concentrating on tasks which are particularly fast-paced?" (yes/no), and (c) "Do you ever feel energized with thoughts racing through your head? If so, during what activities? What are you thinking during these times? Please describe these periods" (free writing). Each criteria answered in the positive direction received a score of 1 point. Like PCL–R items, the 32 thinking errors could be scored 0 ($\leq$ 1 positive criterion question), 1 (2 positive), or 2 (3 positive). The failure to respond to more than one of the criteria questions resulted in omitting the item and prorating the final score.

As expected, ASPD subjects ($M = 23.3$) and students ($M = 5.7$) differed significantly on the PCL–R ($p < .000$). The mean scores for both groups were quite similar to other antisocial and college (nonpatient) populations (Hare, 1991). Interestingly, the one student who produced an elevated PCL–R score (PCL–R $= 20$) was arrested for rape several months after the assessment (Helfgott, 1991). The two groups did not differ significantly on the Cognitive Checklist: ASPDs ($M = 11.7$), students ($M = 10.0$). Correlations were found, however, between PCL–R Factor 1 and CC scores in the ASPD subjects, indicating a strong positive relationship between personality (Factor 1) and cognitive style (CC) that was not evident between behavior (PCL–R, Factor 2) and cognitive style (CC). This finding is consistent with empirical correlations between the *DSM–III–R* narcissistic personality disorder, which includes items such as a sense of entitlement, and the PCL–R Factor 1. Helfgott concluded:

> Significant correlations of the PCL–R and CC tests suggest that the tests may be identifying the same disturbance through different components, and that high scores on both may be a more reliable and accurate indicator of psychopathy than just the PCL–R. This finding provides strong support for Gacono and Meloy's (1988) proposal that personality features, and possibly, as they suggest, defensive operations, may be inferred from conscious cognitive style. (p. 28)

Helfgott (1991) did not find correlations between the other two measures and the Rorschach variables. This probably does not represent a true finding, because a number of problems with the protocols make any conclusions impossible. First, only 17 (42%) of the student protocols and 38 (63%) of the ASPD protocols contained $\geq$ 14 responses, yet all were used in the analysis. As we have previously argued (Gacono & Meloy, 1992; Gacono et al., 1992), ASPD protocols without elevated Lambda may be valid despite low response frequency. Lambda, however, was not analyzed in the Helfgott study. Second, the Rorschach administrator had not been trained in current Comprehensive System administration procedures and scoring criteria (Exner, 1986a). The competent use of the Rorschach test requires several graduate-level courses, many supervised administrations of the instrument, and advanced course work or supervision. The Rorschach administrator for this study had learned the Rorschach through independent self-study, but had not completed one formal graduate course in Rorschach prior to testing subjects. Finally, Gacono's perusal of the ASPD protocols revealed inadequate inquiry for scoring key variables. Sparse inquiry did not allow for scoring certain determinants. Diffuse shading (Y) was overscored at the expense of proper inquiry to allow for the scoring of texture (T), vista (V), and reflections (Fr+rF). Unfortunately, conclusions cannot be made from the Rorschach data gathered in the course of Helfgott's study.

THE "LEVELS" HYPOTHESIS IN ACTION: A SPECULATIVE MODEL

The following hypothetical case example illustrates the relationship between conscious cognitive-behavioral style and unconscious defense processes by discussing the thoughts, feelings, and behaviors of a sexual psychopath prior to, during, and following the rape of a female victim (see also Groth, 1979).

In the beginning sequence of targeting a female victim for rape, the sexual psychopath will unconsciously use projective identification to idealize the potential victim (Gacono, 1992). The victim will usually meet a "goodness of fit" stereotype that is an experiential derivative of the psychopath's previous experience with females, most notably the primary female parental object (Meloy, 1988). Projective identification provides the vehicle for the sexual psychopath (Gacono, 1992) to both externalize and control (Grotstein, 1980) the idealized object representation within the grandiose self-structure. This is usually not a psychotic identification because internal and external perceptual distinctiveness remains. The identification occurs only at an object concept, rather than a perceptual level (Meloy, 1985a, 1988).

The initial stalking of the rape victim is a primary example of the "power thrust" (Yochelson & Samenow, 1977a) that influences most of the cognitive-behavioral style of the psychopath (see Table 10.3). The power thrust combines the psychopath's narcissistic self-perceptions with his need for omnipotent control and, in this case, is expressed through sexual exploitation.

At this phase, the affective state that accompanies the fantasy of omnipotent control is exhilaration. (One 28-year-old, regressed pedophilic sex offender described his experience when breaking and entering with intent to rape as, "The fear inside me was euphoric.") The psychopath may be consciously thinking, "She really wants me," or, "Look how she's looking at me." There is evidence of both corrosion and cutoff in his conscious cognitive-behavioral style as he eliminates from his thoughts any ideational deterrents that would interfere with his grandiose fantasies of power and control or discourage his intent to rape.

The cognitive distortions of the psychopath are supported by his own unconscious projective processes. In all of his interpersonal interactions, projective identification and omnipotent control are defense processes that maintain the grandiose self-structure and prevent the zero state.[11] Inherent within the grandiose self-structure and supported by projective identification is the psychopath's lack of empathy, which includes the joined attitudes of "ownership" and "entitlement" (see Table 10.3). The psychopath relates to others only as a conceptual extension of himself[12] (Meloy, 1985a, 1988).

Yochelson and Samenow (1977a) noted the presence of ego-dystonic cognitive deterrents that often correlated with the initial phases of criminal activity. For example, the sexual psychopath might hear an internal voice stating, "Don't do it," or "This is wrong." These "nonpsychotic hallucinations" are at times able to intrude upon the psychopath's conscious cognitions, and are actually dissociated or severely "split off" introjects (not identifications) of the psychopath's personality. They may suggest borderline personality organization etiologically rooted in acquired trauma or constitutional deficiency (Wycoff, 1993).

When the psychopath makes verbal or physical contact with the victim, reality begins to intrude upon his grandiose fantasies. The victim will quickly become angry or frightened, behaviors contrary to the psychopath's grandiose, power-thrusting fantasies. The psychopath then unconsciously attempts to take back the projective identification of the ideal object to defensively protect his grandiose self-structure. At the same time internal persecutory, malevolent introjects, possibly representations of the actual parent of abuse, are projected onto the victim. The victim is malevolently transformed (Gacono, 1992) into a devalued object and perceived as a threat. Under such circumstances aggression and sadism within the grandiose self-structure may be mobilized and dissociative processes further perceptually distance the psychopath from his victim. Specifically, the psychopath may experience more "aggressive, nonpsychotic hallucinations" commanding him to carry out the act.

At this moment a conscious sense of entitlement is supported by several unconscious defensive mechanisms: (a) The victim has been devalued as an idealized love object and subsequently perceived as a threat; therefore, the psychopath feels entitled to victimize her through acts of sexual sadism that hurt and control (Shapiro, 1981); (b) the psychopath also denies the reality of the actual victim as a whole object deserving of empathy, and denies the monstrosity of his own deeds; and, (c) denial and dissociation occur on an unconscious level enabling the psychopath to maintain his grandiose self-structure, while on a conscious level cutoff and corrosion (suppression) exclude and eliminate any

---

[11]Grandiosity, omnipotent control, and projective identification are evident in Theodore Bundy's subjective description of murder: "You're looking into their eyes. A person in that situation is God! You then possess them and they shall forever be a part of you. And the grounds where you kill them or leave them become sacred to you, and you will always be drawn back to them" (Time-Life Books, 1993, p. 44).

[12]Theodore Bundy's interpersonal relationships epitomized a lack of object ties. "He (Bundy) lived in a world of objects, things to be used or acquired or discarded—but not loved, nor felt for in any substantial way" (Time-Life Books, 1993, p. 15).

cognitions that would interfere with his inflated self-image. The sexual psychopath who is also a serial murderer may use the act of homicide in a regulatory fashion (Gacono, 1992).

With the diminution of autonomic arousal following physical and sexual violence, the multiple defensive processes of omnipotence, devaluation, and dissociation disallow any conscious feelings of empathy (see Tables 10.1 and 10.3). Conscious expression of these defensive processes was expressed by one serial murderer, Angelo Buono, in his statement, "Some girls don't deserve to live" (O'Brien, 1985, p. 117). Dissonant cognitions are eliminated from thought through corrosion and cutoff, clinically expressing the varieties of dissociability and splitting inherent in psychopathic defensive operations (Meloy, 1988).

Helfgott (1992) sought empirical validation for the defensive operations postulated in the aforementioned scenario in a second study. The 1-year interval between her studies (original study, Helfgott, 1991) resulted in attrition of 43 subjects. Thirty-nine ASPD and 18 student control subjects were included in her 1992 study. PCL–R (Hare, 1991) and Cognitive Checklist (Helfgott, 1991) scores were available from prior testing. Fifteen subjects were placed in a primary psychopathy group.

All subjects (in groups of two to four) viewed a 13-minute segment of the 1988 film, *The Accused*, produced by Jaffe/Lansing and Paramount Pictures Corporation, depicting a violent rape. Helfgott was present in the room during all viewings. Other film clips have been used previously to elicit emotional response in the study of cognitive and emotional processes (Davis, Hull, Young, & Warren, 1987). Subjects were instructed to pay careful attention to the film while concentrating on their thoughts and feelings. They were informed that a questionnaire would be completed after the film.

The questionnaire was designed to illicit information for scoring six defenses: splitting, primitive idealization, projective identification, devaluation, omnipotent control, and denial (Helfgott, 1992). It guided subjects in recording thoughts and feelings corresponding to the succession of events in the rape scene. Twelve additional questions elicited verbal manifestations of the primitive defenses. Splitting, for example, was scored when polarized perceptions were evident. "If the subject in one sentence states, 'the woman is a tramp and she was definitely asking for it,' and in the next, 'but as soon as those assholes touched her I realized she was a helpless little girl' he would be scored for splitting" (Helfgott, 1992, p. 159). Individual defenses were rated based on their frequency of occurrence and transposed to checklist scores, ≤ 1 given a 0, 2–4 rated as 1, and > 4 scored as 2. A total defense checklist score was obtained for each subject (ranging from 0 to 12).

Significant correlations were found between cognitive style and splitting, omnipotence, primitive idealization, and devaluation in psychopathic subjects ($N = 15$). Specific defense patterns and their correlations differed depending on level of psychopathy: "Based on this finding, primitive borderline defenses appear to be related to 'criminal' thinking errors in primary psychopaths. This finding supports Gacono and Meloy's (1988) proposal that the defensive process of the psychopath is manifest in and may be inferred from conscious cognitive style" (Helfgott, 1992, p. 212).

The following psychopathic subject's responses were particularly illustrative of how primitive defenses are inferred from conscious-cognitive process:

> This subject's responses contained numerous examples of splitting and omnipotence. Many of his statements blatantly contradicted each other. For example, the subject appeared to intellectually understand what the victim in the scene had experienced with thoughts such as:
>
> "As the men were cheering and chanting I thought she must really feel bad, not just being raped and gang raped, but cheered on by other patrons to go further with it. As each was on top of her I thought she is going to remember each one of them and see to it that she gets them one way or another."
>
> However, when asked to put himself in the place of the victim, his answers were superficial. For example, when asked what he thought the woman was feeling during the rapes he responded:
>
> "I just know I'll catch AIDs, herpes, and shit, get knocked up and all that, and why is no one stopping this?". (Helfgott, 1992, pp. 195–198)

These seemingly sympathetic and understanding statements were contradicted by their superficial tone and the intermixing of contradictory comments expressing enjoyment while viewing the activities in the scene. The predominance of splitting and omnipotence in this subject's questionnaire answers presents a striking picture of the fragmentation and dissociation involved in psychopathic thought. The following are examples of particular defenses found in this subject's responses:

Splitting
"Since it is a true story I didn't like seeing it. I really like seeing tits and ass, it turns me on (while in jail where I can't have sex except with myself). But, rape scenes always make me think of what if it was my family and friends being raped."

Splitting, Denial, and Omnipotence
"I don't like rape or people that rape. However, being in jail for life and seeing females walk around me makes me wonder if some day I might just say fuck it and grab one for myself (but, I won't because everyone would know I'm a scum-bag rapist and I couldn't live with that). I guess if I ever was to rape anyone I would just have to kill them too so they could not tell and to ensure that I would never have to face them. For some reason I think about raping women a lot lately and never did before. I don't think it has anything to do with hurting or humiliating them, more along the line of control or kinky sex."

Primitive Idealization
"She had just the right amount of cheapness and class in her clothes and attitude

. . . she sure can dance."
"She had nice tits."

Omnipotence
"If I was there and stopped the rape she would be so grateful at some later date she might make love to me."

Splitting, Omnipotence
"I wonder if rape victims would pay me to kill the guy here that raped them. Then I thought I wish I could see the whole video again."

Devaluation
"I thought she was a sleaze looking for a hot time." (Helfgott, 1992, pp. 195–198)

This psychopathic subject's responses illustrated some of the psychodynamics and conscious thinking we hypothesized to occur during the commission of a violent rape. As noted by Helfgott (1992),

> Each of the subject's response to questions regarding the man's thoughts at different stages in the film segment (as the woman entered the game room with the man, as they were dancing, as she resisted his advances, as he put her on the pinball machine, as the other men were holding her down, etc.) exactly matched the mental dynamics Gacono and Meloy propose are involved in the psychopath's commission of a violent rape. (p. 198)

Helfgott's (1991, 1992) studies, despite some methodological problems, represent creative attempts to empirically measure the conscious thought and unconscious psychodynamics of the psychopath's personality. They offer models for testing psychodynamic constructs and linking theory with data within the "levels" hypothesis.

PSYCHODYNAMICS AND PSYCHOPHYSIOLOGY

We turn next to another "level": the relationship between unconscious psychodynamics and psychophysiology.

Rorschach Findings (Psychodynamics)

Through a series of studies utilizing the Rorschach test as a psychometric measure of the structure and function of antisocial personality and conduct disorder (Gacono, 1988, 1990; Gacono et al., 1990, 1992; Gacono & Meloy, 1991, 1992; Meloy & Gacono, 1992a; Weber et al., 1992), we found a constellation of variables (as noted in Table 10.4) that discriminate individuals with severe psychopathic traits, as defined by a score of ≥ 30 on the PCL–R (Hare, 1991), from nonpsychopaths (< 30). These Rorschach variables also offer partial

TABLE 10.4
Means, Standard Deviations, and Frequencies for Rorschach
Variables in Antisocial Male Subjects ($N = 43$)

Variable	Mean	SD	Frequency[a]	Mean	SD	Frequency[a]
	Psychopaths ($N = 22$)			Nonpsychopaths ($N = 21$)		
Borderline Object Relations	5.00*	2.39	22	2.24*	2.74	19
Narcissism						
Egocentricity Ratio	.47*	.23	22	.30*	.14	21
Personals	3.32*	2.46	20	1.33*	1.35	14
Anxiety						
Diffuse Shading	.36**	.73	6	2.04**	2.60	15
Coping Index						
D Score	.14	.94	22	−.33	.73	22
Adjusted D	.23	1.02	22	.05	.67	22

[a]Frequencies equal the number of individual subjects who produced at least one response in the given category.
*Mann–Whitney U analysis yielded significant differences for object relations ($p = .0001$), egocentricity ratio ($p = .003$), and personals ($p = .004$). **Chi-square analysis yielded significant differences for diffuse shading ($p < .005$, $X^2 = 8.36$).

psychodynamic validation of the physiological patterns noted in psychopaths (Ogloff & Wong, 1990).

Anxiety level was found to correlate with degree of psychopathy, as psychopathic offenders less frequently produced indices associated with this variable (Y; as noted in Table 10.4) than did nonpsychopathic offenders (Gacono & Meloy, 1991). The adjusted D-score controls for situational factors (Exner, 1986a). D-scores in the positive range signify greater capacities for organizing behavior in a predictable manner, whereas those in the negative range suggest vulnerability to being overwhelmed by stimulus demands and behavioral disorganization (Exner, 1986a). Although no significance was obtained between the groups for D and AdjD (see Table 10.4), trends indicated that psychopaths were more similar to normals than were the nonpsychopaths. The Y and D-score findings suggest that defensive operations in psychopaths are more efficient in protecting the grandiose self-structure from external and internal (anxiety) threat than are those in the nonpsychopaths. Developmentally, Y has also been found to occur less frequently in conduct-disordered youth than dysthymic youth (Weber et al., 1992; also see chapter 3 and Viglione, 1980).

We also investigated the relationship between narcissism and psychopathy through a comparison of Rorschach egocentricity ratios [3r+(2)/R] and personal responses (PER) between two groups of ASPD offenders (Gacono et al., 1990). As noted in Table 10.4, these variables are proportionately greater in psychopaths than nonpsychopathic offenders. Elevations of these indices indicate the grandiosity and omnipotence of psychopaths.

Borderline psychopathology is suggested by the higher proportion of Rorschach primitive object relation indices (Kwawer, 1980) found in psychopaths (as noted in Table 10.4; Gacono & Meloy, 1992). Although psychopaths produced significantly greater numbers of these responses than did nonpsychopathic offenders, Gacono (1990) concluded that all incarcerated felons who met the *DSM–III–R* criteria for antisocial personality disorder would exhibit degrees of borderline personality organization (Meloy, 1988; Meloy & Gacono, 1993).

These Rorschach variables were also compared among male psychopathic ASPD, nonpsychopathic ASPD, narcissistic personality disorders, and borderline personality disorders (Gacono et al., 1992). Psychopaths produced less Y than did the other three groups (Gacono et al., 1992). Although psychopaths produced proportionately greater numbers of PERs (indicative of omnipotence) than did the other groups, their level of narcissism (egocentricity) was the same as the narcissistic personality disorders and significantly greater than the nonpsychopathic ASPDs and borderline personality disorders (Gacono et al., 1992). Psychopaths and borderline personality disordered subjects produced a similar proportion of primitive object relation categories (Kwawer, 1980), with both groups producing significantly more than either the nonpsychopathic ASPDs or narcissistic personality disordered subjects (Gacono et al., 1992).

Links to Psychophysiology

A summary of the recent research concerning the psychophysiology of psychopathy suggests that (a) chronic underarousal, as measured by electrodermal, cardiovascular, and cortical indices, may be causally related to crime (Raine & Dunkin, 1990); (b) in higher social classes, antisocial children are poor conditioners (Raine & Venables, 1981); (c) deficits in skin conductance and heart rate orienting in *passive* attention tasks are causally related to criminality (Raine et al., 1990); (d) psychopaths, however, show enhanced event-related potentials to target stimuli that are motivating and involve *active* short-term attention (Shapiro, Quay, Hogan, & Schwartz, 1988); (e) psychopaths are poor at inhibiting reward-seeking behavior (Newman & Kosson, 1986); (f) subjects elevated on Factor 1 of the PCL–R (aggressive narcissism, emotional detachment) manifest a linear trend between slide valence and startle eyeblink reflex, but a significant quadratic trend between affective and neutral slide valence (Patrick, Bradley, & Lang, 1993); and, (g) there is a psychopathic "coping response" to aversive stimuli that involves heart rate acceleration and lowered skin conductance. This coping response appears to be an inhibitory control mechanism that reduces the impact of premonitory cues (Fowles, 1980; Lykken, 1967; Ogloff & Wong, 1990).

Our findings concerning significant differences in Rorschach measures of anxiety, narcissism, and borderline object relations between psychopaths and nonpsychopaths are convergent with these physiological findings. They suggest that despite being more severely pathological than their nonpsychopathic counterparts, the psychopath functions in a less conflicted manner, free of the disruptive effects of anxiety. These differential physiological and psychodynamic operations can be inferred from the psychopath's response to threat and reward-seeking behaviors.

The chronic physiological underarousal in psychopaths relates dynamically to their shallow, empty affect and proneness to boredom (PCL–R Items 7 and 3). Significantly lower levels of diffuse anxiety (Y) as measured by the Rorschach parallel the chronically lower skin conductance in psychopaths. Low levels of diffuse anxiety would enhance both the peripheral autonomic dampening that occurs in psychopaths when anticipating a threat, and short-term attention in targeted antisocial activities that are reward seeking. Although psychopaths are in general more violent than nonpsychopaths (Hare & McPherson, 1984), lower levels of diffuse anxiety would specifically predispose them to more effective predatory acts of violence, as this psychobiologically distinctive mode of aggression is emotionless, detached, planned and purposeful (Meloy, 1988).[13] Predatory violence is likely to be both intraphysically and behaviorally rewarding for the psychopath. In contrast, affective violence, a psychobiologically distinctive mode of aggression that is emotional, autonomically arousing, and a reaction to a perceived threat, would more closely match an aversive paradigm for the psychopath (Meloy, 1988). Lower levels of peripheral arousal and anxiety, moreover, would facilitate a more focused and adaptive violent response to such an aversive threat.

The psychopath's significantly greater self-absorption (egocentricity ratio) and self-aggrandizement (personals), two aspects of pathological narcissism, also expand our understanding of the physiology research. Self-absorption, by definition, would detract from time attending to external stimuli and hence relate to the psychopath's chronic attentional deficits in passive orienting tasks with no punishment or rewards. However, in active reward-seeking paradigms, including thrill-seeking behavior, self-aggrandizement or grandiosity would cause an inflated evaluation of abilities, as well as enhanced attention and effort. In threatening situations, the coping response would be psychodynamically shaped by the defensive devaluation of a real threat when measured against the psychopath's own grandiosity. This would also dampen any fear response (Patrick et al., 1993). Not only would there be less of a physiological reaction to threat, as evidenced by lower levels of anxiety (Y), but real danger would be both intrapsychically and cognitively rendered less ominous.

Significantly greater amounts of primitive (borderline) object relations implicate both symbiotic merging and narcissistic mirroring as pervasive distortions of the psychopath's object world (Gacono, 1990; Meloy, 1988). Primitive object relations

---

[13]When psychopaths are compared to nonpsychopaths, they (a) are more likely to choose males and strangers as victims, (b) are less likely to act out violently due to frustration or anger, and (c) base aggressive acts on revenge or monetary reward (Williamson et al., 1987; Serin, 1991). These behaviors suggest a greater prevalence of predatory violence among psychopaths.

and grandiosity shape the psychopath's distorted perceptions of both rewarding and threatening situations. Projective-introjective exchanges with a targeted stimulus that was perceived to be rewarding would dynamically allow the psychopath to identify the stimulus as an extension of himself (symbiotic merging) or as a reflection of his grandiose traits (mirroring), thereby increasing attention and effort.

The same primitive object relations, premised on the defense of splitting, facilitate the projection of negative self- and object representations into a threatening stimulus during the coping response. This evacuative process both enhances the psychopath's grandiosity and lessens the perceived impact of a threatening stimulus by devaluing it as "not worth fearing." The defense of projective identification, ubiquitous in psychopaths (Gacono, 1990, 1992), also diminishes the importance of a threatening stimulus by creating an illusion of control over it. Corollary physiological measures of the reward-seeking response and the coping response in psychopaths are convergent with these primitive object relations (Ogloff & Wong, 1990). Actual objects are idealized or devalued as mental representations depending, respectively, on the rewarding or punishing paradigm. Short-term attention is enhanced as the object is idealized; the coping response occurs as the object is devalued.

CONCLUSION

In this chapter we have elaborated on a levels hypothesis for object relations and cognitive-behavioral style by exploring theoretical linkages between object relations and defensive operations and the conscious cognitive-behavioral style of the psychopath. Some preliminary empirical support for this relationship has been offered (Helfgott, 1991, 1992). Rorschach findings also appear to be convergent with the existing psychophysiological research concerning the psychopath, although a relationship between psychodynamic and physiological functioning has not yet been empirically demonstrated. These three avenues of research (biological, unconscious dynamics, conscious thought) suggest coping and orienting responses operating in primary psychopaths that differentiate them from nonpsychopathic criminals. We offer the bridge between cognitive style, psychodynamics, and psychobiological substrates as a hypothetical relationship in need of further empirical validation. We stress the importance of always considering conscious cognitive style, unconscious defensive process, and differential physiological patterning when studying the inner world of the psychopath.

This "levels" approach to understanding psychopathy also points the way toward research with other personality disorders. We think the most promising methodological avenues will involve simultaneous measurement of these levels in experimental and quasi-experimental paradigms, and hope that our work with the Rorschach underscores its importance as a clinical and research instrument in these future endeavors.

The Rorschach Test and The Diagnosis of Psychopathic Personality[1]

Robert M. Lindner
U.S. Public Health Service,
U.S. Penitentiary, Lewisburg, Pennsylvania

The following study represents an attempt to aid in filling a gap in our knowledge regarding the Rorschach Psychodiagnostic Ink-Blot Test. The questions we shall endeavor to answer are: Does the Rorschach lend itself to the diagnosis of psychopathic personality? Can it be used with more than a moderate chance of success to aid in distinguishing the psychopath from other diagnostic classes? Are there any special features of Rorschach records yielded by clinically diagnosed psychopaths which serve to demark these individuals from normals and those in other psychiatric categories?

Theoretically, of course, the answers to the above questions should resolve to a categorical affirmation. If—as some authors (including the writer) have maintained—psychopathic personality is an exclusive rubric delineating a specific psychological type of individual, the Rorschach records of such persons should be separable from others. If it should appear from studies of the type to be presented that no differential patterning for psychopaths is discernable, two possibilities suggest themselves: (1) that so-called psychopaths are not members of a clear-cut diagnostic group so far as basic psychological features are concerned; or (2) that the Rorschach in its present research state is incapable of making so fine a distinction as that required in discriminating the psychopath from other diagnostic classes. In neither case should we be surprised. The diagnosis of psychopathic personality is perhaps the most notorious waste-basket in psychiatry and clinical psychology; and while the Rorschach has had notable success with the employment of the "sign-approach" to diagnosis especially in

---

[1]Originally published in *Journal of Criminal Psychopathology*, July 1943, pp. 69–93. (Footnotes and references have been restyled for the purposes of this book.)

schizophrenia, the psychoneuroses and intra-cranial organic pathology, its staunchest champions would be wary at this time of ascribing to it the power to make diagnostic discriminations requiring almost surgical finesse.

Whereas the history of research and thought about psychopathic personality (known variously as constitutional psychopathic inferiority, constitutional psychopathic state, moral insanity, sociopathy, semantic dementia, anethopathy, moral mania, egopathy, psychic constitutional inferiority, trophopathy, etc.) is a long and confusing one (Cason, 1942), its Rorschach aspects are naturally limited by the comparative novelty of the test. Even so, certain studies bear directly upon the current one, and some may be regarded as collateral. We shall be concerned only with those that have some definite contribution to make to our central problem.

One strikingly apparent and unfortunate gap rests with the fact that Rorschach himself had little to remark about psychopaths, although in his discussions and case presentations a wide variety of diagnostic groups are surveyed, and twenty psychopaths participated in the observations recorded in the original text [Rorschach, 1942]. Boss, in 1931, appears to have been the earliest investigator of this problem. His review of 75 clinically diagnosed psychopaths led him to conclude that the Rorschach records of such psychopaths generally yield the characteristics which follow:[2]

1. CF and C>M and FC.
2. H:Hd and A:Ad increased over normal.
3. W:D and Dd increased over normal.
4. O and Dd increased over normal (with corresponding diminution of P).
5. Many W's but few good M's.
6. W tends to be cheap, vulgar, banal, and frequently appears with CF.
7. Shock is common.
8. Succession is relaxed.
9. Many responses utilizing black-and-white interpretations (Rorschach F (Fb)).
10. Oppositional tendencies (Dzw).

Boss' view of the psychopathic character structure shows:

Very labile and egocentric affectivity, showing inadaptability in the affective sphere. Inability to marshal thought processes, autistic thinking and general loosening of associations. Indifference and disregard for the world outside the ego. Oppositional

---

[2]The writer has transcribed the original symbols after Klopfer and Kelley's *The Rorschach Technique* (1942).

trends. Intensive need of love and sympathy. Aggression. Prey of inner desires and impulses.

From Boss' account it would appear that the records yielded by his psychopaths are related qualitatively with those from hebephrenics and neurotics. The differential diagnosis of psychopathic personality has always been difficult since simple, hebephrenic, and paranoid schizophrenia and some varieties of the psychoneuroses often present similar clinical features.

The Dubitscher study of 1932 reported a survey of 100 male psychopaths [see also Monnier, 1934]. The outstanding features of the Rorschachs of his subjects were:

1. $R <$ in normal subjects.
2. $W >$ in normal subjects.
3. $F-\% <$ in normal subjects.
4. $0\% <$ in normal subjects.
5. $M <$ in normal subjects.
6. Stereotypes = to normal subjects.
7. $D <$ in normal subjects.
8. All intellectual and creative factors $>$ in normal subjects.

For this investigator the overall patterning discloses:

> Poor intellectual control. Heightened affectivity and impulsivity. Inadaptable sociality, externalized by impulsive aggression. Extratensive-egocentric *erlebnistyp*, dilated. Incapacity for imaginative, creative thinking.

The problem seems to have suffered neglect after the Dubitscher study, and in the Beck *Manual* of 1937, we find the author stressing particularly the neurotic character of the records he collected from psychopaths. He also points to the confusion of this group with schizophrenics, the feebleminded, and neurotics, and seems to blame this upon the diagnosis of psychopathic personality *per se* as a miscellaneous category lacking clarification of the personality type it attempts to describe. Binder had observed in 1932 that psychopaths expressed a preference for FY in W, but Beck failed to substantiate this observation. The author of the first American *Manual* also mentioned Oberholzer's reference to the psychopath's tendency to disregard form.

Apart from intermediate studies dealing with subjects whose behavior patterns fall on the borderline of psychopathy or resemble it rather closely [Day, Hartoch, & Schachtel, 19??; Endara, 1937, 1938; Pescor, 1941; Zulliger, 1938], direct assault on the problem within the last few years has been confined to the unpublished material reviewed below and the study now being reported.

When this topic was placed on the writer's research agenda in 1941, Beck was asked for his impressions. Contained in a personal communication and based on inspection of his psychopathic personality Rorschach records, they were:[3]

1. F+(grip on reality) likely to be lower than in the neuroses and higher than in schizophrenia.
2. Z (higher mental processes) likely to be lower than in neuroses. "Psychopathic personalities do not grasp relevance of their activities at the level expected of them."
3. D overemphasized by some psychopathic subjects; a few emphasize Dr (attention to the irrelevant).
4. Or (logic) likely to be reflective of methodicity. "An occasional irregularity occurs, but not enough to account for their unsatisfactory behavior in society."
5. Inner life varies. As many are inclined to be introversive (M > C), as are extratensive (C > M). Some are ambivalent.
6. CF and C> normals.
7. FC appears regularly; "they are capable of mature emotionality."
8. P is average.
9. S (restiveness) bimodal, some showing large amounts, some producing under the average.

In general, Beck holds that psychopaths identify themselves through peculiarities of response and patterns which are "out of step with the rest of the record." He states, somewhat equivocally, that the surest diagnostic sign of psychopathy is that "the Rorschach pattern (of psychopaths) leaves the examiner with the sense of dissatisfaction in its being like that of the schizophrenic without being schizophrenic; or like that of the neurotic without being a neurosis."

Working at the U.S. Penitentiary in Atlanta, Batchellar compared the psychograms-as-wholes (according to the chi-square method) of sixty-five cases showing psychopathic characteristics with 29 non-psychopaths. In this study he found:[4]

1. Underemphasis of W.
2. Overemphasis of Dd.
3. M below expectation.
4. FK (vista) above expectation.
5. C' (Achromatic color) above expectation.

---

[3]Personal communication, quoted with Dr. Beck's permission.
[4]Personal communication quoted with permission of D. E. Batcheller.

From his results, he was able to say that: "The underemphasis of M among psychopaths apparently indicates a greater lack of integration and maturation (than among non-psychopathic inmates)." Further, both his psychopaths and non-psychopaths showed a marked tendency toward infantilism (emotionally).

Perhaps the most complete statement of Batcheller's work with the Rorschach and psychopathic subjects is contained in a statement prepared for oral presentation before the Southeastern Rorschach Conference in the summer of 1942 [Batcheller, 1942]. From a review of the Rorschach records of 59 diagnosed psychopaths, thirteen so-call[ed] "signs" appeared as constants on the basis of frequency. They were:

1. R between 15 and 25.
2. W > 30% of all responses, with consequent underemphasis of d and overall decrease in R below the expectation for a group of persons possessing superior test intelligence.
3. M almost absent (only in 16 of 59 cases was M > 1).
4. FM > M.
5. C > M (with tendency for these two categories to approach each other).
6. CF > FC.
7. F% > 50 (constriction).
8. FK (25 of Batcheller's 59 cases had no FK; 24 had one or more).
9. Tendency toward use of k and K.
10. Color and shading shock.
11. A and Ad responses were numerous (18 of 59 cases gave 50% or more of their responses in this category).
12. Regular appearance of anatomical references.
13. Frequent rejections.

Only seven of Batcheller's 59 psychopathic records yielded less than seven of the above "signs". From his studies he reaches the interesting conclusion that the list of "signs" appear to be a composite of the 9 for psychoneuroses reported by Miale and Harrower-Erickson [1940] and the twenty indices of schizophrenia compiled from research studies of Klopfer and Kelley [1942]. Thus he notes the suggestion that psychopaths "show in reality a psychoneurotic condition super-imposed on a basic schizoid or latent schizophrenic condition, the pattern described and designated by Kisker and Michael as a 'schizo-neurosis'."

There remains another research study for our consideration; that by Geil [1943], dealing with Rorschach examinations of 51 psychopathic criminals. He found them to possess personalities best described as "undeveloped, mal-integrated and mal-functioning," similar to the configuration found in the psychoneuroses. His Rorschach analysis stresses:

Control unrefined, rigid, constrictive. Aggressive and impulsive response characteristics to external stimuli. Insufficient concern with detail and tendency to use
generalized approach. Intellectually inefficient although test level is high. Affectively unadaptive, primitive, egocentric. Color and shading shock. Compulsive
elements in an anxiety configuration.

The current study deals with a comparison of Rorschach records obtained
from two groups of penitentiary inmates under two sets of conditions. The subjects
were 40 psychopaths and 40 "normals." They were given the Rorschach under
group conditions first, and then after a lapse of at least one month, were examined
individually [Lindner, 1943a]. This was done to obtain a measure of reliability
for each subject, to observe whether the "test-yield" would be similar under both
varieties of administration.

Since from the foregoing sections it is evident that much depends on the
criteria by which psychopaths are diagnosed, and that care must be taken to
exclude from the psychopathic group especially the neurotics and schizophrenics,
the choice of subjects was made with extreme caution. In order for an individual
to be placed in the psychopathic group, he was required to conform to the
symptom-complex established in other experimental work and found well adapted
to research on psychopathy [Lindner, 1942]. The checklist (Table [A.1]) contains
most of the signs stressed in the literature of psychopathy, and it was insisted
that both clinically and on the basis of anamneses, the experimental subjects
demonstrate at least 67% (20 out of 30) of the signs noted.

Normal or control subjects were chosen by a random method, the single criterion
being absolute freedom from symptoms of psychopathy, neuroses, or psychoses.
The groups were equated for age, color and intelligence. As can be observed from
an inspection of Table [A.2], the only real difference between the experimental
subjects (psychopaths) and the controls is to be found under "psychiatric status."

After scoring was accomplished, the first step was to determine the reliability
of the results obtained by comparing the performances of both groups under both
conditions. In other words, we ask: Do our subjects tend to give the same results
when they are tested both singly and in groups? The question is answered for
the psychopaths in Table [A.3]. Here we see that only in the W% does there
exist a statistically significant difference in performing, and that in all categories
of response the records of psychopaths remain relatively unchanged. Regardless
of the gross administration conditions of the test, then, our psychopaths yielded
a consistent response pattern, the nature of which will concern us later. At the
same time, we note that certain other categories of response—Dd%, P%, A%,
8–10%, Ad, W, and D%—produce differences in the range of 2, indicating
possibilities of statistical significance, edging toward the critical difference of 3.
In Table [A.4] the operation is repeated with control subjects, and again the
consistency of performing is evident. For the control subjects the only critical
reflection of administrative change is in the content category A%. But—and here

TABLE A.1
Psychopathic Checklist

Symptom	Check if Present
1. Lack of insight	| .....
2. Only verbal acceptance of social demands	| .....
3. Intelligence of normal to superior	| .....
4. Cannot pursue social goals	| .....
5. Defective relationship with community	| ....
6. Rejects authority	| .....
7. Defective judgment	| .....
8. Sexual maladjustment or perversion	| .....
9. Nomadism	| .....
10. Egocentricity	| .....
11. Emotional immaturity	| .....
12. Paranoid tendencies	| .....
13. Failure to profit from experience	| .....
14. Selfishness, etc.	| .....
15. Few emotional ties	| .....
16. Rationalizes easily	| .....
17. Easily distracted	| .....
18. Memory good for remote, poor for recent events	| .....
19. Youthful appearance	| .....
20. Under forty years of age	| .....
21. Extraverted	| .....
22. Impulsive behavior	| .....
23. Frequent contact with the law	| .....
24. Defective parent relationships	| .....
25. Temper tantrums in childhood	| .....
26. Eneuresis	| .....
27. Truancy from school	| .....
28. Dislike of teachers	| .....
29. Runaway from home	| .....
30. Reformatory or juvenile home history	| .....
31. Subject------ ....Group	| .....

a matter of interest is encountered—only three other response categories (R, Ad, and 8–10%) show any sign of possible significance, whereas seven somewhat unstable categories were noted above for the psychopaths. Hence we are drawn to the conclusion that while the performances of psychopaths and control subjects show commendable reliability and are consistent independently of the gross technique of administration, *the psychopathic Rorschach records do tend more toward unreliability than those of controls.* Again, psychopaths are somewhat (although not significantly) less likely to yield consistent Rorschach performance patterns than normal subjects.[5]

---

[5]This was hinted at in a previous paper, Cf. [Lindner & Chapman, 1942].

TABLE A.2
Comparative Personal Data

	Normals[a]	Psychopaths[b]
AGE	26	26
NATIVITY		
a. United States	36	39
b. Foreign Born	4	1
COLOR		
a. White	40	40
b. Negro	0	0
EDUCATION		
a. None	1	0
b. 1–4	0	0
c. 5–8	20	20
d. 9–10	13	12
e. 11–12	4	7
f. Attended First Year College	2	1
INTELLIGENCE		
a. Below Average	0	0
b. Average	31	32
c. Above Average	9	8
PREVIOUS OCCUPATION		
a. None	2	1
b. Unskilled	29	27
c. Skilled	9	10
d. Business	0	1
e. Professional	0	1
CRIMINAL HISTORY		
a. Previous Sentence	30	34
b. None	10	6
PSYCHIATRIC STATUS		
a. Constitutional Psychopathic Inferiority		23
b. Constitutional Psychopathic State, Emotional Instability		9
c. Constitutional Psychopathic State, Inadequate Personality		7
d. Constitutional Psychopathic State, Sexual Psychopathy		1

The next concern was to discover whether any critical differences existed as between psychopaths and controls. The data from the individual examination of subjects were compared first, as shown in Table [A.5].

Even casual observation of [Table A.5] discloses the interesting fact that nowhere was there any statistically significant difference between psychopathic and non-psychopathic subjects. There are suggestions of critical differences in performing in SumC, F%, and the content categories N and Geog.

When we repeat the same statistical maneuver under group conditions, as in Table [A.6], we find that the Dd% achieves a critical ratio of significance, and that those categories tending toward significance are R, k, FC and At.

	Group Test		Individual Test		
	Mean	SD	Mean	SD	D/SigmaD
R.............. 17.		9.8	16.4	9.2	.4
W 6.5		3.9	4.7	2.3	2.5
D 7.3		6.4	7.6	4.6	.2
d 1.5		1.8	2.0	2.0	1.3
Dd .... 1.		1.6	1.4	1.7	.0
S.............. .5		.8	.7	.9	1.1
W% 39.7		21.4	29.5	18.1	3.5
D%........... 35.8		18.9	43.3	12.0	2.1
d% 6.4		8.3	9.4	19.8	.9
Dd%.......... 2.4		3.2	6.0	8.0	2.6
S% 1.6		2.5	2.3	3.1	1.2
M 1.5		1.7	1.1	1.0	1.3
FM 3.1		3.4	3.4	3.0	.5
m 6		1.0	.4	.6	1.1
k.............. .8		1.3	.5	.9	1.5
K.............. .3		.5	.3	.7	.6
FK 5		.7	.3	.6	1.1
F............. 6.4		7.4	8.0	5.9	1.1
F% 33.5		26.5	45.2	21.1	.2
Fc 1.4		1.4	1.3	1.2	.1
c		...	...	...	...
C'............. .2		.5	.2	.5	.2
FC 5		.8	.6	.9	.5
CF 5		.7	.4	.3	1.2
C............. .4		1.0	.2	.6	1.3
Sum C 1.7		2.3	1.0	1.5	1.6
P............. 4.6		2.3	4.5	1.6	.1
P% 23.7		14.5	28.8	5.8	2.4
A%........... 37.8		15.3	48.0	18.3	2.6
8–10% 20.0		11.3	27.0	9.6	2.8
H 1.6		1.5	1.5	.9	.3
Hd 1.2		2.2	.9	1.7	.5
A.............. 6.2		3.8	6.3	3.1	.1
Ad............. 1.0		1.3	2.0	2.0	2.7
Aob............ .5		.7	.6	.8	.9
At 4		1.3	.7	1.0	1.2
Obj 2.8		2.2	2.4	2.5	.6
N 7		.9	.4	.8	1.4
Pl 7		.9	.8	1.1	.5
Geog........... .5		.9	.7	1.0	.6

Group Test Versus Individual Test with Normal Subjects

	Group Test		Individual Test		
	Mean	SD	Mean	SD	D/SigmaD
R	24.0	12.1	17.8	11.7	2.3
W	6.6	4.8	5.7	3.5	1.0
D	7.6	7.7	7.8	7.4	.1
d	2.1	2.5	2.8	3.3	1.1
Dd	1.4	1.8	1.4	1.8	.0
S	.5	.7	.6	1.2	.4
W%	39.2	26.3	29.7	18.3	1.9
D%	32.0	19.0	2.0	14.4	1.8
d%	10.1	9.6	10.1	12.8	.0
Dd%	5.6	5.1	2.7	9.7	1.6
S%	.9	1.6	1.5	2.6	1.2
M	1.7	1.6	1.5	1.4	.7
FM	4.3	3.1	4.6	3.3	.5
m	.7	1.1	.6	1.0	.5
k	.4	.2	.3	.7	.2
K	.1	.4	.2	.6	.8
FK	.4	.7	.4	.9	.3
F	6.4	6.3	7.6	6.5	1.2
F%	29.8	19.9	35.0	23.6	1.1
Fc	1.7	1.4	1.8	1.2	.3
c	...	...	...	...	...
C'	.4	.7	.2	.5	1.1
FC	1.1	1.5	.9	1.2	.5
CF	.7	1.1	.6	.8	.6
C	.8	1.7	.5	1.2	.9
Sum C	2.5	3.6	2.3	2.9	.3
P	4.2	2.0	4.8	1.7	1.3
P%	22.7	16.8	26.7	15.8	1.1
A%	38.8	21.6	43.0	14.4	3.2
8–10%	23.8	10.1	28.4	9.1	2.2
H	1.6	1.7	1.5	1.3	.3
Hd	.8	2.4	1.4	1.9	1.2
A	6.0	3.2	5.9	3.6	.1
Ad	1.4	1.9	2.5	2.4	2.3
Aob	.4	.5	.4	.6	.4
At	1.2	1.6	1.0	1.2	.8
Obj	3.2	2.8	2.7	2.4	.8
N	1.0	1.2	.9	1.3	.3
Pl	.9	1.2	.6	.9	1.4
Geog	.5	1.1	.2	.4	1.8

Psychopaths Versus Normals on Individual Testing

	Psychopaths		Normals		
	Mean	SD	Mean	SD	D/SigmaD
R	16.4	9.2	17.8	11.7	.6
W	4.7	2.3	5.7	3.5	1.5
D	7.6	4.6	7.8	7.4	.1
d	2.0	2.0	2.8	3.3	1.3
Dd	1.4	1.7	1.4	1.8	.1
S	.7	.9	.6	1.2	.1
W%	29.5	18.1	29.7	18.3	.0
D%	43.3	12.0	2.0	14.4	1.4
d%	9.4	19.9	10.1	12.8	.2
Dd%	5.9	8.0	2.7	9.7	1.0
S%	2.3	3.1	1.5	2.6	1.3
M	1.0	1.0	1.5	1.4	1.5
FM	3.4	3.0	4.6	3.3	1.6
m	.4	.6	.6	1.0	1.2
k	.5	.9	.3	.7	1.0
K	.3	.7	.2	.6	1.1
FK	.3	.6	.4	.9	.8
F	8.0	5.9	7.6	6.5	.3
F%	45.2	29.1	35.0	23.6	2.0
Fc	1.3	1.2	1.8	1.2	1.5
c	. . .	. . .	. . .	. . .	. . .
C'	.2	.5	.2	.5	.3
FC	.6	.9	.9	1.2	1.5
CF	.4	.3	.6	.8	1.8
C	.2	.6	.5	1.2	1.9
Sum C	1.0	1.5	2.3	2.9	2.3
P	4.5	1.6	4.8	1.7	.8
P%	28.8	5.8	26.7	15.8	.8
A%	47.6	18.2	43.0	14.4	1.2
8–10%	26.5	9.6	28.4	9.1	.9
H	1.5	.9	1.5	1.3	.1
Hd	.9	1.7	1.4	1.9	1.1
A	6.3	3.1	5.9	3.6	.5
Ad	2.0	2.0	2.5	2.4	1.0
Aob	.6	.8	.4	.6	1.1
At	.7	1.0	1.0	1.2	1.4
Obj	2.4	2.5	2.7	2.4	.6
N	.4	.8	.9	1.3	2.1
Pl	.8	1.1	.6	.9	.9
Geog	.7	1.0	.2	.4	2.8

TABLE A.6
Psychopaths Versus Normals on Group Testing

	Psychopaths		Normals		
	Mean	SD	Mean	SD	D/SigmaD
R 17.0		9.8	24.0	12.1	2.8
W 6.5		3.9	6.6	4.8	.1
D 7.3		6.4	7.6	7.7	.2
d 1.5		1.8	2.1	2.5	1.2
Dd 1.0		1.6	1.4	1.8	1.2
S 5		.7	.5	.7	.4
W% 39.7		21.4	39.2	26.3	.1
D% 35.8		18.9	32.0	19.2	.9
d% 6.4		8.3	10.1	9.6	1.8
Dd% 2.4		3.2	5.6	5.1	3.6
S% 1.6		2.5	.9	1.6	1.4
M 1.5		1.7	1.7	1.6	.6
FM 3.1		3.4	4.3	3.1	1.6
m 6		1.0	.7	1.1	.4
k 8		1.3	.4	.2	2.5
K 3		.5	.1	.4	1.5
FK 5		.7	.4	.7	.5
F 6.4		7.4	6.4	6.3	.0
F% 33.5		26.5	29.8	19.9	.7
Fc 1.4		1.4	1.7	1.4	.9
c . . . . —		—	—	—	—
C' 2		.5	.4	.7	1.1
FC 5		.8	1.1	1.5	2.3
CF 5		.9	.7	1.1	1.3
C 4		1.0	.8	1.7	1.4
Sum C 1.7		2.3	2.5	3.6	1.2
P 4.6		2.3	4.2	2.0	.7
P% 23.7		14.5	22.7	16.8	.3
A% 37.8		15.3	38.8	21.6	.2
8–10% 20.0		11.3	23.8	10.1	1.6
H 1.6		1.5	1.6	1.7	.0
Hd 1.2		2.2	.8	2.4	.7
A 6.2		3.8	6.0	3.1	.3
Ad 1.0		1.3	1.4	1.9	1.0
Aob 5		.7	.4	.5	.6
At 4		1.3	1.2	1.6	2.5
Obj 2.8		2.2	3.2	2.8	.6
N 7		.9	1.0	1.2	1.3
Pl 7		.9	.9	1.3	1.0
Geog 5		.9	.5	1.1	.2

Under each of the two varieties of administration, we have been able to discover only one statistically significant differentiating factor. Translated into concrete terms, and in the light of other computations, we have seen that under conditions of individual testing, psychopathic subjects gave *less responses* to the last three cards, showed a possible *significantly higher F%*, a slight and probably unimportant decrease in Sum C, a few more Geog., and a few less N responses than controls. Where testing was done by a group method, psychopaths yielded a significantly smaller percentage in Dd%, fewer Rs, showed a slight increase in k, a decrease in FC and a few more At responses than control subjects.

The importance of the foregoing is that no real basis of differentiation of psychopaths from controls has yet emerged from this study. The only valid observation these data yield thus far is the wholly interpretive one that the psychopaths seem to react to the group method with some anxiety, while in the individual test situation their control appears to be better.

Utilizing only the means to try to find loci of differential performance we obtain some contradictory data. Under individual examination, psychopaths show an increase over controls in the means of D, Dd, S, F% and Sum C; under group conditions R, W%, Dd, and Sum C show a decrease for psychopaths, while F%, S% and Hd show an increase. The F% is the only factor that consistently gives an increase over the figure for normal subjects.

The approach through the means, then, serves only to underline our previous statement that a basis for differentiating psychopaths from normals has not yet appeared in this study.

When the absolute values of the various categories are considered—as in Figures [A.1, A.2, and A.3]—we find further confirmation for what we have already shown. However, it is true to a certain extent that some *tendencies* are found. Thus, in "Location" or "Manner of Approach" (Fig. [A.1]), psychopaths tend in both forms of testing toward less Ws and to less Ds in individual testing than normals. Fig. [A.2] demonstrates that our psychopaths produced less FM, more F and oddly enough, less quantitatively on the affective side of the graph. As for "Content," no real tendencies differ them from the average. A further factor which does not appear in these figures is the tendency of the normal subjects to produce more R.

Regarding the three figures from an interpretive point of view, we can comment only that in a quantitative sense, the gross personality picture provided by the Rorschach examination is not very different for both groups tested. It is simple, of course, to read into these small differences all sorts of interpretations. The difference of about 10 responses in k between the records of our subjects, even though this amount is spread over 40 cases, can be magnified, and declaration made that psychopaths show more anxiety than normals. This, in view of statements above, would be true, of course, but not sufficiently true to warrant singling it out as a "sign" to be looked for and sought after. It would seem, at least to this writer, that the danger of doing just this is great, and a word of

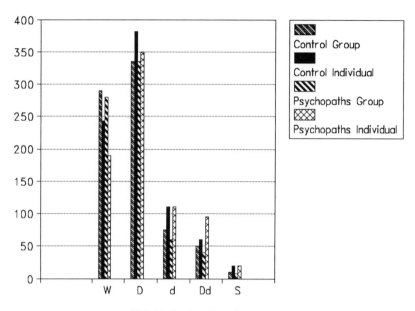

FIG. [A.1].   Location of responses.

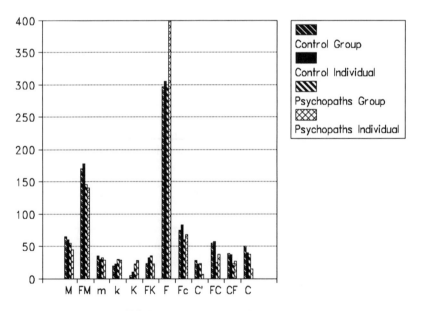

FIG. [A.2].   Determinants of responses.

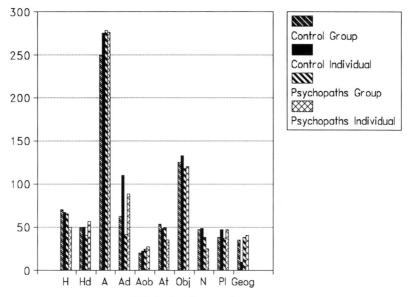

FIG. [A.3]. Content of responses.

caution needs to be inserted here against the tendency of some workers to put their faith in "signs" as a way to quick diagnosis.

So far as the question of shock is concerned, Table [A.7] yields consistent data showing that psychopathic subjects demonstrate less color shock alone, less shading shock alone, more color-and-shading shock, and a higher incidence of no shock at all, than normal subjects. While these data may be more applicable than they appear on cursory inspection, they mean little for differential diagnosis since the shock "sign" is likely to appear in profusion in other diagnostic categories.

The rejection of cards is a reflection both of the attitude of a subject and his ability. Table [A.8] summarizes the results on this score for the current experiment.

In individual testing, Card V is rejected more often by normal subjects, while VI, IX, and X have a higher mortality with psychopaths. In group testing, Cards I, II and VII are refused by normals, while VI, IX and X continue to be avoided by the psychopaths. So it would appear that these three cards, usually considered the most crucial, are avoided by the psychopaths, independently of the conditions of test administration. Whether this avoidance is accounted for by the fact that VI, IX and X stimulate anxiety and have more potency than the others for calling up primitive material, or whether they are rejected simply because they are more difficult, is not known. Hand in hand with this observation, we note the pronounced tendency of the psychopath to reject more cards more frequently than our normals.

TABLE A.7
Incidence and Distribution of Shock

	Individuals				Group			
	N'mls		Psy.		N'mls		Psy.	
	No.	%	No.	%	No.	%	No.	%
Color Shock	14	35.	10	25.	16	40.	13	32.5
Shading Shock	2	5.	1	2.5	2	5.	0	0.
Color and Shading Shock	8	20.	11	27.5	14	35.	16	40.
No Shock	16	40.	18	45.	8	20.	11	27.5

We set out to discover whether the Rorschach could be used to aid in the diagnosis of psychopathic personality. For this reason we undertook a quantitative, comparative study, comparing selected clinical samples of this nebulous disorder with persons who appeared to belong to the vast normal group. The more important of our conclusions can now be stated. According to the survey we have been discussing:

1. Psychopaths give less reliable Rorschach records than normal subjects.

2. No real basis of differentiation of psychopaths from normals emerge when our material is regarded quantitatively.

TABLE A.8
Incidence and Distribution of Card Rejections

	Individuals				Group			
	N'mls		Psy.		N'mls		Psy.	
	No.	%	No.	%	No.	%	No.	%
Card I	2	5.	2	5.	5	12.5	2	5.
Card II	2	5.	3	7.5	5	12.5	1	2.5
Card III	1	2.5	1	2.5	2	5.	1	2.5
Card IV	8	20.	8	20.	9	22.5	8	20.
Card V	4	10.	1	2.5	2	5.	2	5.
Card VI	6	15.	8	20.	7	17.5	10	25.
Card VII	8	20.	9	22.5	10	25.	7	17.5
Card VIII	1	2.5	1	2.5	4	10.	4	10.
Card IX	8	20.	15	37.5	11	27.5	22	55.
Card X	5	12.5	9	22.5	11	27.5	16	40.
No Rejections	23	57.5	11	27.5	18	45.	12	30.
One Rejection	5	12.5	12	30.	7	17.5	8	20.
Two Rejections	6	15.	8	20.	5	12.5	7	17.5
Three Rejections	3	7.5	7	17.5	3	7.5	5	12.5
Four or more	3	7.5	2	5.	7	17.5	8	20.

3. Although some indications of general differentiating tendencies are found, none of them are of sufficient potency, or occur regularly enough, to warrant utilizing them as "signs."

4. Where we have noted tendencies of the psychopathic records to depart from the normal records, none of them have been found to possess qualities of distinction for the exclusive diagnosis of psychopathic personality.

Notwithstanding all that has been shown pertaining to the inadequacy of the quantitative approach, the personal view of the writer, based upon considerable experience, is that the psychopathic personality can be diagnosed with the aid of the Rorschach, that the individual Rorschach record of the psychopath is recognizable, and to a considerable degree unmistakable.

Psychopathic Rorschach records appear to the author to disclose themselves *qualitatively* rather than quantitatively. The "sign" approach, perhaps a technique of value with other disorders, is valueless for psychopathy. The psychopathic character is more variable in its activities than any other. It is just this fluidity that has made this diagnosis the catch-all of psychopathology. In other psychiatric classifications we find the symptoms conforming more or less to a pattern. Each one has a theme, so to speak, that is at the core of the syndrome. This is definitely not the case with psychopathy. Here we are confronted with a hydra-headed category and thrice-confounded by the various aspects of each head. And added to this is the well-established fact that those whom we label psychopathic are, much of the time, free from direct, expressive evidence of psychopathy; it appearing to many observers as a frequently-remissed, explosive, inconstant state [Lindner, 1943b]. To expect inconstancy to yield a repetitious quantitative patterning seems illogical. Were we dealing with a physical matter, we would not expect too much variability in function; but where our concern is with the relative intangibles that are the substance of psychology, we are in the anachronistic position of expecting stability of function from a personality the essence of which we acknowledge to be instability.

Now what are these qualitative aspects of Rorschach performing which disclose the psychopath? The most important seems to be a quality best described by the word *superficiality*. Quantitatively, as has been noted above, the affective side of the psychogram seems to be dominated by the intellective or cognitive side; but a severe examination of actual responses shows this to be false. Frequently the primitive emotionality expressed in pure color or color-form responses appears to be under the dominion of controlled FC responses; but here again a sequence analysis of response delineates a patterning wherein raw and crude chromatic answers are followed by a series of responses denoting inhibition and withdrawal. On the intellective side the same phenomenon is observed, with the anxiety factors apparently succumbing to constricted form elements denoting rigidity and fixity; but actually, on experienced inspection, yielding knowledge of a clinging to reality as an overcompensation for the insecurity just beneath the surface. The same holds for the relationship of the creative and imaginative aspects to reality. On the surface they appear spontaneous, sometimes rich and even luxuriant expressions; but experience shows them to be hesitant and fearful. Although kinesthesis appears in psychopathic records as frequently as in normal records, such answers are of a peculiar stamp and poor in quality. This superficiality is all-pervasive, glossing the records of all psychopaths and so presenting a false-face and misleading the examiner whose experience with psychopathic character-structure is limited. Here we have the reason why the appearance but not the reality of schizophrenia, neuroses, feeblemindedness, or normality confronts and confuses the Rorschach examiner.

A second characteristic of the psychopathic Rorschach records can be characterized by the word *avoidance*. The life of the individual with whom we are concerned is one long struggle to escape self-recognition of his insufficiencies, his limitations, even his own motivations. Thus one outstanding symptom is the lack of insight. In the Rorschach this is manifest by a shying away of all stimuli which threaten to make such disclosures either to self or to the world outside which is represented by the examiner. So it is that those cards which provide the surest vehicles for self-disclosure and either avoided or handled in an obvious, over-banal fashion, and where once a revealing response is given, it is generally followed by an avalanche of ordinary and cheap answers that stand out because they contrast so oddly with the good potential intelligence of such subjects.

A characteristic *explosiveness* is a third feature of most Rorschachs collected from psychopaths. This serves as a signal of aggression and a tension-discharging device. It appears not only when the content of the responses are subjected to close scrutiny, but also in the sequential analysis of test results. Because such explosive responses are transparent and revelatory even to the testee, subsequent answers are found to obey the mechanism of avoidance.

Incompleteness of responses is a fourth aspect of psychopathic Rorschach records. Concepts frequently are found to be somewhat unfinished, or show signs of having been hastily constructed to the extent that a part is missing. This doubtless reflects the well-known and analytically important material that is a psychological component of all histories of psychopaths.

The *egocentricity* of psychopathic records is a final characteristic which this writer has noted. It is betrayed by numerous self-references, by self-involvement in content of material, by symbolistic references such as a point at the core of an object, a central figure surrounded by other constructions, and most of all by the patent identification of the testee with the important figure or thing in a concept.

These five features—*superficiality, avoidance, explosiveness, incompleteness and egocentricity*—have been, in the experience of this writer, invariable features of records he has obtained from psychopathic subjects. They are evident only when the records are approached qualitatively and, for him, have served the same function as the "sign" approach to the diagnosis of other psychiatric classifications. Experience has shown, however, that they must all appear in order to sustain the diagnosis. Together they form a constellation basic to psychopathic personality, reflecting through the Rorschach the essence of the disorder.

REFERENCES TO APPENDIX A

Batcheller, D. E. (1942). *The use of the Rorschach method in a large modern prison.* Paper presented at the Southeastern Rorschach Conference.

Beck, S. J. (1937). *Introduction to the Rorschach method* (Research Monograph No. 1). American Orthopsychiatric Association.

Binder, H. (1932). Die helldunkeldeutungen im psychodiagnostischen experiment von Rorschach. *Schweiz. Arch. Neurol. Psychiat., 30,* 1–67.

Boss, M. (1931). Psychologisch-charakterologishe untersuchungen bein antisozialen psychopathen, mit hilfe des Rorschachschen formdeutversuches. *Ztsch. ges. Neur. und. Psychiat., 133,* 544–575.

Cason, H. (Ed.). (1942). *Summaries of literature on constitutional psychopathy* (5 vols., mimeographed). Springfield, MO.

Day, F., Hartoch, A., & Schachtel, E. (19??). A Rorschach study of a defective delinquent. *Journal of Criminal Psychopathology, 2*(1).

Dubitscher, F. (1932). Der Rorschachsche formendeuteversuch bei erwachsenen psychopathen sowie psychopathischen und schwachsignnigen kindern. *Ztsch. ges. Neur. und Psychiat., 142,* 129–158.

Endara, J. (1937). Psicodiagnostico de Rorschach y delincuencia: Psigramas de dos homicidas reincidentes. *Psiquiat y Criminol, 2,* 45–50.

Endara, J. (1938). A proposito de los examines biopsicologicos en delincuentes. *Arch. Criminol. Neuropsiquiat., 2,* 229–234.

Geil, G. A. (1943). Psychological studies concerning psychopaths. In *Proceedings of the 72nd Congress of the American Prison Association* New York. [Also in *Abstracts of the Symposium on Psychopathy,* Medical Correction Association, mimeographed, p. 11]

Klopfer, B., & Kelley, D. M. (1942). *The Rorschach technique.* Yonkers, NY: World Book.

Lindner, R. M. (1942). Experimental studies in constitutional psychopathic inferiority: Part I. Systemic patterns. *Journal of Criminal Psychopathology, 4*(2), 253–???.

Lindner, R. M. (1943a). A further contribution to the group Rorschach. *Rorschach Research Exchange, 7*(1), 7–15.

Lindner, R. M. (1943b). Homeostasis as an explanatory concept in psychopathy. In *Proceedings of the 72nd Congress of the American Prison Association* New York.

Lindner, R. M., & Chapman, K. W. (1942). An eclectic group method. *Rorschach Research Exchange, 6*(4), 139–146.

Miale, F. R., & Harrower-Erickson, M. R. (1940). Personality structure in the psychoneuroses. *Rorschach Research Exchange, 4,* 71–74.

Monnier, M. (1934). Le test Psychologique de Rorschach. *L'Encephale, 29,* 189–201, 247–270.

Pescor, M. S. (1941). A further study of the Rorschach test applied to delinquents. *Public Health Report, 56*(9), 381–395.

Rorschach, H. (1942). *Psychodiagnostics* (P. Lemkau & B. Kronenberg, Trans.; W. Morganthaler, Ed.). Berne, Switzerland: Verlag Hans Huber.

Zulliger, H. (1938). *Jugendliche diebs im Rorschach-formdeutversuch; eine seelenkundliche und erzieherische studie.* Berne, Switzerland: Haupt.

100 Reflection Responses from 48 Subjects

CARD I

Character-Disordered Felons

1) A pig looking into their reflection like water, like Narcissus. (Inquiry?) Snout, ears, tail, standing up, seeing his exact reflection. (water?) Nothing makes it look like water. Pigs are outdoor animals without access to mirrors, it's a logical conclusion.
W+ Fmᵃ.Fr− A PER, DR1 (omnipotence) (#7;C,M,43,P) (R = 12)[1]

2) A young animal looking at his reflection in a pool of water. I see a baby elephant, ears standing up. A little trunk here. (I?) I saw what I want to see, a baby elephant looking at his reflection. Here is the back, legs, ears, and the face, here's the trunk. (Reflection?) This line separates it and gives the impression of a reflection in water.
W+ 1 Fr.FMᵖo A,Na 4.0 DR1 (omnipotence) (#18;C,F,45,P) (R = 16)

3) (<) A pig, snout and ears, pointing up. (I?) Look like a pig. Anyway you look at it. Here are its hindquarters. Look like its been in a mud-bath. Here's its sty and here's the reflection.
W+ 1 Fr− A 4.0 (#34;5-2;C,M,UNK,P) (R = 23)

4) Absolutely symmetrical. Looks like it could be a caterpillar on a mirror. That's the reflection in the mirror. (I?) Looks like a cocoon.
W+ 1 rF− A 4.0 FAB1 (#35;5-3;C,M,38,P) (R = 13)

---

[1]Comprehensive system scoring is followed by Kwawer (1980) score, if present. The next symbols refer to research number, race, gender, age, presence of primary psychopathy (P), and number of responses in protocol of subject.

5) Looks like a lady. (I?) Looks like she's right up against a mirror. Here's her dress. (Mirror?) Here and like she is leaning up against it. Here is her reflection.
D+ 4 M^p.Fro H,Cg 4.0 (#39;C,F,21) (R = 16)

6) Kind of like a lady facing a mirror or something on her back. (I?) Like I showed you and this is something on her back. Facing the mirror and something on her back.
W+ M^p.Fr– H 4.0 (omnipotence) (#39;C,F,21)

Psychotic Felons

7) (<) This way looks like a rabbit and the bottom of it is reflecting with the shadow on the ground. (I?) The ears, two hind legs right here. Two front legs so close together don't see anything through them. Like it's standing on a rock. (Rock?) Looks like it's round shape of a small boulder or small rock could be a rocky stone next to a small pond or a lake or it cb on the ground reflecting in a small shadow on the pond. The rose looks like a rabbit on this.
W+ Fm^p. Fru A,Na 4.0 Dv1 (#10;C,M,31) (R = 43)

8) It looks like a reflection of one thing from another, got same shapes on both sides. (I?) Other half of one part little it off in places not exactly same. Line down middle, looks like a reflection.
W^v+ r Id 4.0 (#4;C,M,37) (R = 34)

9) (>) Could be a horizon of a plateau. You write like a doctor that takes schooling. (I?) Rocks, like an horizon, crevice is a waterline like a brook, reflects the rocks and stuff.
W^v+ rFu Na 4.0 Dr1 (#45;C,M,24) (R = 20)

CARD II

Character-Disordered Felons

10) (>) An anteater and a reflection underneath the water. (I?) Like he's walking out side of an embankment. Reflection is seen sideways or beneath him.
W+ 1 FM^a.Fru A,Na 4.5 DV1 (#12;C,M,33) (R = 38)

11) A person in a mirror. (I?) This is the person looking at himself in the mirror, body, hand, arm. You know the way you look at yourself in the mirror, you really can't see no mirror there.
W+ 1 M^p.Fr– H 4.5 (#20;B,M,27,P) (R = 22)

12) Looks like a human crawling on ice with his head cut off. (I?) Here's the shadow of ice mirror reflection. Head was here got cut off. Here's the blood. (Blood?) Red, it's dripping.
W+ M^a.Fr.CF.m^a– H,Bl,Na 5.5 MOR,FAB2,DV1 [AGpast], Violent-Symbiosis (#24;C,M,35,P)

13) Two birds looking at each other and got clothes on. This one's looking in the mirror at himself and that's his image he's looking at. (I?) Here's the bird kinda of a bird because he's got a beak. Wouldn't be a personal, this is the other one in the mirror kinda laughing. Just playing in the mirror because he's never seen himself before. (Bird?) Just here, beak. This could be feathers or wing, kinda a Big Bird type thing, not an actual bird that flies.
Dd+ 99 M^P.Fr– (A),Cg 3.0 FAB1,INC1,DR1 (#31;1-008;O,M,34,P) (R = 18)

14) (<) A rabbit standing on a mirror. (I?) Yea, you can see his reflection. Here's his nose and ears and body, and he's just standing there.
Ds+ FM^P.Fro A 4.5 FAB1 (#36;5-4;C,M,38,P) (R = 22)

15) (<) A piece of liver reflected. (I?) Yea, it looks like raw meat. It's all red like raw meat. It's the color mainly.
D+ CF.rFu Fd 5.5 FAB1 (#36;C,M,38,P) (R = 22)

16) If you look this way it could be some sort of animal. Here's the ears, eyes, mouth, feet. This bottom part could be a reflection. (I?) Maybe a baby bear, a reflection.
D+ 6 Fro A P 3.0 (#43;054;C,F,30) (R = 25)

Psychotic Felons

17) Then like this looks like a rhino with a shadow reflecting on the bottom. (I?) I just see a rhino next to the water maybe getting a drink or putting his horn in the water or something.
D+ 6 Fma.Fro A,Na 3.0 (#10;C,M,31) (R = 43)

18) Same thing a little bit of color added to it. This one here is more like a reflection, better practically same on both sides. (I?) Same on both sides.
Wv+ r.C Id 4.5 (#4;C,M,37) (R = 34)

19) (>) Looks like a rabbit. (I?) Jacket rabbit, the body, the legs. Here's the reflection.
D+ 1 Fro A P 3.0 DV1 (#45;C,M,24) (R = 20)

20) A bear and a shadow of a bear in the water. (I?) Mouth and reflection.
D+ 1 Fro A,Na P 3.0 (#45;C,M,24) (R = 20)

CARD III

Character-Disordered Felons

21) Looks like a man, his reflection in the mirror. (I?) Like he's picking up a bag or something. Looking at himself. There's his chest, the head, shoulders, and arms. (Mirror?) There's two.
D+ M^a.Fro H,Id P 3.0 (#28;2-001;B,M,32) (R = 13)

22) Hmm, a male gorilla watching his reflection in a pool. (I?) The slumped over posture. The obvious chest. The thick upper limbs and slim waist. I thought male because of the genitalia. The outer part struck me as an abortion. I saw it in a picture. It makes me feel like an idiot talking about Christmas. The red in the middle I don't get anything from that. Just, something about it. Yea, that's interesting. If one was looking down into a pool you would see themselves, not a reflection. I still see water in the middle. Something about it. Here I get water, a pool or stream.
D+ FMᵖ.Fr+ A,Sx,Na 3.0 DR2,PER (omnipotence, boundary disturbance) (#30;C,M,32,P) (R = 13)

23) Okay, a woman that's had an abortion and she is having difficulty dealing with regrets afterwards. This is great. (I?) As if suddenly they looked in the mirror and saw themselves. Felt sorry for themselves. They realize it takes two to tango. (Abortion?) The red figures, the little bloody fetus. I don't get anything at all from the red in the middle. Interesting.
D+ 1 Mᵖ.Fr.CFo H,Bl,ID 4.0 MOR,DR2 [IMP],[SM],[AGPast] (Violent Symbiosis, Metamorphosis-Transformation) (#30;C,M,32,P) (R = 13)

24) Looks like a woman looking at herself in the mirror. (I?) Head, neck, boobs. Back butt hanging out like she's leaning forward. Head, neck, boobs, butt, purse or bag.
D+ 1 Mᵖ.Fro H,Sx P 3.0 (#41;039;C,F,31) (R = 14)

Psychotic Felons

25) Makes me think of a cave for some reason. (I?) Rocks jutting here, reflection here.
Dds+ 99 rFu Ls 4.5 (#1;C,M,UNK)

26) (>) This way it looks like a mountain landscape. That's it. (I?) I should say that I see it like reflecting in the water. I see it reflecting without the water or so I see it with the water and without the water and I see snow on the mountains. (?) The red doesn't have anything to do with it. (?) The white in between the dark ink.
D+ 1 rF.C'Fo Na 3.0 DR1 (#10;C,M,31) (R = 43)

27) Water coming down, foliage, lake, up, looking down on a valley. (I?) Looking down. Distant water, sun reflecting off water. Heavy foliage, the light and dark. Rain forest, I am seeing in the distance.
Wᵛ+ VF.rF− Na 2.0 (#19;C,F,34) (R = 19)

28) Two people's reflection in the water with a pair of lungs in between, two splots of blood on each side. (I?) This is a person right here. One there and one there. The pair of lungs is in the water. That's the pair of lungs in the water. That's the pair of lungs in the middle. That's a splot of blood. (Lungs?) They just look like or resemble lungs that's how I see them, that's how they are to me.

Ds+ 9 Fr.CFo H,Bl,An 4.0 DV1,FAB2 (omnipotence) (#23;H,M,28) (R = 20)

29) Two men. They're getting water. (I?) This head, hands fat, and legs. These are their buckets, water right here. (Water?) Way it looks like a reflection of shadows on water, a little spring.
D+ Mª.Fro H,Hh,Na P 3.0 (#44;B,M,28) (R = 23)

CARD IV

Character-Disordered Felons

30) (>) From side, oh what was the name, a picture of that Greek god, wings on his feet, these would be black clouds, it's all a reflection. (I?) Head on top, wings rest figure would be black clouds and there's trouble brewing in paradise. (Clouds?) I can think of nothing else that would go along with the picture, stands to reason think of a god or goddess being in a cloud. He's flying into clouds. (Reflection?) Same thing down here. (Trouble brewing?) Black clouds, begets rain. When someone gets angry black clouds. I think of danger or anger. I'm a very angry person sometimes.
W+ Mª.C'F.Fru (H),Cl,Na AB,PER,DR1 [IMP],[AGC],[AGpot] (omnipotence) (#25;C,M,39,P) (R = 13)

Psychotic Felons

31) This way it also reminds me of a fire with black clouds coming up and it's reflecting in the lake like on a stone. (I?) Just looks like a forest fire next to the lake of a brush fire. (?) How dark the clouds are. There's the shoreline there's the bushes or what ever burning and they're all black and there's the smoke going up and it's on a pond or a lake and it's reflecting. (?) The wind's coming up this way and it's rising this way.
W+ C'F.ma.rFo Na,Fi 4.0 [AGC] (#10;C,M,31) (R = 43)

32) (<) That one looks like, I don't know what that looks like. A reflection, not a perfect reflection though, has little flavors in it not very many but has some.
Wᵛ r Id DV1 (#4;C,M,37) (R = 34)

CARD V

Character-Disordered Felons

33) (>) Perhaps an animal jumping in a lake. (I?) Hind leg, tail, front leg something like a buffalo jumping in a lake. Of course he's getting a ten

point here because there's no splash. This is his reflection in the water. (Water?) If you look on a lake on a calm day it's glass smooth. If you can stick something in the water you can see a reflection.

W+ 1 FM^a.Fr– A,Na 2.5 FAB1 (omnipotence) (#11;C,M,20,P) (R = 20)

34) (>) One half would be a snail coming up from a puddle of water. (I?) This would be a reflection of a snail off a puddle of water. Shape of a puddle. Little splash of water here.

W+ 1 FM^a.Fru A,Na 1.0 (#12;5-4;C,M,33) (R = 22)

35) (<) Also, looks like a bird. (I?) Here skimming across the water and the reflection.

W+ 1 FM^a.Fru A,Na 2.5 (#33;5-1;C,M,21,P) (R = 27)

CARD VI

Character-Disordered Felons

36) (>) Gila monster, doesn't really look like one but it's close, reflected in the water, it's swimming. (I?) It has funny things on its back, like dinosaur flaps but more extreme. This is the head, the waterline, and the reflection of it is down here while it's swimming.

D+ 1 FM^a.Fr– A,Na 2.5 INC1,DV1 [AGC] (#9;C,M,29)

37) Why am I seeing the same thing in everything? Looks like more like a reflected image in a mirror with something down the middle. (I?) I don't know couldn't figure out what it was. Nothing comes to mind. Doesn't conform to anything just a blot. (?) I don't see anything in it someone spilled something.

W^v+ r ID 2.5 (#8;C,F,42) (R = 15)

38) (>) Do I have to use my artistic ability today? Perhaps an iceberg like in Alaska. (I?) You have seen the pictures for an Alaskan cruise? What's that glacier giving everyone problems, story reminds me of a picture I saw of it. Has reflection of glacier in the water. (Water?) Separation right here.

W^v+ 1 rFo Na 2.5 PER (omnipotence) (#11;C,M,20) (R = 20)

39) I see a reflection of a sunset and water reflected. (vista used)

Ds+ rFu Na 4.0 (#12;C,M,33) (R = 38)

40) (<) It could be a view from across a pond or a lake with trees and reeds reflected in the water. (I?) This, these little lines look like trees. These lines look like reeds and this cb a forest behind them with a rock and shore at the bottom part of the picture. Looks like a reflection. (Trees?) Small trees or large bushes. (Rock?) different shade then anything else.

W+ 1 Fr.VFo Na 2.5 (#17;4-007;C,M,UNK) (R = 18)

41) It looks like a ship that's been stuck in Alaska, it's all iced over. (I?) It's the boat smoke stack front and back. They hit an iceberg. It splashed water

up, and this is the reflection down here. (Water?) The way it reflects off the boat.

W+ m^p.Fro Sc,Na 2.5 Violent Symbiosis, Engulfment (#24;C,M,35,P)

42) (>) This way early in the morning, guy's out fishing or hunting. Hunting and these here are shrubs, it's on the water, a reflection. (I?) Guy, rifle or fishing rod, this boat, these are shrubs.

W+ M^a.Fru H,Na,Sc 2.5 [AGPot],[AGC] (#25;C,M,39,P) (R = 13)

43) A reflection off the water. (I?) If you're on a lake sometimes and looking at a bank, you will see the reflection on the bank. (?) I think I just described it.

Wv+ rFo Na 2.5 PER (omnipotence) (#32;4-001;C,M,32,P) (R = 19)

44) (>) The bank of a riverbed, some plants and trees reflecting off the water. (I?) More examination—dark spots above the stems, a wet area, flower blossoms, very dark, scrub, chaparral, rocks.

Dd+ rF.TF– Na 2.5 (#35;5-3;C,M,38,P) (R = 13)

45) This might be the reflection off a lake down below. (I?) These look like trees and they are reflected in this lake down here. (Trees?) They're real dense. (Dense?) Covered through, you can't see through. (Lake?) Maybe looking at a picture, it comes out like this, it's rounded. (Reflection?) Like the trees are reflecting off the water down here.

D+ 1 Fru Na 2.5 (#40;035;C,F,36) (R = 14)

46) If you cut half of it off, using the bottom as a shadow. The top would look like a snake. The bottom reflecting the snake. Not so much with the fins. That's all. (I?) Eyeball, fins, body, because the head looks like a snake.

D+ 5 Fru A 2.5 INC1 (#42;C,F,23) (R = 23)

Psychotic Felons

47) This reminds me of a tugboat with a reflection in the water. (I?) Yea. This is the tug boat, the stern and this is the chimney stack with smoke. It's steam powered. (Smoke?) No smoke but it has a chimney on it for smoke.

D+ 1 Fro Sc 2.5 (#10;C,M,31) (R = 43)

48) (<) A reflection, I don't know could be a cloud mass or something. (I?) Same on the top and bottom, Doesn't look like nothing.

Dv+ 1 rFu Cl 2.5 (#4;C,M,37) (R = 34)

CARD VII

Character-Disordered Felons

49) I see two ladies. One lady is dancing and the other is a reflection in the mirror.

W+ 1 M^a.Fro H 2.5 FAB1 (#12;C,M,33) (R = 38)

50) Two women's heads with hats, maybe someone looking in a mirror. (I?) Looking into a mirror, it's the same on both sides, see here is the hat and the nose and chin.
D+ 1 Mp.Fro Hd,Cg P 3.0 (#9;C,M,29)

51) Lady looking in mirror doing hair. (I?) Hair and face. Looks well styled, the shape. (Mirror?) Both the same identical.
W+ 1 Mᵃ.Fru H 2.5 (#16;4-017;C,M,27) (R = 20)

52) It's two people facing each other. I think they're women and they have on a headdress of some kind. (I?) Dressed identical like twins, the head, mouth, nose, it's a person looking in a mirror. That's more the point.
D+ Fr.MPo Hd P 3.0 DR1 (#17;4-07;C,M,UNK) (R = 18)

53) Could be a lady looking in the mirror. (I?) She could be looking in the mirror. (?) The distance looks like she's leaning out to see what's on her hair. Can see one arm here.
D+ 1 MP.Fro Hd P 3.0 DR1 (#22;C,M,46) (R = 21)

54) Maybe a girl dancing in the mirror. (I?) Yea, looking behind her in a mirror. (Mirror?) This side and this side.
W+ Mᵃ.Fru H 2.5 (#26;6-03,C,M,21) (R = 19)

55) A double exposure, duplicate. (I?) Cuz, they are identical like a mirror.
Wv 1 r Id (#27;2-010;C,M,31) (R = 16)

56) It's funny how things come to you. A woman, an old woman, in her seventies. The pioneer era, America, 1860s. Doing nothing in particular. Brings to mind Norman Rockwell. (I?) Jolly woman with ill-fitting dentures. In fact she doesn't have them in. It seems like when they get into their 70s or 80s they get that 'go to hell' attitude. The chin extends. She's looking at her reflection, looking at herself and seeing how terrible she looks without her dentures. She doesn't care.
W+ 1 MP.Fru H,Ay 2.5 DR1,MOR (#30;C,M,32,P) (R = 13)

57) It's a girl looking at herself in the mirror. (I?) Here's her head, here's her arm, and then this part's her body.
W+ 1 MP.Fru H 2.5 (#36;5-4;C,M,38,P) (R = 22)

58) Looks like a little girl with a ponytail looking in the mirror. (I?) Here is the nose or mouth, hair pulled back, ponytail. (?) Here across, it's reflected.
D+ 2 MP.Fro H P 3.0 (#39;024;C,F,21) (R = 16)

59) A person looking in the mirror. "I dream of Jeannie" looking in the mirror. (I?) Headdress from before now with her hair, same face, same body. Instead of 2 it's a reflection in the mirror.
W+ MP.Fru H,Cg 2.5 (#41;039;C,F,31) (R = 14)

60) Well, this one would be, like one of the bar-ladies from the older days, looking at herself in the mirror. Hair, nose, mouth. (I?) feather, mouth, nose, chin, neck, excluding this part.
D+ 2 MP.Fro H P 3.0 (#43;053,C,F,30) (R = 25)

Psychotic Felons

61) I see N, the letter N, and a backwards letter N, mirror image of the letter N. (I?) Right here. These dips here in the square it's a rectangle but it's dipped here and here, it looks like it's typed, a real bold type.
D+ 4 Fru Al 1.0 DV1 (#2;C,M,48)

62) Same thing a reflection, could be clouds. I don't have much to say about this one. (I?) Just what it is.
W^v+ rFo Cl 2.5 (omnipotence) (#4;C,M,37) (R = 34)

63) Something in a mirror. Hard to know with mirrored images, dancing, facing away, but these heads are facing toward each other, swiveled around. Feet, and legs obscured by skirts or they're sitting on the floor. Dancing with one arm out, walk like an Egyptian. (I?) Not visibly obscured, sitting and dancing.
W+ 1 Fr.M$^{a/p}$o H,Ay,Cg P 2.5 DR1 (#6;C,M,38) (R = 40)

64) A forest or something with a brook. (I?) The reflection, the crevice becomes a brook, the reflection.
W^v+ rF− Na 1.0 (#45;C,M,24) (R = 20)

CARD VIII

Character-Disordered Felons

65) Mountain lion climbing on rocks overlooking a lake. (I?) Got it backwards. Some kind of four-legged creature found in the woods. Haven't found them in San Diego. Like at Arrowhead where Father took me. Water line, reflecting of rocks, tree stuck in the water. The animal down here. (Tree?) branches of old tree with thick trunk, seems like it's been uprooted. (Rocks?) more uniform in color, they seem weathered and smooth on the edges. (Water?) Kind of way it reflects.
W+ 1 YF.Fr.FM^{a}o A,Na P 4.5 PER Separation-Division (#11;C,M,20) (R = 20)

66) I see the figure of a bear, maybe from a rock or tree trunk and a reflection on the side of the water or embankment.
W+ 1 Fro A,Na P 4.5 (#2;C,M,48)

67) A lion, a pink tiger walking by a lake. That's all. (I?) Here goes the tiger right there walking on the ground here. That's his reflection and the reflection of the ground. (Ground?) Don't look like nothing to me. I just said ground because what else is it going to be walking on?
W+ 1 Fr.FM^{a}o A,Na P 4.5 INC1 (omnipotence) (#13;1-05;B,M,18,P) (R = 13)

68) Nothing really catches my eye on this. Maybe a few designs look like some kind of animals. (I?) Yea, on both sides could be a reflection on water. Just half way there, cuz they're both exactly the same. (Animals?) Just the way the features just the way he stands. Looks like some kind of animal just the stance. (Water?) Maybe a ripple right there.
D+ Fr.FMᵖo A,Na P 3.0 (#14;O,M,45) (R = 18)

69) Like a bear crossing over a pond with his reflection looking back at him. (I?) He looks down, stepping across the pond.
W+ 1 Fr.FMᵃo A,Ls P 4.5 FAB1 (#15;B,M,30) (R = 15)

70) (>) An animal, beaver or badger, looks like he's walking near a pool and his reflection is in it. Some kind of woodland animal climbing. (I?) I saw a ship but it didn't fit. Primary thing, these animals. And a ship sail but a beaver wouldn't be climbing a ship sail except in the cartoons. When I turned him sideways about to stand on a tree limb. (Water?) Shimmering, feel fluid, not solid, like a mirror image. (Shimmering?) Edges of parts of drawings looks watery. When you look at the edge of the paper.
W+ 1 Fr.FMᵃ.mpo A,Na P 4.5 DR1 (#18;C,F,45,P) (R = 16)

71) Bobcat on the rocks. (I?) These are rocks here. Looks like a reflection off water to put it that way. Four legs he's taking a step. (Rocks?) The colors turquoise rock, here's brown rock, jagged.
W+ Fr.FMᵃ.CFo P A,Na (#24;C,M,35)

72) Looks like a bobcat. These are rocks he's perched on. This must be water down here because there's a reflection of the whole thing. (I?) Bobcat, perfect body of cat, too. Could be rocks, this could be a tree part. (Rocks?) My, I forgot the word, it doesn't look like any tree I've seen. This look like dead part of tree assumed they were rocks. It's a mirrored image.
W+ FMᵖ.Fro A,Na P 4.5 PER,MOR,DR1 (#25;C,M,39) (R = 13)

73) Clearly off the top, I can see two animals that look like tigers or panther. Right here he's stepping on stones and an old tree branch over some water. (I?) Yea, some kind of animal this is the front leg on the tree branch coming out of the water. (Water?) It looks like the tree branch sticks out of the water. Looks like a reflection in the water if you look at it from the top.
W+ Fmᵃ.Fro A,Na P 4.5 (#27;2-02;B,M,32) (R = 13)

74) (>) This one's got two tigers on each end, two cheetahs. This looks really good here. I take it back. This is the water down here and rocks and the tiger crawling here. That looks real. Bout it for this one. (I?) Here's rocks and tiger and his image in the water. (rocks?) Because he's climbing on them. I guess these aren't the color of rocks. The shape too. (Water?) It's duplicated down here and it's backwards or upside down.
W+ 1 FMᵃ.Fro A,Na P 4.5 (#31;1-08;O,M,34,P) (R = 18)

75) Strange each picture has a line in the middle and has somewhat the same reflection. (I?) Center of the card is the same reflection on the other side

not exact but close.

W^v 1 r Id (#32;4-01;C,M,32) (R = 19)

76) Now this looks like an animal. A colorful planet, there's the water down there, with its reflection in the water. It's reaching out from a rock, to a stump, can't figure out why it's going over there. It has its own reason. This is real pretty. (I?) There's the rock here it's reaching over. (Colorful?) Coloring, see the face, eyes. Where the nose comes down. Trying to figure if it went over there just to see its own reflection. (Water?) The reflection makes it look like a reflection.

W+ 1 CF.Fr.FM^{a}o A,Na P 4.5 DR2 (#37;4-03;C,M,43,P) (R = 16)

77) (>) Bear crossing the water. (I?) The bear, land, rocks, and tree. (Water?) The reflection. (Rocks?) Different coloration, bluish gray.

W+ 1 FM^a.Fr.CFo A,Na P 4.5 (#38;4-05;C,M,37,P) (R = 12)

78) (>) Perhaps a mountain lion or bobcat jumping with his reflection in the water. Stone to stone to dead branch, an abstract painting. (I?) Stone to stone, reflection here.

W+ FM^p.Fro (A),Na,Art P 4.5 MOR (#39;C,F,21) (R = 16)

79) (>) If you hold it this way it looks like some kind of animal. Here's its legs, it's stepping over rocks or something. Here's the water, this could be the reflection of it. (I?) Could be a buffalo, ears, now mouth, buffalo don't have much of a neck. (Rocks?) Different colored blotches.

W+ Fma.Fr.CFo A,Ls P 4.5 (#43;054;C,F,30) (R = 25)

Psychotic Felons

80) Animal going over rocks and this is a reflection. (I?) Same image, facing the same way.

D+ 1 Fm^a.Fro A,Ls P 3.0 (#1;C,M)

81) (<) I see a wolf standing on some rocks looking into a pool of water. (I?) This is the wolf. This the rocks this is the wolf standing on the rocks and there's the reflection in the water. (?) The shape of it. (?) Just the reflection.

W+ FM^p.Fro A,Na P 4.5 (#10;C,M,31) (R = 43)

82) Overall, don't look like much. But this look like something like a small fox, dog and rat. It would be a reflection from the other side, also. Nothing that's distinguishable. (I?) A body longer than it is wider. Head, the end of the mouth, four legs, that's pretty much it. Could be dog or rat or lion, looks like reflection of the picture seems split in half, like the animal is walking on the edge of a lake or river.

D+ 1 Fr.FM^{a}o A,Na P 3.0 (#3;C,M,33) (R = 15)

83) Oh, colorful here. Some kind of animal reflection, one thing to another. (I?) Four feet, head, eyes, whiskers.

D+ Fro A P 3.0 DR1 (#4;C,M,37) (R = 34)

84) That's pretty, colors. Bears in the mountains, climbing rocks and going after fishes in the brooks. Why my dad can't stand me cuz I'm a raper. (I?) Cubs, who could shoot them. Could be a wolf stalking like a cat. Bottom is water, reflection. I don't see fishes.
W+ Fr.FM$_o^a$ A,Na P 4.5 DR2 [AGPot] (#11;C,M,20) (R = 20)

85) A dog walking on some rocks with a double image in the water. Upside down like a big cat or something. (I?) This part here, jumping.
W+ FM^a.Fro A,Na P 4.5 (#47;C,M,26) (R = 21)

86) This could be some kind of nocturnal mammal climbing on rocks, trees and reflection in the water. (I?) four legs, head, rocks, vegetation, some living some dead, reflected in H$_2$O.
W+ Fr.FM$_o^a$ A,Na P 4.5 MOR (#48;C,M,26) (R = 16)

87) Looks like two tigers walking along a seashore. (I?) feet, body, like a lake a shoreline, everything is a mirror image.
W+ FM^a.Fro A,Na P 4.5 (#49;C,M,31) (R = 16)

88) (>) Animal going over rocks and this is a reflection. (I?) Same image, facing the same way.
W+ FM^a.Fro A,Ls P 4.5 (#37;C,M,43) (R = 16)

CARD IX

Character-Disordered Felons

89) Oh, I can't think of anything off hand. So I'll have to say a cloud formation. (I?) I looked at it for awhile couldn't come up with anything else. Three different groups here. They are also mirrored. (Groups?) Different colors.
W^v+ CF.rF− Cl 5.5 (#25;C,M,39) (R = 13)

Psychotic Felons

90) (>) I see a beautiful lake, or it could be just a pool of water but it's beautiful. (I?) I just see a lake in there and it's reflecting the clouds. (?) The brightness, the way the water's reflecting the clouds. (?) The colors.
W^v+ r.C Cl,Na 5.5 [IMP] (#10;C,M,31) (R = 43)

91) Well, a couple of seahorses facing each other. (I?) Body, kind of starting at the head, a nose, stomach. Like a mirror image, same on both sides. Just the shape.
D+ 3 FM^p.Fr− A 4.5 (#3;C,M,33) (R = 15)

92) A reflection again, one thing from another. Looks a little bit off. Colors are different on it, wonder how that turned out?
W^v r Id 5.5 (#4;C,M,37) (R = 34)

93) Looks like the sun setting. Not the sun but the clouds and the sun shining on them after it's gone down. The colors. Maybe reflecting on a body of water, the ocean or something. (I?) Well, actually when the sun is going down, the clouds have the coloration of the sun and these don't have any uniform shape, just free flowing like clouds.

D^v+ 2 C.m^p.r– Cl,Na 2.5 (#5;C,M,33) (R = 33)

94) (<) A pond like a broken record. This is fall colors on a tree reflected on a pond. (I?) Three trees, this is the middle it's still green these are pink and orange. That's the water reflection and that's the trees.

W+ 1 rF.CFo Na 5.5 DR1 (#17;C,M) (R = 18)

CARD X

Character-Disordered Felons

95) This looks like a river that has three tributaries, two going off to the side and one in the middle. The one in the middle is taking you to an island with a castle on it. The ones to the side are a dead end. (I?) River, because it sparkles, like a reflection from the castle.

W+ rF.ma– Na,Id 5.5 (#38;002;C,F,27) (R = 44)

Psychotic Felons

96) (<) I see a deer standing next to a river bank with a tree next to him. (I?) This is the deer there's the tree and the whole thing's reflecting into a pool of water. (?) I see antlers, a couple of bugs. These parts look like a couple of caterpillars.

Dd+ 99 FMp.Fru A,Na 4.0 (#10,C,M,31) (R = 43)

97) (<) I see a pool of water reflecting. (I?) I see a pool of water reflecting. It just looks like the double exposure of the ink blot just reminds me of the water. You know how when you paint water to paint the reflection. The double exposure of the ink blot just reminds me of water. (?) Same exact shape opposite each other. It's like when same or parts if have the shape opposite each other is really in water.

W^v r Na (#10;C,M,31) (R = 43)

98) Same thing, reflection of one thing to another, more spread out with colors. (I?) Just the way it looks.

W^v r.C Id (#4;C,M,37) (R = 34)

99) Purplish shape on left, outline of Sweden. Shape and length. Only 8 million people there. The mirrored image. (I?) Shape, I lived there.

D+ 9 rFu Ls 4.5 PER,DR1 (#6;C,M,38) (R = 40)

100) Looks like a cocoon breaking open with a butterfly in the background, with all the colors in the background. (I?) Here's cocoon on both sides. Looks like broken in two, looks like butterfly broken out of it. Colors are reflections of butterfly. Butterfly is not in picture. Bright, sky, clear, you know (?) Springtime now bit past summer. I have been watching them out there flying around the trees.

W+ FMᵃ.C.rF– Ad,Ls 5.5 PER,DR1 Metamorphosis & Transformation, Birth-Rebirth (#21;C,M,43) (R = 11)

References

Acklin, M. (1992). Psychodiagnosis of personality structure: Psychotic personality organization. *Journal of Personality Assessment, 58*(3), 454–463.

Aichhorn, A. (1925). *Wayward youth.* New York: Viking.

American Psychiatric Association. (1952). *Diagnostic and statistical manual of mental disorders.* Washington, DC: Author.

American Psychiatric Association. (1968). *Diagnostic and statistical manual of mental disorders* (2nd ed.). Washington, DC: Author.

American Psychiatric Association. (1980). *Diagnostic and statistical manual of mental disorders* (3rd ed.). Washington, DC: Author.

American Psychiatric Association. (1987). *Diagnostic and statistical manual of mental disorders* (3rd ed., rev.). Washington, DC: Author.

American Psychiatric Association. (1994). *Diagnostic and statistical manual of mental disorders* (4th ed.). Washington, DC: Author.

American Psychological Association. (1993). Adolescence. *American Psychologist, 48*(2). Washington, DC: Author.

Ames, L., Learned, J., Metraux, R., & Walker, R. (1952). *Child Rorschach responses.* New York: Hoeber.

Ames, L., Metraux, R., Rodell, J., & Walker, R. (1974). *Child Rorschach responses* (rev. ed.). New York: Brunner/Mazel.

Ames, L., Metraux, R., & Walker, R. (1959). *Adolescent Rorschach responses.* New York: Hoeber.

Ammons, R., & Ammons, C. (1977). The Quick Test (QT): Provisional manual. *Psychological Reports: Monograph Supplement, 1–11*, 111–161.

Arboleda, C., & Holzman, P. (1985). Thought disorder in children at risk for psychosis. *Archives of General Psychiatry, 42*, 1004–1013.

Archer, R., & Gordon, R. (1988). MMPI and Rorschach indices of schizophrenic and depressive diagnoses among adolescent inpatients. *Journal of Personality Assessment, 52*, 276–287.

Archer, R., Maruish, M., Imhof, E., & Piotrowski, C. (1991). Psychological test usage with adolescent clients: 1990 findings. *Professional Psychology Research and Practice, 22*(3), 1–6.

Arieti, S. (1963). Psychopathic personality: Some views on its psychopathology and psychodynamics. *Comprehensive Psychiatry, 4*, 301–302.

Arkonac, O., & Guze, S. (1963). A family study of hysteria. *New England Journal of Medicine, 266,* 239–242.

Arnold, M. (1986). Dover beach. In *The Oxford dictionary of quotations* (p. 13). New York: Oxford University Press. (Original work published 1850)

Athey, G. (1974). Schizophrenic thought organization, object relations, and the Rorschach test. *Bulletin of the Menninger Clinic, 38,* 406–429.

Auden, W. H. (1989). *Van Gogh: A self portrait.* New York: Paragon House.

Bailey, K. (1987). Human paleopsychology: Roots of pathological aggression. In G. Newmann (Ed.), *Origins of human aggression* (pp. 50–63). New York: Human Sciences.

Barley, W., Door, D., & Reid, V. (1985). The Rorschach Comprehensive System egocentricity index in psychiatric inpatients. *Journal of Personality Assessment, 49,* 137–140.

Barnes, H., & Teeters, N. (1944). *New horizons in criminology.* New York: Prentice-Hall.

Beck, S. (1938). *Personality structure in schizophrenia.* New York: Nervous and Mental Disease Monograph.

Beck, S. (1943). The Rorschach test in psychopathology. *Journal of Consulting Psychology, 7,* 103–111.

Beck, S. (1965). *Psychological process in the schizophrenic adaptation.* New York: Grune & Stratton.

Beck, S., Beck, A., Levitt, E., & Molish, H. (1961). *Rorschach's test: Vol. 1.* New York: Grune & Stratton.

Belter, R., Lipovsky, J., & Finch, A. (1989). Rorschach egocentricity index and self-concept in children and adolescents. *Journal of Personality Assessment, 53,* 783–789.

Bender, L. (1943). The treatment of aggression: Aggression in childhood. *American Journal of Orthopsychiatry, 13,* 392–399.

Benjamin, J., & Ebaugh, F. (1938). The diagnostic validity of the Rorschach test. *American Journal of Psychiatry, 94,* 1163–1178.

Berg, J., Gacono, C., Meloy, R., & Peaslee, D. (1994). *A Rorschach comparison of borderline and antisocial females.* Unpublished manuscript.

Bilmes, M. (1967). Shame and delinquency. *Journal of Contemporary Psychoanalysis, 3*(2), 113–133.

Birnbaum, K. (1914). *Die psychopathischen verbecker* (2nd ed.). Leipzig, Germany: Thieme.

Blatt, S., & Lerner, H. (1983). The psychological assessment of object representation. *Journal of Personality Assessment, 47*(1), 7–28.

Blatt, S., Tuber, S., & Auerbach, J. (1990). Representation of interpersonal interactions on the Rorschach and level of psychopathology. *Journal of Personality Assessment, 54,* 711–728.

Bleiberg, E. (1984). Narcissistic disorders in children: A developmental approach to diagnosis. *Bulletin of the Menninger Clinic, 48*(6), 501–517.

Blos, P. (1979). *The adolescent passage: Developmental issues.* New York: International Universities Press.

Bohm, E. (1958). *A textbook in Rorschach test diagnosis* (A. Beck & S. Beck, Trans.). New York: Grune & Stratton.

Bowlby, J. (1973). *Separation, anxiety and anger.* New York: Basic Books.

Bowlby, J. (1982). *Attachment and loss: Vol. 1. Attachment* (2nd ed.). New York: Basic Books.

Bowlby, J. (1984). Violence in the family as a disorder of the attachment and caregiving systems. *American Journal of Psychoanalysis, 44,* 9–27.

Brittain, R. (1970). The sadistic murderer. *Medical Science and the Law, 10,* 198–207.

Bromberg, P. (1979). The use of detachment in narcissistic and borderline conditions. *Journal of the American Academy of Psychoanalysis, 7*(4), 593–600.

Burgess, A., Hartman, C., Ressler, R., Douglas, J., & McCormack, A. (1986). Sexual homicide: A motivational model. *Journal of Interpersonal Violence, 1,* 251–272.

Bursten, B. (1972). The manipulative personality. *Archives of General Psychiatry, 26,* 318–321.

Bursten, B. (1973). Some narcissistic personality types. *International Journal of Psychoanalysis, 54,* 287–299.

Bursten, B. (1989). The relationship between narcissistic and antisocial personalities. *Psychiatric Clinics of North America, 12*, 571–584.

Butler, P. (1981). *Talking to yourself.* New York: Harper & Row.

Cadoret, R. (1978). Psychopathology in the adopted away offspring of biological parents with antisocial behavior. *Archives of General Psychiatry, 35*, 176–184.

Cadoret, R., & Caine, C. (1981). Environmental and genetic factors in predicting adolescent behavior in adoptees. *Psychiatric Journal of the University of Ottawa, 6*, 220–225.

Cahill, T. (1986). *Buried dreams.* New York: Bantam.

Cameron, D., & Frazer, E. (1987). *The lust to kill: A feminist investigation of sexual murder.* New York: New York University Press.

Campo, V. (1988). Some thoughts on M in relation to the early structuring of character in children. In H. Lerner & P. Lerner (Eds.), *Primitive mental states and the Rorschach* (pp. 619–646). Madison, CT: International Universities Press.

Carlson, R., & Drehmer, D. (1984). Rorschach space response and aggression. *Perceptual and Motor Skills, 58*, 987–988.

Carroll, J., & Weaver, F. (1986). Shoplifters' perceptions of crime opportunities: A process-tracing study. In D. Cornish & R. Clarke (Eds.), *The reasoning criminal: Rational choice perspectives on offending* (pp. 19–38). New York: Springer Verlag.

Chodoff, P. (1982). Hysteria and women. *American Journal of Psychiatry, 139*, 545–551.

Chodorow, N. (1978). *The reproduction of mothering.* Berkeley: University of California Press.

Cirincione, C., Steadman, H., Robbins, P., & Monahan, J. (1992). Schizophrenia as a contingent risk factor for criminal violence. *International Journal of Law and Psychiatry, 15*, 347–358.

Cleckley, H. (1976). *The mask of sanity* (5th ed.). St. Louis, MO: Mosby. (Original work published 1941)

Cloninger, C., & Guze, S. (1970a). Female criminals: Their personal, familial and social backgrounds. *Archives of General Psychiatry, 23*, 554–558.

Cloninger, C., & Guze, S. (1970b). Psychiatric illness and female criminality: The role of sociopathy and hysteria in the antisocial woman. *American Journal of Psychiatry, 127*, 303–311.

Cloninger, C., & Guze, S. (1973a). Psychiatric disorders and criminal recidivism. *Archives of General Psychiatry, 29*, 266–269.

Cloninger, C., & Guze, S. (1973b). Psychiatric illnesses in the families of female criminals: A study of 288 first-degree relatives. *British Journal of Psychiatry, 122*, 697–703.

Coates, S., & Tuber, S. (1988). The representation of object relations in the Rorschachs of extremely feminine boys. In H. Lerner & P. Lerner (Eds.), *Primitive mental states and the Rorschach* (pp. 647–657). Madison, CT: International Universities Press.

Colligan, S., & Exner, J. (1985). Responses of schizophrenics and nonpatients to a tachistoscopic presentation of the Rorschach. *Journal of Personality Assessment, 49*, 129–138.

Coonerty, S. (1986). An exploration of separation-individuation themes in the borderline personality disorder. *Journal of Personality Assessment, 50*(3), 501–511.

Cooper, S., & Arnow, D. (1986). An object relations view of the borderline defenses: A Rorschach analysis. In M. Kissen (Ed.), *Assessing object relations phenomena* (pp. 143–171). Madison, CT: International Universities Press.

Cooper, S., Perry, J., & Arnow, D. (1988). An empirical approach to the study of defense mechanisms: I. Reliability and preliminary validity of the Rorschach defense scale. *Journal of Personality Assessment, 52*(2), 187–203.

Crain, W., & Smoke, L. (1981). Rorschach aggressive content in normal and problematic children. *Journal of Personality Assessment, 45*, 2–4.

Curran, V., & Marengo, J. (1990). Psychological assessment of catatonic schizophrenia. *Journal of Personality Assessment, 55*, 432–444.

Dabbs, J., & Morris, R. (1990). Testosterone, social class, and antisocial behavior in a sample of 4,462 men. *Psychological Science, 1*, 209–211.

Davidow, S., & Bruhn, A. (1990). Earliest memories and the dynamics of delinquency: A replication study. *Journal of Personality Assessment, 54,* 601–616.

Davis, M., Hull, J., Young, R., & Warren, G. (1987). Emotional reactions to dramatic film stimuli: The influence of cognitive and emotional empathy. *Journal of Personality and Social Psychology, 52*(1), 126–133.

DeVos, G. (1952). A quantitative approach to affective symbolism in Rorschach responses. *Journal of Projective Techniques, 16,* 133–150.

Dietz, P., Hazelwood, R., & Warren, J. (1990). The sexually sadistic criminal and his offenses. *Bulletin of the American Academy of Psychiatry and the Law, 18,* 163–178.

Dimmick, G. B. (1935–1936). An application of the Rorschach inkblot test to three clinical types of dementia praecox. *Journal of Psychology, 1,* 61–74.

Eccles, J., Midgley, C., Wigfield, A., Buchanan, C., Reuman, D., Flanagan, C., & MacIver, D. (1993). Development during adolescence: The impact of stage-environment fit on young adolescents' experiences in schools and in family. *American Psychologist, 48*(2), 90–101.

Edell, W. (1987). Role of structure in disordered thinking in borderline and schizophrenic disorders. *Journal of Personality Assessment, 51,* 23–41.

Eichelman, B., Elliott, G., & Barchas, J. (1981). Biochemical, pharmacological, and genetic aspects of aggression. In D. A. Hamburg & M. B. Trudeau (Eds.), *Biobehavioral aspects of aggression* (pp. 51–84). New York: Liss.

Eissler, K. (1949). Some problems of delinquency. In K. Eissler (Ed.), *Searchlights on delinquency* (pp. 3–25). New York: International Universities Press.

Eissler, K. (1950). Ego-psychological implications of the psychoanalytic treatment of delinquents. In *Psychoanalytic study of the child* (pp. 97–121). New York: International Universities Press.

Elizur, A. (1949). Content analysis of the Rorschach with regard to anxiety and hostility. *Journal of Projective Techniques, 13,* 247–284.

Ellis, A. (1962). *Reason and emotion in psychotherapy.* New Jersey: Citadel Press.

Ellis, A. (1993). Reflections on rational-emotive therapy. *Journal of Consulting and Clinical Psychology, 61*(2), 199–201.

Ellis, A., McInerney, J., DiGiuseppe, R., & Yeager, R. (1988). *Rational-emotive therapy with alcoholics and substance abusers.* New York: Pergamon.

Ellis, H. (1927). The conception of narcissism. *Psychoanalytic Review, 14,* 129–153.

Ellison, C. (1991). An eye for an eye? A note on the southern subculture of violence thesis. *Social Forces, 69*(4), 1223–1239.

Ephraim, D., Occupati, R., Riquelme, J., & Gonzales, E. (1993). Gender, age and socioeconomic differences in Rorschach thematic content scales. *Rorschachiana, 18,* 68–81.

Erdberg, P. (1993). The U.S. Rorschach scene: Integration and elaboration. *Rorschachiana, 18,* 139–151.

Erikson, E. (1950). *Childhood and society.* New York: Norton.

Esquirol, J. (1838). *Des maladies mentales.* Paris: Bailliere.

Exner, J. (1969). Rorschach responses as an index of narcissism. *Journal of Projective Techniques and Personality Assessment, 33,* 324–330.

Exner, J. (1973). The self-focus sentence completion: A study of egocentricity. *Journal of Personality Assessment, 37,* 437–455.

Exner, J. (1985). *A Rorschach workbook for the comprehensive system.* Bayville, NY: Rorschach Workshops.

Exner, J. (1986a). *The Rorschach: A comprehensive system: Vol. 1. Basic foundations* (2nd ed.). New York: Wiley.

Exner, J. (1986b). Some Rorschach data comparing schizophrenics with borderline and schizotypal personality disorders. *Journal of Personality Assessment, 50*(3), 455–471.

Exner, J. (1988a). *Alumni newsletter.* Asheville, NC: Rorschach Workshops.

Exner, J. (1988b). Problems with brief Rorschach protocols. *Journal of Personality Assessment, 52,* 640–647.

Exner, J. (1990a). *Rorschach interpretation assistance program, version 2*. Asheville, NC: Rorschach Workshops.

Exner, J. (1990b). *A Rorschach workbook for the comprehensive system* (3rd ed.). Asheville, NC: Rorschach Workshops.

Exner, J. (1991). *The Rorschach: A comprehensive system: Vol. 2. Interpretations* (2nd ed.). New York: Wiley.

Exner, J., Bryant, E., & Miller, A. (1975). *Rorschach responses of some juvenile offenders.* (Workshops Study No. 214, unpublished). Asheville, NC: Rorschach Workshops.

Exner, J., Cohen, J., & Mcguire, H. (1990). *Rorschach scoring program, Version 2*. Asheville, NC: Rorschach Workshops.

Exner, J., Kazaoka, K., & Morris, H. (1979). *Verbal and non-verbal aggression among sixth grade students during free periods as related to a Rorschach Special Score for aggression.* Unpublished manuscript, Workshops Study No. 255, Rorschach Workshops.

Exner, J., Thomas, E., & Mason, B. (1985). Children's Rorschachs: Description and prediction. *Journal of Personality Assessment, 49*(1), 13–20.

Exner, J., & Weiner, I. (1982). *The Rorschach: A comprehensive system: Vol. 3. Assessment of children and adolescents.* New York: Wiley.

Eysenck, H. (1967). *The biological basis of personality.* Springfield, IL: Thomas.

Eysenck, H., & Gudjonsson, G. (1989). *The causes and cures of criminality.* New York: Plenum.

Fagan, T., & Lira, F. (1980). The primary and secondary sociopathic personality: Differences in frequency and severity of antisocial behavior. *Journal of Abnormal Psychology, 89,* 493–496.

Fairbairn, W. (1986). *Psychoanalytic studies of the personality.* New York: Tavistock/Routledge. (Original work published 1952)

Fenichel, O. (1945). *The psychoanalytic theory of neurosis.* New York: Norton.

Fenichel, O. (1953). On the psychology of boredom. In *The collected papers of Otto Fenichel: First series* (pp. 292–302). New York: Norton.

Ferenczi, S. (1930). Autoplastic and alloplastic. In *Final contributions to the problems and methods of psychoanalysis* (p. 221). New York: Basic Books.

Finney, B. (1955). Rorschach test correlates of assaultive behavior. *Journal of Projective Techniques, 19,* 6–16.

Fisher, S., & Cleveland, S. (1958). *Body image and personality.* New York: Van Nostrand Reinhold.

Flor-Henry, P. (1974). Psychosis, neurosis, and epilepsy: Developmental and gender-related effects and their aetiological contribution. *British Journal of Psychiatry, 124,* 144–150.

Flynn, J. (1967). The neural basis of aggression in cats. In D. Glass (Ed.), *Neurophysiology and emotion* (pp. 40–59). New York: Rockefeller University Press.

Flynn, J., & Bandler, R. (1975). Patterned reflexes during centrally elicited attack behavior. In W. Fields & W. Sweet (Eds.), *Neural basis of violence and aggression* (pp. 41–53). St. Louis: Green.

Forth, A., Hart, S., & Hare, R. (1990). Assessment of psychopathy in male young offenders. *Psychological Assessment: A Journal of Consulting and Clinical Psychology, 2*(3), 342–344.

Fowles, D. (1980). The three arousal model: Implications for Gray's two-factor learning theory for heart rate, electrodermal activity and psychopathy. *Psychophysiology, 17,* 87–104.

Frank, L. (1939). Projective methods for the study of personality. *The Journal of Psychology, 8,* 389–413.

Frenkel-Brunswik, E. (1953). Psychodynamics and cognition. In R. Lindner (Ed.), *Explorations in psychoanalysis: A tribute to the work of Theodor Reik* (pp. 38–51). New York: Julian Press.

Freud, A. (1936). *The ego and the mechanisms of defense.* New York: International Universities Press.

Freud, A. (1974). Four lectures on child analysis. In *The writings of Anna Freud: Vol. 1.* New York: International Universities Press. (Original work published 1927)

Freud, S. (1910). Leonardo da Vinci and a memory of his childhood. *Standard Edition, 11,* 63–137.

Freud, S. (1911). Psychoanalytic notes on an autobiographical account of a case of paranoia (dementia paranoides). *Standard Edition, 12,* 9–82.

Freud, S. (1914). On narcissism: An introduction. *Standard Edition, 14*, 69–102.

Friedlander, K. (1945). Formation of the antisocial character. *Psychoanalytic Study of the Child, 1*, 189–203.

Frosch, J. (1983). *The psychotic process*. New York: International Universities Press.

Gabbard, G. (1989). Two subtypes of narcissistic personality disorder. *Bulletin of the Menninger Clinic, 53*, 527–532.

Gabbard, G. (1990). *Psychodynamic psychiatry in clinical practice*. Washington, DC: American Psychiatric Press.

Gacono, C. (1985). Mental health work in a county jail: A heuristic model. *Journal of Offender Counseling, 5*(1), 16–22.

Gacono, C. (1988). *A Rorschach analysis of object relations and defensive structure and their relationship to narcissism and psychopathy in a group of antisocial offenders*. Unpublished doctoral dissertation, United States International University, San Diego.

Gacono, C. (1990). An empirical study of object relations and defensive operations in antisocial personality. *Journal of Personality Assessment, 54*, 589–600.

Gacono, C. (1992). A Rorschach case study of sexual homicide. *British Journal of Projective Psychology, 37*(1), 1–21.

Gacono, C. (in press). Suggestions for the institutional implementation and use of the psychopathy checklists. In S. Hart & R. Hare (Eds.), *Criminal psychopaths: Assessment, patterns of offending, and treatment*. Harcourt Brace & Co.

Gacono, C., & Erdberg, P. (1993, March). Object relations in an antisocial sample. In P. Erdberg (Chair), *Rorschach assessment of object relations*. Paper presented at the Midwinter Meeting for the Society for Personality Assessment, San Francisco.

Gacono, C., & Hutton, H. (1994). Suggestions for the clinical and forensic use of the Hare Psychopathy Checklist–Revised (PCL–R). *International Journal of Law and Psychiatry, 17*(3).

Gacono, C., & Meloy, J. R. (1988). The relationship between cognitive style and defensive process in the psychopath. *Criminal Justice and Behavior, 15*(4), 472–483.

Gacono, C., & Meloy, J. R. (1991). A Rorschach investigation of attachment and anxiety in antisocial personality. *Journal of Nervous and Mental Disease, 179*, 546–552.

Gacono, C., & Meloy, J. R. (1992). The Rorschach and the *DSM–III–R* antisocial personality: A tribute to Robert Lindner. *Journal of Clinical Psychology, 48*(3), 393–405.

Gacono, C., & Meloy, J. R. (1993). Some thoughts on Rorschach findings and psychophysiology in the psychopath. *British Journal of Projective Psychology, 38*(1), 42–52.

Gacono, C., Meloy, J. R., & Berg, J. (1992). Object relations, defensive operations, and affective states in narcissistic, borderline, and antisocial personality. *Journal of Personality Assessment, 59*, 32–49.

Gacono, C., Meloy, J. R., & Heaven, T. (1990). A Rorschach investigation of narcissism and hysteria in antisocial personality disorder. *Journal of Personality Assessment, 55*, 270–279.

Gear, M., Hill, M., & Liendo, E. (1981). *Working through narcissism: Treating its sadomasochistic structure*. New York: Aronson.

Geberth, V. (1990). *Practical homicide investigation* (2nd ed.). New York: Elsevier.

Gerstley, L., McLellan, T., Alterman, A., Woody, G., Luborsky, L., & Prout, M. (1989). Ability to form an alliance with the therapist: A possible marker of prognosis for patients with antisocial personality disorder. *American Journal of Psychiatry, 146*, 508–512.

Gibbs, J. (1982). Personality patterns of delinquent females: Ethnic and sociocultural variations. *Journal of Clinical Psychology, 38*(1), 198–206.

Gilligan, C. (1982). *In a different voice*. Cambridge, MA: Harvard University Press.

Glasser, M. (1986). Identification and its vicissitudes as observed in the perversions. *International Journal of Psychoanalysis, 67*, 9–17.

Glueck, S., & Glueck, F. (1934). *Five hundred delinquent women*. New York: Knopf.

Glueck, S., & Glueck, F. (1952). *Delinquents in the making*. New York: Harper.

Goddard, C., McIntyre, D., & Leech, C. (1969). A permanent change in brain functioning resulting from daily electrical stimulation. *Experimental Neurology, 25*, 295–330.

Goddard, R., & Tuber, S. (1989). Boyhood separation anxiety disorder: Thought disorder and object relations psychopathology as manifested in Rorschach imagery. *Journal of Personality Assessment, 53*(2), 239–252.

Gold, J., & Hurt, S. (1990). The effects of haloperidol on thought disorder and IQ in schizophrenia. *Journal of Personality Assessment, 54*, 390–400.

Goldberg, E. (1989). Severity of depression and developmental levels of psychological functioning in eight-sixteen year old girls. *American Journal of Orthopsychiatry, 59*, 167–178.

Goldstein, W. (1991). Clarification of projective identification. *American Journal of Psychiatry, 148*, 153–161.

Gordon, M., & Tegtmeyer, P. (1982). The egocentricity index and self-esteem in children. *Perceptual and Motor Skills, 5*, 335–337.

Gorlow, L., Zimet, C., & Fine, H. (1952). The validity of anxiety and hostility Rorschach content scores among adolescents. *Journal of Consulting Psychology, 16*, 73–75.

Graham, J. (1990). *MMPI-2: Assessing personality and psychopathology*. New York: Oxford University Press.

Grala, C. (1980). The concept of splitting and its manifestations on the Rorschach test. *Bulletin of the Menninger Clinic, 44*(3), 253–271.

Graysmith, R. (1976). *Zodiac*. New York: Berkeley Books.

Groth, N. (1979). *Men who rape: The psychology of the offender*. New York: Plenum.

Grotstein, J. (1980). *Splitting and projective identification*. New York: Aronson.

Grotstein, J. (1982). Newer perspectives in object relations theory. *Contemporary Psychoanalysis, 18*, 43–91.

Guze, S. (1976). *Criminality and psychiatric disorders*. New York: Oxford University Press.

Guze, S., Woodruff, R., & Clayton, P. (1971a). Hysteria and antisocial behavior: Further evidence of an association. *American Journal of Psychiatry, 127*, 957–960.

Guze, S., Woodruff, R., & Clayton, P. (1971b). A study of conversion symptoms in psychiatric outpatients. *American Journal of Psychiatry, 127*(7), 957–960.

Hackfield, A. W. (1935). An objective interpretation by means of the Rorschach test of the psychobiological structure underlying schizophrenia, essential hypertension, Graves' syndrome, etc. *American Journal of Psychiatry, 92*, 575–588.

Halpern, F. (1953). *A clinical approach to children's Rorschachs*. New York: Grune & Stratton.

Hankoff, L. (1987). The earliest memories of criminals. *International Journal of Offender Therapy and Comparative Criminology, 31*(3), 195–201.

Haramis, S., & Wagner, E. (1980). Differentiation between acting-out and non-acting out alcoholics with the Rorschach and hand test. *Journal of Clinical Psychology, 36*(3), 791–797.

Harder, D., Greenwald, D., Ritzler, B., Strauss, J., & Kokes, R. (1988). The Last–Weiss Rorschach ego-strength scale as a prognostic measure for psychiatric inpatients. *Journal of Personality Assessment, 52*, 106–115.

Hare, R. (1965). Temporal gradient of fear arousal in psychopaths. *Journal of Abnormal Psychology, 70*, 442–445.

Hare, R. (1966). Psychopathy and choices of immediate and delayed punishment. *Journal of Abnormal Psychology, 71*, 25–29.

Hare, R. (1970). *Psychopathy: Theory and research*. New York: Wiley.

Hare, R. (1978). Electrodermal and cardiovascular correlates of psychopathy. In R. D. Hare & D. Schalling (Eds.), *Psychopathic behavior: Approaches to research* (pp. 107–144). New York: Wiley.

Hare, R. (1980). A research scale for the assessment of psychopathy in criminal populations. *Personality and Individual Differences, 1*, 111–119.

Hare, R. (1985). *The psychopathy checklist*. Unpublished manuscript, University of British Columbia, Vancouver, Canada.

Hare, R. (1991). *Manual for the Revised Psychopathy Checklist.* Toronto: Multihealth Systems.

Hare, R., Frazelle, J., & Cox, D. (1978). Psychopathy and physiological response to threat of an aversive stimulus. *Psychophysiology, 15,* 165–172.

Hare, R., Hart, S., & Harpur, T. (1991). Psychopathy and the *DSM–IV* criteria for antisocial personality disorder. *Journal of Abnormal Psychology, 100*(3), 391–398.

Hare, R., & Jutai, J. (1983). Criminal history of the male psychopath: Some preliminary data. In K. Van Dusen & S. Mednick (Eds.), *Prospective studies of crime and delinquency* (pp. 225–236). Boston: Kluner Mijhoff Publishing.

Hare, R., & McPherson, L. (1984). Violent and aggressive behavior by criminal psychopaths. *International Journal of Law and Psychiatry, 7,* 35–50.

Hare, R., McPherson, L., & Forth, A. (1988). Male psychopaths and their criminal careers. *Journal of Consulting and Clinical Psychology, 56,* 710–714.

Harmon, R., Rosner, R., Wiedlight, M., & Potter, C. (1983). Analysis of demographic variables of women evaluated in a forensic psychiatry clinic in 1980 and 1981. *Journal of Forensic Sciences, 28,* 560–571.

Harpur, T., Hare, R., & Hakstian, R. (1989). Two-factor conceptualization of psychopathy: Construct validity and assessment implications. *Psychological Assessment: A Journal of Consulting and Clinical Psychology, 1,* 6–17.

Hart, S., & Hare, R. (1989). Discriminant validity of the Psychopathy Checklist in a forensic psychiatric population. *Psychological Assessment: A Journal of Consulting and Clinical Psychology, 1,* 211–218.

Hartmann, H. (1950). Comments on the psychoanalytic theory of the ego. *The Psychoanalytic Study of the Child, 5,* 42–81.

Hartmann, H., & Lowenstein, R. (1962). Notes on the superego. In *Papers on psychoanalytic psychology* (Psychological Issues, Monograph 14, pp. 141–181). New York: International Universities Press.

Heaven, T. (1988). *Relationship between Hare's Psychopathy Checklist and selected Exner Rorschach variables in an inmate population.* Unpublished doctoral dissertation, United States International University, San Diego.

Helfgott, J. (1991). *A comparison of cognitive, behavioral, and psychodynamic assessments of psychopathy: Integrative measures of understanding the psychopathic personality in criminal and noncriminal populations.* Unpublished master's thesis, Pennsylvania State University, University Park.

Helfgott, J. (1992). *The unconscious defensive process/conscious cognitive style relationship: An empirical study of psychopathic dynamics in criminal and noncriminal groups.* Unpublished doctoral dissertation, Pennsylvania State University, University Park.

Henderson, M., & Kalichman, S. (1990). Sexually deviant behavior and schizotypy: A theoretical perspective with supportive data. *Psychiatric Quarterly, 61*(4), 273–284.

Hertz, M. (1935). Rorschach norms for an adolescent age group. *Child Development, 6,* 69–76.

Hertz, M. (1940). Some personality changes in adolescence as revealed by the Rorschach method. *Psychological Bulletin, 37,* 515–516.

Hertz, M. (1941). Evaluation of the Rorschach method and its application to normal childhood and adolescence. *Character and Personality, 10,* 151–162.

Hertz, M., & Baker, E. (1943a). Personality patterns in adolescence as portrayed by the Rorschach method: II. The color factors. *Journal of General Psychology, 28,* 3–61.

Hertz, M., & Baker, E. (1943b). Personality patterns in adolescence as portrayed by the Rorschach ink-blot method: III. The "Erlebnistypus" (a normative study). *Journal of General Psychology, 28,* 225–276.

Hofer, M. (1987). Early social relationships: A psychobiologist's view. *Child Development, 58,* 633–647.

Holt, R. (1960). A method for assessing primary process-manifestations and their control in Rorschach responses. In M. Rickers-Ovsiankina (Ed.), *Rorschach psychology* (pp. 375–420). Huntington, NY: Krieger.

Holt, S. (1994). *Sadism and psychopathy.* Unpublished doctoral dissertation, California School of Professional Psychology, San Diego.

Horowitz, M. (Ed.). (1991). *Hysterical personality style and the histrionic personality disorder* (rev. ed.). Northvale, NJ: Aronson.

Hull, C. (1952). *A behavior system.* New Haven, CT: Yale University Press.

Inhelder, B., & Piaget, J. (1958). *The growth of logical thinking from childhood to adolescence.* New York: Basic Books.

Ipp, H. (1986). *Object relations of feminine boys: A Rorschach assessment.* Unpublished doctoral dissertation, York University, Toronto.

Jackman, T., & Cole, T. (1992). *Rites of burial.* New York: Windsor.

Jacobson, E. (1964). *The self and the object world.* New York: International Universities Press.

Jarvinen, L. (1977). *Personality characteristics of violent offenders and suicidal individuals.* Finland: Finnish Academy of Science and Letters.

Jenkins, R. (1960). The psychopathic or antisocial personality. *Journal of Nervous and Mental Disease, 131,* 318–334.

Johns, J., & Quay, H. (1962). The effect of social reward on verbal conditioning in psychopathic and neurotic military offenders. *Journal of the American Statistical Association, 65,* 217–220.

Johnson, D., & Quinlan, D. (1993). Can the mental representations of paranoid schizophrenics be differentiated from those of normals? *Journal of Personality Assessment, 60,* 588–601.

Kahn, M., Fox, H., & Rhode, R. (1988). Detecting faking on the Rorschach: Computer versus expert clinical judgment. *J. Personality Assessment, 52,* 516–523.

Kandel, E., & Freed, D. (1989). Frontal-lobe dysfunction and antisocial behavior: A review. *Journal of Clinical Psychology, 45,* 404–413.

Karpman, B. (1941). On the need for separating psychopathy into two distinct clinical types: Symptomatic and idiopathic. *Journal of Criminal Psychopathology, 3,* 112–137.

Karpman, B. (1948). The myth of the psychopathic personality. *American Journal of Psychiatry, 104,* 523–534.

Karpman, B. (1949). The psychopathic delinquent child. *American Journal of Orthopsychiatry, 20,* 223–265.

Karpman, B. (Ed.). (1959). *Symposia on child and juvenile delinquency: Presented at the American Orthopsychiatric Association.* Washington, DC: Psychodynamic Monograph Series.

Karpman, B. (1961). The structure of neurosis: With special differentials between neurosis, psychosis, homosexuality, alcoholism, psychopathy, and criminality. *Archives of Criminal Psychodynamics, 4,* 599–646.

Kazaoka, K., Sloane, K., & Exner, J. (1978). *Verbal and nonverbal aggressive behaviors among 70 inpatients during occupational and recreational therapy.* Unpublished Workshops Study No. 254, Rorschach Workshops.

Kegan, R. (1986). The child behind the mask: Sociopathy as developmental delay. In W. Reid, D. Dorr, J. Walker, & J. Bonner (Eds.), *Unmasking the psychopath: Antisocial personality and related syndromes* (pp. 45–77). New York: Norton.

Kendall, P. (1993). Cognitive-behavioral therapies with youth: Guiding theory, current status, and emerging developments. *Journal of Consulting and Clinical Psychology, 61*(2), 235–247.

Kernberg, O. (1966). Structural derivatives of object relationships. *International Journal of Psychoanalysis, 47,* 236–253.

Kernberg, O. (1967). Borderline personality organization. *Journal of the American Psychoanalytic Association, 15,* 641–685.

Kernberg, O. (1970). A psychoanalytic classification of character pathology. *Journal of the American Psychoanalytic Association, 19,* 595–635.

Kernberg, O. (1974). Further contributions to the treatment of narcissistic personalities. *International Journal of Psychoanalysis, 55,* 215–240.

Kernberg, O. (1975). *Borderline conditions and pathological narcissism.* New York: Aronson.

Kernberg, O. (1982). An ego-psychology and object relations approach to the narcissistic personality. In American Psychiatric Association, *Psychiatry: Annual review* (pp. 510–523). Washington, DC: American Psychiatric Association.

Kernberg, O. (1984). *Severe personality disorders: Psychotherapeutic strategies.* London: Yale University Press.

Kernberg, P. (1981). The hysterical personality in child and adolescent analysis. In E. Anthony (Ed.), *Three clinical faces of childhood* (pp. 27–58). New York: Halsted.

Kernberg, P. (1989). Narcissistic personality disorder in childhood. *Psychiatric Clinics of North America, 12*(3), 671–693.

Kernberg, P. (1990). Resolved: Borderline personality exists in children under twelve. *Journal of American Academy of Child and Adolescent Psychiatry, 29,* 478–482.

Kissen, M. (1986). *Assessing object relations phenomena.* Madison, CT: International Universities Press.

Kleiger, J., & Peebles-Kleiger, M. (1993). Toward a conceptual understanding of the deviant response in the comprehensive Rorschach system. *Journal of Personality Assessment, 60*(1), 74–90.

Klein, M. (1946). Notes on some schizoid mechanisms. *The International Journal of Psychoanalysis, 27,* 99–110.

Klein, M. (1963). *The psychoanalysis of children.* London: Hogarth.

Kline, S. (1992). A profile of female offenders in the Federal Bureau of Prisons. *Federal Prisons Journal, 3*(1), 33–36.

Klopfer, B., & Davidson, H. (1962). *The Rorschach technique.* New York: Harcourt Brace.

Klopfer, B., & Kelley, D. (1942). *The Rorschach technique.* Yonkers, NY: World Book.

Knight, R. (1954). Borderline states. In R. Knight & C. Friedman (Eds.), *Psychoanalytic psychiatry and psychology* (pp. 97–109). New York: International Universities Press.

Kohut, H. (1971). *The analysis of self.* New York: International Universities Press.

Kohut, H. (1977). *The restoration of the self.* New York: International Universities Press.

Kraepelin, E. (1915). *Psychiatrie: Ein lehrbuch* (8th ed.). Leipzig: Barth.

Krafft-Ebing, R. (1965). *Psychopathia sexualis: A medio-forensice study.* New York: Putnam. (Original work published 1886)

Krystal, H. (1978). Trauma and affects. *Psychoanalytic Study of the Child, 33,* 81–116.

Kwawer, J. (1979). Borderline phenomena, interpersonal relations, and the Rorschach test. *Bulletin of the Menninger Clinic, 43,* 515–524.

Kwawer, J. (1980). Primitive interpersonal modes, borderline phenomena and Rorschach content. In J. Kwawer, A. Sugarman, P. Lerner, & H. Lerner (Eds.), *Borderline phenomena and the Rorschach test* (pp. 89–109). New York: International Universities Press.

Kwawer, J., Lerner, P., Lerner, H., & Sugarman, A. (1980). *Borderline phenomena and the Rorschach test.* New York: International Universities Press.

Lane, R., & Chazan, S. (1989). Symbols of terror: The witch/vampire, the spider, and the shark. *Psychoanalytic Psychology, 6*(3), 325–341.

Lanyon, R., & Goodstein, L. (1971). *Personality assessment.* New York: Wiley.

Lasch, C. (1978). *The culture of narcissism: American life in an age of diminishing expectations.* New York: Norton.

Leichtman, M. (1988). When does the Rorschach become the Rorschach? Stages in mastery of the test. In H. Lerner & P. Lerner (Eds.), *Primitive mental states and the Rorschach* (pp. 559–600). Madison, CT: International Universities Press.

Leichtman, M., & Shapiro, S. (1980). An introduction to the psychological assessment of borderline conditions in children: Borderline children and the test process. In J. Kwawer, H. Lerner, P. Lerner, & A. Sugarman (Eds.), *Borderline phenomena and the Rorschach test* (pp. 343–366). New York: International Universities Press.

Lerner, H. (1988). The narcissistic personality as expressed through psychological tests. In H. Lerner & P. Lerner (Eds.), *Primitive mental states and the Rorschach* (pp. 257–297). Madison, CT: International Universities Press.

Lerner, H., & Lerner, P. (1988). *Primitive mental states and the Rorschach.* Madison, CT: International Universities Press.

Lerner, P. (1975). Interpersonal relations. In P. Lerner (Ed.), *Handbook of Rorschach scales* (pp. 324–357). New York: International Universities Press.

Lerner, P. (1991). *Psychoanalytic theory and the Rorschach.* Hillsdale, NJ: Analytic Press.

Lerner, P. (1992). Toward an experiential psychoanalytic approach to the Rorschach. *Bulletin of the Menninger Clinic, 56*(4), 451–464.

Lerner, P., & Lerner, H. (1980). Rorschach assessment of primitive defenses in borderline personality structure. In J. Kwawer, A. Sugarman, P. Lerner, & H. Lerner (Eds.), *Borderline phenomena and the Rorschach test* (pp. 257–274). New York: International Universities Press.

Leura, A., & Exner, J. (1977). *The effects of inquiry after each card on the distribution of scores in the records of young children.* Unpublished Workshops Study No. 247, Rorschach Workshops.

Levitt, E., & Trauma, A. (1972). *The Rorschach technique with children.* New York: Grune & Stratton.

Levy, D. (1950). Psychopathic behavior in infants and children: A critical study of the existing concepts. In B. Karpman (Chair), *American Journal of Orthopsychiatry, 20,* 250–254.

Lewinsohn, P., Hops, H., Roberts, R., Seeley, J., & Andrews, J. (1993). Adolescent psychopathology: I. Prevalence and incidence of depression and other *DSM–III–R* disorders in high school students. *Journal of Abnormal Psychology, 102*(1), 133–144.

Lewis, A. (1974). Psychopathic personality: A most elusive category. *Psychological Medicine, 4,* 133–140.

Lewis, C. (1991). Neurochemical mechanisms of chronic antisocial behavior (psychopathy): a literature review. *The Journal of Nervous and Mental Disease, 179,* 720–727.

Leyton, E. (1986). *Compulsive killers: The story of modern multiple murder.* New York: New York University Press.

Lilienfeld, S., Van Valkenburg, C., Larntz, K., & Akiskal, H. (1986). The relationship between histrionic personality disorder to antisocial personality disorder and somatization disorders. *American Journal of Psychiatry, 143,* 718–722.

Lindner, R. (1943). The Rorschach test and the diagnosis of psychopathic personality. *Journal of Criminal Psychopathology, July,* 69–93.

Link, B., Andrews, H., & Cullen, F. (1992). The violent and illegal behavior of mental patients reconsidered. *American Sociological Review, 57,* 275–292.

Lueger, R., & Gill, K. (1990). Frontal-lobe cognitive dysfunction in conduct disordered adolescents. *Journal of Clinical Psychology, 46,* 696–706.

Lustman, J. (1977). On splitting. *Psychoanalytic Study of the Child, 32,* 119–154.

Lykken, D. (1967). Valins' "emotionality and autonomic reactivity": An appraisal. *Journal of Experimental Research in Personality, 2,* 49–55.

Maas, J. (1966). Cathexes toward significant others by sociopathic women. *Archives of General Psychiatry, 15*(5), 516–522.

Maccoby, E., & Jacklin, C. (1980). Sex differences in aggression: A rejoinder and reprise. *Child Development, 51,* 964–980.

MacCulloch, M., Snowden, P., Wood, P., & Mills, H. (1983). Sadistic fantasy, sadistic behavior and offending. *British Journal of Psychiatry, 143,* 20–29.

Mahler, M. (1958). Autism and symbiosis: Two extreme disturbances of identity. In *The Selected Papers of Margaret S. Mahler* (Vol. 1, pp. 169–181). New York: Aronson.

Mahler, M., Pine, F., & Bergman, A. (1975). *The psychoanalytic birth of the human infant.* New York: Basic Books.

Mahoney, M. (1993). Introduction to special section: Theoretical developments in the cognitive psychotherapies. *Journal of Consulting and Clinical Psychology, 61*(2), 187–193.

Majors, R., & Billson, J. (1992). *Cool pose: The dilemmas of Black manhood in America.* Lexington, MA: Lexington.

Margolis, J. (1992). *Aggressive and borderline-level content on the Rorschach: An exploratory study of some proposed scoring categories.* Unpublished doctoral dissertation, California School of Professional Psychology, Berkeley.

Martinez, B. (1972). *An investigation into the concurrent validity of Cleckley's behavioral descriptions with female sociopaths.* Unpublished master's thesis, University of Denver, Denver.

Mason, B., Cohen, J., & Exner, J. (1985). Schizophrenic, depressive, and nonpatient personality organizations described by Rorschach factor structures. *Journal of Personality Assessment, 49,* 295–305.

Masters, B. (1985). *Killing for company.* New York: Stein & Day.

Maudsley, H. (1874). *Responsibility in mental diseases.* London: King.

McDougall, J. (1980). Narcissus in search of a reflection. In *Plea for a measure of abnormality* (pp. 299–335). New York: International Universities Press.

Mednick, S., Volavka, J., Gabrielli, W., & Itil, R. (1981). EEG as a predictor of antisocial behavior. *Criminology, 19,* 219–229.

Meehl, P. (1962). Schizotaxia, schizotypy, schizophrenia. *American Psychologist, 17,* 827–838.

Meehl, P. (1989). Schizotaxia revisited. *Archives of General Psychiatry, 46,* 935–944.

Meichenbaum, D. (1993). Changing conceptions of cognitive-behavior modification: Retrospect and prospect. *Journal of Consulting and Clinical Psychology, 61*(2), 202–204.

Meichenbaum, D., & Cameron, R. (1974). The clinical potential of modifying what clients say to themselves. In M. Mahoney & C. Thoresen (Eds.), *Self-control: Power to the person.* Monterey, CA: Brooks/Cole.

Meissner, W. (1972). Notes on identification. *Psychoanalytic Quarterly, 41,* 224–260.

Meloy, R. (1984). Thought organization and primary process in the parents of schizophrenics. *British Journal of Medical Psychology, 57,* 279–281.

Meloy, R. (1985a). Concept and percept formation in object relations theory. *Psychoanalytic Psychology, 2*(1), 35–45.

Meloy, R. (1985b). Inpatient psychiatric treatment in a county jail. *Journal of Psychiatry and Law, 14,* 377–396.

Meloy, R. (1986). On the relationship between primary process and thought disorder. *Journal of the American Academy of Psychoanalysis, 14,* 47–56.

Meloy, R. (1988). *The psychopathic mind: Origins, dynamics and treatment.* Northvale, NJ: Aronson.

Meloy, R. (1989). Serial murder: A four book review. *Journal of Psychiatry and Law, 17,* 85–108.

Meloy, R. (1991a). Further comments on projective identification [Letter to the editor]. *American Journal of Psychiatry, 148,* 1761–1762.

Meloy, R. (1991b). Rorschach testimony. *Journal of Psychiatry and Law, 19,* 221–235.

Meloy, R. (1992a). Revisiting the Rorschach of Sirhan Sirhan. *Journal of Personality Assessment, 58*(3), 548–570.

Meloy, R. (1992b). *Violent attachments.* Northvale, NJ: Aronson.

Meloy, R. (1992c). Voluntary intoxication and the insanity defense. *Journal of Psychiatry and Law, 20,* 439–457.

Meloy, R. (in press). Treatment of antisocial personality disorder. In G. Gabbard (Ed.), *DSM–IV treatments of psychiatric disorders.* Washington, DC: American Psychiatric Press.

Meloy, R., & Gacono, C. (1992a). The aggression response and the Rorschach. *Journal of Clinical Psychology, 48*(1), 104–114.

Meloy, R., & Gacono, C. (1992b). A psychotic (sexual) psychopath: "I just had a violent thought . . ." *Journal of Personality Assessment, 58*(3), 480–493.

Meloy, R., & Gacono, C. (1993). A borderline psychopath: "I was basically maladjusted . . ." *Journal of Personality Assessment, 61*(2), 358–373.

Meloy, R., & Gacono, C. (1994). Assessing the psychopathic personality. In J. Butcher (Ed.), *Clinical foundations of personality assessment.* New York: Oxford University Press.

Meloy, R., Gacono, C., & Kenney, L. (1994). A Rorschach investigation of sexual homicide. *Journal of Personality Assessment, 62,* 58–67.

Meloy, R., & Singer, J. (1991). A psychoanalytic view of the comprehensive system "special scores." *Journal of Personality Assessment, 56,* 202–217.

Meyer, G. (1992). Response frequency problems in the Rorschach: Clinical and research implications with suggestions for the future. *Journal of Personality Assessment, 58,* 231–244.

Meyer, G. (1993). The impact of response frequency on the Rorschach constellation indices and on their validity with diagnostic and MMPI–2 criteria. *Journal of Personality Assessment, 60*(1), 153–180.

Meyer, J., & Tuber, S. (1989). Intrapsychic and behavioral correlates of the phenomenon of imaginary companions in young children. *Psychoanalytic Psychology, 6,* 151–168.

Miller, L. (1987). Neuropsychology of the aggressive psychopath: An integrative review. *Aggressive Behavior, 13,* 119–140.

Millon, T. (1981). *Disorders of personality: DSM–III: Axis II.* New York: Wiley.

Milton, J. (1968). *Paradise lost and paradise regained.* New York: American New Library.

Modell, A. (1968). *Object love and reality.* New York: International Universities Press.

Modell, A. (1975). A narcissistic defence against affects and the illusion of self-sufficiency. *International Journal of Psychoanalysis, 56,* 275–282.

Monahan, J. (1981). *The clinical prediction of violent behavior.* Washington, DC: U.S. Government Printing Office.

Monahan, J. (1992). Mental disorder and violent behavior. *American Psychologist, 47,* 511–521.

Moravesik, E. (1894). Das hysterische irresein. *Allg Z fur Psychiatrie, 50,* 117.

Morel, B. (1839). *Traite des degenerescences physiques, intellectuelles et morales de l'espece humaine.* Paris: Bailliere.

Morgan, L., & Viglione, D. (1992). Sexual disturbances, Rorschach sexual responses, and mediating factors. *Psychological Assessment, 4,* 530–536.

Morrison, H. (1978). The asocial child: A destiny of sociopathy? In W. Reid (Ed.), *The psychopath: A comprehensive study of antisocial disorders and behaviors* (pp. 22–65). New York: Brunner/Mazel.

Murray, J. (1992). Toward a synthetic approach to the Rorschach: The case of a psychotic child. *Journal of Personality Assessment, 58*(3), 494–505.

Murstein, B. (1956). The projection of hostility on the Rorschach and as a result of ego threat. *Journal of Projective Techniques, 20,* 418–428.

Neary, A. (1990). *DSM–III and Psychopathy Checklist assessment of antisocial personality disorder in Black and White female felons.* Unpublished doctoral dissertation, University of Missouri, St. Louis.

Newman, J., & Kosson, D. (1986). Passive avoidance learning in psychopathic and nonpsychopathic offenders. *Journal of Abnormal Psychology, 95,* 252–256.

Nunberg, H. (1979). Narcissistic personality disorder: Diagnosis. *Weekly Psychiatry Update Series, 3,* 17.

O'Brien, D. (1985). *Two of a kind: The Hillside Stranglers.* New York: New American Library.

Ogloff, J., & Wong, S. (1990). Electrodermal and cardiovascular evidence of a coping response in psychopaths. *Criminal Justice and Behavior, 17*(2), 231–245.

Ogloff, J., Wong, S., & Greenwood, A. (1990). Treating criminal psychopaths in a therapeutic community program. *Behavioral Sciences and the Law, 8,* 181–190.

Olesker, W. (1980). Early life experience and the development of borderline pathology. In J. Kwawer, H. Lerner, P. Lerner, & A. Sugarman (Eds.), *Borderline phenomena and the Rorschach test* (pp. 411–439). New York: International Universities Press.

Partridge, G. (1930). Current conceptualizations of psychopathic personality. *American Journal of Psychiatry, 10,* 53–99.

Patrick, C., Bradley, M., & Lang, P. (1993). Emotion in the criminal psychopath: Startle reflex modulation. *Journal of Abnormal Psychology, 102*(1), 82–92.

Peaslee, D. (1993). *An investigation of incarcerated females: Rorschach indices and Psychopathy Checklist scores.* Unpublished doctoral dissertation, California School of Professional Psychology, Fresno.

Peaslee, D., Fleming, G., Baumgardner, T., Silbaugh, D., & Thackrey, M. (1992). *An explication of female psychopathy: Psychopathy Checklist scores, Rorschach manifestations, and a comparison of male and female offenders with moderate and severe psychopathy.* Unpublished manuscript.

Perry, W., Viglione, D., & Braff, D. (1992). The Ego Impairment Index and schizophrenia: A validation study. *Journal of Personality Assessment, 59,* 165–175.

Petersen, A., Compas, B., Brooks-Gunn, J., Stemmler, M., Ey, S., & Grant, K. (1993). Depression in adolescence. *Adolescence, American Psychologist, 48*(2), 155–168.

Peterson, C. (1992a). Psychodiagnosis and the regulation of self-esteem: Schachtel's *Experiential Foundations of Rorschach's Test. Journal of Personality Assessment, 59,* 644–648.

Peterson, C. (1992b). A psychotic gynemimetic: I just had a pregnant thought. *Journal of Personality Assessment, 58*(3), 464–479.

Piaget, J. (1965). *The moral judgement of the child.* New York: MacMillan.

Pinel, P. (1801). *A treatise on insanity* (D. Davis, Trans.). New York: Hafner.

Piotrowski, Z. (1957). *Perceptanalysis.* New York: MacMillan.

Piotrowski, C., & Keller, J. (1989). Psychological testing in outpatient mental health facilities: A national study. *Professional Psychology: Research and Practice, 20*(6), 423–425.

Piotrowski, C., & Lewis, N. (1950). An experimental Rorschach diagnostic aid for some forms of schizophrenia. *American Journal of Psychiatry, 107,* 360–366.

Piotrowski, C., Sherry, D., & Keller, J. (1985). Psychodiagnostic test usage: A survey of the Society for Personality Assessment. *Journal of Personality Assessment, 49,* 115–119.

Prentky, R., Burgess, A., Rokous, F., Lee, A., Hartman, C., Ressler, R., & Douglas, J. (1989). The presumptive role of fantasy in serial sexual homicide. *American Journal of Psychiatry, 146,* 887–891.

Prichard, J. (1835). *A treatise on insanity.* London: Sherwood, Gilbert, & Piper.

Pulver, S. (1986). Narcissism: The term and the concept. In A. Morrison (Ed.), *Essential papers on narcissism* (pp. 91–111). New York: New York University Press.

Quality Assurance Project (1991). Treatment outlines for antisocial personality disorder. *Australian and New Zealand Journal of Psychiatry, 25,* 541–547.

Rabin, A. (1979). The antisocial personality—Psychopathy and sociopathy. In H. Toch (Ed.), *Psychology of crime and criminal justice.* New York: Holt, Rinehart & Winston.

Rabinovitch, R. (1949). The psychopathic delinquent child. In B. Karpman (Chair), *American Journal of Orthopsychiatry, 20,* 232–236.

Rader, G. (1957). The prediction of aggressive verbal behavior from Rorschach content. *Journal of Projective Techniques, 21,* 294–306.

Rado, S. (1956). *Psychoanalysis of behavior.* New York: Grune & Stratton.

Raimy, V. (1975). *Misunderstandings of the self.* San Francisco: Jossey-Bass.

Raine, A. (1988). Antisocial behavior and social psychophysiology. In H. L. Wagner (Ed.), *Social psychophysiology and emotion: Theory and clinical applications.* London: Wiley.

Raine, A., & Dunkin, J. (1990). The genetic and psychophysiological basis of antisocial behavior: Implications for counseling and therapy. *Journal of Counseling and Development, 68,* 637–644.

Raine, A., & Venables, P. (1981). Classical conditioning and socialization—A biosocial interaction. *Personality and Individual Differences, 2,* 273–283.

Raine, A., Venables, P., & Williams, M. (1990). Autonomic orienting responses in 15-year-old male subjects and criminal behavior at age 24. *American Journal of Psychiatry, 147*(7), 933–937.

Rapaport, D. (1951). *Organization and pathology of thought.* New York: Columbia University Press.

Rapaport, D., Gill, M., & Schafer, R. (1945). *Diagnostic psychological testing* (Vol. 1). Chicago: Year Book Publishers.

Rapaport, D., Gill, M., & Schafer, R. (1946/1948). *Diagnostic psychological testing.* New York: International Universities Press.

Rausch de Traubenberg, J., & Boizou, M. (1980). Pre-psychotic conditions in children as manifested in their perception and fantasy experiences on Rorschach and thematic tests. In J. Kwawer, H. Lerner, P. Lerner, & A. Sugarman (Eds.), *Borderline phenomena and the Rorschach test* (pp. 395–409). New York: International Universities Press.

Raychaudhuri, M., & Mukerji, K. (1971). Homosexual-narcissistic "reflections" on the Rorschach: An examination of Exner's diagnostic Rorschach signs. *Rorschachiana Japonica, 12*, 119–126.

Redl, F., & Wineman, D. (1951). *Children who hate: The disorganization and breakdown of behavior controls.* New York: Free Press.

Regier, D., & Robins, L. (1991). *Psychiatric disorders in America.* New York: Free Press.

Reich, A. (1960). Pathological forms of self-esteem regulation. In K. Eissler et al. (Eds.), *Psychoanalytic study of the child* (Vol. 15, pp. 215–232). New York: International Universities Press.

Reid, W. (Ed.). (1978). *The psychopath: A comprehensive study of antisocial disorders and behaviors.* New York: Brunner/Mazel.

Reiner, B., & Kaufman, I. (1974). *Character disorders in parents of delinquents.* New York: Family Services Association of America.

Reis, D. (1972). The relationship between brain norepinephrine and aggressive behavior. *Res Publication Association Res Nervous Mental Disease, 50*, 266–297.

Reis, D. (1974). Central neurotransmitters in aggression. *Res Publication Association Res Nervous Mental Disease, 52*, 119–148.

Ressler, B., Burgess, A., & Douglas, J. (1988). *Sexual homicide: Patterns and motives.* Lexington, MA: Lexington.

Revitch, E. (1965). Sex murder and the potential sex murderer. *Diseases of the Nervous System, 20*, 640–648.

Revitch, E., & Schlesinger, L. (1981). *Psychopathology of homicide.* Springfield, IL: Charles C. Thomas.

Rice, M., & Harris, G. (1992). A comparison of criminal recidivism among schizophrenic and nonschizophrenic offenders. *International Journal of Law and Psychiatry, 15*, 397–408.

Rice, M., Harris, G., & Cormier, C. (1992). An evaluation of a maximum security therapeutic community for psychopaths and other mentally disordered offenders. *Law and Human Behavior, 16*, 399–412.

Richards, H. (1993). *Therapy of substance abuse syndromes.* Northvale, NJ: Aronson.

Rickers-Ovsiankina, M. (1938). The Rorschach test as applied to normal and schizophrenic subjects. *British Journal of Medical Psychology, 17*, 227–257.

Riquelme, J., Occupati, R., & Gonzales, E. (1991). *Rorschach: Estudio de contenidos. Datos normativos para de sujetos no pacientes di Caracas y su area metropolitana. Aportes al sistema comprensivo de Exner* [Rorschach: Study of the content. Normative data for nonpatient subjects from the greater Caracas area. According to Exner's Comprehensive System]. Unpublished raw data.

Rivers, L. (1993). *Cognitive, behavioral, and emotional impulse control in violent offenders, nonviolent offenders, and male controls. Unpublished doctoral dissertation.* California School of Professional Psychology, San Diego.

Robertson, R., Bankier, R., & Schwartz, L. (1987). The female offender: A Canadian study. *Canadian Journal of Psychiatry, 32*, 749–755.

Robins, L. (1966). *Deviant children grown up: A sociological and psychiatric study of sociopathic personality.* Baltimore: Williams & Wilkins.

Robins, L. (1970). The adult development of the antisocial child. *Seminars in Psychiatry, 2*, 420–434.

Robins, L. (1972). Follow up studies of behavior disorders in children. In H. Quay & J. Werry (Eds.), *Psychopathological disorders of childhood* (pp. 414–446). New York: Wiley.

Rogers, R., & Cavanaugh, J. (1983). Usefulness of the Rorschach: A survey of forensic psychiatrists. *The Journal of Psychiatry and Law, 11*, 55–67.

Rorschach, H. (1942). *Psychodiagnostics*. New York: Grune & Stratton. (Original work published 1921)

Rosanoff, A. (1938). *Manual of psychiatry and mental hygiene*. New York: Wiley.

Rose, D., & Bitter, E. (1980). The Palo Alto Destructive Content Scale as a predictor of physical assaultiveness in men. *Journal of Personality Assessment, 44*, 223–233.

Rosse, R., Miller, M., & Deutsch, S. (1993). Violent antisocial behavior and Wisconsin Card Sorting Test performance in cocaine addicts [Letter to the editor]. *American Journal of Psychiatry, 150*(1), 170–171.

Rothstein, A. (1984). *The narcissistic pursuit of perfection*. New York: International Universities Press.

Rubenstein, A. (1980). The adolescent with borderline personality organization: Developmental issues, diagnostic considerations, and treatment. In J. Kwawer, H. Lerner, P. Lerner, & A. Sugarman (Eds.), *Borderline phenomena and the Rorschach test* (pp. 441–467). New York: International Universities Press.

Rubenstein, A. (1988). Adolescence, self-experience, and the Rorschach. In H. Lerner & P. Lerner (Eds.), *Primitive mental states and the Rorschach* (pp. 665–680). Madison, CT: International Universities Press.

Rush, B. (1812). *Medical inquires and observations upon diseases of the mind*. Philadelphia: Kimber & Richardson.

Russ, S. (1988). The role of primary process thinking in child development. In H. Lerner & P. Lerner (Eds.), *Primitive mental states and the Rorschach* (pp. 601–618). Madison, CT: International Universities Press.

Ryan, R., Avery, R., & Grolnick, W. (1985). A Rorschach assessment of children's mutuality of autonomy. *Journal of Personality Assessment, 49*, 6–12.

Saccuzzo, D., Braff, D., Sprock, J., & Sudik, N. (1984). The schizophrenia spectrum: A study of the relationship among the Rorschach, MMPI, and visual backward masking. *Journal of Clinical Psychology, 40*, 1288–1294.

Sanders, M., Dadds, M., Johnston, B., & Cash, R. (1992). Childhood depression, and conduct disorder: I. Behavioral, affective, and cognitive aspects of family problem-solving interactions. *Journal of Abnormal Psychology, 101*(3), 495–504.

Santostefano, S., Rieder, C., & Berk, S. (1984). The structure of fantasied movement in suicidal children and adolescents. *Suicide and Life-Threatening Behavior, 14*, 3–16.

Savage, G. (1881). Moral insanity. *Journal of Mental Science, 27*, 147–155.

Schachtel, E. (1951). Notes on Rorschach tests of 500 juvenile delinquents and a control group of 500 non-delinquent adolescents. *Journal of Projective Techniques, 15*, 144–172.

Schachtel, E. (1966). *Experiential foundations of Rorschach's test*. New York: Basic Books.

Schacter, D. (1992). Understanding implicit memory; a cognitive neuroscience approach. *American Psychologist, 47*(4), 559–569.

Schafer, R. (1948). *The clinical application of psychological tests*. New York: International Universities Press.

Schafer, R. (1954). *Psychoanalytic interpretation in Rorschach testing*. New York: Grune & Stratton.

Schafer, R. (1968). *Aspects of internalization*. New York: International Universities Press.

Schafer, S. (1969). *Theories in criminology: Past and present philosophies of the crime problem*. New York: Random House.

Schroeder, M., Schroeder, K., & Hare, R. (1983). Generalizability of a checklist for the assessment of psychopathy. *Journal of Consulting and Clinical Psychology, 51*, 511–516.

Seidman, L. (1983). Schizophrenia and brain dysfunction: An integration of recent neurodiagnostic findings. *Psychological Bulletin, 94*, 195–238.

Serin, R. (1991). Psychopathy and violence in criminals. *Journal of Interpersonal Violence, 6*, 423–431.

Serin, R. (1992). The clinical application of the Psychopathy Checklist–Revised (PCL–R) in a prison population. *Journal of Clinical Psychology, 48*(5), 637–642.

Shapiro, D. (1965). *Neurotic styles*. New York: Basic Books.

Shapiro, D. (1981). *Autonomy and rigid character*. New York: Basic Books.

Shapiro, S., Quay, H., Hogan, A., & Schwartz, K. (1988). Response perseveration and delayed responding in undersocialized conduct disorder. *Journal of Abnormal Psychology, 97*, 371–373.

Shengold, L. (1988). *Halo in the sky: Observations on anality and defense*. New York: Guilford.

Sherman, M. (1960). *A Rorschach reader*. New York: International Universities Press.

Shipley, W. (1940). A self-administering schedule for measuring intellectual impairment and deterioration. *Journal of Psychology, 9*, 371–377.

Simon, M. (1985). The egocentricity index and self-esteem in court ordered psychiatric evaluations. *Journal of Personality Assessment, 49*, 437–439.

Simon, R., & Sharma, N. (1979). Women and crime: Does the American experience generalize? In F. Adler & R. Simon (Eds.), *Criminology of deviant women* (pp. 391–400). Boston: Houghton Mifflin.

Sims, A. (1992). Women's prisons: Their social and cultural environment. *Federal Prisons Journal, 3*(1), 44–48.

Skoler, G. (1988). *Saviors of the nation, assassins of the self: Psychodynamic characteristics of presidential threateners and other secret service cases*. Unpublished doctoral dissertation, University of Nebraska at Lincoln.

Smith, A. (1994). *Juvenile psychopathy: Rorschach assessment of narcissistic traits in conduct-disordered adolescents*. Unpublished doctoral dissertation, California School of Professional Psychology, Alameda, CA.

Smith, K. (1980). Object relations concepts as applied to the borderline level of ego functioning. In J. Kwawer, A. Sugarman, P. Lerner, & H. Lerner (Eds.), *Borderline phenomena and the Rorschach test* (pp. 59–87). New York: International Universities Press.

Solomon, R. (1977). *The passions*. Garden City, NY: Anchor.

Sommer, R., & Sommer, D. (1958). Assaultiveness and two types of Rorschach color responses. *Journal of Consulting Psychology, 22*, 57–62.

Sontag, L. (1959). Defenses in delinquent behavior. In B. Karpman (Ed.), *Symposia on child and juvenile delinquency* (pp. 233–239). Washington, DC: Psychodynamic Monograph Series.

Spalt, L. (1980). Hysteria and antisocial personality: A single disorder? *The Journal of Nervous and Mental Disease, 168*(8), 456–464.

Spearman, C. (1927). *The abilities of man: Their nature and measurement*. New York: MacMillan.

Spiegel, R. (1966). Anger and acting out: Masks of depression. *American Journal of Psychotherapy, 21*, 597–607.

Spitz, R. (1949). The psychopathic delinquent child. In B. Karpman (Chair), *American Journal of Orthopsychiatry, 20*, 240–248.

Stoller, R. (1974). Symbiosis anxiety and the development of masculinity. *Archives of General Psychiatry, 30*, 160–172.

Stoller, R. (1975). *Perversion: The erotic form of hatred*. Washington, DC: American Psychiatric Press.

Stolorow, R. (1975). Toward a functional definition of narcissism. *International Journal of Psychoanalysis, 56*, 441–448.

Stone, H., & Dellis, N. (1960). An exploratory investigation into the levels hypothesis. *Journal of Projective Techniques, 24*, 333–340.

Storment, C., & Finney, B. (1953). Projection and behavior: A Rorschach study of assaultive mental hospital patients. *Journal of Projective Techniques, 17*, 349–360.

Strachan, C. (1993). *The assessment of psychopathy in female offenders*. Unpublished doctoral dissertation, Department of Psychology, University of British Columbia, Vancouver, Canada.

Strachan, C., Williamson, S., & Hare, R. (1990). *Psychopathy and female offenders*. Unpublished data, Department of Psychology, University of British Columbia, Vancouver, Canada.

Sugarman, A. (1980). The borderline personality organization as manifested on psychological tests. In J. Kwawer, P. Lerner, H. Lerner, & A. Sugarman (Eds.), *Borderline phenomena and the Rorschach test* (pp. 39–57). New York: International Universities Press.

Sugarman, A., Bloom-Feshbach, S., & Bloom-Feshbach, J. (1980). The psychological dimensions of borderline adolescents. In J. Kwawer, P. Lerner, H. Lerner, & A. Sugarman (Eds.), *Borderline phenomena and the Rorschach test* (pp. 469–494). New York: International Universities Press.

Svrakic, D. (1989). Narcissistic personality disorder: A new clinical systematics. *European Journal of Psychiatry, 3,* 199–213.

Sykes, G., & Matza, D. (1957). Techniques of neutralization: A theory of delinquency. *American Sociological Review, 22,* 664–670.

Taulbee, E., & Sisson, B. (1954). Rorschach pattern analysis in schizophrenia: A cross-validation study. *Journal of Clinical Psychology, 10,* 80–82.

Teicholz, J. (1978). A selective review of the psychoanalytic literature on theoretical conceptualizations of narcissism. *Journal of the American Psychoanalytic Association, 26,* 831–861.

Thiesen, J. (1952). A pattern analysis of structural characteristics of the Rorschach test in schizophrenia. *Journal of Consulting Psychology, 16,* 365–370.

Thomas, T. (1987, March). *A Rorschach investigation of borderline and attention deficit disorder children.* Paper presented at the Midwinter meeting of the Society for Personality Assessment, San Francisco.

Time-Life Books. (1993). *Serial killers.* Alexandria, VA: Author.

Towbin, A. (1959). Hostility in Rorschach content and overt aggressive behavior. *Journal of Abnormal and Social Psychology, 58,* 312–316.

Tuber, S. (1983). Children's Rorschach scores as predictors of later adjustment. *Journal of Consulting and Clinical Psychology, 51,* 379–385.

Tuber, S. (1989a). Assessment of children's object representations with the Rorschach. *Bulletin of the Menninger Clinic, 53,* 432–441.

Tuber, S. (1989b). Children's Rorschach object representations: Findings for a non-clinical sample. *Psychological Assessment, 1,* 146–149.

Tuber, S. (1992). Empirical and clinical assessments of children's object relations and object representations. *Journal of Personality Assessment, 58*(1), 179–197.

Tuber, S., & Coates, S. (1989). Indices of psychopathology in the Rorschachs of boys with severe gender-identity disorder. *Journal of Personality Assessment, 53,* 100–112.

Tuber, S., Frank, M., & Santostefano, S. (1989). Children's anticipation of impending surgery. *Bulletin of the Menninger Clinic, 53,* 501–511.

Tucker, D. (1981). Lateral brain function, emotion and conceptualization. *Psychological Bulletin, 89,* 19–46.

Tuovinen, M. (1974). Depression sine depressione: An aspect of the antisocial personality. *Dynamische Pscychiatrie, 7*(1), 19–31.

Urist, J. (1977). The Rorschach test and the assessment of object relations. *Journal of Personality Assessment, 41*(1), 3–9.

Vaillant, G. (1975). Sociopathy as a human process. *Archives of General Psychiatry, 32,* 178–183.

van der Kolk, B. (1987). *Psychological trauma.* Washington, DC: American Psychiatric Press.

van Gogh, V. (1889). *Death's head moth* [Vincent van Gogh Museum, Amsterdam]. In van Gogh 1993 engagement calendar. New York: Abberville Press.

Venables, P. (1988). Psychophysiology and crime: Theory and data. In R. Moffitt & S. Mednick (Eds.), *Biological contributions to crime causation* (pp. 3–13). Dordrecht, Holland: Martinus Nijhoff.

Viglione, D. (1980). *A study of the effect of stress and state anxiety on Rorschach performance.* Unpublished doctoral dissertation, Long Island University, Brooklyn, NY.

Viglione, D. (1990). Severe disturbance or trauma-induced adaptive reaction: A Rorschach child case study. *Journal of Personality Assessment, 55*(1&2), 280–295.

Waelder, R. (1933). The psychoanalytic theory of play. *Psychoanalytic Quarterly, 2,* 208–224.

Wagner, E., & Hoover, T. (1972). Behavioral implications of Rorschach's human movement response: Further validation based on exhibitionistic Ms. *Perceptual and Motor Skills, 35*, 27–30.

Waldo, G., & Dinitz, S. (1967). Personality attributes of the criminal: An analysis of research studies, 1950–1965. *Journal of Research in Crime and Delinquency, 4*(2), 185–202.

Walker, N. (1987). *Crime and criminality: A critical introduction.* New York: Oxford University Press.

Walker, R. (1951). A comparison of clinical manifestations of hostility with Rorschach and MAPS test performance. *Journal of Projective Techniques, 15*, 444–460.

Walsh, D. (1986). Victim selection procedures among economic criminals: The rational choice perspective. In D. Cornish & R. Clarke (Eds.), *The reasoning criminal: Rational choice perspectives on offending* (pp. 39–52). New York: Springer Verlag.

Ward, D., Jackson, M., & Ward, R. (1969). Crimes of violence by women. In D. Mulvihill & M. Tumin (Eds.), *Crimes of violence* (pp. 843–909). Washington, DC: U.S. Government Printing Office.

Watkins, C. (1991). What have surveys taught us about the teaching and practice of psychological assessment? *Journal of Personality Assessment, 56*(3), 426–437.

Watkins, J., & Stauffacher, J. (1952). An index of pathological thinking on the Rorschach. *Journal of Projective Techniques, 16*, 276–286.

Watson, R. (1985). *A re-evaluation of the "reflection response" in adolescent psychiatric inpatients.* Unpublished doctoral dissertation, Illinois School of Professional Psychology, Chicago.

Weber, C. (1990). *Analysis of attachment through texture, human movement and human content Rorschach variables in inpatient conduct disordered and dysthymic adolescents.* Unpublished doctoral dissertation, United States International University, San Diego.

Weber, C., Meloy, J., & Gacono, C. (1992). A Rorschach study of attachment and anxiety in inpatient conduct-disordered and dysthymic adolescents. *Journal of Personality Assessment, 58*(1), 16–26.

Wechsler, D. (1981). *Wechsler adult intelligence scale–revised.* New York: Psychological Corporation.

Weiner, I. (1964). Differential diagnosis in amphetamine psychosis. *Psychiatric Quarterly, 38*, 707–716.

Weiner, I. (1965). *Rorschach clues in the differential diagnosis of amphetamine psychosis.* Paper presented at the meeting of the Eastern Psychological Association, Atlantic City, NJ.

Weiner, I. (1966). *Psychodiagnosis in schizophrenia.* New York: Wiley.

Weiner, I. (1975). Juvenile delinquency. *Psychiatric Clinics of North America, 22*, 673–684.

Weiner, I. (1982). *Child and adolescent psychopathology.* New York: Wiley.

Weiner, I. (1991). Conceptual issues in the Rorschach assessment of criminality and antisocial personality. *Rorschachiana XVII*, 31–38.

Weiner, I., & Del Caudio, A. (1976). Psychopathology in adolescence: An epidemiological study. *Archives of General Psychiatry, 33*, 187–193.

Weiner, I., & Exner, J. (1991). Rorschach changes in long-term and short-term psychotherapy. *Journal of Personality Assessment, 56*, 453–465.

Weiner, I., Levy, D., & Exner, J. (1981). The Rorschach EA-ep variable as related to persistence in a task frustration situation under feedback conditions. *Journal of Personality Assessment, 45*, 118–124.

Westen, D. (1991). Clinical assessment of object relations using the TAT. *Journal of Personality Assessment, 56*, 56–74.

Wheeler, W. (1949). An analysis of Rorschach indices of male homosexuality. *Journal of Projective Techniques and Rorschach Research Exchange, 13*, 97–126.

Williamson, S., Hare, R., & Wong, S. (1987). Violence: Criminal psychopaths and their victims. *Canadian Journal of Behavioral Science, 19*(4), 454–462.

Willock, B. (1986). Narcissistic vulnerability in the hyperaggressive child: The disregarded (unloved, uncared for) self. *Psychoanalytic Psychology, 3*, 59–80.

Willock, B. (1987). The devalued (unloved, repugnant) self—A second facet of narcissistic vulnerability in the aggressive, conduct-disordered child. *Psychoanalytic Psychology, 4,* 219–240.

Wilson, A. (1985). Boundary disturbance in borderline and psychotic states. *Journal of Personality Assessment, 49,* 346–355.

Wilson, J., & Herrnstein, R. (1985). *Crime and human nature.* New York: Simon & Schuster.

Winnicott, D. (1958a). The antisocial tendency. In *Collected papers: Through paediatrics to psychoanalysis.* New York: Basic Books. (Original work published 1956)

Winnicott, D. (1958b). Hate in the counter-transference. In *Collected papers: Through paediatrics to psychoanalysis.* New York: Basic Books. (Original work published 1947)

Wirt, R. (1956). Ideation expression of hostile impulses. *Journal of Consulting Psychology, 20,* 185–189.

Wishnie, H. (1977). *The impulsive personality.* New York: Plenum.

Wong, S. (1988). Is Hare's Psychopathy Checklist reliable without the interview? *Psychological Reports, 62,* 931–934.

World Health Organization. (1990). *International classification of diseases and related health problems* (10th ed.). Geneva, Switzerland: Author.

Wulach, J. (1983). August Aichhorn's legacy: The treatment of narcissism in criminals. *International Journal of Offender Therapy and Comparative Criminology, 27*(3), 226–234.

Wulach, J. (1988). The criminal personality as a *DSM–III–R* antisocial, narcissistic, borderline, and histrionic personality disorder. *International Journal of Offender Therapy and Comparative Criminology, 32*(3), 185–199.

Wycoff, A. (1993). *Sexually abused and nonabused borderlines: Differentiating groups through psychological testing.* Unpublished doctoral dissertation, California School of Professional Psychology, San Diego.

Yochelson, S., & Samenow, S. (1977a). *The criminal personality: Vol. 1. A profile for change.* New York: Aronson.

Yochelson, S., & Samenow, S. (1977b). *The criminal personality: Vol. 2. The change process.* New York: Aronson.

Zachary, R. (1986). *Shipley Institute of Living Scale: Revised manual.* Los Angeles: Western Psychological Service.

Author Index

Subject Index

A

Adolescent(s)
  antisocial pattern for, 45–46
  conduct-disordered,
    comparison of dysthymia and, 54–55,
      56*f*, 57
    Rorschach study and, 53–54
  conduct-disordered, sample, 57, 58–60*t*, 60,
    61–62*t*, 63–64*t*, 65–70, 67*t*, 68*t*
  identity issues and gender of, 50–53
  psychopathic, 46–49, 53–54
    case of, 71–73
    Rorschach study of, 73, 74–77*t*, 77*t*, 78*t*,
      79–86*t*, 87*t*, 88*t*, 89–92
    reflection responses for, 242*f*
  Rorschach studies of, 49–53
Adult male antisocial personality disorder,
  Rorschach perspective of, 149–157
Affect tension, for sexual homicide
  perpetrators, 288–289, 296, 300
Affects
  for antisocial personality disordered adult
    males, 161, 164
  for conduct-disordered adolescents, 60,
    65–66
    females, 63*t*
    males, 61*t*

for conduct-disordered children, 22, 23*t*, 25
for female offenders, in relationship to
  PCL-R scores, 100–101
for psychopathic male, 169
for schizophrenic antisocial personality
  disordered males, 197, 201
for sexual homicide perpetrators compared
  to psychopaths, 306*t*
Aggression
  in antisocial personality disordered male,
    153
  categories of, 263, 264–265*t*, 266
  in conduct-disordered adolescents, 67*t*
  in conduct-disordered children, 13
  differential expressions of, 52
  in female sexual psychopath, 138
  pregenital, in sexual homicide perpetrators,
    292, 303
  in psychopathic adolescents, 46–47
  psychopath's perception of, 277
  Rorschach study and, 260–263, 261*t*
  sexual, relationship between rehearsal
    fantasy and, 284–285, 285*f*
Aggression responses, 259–260, 276–278
  frequency of, 261*t*
  idiographic understanding of, 273–276
  interjudge reliability of, 266–267
  nomothetic applications of, 267*t*, 267–268,
    269*t*, 270, 270*t*, 272–273